68000 Microcomputer Systems

Designing and Troubleshooting

68000 Microcomputer Systems

Designing and Troubleshooting

Alan D. Wilcox, Ph.D., P.E.
Bucknell University

Prentice-Hall, Inc.
Englewood Cliffs, New Jersey 07632

Library of Congress Cataloging-in-Publication Data

Wilcox, Alan D., (date)
68000 microcomputer systems.

Includes bibliographies and index.
1. Motorola 68000 (Microprocessor) I. Title.
QA76.8.M6895W55 1987 004.165 86-18735
ISBN 0-13-811399-8

Editorial/production supervision and
interior design: Linda Zuk, WordCrafters Editorial Services, Inc.
Cover design: 20/20 Services, Inc.
Manufacturing buyer: Rhett Conklin

Printed in the United States of America
10 9 8 7 6 5 4 3 2 1

ISBN 0-13-811399-8 025

Prentice-Hall International (UK) Limited, *London*
Prentice-Hall of Australia Pty. Limited, *Sydney*
Prentice-Hall Canada Inc., *Toronto*
Prentice-Hall Hispanoamericana, S.A., *Mexico*
Prentice-Hall of India Private Limited, *New Delhi*
Prentice-Hall of Japan, Inc., *Tokyo*
Prentice-Hall of Southeast Asia Pte. Ltd., *Singapore*
Editora Prentice-Hall do Brasil, Ltda., *Rio de Janeiro*

This book is dedicated to my father, Roy F. Wilcox,
whose faith and confidence encouraged
and supported me throughout the project,
and to the memory of my mother, Esther W. Wilcox,
who always delighted in her son's achievements.

Contents

About the Author

Alan D. Wilcox is associate professor of Electrical Engineering at Bucknell University. Since coming to Bucknell in mid-1983, he has taught courses in computer programming, digital logic, and computer system design.

Professor Wilcox received his Ph.D. in electrical engineering in 1976, his M.E.E. in 1974, and his M.B.A. in 1972, all from the University of Virginia. He received his B.E.E. from Rensselaer Polytechnic Institute in 1965. He is a licensed Professional Engineer and has been involved with computers since the mid-1960s. His current technical interests are microprocessor architecture, troubleshooting, and multitasking-multiprocessing computer systems. He is a member of the IEEE, ACM, ASEE, and Eta Kappa Nu.

Before joining Bucknell, Dr. Wilcox worked in Virginia with E-Systems as a principal engineer doing advanced development of digital speech-enhancement hardware. Earlier, he was a project manager with Weston Controls and was responsible for microprocessor software development for nuclear instrumentation.

Dr. Wilcox may be contacted at 60 South 8th Street, Lewisburg, PA 17837. Telephone (717) 523-0777.

Preface

ABOUT THIS BOOK

This book is about the Motorola MC68000 microprocessor and how to design a 16-bit computer system around it. The principles and techniques presented in this book can be applied directly to the design, construction, and troubleshooting of your own 68000 design project. The purpose of this book is to help you learn these principles and techniques by guiding you through a complete 68000 design project. You can build your system based on the design presented in the book, or you can easily modify the specifications and build a system that meets the unique requirements of your own project.

Sound hardware design is a primary objective of this book. Applied engineering design principles are introduced and developed to establish a solid foundation for a practical, well-documented design that meets specifications. Sound software design, while certainly as important as hardware design, is not emphasized in this book. The necessary software can be developed using the same design principles that apply to hardware. Because the proper software is so essential to computer system design and testing, however, a number of simple programs are presented. If you wish, you can easily add to these programs by writing your own software using Motorola firmware or by using a host computer system with 68000 capabilities.

The emphasis in this book is on the engineering design required to build and test a 68000 microcomputer system. Certainly the newest 32-bit 68020 or the virtual-memory 68010 could just as easily be the main focus, but the idea here is to lay a foundation for the future. The 68000 is powerful, inexpensive, and easily understood: it can be used effectively as a generic design illustration. Then, with the experience and confidence gained by completing this 68000 system, you can go on to design a truly exotic system using the very latest microprocessors available today and in the future.

Planning and scheduling are vitally important aspects of an engineering project. Finishing the design and prototyping in a reasonable time requires attention to many nontechnical details. Without proper attention, even the best technically perfect project can turn out poorly. Consequently, the book stresses project planning and how to schedule a realistic completion date for the project.

The 68000 microcomputer system featured here can be designed, built, and tested without using sophisticated and expensive development equipment. This depends directly on a well-planned system design that can be built and tested by modules. The 68000 is the heart of the system, and it can be made to operate in a freerunning mode very simply. While the 68000 module freeruns, it can be used to test each circuit module you add to the system. This modular-development technique virtually guarantees that your microcomputer project will be a success.

WHO SHOULD USE THIS BOOK

Written especially for the advanced electrical engineering student and for the practicing computer hardware engineer, this book focuses on developing a systematic design technique for using the 68000 microprocessor. To fully profit from the material, an introductory digital systems course covering combinational and sequential analysis and design is required background.

If you are a student, the systematic design technique in this book will be especially valuable in your classroom and laboratory. The design method, illustrated with circuit design examples, is applied to a complete 68000 system design project. The various examples may be built and tested in laboratory exercises, or a complete 68000 system can be designed to your requirements following the textbook example. Emphasis is placed on modular hardware development so that your designs can be flexible and easily adapted to your needs.

If you are a practicing computer engineer, you will benefit by studying the design technique and example designs using the 68000. Having a system already designed to use as an example can make the design of your own special-purpose 68000 system much easier. If you already have a 68000 product and need to add extra features, this book will help you understand how to do it. In addition, the book covers often-overlooked details of system timing, worst-case components, and designing to avoid test and manufacturing problems.

Whether student or engineer, you will learn engineering analysis and design principles. You will learn how to design methodically a 68000 computer system that *always* works, even when production components are used and the system is operated in the worst temperature extremes from freezing to oven. After studying the examples and building your 68000 computer, you will have a CPU board that can be used by itself for program development and testing or used as part of a larger system. Depending on the design options you select, it will have one or two serial ports for a console and modem, or perhaps it will be a board for use in an IEEE Std-696 (S-100 bus) system.

HOW TO USE THIS BOOK

The book can be used as the primary text in laboratory-oriented microprocessor courses* dealing with the 68000. Because of its heavy emphasis on hardware design and laboratory application, the book can also be used to supplement a theory-only computer architecture or programming course.

The book can also be used as a design guide to help in planning and building 68000-based products. It includes the basic information you need to design using memory and interface devices found in a typical system. The documentation standards will also be a good guide for you to use in your designs so you can easily modify your system in the future.

Finally, if you are studying the 68000 alone, the book can be used to guide the construction of your own 68000 system. Enough details are presented so that you can build and test a working system on a solderless breadboard with full confidence in the results. Later, depending on your interests and needs, you can expand your system to include more hardware and more complex software. If you opt for building the IEEE Std-696 version, you can use the CPU along with a commercial disk controller board to boot a full disk operating system (DOS).

BUS SELECTION

When you design your 68000 system, you may choose to design the CPU, memory, and I/O all on one board—much like the Motorola Educational Computer Board (ECB), for example. If you want contact with devices other than those already on your board, then you must provide some path for them to communicate. That path, or bus, is most useful if it conforms to some public standard so that it can be used with devices manufactured by a number of vendors. The IEEE Std-696 or S-100 bus is one such standard: it provides for 8- or 16-bit data, address, and control between a CPU board, memory, I/O, and other peripherals.

There are many bus standards and proposed standards. The VME bus, IBM PC bus, Multi-bus I and II, STD bus, and the S-100 bus are just some of the most frequently used buses. As processors with wider data paths become more popular, the competition between the 32-bit VME bus and Multi-bus II will intensify. Which bus should you use? Or, more to the point, should you use a bus at all?

The IEEE Std-696 bus was chosen as the standard for this book for several reasons. First, the IEEE specifications are not overwhelming for a student: the total system *can* be comprehended. Working out an engineering design that meets an industry specification is a valuable experience for a neophyte engineer. Second, the design work in this book does not require a large equipment budget; the S-100 bus is inexpensive and a perfect match in that regard. In fact, most S-100 bus equipment can now be obtained for next to nothing

*See Appendix I for teaching notes and course design.

because of a perceived movement in the industry to the more powerful "performance" buses. There is no doubt that the days of the S-100 bus are numbered: in a dynamic industry like computers, nothing remains static. The important issue, then, is to focus on the principles of bus design rather than the specifics of just one bus.

If you want to design a 68000 CPU board to put on the VME bus, you can do it with the background you will get in this book. If you want to design with an MC68020, the engineering principles you learn from the 68000 will help you become productive quickly. Once you have the engineering techniques, you can design to meet the specifications required for any bus.

REQUIRED SUPPORT MATERIAL

Learning how to design a 68000 computer system is an active process. You must get involved in designing, building, and testing hardware: reading *about* the 68000 is insufficient. Consequently, in addition to this book, you need reference data, test equipment, hardware, and software. If you have a laboratory with sophisticated equipment, you can use it to great advantage; however, this book is designed so that expensive equipment is not necessary. The modular approach of bringing up a freerunning 68000 requires very little investment for a successful project.

Books

The 68000 data manual is an absolute requirement to benefit from the text. If you intend to do software development, the 68000 programmer's reference manual is also necessary. The Motorola Educational Computer Board manual is definitely worth having because it provides a good example of 68000 design and hardware documentation. If you are building an IEEE Std-696 CPU board, then you must have a copy of IEEE Std-696. Also, get a copy of the Libes and Garetz book: it gives valuable insight and clarification to many topics treated in the Standard.

Test Equipment

There are only several pieces of test equipment required to build the 68000 board. The essentials are a logic probe, a volt-ohm-meter, and a dual-trace oscilloscope with at least a 40 MHz bandwidth. The "nice to have" equipment includes the Fluke 9010A Troubleshooter (with 68000 pod) and a logic analyzer. If you have the option, be sure to set up your logic analyzer so it can print a hardcopy of timing diagrams; a record of timing diagrams is extremely important material to retain in your lab notebook.

Firmware, Software

The TUTOR EPROM set from Motorola is essential to quickly bringing up the 68000 so it can communicate through a serial I/O port. Without TUTOR, a crude monitor can be written and placed in EPROMs using a host computer, but it will take time. The emphasis in this book is on hardware, and the TUTOR EPROM set is simply another component that gets designed into the system. See Chapter 14 for a discussion of TUTOR and its applications.

If you intend to do substantial software development once your 68000 board is running with TUTOR, you will probably benefit from a cross-assembler operating on a host computer. Quelo, Inc. has been quite active in developing a powerful set of tools that can be used on CP/M-80 machines or on IBM PCs. There is also a public-domain version of the Quelo cross-assembler available.

Hardware

The Motorola Educational Computer Board (ECB) is highly desirable for a complete learning experience. Being able to test a working system and experiment with it is important while learning design principles. In the academic setting, the ECB can be obtained either through Motorola's educational grant program or at a discount directly from Motorola. In the industrial environment, the ECB will save many weeks of engineering frustration: at a price much less than a single week's engineering salary, the payoff is easy to justify. If you are studying the 68000 alone, you can get by without the ECB; some of the inconveniences of not having the ECB could be helpful in learning more about the 68000.

The hardware required for the 68000 project itself consists of standard LS-TTL off-the-shelf components. A solderless breadboard, the largest you can find, will do for prototyping the 68000. They work well for speeds to 8 MHz or so and simplify the experimenting part of learning the 68000. If you are building an IEEE Std-696 version, you should use an S-100 wire-wrap protoboard.

Development of an IEEE Std-696 CPU board requires an S-100 frame. The minimum is an old motherboard with a power supply; the desirable is a frame with memory, I/O using 6850s, and a disk controller board. For test, the Jade Bus-Probe is helpful in solving bus problems; it needs to be modified for single-stepping to be fully useful, though.

AVAILABILITY OF SUPPORT MATERIAL

Books

IEEE Standard-696 Interface Devices, 1983. Obtain from the IEEE Service Center, 445 Hoes Lane, Piscataway, NJ 08854. (201) 981-0060.

LIBES, SOL, and MARK GARETZ. *Interfacing to S-100/IEEE-696 Microcomputers.* Osborne/McGraw-Hill, 1981.

MC68000 16-bit Microprocessor Data Manual, and *MC68000 Educational Computer Board User's Manual,* MEX68KECB/D2, 2nd Edition, 1982. Motorola Literature Distribution Center, 616 West 24th Street, Tempe, AZ 85282. (602) 994-6561.

M68000 8/16/32-bit Microprocessor Programmer's Reference Manual. 5th Edition, Prentice-Hall, 1986. Obtain from local bookstore or Motorola.

Test Equipment

Jade Computer Products, 4901 W. Rosecrans, Hawthorne, CA 90250. (213) 973-7707 (The S-100 Bus Probe.)

John Fluke Manufacturing Company, Everett, WA 98206. (206) 347-6100. (9010A Micro-System Troubleshooter.)

Hewlett-Packard, PO Box 10301, Palo Alto, CA 94303. (HP-1631D logic analyzer.)

Cross-Assemblers

Quelo, Inc., 2464 33rd Avenue West, Seattle, WA 98199. (Cross-assemblers for 68000–68020.)

SIG/M Public Domain Software, Box 97, Iselin, NJ 08830. (The Quelo V1.9 public domain cross-assembler is available in Volume SIG/M-92.)

Firmware, Software

A pair of MCM68A364 ROMs as in the Educational Computer Board (ECB). Price $100.* Order part numbers

51AW4129B24	(odd ROM)
51AW4129B25	(even ROM)

Motorola Communications and Electronics, Inc.
Phoenix Repair Depot
1711 West 17th Street
Tempe, Arizona 85281
Telephone: 602/994-6472

The license and source code listing of TUTOR (except for the one-line assembler source). Price $125. Order M68KTUTOR-D4 from any Motorola distributor (Pioneer, Schweber, etc.). No ROMs included.

The license and source code listing of TUTOR. Price of $400 gets code on VERSAdos disk. Order M68KTUTORS from any Motorola distributor.

Tiny BASIC software. Contact

Gordon Brandly
R.R. 2
Fort Saskatchewan, AB
Canada T8L 2N8

*All prices as of spring 1986.

Hardware

Solderless breadboard. Global Specialties PB105; AP Products ACE-236.

Educational Computer Board with TUTOR ROMs is available from any Motorola distributor. Price $495. Order MEX68KECB.

If you are affiliated with a school or university, contact Motorola directly for donations and grants at:

Motorola Technical Operations
University Support Program, HW-68
PO Box 2953
Phoenix, Arizona 85062
Telephone: 602/244-6777

ACKNOWLEDGMENTS

This book is the result of much help from a number of friends, most of whom are my students at Bucknell. I would like to thank several in particular—Donna Kidd, Debbie Polstein, Jim Beneke, and Mark Luders. They put in many hours of editing and proofreading the original manuscript used in classes. I certainly appreciate their enthusiastic support urging me on throughout this project! Mark Luders served as my Teaching Assistant for the 68000 course, and he worked many long hours making sure that the class and laboratory were always prepared properly. Kanwalinder Singh, a graduate student in electrical engineering, was one of the first participants in the 60000 course; his CPU design in Appendix C is an example of student excellence, and I thank him for his permission to use it. I also thank Diane Goodling, my assistant at the word processor, for typing the manuscript.

Finally, I thank the folks at Prentice-Hall: Bernard Goodwin for his vigorous and positive faith in the 68000 project as it first began; my editor, Tim Bozik, for his interest and help in carrying the project through to completion; and my production editor, Linda Zuk, for her diligent attention to details and for bringing this all together.

A.D.W.

Introduction

There is a large gap between the engineering design usually studied in school and the actual practice of engineering in industry. This book is unique because it integrates the principles of engineering design with practical hands-on experience in the real world. It does so by presenting design techniques and then using them to design, build, and test a major computer system. After describing the computer system as a whole, the student can develop the computer module by module. This sequence of designing, building, and testing not only assures success in the project, but also builds student confidence. The constant interplay between design and test develops a feel for the realities of engineering design.

68000 Microcomputer Systems: Designing and Troubleshooting is divided into two main components: Part I is engineering design and Part II is system design and construction. The first develops problem solving, project planning, design techniques, and documentation standards for the rest of the book. It culminates with a detailed comprehensive design example. The second presents a 68000 project plan and shows how the project design can be successfully completed to meet specifications. It illustrates the design implementation by describing the construction of a working system and by showing how to test it for correct performance.

Chapter 1 introduces the concept of designing to meet customer needs. Engineering design involves two steps in meeting these needs: first, the project must be defined and planned; and second, the project must be implemented. Problem solving is introduced as a tool to help identify the customer requirements as well as to help in all phases of the design process. The interplay of problem solving and project planning is essential to assemble the mini-proposal at the end of the chapter. The mini-proposal is the guiding document that contains the project definition, objectives, strategy, and step-by-step plan of action with a time schedule. The plan given in the mini-proposal is then used in Chapter 2 to complete a full project implementation. This implementation, beginning with the analysis of the specifications and constraints, covers the technical design of the product on paper and the construction of a working prototype.

Chapter 3 provides the rules and guidelines on designing a technically sound digital circuit. Signal levels, loading, timing, and noise are covered in detail because of their importance in building a successful 68000 system. The material is presented to supplement, not replace, the information contained in an introductory course in digital logic design. A number of heuristics, or rules of thumb, are also included to moderate the technical paper design with a measure of common-sense reality.

Chapter 4 covers the essentials of recording the project in a lab notebook and of documenting the final design. Drawing guidelines for documentation are covered in Chapter 4; standards for the schematic diagrams are given in Appendix A. Rather than describe a "project report" or an in-house technical report, Chapter 4 presents the outline of a "technical manual" as the final system documentation. The reason for the technical manual is simple: far too many excellent designs have become absolutely useless without proper operating and service information. Lack of a comprehensive technical manual can spell disaster in the marketplace. A sample technical manual that illustrates the ideas in Chapter 4 is in Appendix B.

Chapter 5 is the culmination of the treatment of engineering design. This chapter illustrates the application of project planning and implementation to an actual design project. The secondary purpose of the chapter is to introduce the IEEE Std-696 bus and explain how to use it, or any standard, in a product design. There is no need to actually construct the clock: the 68000 project does not require it in the system. The design approach taken in the Chapter 5 project can be used as a model for designing the complete 68000 computer system.

Chapter 6 gives an overview of the complete 68000 computer system and a description of its requirements. Its purpose is to show you how to plan the 68000 project so that you have a useful guide to future hardware and software development. This guide, or project plan, defines the scope of your project and its objectives, states the strategy to reach the objectives, and sketches a plan of action to finally build and test the product. Although the IEEE Std-696 bus is used in the project plan, there is no reason not to change to another bus (or no bus at all) if you wish: the integrity of the following chapters will not be affected by such a substitution. The exercises at the end of Chapter 6 are intended to give direction to a design similar to the Educational Computer Board.

Chapter 7 is a descriptive overview of the 68000. Its purpose is to study the features of the 68000 and to examine typical data taken using a working 68000 CPU board. This overview is not intended to take the place of the product technical manual; it should, however, be useful clarification of some of the more difficult technical areas. The emphasis is on timing diagrams: it is extremely important to understand the 68000 read and write bus cycles. The success of the entire 68000 design will depend on this understanding!

The material in Chapter 8 deals with testing and troubleshooting. Much can be learned about the 68000 by testing a working system using all available test equipment. One can go just so far looking at data sheets and timing diagrams: real understanding comes only after putting the equipment on the lab bench and testing it. The approach taken in this chapter is to complete a thorough test of the Motorola Educational Computer

Board (ECB); if you do not have the ECB, Chapter 8 does illustrate the test results you would have seen. Troubleshooting strategy is presented for two situations: first, the circuit worked at some time in the past; and second, the circuit is new and never worked at all. Finally, the chapter considers how to design for testability; this is especially important because the 68000 system you design must be easy to test.

Chapter 9 presents the minimum 68000 computer system and shows how to get it running. The material in this chapter covers the design of each required system module and how each can be tested. This chapter is a milestone for the reader building his or her own system: seeing the 68000 run for the first time is an exciting moment! In addition to the minimum system, an IEEE Std-696 version is also presented in this chapter. A simple single-step circuit is included at the end of the chapter and should be used in the prototype 68000; it is extremely useful in testing and troubleshooting the rest of the system.

Once the processor runs, Chapter 10 illustrates how to design memory into the system. All the previous study on the 68000 timing diagrams is needed here: reliable memory operation requires close attention to processor speed and memory access times. Erasable Programmable Read Only Memories (EPROMs) and static Random Access Memories (RAMs) are presented and used in the 68000 design. Worst-case design and maximum clock speed for both reading and writing data are considered. This chapter stresses strongly that the engineer must design carefully to have reliable memory operation.

Chapter 11 shows how to add a serial input/output (I/O) port to the 68000 system. This chapter is a second major milestone, because now the 68000 can finally become useful. Up to now, most of the effort has been hardware design; the only software required was programmed into EPROMs to test various modules being developed. If the TUTOR EPROM set is installed, some useful programs can be written to test new circuits being added or to test more thoroughly the existing system. Without TUTOR, the alternative is either to write your own monitor program or to write a disk-boot program to load a DOS. Whatever your situation at this point, you have a fully functional 68000 computer system.

The last major 68000 topic, exception processing, is covered in Chapter 12. While this material is necessary to take advantage of the 68000's power, it can be treated lightly if desired. The 68000 can deal effectively with a number of different system abnormalities, and proper hardware and software can be useful in your own system. At a minimum, especially if you have TUTOR installed, the circuit for a non-maskable interrupt (*NMI*) should be included. The *NMI* is as important for software debugging as the single-step circuit is for hardware troubleshooting.

Chapter 13 treats the 68000 interface with the IEEE Std-696 bus. Because the 68000 is an asynchronous processor, and the bus itself is synchronous, this interface presents an interesting design challenge. The solution to this problem can be generalized to solve the problem of how the 68000 might be interfaced to any other bus. Understanding the 68000 timing diagrams and close attention to bus specifications are required to complete the bus interface design.

Chapter 14 pulls together a number of the software issues that are related to the hardware development of the 68000. Several software possibilities are considered for using the hardware and communicating with a host computer. The host, for example, can be used with a cross-assembler program to generate executable 68000 code; this code can be downloaded to your 68000 board for testing or normal execution. A high-level language can also be placed in EPROMs and installed permanently in your CPU board if desired. As mentioned earlier, you might want to write your own monitor program or a disk boot program to load a DOS.

The appendix contains a number of important reference items to help design the 68000 system. Data sheets on several of the memory and I/O integrated circuits are included for convenience; data on the 68000 is not included because you must have the *complete* data manual for serious design. The reality of design engineering includes a desk with many data manuals open at the same time. The appendix also contains full documentation on the author's IEEE Std-696 system as well as a copy of a student technical manual.

After you finish this book, you will have a good understanding of engineering design and will know how to design and troubleshoot a microcomputer system. You will know facts about the 68000 and have a grasp of how to use it effectively in a system. After designing and building your own 68000 microcomputer system, you will have the confidence to tackle major engineering jobs. In short, you will have a solid foundation in the theory and practice of engineering.

68000 Microcomputer Systems

Designing and Troubleshooting

ONE

Engineering Design
A Creative Activity that Requires Planning

Digital design can be fun! How else can you enjoy building a piece of complex equipment and expect to have it working in several days? If the entire circuit has not already been described in some magazine or book, you can always take parts of the circuit from several sources and piece together a complete design ready to build. Give it a quick ''smoke test'' to see if you have wired it correctly, and then connect it to your home computer. Moreover, after a few quick patches, you can type a program from your favorite magazine and run it in a matter of hours. Give it the ''big bang'' test to see if you have put all the code together correctly, and then congratulate yourself on a successful project.

Do you see a bit of yourself in this? We all experience this scenario for many design projects, and the approach seems to work. It has survived the test of time to become an almost traditional way of developing new hardware and software products. Although not the most efficient way of doing a project, it does appear to get the job done.

Getting the job done is certainly important, but have you really done a proper engineering design? You might have been creative and solved the problem but not practiced sound engineering design along the way. The ''product'' is one of a kind and probably unsuitable for another person to build or for a company to manufacture.

Whether you are a student about to start a major design project or a professional engineer on the job, this hobbyist technique is clearly not satisfactory. You need a systematic way to approach engineering design so that you can complete your project on time and within your budget; in addition, your design must meet all specifications. In short, you must plan your project and plan it well.

1.1 DESIGN OVERVIEW

Engineering design is the creative process of identifying needs and then devising a product to fill those needs. As shown in Figure 1.1, engineering design is the central activity in

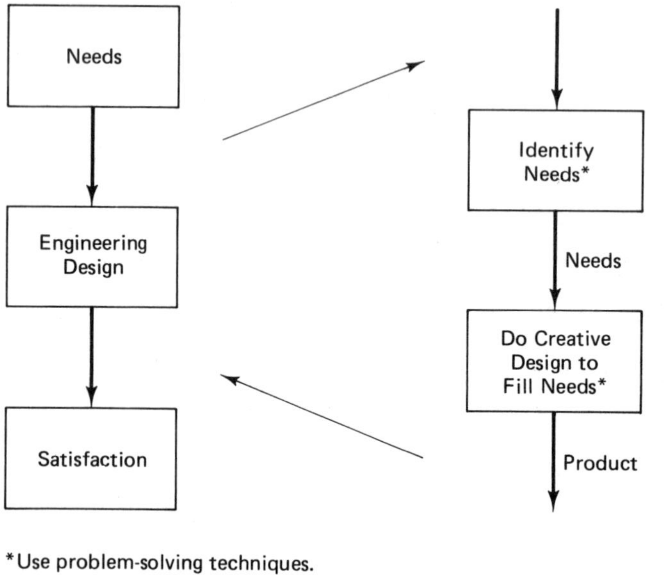

Figure 1.1 Engineering design is the central activity in meeting needs. It involves identifying the needs and then doing a creative design to fill them; both require problem-solving techniques.

meeting needs; these needs may be yours or a customer's. If you understand the requirements involved, then you can develop a creative design to satisfy them.

Figure 1.2 shows two parts of the creative design process. The first part of the process is a project plan outlining the various needs and reducing them to a set of specifications. The project plan is an administrative tool used to identify the various tasks and when to do them. The second part, the project implementation, is the process of designing and developing the final product. Both the project plan and the project implementation are necessary for an orderly product development.

In the context of engineering design, the project plan leads to a set of specifications and tasks. In a sense, you can consider it a nontechnical document because it includes more concepts than technical detail. However, it should not be overlooked. The project plan may be easily summarized and put into the form of a proposal, which is an outline of intended work for a complete project. The proposal functions as a road map for the entire creative design effort, making the difference between project success and failure.

The project implementation, on the other hand, involves the technical activity you would expect in a design project: specifications, hardware and software design and development, documentation, prototype construction, and testing. You can see that the hobbyist technique is only a small part of this implementation and consequently overlooks many essential aspects of the project. Because of these many details, the next chapter is devoted to doing the project implementation.

Both parts of the creative design process require problem solving. It is a problem to determine the information that you need to set the design specifications. Likewise, it is an equally substantial problem to design the product. Both can be addressed by the same problem-solving techniques.

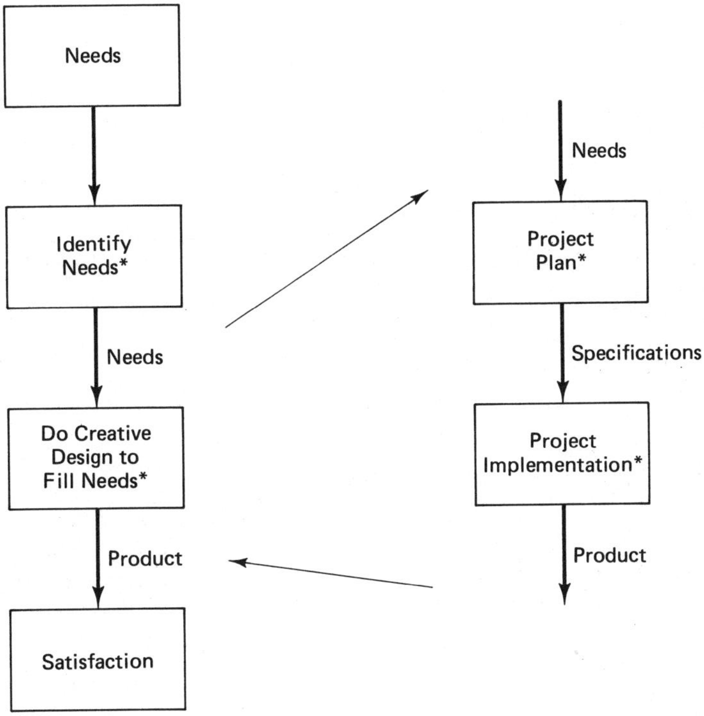

Figure 1.2 The essential first part of a creative design is to complete the project plan. The project plan producess the specifications that describe what product is needed so it can be designed and built.

1.2 PROBLEM SOLVING

Problem solving is the process of determining the best possible action to take in a given situation. This process requires identification of the problem and a description of its causes. Then it makes a systematic evaluation of various alternative solutions until one can be selected as the best. Although you have used problem-solving techniques in one form or another for years, you probably have not looked at them closely.

An outline of a problem-solving method suitable for engineering design is shown in Figure 1.3. It is important to note that this method is not limited to identifying the needs of a customer. It can be used in working through both the project plan and the project implementation. The general problem-solving activities of analysis, synthesis, evaluation, decision making, and action are the essence of engineering design.

Assume for now that you have a customer with a particular technical difficulty. Knowing this customer and his (or her) needs is essential to defining the problem. Who is

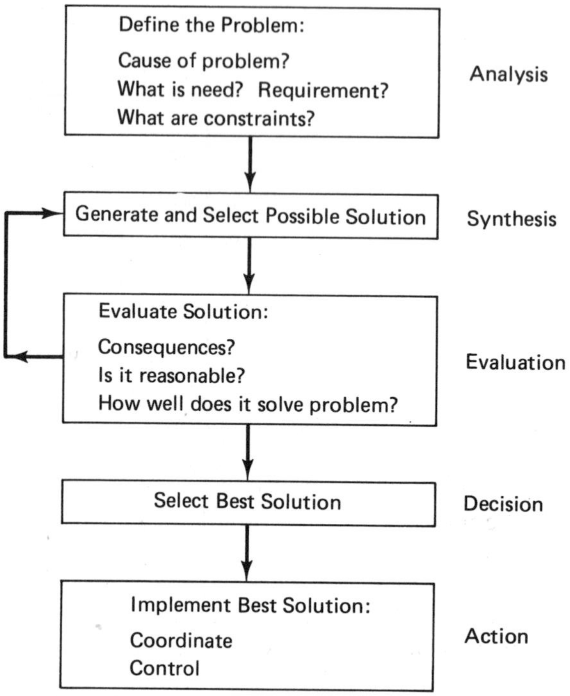

Figure 1.3 General problem-solving steps in defining a problem and evaluating a number of possibilities until a best solution can be selected. The best solution is never perfectly satisfactory because it is a balance between needs and constraints.

the customer? What does he do? What is most important to him in his work? What is least important? What caused his problem? When seeking to define the problem better, be sure to separate the causes of the problem from its effects.

Suppose, for example, that the owner of a local metal-working shop has asked you for your advice on buying a computer. Would you immediately tell him that he needs a Brand-X computer? Of course not. You would begin to ask questions to determine what he wants it to do. Maybe he wants to simplify his job scheduling and inventory management so that he has more free time to plan his future business. Maybe he wants to put all of his accounting on a computer so that he can have quick monthly reports. Maybe a friend has told him that a computer will help business, and "everybody needs a computer to be competitive." What you are doing is analyzing the situation and defining the problem. Remember, if you do not grasp the problem, then any solution will do. This is simply another way of saying, "If you don't know where you're going, then any road will take you there."

How do you find the information necessary to know the customer and his needs? Ask him! If he thinks you can help solve his current problem, he will be more than willing to tell you every problem his company ever had. Understanding his day-to-day operations is vital to defining the problem and its cause.

By the time you understand the problem and its cause, you are also likely to have some ideas on solutions. Make a list of possible solutions, select one, and evaluate its effectiveness. What consequences would you expect from this solution? Any decision you make will have both favorable and unfavorable consequences.

For example, if you were to select Brand-Y computer to solve an accounting problem, you might find these consequences:

1. Computer hardware price reasonable.
2. Software price not too high.
3. This computer might be discontinued soon.
4. Software might do the accounting now.
5. Software might not do for a growing business.

Some consequences look good, while some seem to argue against Brand-Y. What do you do about a list of consequences like this? Set it aside for now and analyze Brand-Z and any other appropriate brands. Perhaps you might compare the brands by constructing a chart or developing a set of standard test programs.

While selecting and evaluating possible solutions to the problem, notice that you are gaining a deeper understanding of the problem. You are also reaching for solutions that you never thought of when you started. You are using facts and concepts to synthesize new ideas. In other words, you are being creative.

Finally, after gathering information and comparing various alternatives, you are ready to make a decision. Any decision, however, involves compromise. After comparing various computer brands, you may find two equally satisfactory choices. What do you do? How do you quantify your preference for the color of Brand-X, or the shape of Brand-Y? The final decision becomes a feeling or preference, an intangible that you cannot define.

After making a decision, you must take action. As in Figure 1.3, the best solution is implemented, coordinated, and controlled. You accomplish this through project management. In the simple computer-selection example, if you were asked for advice on which computer to buy, then your job is done when you give the advice; no real action or project work is involved. On the other hand, if you were asked not only to make a selection, but also to purchase, install, and service the equipment, then you would have a project to implement. This project would require proper planning and close supervision to ensure its success.

1.3 PROJECT PLANNING

A project is a single job that can be accomplished within a specified time and within a certain budget. How this project actually gets done depends on your project plan. The project plan outlines the various needs and reduces them to a set of specifications. It also helps you to identify and schedule the various tasks.

What does this idea of a project plan mean to you, the student or engineer, as you begin designing a piece of hardware or programming a computer system? First, it means that you have an orderly way to conceptualize the confusing array of information. Second, it means that you have an orderly way to complete the project. The project plan is the management tool that helps you do your job.

Look at the project-planning steps outlined in Figure 1.4. How can this outline help you do a better job? Instead of thinking of the project deadline as next year, think of it as next week. Go through the steps of the outline and make a list of the things you should do each of the next five days so that your "one-week" project is a success.

The first step in Figure 1.4 is to define the project. This is a statement of the goals you are trying to accomplish. Think of it as the big picture describing your project. For example, suppose you are to design and build a microcomputer-based temperature monitor. You might write your project definition:

> My project is to design, build, and test a meter that I can use to measure and record air temperature.

At this point, you are saying nothing about its performance (such as temperature range or accuracy); nor are you saying how you intend to build it (do you really need a microcomputer?). Avoid locking yourself into a project goal that is too specific; stick to the big picture.

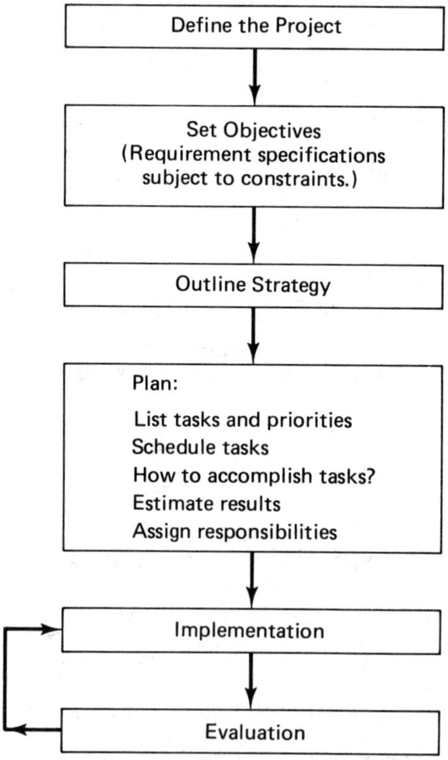

Figure 1.4 General outline of steps to follow when planning a project.

You get specific in the next step when you set your objectives. Your objectives should be specific measurable outcomes of your work. This is where you get into details about the performance of the device you are designing. The objectives are stated in several dimensions: required performance, time to complete, and total cost. For example, you might set these objectives:

> By the end of this month, my meter will be completely built and tested. It will perform to these specifications:
>
> Temperature range −40 to +100°C,
> Accurate to within 1°C,
> Display either Fahrenheit or centrigrade temperature,
> Display minimum and maximum temperatures during last 24 hours,
> Calculate and display 24-hour average temperature,
> Calculate and display daily heating degree days.
>
> In addition to these performance requirements, the meter will be portable and capable of battery operation. Parts for the prototype will cost less than $150.

After you have some solid objectives to work toward, you need to outline your strategy; that is, your concept of how to reach your objectives. Keep in mind that your strategy is your idea of how to achieve the objectives, not the details for actually achieving them. To reach the temperature meter objectives, you might form this strategy:

> To attain my objectives, I will breadboard a prototype model of the analog circuitry with the temperature sensor on the breadboard. Once I understand how it should work, then I will add an analog-to-digital converter plus an interface to a small microcomputer board. I should be able to handle all the calculations and display functions with the microcomputer. After I have it working properly, I will make a prototype printed-circuit board for the customer to evaluate.

This strategy is unique to you and your choice of a design solution. Relate this to what you just learned about problem solving. Your problem is to meet the required design objectives. A possible solution is to start with the breadboard, develop a working circuit, and then build a circuit board. Another possible solution might be to do a complete design on paper first, breadboard it, and then interface it to the microcomputer. Which approach you choose as a best selection depends entirely on you and your work habits. Thus, your strategy is a statement of how you intend to implement the best solution.

You implement your solution by using a plan. Depending on the size of the project, you may find the plan ranging from a simple list of tasks to a complex set of schedules involving many different engineers and departments within your school or company. For our purposes here, we will assume that the implementation is going to involve only one person: yourself.

The best place to start with your plan is to look closely at your strategy and list the major tasks. Early in the project you may not know all your tasks, but you can begin by listing the major tasks chronologically. Under each major task, you probably will think of some subtasks that are also necessary. Some of the major tasks will be high-priority items and must be listed. For example, you must have a breadboard and you must test the circuit for proper operation. Consider this as a possible plan to implement your strategy:

1. Get a breadboard and power supply for the prototype.
2. Look for articles and designs on temperature measurement.
3. Select temperature sensor and A/D for first design.
4. Sketch tentative circuit and calculate circuit values.
5. Build the analog circuit and take measurements.
6. Connect the analog circuit to the A/D converter.
7. Test the circuit completely for proper performance.
8. Design the microcomputer interface logic.
9. Connect the microcomputer and test the interface.
10. Write a simple program to read the temperature.
11. More programs and tasks I cannot estimate now.

Can you start work with this list of tasks? Probably you can. However, you might want to consider how long each will take to complete. If you want to finish the project in a month, when must you complete each task? If you spend the first two weeks on only a few tasks, then you will probably not finish the project in time. You need to set your own deadline for each task.

One way of scheduling is to estimate how many days each task will take and when you should be done with each. As you work your schedule, though, you may lose track if you get ahead or fall behind schedule. You may want to use a bar chart graphical presentation of your schedule as shown in Table 1.1.

TABLE 1.1 BAR-CHART SCHEDULE OF TASKS NEEDED TO BUILD A SIMPLE TEMPERATURE METER.

	Week Beginning			
			March	
Tasks to Do	3	10	17	24
Get breadboard, etc.	**			
Get articles	***			
Select sensor and A/D	****			
Sketch circuit	*****			
Build analog and test	*********			
Connect analog and A/D		********		
Test completely		******		
Design interface		****		
Connect microcomputer			****	
Write simple program			*******	
Write more programs			*********	
Unknown extra tasks				*******

The bar chart is one of the easiest ways to manage your work schedule as you progress through your project. The chart shows not only the tasks you listed when you started your plan, but also when you will actually start and finish each one. The chart also shows overlapping tasks at a glance. One task might depend on another, as shown in Table 1.1 by the arrow between designing the interface and connecting the microcomputer; when you see the arrow, you know that you must finish one task before starting the other. You can make the chart as simple or as complex as you wish, but remember that you must work from it. It should be usable and easy to modify if you get ahead or behind.

The "unknown extra tasks" designation at the end of the chart reminds you that the chart must be flexible and will be modified as you go along. At the start, you do not know of all the things you need to do or how long each will take. The best you can do is estimate.

As you complete your schedule, think about how you will accomplish each of the tasks. What results do you expect as you go along? Anticipate problems and act as soon as possible. For example, if you think you might need precision components for the accuracy specified, then complete that part of the design early and order the parts so that they will be available when you need them in the circuit. Plan ahead! Also, think of contingency plans so that your project is not in jeopardy if, for example, your precision parts are unavailable.

Once you have a plan and a tentative schedule put together, implement it. Get to work! The implementation part of Figure 1.4 goes hand in hand with evaluation. Because the evaluation is done as you work on your project, you know how closely you are following your plan. Are your results meeting your objectives? Are you getting ahead or behind schedule? You should rethink and modify your schedule to reflect changes. If your project is in trouble, have you asked for help?

Your project manager will want to know how well you are keeping to your schedule and whether you need help with any problems. Normally, you would update management

TABLE 1.2 SAMPLE PROGRESS REPORT COVERING THE SECOND WEEK OF THE TEMPERATURE-METER PROJECT

PROGRESS REPORT
Temperature Project—Week 2

Current status:	The analog design has been completed and successfully tested. There have been no delays and I am on schedule.
Work completed:	During the week since the last report, I completed building and testing the analog circuit. I used the temperature sensor and measured the output of its amplifier and plotted a graph of its response. I connected the A/D converter and tested its performance by varying the temperature sensor voltage.
Current work:	During the last day of this week I started work on the interface design and I am now in the middle of connecting it to the microcomputer board.
Future work:	During the third week I plan to finish the connection to the microcomputer board and to write a program to test the A/D. Then I plan to write a more complex program to display the temperature in both centigrade and Fahrenheit.

MINI-PROPOSAL
Temperature Monitor

Project definition:	The goal of this project is to design, build, and test a meter that can be used to measure and record air temperature.
Project objectives:	At the end of four weeks, the temperature monitor will be completely built and tested. It will perform to these specifications: Temperature range −40 to +100°C Accurate to within 1°C Display either Fahrenheit or centigrade temperature Display minimum and maximum temperatures during last 24 hours Calculate and display 24-hour average temperature Calculate and display heating degree days In addition to these performance requirements, the meter will be portable and capable of battery operation. Parts for the prototype will cost less than $150.
Strategy to achieve objectives:	The analog circuitry and temperature sensor will be prototyped on a temporary breadboard until its operation is fully understood. An analog-to-digital converter plus interface circuit will be added to work with a microcomputer system. After the data is being properly read by the computer, a number of display and calculation programs will be written.
Plan of action:	The various tasks needed to implement the strategy are as follows: Get prototype breadboard and power supply Look for articles and designs on temperature measurement Select temperature sensor and A/D Sketch tentative circuit and calculate circuit values Build analog circuit and take measurements Connect analog circuit to the A/D converter Test the circuit completely Design the microcomputer interface logic Connect microcomputer and test interface Write simple program to read temperature Programs and tasks I cannot estimate now The schedule necessary to finish the project in the required four weeks is attached. [Refer to Table 1.1 for schedule]
Reporting:	Weekly progress reports will be made. At the end of the project a complete engineering design and working prototype will be presented.
Budget:	Initial funding of $150 is necessary to purchase the prototype analog parts and the microcomputer.
Evaluation:	Verification of how well the prototype meets the design specifications subject to the constraints will be made weekly and at the end of the project. The final evaluation will be conducted by the design engineer and the customer.

with a monthly progress report. If you are in school, your professor may require several progress reports during the semester. A progress report can take many forms depending on individual preferences, company policy, or customer requirements. In its simplest form, a progress report describes the current status of your project, the work completed, the work in progress, and your plans leading up to the next report. You should attach a copy of your schedule and mark your progress in each task. A sample progress report is shown in Table 1.2.

As you near the end of your project, you should be evaluating how well you are meeting all of your objectives. Review your progress reports and your schedule. Decide what last-minute action is necessary to correct any difficulties. Leave enough time at the end of the schedule to summarize your project and report on your technical accomplishments.

You can easily summarize all the steps of your project plan in the form of the "mini-proposal" shown in the box. It defines your proposed project, what you want to achieve, and how you plan on doing it. This mini-proposal is abbreviated and illustrates only the major topics you should include in a full proposal. If you are a student, you might find this proposal very useful to focus your project and win financial support to build it. If you are a professional engineer, the proposal is necessary to describe a project to a potential customer. Likewise, a proposal is valuable to gain support for possible areas of new-product development.

1.4 SUMMARY

Computer hardware and software can be easily designed and patched together to work. Usually this hobbyist technique seems to get the job done, but the "design" is probably unsuitable for another person to build. You need a systematic way to approach engineering design so that your product meets specifications and manufacturing requirements.

This systematic approach to engineering design requires that you understand whose needs are involved. Will the product meet your need or your customer's need? Engineering design is the creative process of devising a product to fill customer needs; it closes the gap between customer needs and customer satisfaction. You must use problem-solving skills to find the customer's needs and to design the product properly. If you fail to design the product with your customer in mind, it may work perfectly but be completely useless.

The problem-solving approach is applicable to many situations in addition to the case of determining the customer needs. The steps of defining the problem, selecting a possible solution, evaluating the solution, generating another possible solution, and selecting the best one of many possibilities can be used anywhere. The general problem-solving activities of analysis, synthesis, evaluation, decision making, and action constitute the essence of engineering design.

Problem-solving skills are necessary if you are to know what to do, what decision to make, what road to take, what product to build. But how you carry out a decision requires an understanding of how to plan a project. You must define the project clearly and set objectives. You must devise a strategy and plan your action so that you can complete the project in a reasonable time. You summarize all this in the proposal, in which you describe the various design tasks that go into the final product.

EXERCISES

1. An old family friend just graduated from law school and started working at a local law office. The two attorneys at the firm asked your friend to find a way to automate the typing of legal documents. Using their electric typewriter for all letters and drafts had become increasingly unsuitable as their workload increased over the last several years. Knowing your interest in computers, your friend called you yesterday and asked if a computer is worth investigating.
   - **a.** Who is the customer?
   - **b.** What does the customer need for satisfaction?
   - **c.** Define the problem.
   - **d.** What constraints are there?
   - **e.** List three possible solutions to the problem.
   - **f.** Make a selection. How would you justify it to the customer?
   - **g.** Who is responsible if your idea proves disastrous? Who is responsible if your idea is a great success?
2. Rather than move into a new house, you and your family are going to refurbish your present home. The heating system has been in need of constant repair every year and probably should be replaced if you plan on keeping the house. The winter heating season begins in about two months. Make realistic assumptions based on your past experience.
   - **a.** Define the problem and constraints.
   - **b.** List three possible solutions to the problem and the factors you must consider in making a decision.
   - **c.** Which solution would you choose? Why?
   - **d.** List the tasks needed to implement your solution.
3. Make the temperature-monitor mini-proposal into a proposal to create a device to monitor the local 115 VAC line voltage. There have been a number of complaints that the voltage drops down briefly (how briefly?) when the building's heat pump turns on. This drop is alleged to cause a problem with any computers that are running at the time. You want to find the maximum and minimum voltages as well as the time of day they occurred.
4. Your manager at the Wheel Works just walked into your office to tell you about a new product idea from the marketing department. The idea is to install an electronic water-level indicator on the company's 200-gallon standard steel tank. Besides being able to delete the glass-tube level indicator on the side of the tank, an electronic indicator might even be adapted later to turn on an inlet valve automatically when the water level drops during usage.
   - **a.** Define the problem. Make assumptions about the system.
   - **b.** Make a mini-proposal describing a creative solution.

FURTHER READING

ROBERTSHAW, JOSEPH E., STEPHEN J. MECCA, and MARK N. RERICK. *Problem Solving: a Systems Approach*. New York: Petrocelli, 1978. (QA 402.R6.)

RUBINSTEIN, MOSHE F. *Patterns of Problem Solving*. Englewood Cliffs, NJ: Prentice-Hall, 1975.

RUBINSTEIN, MOSHE F., and KENNETH PFEIFFER. *Concepts in Problem Solving*. Englewood Cliffs, NJ: Prentice-Hall, 1980.

WICKELGREN, WAYNE A. *How to Solve Problems*. San Francisco: Freeman, 1974.

TWO

Project Implementation

Bring Ideas to Reality

When you examined engineering design in the last chapter you saw how your needs or your customer's needs could be satisfied. First you used problem-solving techniques to identify needs. Then, after you identified the needs, you prepared a project plan that you developed and summarized in the form of a mini-proposal. This proposal outlined all the necessary work and completion dates for each task.

This chapter shows how to use the proposal to complete the project implementation step shown in Figure 2.1. This step is important because it is a systematic way of finishing the project design within the given time and financial constraints. The approach presented here is just one of many ways to tackle the project implementation, and it may be easily modified to your own particular requirements. The focus is on the method of design rather than on the details of digital circuit design or computer programming.

As indicated in Figure 2.1, the specifications are used in the implementation phase of the engineering design to produce a product meeting your needs or a customer's needs. The project implementation involves two major steps: the technical design and the construction of a prototype. In the technical design step the circuit is created on paper; in the construction phase, the prototype (a working model) is built and tested.

When you look at the temperature monitor mini-project in Chapter 1, you can see the evidence of some technical design work. Although the proposal is an administrative planning document, it contains enough technical effort to establish a set of reasonable specifications and a realistic work schedule. Most of this design was conceptual, and unless you had built something similar in the past, you did not do enough detailed design to be absolutely certain of the results. Consequently, your strategy might be inadequate. However, the mini-proposal does establish some feasible specifications and does provide a useful working document for the full design effort.

Although the mini-proposal is adequate to develop your small project, a typical industrial or government proposal needs a substantial design content. If your company is

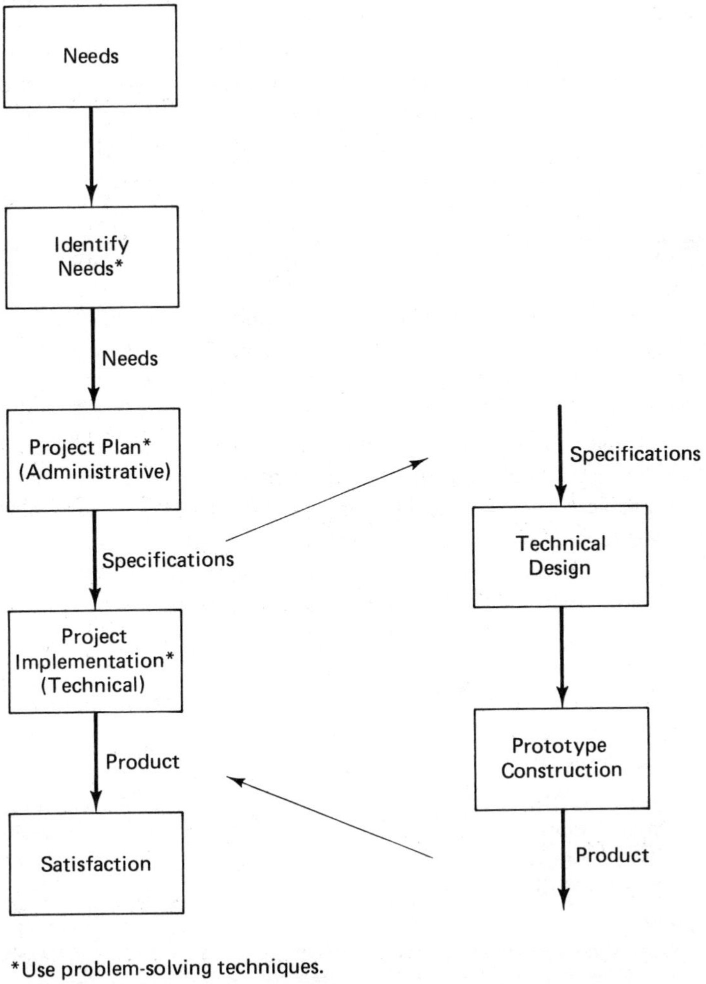

Figure 2.1 Engineering design involves identifying the needs of either you or your customer. Using problem-solving techniques, you can develop a project plan describing the specifications of the needed product. Then, using these specifications, you can implement a project to build the product.

competing for a manufacturing contract, most of the design work, including the completed prototype, will probably be done before the proposal is finalized. You must be certain of your design and be able to estimate closely how much time will be needed to deliver a final product. If your company hopes to make a profit, there is little latitude for errors and radical design changes once the contract has been signed.

For your purposes in learning engineering design, once you have a documented and tested prototype you will consider your engineering complete. However, a prototype that works and meets specifications is by no means a finished job if you are doing the project in industry. If your project is research-oriented, resulting in patents and further research, the prototype is only the beginning. Likewise, if your project is directed toward production, you have much follow-up work to do. For example, your design documentation will be used by drafting personnel to make assembly drawings and schematics. Also, you will be coordinating your project with other electrical, mechanical, production, test, and quality-control engineers so that the final design can be manufactured successfully.

2.1 PROJECT OVERVIEW

The proposal provides an overall plan for the full project implementation. It establishes the project definition, its objectives, and a strategy for meeting those objectives; then it details a plan of action with a schedule for completion. These activities are shown in the left column of Figure 2.2; the corresponding activities in the project implementation are shown in the right column. The planning to set your project's goal and objectives completed the first step of the project implementation. The strategy you developed to solve the design problem was your design concept. The list of tasks and their completion schedule was your technical design combined with prototype construction. On the surface, you might think that these are almost the same. There is a difference: when you carry out the project, you are *doing* the technical design and the prototype construction rather than *talking* about doing it.

Project Plan (Mini-Proposal)		Project Implementation
Project Definition Goal of the project		
Project Objectives Specifications Constraints Assumptions	→	Analysis Specifications Constraints Assumptions
Strategy Idea of how to solve the design problem.	→	Synthesis Generate design concept
Plan of Action List tasks (design, build, test) Schedule tasks	→	Technical Design Do various tasks
		Evaluation and Decision
		Prototype Construction
		Evaluation
		Documentation

Figure 2.2 The project plan leads directly into the project implementation. Both are closely related throughout the project.

Figure 2.3 shows the overall activities involved in the project implementation. Accomplishing each of these requires a number of steps and may appear somewhat confusing at first. The design sequence is one way of simply visualizing the process you use when designing a product. The major design activities and typical tasks are:

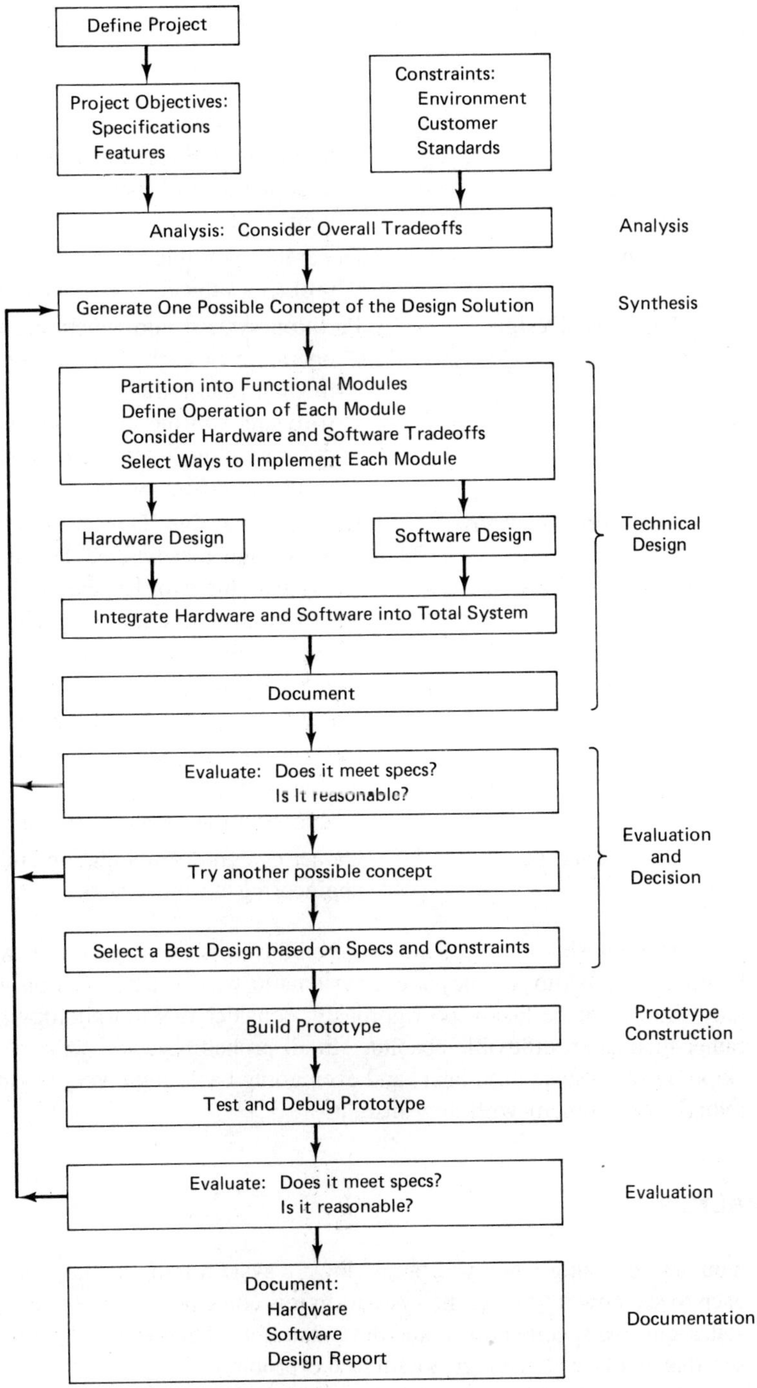

Figure 2.3 Activities involved in implementing a project.

Analysis	Consider the product specifications and features. Allow for constraints related to environment, customer limitations, industry standards. Balance overall tradeoffs between specifications and constraints.
Synthesis	Generate a possible concept of a solution to the design problem subject to the constraints.
Technical Design	Partition system into functional modules and define operation of each. Select ways to implement each module; make tradeoff between hardware and software. Do the circuit design and computer programming, integrate into the system, and document the design so far.
Evaluation/Decision	Review the design. Does it meet the specifications? Is the design reasonable? Try another design and compare the two. Repeat until you can select a best compromise that meets specifications subject to the constraints.
Construction of Prototype	Build a prototype system. Test it and correct any hardware and software errors.
Evaluation	Review the system as built. Does it perform as designed? Does it meet specifications? Is it a reasonable solution to the problem?
Documentation	Gather design documentation and prepare a complete engineering design report.

These design activities are based on the work in the proposal, which by now should be complete. Although they are a systematic way to deal with project implementation, they should not be taken too rigorously: consider this morphology as a guide to design rather than as an inflexible absolute. In all probability, you will do a little of each step, skipping some steps until later, and even going back to the very beginning on occasion to rethink the problem with new insight.

2.2 ANALYSIS

You are analyzing when you break down a system into its component parts and examine each to see how it fits into the system. In this context, you are breaking down the problem statement, the specifications, and the constraints. Then you look closely at each of them to see that it fits well enough to solve the problem.

Begin your design analysis by studying the problem statement as given in the proposal. Investigate the background that led to the problem, and then paraphrase the problem in a sentence or two to ensure that you fully understand it. Review the product features and see if they are consistent with each other and with the specifications. Step back a moment, look at the total situation, and imagine that you have the product already completed as specified. Would it solve the problem? If so, is the solution reasonable? Does it make sense?

The specifications you accept at the start of the project will be your criteria for selecting among the design alternatives. Because the specifications are a statement of your design objectives, they must be as specific as possible so that you know when your design is good enough to start building it. Overengineering a product is perhaps as bad as underengineering: the product never gets built. As you examine the specifications, identify the top-priority requirements and be prepared to consider them first as you solve the design problem.

Resolve any problems with the specifications. Ideally, the specifications should describe the product exactly, but often a product might be overspecified. Trying to meet unnecessary specifications adds extra engineering and complexity to the final product. Similarly, specifications can be ambiguous. Ambiguity results when the writer uses poorly defined or imprecise terms. Specifications can also contradict each other, so that a design solution meeting one requirement would never meet the other.

Review each of the constraints or limits imposed on the product. Are they necessary and realistic, or could some of these limitations be relaxed? Find out how much room you have to work in before you get too involved. For example, if one of your constraints is that the product must be battery-operated and run for 72 hours at full load, find out whether 48 hours would solve the problem. Why? Because the extra battery life might add to the product cost, complexity, and design time. If you know which constraints are flexible, then you can ask for relaxation of certain limitations if necessary.

Some constraints, however, are absolutes. For example, various IEEE standards have been agreed upon concerning certain aspects of electrical design. If you are designing a product that must meet IEEE Std-696, then your design cannot deviate from the limits written in the standard. If your design does not meet the standard on all points, then your product might not work properly with other units in the system. If that happens, then the customer will be inclined to blame any system malfunctions on your product even though your violation might have been inconsequential.

Although standards can at times be an inconvenience, they do make the design job easier because you have a ready-made design outline before you even start. For example, IEEE Std-696 describes the physical and electrical specifications of a circuit board intended for use in a computer system. If you know that your design must conform to this standard, then you immediately know what physical space and what voltages are available for your circuit: the environment for your design will be an enclosure with a maximum of 22 connected devices. As you study the standard and begin to visualize your creation, you can work more easily toward a tentative design solution.

In addition to the explicit constraints, you are working within the implied constraints of a set schedule and limited financial resources. These implied constraints are likely to affect your design decisions substantially. If you had all the time you wanted to complete a design, it would be a masterpiece. If only you had some extra finances, or the customer were willing to pay more, you could do a truly wonderful work of art. Think of the time/money limit as part of the engineering challenge: you would like to design the right product at a reasonable price in time to be useful.

With a set of workable specifications and standards, consider the tradeoffs that you should make between them. When you analyze the specifications, you consider whether each specification is consistent with the next; you consider each of the constraints in a similar manner. You also should investigate an overall tradeoff between specifications and constraints. Consider the battery-life constraint: perhaps you find that the 72-hour life is a "must," but that you can reduce product cost by modifying the specification in another area. The longer battery life might be required, but nothing is said in the specifications about a trickle-charge being used to recharge the batteries constantly before "battery-only" operation. If you can keep the batteries fully charged, then perhaps they can be the same size as the 48-hour-life batteries and still run for 72 hours. You might not be able to make the tradeoff even though the specification is "quiet" about recharging; on the other hand, you might be able to negotiate a specification requiring charging before use. It depends on the application and all the other variables involved.

The analysis of specifications is never complete. After completing all the steps to implement a project, you will find that another iteration of the analysis improves your understanding. Even though you understood the problem, the objectives, and the constraints, another look can add substantially to the success of your work. In design, you never fully know the situation.

2.3 SYNTHESIS

In the synthesis portion of implementing your project, you are seeking to create and define one concept of the problem solution. Your initial strategy in the proposal described one concept that you believed would work, and from there you developed a project plan. After a complete analysis, you might refine that concept to synthesize a better approach.

As you conclude your analysis, you will also have a number of other ideas for solving the problem. Write them all down even though some of them seem extreme or impractical. Sketching each of your ideas helps you to visualize a potential solution to a design problem. Sort through this assortment of design ideas and pick one that you think will best meet the specifications. This idea might very well be the concept that you use for your final product design; however, you may yet discover a better one. At this point, you make your selection expecting to do a technical design and then an evaluation. You might do several designs before final selection, and each time you go through a design you will have better ideas on how to solve the original problem. This iteration helps refine your concepts into better designs.

Using the concept that best fits the specifications, begin by sketching a block diagram of the system. You can do the block diagram easily by asking what the total system does and drawing one big block with an input and an output. Then look inside the block and draw several small blocks that describe how to use the input to create the output. This is a top-down design approach similar to the software concept of writing a program by starting with the top level module followed by writing its support modules. Consider the temperature monitor from the last chapter where you saw a mini-proposal containing specifications and a plan for design. For the monitor, draw one big box with temperature as an input and display as an output. Then, to obtain the smaller blocks inside, look at the mini-proposal strategy. The strategy (concept) includes a sensor, an analog-to-digital (A/D) converter, an interface, and a microcomputer. You can draw the block diagram of this system as shown in Figure 2.4 to express your strategy for solving the measurement problem.

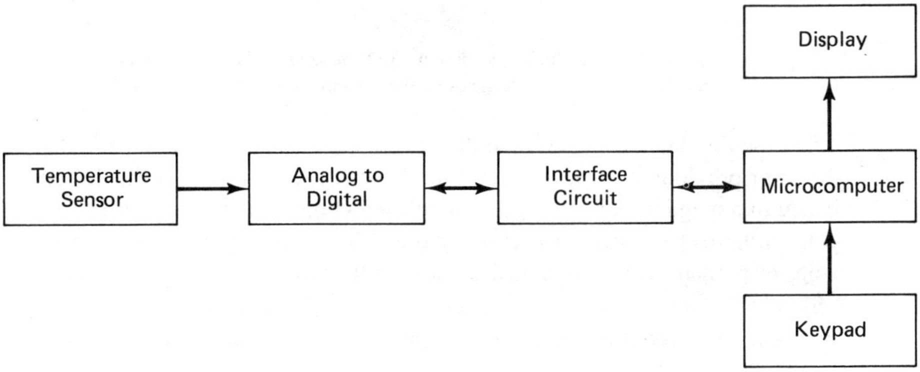

Figure 2.4 Block diagram of the temperature-measurement system. This is a result of partitioning into functional modules.

2.4 TECHNICAL DESIGN

The technical design phase begins with the block diagram of the desired system and finishes with the hardware and software description of the product. The design is on paper in sufficient detail to fully predict how well the product will meet the specifications. For this reason, all your circuit designs and computer programs must be well-documented.

As you draw each of the blocks in the system, you are in effect partitioning the system into functional modules. Each module has a purpose, and you should define each according to its operation, inputs, and outputs. For example, the purpose of the A/D block is to convert an analog voltage to an equivalent digital value. To operate properly, it must be told when to do a conversion, and it must be able to notify the computer when it finishes.

When you partition the system into modules, you actually imply a tradeoff between hardware and software. According to the product concept, the temperature monitor will acquire data and pass it without modification to the computer. If any corrections must be made to compensate for nonlinearities in a thermocouple, for example, the solution must implement them in software. Another concept for solving the measurement problem might have done the compensation in hardware before the A/D converter. Consider the various tradeoffs as you review the design.

The next step in the design is selecting a way to implement each module. Draw a block diagram for each of them to the same level of detail as shown in Figure 2.5 for the

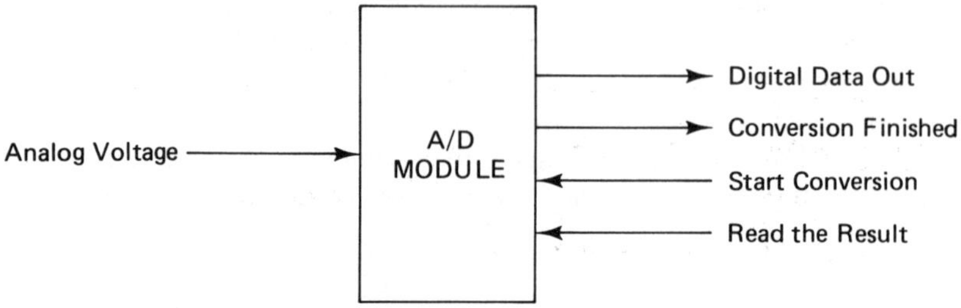

Figure 2.5 The analog-to-digital (A/D) module. This sketch expresses more detail than the overall block diagram of the system shown in Figure 2.4.

A/D module. Then for each module, see if you did a similar design in the past. Can you use your previous work in your current design? Likewise, see if the design has been published in a magazine, book, or manufacturer's application note. For example, how would you implement the A/D converter module? You could build it using transistors and op-amps or perhaps use a single LSI device for the whole A/D function. Suppose you find an LSI chip that meets your accuracy and response-time requirements. In this case you might sketch a rough circuit design like Figure 2.6 to use for the A/D module.

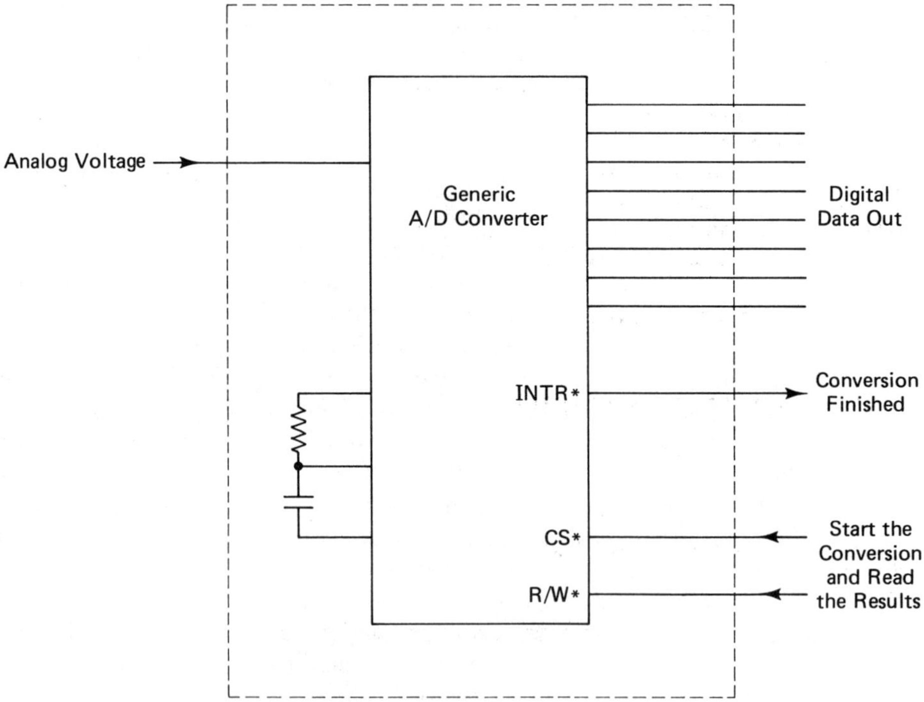

Figure 2.6 An LSI implementation of the A/D Module. This is a rough circuit that needs additional design effort to be operational.

Once you have all the modules roughly sketched, then you can design the detailed circuit. The hardware design at this point is completed to the final circuit with all the components and their interconnections shown in detail. Actual parts should be selected and fully documented. The design should be in accordance with any design rules that have been set for the project. The software design is also done in like detail from the top-level functions down to flow charts and code if possible.

As you design the hardware and software, watch that they parallel one another in their development. Although shown in Figure 2.3 as separate activities, hardware and software design are done concurrently if possible. This is because they must work together when both are integrated into the final system.

Documentation is vital to the success of the hardware and software design. Throughout the analysis, synthesis, and technical design stages of your project implementation you should be maintaining a laboratory notebook. The lab book serves as a permanent reference document of your ideas, plans, and designs as you work through the project. As you make design decisions, you should record the rationale for each decision in the lab book. Also, include in the lab book all the information to make design decisions and to formalize a final design.

2.5 EVALUATION AND DECISION

The evaluation following the technical design stage is intended to see if the hardware and software will perform together as a system and meet the specifications. The evaluation should also reveal what the expected performance should be if the system were actually built.

Suppose you have recently finished a complete paper design of the temperature monitor using the functional modules illustrated in Figure 2.4. You would like to know if your design will meet or exceed the required specifications given in the mini-proposal at the end of Chapter 1. Consider, for example, the requirement for accuracy to within 1° C. To find out how well you meet this accuracy specification, you get the worst-case performance data on the temperature sensor and A/D converter from the manufacturer's data sheets. Also, ask yourself where other errors could come into the system, estimate their size, and add the errors. Your answer will not be exact, but it will be useful. Did it come out to an overall accuracy of 1° or several degrees? If it came out too high, you know you have more design work ahead to improve accuracy.

For each of the product specifications, you might want to make a small chart like Figure 2.7 to help you compare the performance of each design. Include cost, development time, and other possible requirements in addition to the specifications. After you have done one or two designs, you will sense what to expect for a final product and whether or not the original requirements were reasonable for the price. You might find that no design can be completed within your budget in the time available. What do you do then? Perhaps you need to rethink your approach entirely: delete the microcomputer and implement the logic with LSI components. Perhaps you need another meeting with your

	Design 1	Design 2
Specification		
Range −40° to +100°C	−40° to +90°C	−40° to +100°C
Accuracy within 1°C	2°	1°
Display Fahrenheit and centigrade	F only	Both OK
Min/Max temperature reading	yes	yes
Average temperature	yes	yes
Heating degree-days	no	yes
Portable	yes	yes
Cost	$60	$200
Time to develop final prototype	3 weeks	6 weeks
Special test equipment required?	no	logic analyzer

Figure 2.7 A simple chart with the mini-project specifications showing how one design compares with another.

customer to review what you can deliver versus the specification that is required; there may be room for negotiation.

The evaluation process goes on continually as you perform the technical design and documentation. As you begin your design, you might find that a particular technical approach cannot meet the specifications. Rather than waste time carrying the design further, estimate its performance, put it in the comparison table, and work up another possible solution to the design problem. Doing this speeds up your technical design substantially, and you have a more diverse selection of alternatives for comparison.

After you complete several designs, your comparison chart will help you decide which design to build as a prototype. The specifications are your decision criteria. Given two designs that meet the specifications equally, you then consider minimum cost, maximum features, maintainability, reliability, and other values important to you or your customer. The actual selection you make, however, should meet the required specifications.

2.6 PROTOTYPE CONSTRUCTION

The purpose of building a prototype is to demonstrate that your paper design is correct and to uncover any oversights that might hinder the product's performance. You can easily use your completed prototype in a number of different experiments to adjust the design and verify its performance.

When you build your prototype, build it module by module. This holds whether you use wire-wrap, a prototype board, or solder for your actual construction. Hardware can be constructed and tested one module at a time just as you might write a computer program one module at a time. The reasoning is this: if you build one small module, apply power, and test it fully for proper operation, then you can use it as part of a larger subsequent module. If any problems develop with the larger module, then you know the difficulty is probably in the circuit you just added. This modular approach to building and testing hardware is far easier than wiring the entire circuit and then trying to diagnose an elusive malfunction in the system.

After you have an operational prototype, test it fully over all the ranges of the specifications. Find and fix any problems that occur as you test the unit. Keep accurate notes in your lab book; it is especially important when you are testing and debugging the prototype. Be able to explain why the unit behaves as it does. Does it perform the way you designed it?

2.7 EVALUATION AND DOCUMENTATION

The evaluation following construction of the prototype is intended to demonstrate that the hardware and software do in fact work together properly and meet the specifications. Unlike the evaluation you did on the prototype, this more formal evaluation will probably involve other persons from different departments in your company. In addition, depending on the product and the arrangements, the customer might receive a copy of the test results.

The results of the prototype testing should prove the merit of your design concept and its implementation. If something was overlooked or a specification changed late in the design cycle, then you might have to redesign even now. Figure 2.3 shows the evaluation going back to start with another concept, but in reality you go back only as far as necessary to correct the problem.

While the prototype is being tested, you should be finishing your final design documentation on the project. Review your lab book and outline your technical design report. Plan on covering the design concept, the reasons for your technical choices, the hardware and software design, the prototype construction, and the operation of the prototype. Besides treating the design details, you should also include a description of how to test the unit and what results should be expected. Later, when your design goes into production, either you or a test engineer will need this test information to write the test plan for the manufactured units.

2.8 SUMMARY

Chapter 2 shows how to finish the project systematically by following a number of engineering design steps in sequence. First, identify needs by using problem-solving techniques, and then prepare a project plan. You can summarize the plan in the form of the mini-proposal. The proposal outlines each task and its completion date and can be used to guide the project implementation. Using the specifications and design concept in the proposal, you can complete the project within the given time and financial constraints.

The activities of analysis, synthesis, technical design, evaluation/design, prototype construction, and evaluation/documentation are presented as a flowchart in Figure 2.3. The sequence is one way of approaching the project implementation and may be easily modified to suit your own needs. View the various activities as guides to aid your design rather than as restraints. You will probably begin each step and then on occasion return to the start to rethink with a new understanding of your project.

When you analyze, you are breaking down the problem statement, the specifications, and the constraints to see how well they fit together to solve the problem. Because your planned design must meet the specifications, resolve any problems with them such as ambiguity, contradiction, and overspecificity; resolve any similar problems with the stated constraints as well. If you are designing to conform to a particular industry standard, be sure that your specifications are consistent with its requirements.

In the synthesis portion of the project implementation, you are attempting to create and define one concept of the problem solution. After considering a number of ideas, pick one concept that appears likely to fulfill your specifications the best. Then sketch a block diagram that expresses this concept.

You use this block diagram in the technical design phase to complete a paper design of your project. Each block in the diagram is a functional module; you can describe each according to its operation, inputs, and outputs. Select how you can implement each module in hardware and software, and then design the circuit and program in detail.

The evaluation following the technical design is intended to see if the hardware and software will perform together as a system that meets the specifications. Make a comparison chart to establish which of your design alternatives is most satisfactory. When you have several possibilities, use the specifications as your criteria to decide which design to build as a prototype.

The purpose of building the prototype is to demonstrate that your paper design is correct and to uncover any oversights that might adversely affect the product's performance. Construct the prototype module by module so that you can test each section as you build it. When you have all the modules interconnected, fully test and debug your finished prototype.

The final evaluation after you debug the prototype is intended to demonstrate that the hardware and software work together as a system and that they meet specifications. The documentation should result in a technical design report during this phase of the project. This report should cover design concept, reasons for your choices, and the design, construction, and operation of the prototype.

EXERCISES

1. During the heating season, fuel-oil distributors make customer deliveries based on how cold the weather has been rather than filling tanks on a weekly or biweekly basis. Needless frequent deliveries increase costs, so it is desirable to wait until the customer tank is nearly empty before filling it. Ideally, a typical 275-gallon tank should be refilled when it gets to within 20 to 50 gallons of being empty.

   Hot-Spot Oil company presently estimates a "k-factor" for each customer to help decide when to deliver oil. The k-factor is an empirical number of degree-days of heating the customer gets from each gallon of oil. Heating degree-days equal 65 minus the average temperature during 24 hours; for example, if the average temperature yesterday was 20°, then 45 degree-days of heating were required. Suppose Hot-Spot estimated Jack Smith's house at $k = 5$ degree-days per gallon: the 45 degree-days of heat required yesterday used 45/5, or 9 gallons of oil.

   If Hot-Spot Oil can keep data on daily heating degree-days, then they can estimate how much oil Jack Smith is using, If Jack has a 275-gallon tank, then that means he can heat for a maximum of 275 times 5, or 1375 degree-days. If each day averages 20°, then Jack will run out of oil in about 30 days (1375/45 = 30+). To be on the safe side, Hot-Spot will probably deliver about 5 days before they estimate Jack will run out of oil. This is equivalent to about 1100 degree-days accumulated since the last delivery.

Hot-Spot Oil came to you recently, and you both worked out some specifications for a way to calculate yesterday's number of degree-days each morning when they come to work. For Jack and their other customers, they can total the degree-days and figure out when to make deliveries. The specifications you worked out are: measure temperature from −40 to +70°F, calculate the average temperature from 8 A.M. to 8 A.M., calculate the number of degree-days, and display the result for them to write down.

a. Define the problem.

b. List the specifications above and add three more specifications you might want to include for a better definition of the job.

c. List three constraints.

d. List three possible ways to solve the problem.

e. Do a rough sketch of each way you listed.

f. Select the best approach and do a block diagram of the system.

g. Using your block diagram, partition the system by function.

h. Do a detailed block diagram of each module.

i. Do the circuit design for at least one module.

j. Describe how you would build your prototype.

k. Describe an alternative way to construct the prototype.

2. Make up a problem and specify a product that you can design. Do a rough mini-proposal and then all the implementation steps from problem definition through prototype description (steps a–k in Problem 1). Polish the mini-proposal after completing these steps. Your deliverable to the customer is a completed mini-proposal.

Pick an interesting topic from either your own background or the following list of ideas:

Computer-controlled speech synthesizer
Programmable music organ
Waveform generator
ASCII display of serial or parallel data
Joystick or mouse for computer cursor control
Printer buffer
Clock with alarm
Data modem
Morse code generator
Programmable power supply

FURTHER READING

ARTWICK, BRUCE A. *Microcomputer Interfacing*. Englewood Cliffs, NJ: Prentice-Hall, 1980. (TK 7888.3.A86)

ASIMOW, MORRIS. *Introduction to Design*. Englewood Cliffs, NJ: Prentice-Hall, 1962. (TA 175.A83)

CAIN, WILLIAM D. *Engineering Product Design*. London: Business Books Limited, 1969. (TA 174.C3)

COMER, DAVID J. *Digital Logic and State Machine Design*. New York: Holt, Rinehart and Winston, 1984. (TK 7868.59C66)

DAVIS, THOMAS W. *Experimentation with Microprocessor Applications*. Reston VA: Reston Publishing, 1981.

FLETCHER, WILLIAM I. *An Engineering Approach to Digital Design*. Englewood Cliffs, NJ: Prentice-Hall, 1980. (TK 7868.D5F5)

GREGORY, S. A. *Creativity and Innovation in Engineering*. London: Butterworth, 1972. (TA 174.C7X)

HARMAN, THOMAS L., and BARBARA LAWSON. *The Motorola MC68000 Microprocessor Family: Assembly Language, Interface Design, and System Design*. Englewood Cliffs, NJ: Prentice-Hall, 1985. (QA 76.8.M6895H37)

HAYES, JOHN P. *Digital System Design and Microprocessors*. New York: McGraw-Hill, 1984. (TK 7874.H393)

KLINE, RAYMOND M. *Structured Digital Design*. Englewood Cliffs, NJ: Prentice-Hall, 1983.

ROBERTSHAW, JOSEPH E., STEPHEN J. MECCA, and MARK N. RERICK. *Problem Solving: a Systems Approach*. New York: Petrocelli, 1978. (QA 402.R6)

SHORT, KENNETH L. *Microprocessors and Programmed Logic*. Englewood Cliffs, NJ: Prentice-Hall, 1981. (QA76.5.S496)

WINKEL, DAVID, and FRANKLIN PROSSER. *The Art of Digital Design*. Englewood Cliffs, NJ: Prentice-Hall, 1980. (TK 7888.3W56)

THREE

Design Rules and Heuristics

Guidelines and Common Sense

In the first chapter, after you identified needs, you prepared a project plan that you summarized in the form of a mini-proposal. This proposal outlined all the necessary work and completion dates for each task. Then, in the second chapter, you used the proposal to do the project implementation by starting with the specifications in the proposal. First you completed a technical design on paper, and then you built a working prototype; as you did this implementation, you were following the general activities shown in Figure 2.3.

This chapter provides guidelines for doing the technical design on paper before actually building the prototype. These guidelines or design rules are the conventions established to do an orderly design that is not only technically sound but also consistent with the designs of team members working on the same project. In addition to providing technical guidelines, this chapter presents a number of heuristics, or rules of thumb, that may be applied to the design process. These heuristics serve to moderate the technical paper design with a measure of common-sense reality.

The technical design you did in Chapter 2 involved using a block diagram of one particular concept. Before building a prototype, you expected to go through a design of several different concepts, and you hoped that one of them would meet the specifications subject to the constraints. When you did the technical design using your block diagram, you probably did it rather haphazardly and did not concern yourself with following any particular rules: if the numbers worked together, then you were happy enough to finish.

When you follow design rules, however, your work goes easier and is more orderly. For these rules to make sense though, some additional detail beyond the original ideas in Figure 2.3 might be helpful. Figure 3.1 shows how the technical design can be expanded and used to go from a block diagram to a complete paper design. Starting with the concept, you can partition your system into functional modules and describe the purpose and function of each module. At the same time, you can decide on how to split the various functions between hardware and software. Then, for each hardware and software module,

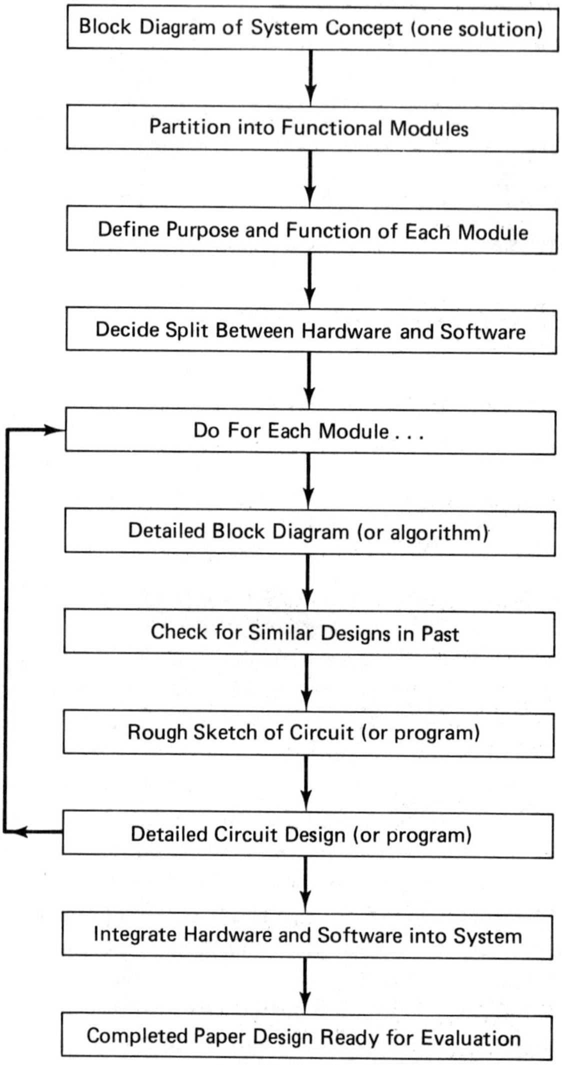

Figure 3.1 An expanded form of the technical design first presented in Figure 2.3

you can draw a block diagram or write an algorithm and do a detailed circuit design or working program. The design rules in this chapter typically apply when you do the detailed circuit design or the program.

Heuristics, on the other hand, apply anywhere in design engineering from the original problem-solving steps through to the detailed circuit design. Heuristics are techniques or rules of thumb that help solve a problem, but are not themselves technically justifiable. They are a blend of past experience, logic, common sense, and nonsense that gives the engineer some direction in solving the problem at hand.

3.1 TECHNICAL DESIGN RULES

After you have a block diagram of your intended circuit, you will probably want to quickly check some of your previous work for similar designs. Many times you can locate a useful circuit in your own notes, in a magazine, or in a text and save some time for extra effort on the more unique parts of your design job. This is not to say, however, that you can simply select a handy circuit and put it in your system without analysis; even if the circuit appears to fit exactly, you should always verify that it does indeed meet your specifications.

Based on your understanding of the circuit requirements, draw a rough sketch of the circuit. At this point, the idea is not necessarily to have a working circuit. You want to get an idea of the ICs involved and how they all fit together in the module. Pinpoint areas you think are difficult or might cause problems later in your design.

Finally, using the rough sketch as a guide, do a detailed circuit design. As you work on the design, you might be unsure how a particular device works; find out—take it to the lab with the data book and try it out. While you do the design work, review the following design rules as a guide. The rules will help you transform the rough circuit sketch into a technically sound design. In addition, if you are working with other designers on a large project, the design rules will help maintain consistency so that the various systems modules will work together.

3.1.1 Hardware Design Rules

Most of the digital logic devices you will use in your design work will be either TTL or CMOS family components. There are a number of advantages and disadvantages associated with each family, and the decision to use one, the other, or a combination of both depends on a number of factors. Generally, if you want speed, then you select TTL; if you want noise-immunity and low-power battery operation, then you select CMOS.

Both TTL and CMOS families simplify the digital design process considerably by allowing the connection of the digital circuit in building-block fashion; that is, a particular logical function can be quickly designed by simply interconnecting the appropriate logic gates to each other. Gates in the same family can be freely connected without concern about how the gates work internally; when using LSI devices, this freedom saves considerable design time.

When gates in the same family are connected, one concern is that proper logic signal levels must be maintained as additional gates are interconnected. Within the TTL family, for example, a logic LOW may be between 0 and 0.8 V and a logic HIGH may be between 2.0 and 5 V. The addition of more and more gates to the output of a single device will tend to cause the LOW to go up and the HIGH to come down. Thus, if the circuit is overloaded, the LOW and HIGH might become 1 V and 1.9 V, respectively; these levels might not be recognized properly as LOW and HIGH later in the system and cause malfunctions.

When gates from different logic families are connected, maintaining the proper signal levels is even more critical. Within the CMOS family, if the devices are connected to a

5-V supply, a logic LOW may be between 0 and 1.5 V, and a logic HIGH may be between 3.5 and 5 V. You can see that the CMOS logic LOW does not match with TTL: if the CMOS device outputs 1.5 V as a LOW, there is a strong likelihood that a TTL input will misinterpret it as a logic HIGH. Usually the TTL and CMOS parts can be interfaced easily, but you must pay close attention to design for the proper signal levels. While TTL devices can easily drive CMOS, the typical CMOS gate does not have the drive capability to connect directly to TTL.

In the context of your design work in this book, TTL parts will be used almost exclusively. Consequently, most of the design rules are related to design in the one family, and very little attention is given to interfacing or using CMOS. If you have a design requirement for CMOS, gather component data and design following the same general principles as you would using TTL.

Timing is another important issue in hardware design. It takes a finite length of time for signals in a digital system to get to their destination, and special care must be taken to consider all aspects of signal propagation. Problems with clock skew, setup times, and hold times should be resolved before the circuit design is finalized.

Synchronous sequential circuits should be used in your system design. Using clocked sequential circuits helps make your design considerably easier because you can draw timing diagrams and relate the state transitions to clock pulses. These timing diagrams can be used in troubleshooting your circuit as well as in design. In general, noise is always a problem, but with a synchronous device, noise present at the input is ignored unless it comes at just the instant the clock pulse arrives.

In contrast, asynchronous sequential circuits operate without a clock: input signals ripple through the system, set and reset flip-flops, and produce an output at some unpredictable future time depending on the system propagation delays. Also, because signals can happen any time in the asynchronous circuit, it is prone to being upset by noise in the system. For example, a noise burst between clock pulses in a synchronous system would be ignored, but in the asynchronous system the noise could cause a number of flip-flops to change state and cause a system malfunction.

Use worst-case specifications for your components when you do hardware design. For example, when you estimate the power requirements for your circuit, add up all the worst-case specified values to obtain an upper bound on your power needs. When you do your timing diagrams, the worst-case propagation delays in your analysis to help estimate circuit speed.

Signal levels and loading. When you examine the data sheets for TTL parts, you find that there are two different logic device outputs available: totem-pole and open-collector. The difference is that the open-collector device does not have an internal pull-up resistor. Compare the outputs of the circuits shown in Figure 3.2. Most of your digital circuits can be done entirely with totem-pole devices; however, if you need to connect the outputs of several devices (as to a bus or in a wired-OR), then you use an open-collector device. Both of these TTL devices have the same input characteristics and both should be treated as logical equivalents when you do a logic diagram.

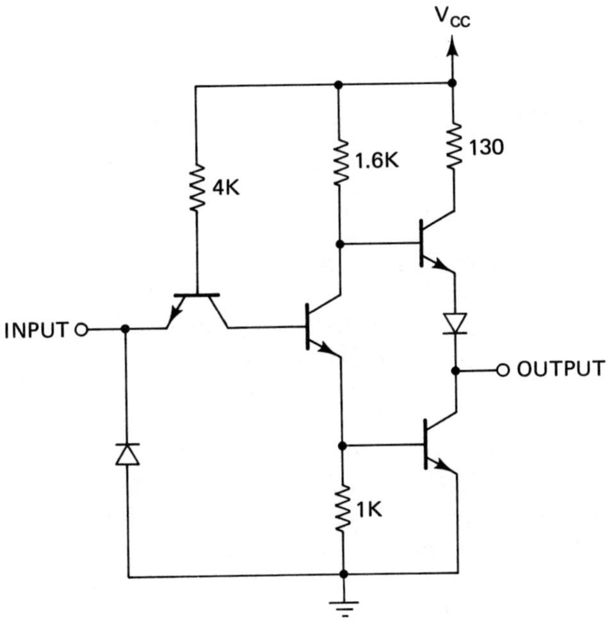

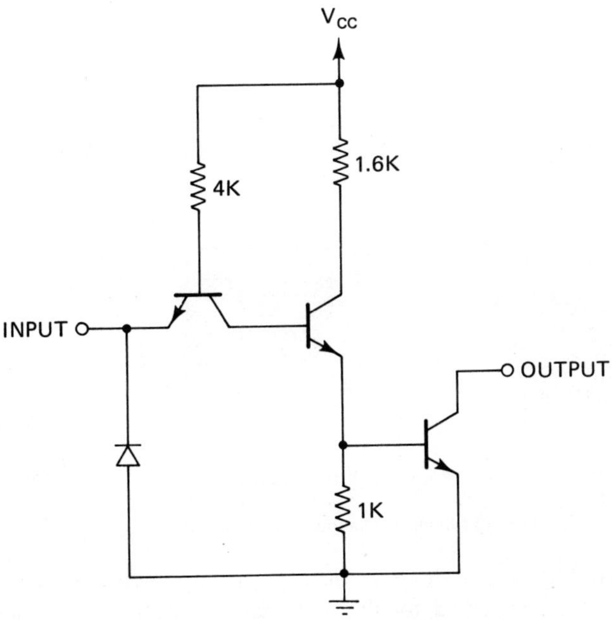

Figure 3.2 Circuits of typical TLL Devices. (a) 7404 totem-pole output, (b) 7405 open-collector output. (Courtesy Texas Instruments, Inc.)

The voltages corresponding to the logic LOW and HIGH are given by the TTL specifications for V_{IL}, V_{IH}, V_{OL}, V_{OH}. These voltages are typically given by

V_{IL} = 0.8 V = the maximum input voltage that will be interpreted as a logic LOW.

V_{IH} = 2.0 V = the minimum input voltage that will be interpreted as a logic HIGH.

V_{OL} = 0.4 V = the maximum logic LOW output voltage.

V_{OH} = 2.4 V = the minimum logic HIGH output voltage.

Visualize a single 7404 inverter gate. Any input voltage from 0 to V_{IL} (0.8 V) will be interpreted as a logic LOW and cause a logic HIGH output; this logic HIGH output can be anything from 5 V down to V_{OH} (2.4 V). Similarly, any input voltage from V_{IH} (2.0 V) up to 5 V will be interpreted as a logic HIGH and cause a logic LOW output; this logic LOW output can range from 0 to a maximum of V_{OL} (0.4 V). The typical output voltages will probably be above 3.4 V for a HIGH and less than 0.2 V for a LOW.

These voltages are illustrated in Figure 3.3. Notice that an input voltage between 0.8 and 2.0 V is not defined; any input voltage in this range will cause an unpredictable output. If the input voltage is below V_{IL} or above V_{IH}, then the device is guaranteed to interpret the input correctly as a LOW or HIGH, respectively. Likewise, an output logic LOW will be below 0.4 V and an output logic HIGH will be above 2.4 V. Any output voltage between 0.4 and 2.4 V is guaranteed not to occur unless the device is overloaded.

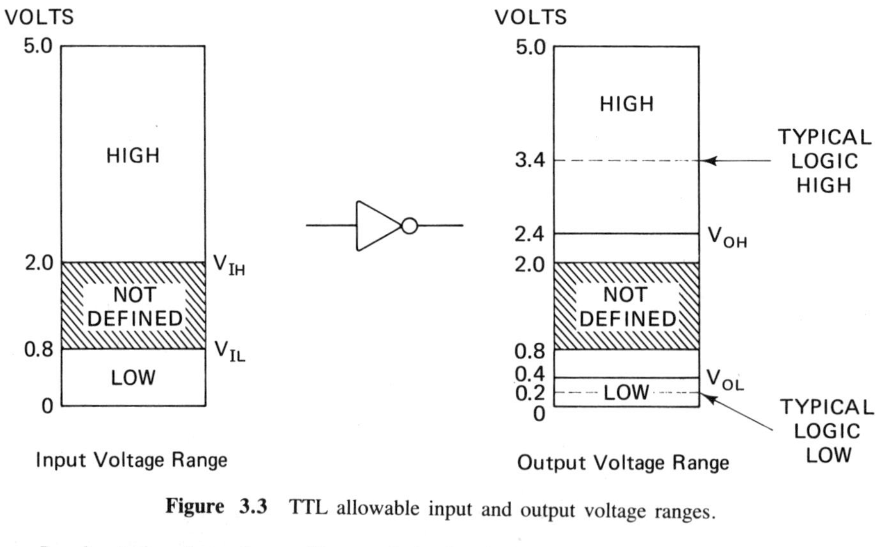

Figure 3.3 TTL allowable input and output voltage ranges.

Look at the data sheet, Figure 3.4, for information on the positive NANDs and inverters. Notice that currents are specified for the inputs and outputs of the gates:

I_{IL} = current flowing out of an input when LOW (V_{IL}) applied.

I_{IH} = current flowing into an input when HIGH (V_{IH}) applied.

recommended operating conditions

		SN5400			SN7400			UNIT
		MIN	NOM	MAX	MIN	NOM	MAX	
V_{CC}	Supply voltage	4.5	5	5.5	4.75	5	5.25	V
V_{IH}	High-level input voltage	2			2			V
V_{IL}	Low-level input voltage			0.8			0.8	V
I_{OH}	High-level output current			– 0.4			– 0.4	mA
I_{OL}	Low-level output current			16			16	mA
T_A	Operating free-air temperature	– 55		125	0		70	°C

electrical characteristics over recommended operating free-air temperature range (unless otherwise noted)

PARAMETER	TEST CONDITIONS†	SN5400			SN7400			UNIT
		MIN	TYP‡	MAX	MIN	TYP‡	MAX	
V_{IK}	V_{CC} = MIN, I_I = – 12 mA			– 1.5			– 1.5	V
V_{OH}	V_{CC} = MIN, V_{IL} = 0.8 V, I_{OH} = – 0.4 mA	2.4	3.4		2.4	3.4		V
V_{OL}	V_{CC} = MIN, V_{IH} = 2 V, I_{OL} = 16 mA		0.2	0.4		0.2	0.4	V
I_I	V_{CC} = MAX, V_I = 5.5 V			1			1	mA
I_{IH}	V_{CC} = MAX, V_I = 2.4 V			40			40	μA
I_{IL}	V_{CC} = MAX, V_I = 0.4 V			– 1.6			– 1.6	mA
I_{OS}§	V_{CC} = MAX	– 20		– 55	– 18		– 55	mA
I_{CCH}	V_{CC} = MAX, V_I = 0 V		4	8		4	8	mA
I_{CCL}	V_{CC} = MAX, V_I = 4.5 V		12	22		12	22	mA

† For conditions shown as MIN or MAX, use the appropriate value specified under recommended operating conditions.
‡ All typical values are at V_{CC} = 5 V, T_A = 25°C.
§ Not more than one output should be shorted at a time.

switching characteristics, V_{CC} = 5 V, T_A = 25°C (see note 2)

PARAMETER	FROM (INPUT)	TO (OUTPUT)	TEST CONDITIONS	MIN	TYP	MAX	UNIT
t_{PLH}	A or B	Y	R_L = 400 Ω, C_L = 15 pF		11	22	ns
t_{PHL}					7	15	ns

NOTE 2: See General Information Section for load circuits and voltage waveforms.

TEXAS INSTRUMENTS
POST OFFICE BOX 225012 • DALLAS, TEXAS 75265

Figure 3.4 (Courtesy Texas Instruments, Inc.)

recommended operating conditions

		SN54LS00			SN74LS00			UNIT
		MIN	NOM	MAX	MIN	NOM	MAX	
V_{CC}	Supply voltage	4.5	5	5.5	4.75	5	5.25	V
V_{IH}	High-level input voltage	2			2			V
V_{IL}	Low-level input voltage			0.7			0.8	V
I_{OH}	High-level output current			− 0.4			− 0.4	mA
I_{OL}	Low-level output current			4			8	mA
T_A	Operating free-air temperature	− 55		125	0		70	°C

electrical characteristics over recommended operating free-air temperature range (unless otherwise noted)

PARAMETER	TEST CONDITIONS †			SN54LS00			SN74LS00			UNIT
				MIN	TYP‡	MAX	MIN	TYP‡	MAX	
V_{IK}	V_{CC} = MIN,	I_I = − 18 mA				− 1.5			− 1.5	V
V_{OH}	V_{CC} = MIN,	V_{IL} = MAX,	I_{OH} = − 0.4 mA	2.5	3.4		2.7	3.4		V
V_{OL}	V_{CC} = MIN,	V_{IH} = 2 V,	I_{OL} = 4 mA		0.25	0.4		0.25	0.4	V
	V_{CC} = MIN,	V_{IH} = 2 V,	I_{OL} = 8 mA					0.35	0.5	
I_I	V_{CC} = MAX,	V_I = 7 V				0.1			0.1	mA
I_{IH}	V_{CC} = MAX,	V_I = 2.7 V				20			20	μA
I_{IL}	V_{CC} = MAX,	V_I = 0.4 V				− 0.4			− 0.4	mA
I_{OS}§	V_{CC} = MAX			− 20		− 100	− 20		− 100	mA
I_{CCH}	V_{CC} = MAX,	V_I = 0 V			0.8	1.6		0.8	1.6	mA
I_{CCL}	V_{CC} = MAX,	V_I = 4.5 V			2.4	4.4		2.4	4.4	mA

† For conditions shown as MIN or MAX, use the appropriate value specified under recommended operating conditions.
‡ All typical values are at V_{CC} = 5 V, T_A = 25°C
§ Not more than one output should be shorted at a time, and the duration of the short-circuit should not exceed one second.

switching characteristics, V_{CC} = 5 V, T_A = 25°C (see note 2)

PARAMETER	FROM (INPUT)	TO (OUTPUT)	TEST CONDITIONS		MIN	TYP	MAX	UNIT
t_{PLH}	A or B	Y	R_L = 2 kΩ,	C_L = 15 pF		9	15	ns
t_{PHL}						10	15	ns

NOTE 2: See General Information Section for load circuits and voltage waveforms.

TEXAS INSTRUMENTS
POST OFFICE BOX 225012 • DALLAS, TEXAS 75265

Figure 3.4 (continued) (Courtesy Texas Instruments, Inc.)

recommended operating conditions

		SN5404			SN7404			UNIT
		MIN	NOM	MAX	MIN	NOM	MAX	
V_{CC}	Supply voltage	4.5	5	5.5	4.75	5	5.25	V
V_{IH}	High-level input voltage	2			2			V
V_{IL}	Low-level input voltage			0.8			0.8	V
I_{OH}	High-level output current			– 0.4			– 0.4	mA
I_{OL}	Low-level output current			16			16	mA
T_A	Operating free-air temperature	– 55		125	0		70	°C

electrical characteristics over recommended operating free-air temperature range (unless otherwise noted)

PARAMETER	TEST CONDITIONS†	SN5404			SN7404			UNIT
		MIN	TYP‡	MAX	MIN	TYP‡	MAX	
V_{IK}	V_{CC} = MIN, I_I = – 12 mA			– 1.5			– 1.5	V
V_{OH}	V_{CC} = MIN, V_{IL} = 0.8 V, I_{OH} = – 0.4 mA	2.4	3.4		2.4	3.4		V
V_{OL}	V_{CC} = MIN, V_{IH} = 2 V, I_{OL} = 16 mA		0.2	0.4		0.2	0.4	V
I_I	V_{CC} = MAX, V_I = 5.5 V			1			1	mA
I_{IH}	V_{CC} = MAX, V_I = 2.4 V			40			40	μA
I_{IL}	V_{CC} = MAX, V_I = 0.4 V			– 1.6			– 1.6	mA
I_{OS} §	V_{CC} = MAX	– 20		– 55	– 18		– 55	mA
I_{CCH}	V_{CC} = MAX, V_I = 0 V		6	12		6	12	mA
I_{CCL}	V_{CC} = MAX, V_I = 4.5 V		18	33		18	33	mA

† For conditions shown as MIN or MAX, use the appropriate value specified under recommended operating conditions.
‡ All typical values are at V_{CC} = 5 V, T_A = 25°C.
§ Not more than one output should be shorted at a time.

switching characteristics, V_{CC} = 5 V, T_A = 25°C (see note 2)

PARAMETER	FROM (INPUT)	TO (OUTPUT)	TEST CONDITIONS	MIN	TYP	MAX	UNIT
t_{PLH}	A	Y	R_L = 400 Ω, C_L = 15 pF		12	22	ns
t_{PHL}					8	15	ns

NOTE 2: See General Information Section for load circuits and voltage waveforms.

Figure 3.4 (continued) (Courtesy Texas Instruments, Inc.)

recommended operating conditions

		SN54LS04			SN74LS04			UNIT
		MIN	NOM	MAX	MIN	NOM	MAX	
V_{CC}	Supply voltage	4.5	5	5.5	4.75	5	5.25	V
V_{IH}	High-level input voltage	2			2			V
V_{IL}	Low-level input voltage			0.7			0.8	V
I_{OH}	High-level output current			− 0.4			− 0.4	mA
I_{OL}	Low-level output current			4			8	mA
T_A	Operating free-air temperature	− 55		125	0		70	°C

electrical characteristics over recommended operating free-air temperature range (unless otherwise noted)

PARAMETER	TEST CONDITIONS †	SN54LS04			SN74LS04			UNIT
		MIN	TYP ‡	MAX	MIN	TYP ‡	MAX	
V_{IK}	V_{CC} = MIN, I_I = − 18 mA			− 1.5			− 1.5	V
V_{OH}	V_{CC} = MIN, V_{IL} = MAX, I_{OH} = − 0.4 mA	2.5	3.4		2.7	3.4		V
V_{OL}	V_{CC} = MIN, V_{IH} = 2 V, I_{OL} = 4 mA		0.25	0.4			0.4	V
	V_{CC} = MIN, V_{IH} = 2 V, I_{OL} = 8 mA					0.25	0.5	
I_I	V_{CC} = MAX, V_I = 7 V			0.1			0.1	mA
I_{IH}	V_{CC} = MAX, V_I = 2.7 V			20			20	μA
I_{IL}	V_{CC} = MAX, V_I = 0.4 V			− 0.4			− 0.4	mA
I_{OS} §	V_{CC} = MAX	− 20		− 100	− 20		− 100	mA
I_{CCH}	V_{CC} = MAX, V_I = 0 V		1.2	2.4		1.2	2.4	mA
I_{CCL}	V_{CC} = MAX, V_I = 4.5 V		3.6	6.6		3.6	6.6	mA

† For conditions shown as MIN or MAX, use the appropriate value specified under recommended operating conditions.
‡ All typical values are at V_{CC} = 5 V, T_A = 25°C.
§ Not more than one output should be shorted at a time, and the duration of the short-circuit should not exceed one second.

switching characteristics, V_{CC} = 5 V, T_A = 25°C (see note 2)

PARAMETER	FROM (INPUT)	TO (OUTPUT)	TEST CONDITIONS	MIN	TYP	MAX	UNIT
t_{PLH}	A	Y	R_L = 2 kΩ, C_L = 15 pF		9	15	ns
t_{PHL}					10	15	ns

NOTE 2: See General Information Section for load circuits and voltage waveforms.

Figure 3.4 (continued) (Courtesy Texas Instruments, Inc.)

I_{OL} = current flowing into an output when it is LOW.

I_{OH} = current flowing out of an output when it is HIGH, or leakage current going into a turned-off open-collector output with a specified HIGH output voltage applied.

A sketch with arrows indicating current directions is shown in Figure 3.5 for the 7404 and 74LS04. The spec-sheet treats current as positive if it enters the devices, and negative if it comes out; the arrows in the sketch give the actual direction of the current. If you draw sketches with arrows, then your analysis will make more sense and be easier to understand.

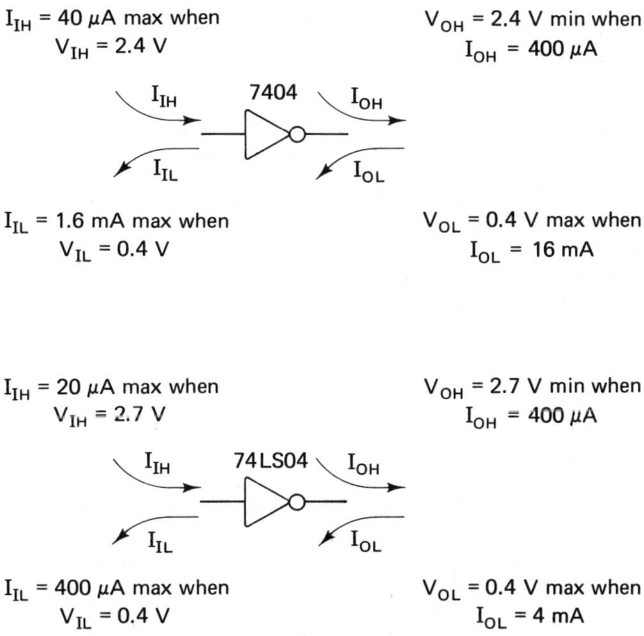

Figure 3.5 Currents and voltages specified for 7404 and 74LS04.

Designing With Totem-Pole Devices. Although it is simple to interconnect totem-pole devices, you must always consider both the currents and the voltages involved. As more gates are connected onto the output of a single device, more current flows and causes the logic HIGH to drop down and the LOW to go up. If too many loads are connected, then the output logic level does not meet the required 0.8 and 2.0 V. Consider these TTL example circuits:

Example 1

Connect two 7404 inverters to the output of a single 7404. Suppose the input to "a" is LOW, so its output is HIGH at a level of at least V_{OH}. The current I from "a" flows into the two inputs, each of which require a maximum of I_{IH}, for a total of 80 μA. This is a light load on "a," and the output voltage V_{OH} stays above the 2.4 V minimum.

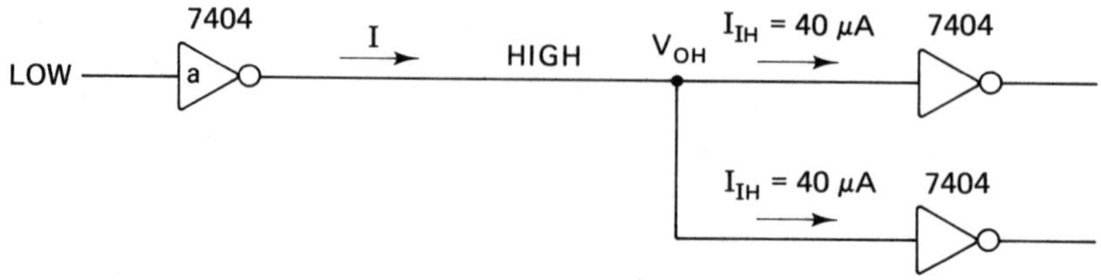

If you connect ten 7404s to the output of "a," then the total current, I_{OH}, required will be 10 × 40 μA or 400 μA maximum. This load tends to pull the output voltage, V_{OH}, down to 2.4 V in the worst case. If more than ten loads are put on the single 7404 gate, then the output voltage will go lower still, and finally go below 2 V; when this happens, the loads will not operate reliably because their input voltage is below their required V_{LH} logic HIGH.

Example 2

Connect two 7404 inverters to the output of a single 7404. Suppose the input to "a" is HIGH, so its output, V_{OL}, is LOW. The current I_{IL} flows from the two inputs, each of which requires a maximum of I_{IL}, for a total of 3.2 mA. This is a light load on "a," and the output voltage V_{OL} stays below the 0.4 V maximum for a LOW.

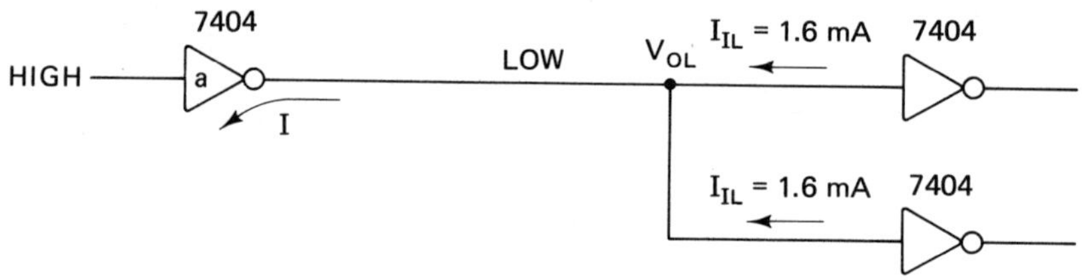

If you connect ten 7404s to the outut of "a," then the total current, I_{OL}, required will be 10 × 1.6 mA, or 16 mA maximum. This load tends to pull the output voltage, V_{OL}, up to 0.4 V in the worst case. If more than ten loads are put on the single 7404 gate, then the output voltage will go higher still, and finally be above 0.8 V; the loads will not operate reliably because their input voltage is above their required V_{IL} logic LOW.

Therefore, you can see that after considering both the HIGH and LOW logic cases, a maximum of ten gates can be connected to a single 7404 inverter. This is referred to as a "fanout" of ten. By following a similar line of reasoning, you can calculate a fanout for each of the logic gates you select for your system.

Designing with Open-Collector Devices. Open-collector TTL components do not have the active pull-up of the totem-pole devices. If you connected a 7405 inverter with an LED on the output as shown in Figure 3.6(a), you would see nothing, even when you might expect an active HIGH. If you changed the circuit slightly plus added an external pull-up resistor as shown in Figure 3.6(b), then the circuit would perform correctly. Consider the output transistor as an on-off switch: when on, the LED is at ground potential and lights; when off, the LED circuit is open and it remains unlighted.

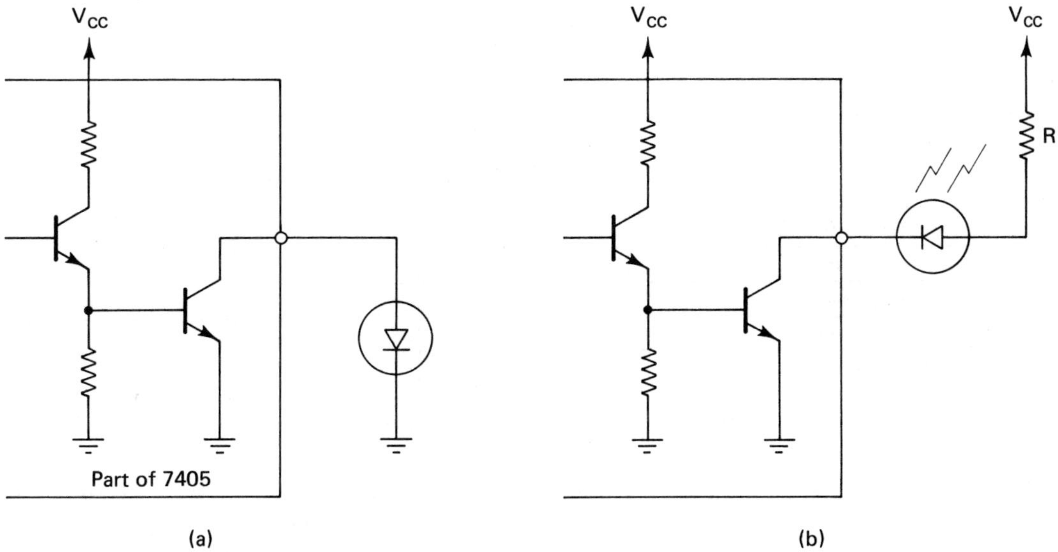

Figure 3.6 A pull-up resistor must be used on the output of the open-collector IC.

The logic levels that correspond to a logic LOW and HIGH are the same as the normal TTL specifications. They are

$$V_{IH} = 2.0 \text{ V} \qquad V_{OH} = 2.4 \text{ V}$$

$$V_{IL} = 0.8 \text{ V} \qquad V_{OH} = 0.4 \text{ V}$$

If you look at the data sheet in Figure 3.7 for the 7405, however, you see that the sign given for the output current is different. This results in the voltages and currents shown in Figure 3.8. Compare this sketch with the totem-pole situation in Figure 3.5.

Instead of being able to source current, the open-collector device has an ouput leakage current I_{OH}, which is defined:

I_{OH} = leakage current going into a turned-off open-collector output with a specified HIGH output voltage applied.

To find a value for the external pull-up resistor, you need to examine the circuit when it is a logic LOW and then examine it again when it is a logic HIGH. When you do this, you find a minimum and maximum value for the resistor. Pick some compromise resistance that allows you maximum response speed but does not draw too much current.

recommended operating conditions

		SN5405			SN7405			UNIT
		MIN	NOM	MAX	MIN	NOM	MAX	
V_{CC}	Supply voltage	4.5	5	5.5	4.75	5	5.25	V
V_{IH}	High-level input voltage	2			2			V
V_{IL}	Low-level input voltage			0.8			0.8	V
V_{OH}	High-level output voltage			5.5			5.5	V
I_{OL}	Low-level output current			16			16	mA
T_A	Operating free-air temperature	– 55		125	0		70	°C

electrical characteristics over recommended operating free-air temperature range (unless otherwise noted)

PARAMETER	TEST CONDITIONS†			MIN	TYP‡	MAX	UNIT
V_{IK}	V_{CC} = MIN,	I_I = – 12 mA				– 1.5	V
I_{OH}	V_{CC} = MIN,	V_{IL} = 0.8 V,	V_{OH} = 5.5 V			0.25	mA
V_{OL}	V_{CC} = MIN,	V_{IH} = 2 V,	I_{OL} = 16 mA		0.2	0.4	V
I_I	V_{CC} = MAX,	V_I = 5.5 V				1	mA
I_{IH}	V_{CC} = MAX,	V_I = 2.4 V				40	μA
I_{IL}	V_{CC} = MAX,	V_I = 0.4 V				– 1.6	mA
I_{CCH}	V_{CC} = MAX,	V_I = 0 V			6	12	mA
I_{CCL}	V_{CC} = MAX,	V_I = 4.5 V			18	33	mA

† For conditions shown as MIN or MAX, use the appropriate value specified under recommended operating conditions.
‡ All typical values are at V_{CC} = 5 V, T_A = 25°C.

switching characteristics, V_{CC} = 5 V, T_A = 25°C (see note 2)

PARAMETER	FROM (INPUT)	TO (OUTPUT)	TEST CONDITIONS		MIN	TYP	MAX	UNIT
t_{PLH}	A	Y	R_L = 4 kΩ,	C_L = 15 pF		40	55	ns
t_{PHL}			R_L = 400 Ω,	C_L = 15 pF		8	15	ns

NOTE 2: See General Information Section for load circuits and voltage waveforms.

Figure 3.7 (Courtesy Texas Instruments, Inc.)

recommended operating conditions

		SN54LS05			SN74LS05			UNIT
		MIN	NOM	MAX	MIN	NOM	MAX	
V_{CC}	Supply voltage	4.5	5	5.5	4.75	5	5.25	V
V_{IH}	High-level input voltage	2			2			V
V_{IL}	Low-level input voltage			0.7			0.8	V
V_{OH}	High-level output voltage			5.5			5.5	V
I_{OL}	Low-level output current			4			8	mA
T_A	Operating free-air temperature	– 55		125	0		70	°C

electrical characteristics over recommended operating free-air temperature range (unless otherwise noted)

PARAMETER	TEST CONDITIONS†			SN54LS05			SN74LS05			UNIT
				MIN	TYP‡	MAX	MIN	TYP‡	MAX	
V_{IK}	V_{CC} = MIN,	I_I = – 18 mA				– 1.5			– 1.5	V
I_{OH}	V_{CC} = MIN,	V_{IL} = MAX,	V_{OH} = 5.5 V			0.1			0.1	mA
V_{OL}	V_{CC} = MIN,	V_{IH} = 2 V,	I_{OL} = 4 mA		0.25	0.4		0.25	0.4	V
	V_{CC} = MIN,	V_{IH} = 2 V,	I_{OL} = 8 mA					0.35	0.5	
I_I	V_{CC} = MAX,	V_I = 7 V				0.1			0.1	mA
I_{IH}	V_{CC} = MAX,	V_I = 2.7 V				20			20	µA
I_{IL}	V_{CC} = MAX,	V_I = 0.4 V				0.4			– 0.4	mA
I_{CCH}	V_{CC} = MAX,	V_I = 0 V			1.2	2.4		1.2	2.4	mA
I_{CCL}	V_{CC} = MAX,	V_I = 4.5 V			3.6	6.6		3.6	6.6	mA

† For conditions shown as MIN or MAX, use the appropriate value specified under recommended operating conditions.
‡ All typical values are at V_{CC} = 5 V, T_A = 25°C.

switching characteristics, V_{CC} = 5 V, T_A = 25°C (see note 2)

PARAMETER	FROM (INPUT)	TO (OUTPUT)	TEST CONDITIONS		MIN	TYP	MAX	UNIT
t_{PLH}	A	Y	R_L = 2 kΩ,	C_L = 15 pF		17	32	ns
t_{PHL}						15	28	ns

NOTE 2: See General Information Section for load circuits and voltage waveforms.

Figure 3.7 (continued) (Courtesy Texas Instruments, Inc.)

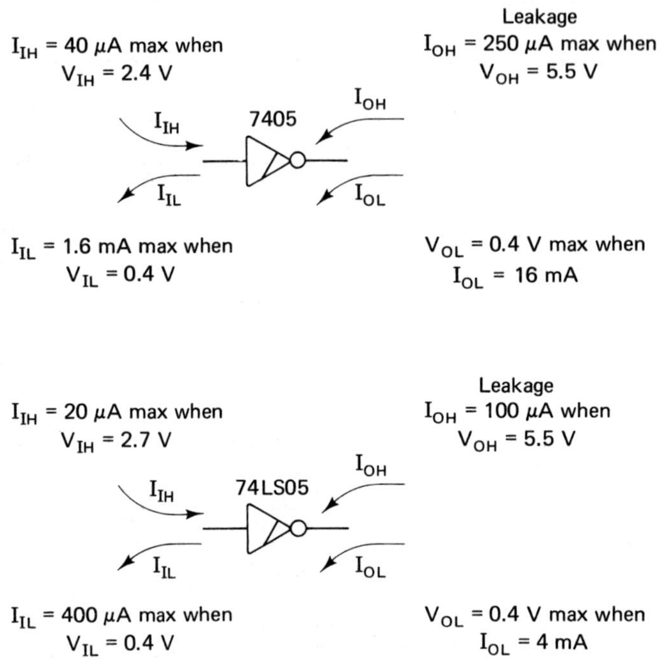

Figure 3.8 Currents and voltages specified for the 7405 and 74LS05 open-collector ICs.

Consider these example problems:

Example 3

You are given a circuit with a 7405 open-collector inverter connected to a 7404. What value pull-up resistor should you specify?

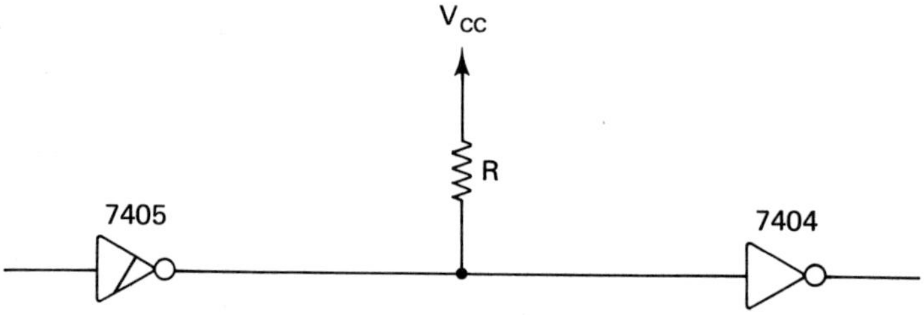

(a) For a logic LOW at the output of the 7405, you would expect currents and voltages:

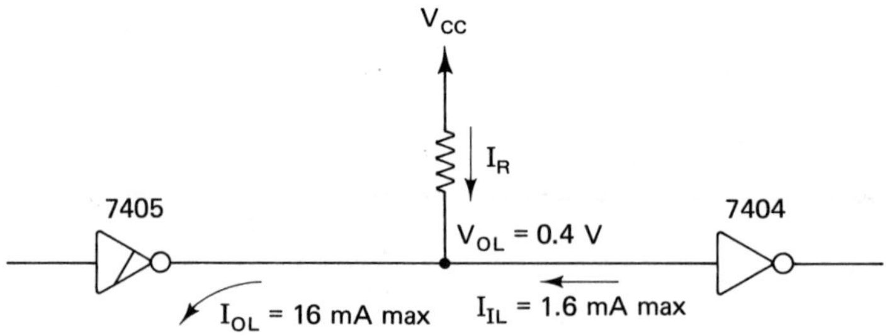

If you design for the maximum I_{OL} into the 7405, then the current through the resistor is

$$\begin{aligned} I_R &= I_{OL} - I_{IL} \\ &= 16 - 1.6 \text{ mA} \\ &= 14.4 \text{ mA} \end{aligned}$$

With the 7405 sinking 16 mA, its output voltage will rise to a maximum of $V_{OL} = 0.4$ V. The voltage across the resistor is

$$\begin{aligned} V_R &= V_{CC} - V_{OL} \\ &= 5 - 0.4 \\ &= 4.6 \text{ V} \end{aligned}$$

and this makes the minimum resistor value

$$\begin{aligned} R_{\min} &= 4.6 \text{ V}/14.4 \text{ mA} \\ &\approx 320 \ \Omega \end{aligned}$$

(b) Do a similar calculation for a logic HIGH at the 7405 output:

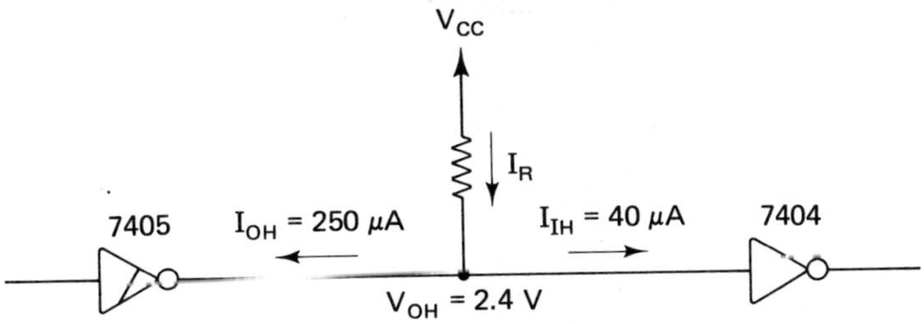

The current through the resistor is

$$\begin{aligned} I_R &= I_{OH} + I_{IH} \\ &= 250 + 40 \ \mu\text{A} \\ &= 290 \ \mu\text{A} \end{aligned}$$

and the voltage across the resistor is

$$\begin{aligned} V_R &= V_{CC} - V_{OH} \\ &= 5 - 2.4 \\ &= 2.6 \text{ V} \end{aligned}$$

so the maximum value of the resistor is

$$\begin{aligned} R_{\max} &= 2.6 \text{ V}/290 \ \mu\text{A} \\ &\approx 8970 \ \Omega \end{aligned}$$

(c) Select some value of resistor between the two extremes. When the resistor is small, you gain better circuit speed at the expense of the added current when the 7405 output is at a logic LOW. For a large resistor, you save current but lose some speed on the rising edge of a pulse from the 7405. You might select a value of $R = 2.2$ KΩ as a possible compromise.

Example 4

Consider a typical situation you might encounter when you decode an address. The circuit partially decodes the address bus using a wired-AND circuit. When the proper address appears on A7, A6, and A5, the output is asserted. Suppose that the switches are set to "101" so that any address in the range 101x xxxx (that is, AO through BFhex) will cause a chip-select (CS) response. In the wired-AND, all the 74LS136 outputs must be off (logic HIGH) so the resistor can pull up CS. If just one of the 74LS136 outputs go LOW, then that is sufficient to negate CS.

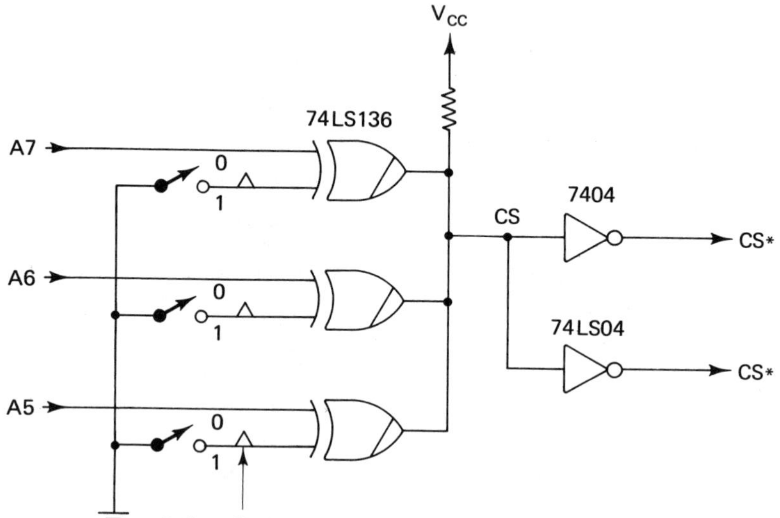

(a) Examine Figure 3.9 to get the following 74LS136 data-sheet information:

I_{OH} = 100 μA max leakage into open-collector when V_{OH} = 5.5 V,

V_{OL} = 0.4 V max when I_{OL} = 4 mA,

V_{OL} = 0.5 V if I_{OL} = 8 mA.

Draw the circuit for a logic LOW at CS:

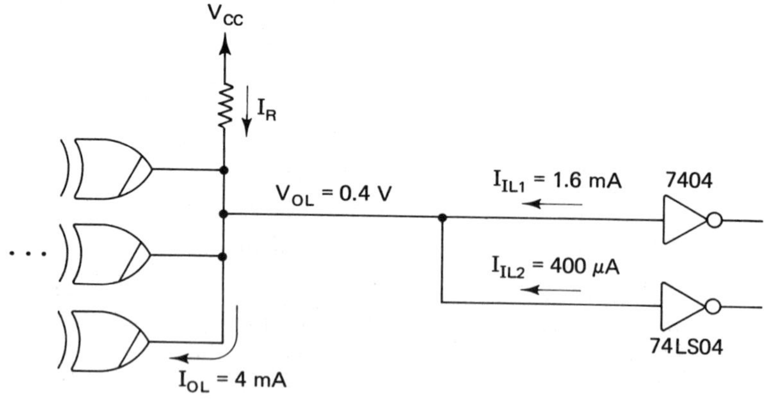

TYPES SN54LS136, SN74LS136
QUADRUPLE 2-INPUT EXCLUSIVE-OR GATES
WITH OPEN-COLLECTOR OUTPUTS

absolute maximum ratings over operating free-air temperature range (unless otherwise noted)

Supply voltage, V_{CC} (see Note 1)	7 V
Input voltage	7 V
Operating free-air temperature range: SN54LS136	−55°C to 125°C
SN74LS136	0°C to 70°C
Storage temperature range	−65°C to 150°C

NOTE 1: Voltage values are with respect to network ground terminal.

recommended operating conditions

	SN54LS136			SN74LS136			UNIT
	MIN	NOM	MAX	MIN	NOM	MAX	
Supply voltage, V_{CC}	4.5	5	5.5	4.75	5	5.25	V
High-level output voltage, V_{OH}			5.5			5.5	V
Low-level output current, I_{OL}			4			8	mA
Operating free-air temperature, T_A	−55		125	0		70	°C

electrical characteristics over recommended operating free-air temperature range (unless otherwise noted)

PARAMETER		TEST CONDITIONS†		SN54LS136			SN74LS136			UNIT
				MIN	TYP‡	MAX	MIN	TYP‡	MAX	
V_{IH}	High-level input voltage			2			2			V
V_{IL}	Low-level input voltage					0.7			0.8	V
V_{IK}	Input clamp voltage	V_{CC} = MIN,	I_I = −18 mA			−1.5			−1.5	V
I_{OH}	High-level output current	V_{CC} = MIN, V_{IL} = V_{IL} max,	V_{IH} = 2 V, V_{OH} = 5.5 V			100			100	μA
V_{OL}	Low-level output voltage	V_{CC} = MIN, V_{IH} = 2 V, V_{IL} = V_{IL} max	I_{OL} = 4 mA		0.25	0.4		0.25	0.4	V
			I_{OL} = 8 mA					0.35	0.5	
I_I	Input current at maximum input voltage	V_{CC} = MAX,	V_I = 7 V			0.2			0.2	mA
I_{IH}	High-level input current	V_{CC} = MAX,	V_I = 2.7 V			40			40	μA
I_{IL}	Low-level input current	V_{CC} = MAX,	V_I = 0.4 V			−0.8			−0.8	mA
I_{CC}	Supply current	V_{CC} = MAX,	See Note 2		6.1	10		6.1	10	mA

†For conditions shown as MIN or MAX, use the appropriate value specified under recommended operating conditions for the applicable type.
‡All typical values are at V_{CC} = 5 V, T_A = 25°C.
NOTE 2: I_{CC} is measured with one input of each gate at 4.5 V, the other inputs grounded, and the outputs open.

switching characteristics, V_{CC} = 5 V, T_A = 25°C

PARAMETER¶	FROM (INPUT)	TEST CONDITIONS		MIN	TYP	MAX	UNIT
t_{PLH}	A or B	Other input low	C_L = 15 pF, R_L = 2 kΩ, (See Note 3)		18	30	ns
t_{PHL}					18	30	
t_{PLH}	A or B	Other input high			18	30	ns
t_{PHL}					18	30	

¶t_{PLH} = propagation delay time, low-to-high-level output
t_{PHL} = propagation delay time, high-to-low-level output
NOTE 3: See General Information Section for load circuits and voltage waveforms.

TEXAS INSTRUMENTS
POST OFFICE BOX 225012 • DALLAS, TEXAS 75265

Figure 3.9 (Courtesy Texas Instruments, Inc.)

For the moment, assume that just one 74LS136 is on: any current flowing in the circuit will not be shared by any of the other 74LS136 gates. The current through the resistor is

$$I_R = I_{OL} - I_{IL1} - I_{IL2}$$
$$= 4 \text{ mA} - 1.6 \text{ mA} - 400 \ \mu\text{A}$$
$$= 2 \text{ mA}$$

When the 74LS136 sinks 4 mA, its output voltage rises to a maximum of $V_{OL} = 0.4$ V. Thus, the voltage across the resistor is $V_{CC} - V_{OL}$ or 4.6 V, so the resistor value is

$$R_{\min} = 4.6 \text{ V}/2 \text{ mA}$$
$$= 2300 \ \Omega$$

If you allow the 74LS136 to sink 8 mA (resulting in $V_{OL} = 0.5$ V), then you find

$$R_{\min} = 4.5 \text{ V}/6 \text{ mA}$$
$$= 750 \ \Omega$$

If you assume that two or three of the 74LS136s might normally be LOW and sharing the 8 mA, then the V_{OL} will be below 0.4 V. This might not be a valid assumption, so it should be verified.

(b) Draw the circuit for a logic HIGH at CS:

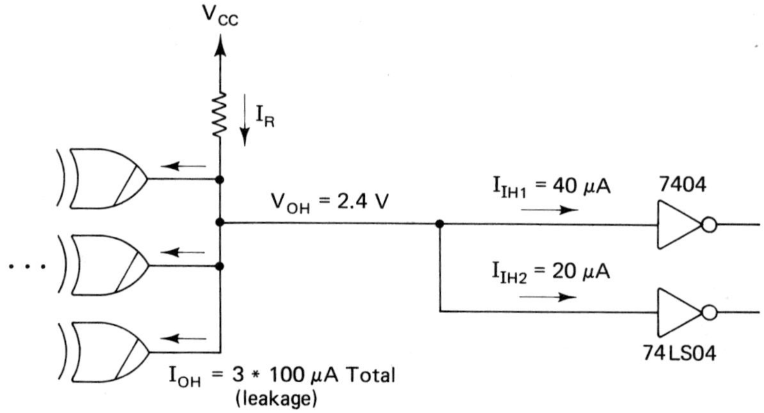

The current through the resistor is

$$I_R = I_{OH} \text{ (total)} + I_{IH1} + I_{IH2}$$
$$= 300 \ \mu\text{A} + 40 \ \mu\text{A} + 20 \ \mu\text{A}$$
$$= 360 \ \mu\text{A}$$

and the voltage across the resistor is

$$V_R = V_{CC} - V_{OH}$$
$$= 5 - 2.4$$
$$= 2.6 \text{ V}$$

so the resistor value is

$$R_{max} = 2.6\text{ V} / 360\ \mu\text{A}$$
$$= 7220\ \Omega$$

(c) Select some resistor vaue between the minimum and maximum based on speed and power. You might select 2.2 KΩ simply because it works and you have a large stock of them to use.

At some point in the design and development cycle, you should verify your circuit performance with oscilloscope measurements. For the present, you at least have a design within required logic-level specifications.

Rules on Loading and Pull-Ups

1. Use worst-case specifications over operating temperature.
2. Measure actual signal and current levels and compare with design values.
3. Connect unused inputs to V_{CC} through a 1 KΩ resistor. LS-TTL devices, which have internal diodes, can be connected directly to V_{CC}.
4. Examine the loading capabilities of all devices and provide buffering as required.
5. Connect a maximum of ten 74xx inputs to any single 74xx output.
6. Connect a maximum of ten 74LSxx inputs to any single 74LSxx output.
7. Connect a maximum of 20 74LSxx inputs to any single 74xx output. However, double-check the I_{IL} and I_{IH} 74LSxx inputs because they do not all present the same load to a source.
8. Connect a maximum of three 74xx inputs to any single 74LSxx output.
9. Consider open-collector devices if you need wired-AND and OR functions, external relay capability, or bus-interface capability.
10. When you use open-collector devices, calculate a minimum and a maximum pull-up resistance. Then make a selection based on speed and power constraints.

Timing. You find that there is substantially more information in the TTL data sheets than just signal levels and loading: you also find details on signal propagation. The finite time that signals take as they go from one part of your circuit to another can have a profound impact on the performance of your design. The delays in your circuit set a maximum speed for reliable performance, and you need to know how to calculate what that speed is under worst-case conditions.

Propagation Delay. The propagation delay is the time a signal takes to go through a gate or array of gates. If you consider a simple 7404 inverter and drive it with a single pulse, you have a time delay for the output to go high and another delay for the output to go low:

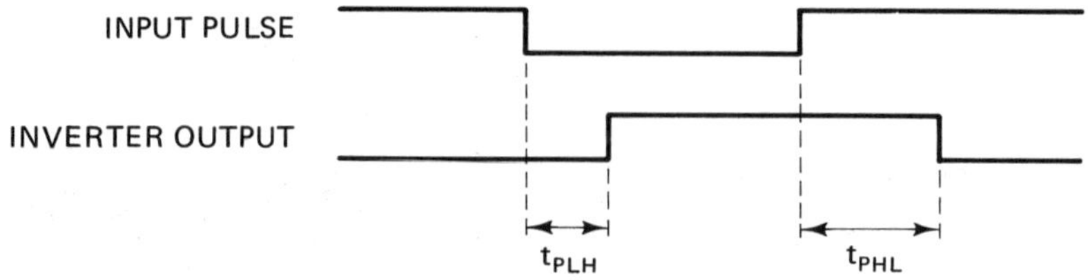

Examine Figures 3.4 and 3.7 to find the propagation times for the 7404, 74LS04, 7405, and 74LS05. Typical and worst-case times are given for both low-to-high and high-to-low output transitions.

You can summarize this data sheet information for the totem-pole and open-collector inverters:

	t_{plh} (ns)		t_{phl} (ns)	
	Typical	*Worst-case*	*Typical*	*Worst-case*
7404	12	22	8	15
74LS04	9	15	10	15
7405 (open col)	40	55	8	15
74LS05 (open-col)	17	32	15	28

In general, if you want to get an estimate of the time it takes a signal to go through your circuit, average t_{plh} and t_{phl} for each device. For example, the average 7404 typical propagation time is 10 ns. For several such gates in series, add the times for each. If you need a worst-case estimate, use the higher worst-case value of t_{plh} or t_{phl}. Thus, the 7404 worst-case propagation time is 22 ns; the worst case for two in series is 44 ns.

The propagation times given in the charts are based on specific test circuits. Compare your circuit to the test circuit to see whether you might expect similar propagation times. For example, the 74LS05 times are taken using the test circuit shown in Figure 3.10. Notice that the t_{phl} for the open-collector 7405/LS05 devices are similar to the

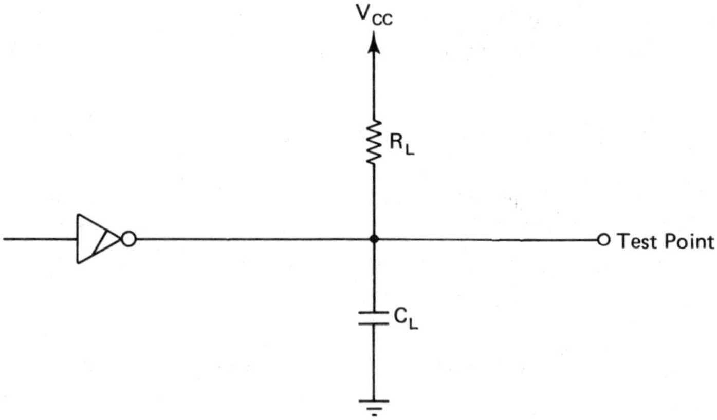

Figure 3.10 Load circuit for open-collector outputs. (Courtesy Texas Instruments, Inc.)

totem-pole gates. This is because the output transistor is quite effective in discharging the load capacitor in a short time. However, the t_{plh} depends primarily on how fast R_L can provide enough charging current for C_L to get the output voltage HIGH. If you need to speed up the propagation time of open-collector devices, you can consider making the pull-up resistor a lower value. In doing that, however, watch not to exceed the maximum I_{OL} for the device; if you go too far, then the output voltage will become higher than V_{OL} and will cause errors in your logic.

The propagation delay through a complete system is an important design consideration. Suppose you have a signal being propagated through a number of gates and need to know how long it takes to get to its destination. Add up each of the worst-case delays, as in this example problem:

Example 5

Look at the address decoder in Example 4 and estimate how long it will take to establish CS* after receiving a valid address.

Solution. See Figure 3.9 for the 74LS136 data-sheet information: $t_{plh} = t_{phl} = 18$ ns typical, 30 ns maximum when R = 2000 Ω and C = 15 pF load.
With the 2.2 KΩ pull-up resistor and two gates loading the 74LS136, you expect that the 30 ns worst-case time is reasonable. Add the 22 ns worst-case time through the 7404 inverter, and you conclude that CS* is valid about 52 ns after a valid address. Typically, however, you expect a propagation time of 18 + 10, or 28 ns.

Clock Timing. In a large digital system, there are many sequential devices interconnected that need synchronization using the same clock signal. If your clock has a single 7404 or other 74xx output device, it cannot drive more than 10 74xx loads; however, there are several ways to boost the drive capability of your clock. The first way, as shown in Figure 3.11(a), is to parallel the gate inputs and outputs of a single package; avoid using separate packages because the different switching times will cause problems with noise transients. The second way, Figure 3.11(b), is to use a clock driver such as the 7437 to provide a drive for up to 30 74xx loads. For still more drive capability, multiple sections of a 74S37 can be used as in Figure 3.11(c).

When you divide the clock load between two or more drivers as in Figure 3.11(c), then you cause a potential clock skew problem in your system. Clock skew is the difference in time between two clock signals. Suppose your system clock goes to two 7404 inverters, each of which goes to two different parts of your system. As shown in Figure 3.12, one 7404 has 3 loads, and the other has a full 10 loads. Both 7404s are different and have propagation times that can be from the worst-case 22 ns to better than the typical 10 ns. Even if the gates are identical, the difference in loading affects the propagation times. Consequently, you might find a clock skew of 12 ns or more between the two clock circuits.

You might improve the circuit by changing from the 7404 to the Schottky 74S04, which has a worst-case propagation time of 5 ns. The resulting clock skew would be less than 5 ns, typically less than 3 ns. The tradeoff you make in going to a Schottky device is

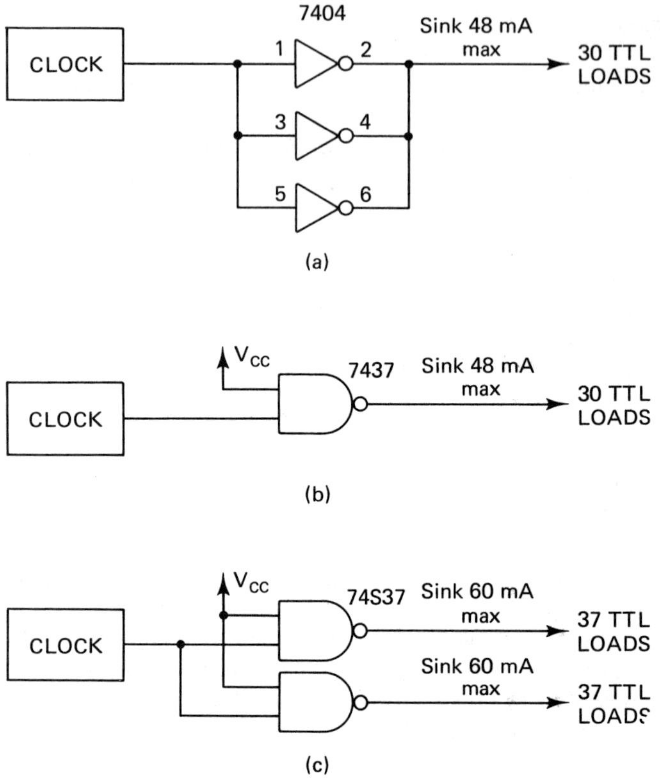

Figure 3.11 Several clock driver circuits.

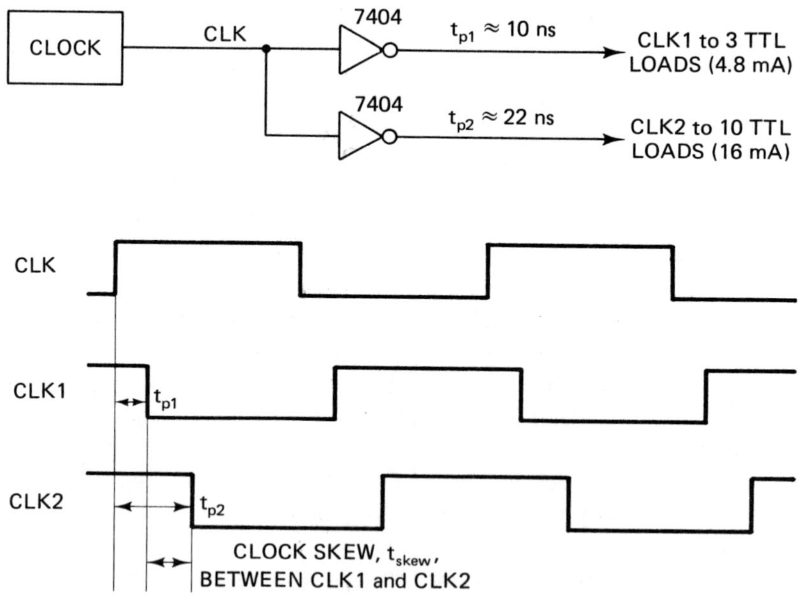

Figure 3.12 Clock with two clock drivers that cause a skew between CLK1 and CLK2.

an approximate doubling of the supply current to power the IC. If you have a fairly simple system, you probably would not notice the skew at all and have no need to resort to a 74S04. If you use a Schottky device, watch that you do not cause problems with noise: the very fast switching speeds can not only affect the 5 V supply but can also couple energy into adjacent circuits.

Sometimes a complementary clock is needed in the system, as depicted in Figure 3.13. Using a simple 7404 inverter to obtain an inverted clock could cause a clock skew of up to 22 ns. However, the 74265 quad complementary-output circuit provides the two clocks with a typical skew of 0.5 ns and a maximum skew of 3 ns.

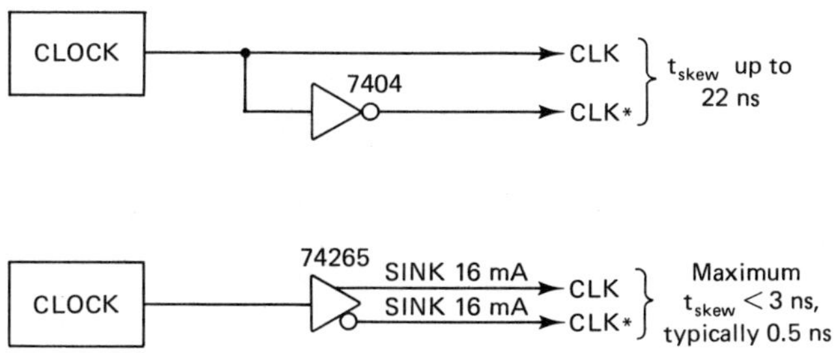

Figure 3.13 Rather than using a 7404 to get a complementary clock signal, use a device designed for a minimum output skew.

Setup and Hold Times. Each pulse of the system clock signals the beginning of a number of events in a digital circuit. It takes a finite time for each event to propagate through the system to get all the devices ready for the next clock pulse. That is, the proper data must be present for a certain time before the clock pulse arrives. You can define this as the "setup time."

> *Setup Time* is the time interval preceding the clock pulse that a clocked device must have valid input data. A negative setup time means that valid input data may be applied after the clock pulse and still be properly recognized.

Likewise, it takes some time after the clock pulse arrives for the input data to be acted upon by a sequential device. This is referred to as the "hold time."

> *Hold time* is the time interval after the clock pulse that a clocked device must have valid input data. A negative hold time means that the input data may be removed prior to the clock pulse and still be properly recognized.

There are also requirements on the duration of the clock pulse itself. Normally, most of the flip-flops you will use in your TTL designs will be edge-triggered. That is, the clock transition from LOW to HIGH (positive edge) or from HIGH to LOW (negative edge) determines the exact moment to change state. Although the clock edge triggers the flip-flop, the clock pulse must remain high or low for a certain time. Consequently, the required pulse width is specified in the device data sheet.

Pulse width is the time between the leading and trailing edges of a pulse. A width may be specified for either or both of the high and low portions of the clock cycle.

Example 6

What are the requirements for setup and hold times of the 7474 D flip-flop? What is its maximum clock speed? How does this relate to the propagation time?

Solution. When you examine the data for the positive-edge-triggered 7474, you find:

t_{su}	20 ns	setup time
t_h	5 ns	hold time
t_w	30 ns	pulse width, clock high
	37 ns	pulse width, clock low
t_{plh}	14 ns	typical propagation time
	25 ns	worst case
t_{phl}	20 ns	typical propagation time
	40 ns	worst case

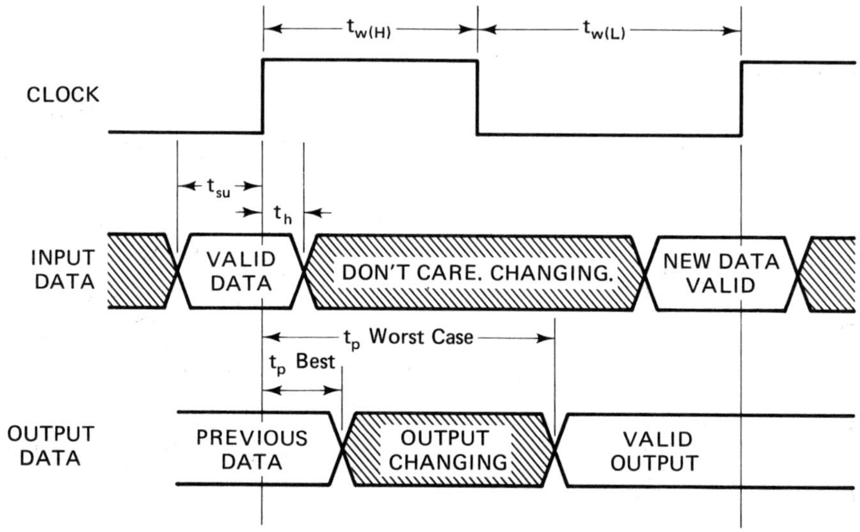

If you add the clock pulse-width times specified (30 and 37 ns), you can calculate the 7474 maximum clocking frequency. In this case, the times add to 67 ns, which corresponds to 15 MHz.

Example 7

Clock-speed calculation: How fast can the clock run and still drive this circuit reliably?

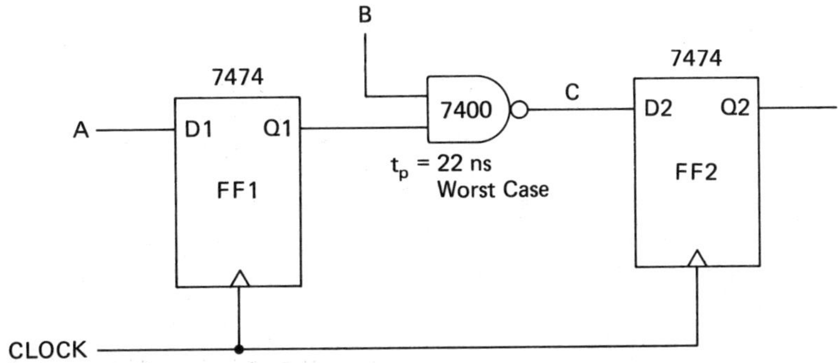

Solution. Assuming that input A setup and hold times are met and that input B is not changing, you can add the worst-case times through each of the devices and draw the timing diagram.

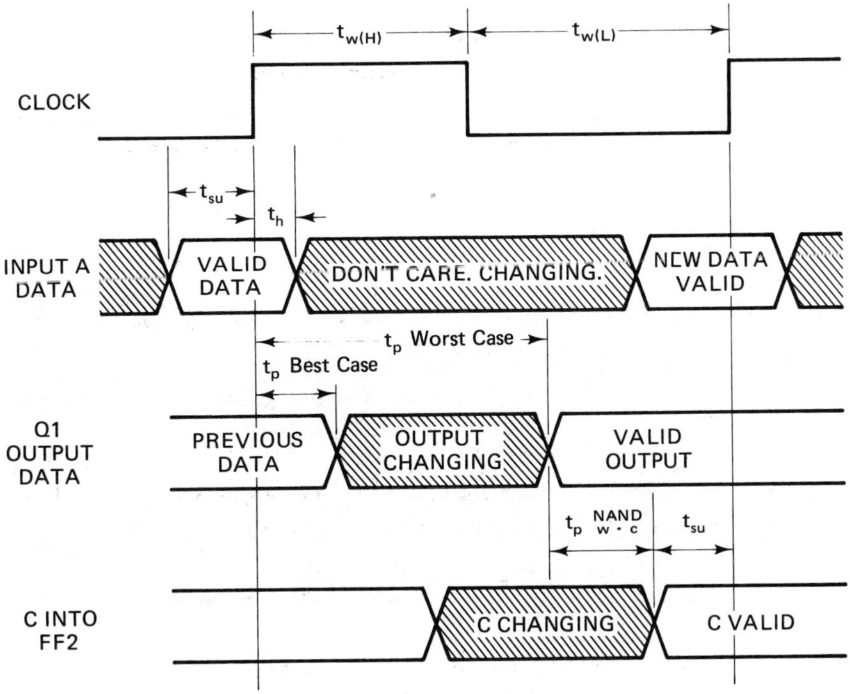

Q1 output: propagation delay	40 ns
NAND output C	22 ns
Setup time for input D2	20 ns
Total	82 ns

Therefore, the maximum clock speed should be less than 1/82 ns or about 12 MHz. Suppose that there are five NAND gates between the flip-flops instead of one. The 22 ns above would be 5 × 22 or 110 ns for a total of 170 ns. The maximum clock would then be just under 6 MHz. Anything faster might not operate reliably. In general, you can calculate the maximum clock speed using the worst-case propagation through the *longest* signal path.

Example 8

Example clock-skew calculation: What is the maximum tolerable clock skew for the following circuit?

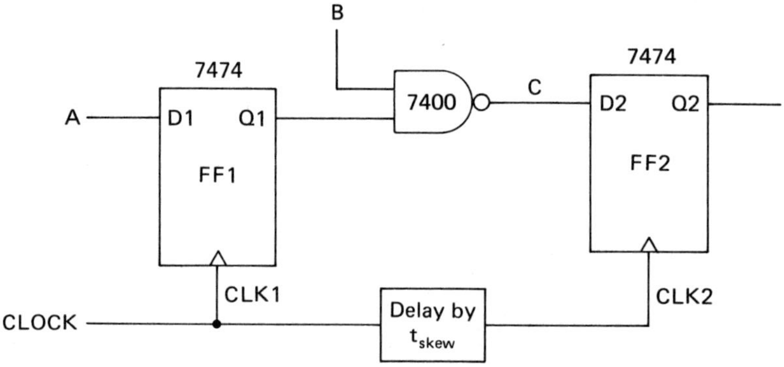

Solution. Draw the timing diagram as before to obtain the arrival time of the data at output C of the 7400. When you calculate the maximum skew, however, use the *fastest path* between the two flip-flops; *the worst-case propagation time for the NAND is actually the favorable case*. You can estimate the fastest time as the value given in the data sheet as typical; or to be conservative, you might estimate a still faster time for the NAND.

If the maximum clock-skew time is exceeded, then you will be clocking the second flip-flop when the NAND output C could be in a state of change. The maximum clock skew is the best propagation time through the first flip-flop plus the best time through the NAND minus the hold time of the second flip-flop.

$$\begin{aligned}\text{Max } CLK2 \text{ skew} &= t_p \text{ (best thru } FF1) + t_p \text{ (best thru NAND)} - t_{\text{hold}} \text{ (max } FF2) \\ &\approx 14 \text{ typ} + 7 \text{ typ} - 5 \text{ typ} \\ &\approx 16 \text{ ns or less}\end{aligned}$$

Rules on Clocks and Timing

1. Estimate propagation time by taking the total of all the worst-case times in the data path.
2. Estimate typical propagation times by taking the average of t_{phl} and t_{plh}.
3. Adjust estimated times depending on how heavy the load capacitance is when compared to the load used to obtain data-sheet times.

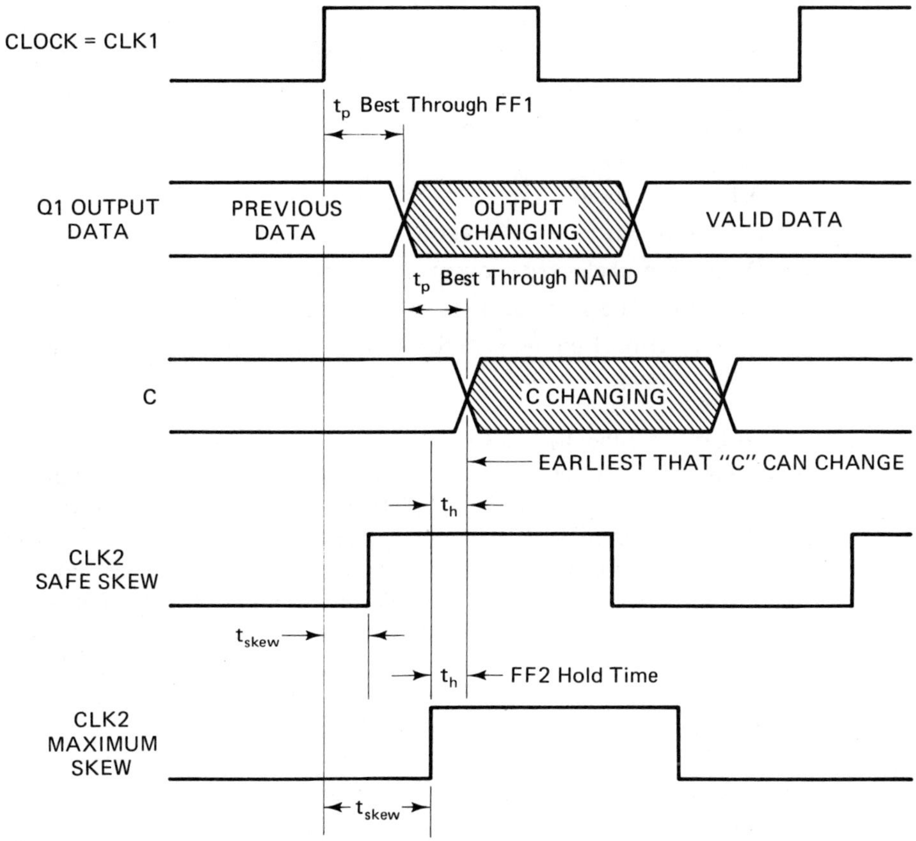

4. Calculate the maximum clock speed using the longest signal path between two flip-flops (or similar clocked devices). Use the worst-case propagation times for logic gates along the path.
5. Calculate the maximum allowable clock skew using the shortest path between two flip-flops (or other clocked devices). Use the fastest propagation times for any logic gates along the path.
6. Verify that clock speed is not excessive.
7. Verify clock skew through the system.
8. Use pull-up resistors on any unused logic gate inputs to avoid degradation in package propagation time. Doing this will ensure best switching times and minimum noise susceptibility.
9. Verify that clock high and low times are met. This might be part of the duty-cycle specification on a DIP clock you buy as a complete unit.
10. Verify that setup and hold times are being met.
11. Review the timing diagrams related to all LSI devices.

12. Use processor wait-states if necessary to slow the system down for certain operations rather than run the risk of sometimes having a system failure.
13. Select or design a clock for a fast rise time to minimize skew.
14. Shield the clock line or keep it physically isolated or at right angles from other logic paths if possible.
15. All devices should respond to the same clock. Tie all clock inputs together.
16. Do not use an inverter to get a complementary clock signal.
17. Do not use unclocked sequential devices.
18. Do not operate logic at its maximum speed.
19. Find the critical timing path that has the longest propagation delay and verify that system timing is proper.

Noise. All the TTL devices you use in your designs are susceptible to possible malfunction because of noise. This noise is a corruption of the logic signal levels so that, for example, a signal with a logic HIGH might be misunderstood as a logic LOW.

The noise margin is the maximum voltage disturbance that can be added to the input of a gate; any disturbance greater than the margin might cause an unwanted change in output. When you first examined the TTL allowable input and output voltage ranges in Figure 3.3, you noticed that the TTL outputs are specified less than 0.4 V and greater than 2.4 V. The inputs, however, accept less than 0.8 V or greater than 2.0 V. This difference is referred to as the "noise margin." For the TTL logic levels, the noise margin is 0.4 V.

You can see how noise affects the signal, as shown in Figure 3.14. This noise is superimposed on the desired signal and could cause an unwanted change in the output. Notice that the noise is high-frequency spikes, or glitches. In (a), a brief burst of noise exceeding 0.8 V caused a momentary transition in the output (b); likewise, an instantaneous drop below 2.0 V in (a) caused a brief output transition in (b). To respond to such a sudden noise impulse, the logic device must have been quite fast (say a 74S04). In general, if your logic family is slow, then it will not be prone to respond to high-frequency noise. It will, however, still respond to excessive lower-frequency noise.

Noise in the digital system can come from many sources. One of the primary sources of TTL noise comes through the +5 V supply lines; this noise is caused by various gates switching from one logic level to another. When you first examined totem-pole devices, you saw the two output transistors as an advantage to boost the device speed: turning on one or the other could quickly change the state of the output. In reality, the two transistors are both on for a brief instant when they switch, and this causes a heavy current surge from the power supply. Unless the power supply and wiring to the TTL device is substantial, the supply voltage V_{cc} at the device will drop. This causes drops at nearby ICs and might cause misinterpretation of data levels. To help mitigate the switching noise, decoupling capacitors are used near every several IC packages. Typically, a 0.01 μF capacitor is used for two ICs; this capacitor value is not critical, nor is it critical to use a capacitor for every two devices. Some designs use decoupling capacitors between V_{cc} and ground built into the IC sockets themselves.

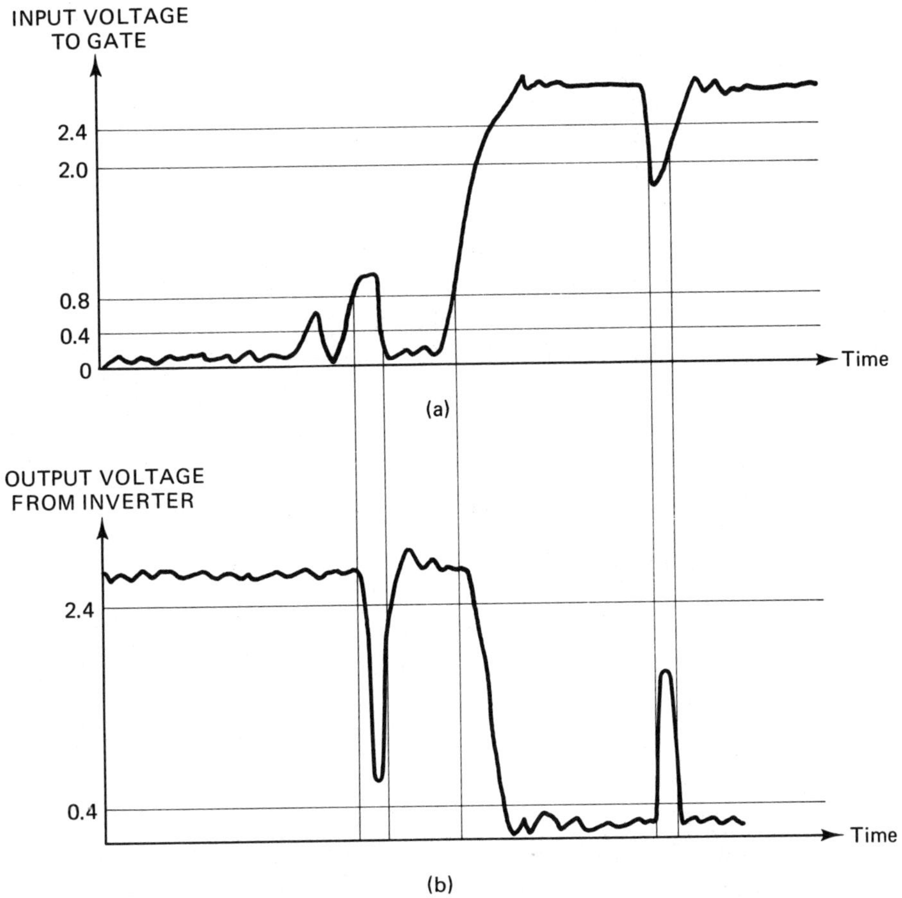

Figure 3.14 The effect of noise on a typical TTL gate. (a) The noisy input to an inverter with two noise bursts exceeding the noise margin. (b) The possible output of the same inverter. Drawing assumes zero propagation delay and that the gate switches immediately on entering the transition region.

Another source of noise is the clock itself. One desirable feature of the clock is that it have a fast risetime to cut down on clock skew problems. However, this fast transition can be easily radiated and cause crosstalk, or extraneous signals in nearby circuits. Shielding the clock lines or using twisted-pair cable can help, but on a circuit board a good layout is most effective in minimizing the crosstalk. Rather than run the clock near data lines, keep it separate; if possible, run the clock on the opposite side of the board at right angles to any data lines.

Rules on Noise

1. Tie unused gate inputs to V_{cc} or use pull-up resistors.
2. Assert communication lines to the system low-true for best noise immunity.
3. Use 0.01 μF decoupling capacitors every two or three ICs.
4. Design with the slowest acceptable logic family.
5. Keep clock lines away from data lines.
6. Use a ground plane and heavy ground and power leads.
7. Keep connections to all parts as short as possible.
8. Use wide, low-impedance conductors on PC boards.
9. Avoid crosstalk with twisted-pair or shielded cable.
10. If using double-sided PC board, run circuits perpendicular to each other on the top and bottom. Use ground and power planes if using multilayer boards.
11. Shield the clock line or keep it isolated from other circuits.
12. Verify that the noise level is less than the design margin.

General Design Rules

1. Design for testability: include push-to-test or self-test capability.
2. Do modular system design so circuits can be developed and debugged by stages.
3. Design and test the power supply module first.
4. Design utility modules such as bus buffers and address decoders early.
5. Use mixed logic symbols in all schematics for quick comprehension.
6. Examine all LSI devices to see if buffering should be provided.
7. Watch for possible bus contention problems.
8. Use worst-case specifications.
9. Use proven circuits; save your time for creative problem solving.
10. Verify that the system works over a reasonable temperature range even if there is no explicit temperature specification.

3.1.2 Software Design Rules

Regardless of the language or processor you use, your programs can be treated the same as hardware; that is, programs can be interconnected and used as building blocks to solve a particular problem. Visualize a program as you would an LSI device: it has inputs, outputs, and performs a particular function in the system. In the same sense, your programs can be modularized and used to save substantial design time as your project evolves.

In order to make your programs into modules that you can call as needed, you should do a top-down design of your software just as you did your hardware design. This design can be easily drawn in the form of a structure chart, as shown in Figure 3.15.

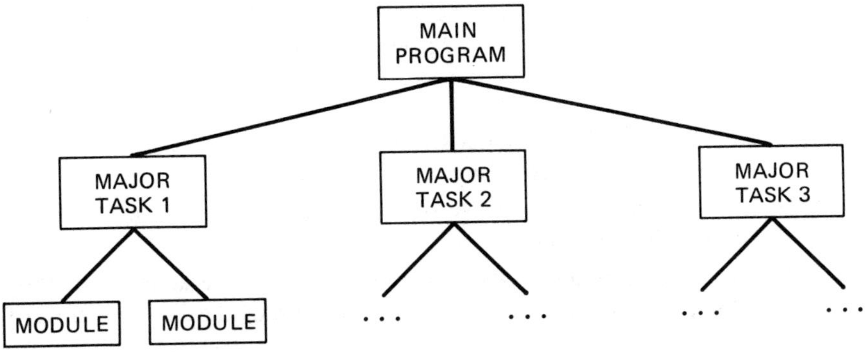

Figure 3.15 The form of the structure chart used in a top-down program design.

Consider each block as a functional module within the system and define the purpose of each. Start with the purpose of the main program: what does it do and what are its inputs and outputs? Then, for the main program to accomplish its purpose, a number of supporting tasks are necessary. The process becomes more detailed as you get down to the next level in the structure chart.

The easiest way to visualize the decomposition process into modules is to think of the main program as in the form of a menu of tasks that can be selected. Each of the tasks is a subroutine within the program and can be selected from the menu for execution. Once a task has been selected, it needs to call on a number of supporting modules or routines during execution.

If you think of each of the blocks of the structure chart as subroutines, you can see the advantage of making each module as straightforward and specific as possible. With one function per module, you can combine them in just the same fashion as you design hardware. Not only that, but you can write the code for the module and thoroughly test it before "building" it into the larger body of the main program.

Rules on software design

A module should:

1. Have one purpose.
2. Be as general as possible for use in other applications.
3. Be reliable. (Provide worst-case test data to demonstrate.)
4. Have a length less than two pages.
5. Contain one statement maximum per line of program.
6. Have one entry point and one exit point.
7. Be internally documented with ample comments.
8. Contain a heading with: name of module, date, revision number; list of external

modules and variables; public labels and variables; description of input and output variables; and note of any registers that are changed during a call to the module.

In general:

1. All constants should be EQUated at the beginning of the main program or in a library related to the appropriate module.
2. Routines, parameters, labels, storage area, and all calling procedures should be consistent with each other.
3. Avoid absolute addresses if possible. Use relative addressing. Program for easy relocation of module. Ideally, your module should execute wherever you place it in memory.

3.2 DESIGN HEURISTICS

Your design up to this point has probably been somewhat conventional: define the problem and specifications, synthesize several possible solutions to the problem, select the best solution, and then implement it. Although these are the general steps in the engineering design process, they seem somewhat pedestrian and lack vigor. Where is the creativity and flexibility to innovate?

In reality, when you first begin a design task, you do not understand the problem. You cannot decide which specifications are critical to the design or even decide which job to do first. Why not follow some rule of thumb, or heuristic, that can help you get moving in the right direction as you feel your way into a better understanding of the problem?

By its very nature, a heuristic is a guide based on past experience and common sense. A heuristic is not a rule that can be conclusively proven, because the heuristic might not even be correct in certain situations. Therefore, when you use heuristics to help speed your design work, remember that they do not guarantee a correct answer and that you must still work out a proper design. The advantage of the heuristic is in helping you decide on which design might be worth your time and effort.

The following list of heuristics are a collection of useful rules for general engineering as well as digital design. Some are obvious, some are obscure, but many should be useful.

3.2.1 Engineering Heuristics

1. Don't reinvent the wheel: read data sheets and application notes.
2. Reduce your problem to something you've already solved before.
3. If you can't meet the specs, negotiate; don't hide the problem.
4. Always have an answer; you have to start somewhere.
5. Change one variable at a time when you adjust your design.
6. Develop circuits and programs module by module; debug as you go.
7. Build a quick simple circuit for experimentation; understand it.

8. Keep your designs simple.
9. Use LSI devices whenever possible.
10. Talking aloud to yourself helps spot errors.
11. If you find you made a mistake, figure out why.
12. Solve the right problem.
13. Act rather than react: don't spend your day fighting fires.
14. Read the fine print at the bottom of data sheets.
15. When in doubt, don't guess; look it up and be sure.
16. On time management:
    Keep a daily do-it list with priorities for each task.
    Do critical or difficult tasks as soon as possible.
    Schedule unfinished tasks for a definite day in the future.
    Keep a time log of your work and review your progress.
    Don't procrastinate—a project gets late one day at a time.

3.3 SUMMARY

Design rules are the procedures or conventions established to direct your project. These design guidelines, rather than being confining, can help make your design effort more orderly and technically sound. They also help make your work consistent with the designs of other team members working on the same project. This is important so that you can complete your project within your available time and budget.

One of the nice features of digital design is that the circuits can be easily connected in building-block fashion. When you work out a logic function, for example, you can usually implement it by simply interconnecting the required gates. When you do this, however, you must be careful to stay within the TTL signal level and loading specifications. You must consider how many totem-pole devices you can connect before the signals become too degraded; likewise, you must calculate the size pull-up resistor for open-collector devices so that its output is satisfactory.

Timing is one of the most important issues in designing your digital system. When you include propagation time in your design, you find that it can affect a number of different parts of your circuit. This becomes especially critical when you select a clock frequency that pushes the system to its speed limit. Because not all components perform the same, one circuit might work at a high speed while another might not. For all your designs, therefore, be sure to design for the worst-case component tolerances.

Noise can cause a number of strange malfunctions at odd times during circuit operation. The noise can come from external sources or from inside the digital system itself. The best design approach to take is to design so that you have a noise margin in your logic levels. For example, design your gates for an output LOW of less than 0.4 V; that way, any inputs connected to it will not mistake it for a logic HIGH unless the output exceeds a total of 0.8 V.

Software can be designed following the same general approach that you use when you design hardware. You can do a top-down modular program design just the same as you would design using LSI devices in a hardware system. Each of the modules has an input, an output, and performs a special function. A structure chart is an easy way to visualize how the various software modules in the system relate to one another. As you write each of the modules, you can test and debug them as you go, just the same as you test and debug hardware.

Engineering heuristics are rules of thumb or guides that you can use in a somewhat intuitive sense to solve engineering problems. They cannot be proven, and some might not even work in any particular situation. They can, however, speed your design work by giving you a feel for what might be important in the design. At the very least, heuristics can usually get your initial calculations approximately correct. Instead of getting bogged down in a deep theoretical design issue, you can speed your work with the common-sense reality of the heuristic.

By applying both technical design rules and engineering heuristics, you can work much more effectively to finish a design problem. The guidelines will help you do a technically sound design that is consistent with the design work of other team members. They will help make the work go faster and, as you use more heuristics, make design engineering an enjoyable challenge to your creativity.

EXERCISES

1. What is the maximum operating temperature for a 7404? Express it in Fahrenheit as well as centrigrade.
2. What is the maximum worst-case supply current required by a 7404 package? Compare this to the worst-case 74LS04.
3. Suppose the output of a 74LS00 is accidentally shorted to ground, and your circuit causes the device to try switching to a HIGH output.
   a. How much current will flow maximum?
   b. Which way?
   c. How long?
4. Consider the circuit in Example 3. Suppose you built the circuit and accidentally forgot to hook up the pull-up resistor. Will the circuit function? How well or poorly? Build up a quick test circuit to see what happens. Explain your answers. Hint: This problem is *not* as trivial as it might appear.
5. Ten LS gates are connected to the output of a single 74LS04, but you need to add two more LS gates because of a circuit change.
   a. Predict the effect on the logic HIGH and logic LOW at the output of the 74LS04.
   b. Can you use the circuit as is, with 12 gates connected?
      What compromises are you making?
   c. Suppose you decide not to connect 12 gates to the 74LS04. What alternatives are open to you? Sketch a circuit and defend its technical merit. State your assumptions and justify them.

6. You want to connect a 7407 output to the RESET* input of a 68000 microprocessor.
   a. Calculate a minimum and maximum value for a pull-up resistor. Assume the 68000 input looks like a 74LS04.
   b. Assume three LS gates are also connected to RESET*. Calculate a minimum and maximum pull-up resistor. Make a choice.
   c. Why not use a totem-pole device instead of the open-collector 7407?
   d. Suppose the 68000 executes the RESET instruction and the RESET* pin is suddenly pulled LOW (V_{OL} = 0.5V when I_{OL} = 5mA). Calculate 6b once again.
7. Consider text Example 3 of the 7405 connected to a 7404: the two resistances were calculated at 320 and 8970Ω. You decide to try saving current by using an 8.2K pull-up.
   a. Calculate the risetime as the output goes from low to high. (Assume that C = 5pF load.)
   b. What is the risetime for a 330Ω pull-up resistor? (Assume that C = 5pF load.)
   c. Your system runs on a 12 MHz clock. Sketch a clock cycle and a "compromise" signal from the 7405. What value resistor will suffice to produce a reasonable signal?
8. Four 7400 gates are in series in a signal path you traced in a digital system.
   a. What is the worst-case propagation delay? Typical?
   b. You see that each gate output only has two 7400 loads. Estimate the worst-case propagation delay.
9. The worst-case delay in Problem 8b is not acceptable. You must have your signal guaranteed valid within 20 ns to assure enough setup time for the following clocked device.
   a. What can you do?
   b. What tradeoffs are you required to make?
10. How fast, worst-case, can you clock a 74LS109A?
11. Sketch the clock, input data, and output data for the 74LS109A by following the pattern in Example 6. Assume a 16 MHz clock and draw approximately to scale.
12. You have a circuit similar to Example 7 except that you have an 74LS109A instead of a 7474. How fast can the clock run?
13. Suppose you modified your design and could run the 74LS109A at 8 MHz in the circuit in Example 8. How much skew can you allow in the clock circuit?
14. Explain how a Schmitt-trigger device such as the 74LS14 could help prevent noise disturbances in a circuit.

FURTHER READING

COMER, DAVID J. *Digital Logic and State Machine Design*. New York: Holt, Rinehart and Winston, 1984. (TK 7868.S9C66)

FLETCHER, WILLIAM I. *An Engineering Approach to Digital Design*. Englewood Cliffs, NJ: Prentice-Hall, 1980. (TK 7868.D5F5)

FORBES, MARK, and BARRY B. BREY. *Digital Electronics*. Indianapolis, IN: Bobbs-Merrill Educational Publishing, 1985.

HAYES, JOHN P. *Digital System Design and Microprocessors*. New York: McGraw-Hill, 1984. (TK 7874.H393)

KLINE, RAYMOND M. *Structured Digital Design*. Englewood Cliffs, NJ: Prentice-Hall, 1983.

PEATMAN, JOHN B. *Digital Hardware Design*. New York: McGraw-Hill, 1980.

The TTL Data Book. Vol 2. Dallas, TX: Texas Instruments, Inc., 1985.

WIATROWSKI, CLAUDE A., and CHARLES H. HOUSE. *Logic Circuits and Microcomputer Systems*. New York: McGraw-Hill, 1980. (TK 7868.L6W5)

WINKEL, DAVID, and FRANKLIN PROSSER. *The Art of Digital Design*. Englewood Cliffs, NJ: Prentice-Hall, 1980. (TK 7888.3W56)

FOUR

Design Documentation

Putting Ideas on Paper

When you begin your project, you have many ideas for solving the various parts of your design problem. At the beginning of your work, you should outline your project goals, objectives, strategy, and plan in a mini-proposal. Is this the end of the paperwork? No, you know that either your manager or your professor expects a report of some kind at the end of the project. How can you be ready to easily prepare a report on your work?

This chapter demonstrates how to record your daily progress systematically and how to document the final results of your project. This documentation is important because someone else such as team members, manager, professor, or customer needs to understand and to use your design or product. You benefit as well: as you record your progress each day, you can review your work and learn from your mistakes. A daily review gives a better direction to your work.

You can record your daily progress most effectively by using a laboratory notebook. The lab book records what design and testing you do each day. In a larger sense, it contains everything about your project from its conception to the final report. There are many ways to keep a lab book, but the most important point to remember is that it is your "idea book," where you jot down your thoughts each day as your work progresses.

You can fully document your final results in the form of a technical design report to an engineering manager, a design report to a customer, or a semester project report. We will use the form of a technical manual because it contains all the information needed to install, operate, understand, and troubleshoot a product.

In order to present your design information clearly and consistently, you should follow the drawing guidelines given in the Appendix when you prepare your technical manual. This chapter will help you explain the drawings you prepare for hardware designs as well as for software designs.

4.1 LABORATORY NOTEBOOK

Your laboratory notebook is your workbook where you record the tasks you do each day. All your ideas and thoughts on your project should be included in it, beginning with the project conception, through the written proposal, and ending with the final report. Consider it your "idea book" where you write down everything that seems even remotely useful.

Physically, your lab book should be a bound notebook with numbered pages; it should not be a loose-leaf notebook because pages can be removed and easily lost. All writing should be in ink rather than in pencil. Date each page as you use it, and if you are involved with some patentable ideas, have a colleague witness and sign the pages with you. This is important because your lab book is evidence if you ever need to prove in court when you first worked on an invention.

Because your lab book is so special in this regard, be careful never to remove pages or obliterate any material. If you make an error, never erase it or blank it out: line it out and place the correct data beside the error. If a page is in error, put a large "X" through the page. Later, as you review your progress, you can see your errors and perhaps avoid making the same kind of mistake in the future.

Your laboratory notebook should be neat. However, never take data on a scrap piece of paper with the idea of later copying it neatly into the lab book. Loose paper gets lost easily; even if not lost, copying into the lab book might cause errors. Your lab book must always contain original data.

When you write in the lab book, do most of your work on the right-hand pages. Save the left-hand pages for graphs, for equations you might want to find easily, or for marginal notes of any kind. As you work on some of the creative parts of design, you might find the left pages useful for rough sketches of your ideas.

You might find it helpful to tape photocopies of manufacturers' data sheets in your lab book so you can easily refer to the information. In addition, you might need to use your lab book in several years when you do a similar design; by that time, the data manual you used originally might be replaced or lost. Your lab book should be as complete a record as possible of all that goes into your design; it should be able to stand alone.

If you find a technical article that is especially relevant to the lab work you are doing, tape it into your lab book for easy reference. Be sure to note its bibliographic information. Generally, however, you will find it more helpful to collect relevant articles and file them by topic rather than putting them in the lab book. Depending on the nature of your project, you might want to keep the lab book and the article files together and not mix the articles in with any others you might be saving.

The organization you follow when you actually enter information in your lab book depends on the nature of the problem. If you have a short "experiment" to perform, you will find the outline shown in Table 4.1 helpful. Notice that it follows the pattern of problem solving presented in Chapter 1. Does it make sense to use Table 4.1 for a large project that might take weeks to complete? Yes, because with a sizable job, it is easy to lose sight of your objectives and to waste time working on some minor detail. As with any design work, the outline is only a guide and should be modified to fit your particular situation.

TABLE 4.1 AN OUTLINE OF A TYPICAL LABORATORY EXPERIMENT.

Problem Statement	Briefly state an overview of what you are trying to accomplish. What is the problem or purpose of the experiment. Significance?
Objectives	List specific measurable outcomes of your experiment.
Background	Outline of relevant theory or practice. Include references for sources of information.
	Relate present problem to past work.
	Do an analysis of the present problem. (Do diagrams, equations, derivations, simulations.)
	What results are expected? (The analysis should give preliminary answers to each of your objectives stated above.)
Experiment Design	Plan how to obtain the data necessary to verify or disprove your analysis.
	Sketch equipment configuration and test circuits you need to attain each objective above.
Experiment	For each objective, connect equipment in accordance with your plan and make measurements and observations. Put your data in tables if appropriate.
	Note the model and serial number of the equipment you actually use for the experiment in case you need to verify data or expand the scope of your experiment later.
Evaluate Results	Analyze the data collected. What does the data indicate? Plot graphs of data if appropriate. Are there interrelations that explain what happened?
	For each objective, interpret the results and compare with the expected results. Why are there any differences between actual and expected?
Conclusions	What is your answer to the original problem?

If you begin your lab book with your original project concept and thoughts leading up to your proposal, then you will be able to focus quite clearly on your objectives. Break up a large project into manageable smaller tasks, work each task as shown in Table 4.1, then write a short summary for each task as you complete it. Each of these summaries can be used later as part of your progress reports or as part of the final project report.

Keeping your lab book neat and complete takes time. However, that time is well worth the effort. In addition to its value as a record of your designs and data, it is your daily idea book of useful information.

4.2 TECHNICAL MANUAL

The final results of your project can be reported in a number of ways depending on the reader and how the report will be used. A report intended for management, for example, will be different from a report directed primarily to engineers. A report in the form of a technical manual for engineers will be adopted for our use here because of its technical completeness. We will not be concerned with trade secrets and whether or not the product design is proprietary; delete sections your company normally withholds.

As shown in Table 4.2, the complete technical manual contains the information nec-

TABLE 4.2 AN OUTLINE OF THE MAJOR SECTIONS OF A TECHNICAL MANUAL.

Title Page	Title of project or product, author, date.
Introduction	Purpose of the product: What problem was solved? Importance: Background information and how the product relates to prior designs. Features: Description of unit and how it solves the problem.

Installation	System Configuration
	  Hardware setup and requirements
	    Equipment interconnections
	    Switch and jumper settings
	      Location drawing of switches and jumpers
	      Function table of switches and jumpers
	    Connectors
	      Location and assignments
	      Table of signals at each connector
	  Software organization and requirements
	    Memory map
	    I/O map
	  System checkout instructions

Operation	Operating instructions Operating Difficulties (How to Resolve)

Circuit Description	Theory of Hardware Operation
	  Block diagram of system and modules
	  Explanation of functional modules
	  Timing diagrams

Software Description	Theory of Software Operation
	  Structure Chart of System
	  Description of Algorithms
	  Flowcharts

Troubleshooting	Explanation of How to Troubleshoot Product
	  Chart of symptoms and possible causes
	  Sample hardware and software test-data readings

References	Documents Related to the Product
Appendix	Specifications Schematic Diagram Component Layout Jumper and Switch Index Parts List Data on LSI Devices Program Listings

essary to install, operate, understand, and troubleshoot the product. This information comes from the laboratory notebook and related material. If the lab book was written with short summaries at the end of each major task, then they can be used in the technical manual with only a little revision.

When you write the technical manual, design it so that the reader can use it efficiently. Your purpose in writing the report is to provide the reader with enough information to set up, use, and fix your product. If the material is arranged logically and facts can be found easily, then your manual will be effective and helpful. Remember, your reader probably has no previous experience with your product, and those points that are obvious to you might be quite obscure to someone else.

In Table 4.2, the *introduction* is intended to clarify the rationale behind your product. It presents the nature of the problem addressed and how your product solves the problem. Any relevant background information and how your product relates to it should be discussed. Give a brief description of your product including its features and limitations. Your introduction should provide enough information so that a reader can determine if your product will solve his or her particular need.

The *installation* section should provide all the information needed to connect and test your product for proper operation. Sketches are useful to illustrate the equipment setup and to show the settings for any switches and jumpers. Consider the possibility of putting in a very brief ''hook-it-up-quickly'' section; this is for the reader who skips the instructions unless the product fails to work as expected.

A special section of the installation instructions should cover system checkout. Illustrate several different software and hardware configurations and how the equipment responds for each setup. If the installer has been having difficulty, an indication of correct performance will be quite valuable.

The *operation* section covers all the details of how to use your product. You might find a tutorial section and a reference section helpful in explaining the operation of your system. The tutorial section will aid the inexperienced user by illustrating some practical instructions on each of the product features; the reference section will help the knowledgeable user find needed information quickly. If you are doing a major product, the tutorial and reference sections may be easily separated from the technical manual and used alone by a nontechnical operator. Include a section on how to resolve operating difficulties. For example, if the user makes a single incorrect datum entry, explain how it can be corrected without reentering all the data.

The *circuit description* section explains all the technical aspects of your hardware. After an overview of the product, present a block diagram of the system and its division into various functional modules. Show each of the modules individually and explain how each operates. If appropriate, include timing diagrams and segments of the circuit diagram to help the reader understand the design. By explaining the hardware design in detail, the technical reader can repair the equipment himself rather than send it back to the manufacturer if service is required.

The *software description* presents the system programs and how they work together with the hardware. A program structure chart, or a flowchart equivalent, can help the reader understand system functions easily. Include a description of the algorithms and their flowcharts as necessary. By providing these details, the user can correct any software bugs and keep the system running. Depending on the reader and the nature of the system, you might include program listings in the appendix of your manual.

The *troubleshooting* portion of your technical manual is also intended to help the technical reader repair your product. The most helpful information you can give is a chart describing various symptoms of hardware and software malfunctions. For each of the symptoms, give a list of several possible causes and how to fix them. Keep it brief: a checklist at the workbench is far more valuable than page upon page of theory. Show several test setups, and give a number of typical voltage and oscilloscope patterns at critical points.

Much of the troubleshooting outline can come from your own experience in getting the prototype working properly. You probably already know which parts are critical and what the symptoms are if they fail. Additional information can be gathered for high-risk parts by replacing a good part with a defective one and noting the effect on the product. Open some critical circuits or cause some shorts in signal paths for additional troubleshooting data. If your system uses a microprocessor, include diagnostic programs to test various modules such as memory, I/O, and any external devices connected to the system.

The *references* section cites all the documents related to your product. The idea is for the reader to know what other material must be included with the design manual for a complete documentation package. You may also want to cite reference articles or tutorials for the reader to study.

TABLE 4.3 A SAMPLE OUTLINE OF A SOFTWARE DOCUMENTATION PACKAGE.

Problem Statement	Concise statement of the problem. Include a description of input variables required and outputs that will be provided by program.
Program Description	Overview: The approach to the problem's solution. Describe the strategy used to solve the problem. Include equations.
	Assumptions: What assumptions were made about the problem or the solution method?
	Variable List: Include list of names and descriptions of each of the input, process, and output variables.
	Data Structures: Sketch how the data is represented. This might be on several levels of abstraction: the problem level, the system level, and the machine level.
	Limitations: What parts of the problem are not programmed completely? How does the program handle undesired events such as out-of-range data or system faults? Areas that need more design in the future?
Program Design	Structure Chart: Describe the overall plan of how the program is constructed.
	Algorithms: Use pseudo-design language (PDL) to describe how the program works.
	Flow Chart: Illustrate portions of the program with a simple flow chart.
Program Listing	Provide a complete listing of the program. The program should be internally documented and start with a heading containing the name and function of the program, your name, and the date. Include comments to explain each major section of code. Tell how to compile and link all the program modules together.
Test Data and Results	Provide sample output that will illustrate correct operation of the program for normal and abnormal inputs. Include test data verifying the program at its design limits.

The *appendix* includes all the charts, tables, diagrams, programs, and background material related to your design. It is a collection of vital information required to describe and completely build the product.

When you assemble the technical manual, you can easily delete the software details and put them in a separate document. An outline of a typical software documentation package is shown in Table 4.3. For many products, it is convenient to give a brief explanation of the software in general and then refer the reader to a software manual. Because software tends to be updated with new revisions more frequently than hardware, a separate manual is easier to keep in order. This is especially true in a large project where different groups of designers are responsible for hardware and software.

4.3 DRAWING GUIDELINES

Drawing guidelines help you present your design clearly and consistently in a form other technical people will easily understand. As you saw in Table 4.2, a number of different drawings and tables are used to document a project. One of the most important drawings is the schematic diagram. The schematic diagram illustrates how your circuit is wired. It shows the logic gates, switches, connectors, memory, and all other devices that are connected in your design. Appendix A gives the guidelines to use when drawing the schematic.

Note that the schematic is oriented toward board-level rather than system-level documentation. For example, suppose you have a system with several printed circuit boards (PCBs) connected together. Each of the PCBs would be documented with schematics as in Appendix A. The system-level documentation would involve a different schematic showing the wiring that connects the PCBs to each other and to any external devices such as switches, lights, or power supplies. It would show the PCBs as functional blocks rather than display the details of each board.

The component-layout drawing is used with the schematic diagram to pinpoint where each part is located physically on the PCB. It should show the location of each IC and indicate all switch, jumper, and connector locations. If there are many switches and jumpers, a duplicate component-layout drawing with highlighted switch and jumper locations would be useful. The drawing should be drawn reasonably close to scale so that it appears the same as the board. Each part should be designated by its part number (U1, U2, etc.) and type (7400, 7404, etc.) for easy use at the workbench.

4.4 EXAMPLE TECHNICAL MANUAL

An example technical manual will be helpful in pulling together the ideas of this chapter. For example, consider the temperature monitor described in the Chapter 1 mini-proposal. How should this project be documented? One approach using Table 4.2 is shown in Appendix B. Because of the project's small size, not all the elements of Table 4.2 are present; however, you can install, operate, understand, and troubleshoot using the information given.

4.5 SUMMARY

All of your engineering work requires documentation of some kind to record your progress and to explain your final results. This is important because others need to understand and use your design or product.

Your primary documentation is the laboratory notebook. It contains everything related to the project: the initial ideas on a problem solution, the rough mini-proposal, the block diagrams, the hardware and software designs, and all your sketches and notes. Keeping the lab book well organized is important, and Table 4.1 outlines an approach for performing the lab work as a series of experiments. The lab notebook provides all the information you need for any reports on your project. It also contains the data to write a complete technical manual on the product.

A technical manual is one way of preparing a final report on a project. Its focus is on the user of the product and it illustrates setting up, operating, and troubleshooting the product. The technical manual can be organized in a variety of ways. Table 4.2 shows an outline of the major sections in one form of a technical manual. Several parts of the manual can easily be written as separate documents. For example, the operating instructions can be written in a small booklet kept with the product. Similarly, because of its many possible revisions, software documentation may be kept in its own separate binder.

All the schematics in the technical manual should be prepared according to drawing guidelines as shown in Appendix A. This is necessary because the design will be used by a number of technical people, and a standard format will not only help their understanding but also will reduce the chance of errors.

The example technical manual on the temperature monitor is intended to illustrate the documentation concepts in the chapter. Although abbreviated, this example is sufficient to help a user set up and use the equipment.

By systematically recording your daily work and documenting the results of your project, you will be able to explain your work clearly to others. In addition, you can review your progress and learn from your past mistakes. As you do the review, you may find a better direction for your work and perhaps even discover some new ideas for future product development.

FURTHER READING

BROWNING, CHRISTINE. *Guide to Effective Software Technical Writing*. Englewood Cliffs, NJ: Prentice-Hall, 1984.

FLETCHER, WILLIAM I. *An Engineering Approach to Digital Design*. Englewood Cliffs, NJ: Prentice-Hall, 1980. (TK 7868.D5F5)

SHERMAN, THEODORE A., and SIMON S. JOHNSON. *Modern Technical Writing*. 4th Edition. Englewood Cliffs, NJ: Prentice-Hall, 1983.

WEISS, EDMOND H. *The Writing System for Engineers and Scientists*. Englewood Cliffs, NJ: Prentice-Hall, 1982. (T11.W44)

FIVE

Clock Design Example
Reality

As you studied the first four chapters, your work was fairly structured and your designs were virtually guaranteed to perform properly. When you analyzed the customer needs and prepared a mini-proposal to outline your project plan, you were sure your plan would work. In the second and third chapters you used the proposal to complete a technical design on paper and to build a working prototype; you were sure this would work too. Why? Because you were both the customer and the designer: you could change the rules. If a feature became particularly difficult, you eliminated it from the requirements and made sure of a satisfactory design. Likewise, although your design had to adhere to certain technical standards (as in Chapter 3), you did not have to design to meet a formal industry or military standard. Consequently, your designs could be done easily and successfully.

The reality is that you must do your engineering in accordance with a number of technical standards. Which standards apply in any given situation depends on the customer and his or her requirements. For example, suppose your customer has a computer system that conforms with IEEE Std-696 (S-100 bus) and needs an added function in the system. Your design must either comply with the standard or run the risk of causing system malfunctions or complete system failure. Suppose your customer is the military and you would like to supply a circuit to be added to a radio transmitter. To have even a slight hope of proper operation, you would have to design your circuit to meet all of many applicable military standards and specifications. If your design does not meet the requirements in all points, then there could be system failures with drastic consequences.

Even though standards tend to be confining at times, they do ease the design burden considerably. When you design to meet a standard, many technical details are clearly outlined and do not require extra design time on your part. For example, in IEEE Std-696, a standard 100-conductor bus is defined with certain signals on particular lines in the bus. Thus, you do not need to design a connector and the location of certain signals. In addition to the physical configuration, a bus protocol is specified that helps you communicate with other devices in the system. Therefore, you do not need to spend design time figuring out bus protocol. The design effort, while complex in a sense, does become easier when you can use the standard.

The primary purpose of this chapter is to illustrate the complete design sequence from need identification through documentation. The secondary purpose is to introduce the IEEE Std-696 and how you use it when you design a product. To apply your knowledge of planning and implementation, you will design a clock that meets the IEEE Std-696. As you work through the design you will begin to understand engineering more fully and also learn how to design using an industry standard.

After you work through the clock design example, you should be able to develop the more complex design required for the 68000 microcomputer system. Also, you can use your clock design as a full-scale realistic design guide to help you meet the bus standard. After you finish this chapter, you will be able to construct a prototype circuit board and document it fully. This chapter will help you integrate all you know so far and prepare you for your 68000 design project.

5.1 NEED IDENTIFICATION

For our purposes, suppose you are a design engineer in a small design and manufacturing company and that you work directly with customers. A customer will normally meet with the sales and engineering managers first, and then you will be assigned to handle all the details of the project. When you first meet the customer, about all you can be sure of is that your company management thinks you can solve the customer's problem. Your role is to find out what the customer needs and then work out a solution to the problem. Although the customer will probably pay for a portion of your engineering time, assume your company expects to profit by building and selling several hundred units of the circuit you design.

On first meeting and talking with your customer, you find that he needs a real-time clock that will operate in an S-100 (IEEE Std-696) computer system running at the maximum system clock speed of 6 MHz. The clock should be able to keep time and date as well as provide a means of interrupting the system on either a regular basis or at a predetermined point in time. It should maintain an accuracy within ten seconds per month with or without system power. Except for initially setting the time and date, the operator should not have to interact with the clock in any way.

The clock should operate as a slave on the bus without affecting normal system operation; likewise, there should be no changes required in the system software. Data transfer between the clock and system should use I/O-mapped ports. The handshaking should use the S-100 RDY line, and because the processor operates at 6 MHz, some wait states may be used if necessary. Clock interrupts to the system should be switchable to use any of the S-100 vectored-interrupt lines.

Although the customer is planning to write his initial programs to poll the clock for the time, the clock should be able to use any of the vectored-interrupt lines to implement a future real-time multitasking executive. In the long term, this could involve multiprocessing with a new 6 MHz 68000 CPU board in the system. For the near term, however, the software will only set and display the time and service interrupts.

During these discussions with the customer, you discovered that he was really looking for two things: first, a clock in his system so that he could have a "time" function in his programs, and second, a future capability to use the clock interrupts in an advanced system being planned. If your clock design is a success, then there is a high probability that your company will have the contract to develop the advanced system as well.

5.2 PROJECT PLAN

At this point, you have a good idea of what your customer wants, and already you have a few ideas on how you can do the clock design. Before going out to the lab bench to build some models, plan your project! You have a job to do, so make a mini-proposal for your own use to keep you on target as you do the project. Put this mini-proposal directly into your lab notebook as you start work.

First, write your project definition as you understand it. Capture the essence of the big picture:

Project Definition

The goal of my project is to design, build, and test a prototype real-time clock board meeting the IEEE Std-696.

Next, write your project objectives. These are the specific measurable outcomes of what you intend to accomplish by the end of your project. Allowing at least a page or more in your lab book, you can write these objectives as your product specifications.

Project Objectives

Time: hour, minute, second
Calendar: day of week, date, month, year
Periodic interrupts: 100 ms and 1 s
Wake-up interrupts at preset times
Accuracy 0.01 %
Operating temperature 20 to 40°C
Power supply: +8 V (200 mA, rechargeable battery)
Meet IEEE Std-696
Use readily available parts, easy to build and test
No system hardware or software changes required

Once you have your project defined and have a set of objectives written in your lab book, figure out the strategy of how you can do the job. Avoid getting into the details of how to reach objectives, even if you think you know the answers. When you write the strategy, double space and allow yourself a full page in your lab book. Remember, this is a working document that you will want to refer to as you go along.

Strategy

The strategy of how to meet the clock objectives is to do a complete design on paper of the entire clock. This will be followed by building a prototype and testing it as each module is completed.

Finally, make your plan of action to get the project accomplished. Go through your strategy and find major items that need to be done and write yourself a ''do-it'' list. Refer to Chapter 1 and outline a step-by-step plan in your lab book along with your best estimate of how long each step will take. Sketch a tentative bar chart of the various tasks so you have some deadlines to meet.

Notice the sequence you followed when you started the clock project. After identifying the customer's needs, you wrote a project plan in your lab book that contained:

- Project Definition (the goal)
- Project Objectives (requirements and constraints)
- Strategy (how to reach objectives)
- Plan (action needed to implement strategy)

Now that you know where you should go, you can begin the implementation of the project. Remember that doing the planning as you start the project might seem like lost time, but in reality you are saving time by focusing your overall effort directly on the problem.

5.3 PROJECT IMPLEMENTATION

As you learned in Chapter 2, the project implementation involves two major steps: the technical design and the construction of a prototype model of the circuit. The technical design phase is when you do a complete paper design of the project; the construction phase is when you build a first unit and test it for proper operation.

5.3.1 Technical Design

When you begin the technical design, you should analyze the constraints and the specifications you intend to meet. Review the standards that you expect to use in your design and see that you understand what will be required; be sure to work from the standard itself and not someone else's summary of it. You want to synthesize a design concept that is a best balance between the required specifications and the various constraints.

First, analyze the product specifications in detail and categorize each requirement by function. Try to describe what your clock board is supposed to do; when you do this, avoid any statement about how to do it. You might use this list when you divide up the product by function:

1. What does the clock board do?
2. How well must it perform?

3. What system interactions are required?
4. What operator attention is needed?
5. What hardware interface is required?

After you complete answering these questions, probably you will have a functional specification similar to Figure 5.1. This specification describes the product as you see it at the moment. As you synthesize a solution to the design problem, you will add more technical details later that describe the actual circuit as it evolves.

Functional Requirement	Keep time: hour, minute, second Keep calendar: day, date, month, year Provide periodic interrupts to system Provide wake-up interrupts to system
Performance Requirement	Maintain 0.01% accuracy Operate between 20 and 40°C Use less than 200 mA at 8 V supply
System Interaction	Operate with 6 MHz system bus Assert interrupts when required Set interrupt modes
Operator Interaction	Set initial time and date Inquire for time and date Set interrupt modes
Hardware Interface	Compatible with IEEE Std-696 Operate as slave on the bus

Figure 5.1 The initial functional specification of the clock board. More details will be added as the design develops.

Next, sketch a system block diagram and then do a top-down design of the modules within the system. You might begin with a sketch of the system as shown in Figure 5.2(a). After seeing the board in its proper frame of reference, go into more detail as in Figure 5.2(b). Ask yourself what the board needs for inputs (power, someone to set the time at least once, etc.) and what it provides as outputs (time, interrupts, etc.). Note that these inputs and outputs match the functions you described in the functional specification in Figure 5.1.

At this point you can combine both sketches in Figure 5.2 to begin the block diagram of the clock board as shown in Figure 5.3. Now you are synthesizing a concept for the solution to the design problem. One possible concept is to use a CMOS LSI clock such as the National MM58167A real-time clock. The advantage of using CMOS is that you can operate the clock with a small battery over extended periods of time.

The block diagram for the system designed around this clock IC is shown in Figure 5.4. The design using this clock IC can be partitioned into several major modules that include the clock, address decoder, data-bus interface, interrupt switches, and power supply. Once divided into modules, the hardware can be easily designed in much the same way software is developed; that is, the hardware design can be done top-down, bottom-up, or most critical first.

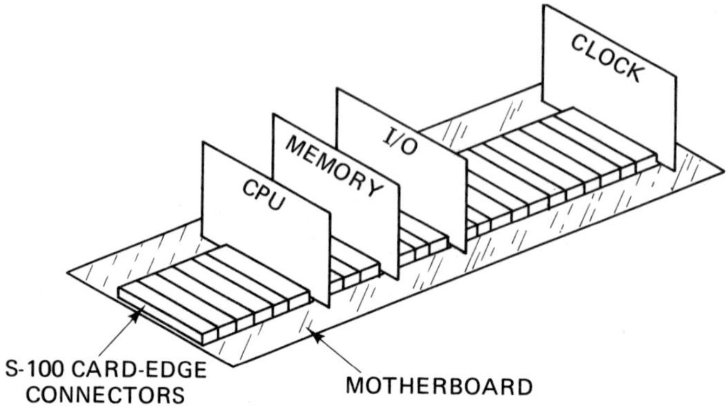

(a)

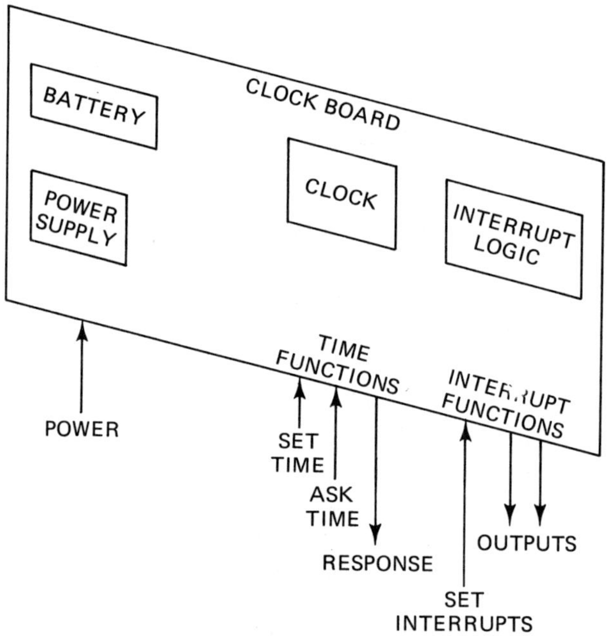

(b)

Figure 5.2 One way to begin the technical design is to draw some quick sketches. (a) Show the proposed clock board in the system. (b) Sketch the clock board showing its major inputs, outputs, and functions.

The appropriate design method in this case is to consider the most critical section first. Everything depends on the clock IC, and its requirements should be considered before all else. The block diagram of the MM58167A, Figure 5.5, shows that the IC uses 5 address lines (32 different addresses) and a chip select, has a single bidirectional data bus and separate read/write controls, two interrupt outputs, and a power-down control. Each

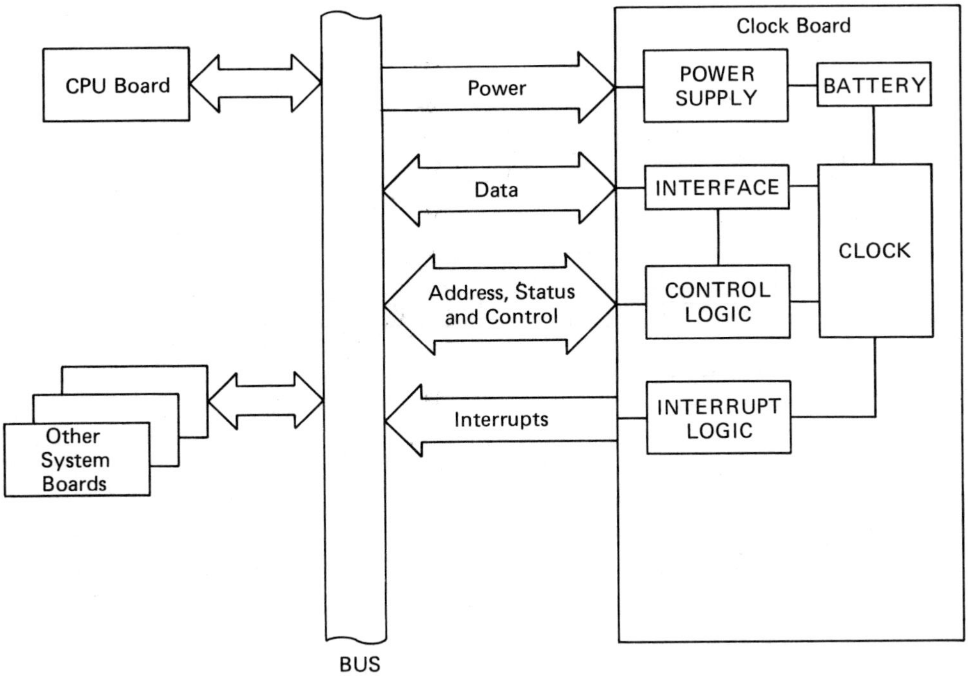

Figure 5.3 Block diagram of the system plus some rough detail on the clock board design.

of these requirements can be designed individually at this point and result in the implementation shown in the circuit schematic in Figure 5.6.

When you use I/O mapping (as opposed to memory mapping) for the clock data transfer, you have a maximum of 256 ports. Only the lower eight bits of the address bus need decoding, and five of these are internally decoded by the clock IC. For maximum flexibility, you can use DIP switches to select the three most significant bits of the I/O address. The output of the decoder is used as a chip-select for the clock and is used by the read/write qualifier circuit.

The S-100 data bus in-and-out lines are buffered with a pair of 74LS244s connected directly to the clock IC. The buffer for data-in (DI from the processor's viewpoint) is strobed using the I/O read qualifiers pDBIN, sINP, and the chip-select CS. The data-out buffer is strobed using pWR*, sOUT, and the chip-select CS. During a typical read bus cycle, for example, the proper address is placed on the address bus, sINP asserted, and then pDBIN asserted to strobe the DI buffer and the clock RD* input. In the typical write bus cycle, the address is put on the bus, sOUT asserted, and then pWR* asserted to strobe the DO buffer and the clock WR* input.

Timing. A basic read or write bus cycle has three bus states (BS1, BS2, and BS3), each of which takes 167 ns in a 6 MHz system; consequently, a bus read or write

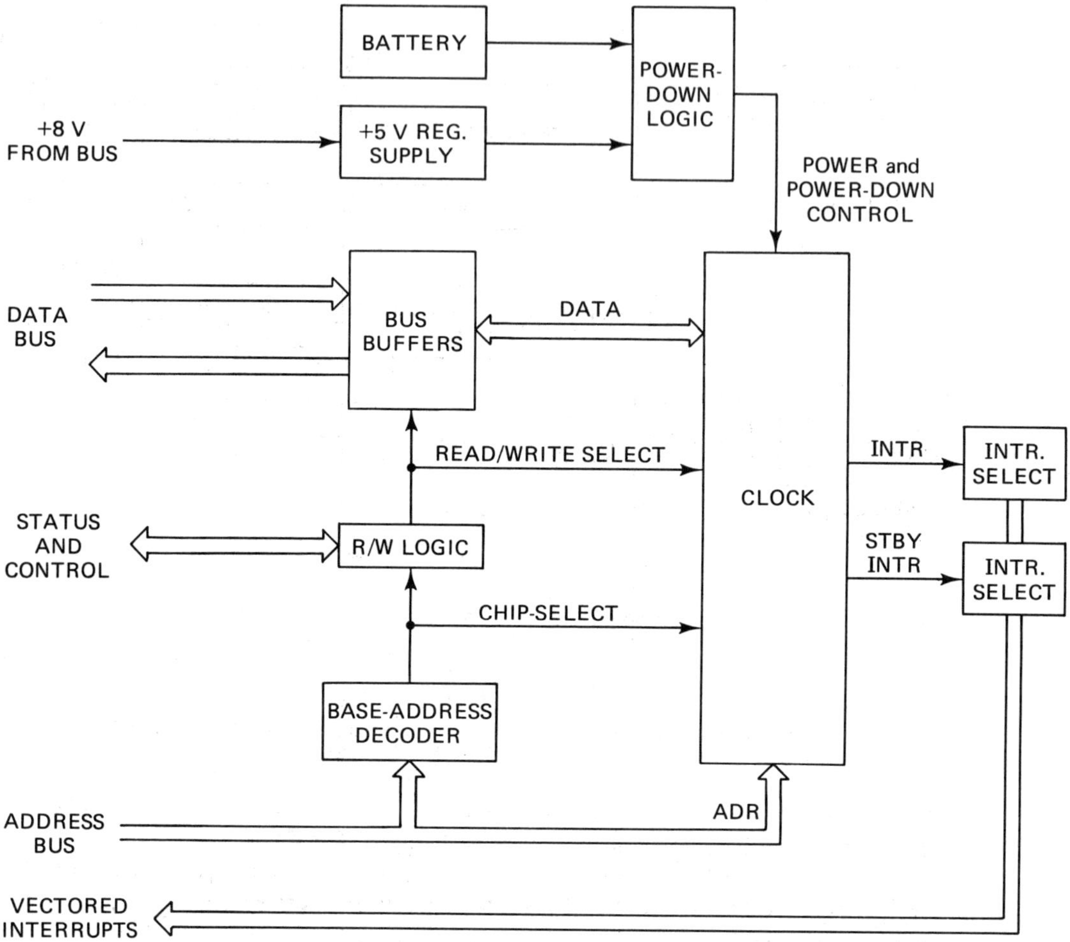

Figure 5.4 Block diagram of real-time clock board.

normally completes within 500 ns. However, for I/O devices that require substantial access times, the bus cycle can be extended by adding a number of wait states, as in Figure 5.7. To find out if wait states are required during any read or write bus cycle, the bus master (the CPU) samples the RDY line at the rising edge of the system clock in Bus State 2 (BS2). If the RDY line is found low, then a wait state (BSw) is inserted immediately after BS2; if the RDY line is still low a bus state later, then yet another wait state is inserted. Wait states continue to be added until RDY finally goes high; at that point, the bus cycle concludes with BS3.

The MM58167A clock requires wait states in the bus cycle because of its slow access time. For a clock-read operation, the time required from a valid address until the output data is valid might range from 500 ns to the specified maximum of 1050 ns, far

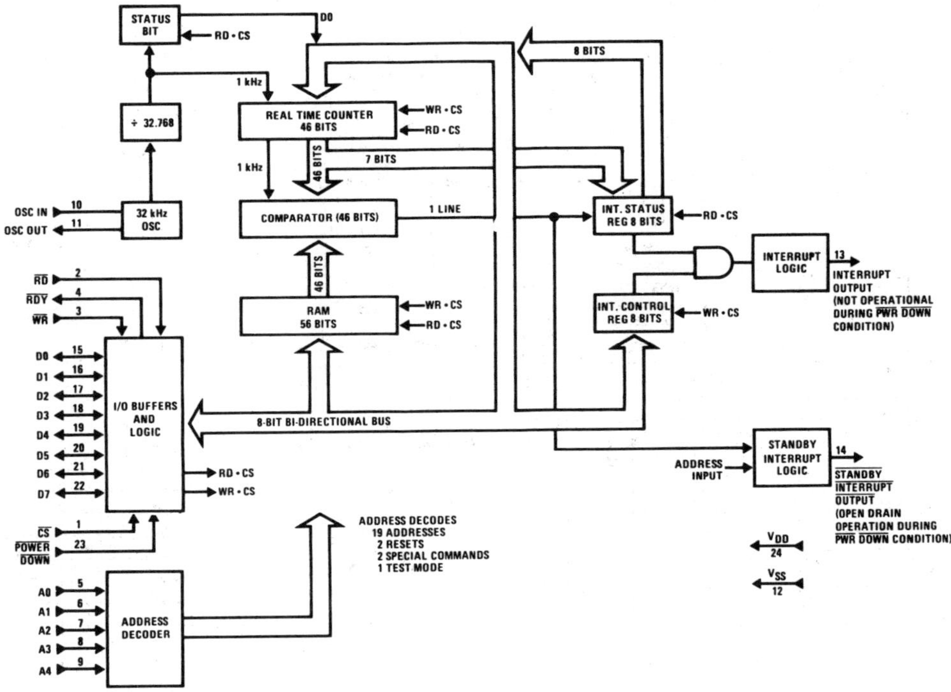

Figure 5.5 Block diagram of the MM58167A real-time clock. (Courtesy National Semiconductor Corporation)

longer than the time required for a normal bus cycle (i.e., 167 ns $\times$ 3 = 500 ns). The read cycle of a typical 6 MHz IEEE-696 system is shown in Figure 5.7, with approximate times to scale. Notice that the example timing diagram includes a total of three wait states to make up for the slow access time.

The normal S-100 requirement is that the RDY line be low at the end of BS1 if waits are required in a bus cycle. In the clock case, however, this is impossible: the clock is not even being read until BS2, so it cannot respond until about a cycle later. In a case like this, the CPU board itself has to add in a wait state automatically if an I/O access is being made. Doing so allows the clock to have until the end of BS2 to get RDY pulled low. As shown in Figure 5.7, the clock holds RDY low to get two more wait states in the bus cycle. When the clock data is finally valid, the RDY line is allowed to go high, and the data is read by the processor in BS3. To finish BS3, pDBIN is negated, which raises the clock RD* input, and the address deselects the clock.

Figure 5.8 shows actual bus timing data using a Z-80 CPU board as bus master. The CPU has been set to add in a single wait state. RDY is pulled low by the clock about 50 ns after the start of BS2; this is 167 minus 50 or about 120 ns before it *must* be low. The IEEE Std-696 calls for a 70 ns setup time before the rising edge of the next system clock, so you can see there is about 120 minus 70 or 50 ns margin here. That is, if RDY were later by more than 50 ns, then RDY would not meet the standard's setup-time

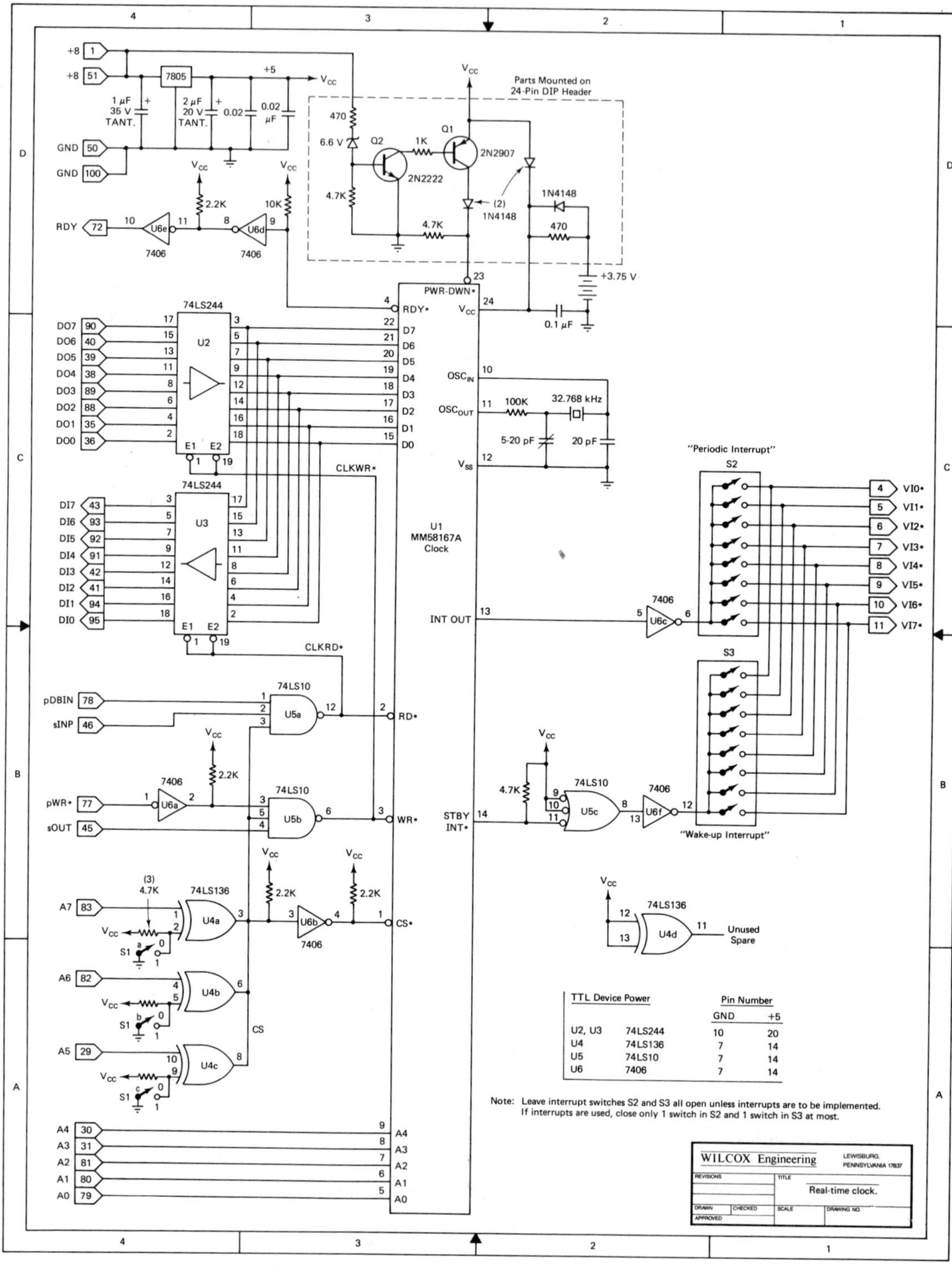

Figure 5.6 Real-time clock schematic drawn on zonal-coordinate paper.

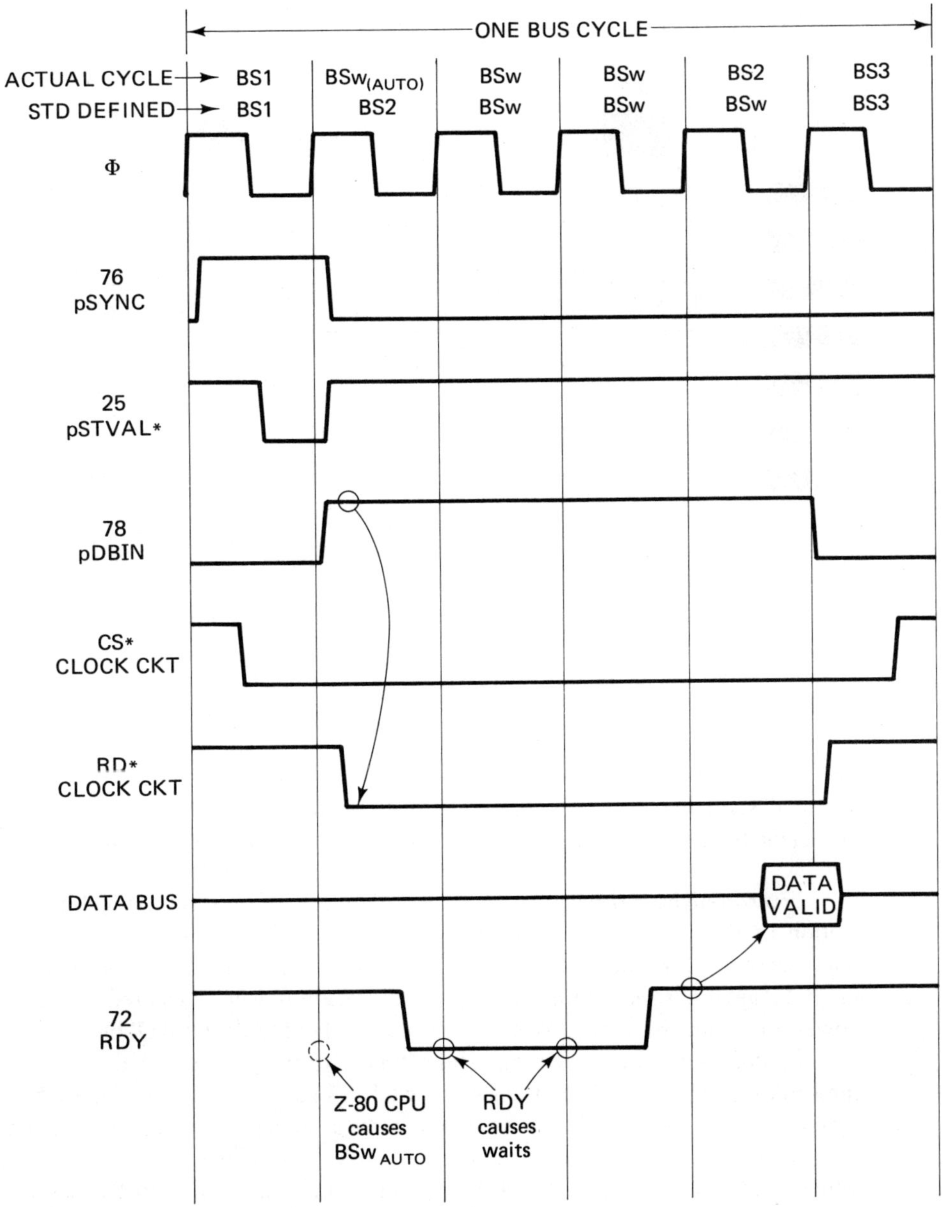

Figure 5.7 Read bus cycle for the clock. As drawn, one wait is caused by the Z-80 CPU board; the others by the clock RDY line.

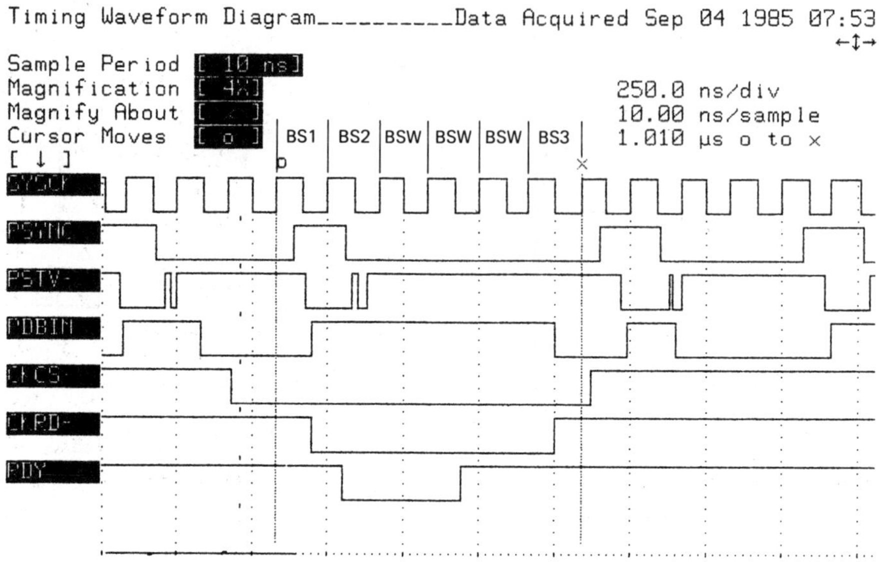

Figure 5.8 Actual bus data using a commercial Z-80 CPU board.

specification. Your system would probably work even if the setup time were reduced to, say, 20 ns, but you would not be able to guarantee a general-case performance.

The write bus cycle timing requirements for the clock are quite similar to the read later by more than 50 ns, then RDY would not meet the standard's setup-time timing described above. As in the read, a total of two wait states must be included to allow sufficient time for RDY to be pulled low during the write operation.

Power-down design. The power-down design is quite critical in the actual operation of the clock. If PWR-DWN* is not asserted to a low-voltage level at least a microsecond before the system power is removed, then the contents of the clock memory might be anything (or nothing) when normal system power is restored. Further, when the power does come back on, PWR-DWN* must be held LOW until all bus signals are valid.

A common way of accomplishing this is to use a zener diode to set a reference threshold voltage to control a transistor switch. Consider the circuit, Figure 5.6, when the system is off: Q1 and Q2 are both off. When the system power comes on, nothing happens until the system bus voltage reaches about 6.6 V. Then the zener conducts, turns on Q2, which then turns on Q1. When Q1 goes on, voltage is applied to PWR-DWN*, which activates the clock chip for normal operation. A system bus voltage greater than 6.6 V is enough to allow near-normal output from all 5 V regulators, so all bus signals should be valid by this time. When the system is turned off, the system voltage drops down gradually enough so that when it passes below 6.6 V, the zener and Q1/Q2 can drop the PWR-DWN* to a low voltage before the bus signals b ecome invalid.

A small 3.75 V, 20 mAH NiCad rechargeable battery is used to maintain clock operation when system power is off. Specified current consumption of the clock is on the order of 10 to 20 μA using the battery with series-blocking diode. The 470 Ω resistor provides a trickle charge of 0.5 mA to about 2 mA depending on the state of the battery and component tolerances. For an average of several hours a day use, this resistor keeps the battery charged between 3.8 V and 4.15 V with no difficulties.

Logic circuits. IEEE Std-696 (Sec. 3.7) states that a card may not source more than 0.5 mA at 0.5 V nor sink more than 80 μA at 2.4 V on most system signal lines. The effect of this is that only one LS-TTL gate per card can be connected to each line of the address bus. The address decoder uses a 74LS136 exclusive-or, which sources a worst-case maximum of 0.8 mA at 0.4 V. This should cause no operational problems in any practical sense, and the appropriate design tradeoff is to use the 74LS136 rather than add extra hardware to buffer the address bus to be strictly within the specification. You might want to check with your customer to verify that this tradeoff will not cause a problem later in the system.

The pull-up resistors for the open-collector 7406 are selected to maintain proper logic levels and currents. The design tradeoff is to let the various resistors be high for lower current consumption, or to let them be low for more speed at the expense of the current. As drawn in Figure 5.6, the pull-up resistors are designed for as much speed as possible.

The clock standby-interrupt output can be used to implement the "wake-up" interrupt specification; to do this, an extra noninverting gate is needed. The spare 74LS10 and the last spare 7406 gate can be used to get this output from the clock board without adding another package. This particular output does not have the flexibility of the programmable output, but is useful to indicate a match between real time and a preset time for a wake-up alarm.

5.3.2 Prototype Construction

The second half of the project implementation is the construction of the prototype model of the circuit. Although the paper design is done and appears correct, you still must build the prototype and demonstrate its proper operation. In the technical design, it is easy to overlook some specifications, and your prototype will help you find and correct these oversights.

First do a rough sketch of where the major functions will be physically located on the prototype circuit board. Then build the prototype module by module, much as you did the technical design by modules or functions. In the design phase, the most critical section was the clock, and you did its circuit first. After the clock, you did the address decoding, bus control, interrupts, and power-down. When you build, however, construct from the bottom-up so you can debug as you go along.

What you would like to have as you build the prototype is a working, error-free circuit that can help you catch flaws in your paper design. Start with a simple but necessary function on the clock board: the power supply. All the parts on the board need power, so build that module first and check it out. Once you have power available, then you can do the address decoder and check it out too. Next, do the bus buffers and continue with the rest until you have a complete circuit.

How do you do the testing and then the debugging if there is a problem? Test the first module, the power supply, with a multimeter for shorts when you finish its wiring. Then plug the board into an S-100 system and turn on the system power. Measure the +5 V from the regulator and see that it appears at the proper places on your prototype board. If you find a problem with your supply, trace the circuit back to see that the system +8 V is coming into your circuit. If it is, with only the 7805 regulator in the supply, then either the 7805 is defective or its output is shorted. You should have found the short earlier with the multimeter, so fix the regulator. When all is satisfactory, turn off the system, remove the board, and start wiring the next section.

Build and test the address decoder next. Wire up the four logic gates that produce the clock chip-select CS*. Set the three switches to a clear I/O port address (A0 hex, for example) and plug the board back into the system. Apply power and boot up your system as you do normally. If your system cannot boot, the problem must be related to the A7 through A0 address inputs you connected on the clock board. Use your logic probe and check to see if one or more of the address lines is being held high or low. If the system booted normally, use the logic probe and check for CS*. You should find activity here because the address bus hits the address A0 (and all the combinations of 101x xxxx) many times each second.

Following the same approach, build and test the read-and-write strobe qualifier circuits RD* and WR*. Boot your operating system and use the logic probe to make sure CS* still has activity. Check RD* and WR*: they should be negated (i.e., HIGH). Using your operating system debugging program (for example, CP/M's DDT), execute a small one-line program that will assert RD*. If your system is running with a Z-80, you might execute an instruction

```
IN A, (A0)
```

This will cause the Z-80 to place A0 on the address bus and then read the data at that I/O port into the accumulator. Relate your circuit to the read bus cycle in Figure 5.7: the combination of pDBIN and sINP and the correct address will cause RD* to go LOW just once. You should see this pulse on your logic probe as you execute the instruction. You can do a similar test for WR* by executing the instruction

```
OUT (A0),A
```

This will cause the Z-80 to send the accumulator data out to the I/O port A0. Each time you execute this instruction you should see the pulse on your logic probe.

If you already have an IEEE Std-696 68000 CPU board in operation, you know that it does memory-mapped I/O. That is, rather than IN or OUT, the 68000 normally exchanges data with other system devices by reading or writing to memory addresses. A certain block of the 68000's 16 Mb address space should be decoded on your 68000 board for I/O purposes. For example, suppose the address range FF0000 to FFFFFF hex is designated for I/O devices. You could expect that the S-100 sINP and sOUT would respond properly and you could write your test code just as you would for memory accesses. For example, you might use

```
MOVE.B $FF00A0,D0
```

to do a read from port A0. The data would be stored in D0. Then use

```
MOVE.B D0,$FF00A0
```

to write D0 data out to port A0.

After you have RD* and WR* working properly, you can build and test the data bus buffers. With nothing in the clock socket, you will not be able to read or write actual data. You will, however, be able to boot your system and see that the buffers are being properly strobed when you execute the same programs you used to test RD* and WR*. If you want, you can test for proper reading by temporarily connecting arbitrary logic HIGH and LOW values to the data lines at the empty clock socket: execute an IN A,(A0) and see if you read the correct data into the Z-80 A register. Remove the temporary wires and execute an OUT (A0),A instruction to check if data is getting to the clock socket. When you do this instruction, you should be able to use your logic probe to see a pulse at each data pin on the socket.

Finish the rest of the clock board following the same approach: build a module, test it, build another module, and test it too. When you have the board finished, you will fully understand how it works and will be confident of how well it meets the specifications. Notice that the only test equipment you needed to get the clock board in operation was your multimeter and logic probe. You might have used an oscilloscope and executed scope-loop programs to check the various timing waveforms and be sure they were within specifications.

For illustration in this chapter, the entire real-time clock was prototyped on a Vector 8800V wire-wrap board as shown in Figure 5.9. The interrupt switches (S3) for the wake-up interrupt are located beside the main interrupt switches (S2). Less than a third of a standard S-100 board is required for all the circuits. The transistor power-down circuit is wired on the 24-pin component-carrier at the lower-left edge of the board by the battery. Plastic "wrap-ID" panels were used on the back of the board for each IC socket to make component and pin identification easier.

5.4 DOCUMENTATION

When you started the clock project, you began by writing your project definition, objectives, and strategy in your lab notebook. After writing out a step-by-step plan of action, you did all your circuit design in the notebook. Then, as you started building and testing the prototype, you put more information in your lab book. By the time you had a working prototype meeting specifications, your lab book probably became quite full with everything in it. Of all the information, the most important is your test data and your notes on how you corrected any problems.

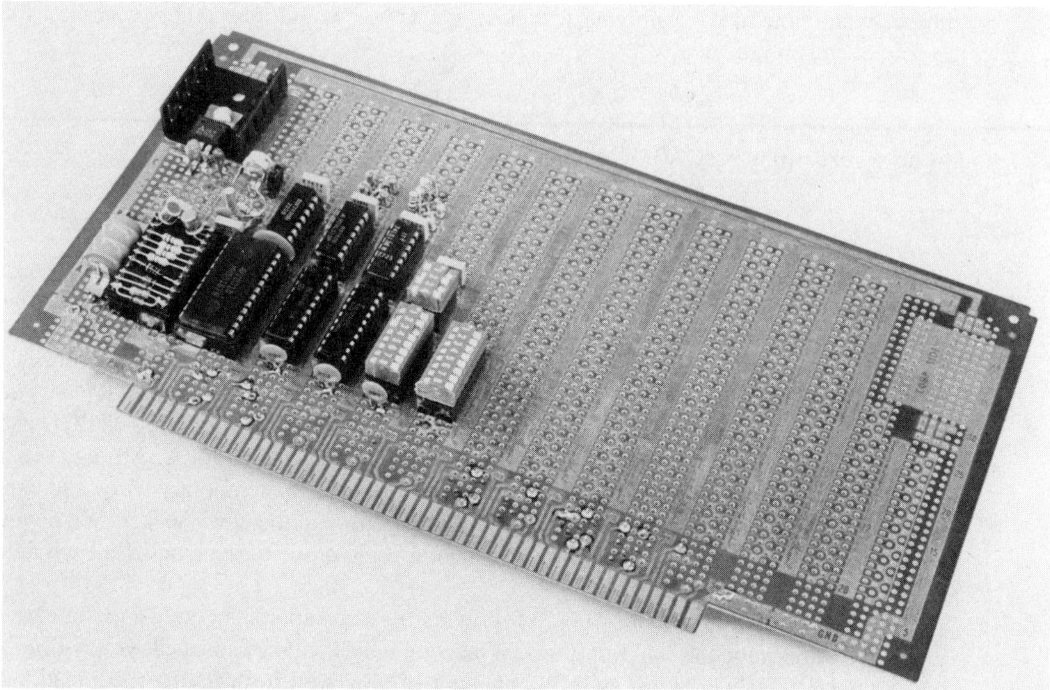

Figure 5.9 Prototype model of the real-time clock.

What you do next really depends on your actual situation. If your customer (hypothetically described earlier in Section 5.1) wants to try the prototype in his system so he can write some software for it, then all you may need to give him is a single sheet showing the address and interrupt switch settings. More likely, however, you will need to provide more information than that.

Suppose you learn that the design is entirely satisfactory and that your company will probably sell several hundred of the clock boards. The information in your lab book will be necessary so you can provide sketches for your drafting personnel and a parts list for purchasing. As your board finally moves into manufacturing, you will need to verify production test data with your original design. If you were diligent in keeping your lab book up to date, then you should have no problems.

A manual of some type will be shipped with the clock boards you sell. For the moment, assume that a full technical manual is required. Refer to Table 4.2 and start assembling your information. All the data you need should be in your lab book and only needs to be organized and explained.

5.5 SUMMARY

Your work during the first four chapters was structured enough so that your designs would perform properly. Other than making sure that your circuits were technically correct, you did not need to follow any particular industry or military standards. In reality, though, you know that you must not only design a technically correct product that satisfies the customer's needs, but you must also design to standards.

Standards can substantially ease your design burden. The idea behind the standards is to have uniformity and interchangeability of system subassemblies, and this means that many technical details are already set. You do not need to spend time doing design that the standard has already covered. You do, however, have the obligation to study and understand the standard so that you can use it properly.

An ideal way to learn about a standard is to do a design with it. The purpose in doing the clock board project is to see how to do a complete design using the IEEE Std-696. This particular standard has been successfully implemented on a number of machines, and you can test out your circuit easily using one of them as a test bed.

Just as you would begin any design project, when you design with a standard you start with the need identification and project plan. Write down the project definition, objectives, and strategy in your lab notebook. Then move on to a complete paper design and the construction of the prototype.

Most of your work with the standard is during the technical design phase when you examine how your circuit should interface with the system. If you begin with a top-down approach of defining various functions that your board needs to perform, then you can quickly sketch a useful block diagram of the board. Deal with the most critical section as soon as you have a block diagram: examine the clock itself and what support circuits it needs. Then you can design the necessary interface modules to meet the standard.

The most critical issue when you design with the IEEE Std-696 is the timing of signals. Depending on the type of input or output instruction the CPU performs, the bus signals behave in a unique way to complete the I/O required. You must sketch your timing diagrams and examine them closely to be sure that your circuit will be able to respond properly. In the clock design, for example, you found that the clock board could not respond quickly and that wait states were necessary for proper operations. Without a timing diagram, the need for wait states would not have been clear at all.

When you construct your prototype clock, do it bottom-up so you can test and debug along the way. Build the power supply section first because all the modules depend on it for their power. After you finish the supply, build the address decoder and test it for proper operation. You can build and test the whole clock board this way so that when you test the last module, you are confident you have a satisfactory product.

Your lab notebook is the central focus of your project documentation. All your project plan notes and technical design work is recorded here. Perhaps most importantly, the data you took when you tested each prototype module is there along with notes on how you corrected problems you encountered during testing.

After the prototype is built and tested, you need to document your work for others involved in the project. Perhaps you need only make a brief summary of the design for use in your own department. Maybe you need to extract more information from your lab book and put together a full technical manual, as you learned in Chapter 4.

By now you should be fully capable of developing the engineering design plan for a 68000 microcomputer system. Naturally, a 68000 project will be more complex, but your approach will make the difference. You know that you can plan, design, build, and test in small steps that will finally get the job done successfully.

EXERCISES

1. One of your first engineering assignments with your company is designing a clock to run with a Z-80. The customer would like you to design a small Z-80 system with a clock connected directly to it; no bus interface is required. Write a project plan. In your plan, include the project definition, objectives, strategy, and the plan for implementation. Make assumptions as needed.
2. Sketch a block diagram of the Z-80 and clock system. Hint: see the MM58167A data sheet for application notes.
3. Discuss the merits of I/O mapping versus memory-mapped addressing of the clock board. Make an engineering decision and explain your rationale.
4. Sketch the Z-80 read cycle timing diagram (memory or I/O depending on your choice in Problem 3). Sketch the MM58167 read cycle timing diagram aligned under it on the page.
5. Assume that the Z-80 runs at 2 MHz. Will it read the data correctly from the clock IC? If the Z-80 runs at 6 MHz instead of 2 MHz, will the data be correct? What must be done?
6. Do Problem 4 for the write cycle timing.
7. Do Problem 5 for the write cycle case.
8. Explain the steps you would take in constructing a prototype of the Z-80 with MM58167 clock.
9. How would you test the prototype?
10. Write a two-page technical manual describing your computer board with the clock connected to it.

FURTHER READING

CALAWAY, J.L., and B. HILL. "CP/M, Your Time Has Come." *BYTE* (May 1982): 479–93.

CIARCIA, STEVE. "Everyone Can Know the Real Time." *BYTE* (May 1982): 34–58.

HASSEBROCK, GLEN E., JR. "The Hayes Chronograph, an H-89, and CP/M." *Remark* 35 (Dec. 1982): 9–14.

IEEE Standard 696 Interface Devices. New York: IEEE, 1983.

LIBES, SOL, and MARK GARETZ. *Interfacing to S-100/IEEE-696 Microcomputers*. Berkeley, CA: Osborne/McGraw-Hill, 1981.

MM58167A Microprocessor Real Time Clock. National Semiconductor Data Sheet, July 1984.

POE, ELMER C., and JAMES C. GOODWIN. *The S-100 and Other Micro Buses*. Indianapolis, IN: Howard W. Sams & Co., 1981.

The TTL Data Book. Vol. 2. Dallas, TX: Texas Instruments, Inc., 1985.

WILCOX, ALAN D. "Designing a Real-Time Clock for the S-100 Bus." *Dr. Dobb's Journal*, 10 (7): July 1985, 56–90.

SIX

System Planning and Design

The Big Project

As you begin the big project, you can almost see your 68000 board all wired and operating in a complete system. Then the doubts begin as you wonder if you know enough to do the design or even enough to build and test it. This is how it is with a challenging project: you are never quite sure of success until the design is finished and you see that it works. Although the 68000 project is a big challenge and cannot be done easily, it can be done.

This chapter shows how to plan the complete 68000 project so that it will be a success. The promise of Chapter 5 was that, after working through the clock design example, you would be able to develop the engineering design for the 68000. The key, of course, is the plan. You can use the clock design as an example while you make the 68000 plan. Just as you did before, start by identifying needs and then defining the project and its objectives. After you decide on a strategy, make your plan of action.

When you did the clock board, writing the project definition objectives and strategy probably seemed like simple busywork. Why bother writing it all down when you could keep it in your head? The plan of action with a task list and a schedule probably seemed the same. Why bother doing all that for such an easy plan? The answer is so that you would have some practice making a project plan and so that you would have an example to follow. You cannot finish the 68000 project without careful planning and without watching your schedule.

6.1 NEED IDENTIFICATION

Assume the scenario as in Chapter 5 and suppose that you are a design engineer in a small company. Your clock design was a success, and now your company has a contract to develop a 68000 computer system. Your role is to identify what the customer needs and then go ahead with the design and construction of the prototype computer board.

On meeting with your customer, you find that he wants a 68000 computer board that will operate on an S-100 bus (IEEE Std-696) at 6 MHz. At the present time, the customer has a 6 MHz Z-80 CPU board running under CP/M 2.2 and wants to upgrade the system. As you understand him, the purpose in the upgrade is so his simulation programs and other applications programs can run faster. If the new board has a substantial speed improvement over the old model, he believes he will be able to sell a number of them to his customers who are already using his Z-80 CPU boards.

An important factor in marketing the new boards is the issue of software compatibility. How can he convince his customers to buy a new 68000 board when they cannot use their existing software? Is there some way to run their existing Z-80 applications programs by using a slave Z-80 running as a task under the control of the new 68000 board? Then, over a period of months, the most critical programs could be converted to 68000 code for faster execution. This way he could help his customers phase in the 68000 board while at the same time avoid making their Z-80 programs obsolete.

To help you develop the new 68000 CPU board, your customer is willing to lend you one of his Z-80 systems. You will have, in addition to your normal lab equipment, an IEEE Std-696 system that has the S-100 motherboard and power supply, a disk-controller card, an I/O card, and a 64K static memory board. There are many empty slots in the cabinet for you to insert your new 68000 board when you have it ready to try out. If you need more memory, your customer has several more 64K static memory boards, all with extended-addressing capability.

6.2 PROJECT PLAN FOR THE 68000 CPU

Based on all that you know about your customer and his needs, you can now put together the project plan for the 68000. This plan takes the form of the mini-proposal that you learned in Chapter 1 and used again in Chapter 5 with the clock project. The 68000 project plan you do in this chapter is just the plan itself; the implementation of the plan will take the rest of the book to complete.

I. Project Definition.

The goal of this project is to design, build, and test a prototype 68000 CPU board that meets IEEE Std-696.

II. Project Objectives.

CPU software requirements:

Monitor in EPROM that will control the 68000. It should be able to read and change memory and registers as well as trace and execute programs. It should provide a means of downloading programs from a host system.

BASIC programming language in EPROM.

Disk operating system that will boot from a disk and provide normal system utilities and languages.

CPU hardware requirements:

- Use MC68000 microprocessor
- Be able to run using MC68010 microprocessor
- Conform to IEEE Std-696 (S-100 bus)
- On-board memory
  - Two 28-pin sockets for static RAM (6116 or 6264)
  - Two 28-pin sockets for EPROM (2716, 2732, 2764, or 27128)
- I/O data transfer by memory-mapping; I/O-mapping above FF0000 hex
- Clock speed 6 MHz
- Wait generator to select 1 to 8 wait states
- Reset circuit to provide stack pointer and program counter for 68000
- Bus-error watchdog timer circuit
- Build with easy-to-find parts

Testing and maintenance requirements:

- Single-step circuit with control switches on CPU board
- LED to indicate 68000-halted condition
- Switch to set on-board memory anywhere in 16 Mb range of 68000
- Freerun capability
- Self-testing capability

III. Strategy to Achieve Objectives.

The overall strategy will center on a sequence of design, build, and test; this sequence will be used to develop each module of the CPU until the prototype board is complete. To support this strategy, the 68000 will be configured in a freerunning mode until the hardware is ready for the monitor EPROM. The routines in the monitor EPROM will be used to aid the testing as more hardware modules are added to the board. Finally, the monitor EPROM will control the 68000 to load a disk operating system (DOS).

IV. Plan of Action.

Review background information:

- Review Motorola application notes and technical manuals
- Review trade and technical articles on 68000 design
- Study designs of existing 68000 boards
- Study designs of S-100 bus boards

Order prototyping parts:

- Prototype board or wire-wrap board

- Clock oscillator
- ICs not on hand already

Study IEEE Std-696 in detail:
- What signals are required of a bus master?
- How to derive the required signals?
- Synchronization of bus states with 68000 states

System design:
- Draw block diagram of system
- Consider hardware/software tradeoffs
- How does the bus interface standard affect this?

Hardware design:
- Identify critical modules
- Draw block diagrams of each module
- Do logic diagrams, timing diagrams
- Build and test each module

Software design:
- Top-level system design
- Memory map and how modules all fit together

Document the system (from lab book details)

Test the completed board in the system

Evaluate how well the board meets system specifications

6.3 GENERAL STRATEGY

If you have been following the approach described in the Chapter 5 clock design, you know that implementation of the plan is next. When you did the clock, you did a complete paper design before you started building and testing the prototype. For a project the size of the 68000, however, there are just too many unknowns that prevent doing a complete paper design before construction.

A reasonable solution to this problem is to design the system by modules and do the construction and testing of each module immediately. After you design a module, build it on a prototype board, test it as completely as possible, and move on to design another module.

This sounds easy enough, but there is a slight difficulty: how do you know which module comes next? In Chapter 2, the technique was to partition the system into modules by drawing a system block diagram; then, using a top-down approach, the system diagram could be divided into manageable modules. At this point in the 68000 project, you have information on the system and understand some of the requirements the CPU board has to meet. You can draw the system diagram along the lines of Figure 6.1. After you have the

Project Schedule

Week Beginning	Jan 6	13	20	27	Feb 3	10	17	24	Mar 3	10	17	24	Apr 7	14	21	28
Tasks to Do																
Review background info	* *	* * * *	* * * *													
Order prototype parts		* * * *														
Study IEEE Std-696		* *	* * * *	* * * *	*											
System design			* * * *	* *												
Design, build, test			*	* * *	* * * *	* * * *	* * * *	* * * *	* * *	* * * *	* * *	* * * *	* * * *			
Software design					*	* * * *	* * * *	* * * *	* * *	* * * *	* * *	* * * *	* * * *	* * * *	* * *	
Document system												* * * *	* * * *	* * * *	* * * *	* * * *
Test completed board														* * * *	* *	
System evaluation															* * * *	* * * *

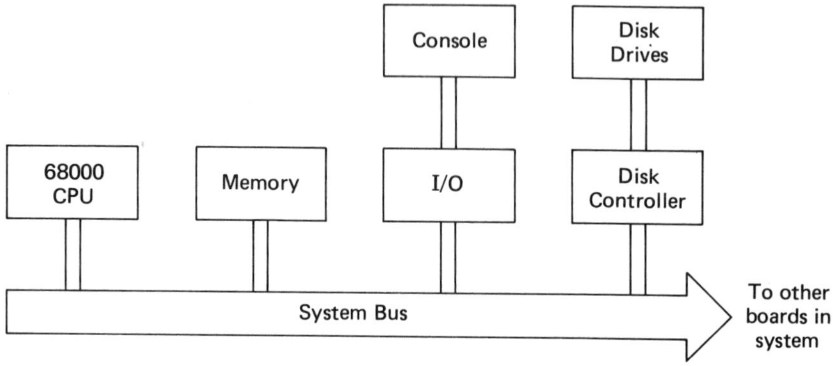

Figure 6.1 Block diagram of the computer system.

CPU board in perspective, review the specifications and go into more detail. A rough sketch of the board modules might look like Figure 6.2; this is not a complete block diagram yet, however.

If you use Figure 6.2, can you guess which module is first, second, third? Suppose you do the power first—an essential circuit and easy to design, build, and test. How can you design the power supply without knowing how heavily it will be loaded? Just make a reasonable guess and hope you were close enough? Probably this is the best choice for the prototype, because you do not know exact loading until the design is completed.

Consider designing and building the clock and the reset circuitry next. The 68000 has to have both of them, and they can be done quite simply. Do you see the essential strategy here? Design, build, and test—gradually building a foundation for more complicated modules that come later. Constantly check for proper operation of each module as you add it in; check the previous modules to be certain they still work.

Designing for testability means that you engineer a product so that it can be easily tested. If you were to do your design from start to finish on paper and build it all at once, you would probably have problems testing for proper operation. This is the situation a service technician might be in when troubleshooting a customer's board: how can it be tested easily? In contrast, if you do your design so that it can be built and tested by modules, chances are good that the final product will be easy to test and service. Why is that? Each of your modules was tested, and you provided for it in the initial design.

As an example of designing for testability, suppose you prepare a circuit to single-step the 68000. Normal system operation is for the 68000 to keep running; being stopped indicates some error, and the watchdog timer alerts the system. To avoid having the timer cause an alarm, you design your circuit so that the timer is disabled if you are in a single-step mode. If you were not building and testing during your design, you could overlook this simple timer-defeat logic.

In fact, your entire design is based on testability. The 68000 board can be built and tested with common lab equipment: multimeter, logic probe, and oscilloscope. If you did not build and test your modules as you went along, you would need more powerful tools such as a logic analyzer or an in-circuit emulator for success. You can see the parallel here

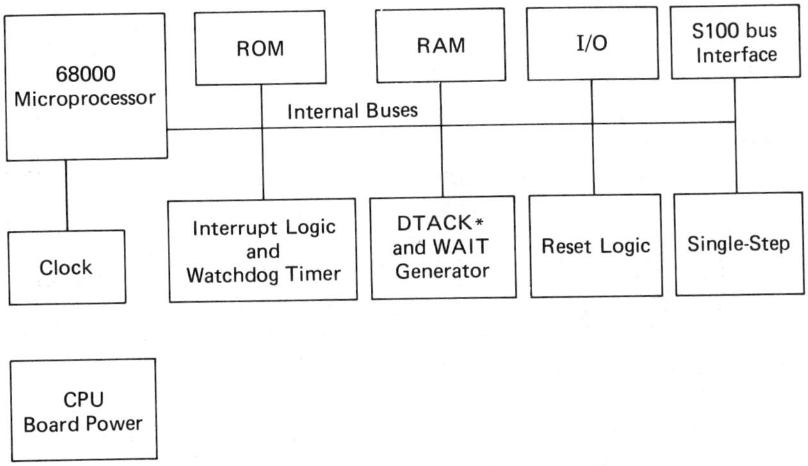

Figure 6.2 Some of the major functions on the CPU board.

with software development: if you develop and write programs in modules, then getting the complete program to work is simple. On the other hand, if you write the whole program at once, then you need sophisticated debugging tools to straighten out a host of interacting program bugs.

The cornerstone is being able to accomplish module testing with an oscilloscope is the ability to freerun the processor. To freerun a processor, you disable the memory-to-CPU feedback loop and provide a no-operation (NOP) instruction every time the microprocessor reads an instruction. The result is that the processor continually cycles through its address range over and over, reading and executing a NOP instruction. Because the instructions are all the same and are repeating, you can easily synchronize an oscilloscope to look at all the processor's address and control lines.

The circuit that implements this freerunning mode is called the "kernel." The kernel is the absolute minimum circuit: if it will not run, then the system cannot function. Put another way, if you have the microprocessor kernel running, then your system has a chance of working. *You can use the free-running kernel as a means of testing all the additional circuits you design and build on your CPU board.*

6.4 SUMMARY

The 68000 project is considerably larger than the clock example in the last chapter, and yet it can be successfully completed by using a plan. It all begins with customer needs; after you understand what is wanted, you can define the project and set specific objectives. The objectives are the product specifications, and they will influence your activity throughout the whole project.

How you actually reach your objectives by building a board that meets specifications depends on your strategy. Rather than following the previous strategy of a complete paper design followed by the building and testing, you might consider an incremental design/build/test strategy that takes smaller steps. By doing this, not only do you avoid being overwhelmed by a huge project, you also develop an easy-to-test system. If you keep module testing in mind as you design, the development of the whole system will be much easier.

Part of designing for testability involves the idea of freerunning the processor so that it constantly cycles over its address range. This allows you to use your oscilloscope to look at the various parts of the system as you refine your design. The minimum circuit that implements the freerunning is the kernel.

Your project plan of action is along the same lines as the clock in Chapter 5: write a do-it list of the tasks that you should complete and a rough schedule to make sure you have time to finish. The plan presented in this chapter has the detail you want for the project; less detail would be too little help in staying on target, and more detail would be unrealistic without experience. As the job progresses, you can keep a daily or weekly list of current tasks you need to follow.

Make a point of checking your schedule of tasks on a daily basis. If you find a particular module extremely difficult, do another one instead if possible; as you do more of the board, your understanding will improve, and you can come back to the troublesome module with a fresh view of how it should work. When you work your schedule, consider this: *a project gets late one day at a time.*

EXERCISES

Note: This sequence of exercises is intended to give direction to the design work that comes in the following chapters. If you intend to build the 68000, write your answers to these exercises in your lab notebook for ready reference during the design and construction.

1. You were asked recently to design a 68000 system and build a prototype model on a solderless breadboard. The customer wants to see if your prototype will be a feasible approach to logging data and performing statistical analysis. Write an outline of what you think the 68000 board might be able to do for him. Write a list of questions you have about uncertain aspects of the project.
2. Suppose you met with the customer and now have a clear idea of the project. Write the project definition as you understand it.
3. List the software requirements (objectives) of the project. Assume that you have the TUTOR EPROM set available to use in your prototype.
4. List the hardware requirements of the project. Assume that you do *not* have a requirement to interface to the IEEE Std-696 bus.
5. List the testing and maintenance requirements. Assume that you have only a logic probe, a multimeter, and a dual-trace oscilloscope.
6. Describe the strategy you will follow to meet your objectives.
7. Write out your plan of action. Include contingency plans so that your project does not get held up by temporary parts shortages or design difficulties.

8. Assume that your whole project must be completed within 12 weeks; at the end of the project, you will make a technical presentation to the customer and deliver your prototype with a complete technical manual. Sketch a schedule showing your plan of work for each of the next 12 weeks.

FURTHER READING

LOCK, DENNIS. *Project Management.* Toronto, Canada: Coles Publishing Company, Ltd., 1980.

RAY, MARTYN S. *Elements of Engineering Design.* London: Prentice-Hall International, UK, Ltd., 1985. (TA 174.R37)

WILCOX, ALAN D. "Bringing Up the 68000—A First Step." *Doctor Dobb's Journal* 11(1): Jan 1986, 60–74.

SEVEN

An Overview of the 68000

At the beginning of a large project, one of the most difficult tasks is knowing where to start. Even if you did a similar project a year ago, somehow the beginning of a new job feels a bit unsettling. In the case of the 68000 design project, the initial steps appear even more uncertain. If you had already done a similar design last year, wouldn't that help you get off to an easier start?

A feature common to all projects is a review of what has already been done. If you had direct experience with the 68000 already, then you would know some of its features and how to use it. Without that first-hand experience, however, you rely on many others to explain the issues and important details. For example, your first steps in the project plan involve a review of the application notes and technical manual.

The purpose of this chapter is to study the features of the 68000 and to examine some typical data taken with an actual single-board design. The intent is not to take the place of the product technical data manual. In fact, as a general rule, when in doubt about any point on the operation of the 68000, always refer to the manufacturer's technical information.

In the last chapter the 68000 was described in the context of a processor on a CPU board with memory and some means of I/O capability, much along the lines of Figure 7.1. It meets the outside world through connections referred to as buses, which are multi-wire signal paths into and out of the processor. When you look inside the 68000 to learn more about the signals, it helps to consider a *software* description and also a *hardware* description of the processor.

Also, you can describe the 68000 as either a 32- or 16-bit processor depending on your point of view. Because the 68000 has internal 32-bit registers and instructions that

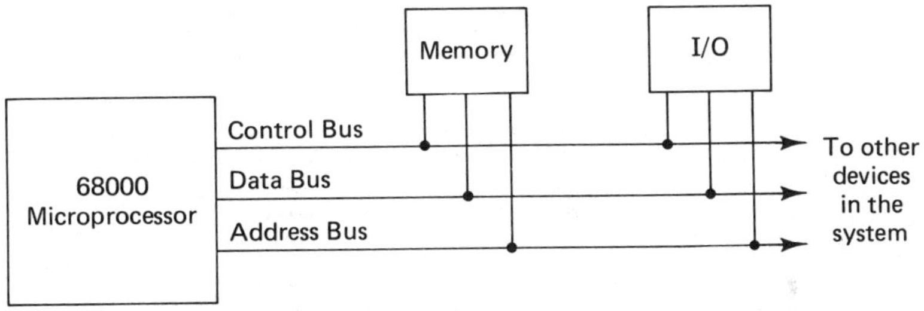

Figure 7.1 Block diagram of a 68000 computer.

move 32 bits, you can think of it as a 32-bit processor. However, because all data transfers outside the processor are 16 bits and because the internal ALUs are 16 bits, you can properly regard it as a 16-bit machine. If your application requires a full 32-bit data bus, you should consider the MC68020.

7.1. SOFTWARE ISSUES

A programmer's view of the 68000 is shown in Figure 7.2. You can see that its architecture is oriented around the register. There are

8 Data Registers	D0–D7	(8, 16, or 32 bits)
9 Address Registers		
7 General Purpose	A0–A6	(32 bits)
1 User Stack Pointer (USP)	A7	(32 bits)
1 Supervisory Stack Pointer (SSP)	A7′	(32 bits)
1 Program Counter	PC	(32 bits)
1 Status Register	SR	(16 bits)

The data registers can be used to manipulate either 8-, 16-, or 32-bit data. Transfers involving 8 bits are byte operations, while the 16- and 32-bit operations are word and long-word operations, respectively. The 68000 also supports 1- and 4-bit (BCD) data types involving the data registers.

The address registers are intended for address operations and generally cannot be used to manipulate data. Although they are internally 32-bits wide, the 68000 uses only the lower 24 bits when addressing external memory. These 24 bits provide an address range of 2^{24} (16M) bytes of memory.

There are two stack pointers, one for the "supervisor" (A7′ or SSP) and another alternate pointer for the "user" (A7 or USP). The 68000 executes program instructions in either user or supervisor mode; only one mode can be active at a time. The mode is a state of privilege to provide security within an operating system. When the 68000 is in user mode, only the user stack pointer is available, and certain instructions cannot be executed.

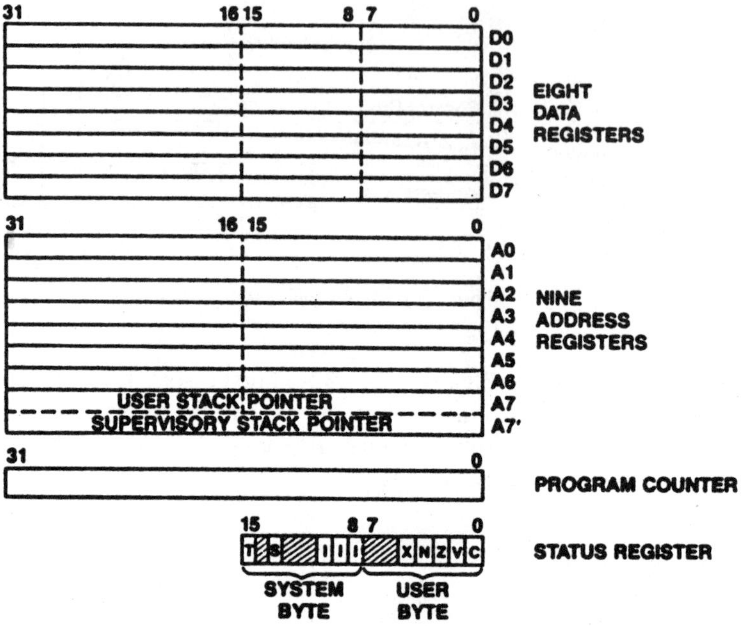

Figure 7.2 Programming model of the 68000. (Courtesy Motorola, Inc.)

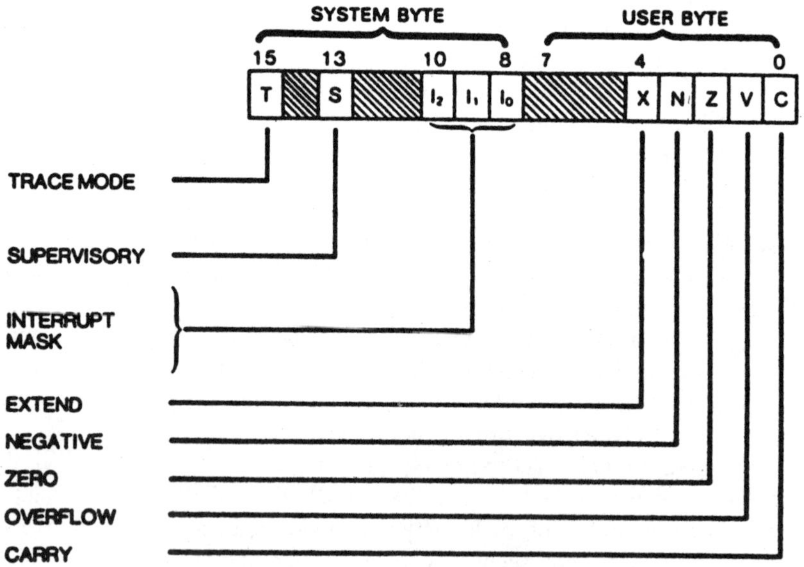

Figure 7.3 Status Register. (Courtesy Motorola, Inc.)

This prevents a user from accessing restricted blocks of memory, for example. The user mode also protects the system from being stopped or modified maliciously.

The program counter is 32 bits internally but 24 bits externally; if you push the program counter on the stack, however, you push all 32 bits. The PC always points to executable code on an even address. This is because all memory bus cycles that fetch an op-code are word operations. If you try to read 16 bits from an odd address, then the 68000 will begin exception processing to recover from the error.

The status register shown in Figure 7.3 is divided into two sections: the system byte and the user byte. When the 68000 is in the supervisor mode, both bytes may be read and modified. When in the user mode, both bytes may be read; however, only the lower 8 bits may be changed. Thus the user can have the usual status flags for programs but cannot alter the state of the system itself. If the processor is in the supervisor state, the S-bit is set to 1 in the status register. If the T-bit is set, then the 68000 is in the trace mode: after each instruction the processor will perform exception processing. The interrupt mask determines the level of interrupt that will be serviced.

The best way to view memory is to think of 16-bit words as shown in Figure 7.4. You probably already visualize memory as an 8-bit wide array, even though the memory is physically identical; now take it twice as wide. For example, suppose address ADR1 in the figure is address 100; you can reference the even data at address 100 and the odd data at 101. Likewise, you can refer to the word at address 102. If ADR2 = 200, you can read a long word at 200 and then read more data at 204 and the following addresses.

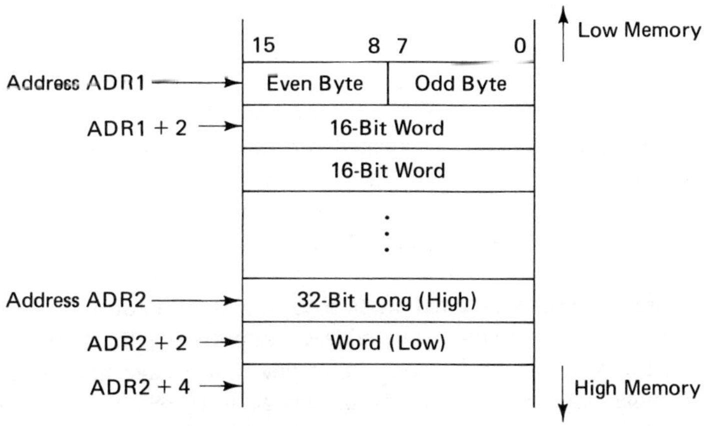

Figure 7.4 Memory showing bytes, words, and long words.

The rules for accessing memory can be summarized:

- Bytes can be written or read from memory on either even or odd addresses.
- Words and long words can only be accessed on even addresses.
- Program op-codes can only be read on word addresses.

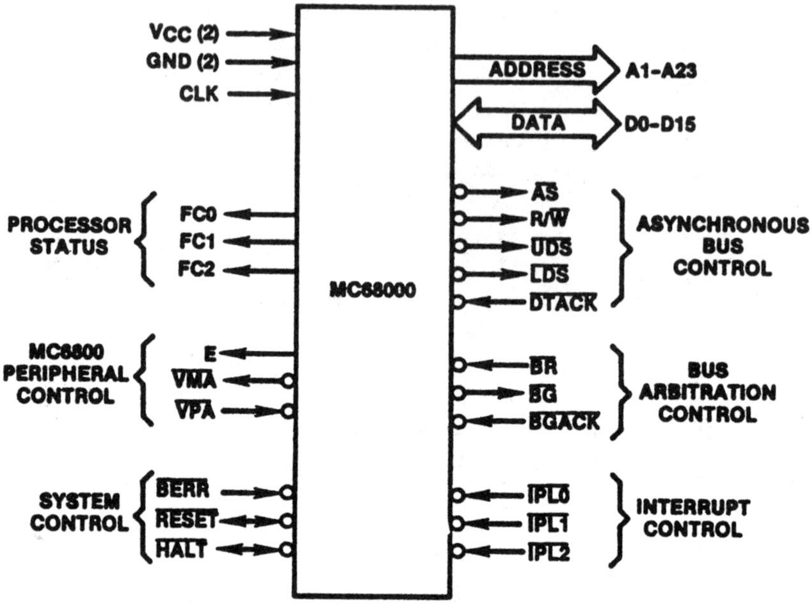

Figure 7.5 Input and output signals divided by function. (Courtesy Motorola, Inc.)

7.2 HARDWARE FEATURES

The 68000 input and output signals can be divided into several major functions, as shown in Figure 7.5. Notice that most of the control signals are written with an overbar. The bar is equivalent to the * suffix and indicates that the signal is asserted, or made true, when low. Likewise, the signal is negated, or made false, when high. For example, $\overline{AS}$ is equivalent to AS* and is read "address strobe star."

7.2.1 Asynchronous Bus Control

The address strobe is asserted when a valid address is on the address bus (A_{23} to A_1). There is no A_0 least-significant address output from the 68000: it is internal to the processor. If you assume A_0 is zero, then you always have an even address. In Figure 7.6, for example, you can read the 16-bit words at address 0 and 2 without using A_0. As shown, you would read 0000 first and then $0444 next.

The 68000 always reads on an even address when fetching instructions, so A_0 is unnecessary for program execution. There are many times, however, when you want to access data in bytes rather than in whole 16-bit words. The upper data strobe (UDS*) and lower data strobe (LDS*) control whether you access either the even (upper), the odd (lower) data byte, or both bytes together. Table 7.1 shows the relationship between these signals. The R/W* line controls whether the memory access is a read or write. For example, suppose you want to read memory location 3. From Table 7.1 you find that UDS*

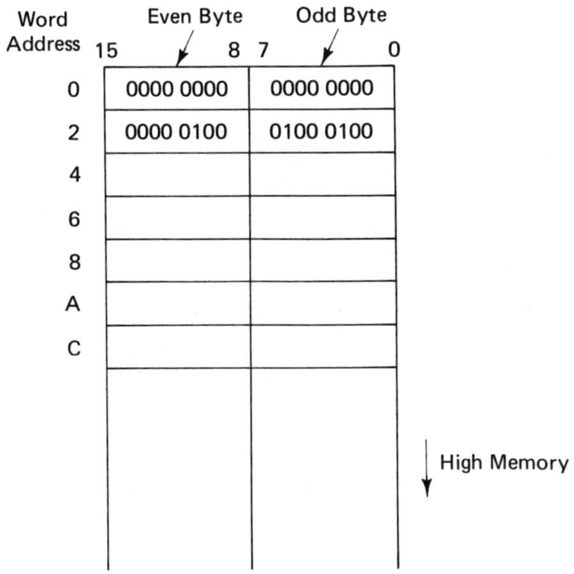

Figure 7.6 Memory map organized into 16-bit words.

TABLE 7.1 DATA BUS ACCESS CONTROL

	UDS*	LDS*	R/W*	EVEN D8–D15	ODD D0–D7	
	HIGH	HIGH	—	NO VALID DATA	NO VALID DATA	
READ	LOW	LOW	HIGH	VALID DATA BITS 8–15	VALID DATA BITS 0–7	16-Bit READ
READ	HIGH	LOW	HIGH	NO VALID DATA	VALID DATA BITS 0–7	8-Bit READ
READ	LOW	HIGH	HIGH	VALID DATA BITS 8–15	NO VALID DATA	8-Bit READ
WRITE	LOW	LOW	LOW	VALID DATA BITS 8–15	VALID DATA BITS 0–7	16-Bit WRITE
WRITE	HIGH	LOW	LOW	VALID DATA* BITS 0–7	VALID DATA BITS 0–7	8-Bit WRITE
WRITE	LOW	HIGH	LOW	VALID DATA BITS 8–15	VALID DATA* BITS 8–15	8-Bit WRITE

*SHADED AREAS ARE A RESULT OF CURRENT IMPLEMENTATION AND MAY NOT APPEAR ON FUTURE DEVICES.

(Courtesy Motorola Inc.)

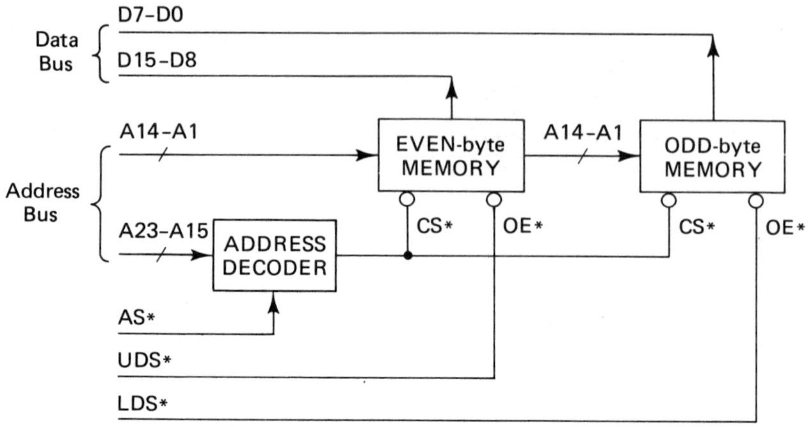

Figure 7.7 One way to design memory for byte or word read operations. As shown, the address decoder will select the memory when the proper 16K block address is on A23-A15.

will be high (negated), LDS* will be low (asserted), and R/W* will be high for the read.

You can use the upper and lower data strobes when you design your memory, as shown in Figure 7.7. Notice that the address strobe qualifies the address bus selection so that the memory is not inadvertently selected until the address is valid. Compare the operation of this circuit with Table 7.1. See, for example, that if you assert UDS* when CS* is true, then you read the even (upper) 8 bits of data.

The DTACK* input to the 68000 is data transfer acknowledge and is used to indicate that the data read or write is completed. The 68000 will pause during every bus cycle and wait for DTACK* from the external device being addressed. As soon as DTACK* is received, the 68000 will finish its cycle normally; if the external device fails to return DTACK*, then the 68000 continues to wait . . . and wait . . . until perhaps a timer signals the fault. While DTACK* allows you to design a completely asynchronous bus with widely differing access times, it does require the addressed device to respond with a DTACK* signal (or valid peripheral address, VPA*, if it is a synchronous 6800 family device).

7.2.2 Processor Status

The 68000 status is available on the function code pins FC0, FC1, and FC2. As shown in Table 7.2, the function codes indicate what bus activity is currently in progress. These outputs are valid whenever AS* is true. A typical 68000 operation is fetching an instruction from memory, so the function code will indicate "program." For example, if the status register S bit is 1, then the current read is "supervisor program." If the memory access is to read data or operands, then the function code will be either supervisor or user data depending on the S bit.

TABLE 7.2 FUNCTION CODE OUTPUTS INDICATING THE 68000 STATE (USER OR SUPERVISOR) AND THE CYCLE TYPE.

Function Code Output			Cycle Type
FC2	FC1	FC0	
Low	Low	Low	
Low	Low	High	User Data
Low	High	Low	User Program
Low	High	High	

Function Code Output			Cycle Type
FC2	FC1	FC0	
High	Low	Low	
High	Low	High	Supervisor Data
High	High	Low	Supervisor Program
High	High	High	Interrupt Acknowledge

(Courtesy Motorola Inc.)

7.2.3 System Control

The system control inputs to the 68000 are used to either reset or halt the processor, or in the case of BERR*, to indicate that a bus error has occurred.

The RESET* line can be either an input or an output. If you are powering up the 68000 you must initialize the system by holding RESET* and HALT* both low for 100 ms. Asserting HALT* by itself will cause the processor to stop after the current bus cycle. The 68000 can assert RESET* as an *output* by executing the reset instruction; this does not reset the 68000 itself and can be used to reset slave devices connected to the processor.

The BERR* input signals the 68000 that there is a problem with the current bus cycle. For example, if DTACK* did not get returned on a memory read cycle, the processor would be hung indefinitely. If a timer is connected to the bus and asserts BERR* after a suitable delay, then the processor can try to recover from the error.

7.2.4 Interrupt Control

The interrupt priority level (IPL) inputs on the 68000 tell the processor that an interrupt is pending and its priority. The decoding of the priority level is done internally. The highest priority is level 7 (all 3 inputs low), which is a nonmaskable interrupt. Any interrupts less than a level 7 are maskable depending on the status register bit pattern. When all three inputs are high, no interrupt is being requested.

7.2.5 Bus Arbitration

The bus request (BR*) input, the bus grant (BG*) output, and the bus-grant acknowledge (BGACK*) inputs arbitrate whether the 68000 or another device on the bus will have bus control. For example, suppose a DMA controller is connected to the data, address, and control buses; when it needs to access memory, it cannot do so until the 68000 gives up its control of the bus. The orderly completion of the current instruction and passage of control over to the DMA controller is referred to as "arbitration."

7.2.6 6800 Peripheral Control

The enable (E) output, valid peripheral address (VPA*) input, and the valid memory address (VMA*) output are used to interface the asynchronous 68000 with the synchronous 6800-family of peripheral devices. Whenever a 6800-type device is detected, the 68000 modifies its bus cycle so it uses VPA* and VMA* rather than DTACK* to complete the transfer.

7.3 BUS OPERATION

When you write a program for the 68000, you use assembly-language statements or some high-level language to describe the flow of your algorithm. You rarely, if at all, need to concern yourself with the binary machine code that the 68000 uses when it executes your program. You probably recognize your assembly listing as a program that looks like this:

Program counter	*Machine code*	*Instruction*	*Operand*	*Comments*
1000	4241	CLR.W	D1	Clear register D1
1002	103C0006	MOVE.B	#6,D0	Put 6 in register D0
1006	4E71	NOP		No operation
1008	60F6	BRA.S	$1000	Loop back

Your concern when you review the listing is that you include the proper program statements and that you located your program in a valid memory location. Depending on your system, you might not even need to consider where the program goes in memory.

To understand how the 68000 treats a program like this simple CLR and MOVE example, look at the machine code as it appears in the memory map in Figure 7.8. The 68000 will read the program in 16-bit words, always starting at an even address; in this case, the 68000 will read the instruction $4241 at memory location $1000. Then it reads the MOVE instruction at $1002 and its operand $0006 at $1004. Each 16-bit read operation requires a bus cycle; the program shown requires five[1] bus cycles to be read completely. The relationship between bus and instruction cycles is shown in Figure 7.9.

The 68000 is an asynchronous processor in that the individual bus cycle can be any duration depending on how long memory or a peripheral device takes to return DTACK* (or VPA*). In Figure 7.10, the bus cycles are shown relative to the 68000 clock and are all the same length: eight clock states. If DTACK* responds slowly, the 68000 inserts wait states into the individual bus cycle as necessary. Consequently, because the bus cy-

[1]In actual operation, a sixth bus cycle occurs after the BRA instruction. This is due to the 68000 prefetch and will be explained shortly.

	(EVEN Byte)	(ODD Byte)
$1000	42	41
1002	10	3C
1004	00	06
1006	4E	71
1008	60	F6

Figure 7.8 The hex machine code of a simple program in memory

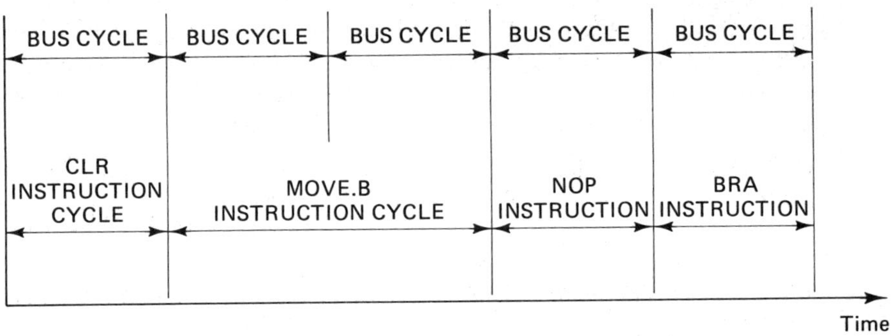

Figure 7.9 Relationship between bus cycles and instruction cycles.

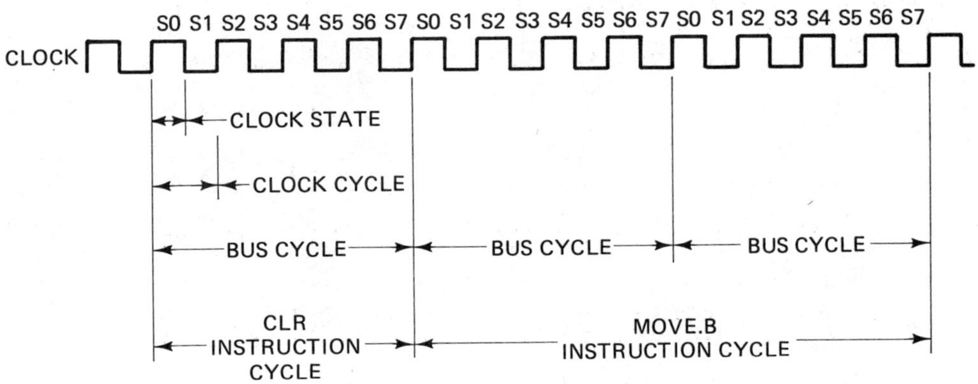

Figure 7.10 Timing diagram for two instruction cycles.

cles can have difficult durations, you would think of them as being asynchronous. Within the bus cycle, however, timing is synchronous: everything that happens corresponds closely with the 68000 clock rising or falling edges.

You can summarize the events in Figure 7.10 as follows:

Instruction Cycle	The time during which the 68000 reads and executes a complete instruction.
Bus Cycle	The time during which the 68000 does a byte/word read or write. A read/modify/write operation also takes one bus cycle.
Clock Cycle	Time from positive-edge to positive-edge of the 68000 clock; same as clock period. There are a minimum of four clock periods in a read or write bus cycle.
Clock State	Half of the clock cycle.

Examine the CLR/MOVE program again closely. Each of the bytes corresponding to the program appears in the Figure 7.8 memory map. Suppose you use software to single-step your 68000 through the program: you will see the program counter going from 1000 to 1002 to 1006 to 1008 and back again. Try this sequence again, but use hardware to look at the 68000 address bus and data bus during each instruction: first you see a single bus cycle for the CLR and then two bus cycles for the MOVE. The rest of the sequence you get looks like this:

Address	*Data bus*	*Corresponding instruction*
$1000	$42 41	CLR.W D1
1002	10 3C	MOVE.B #6, D0
1004	00 06	
1006	4E 71	NOP
1008	60 F6	BRA.S $1000
100A	12 34	(1234 is arbitrary memory contents)
1000	42 41	CLR.W D1
1002	10 3C	(continue the looping)
etc.	etc.	

Where did the data $1234 at location $100A come from? If you examine memory, these two bytes (or whatever chanced to be in memory) are there, but why did the 68000 read them if they are after the branch-to-start instruction? The 68000 always does an instruction prefetch—it reads the next instruction word while it executes the current instruction. This pipelining of the next operation speeds overall processor performance. In the case of this branch, however, the fetch is superfluous and is discarded by the 68000.[2]

[2]This can be very time-inefficient for a tight loop instruction. The MC68010 has an optimized loop mode in which the next instruction is not fetched until the loop is complete. The result is halving the loop execution time.

Normally, you need only know that prefetch is being done when you single-step using hardware and watch the data bus and address bus. However, you need to consider prefetch if you want to know where the program counter is pointing when you calculate a branch displacement. Look at the code for the branch back to \$1000: 60 F6. The F6 is the 8-bit 2's complement displacement that is added to the current PC to get the new PC.

Current PC =	\$0000 100A	(when prefetch was executed)
Displacement =	\$FFFF FFF6	(sign extended)
New PC =	\$0000 1000	

In general, as you start each instruction (regardless of the size of the instruction), you can expect the PC to be 2 bytes ahead of the op-word location. The PC does *not* necessarily point to the next instruction to be executed.

Read bus cycle. When a program is being executed, the 68000 reads the contents of even memory locations in sequence; all the bus cycles read 16-bit words. The flow of events during the bus cycle is shown in Figure 7.11. The timing diagram is given in Figure 7.12.

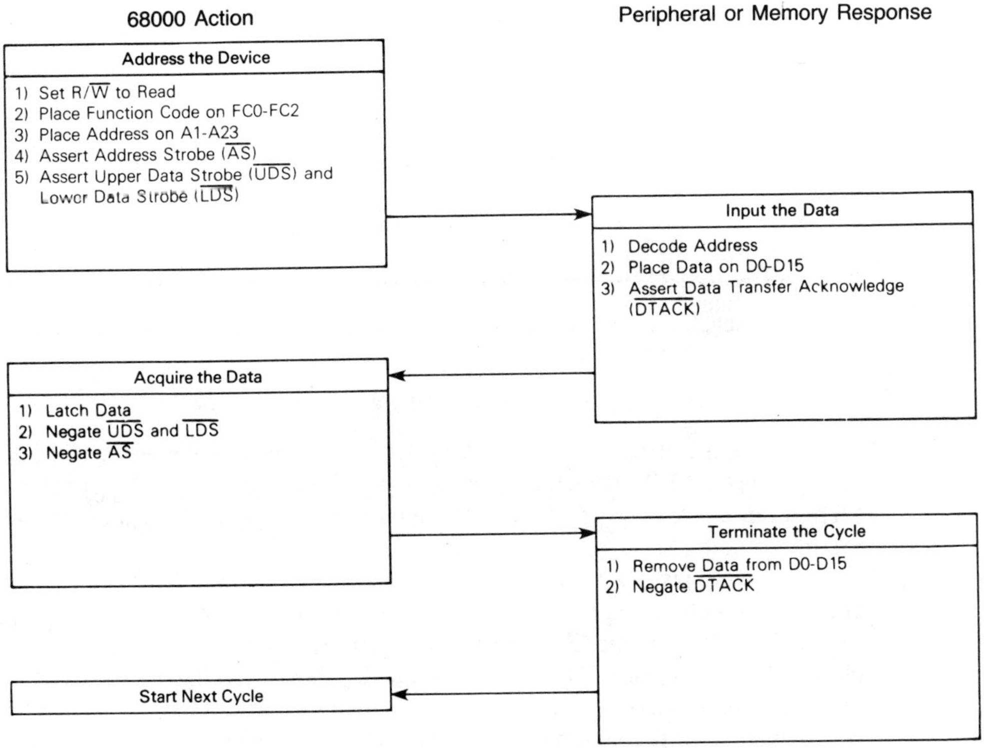

Figure 7.11 Flow of events during a word read bus cycle. (Courtesy Motorola, Inc.)

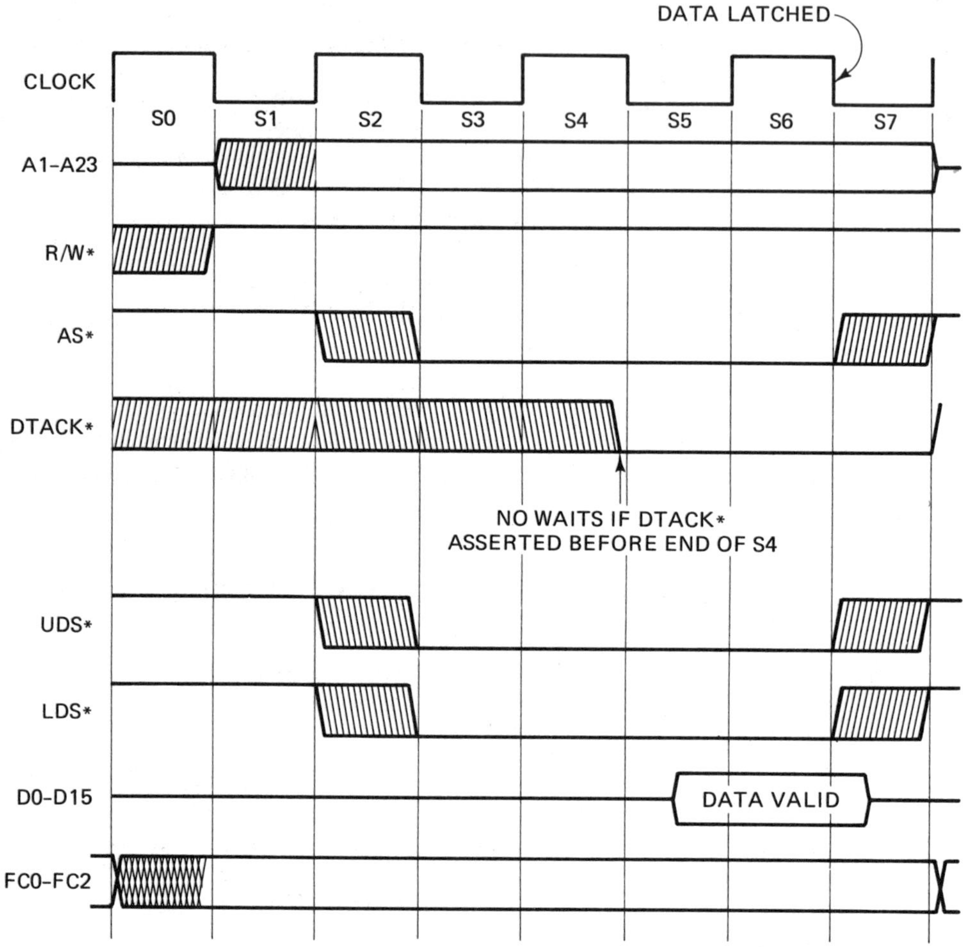

Figure 7.12 Timing of the read bus cycle.

Notice that there are four clock cycles (eight states) in the bus cycle. Suppose this bus cycle is the CLR instruction. How long does it take to execute? If your clock runs at 4 MHz, each clock cycle is 250 ns. The total time is 4 × 250 ns, or 1 μs, to clear the register.

Knowing just your clock speed, you can easily calculate the execution time of your entire program by using the information contained in the manufacturer's data manual. In Figure 7.13, look up the CLR instruction. Your program used the CLR.W instruction to clear 16 bits of register D1, so you can quickly find the entry 4(1/0) in the chart. This instruction involves one read bus cycle for a total of four clock cycles or 1 μs at 4 MHz. Notice that the CLR.L involves one read bus cycle too, but takes a total of six clock cycles to complete; the extra states appear after the following fetch bus cycle when the CLR.L is executed.

Instruction	Size	Register	Memory
CLR	Byte, Word	4(1/0)	8(1/1)+
	Long	6(1/0)	12(1/2)+
NBCD	Byte	6(1/0)	8(1/1)+
NEG	Byte, Word	4(1/0)	8(1/1)+
	Long	6(1/0)	12(1/2)+
NEGX	Byte, Word	4(1/0)	8(1/1)+
	Long	6(1/0)	12(1/2)+
NOT	Byte, Word	4(1/0)	8(1/1)+
	Long	6(1/0)	12(1/2)+
Scc	Byte, False	4(1/0)	8(1/1)+
	Byte, True	6(1/0)	8(1/1)+
TAS	Byte	4(1/0)	10(1/1)+
TST	Byte, Word	4(1/0)	4(1/0)+
	Long	4(1/0)	4(1/0)+

+ add effective address calculation time

Figure 7.13 Chart of instruction execution times. The figures are the number of clock cycles followed by (r/w): "r" gives the number of read clock cycles and "w" the number of write clock cycles. (Courtesy Motorola, Inc.)

Many peripherals and memory devices cannot respond to the read bus cycle quickly enough. For example, suppose the 68000 clock is 10 MHz: the total bus cycle time can be as short as 400 ns. There is no way of using an EPROM with an access time of, say, 450 ns unless the 68000 waits for it to respond. The mechanism used to slow the 68000 is simply to delay returning DTACK*. As shown in Figure 7.14, the processor inserts wait states directly after S4 until DTACK* is detected on a *falling* edge of the clock. The waits are always added in pairs; two wait states equal the time of one clock cycle. During the wait states, all 68000 bus signals are held constant. If you implement a single-stepper circuit using DTACK* like this, you can use a simple logic probe to check all the bus signals.

The read-byte bus cycle is identical to the read-word bus cycle except for the upper and lower data strobes. Refer to Table 7.1 again: the 16-bit read is done with both UDS* and LDS* asserted. If you want to read a single byte of memory at an even address, only UDS* need be asserted. Likewise, to read an odd address, assert only LDS*. In all cases, however, AS* is asserted until the end of the bus cycle.

Write bus cycle. As in the case of the read bus cycles, the 68000 follows the same general sequence of events and takes a minimum of four clock cycles to complete. This sequence is shown in Figure 7.15 with timing in Figure 7.16. The most noticeable difference between the two is that the R/W* control line is set low for the write.

There is one other significant difference between read and write timing that you should consider: the upper and lower data strobes are delayed by one clock cycle. For a word write, both are asserted at the same time but one clock cycle behind AS*, as shown in Figure 7.16. The reason for the cycle delay is so that system RAM ICs can be selected before they receive a write strobe; you cannot select a RAM chip and assert its write-enable control simultaneously.

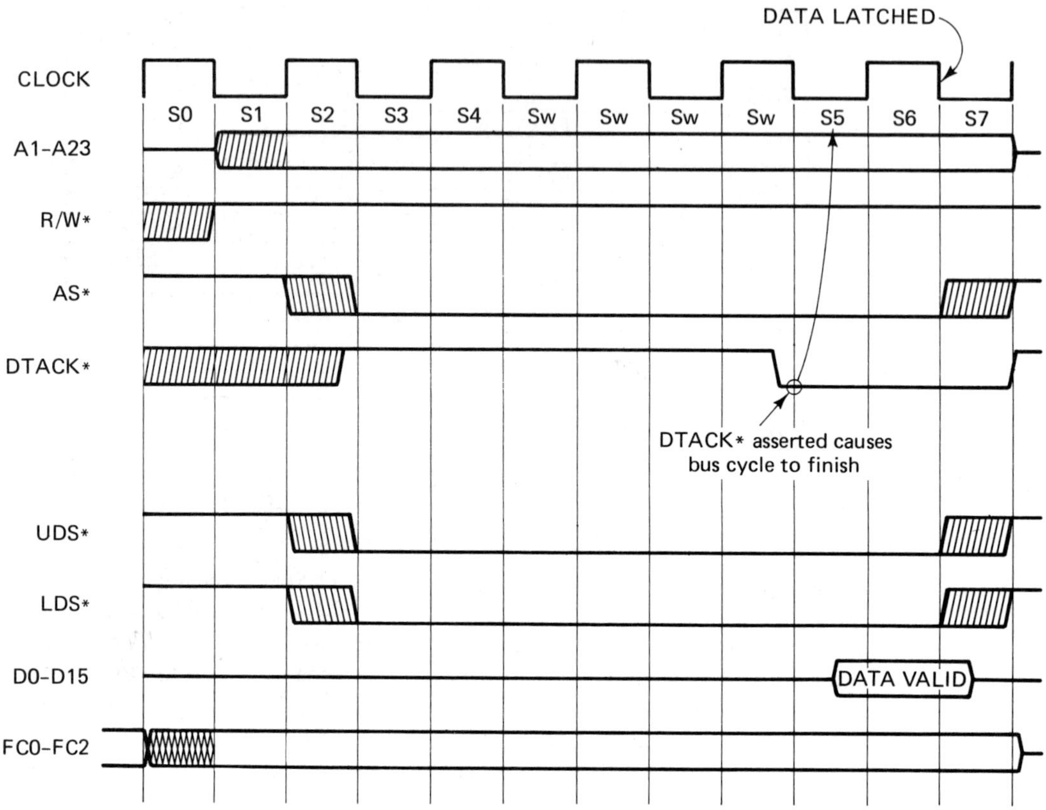

Figure 7.14 Timing of the read bus cycle with wait states.

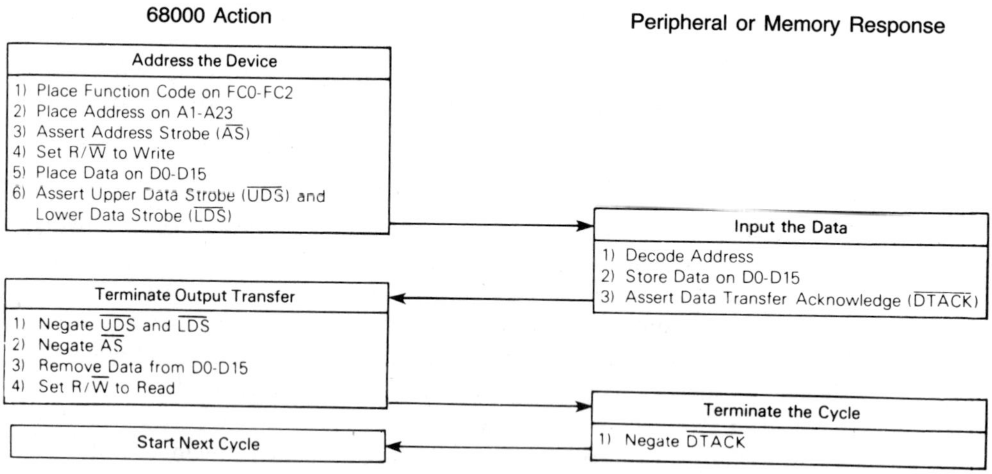

Figure 7.15 Flow of events during a word write bus cycle. (Courtesy Motorola, Inc.)

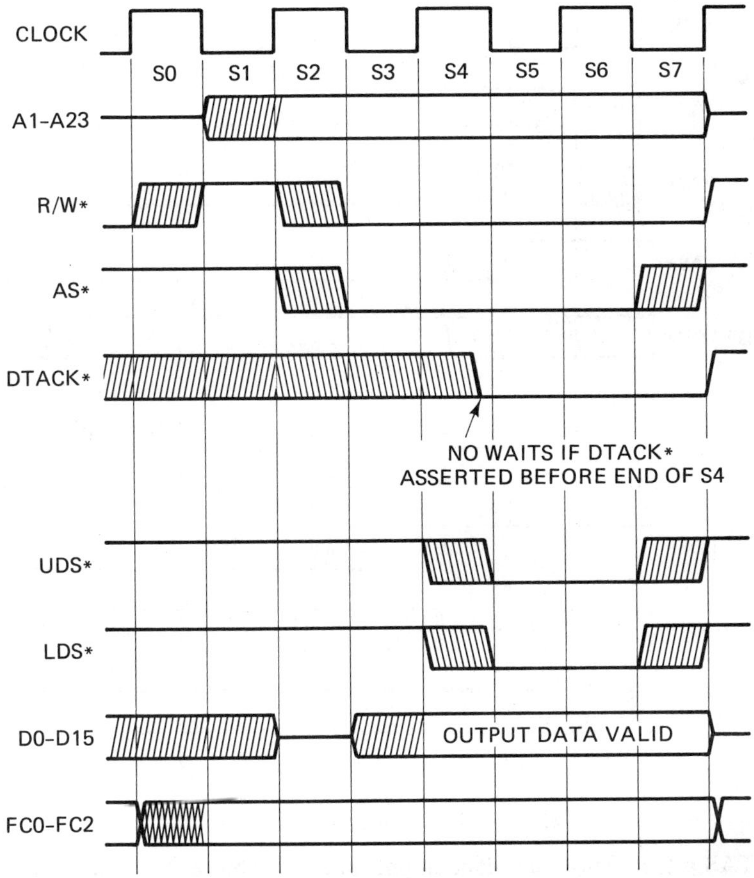

Figure 7.16 Timing of the write bus cycle.

The 68000 inserts wait states directly after S4 if DTACK* has not been asserted by the falling clock edge. The timing in Figure 7.17 shows that waits are added in pairs, the same as the read bus cycle.

The write-byte bus cycle is identical to the write-word cycle except for the data strobes. If you refer back to Table 7.1, you can see that to write a single byte to an even memory address, you need to assert UDS*; similarly, to write an odd address, assert LDS*. The table also indicates that valid data appears on both the even and odd data bus lines at the same time. Because this data might not be provided in future 68000 implementations, you should not use it in your design; by the same token, do not let its presence cause a problem.

Read-modify-write cycle. The read-modify-write cycle is used only by the test-and-set (TAS) instruction to implement a semaphore in a multiprocessor system. The idea is to check a designated effective address to see if the high-order bit is set: if not set, then

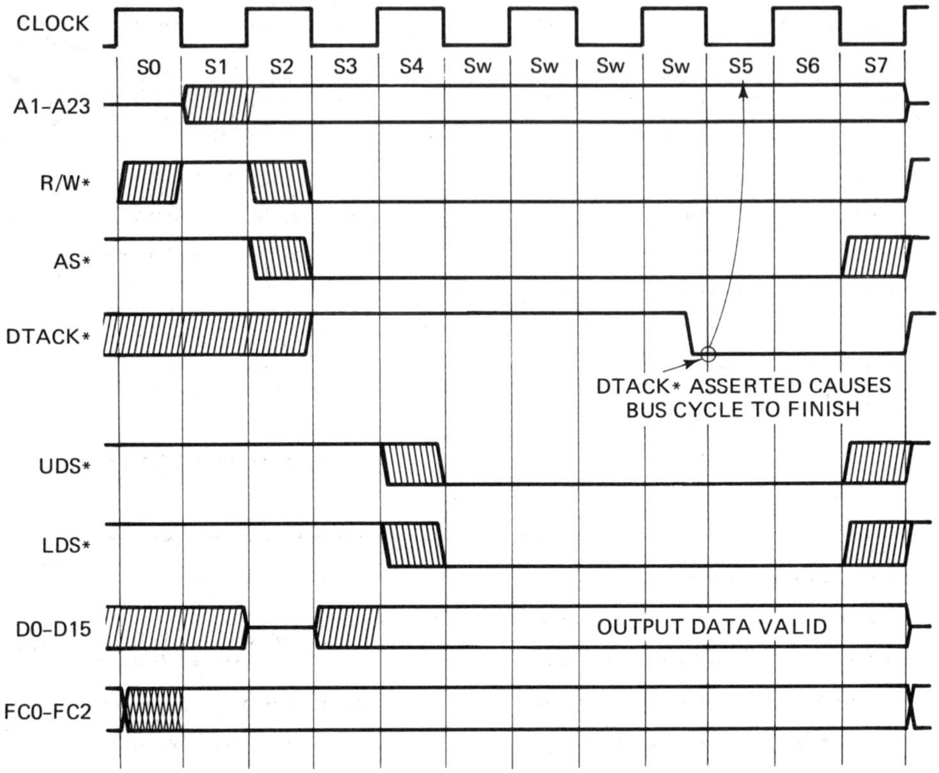

Figure 7.17 Timing of the write bus cycle with wait states.

TAS sets it. This is all done in one *indivisible* bus cycle. When the high bit is tested by another processor (P2) seeking, say, common memory, while the first processor (P1) is using it, P2 finds the bit set and avoids the common memory until P1 is finished and has reset the semaphore back to zero. If the TAS instruction were not indivisible, it is possible that the second processor could check the semaphore between the first's test-and-set and find it not set. Both processors might then claim the resource and cause errors in the system.

The 68000 AS* is used to make the TAS instruction indivisible. For a normal read followed by a write operation, the AS* is negated at the end of the read, and then asserted again for the write. During a TAS, however, AS* is continuously asserted to indicate to the entire system that a bus cycle is in progress. Only truly urgent events (such as an external reset, a bus error, or an address error) can cause the 68000 to abort a bus cycle before its normal completion. The sequence of events in the TAS is shown in Figure 7.18 and its timing diagram in Figure 7.19.

You can see in Figure 7.19 that DTACK* is returned as usual when testing the bit; a second DTACK* acknowledges the following write operation. Because AS* is constantly asserted for the TAS, you cannot use it to synchronize the read/write sequence in your system. This means that you cannot use AS* as a universal start-of-bus-cycle signal.

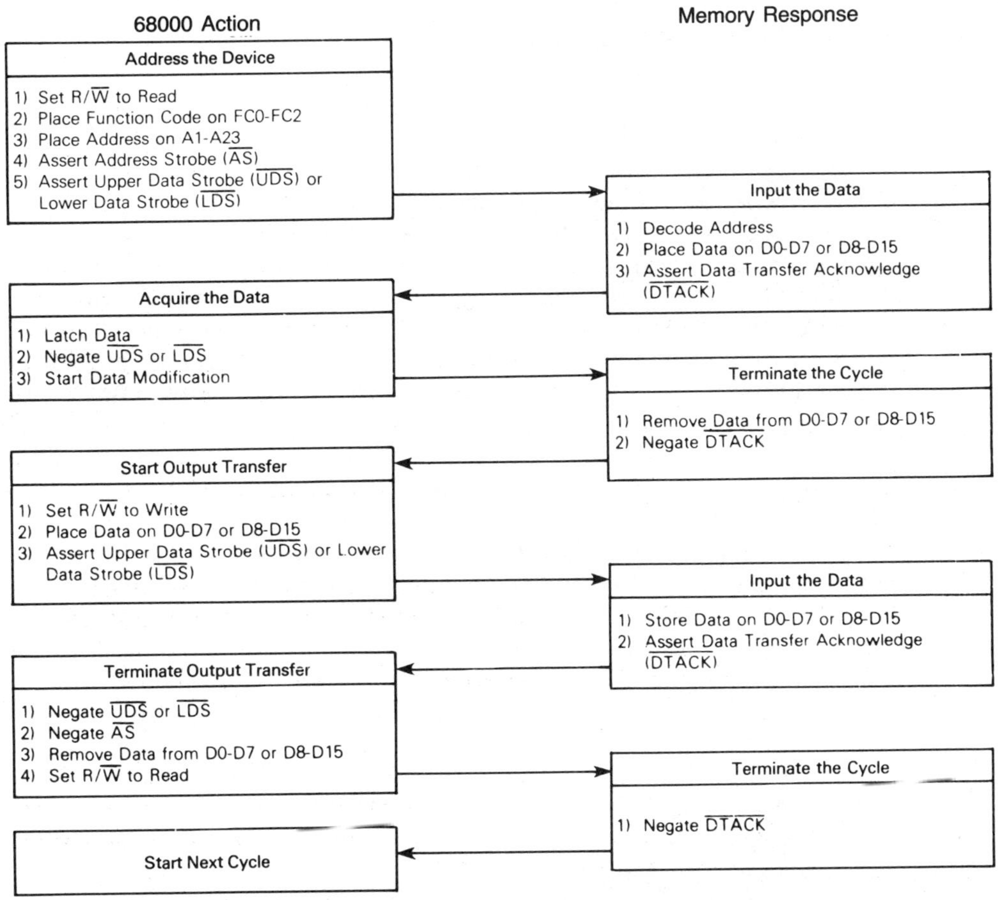

Figure 7.18 Read-Modify-Write cycle flowchart. (Courtesy Motorola, Inc.)

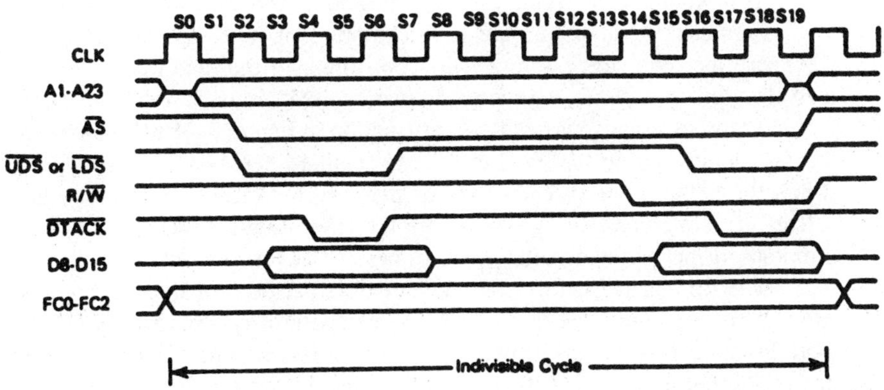

Figure 7.19 Read-Modify-Write cycle timing diagram. (Courtesy Motorola, Inc.)

7.4 EXAMPLE TIMING DIAGRAMS

Figures 7.20 through 7.25 show actual timing diagrams obtained from the 6 MHz CPU board that you will be building. The diagram at the top of each figure is 1X magnification for an overview of events; the lower figure is a 2X or 4X magnification of the same sequence. The sequence of interest is marked with an "o" to start and an "x" to finish.

For example, Figure 7.20 shows a bus cycle that reads an I/O address. The system monitor program is being executed at the moment, and it repeatedly checks I/O to see if there is a console key press. The CPU board has been set to insert eight waits in any I/O bus cycle so the I/O port, which uses 6850 ACIAs, has time to respond. ("Wait" as used in this context refers to a "wait cycle" made up of two 68000 wait states.) Looking at the expanded diagram, you can see that when DTACK* is found asserted (low) on a falling clock edge, the 68000 immediately concludes the bus cycle with states S5, S6, and S7.

The function code has been decoded as sM1 = FC0′ • FC1 to indicate when either a user or a supervisor program is being accessed. Notice that the 68000 is not in a program cycle when the I/O port is being read.

Notice also the data strobes. Both are asserted (low) for the program bus cycles, but only one is low for the I/O operation. You can conclude that the 68000 is reading an 8-bit byte rather than reading a whole 16-bit word from I/O. Can you tell from the diagram if the byte is on an even or odd address? Look back at Table 7.1 and check your answer.

Compare this with the data in Figure 7.21. A simple read of an even byte of memory is being done repeatedly. There are no waits involved in this operation, so the memory read is completed at full speed: four clock cycles.

Look at the timing in the upper view in Figure 7.21 again. It repeats over and over every 22 clock cycles or 3.67 μs (approximately). This means you can view the timing diagram using an oscilloscope synchronized to trigger on sM1; you should have a perfectly stable pattern. The program is

```
1000   MOVE.B   $1100,D0
1004   JMP.S    $1000
```

You would refer to this as a "scope-loop" program when you test the processor.

Figures 7.22 and 7.23 are both examples of write operations using scope loops. Compare the data strobe timing with the timing in the read operation. Both writes are outside user or supervisor program space, so sM1 is not asserted.

The read-modify-write (TAS) instruction in Figure 7.24 can also be examined using a scope-loop. Within the TAS execution (marked between "o" and "x") you can see when the 68000 read an even byte of memory ("tested" it) and then later wrote to it ("set" it). Note that AS* is asserted for the entire sequence to prevent any external interruptions to the bus cycle; the data strobes, however, are active.

The timing in Figure 7.25 shows the actual boot of the system monitor program starting from a reset. The first four bus cycles after a system reset (RESET* and HALT* both low) are 16-bit reads of two long words: first the supervisor stack pointer (SSP) and then the program counter (PC). With the memory contents shown, the processor reads the SSP = $444 and the PC = $FD 0146. Then, beginning at address $FD0146, the 68000

READ I/O
NEEDING 8 WATTS

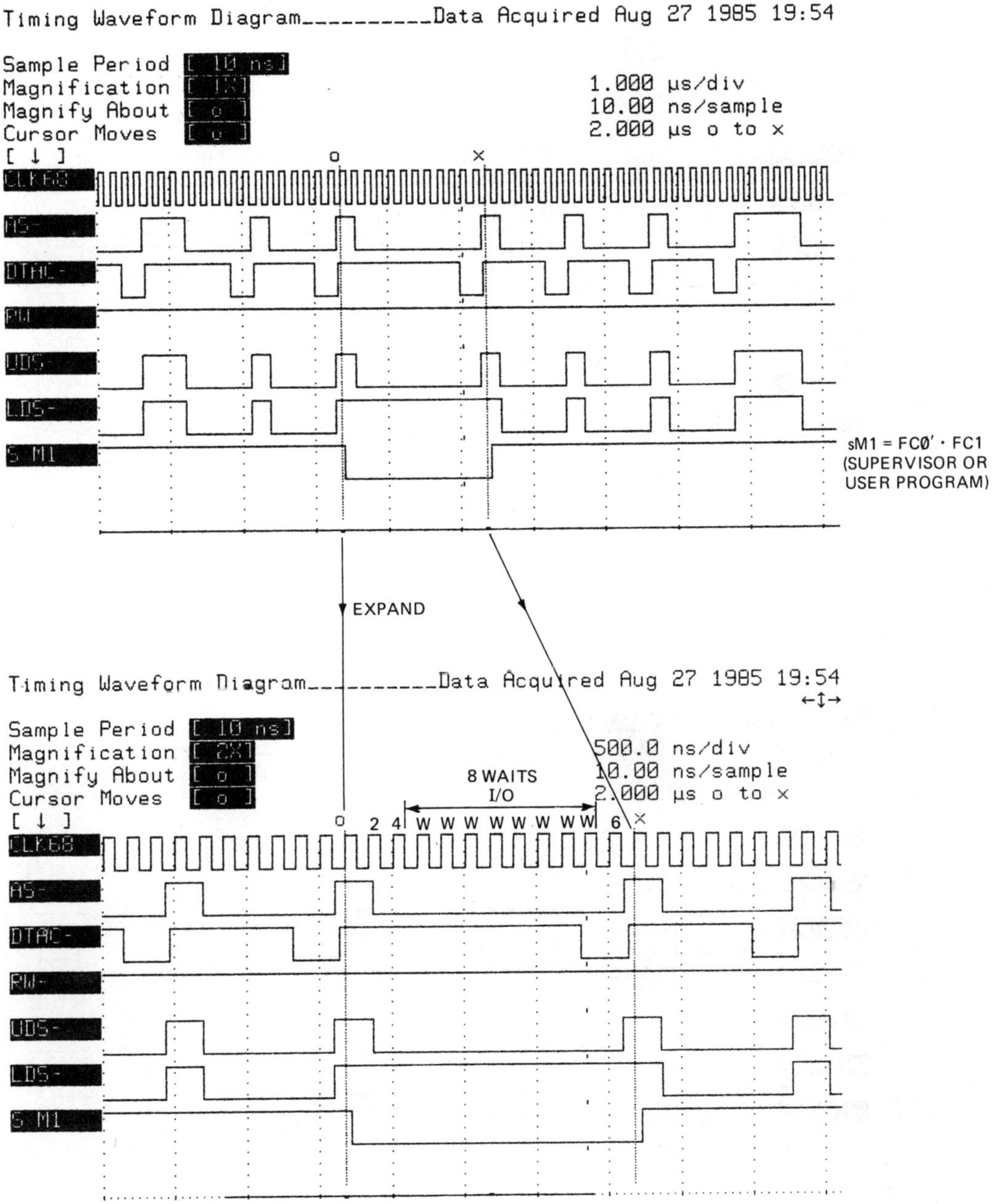

Figure 7.20 Timing diagram of read I/O needing 8 waits.

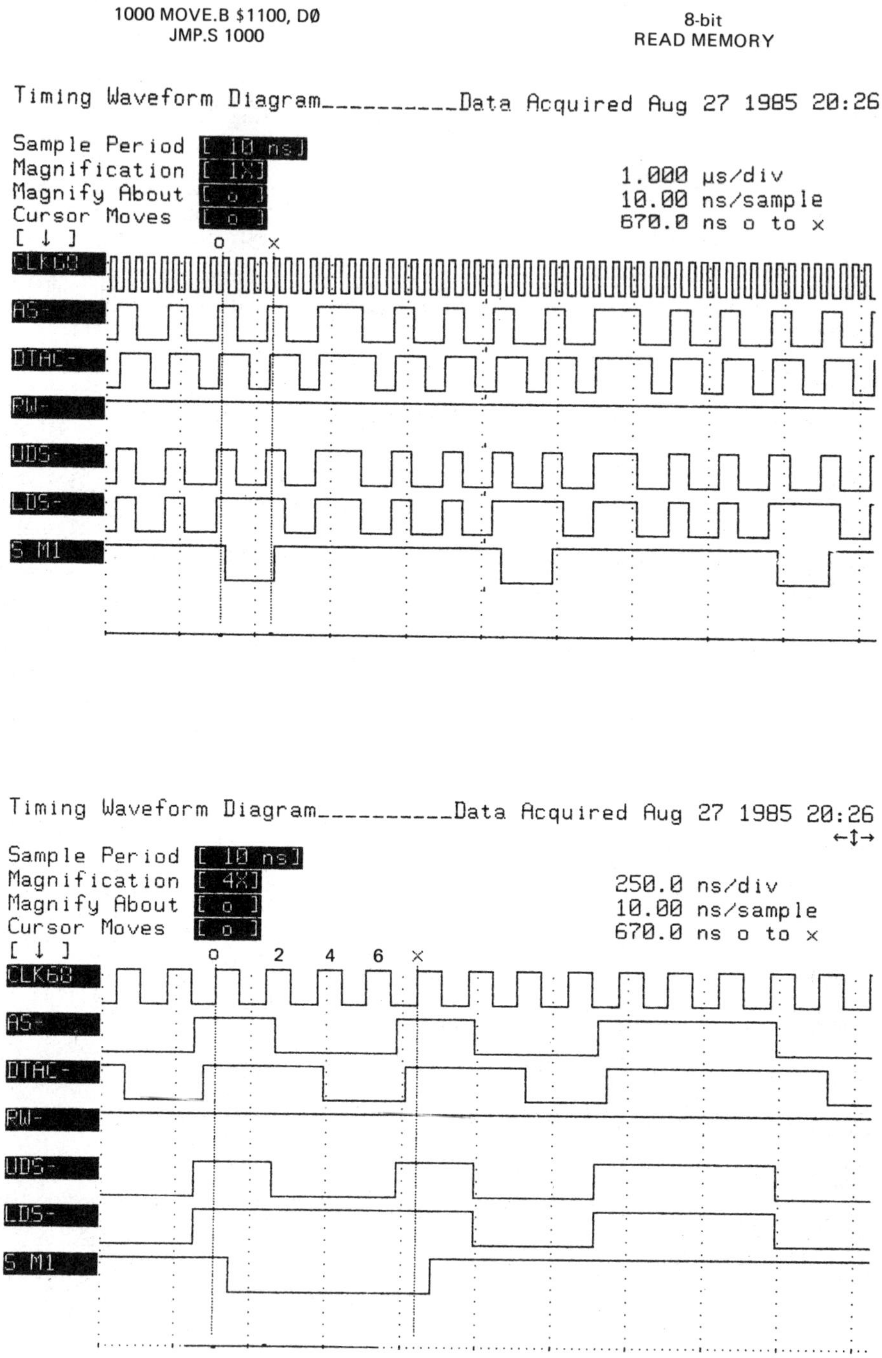

Figure 7.21 Timing diagram of a byte memory read.

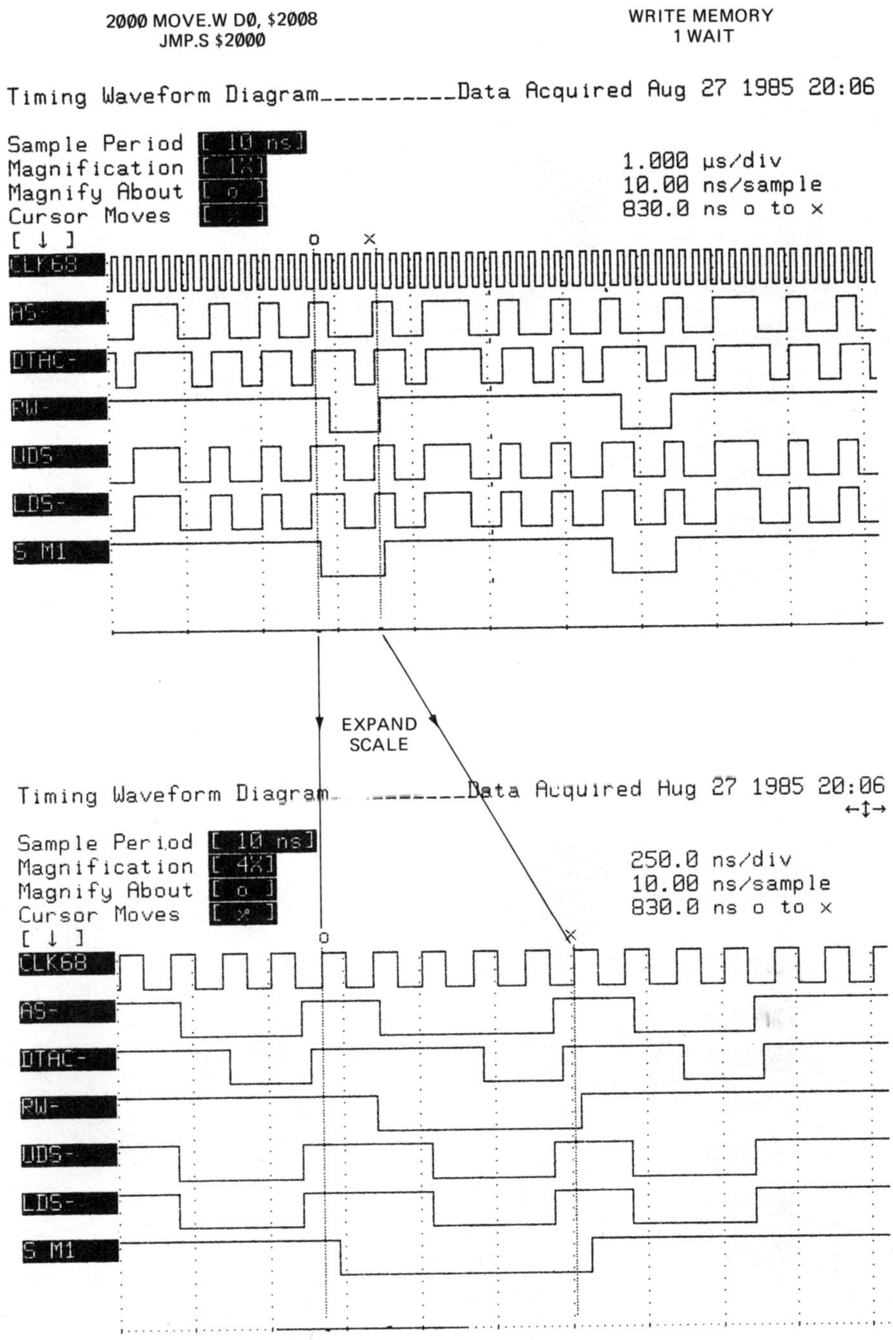

Figure 7.22 Timing diagram of a word write with one wait.

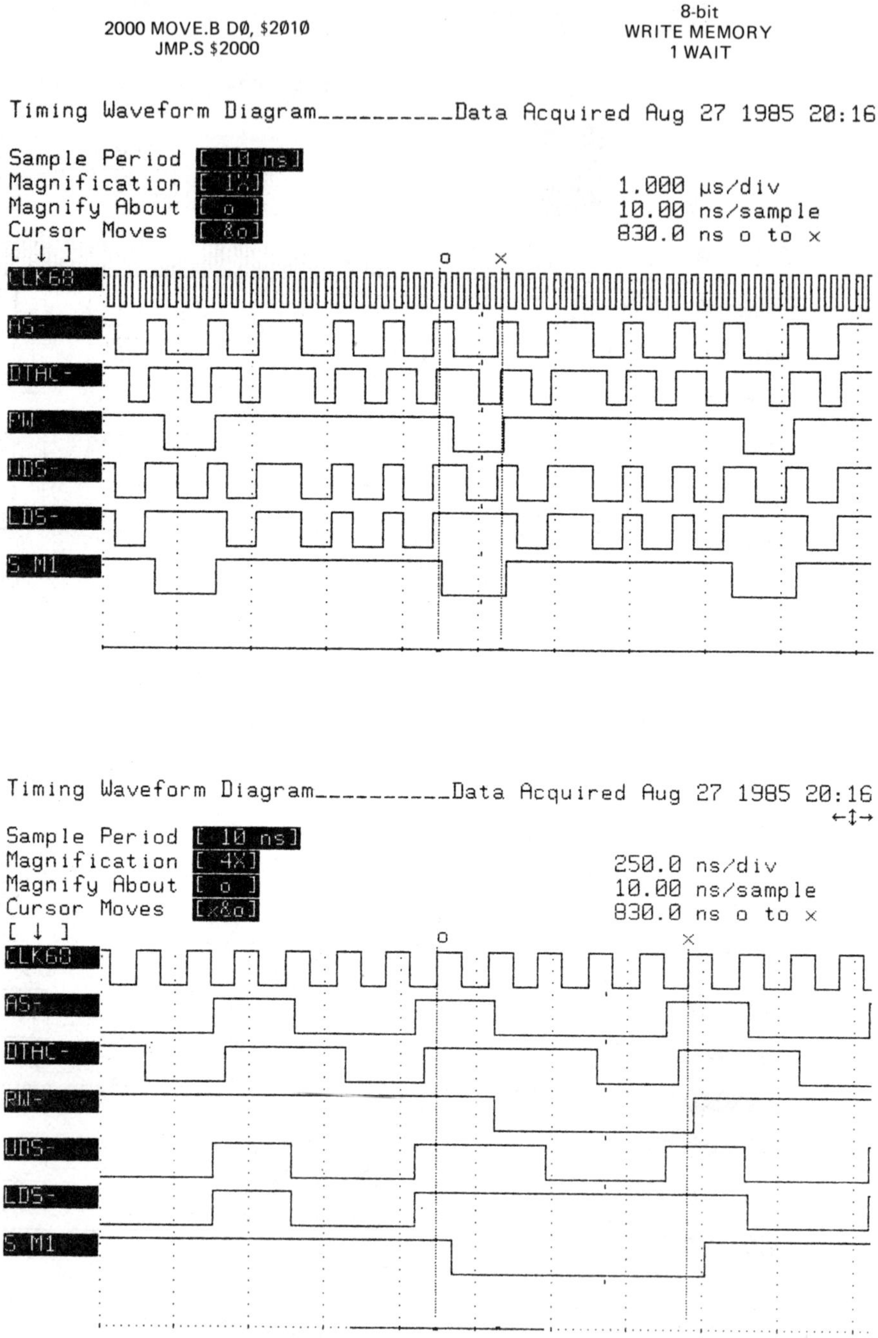

Figure 7.23 Timing diagram of a byte write with one wait.

1000 TAS.B $2000
JMP.S 1000

TAS

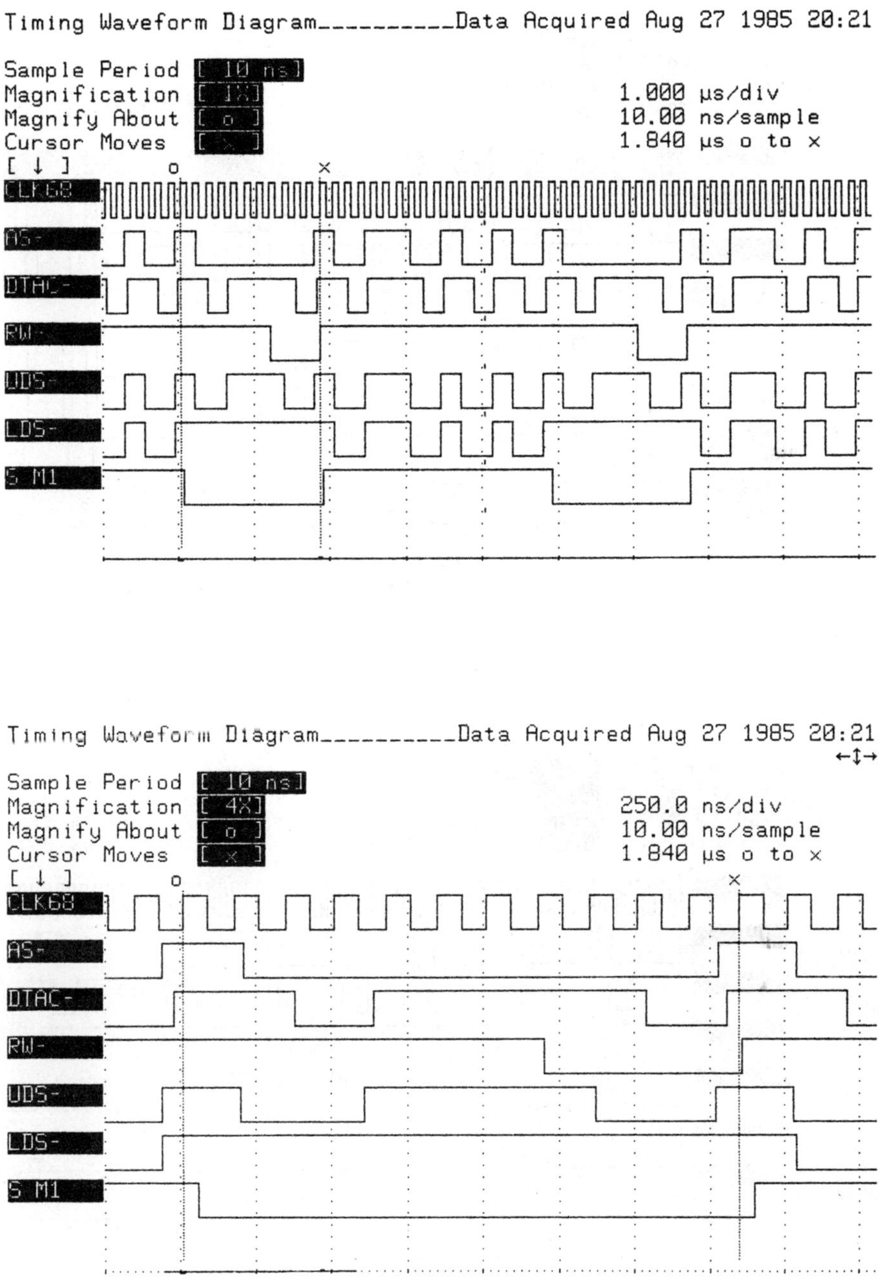

Figure 7.24 Timing diagram of the TAS instruction.

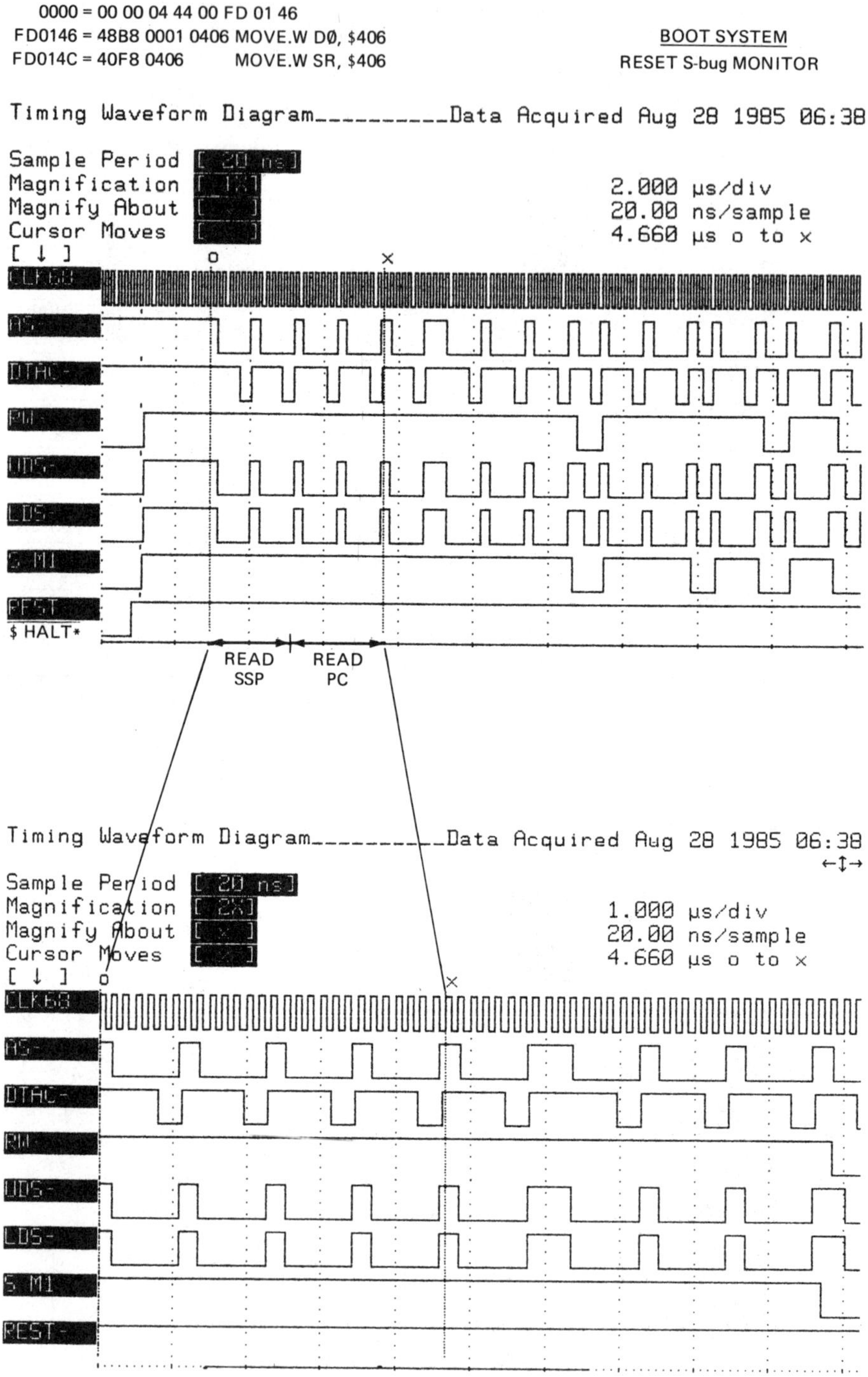

Figure 7.25 Timing diagram of the first bus cycles after a processor reset. The contents of memory starting at address 0 are 00 00 04 44 00 FD 01 46 hex.

does three 16-bit reads for the first instruction and then one 16-bit prefetch. On the ninth bus cycle following reset, the first instruction is executed to do a 16-bit write from D0 to memory location $406.

Pay particular attention to the reset sequence. The 68000 reads memory location 0 for its SSP and 4 for its PC when reset. The SSP and PC are in EPROM and do not *normally* respond to a memory read of address 0. As constructed, the actual system has 128K static RAM starting at memory 0, and EPROM is decoded at $FD 0000 and up. You must provide a special boot circuit that enables EPROM (and disables RAM) for the first four bus cycles after a reset.

7.5 SUMMARY

As you begin a major project, a review of past work in the field can be helpful. To understand what others have done with the 68000, you should go over application notes and study the relevant technical manuals. You can think of the 68000 as just one small piece of a large computer system. As you look closer, you find that you can describe the 68000 from either a software or a hardware viewpoint.

If you approach the 68000 as a programmer, you can describe it as a 16-bit processor with eight 32-bit data registers, seven 32-bit address registers, two stack pointers, a program counter, and a status register. The 68000 can operate in either a supervisor mode with full system control, or in a user mode with restricted privileges. You can read and write to registers or to memory. Memory operations can be done using 8-bit bytes, 16-bit words, or 32-bit long words.

From the hardware designer's viewpoint, however, you might think of the 68000 as an asynchronous processor with a data bus, an address bus, and a control bus. The various control lines to the processor can be divided by function and deal with control of the asynchronous bus, processor status, system control, interrupt control, bus arbitration, and 6800 peripheral control.

Instructions are fetched and executed by the 68000 by using one or more bus cycles. A read or write bus cycle is made up of at least four clock cycles plus any extra cycles to wait for slow memory or other peripherals. The actual execution time depends on the instruction; an instruction such as division, for example, can take over 150 clock cycles before the processor is ready to start another cycle. During any extended execution time, the bus is idle.

The 68000 uses a prefetch mechanism to enhance its performance; that is, while the processor executes one instruction, it goes ahead to read the next instruction and keeps it internally until needed. If you use hardware single-stepping, you can easily see the sequence of events as prefetch occurs.

All read and write bus cycles are at least four clock cycles long. Both read and write have the same timing within the bus cycle except for the data strobes. The write data strobes are a clock cycle later so that read/write memory can be selected before being write-enabled.

The example timing diagrams can give a better understanding of the bus cycles in an actual system. You can see the effect of waits on the bus cycle time for both read and write operations. You can also see how the TAS instruction works and how the 68000 system acts when reset. The reset sequence is especially important, and must be designed carefully.

EXERCISES

1. List the various registers used in the 68000 and give a brief description of what each one does.
2. How many bits are represented in the address registers? How many bits appear on the address bus? Explain the difference and how it can be handled.
3. Where is the least-significant bit of the address bus? When would you want to use it? How can you access it?
4. Describe the stack pointers. How can they both be used?
5. Does the PC point to executable code? On an even or odd address? What happens if there is a problem?
6. Explain the operation of DTACK*. What happens if it never gets asserted?
7. What is bus arbitration? When would you use it?
8. Is DTACK* used if synchronous peripherals are being accessed?
9. Explain the relationship between clock, bus, and instruction cycles.
10. Explain prefetch. Refer to the 68000 data manual and see what conditions are mentioned.
11. Describe the read bus cycle. Sketch a typical read. Sketch the bus cycle for a CLR.L instruction. If the 68000 runs at 8 MHz, how long does this instruction take to execute?
12. Suppose two waits (time of two clock cycles) are associated with an op-code fetch. How long does the CLR.L instruction in Problem 11 take to execute? Sketch the bus cycle.
13. Describe the write bus cycle and sketch a typical write.
14. Sketch the instruction cycle for CLR.W $1000. What does this instruction do? How long will it take using an 8 MHz clock?
15. Sketch the TAS instruction and explain how it works.
16. Examine the timing diagram in the 68000 data manual for the following. Assume an 8 MHz 68000 that is running with a 4 MHz clock. Show bubble numbers in your answers. For a read bus cycle:
    a. AS* is asserted how long (min/max) after the start of S2?
    b. When is AS* negated?
    c. What minimum setup time must be provided for DTACK*?
    d. When should DTACK* be negated?
17. Do Problem 16, but assume a write bus cycle.
18. In the write cycle, when do the data strobes go low? High?
19. What control signal is used to make the TAS instruction indivisible? Why is it important?
20. If you have an Educational Computer Board, write a scope loop program and examine the bus cycles. Does it match your expected pattern? Do the execution times match?

21. Do the CLR.W $1000 from Problem 14 in a scope-loop. How long does it take with the 4 MHz ECB? Sketch the bus cycles and see if you can verify your diagram using a scope or logic analyzer.

FURTHER READING

ALEXANDRIDIS, NIKITAS A. *Microprocessor System Design Concepts.* Rockville, MD: Computer Science Press, 1984.

ANDREWS, MICHAEL. *Self Guided Tour Through the 68000.* Reston, VA: Reston Publishing Co., Inc., 1984.

HARMAN, THOMAS L., AND BARBARA LAWSON. *The Motorola MC68000 Microprocessor Family: Assembly Language, Interface Design, and System Design.* Englewood Cliffs, NJ: Prentice-Hall, 1985.

KANE, GERRY. *68000 Microprocessor Handbook.* Berkeley, CA: Osborne/McGraw-Hill, 1981.

"MC68000 16-BIT MICROPROCESSOR DATA MANUAL." Austin, TX: Motorola Semiconductor Products, Inc.

"MC68000 EDUCATIONAL COMPUTER BOARD USER'S MANUAL," MEX68KECB/D2. 2nd Edition. Tempe, AZ: Motorola Literature Distribution Center, 1982.

RAFIQUZZAMAN, MOHAMED. *Microprocessors and Microcomputer Development Systems.* New York: Harper & Row, 1984.

WILLIAMS, STEVE. *Programming the 68000.* Berkeley, CA: Sybex, Inc., 1985.

EIGHT

Testing and Troubleshooting

Now that you have had a chance to see the software and hardware features of the 68000, you should be almost ready to build your CPU board. If you were to build the board right now, do you know how to test it to show that it works? Or, suppose you built the board and it failed to do what you thought it should: how could you get it working?

Knowing the facts of the 68000 is not enough to get a successful CPU board running. You also need to know how to test the board for correct operation. You also need to know how to fix it by being able to correct anything from a simple failure to meet a test specification, to an intermittent board, to a completely dead board.

This chapter will help you understand the 68000 better by testing a working processor board. Because you are using the 68000 in a system, you can get a deeper understanding of how it relates to other modules and their relative importance. You will also learn about digital test equipment in this chapter and how you can use it to troubleshoot a malfunctioning processor board.

8.1 TEST EQUIPMENT

The test equipment you use in the 68000 project, or any design project, depends on the complexity of the design. A microprocessor board can get quite involved, and usually a logic analyzer is a necessity for the hardware engineer developing a prototype. One of the first rules of design is to "keep it simple," and perhaps you might modify this to read, "keep it simple enough to test simply."

The original design and development of the 68000 board in this book was done with a logic analyzer. However, any subsequent CPU boards based on the original design can be tested with less sophisticated equipment. Certainly, if you have a logic analyzer, it can usually save you considerable time and also help you understand the interaction of many signals within the system.

The following list of test equipment describes some of the tools you will use to build your 68000 system. It is not a comprehensive listing, but it is intended to give you a flavor of the broad range of test and troubleshooting possibilities.

8.1.1 Light-Emitting Diode

Follow the principle of using the simplest possible tool for each task: if you want to know if a logic level is high or low, the LED shown in Figure 8.1 is as simple as you could want. It is so simple you can build it into your prototype (or even production model) and leave it there. For example, you can use an LED circuit like this to indicate at a glance whether your processor is running or halted.

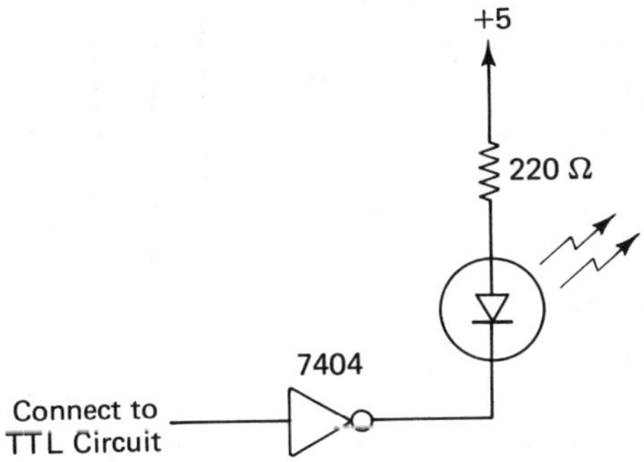

Figure 8.1 An LED logic-level indicator.

8.1.2 Volt-Ohm-Meter

The volt-ohm-meter, or VOM, is a necessary piece of test equipment for any project. When you build a circuit, you can use it to check for opens or shorts as well as to "buzz" the connections to make sure your wiring is correct. You can also check power supply voltages and measure the current your board requires.

8.1.3 Logic Probe

The logic probe is also a required tool for any digital test or troubleshooting. With it, you can tell if a circuit node is high, low, or in a three-state high-impedance condition. Usually, most logic probes have a "pulse catcher" of some sort: a simple flip-flop circuit that will trigger if even a short pulse is present at a node. If the logic probe is connected to the system clock, or any other rapidly changing signal, it will flash high-low over and over or give some similar indication of oscillation.

If you connect a logic probe to the bus of a microprocessor, you would expect to see it oscillate. Consequently, the logic probe is virtually useless in testing an operating processor unless either the processor is stopped or the probe is synchronized to the system. In the latter case, suppose you wanted to check the logic levels on the data bus; if the probe were enabled *only* when the data bus has valid data, then it would work. The Fluke 9010A Troubleshooter uses its logic probe like this to test synchronously.

8.1.4 Oscilloscope

Usually the oscilloscope is not thought of as a digital testing tool. Virtually all analog design and development engineering requires an oscilloscope, but it has been generally replaced by the logic analyzer in digital work. However, you will find that the oscilloscope is just as valuable in digital design as the logic analyzer if you can work within a few restrictions.

You know that an oscilloscope requires a constantly repeating test pattern so you can synchronize the horizontal sweep. For example, if you have a 1 MHz sine wave that you want to display, you know the single sine repeats every 1 μs; if your oscilloscope sweeps at a rate of once per microsecond, then you see a sine wave on the screen. This is your restriction on using an oscilloscope on a digital device: whatever you want to display has to repeat at a rate within the sweep capability of the oscilloscope.

Suppose you would like to see some timing diagrams similar to the logic analyzer prints shown in Chapter 7. If you use a dual-trace scope connected as shown in Figure 8.2, you should be able to see a stable pattern if each bus cycle is identical to the next. To get a stable pattern, the sequence must repeat.

Even a quick glance at any of the timing diagrams in Chapter 7 shows that the bus cycles are all different lengths. As a program executes, some instructions are I/O, some are program, some are memory writes—all different. Your scope display connected as in Figure 8.2 would not be stable. However, if you were to execute a *very* short program (a simple instruction plus a jump back to do the instruction over again), then you could synchronize the scope for a stable pattern.

The scope loop, a simple looping program, is your key to making the oscilloscope a useful digital test and troubleshooting tool. You can lock in on the repeating pattern of pulses as the 68000 executes the program over and over. If you use the top channel as

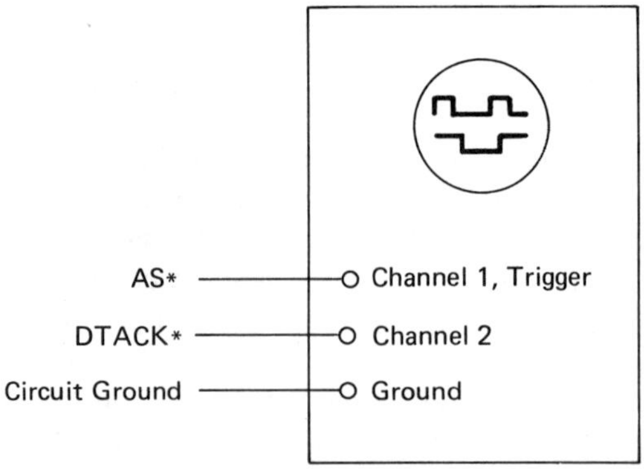

Figure 8.2 Connecting a dual-trace oscilloscope to display the address strobe (AS*) on the upper trace and data acknowledge (DTACK*) on the lower trace.

trigger and to show AS*, you can easily look at any of the other 68000 signals and see immediately what they do during the looping operation. The disadvantage, of course, is that you have only two (or perhaps four) channels, and you cannot see all the controls at once as with a logic analyzer. You do have the distinct advantage of simplicity, and that means less chance for error and less time spent in finding an answer to a problem.

The scope loop requires you to execute a program on the 68000. You must have a running system with memory, I/O, and a monitor program to control entry and execution of programs. When you first build a 68000 system, you have none of this, and yet this is when you need the oscilloscope the most. What can you do? The absolute minimum system is the freerunning processor: it continuously reads a no-operation (NOP) instruction and steps to the next address to read another NOP. With the freerunning system in a loop, you can easily connect your oscilloscope to see all the controls and address lines of the 68000.

8.1.5 In-Circuit Emulator (ICE)

The Fluke 9010A Troubleshooter shown in Figure 8.3 is a portable service instrument to test and troubleshoot microprocessor-based equipment. Unlike the oscilloscope, which observes the unit under test (UUT), the Fluke is an active participant in the system being developed. Rather than watching the processor and then displaying data, the Fluke actually becomes part of the system and takes control. For example, if you have your system ready to test, but you have not yet connected memory, you can use the Fluke to run a small scope-loop.

The troubleshooter is connected to your system as shown in Figure 8.4 by using an interface pod plugged into your 68000 socket. Your system will be able to run normally but will be under the control of the 9010A. The troubleshooter emulates the 68000 your system requires, and because it is in your circuit, it can run diagnostics to find problem areas. In general, the ICE is a valuable engineering tool because it can run by itself and help you develop your system module by module.

The Fluke 9010A can be utilized in one of several operating modes:

- Immediate — The tester responds to keyboard selections immediately.
- Program — A sequence of test instructions is stored in the 9010A internal RAM.
- Execution — Steps in a stored program are executed automatically.

The immediate operating mode will be most useful when you build up your 68000 system; the other modes are more useful for routine testing and production testing. When in the immediate mode, you can do all the operations shown in Tables 8.1, 8.2, 8.3.

You will find your most frequently used commands in Table 8.1. The tester can be used to learn and display the addressing information for a properly operating UUT. It does this by writing 64-byte blocks across the specified address range and then deciding the memory allocations based on the following:

Figure 8.3 9010A Micro-system troubleshooter. (Courtesy John Fluke Mfg. Co., Inc.)

- If the address is decoded and readable but not writable then it is ROM.
- If the address is decoded and the 64-byte block can be read back after writing, then it is RAM.
- If at least one bit of an address is write-readable, then it is I/O.

The built-in tests in Table 8.1 are your most useful diagnostic tools. While the learning-viewing feature seems convenient, it has a number of limitations; besides, you should already know the memory map of a system you want to test. Each of the tests can be performed separately or all together automatically.

The first, bus testing, checks the system for shorts or opens in the data, address, and control buses. When you first bring up the microprocessor in a freerunning mode, you can use the bus test. Remember, though, to disable the NOP being jammed on the data bus so that the tester can properly check the data lines.

As you add more circuits to your system, the 9010A can be more helpful by testing the ROM and RAM modules. Before you write any test programs for your 68000, you can check to see that your RAM is functioning properly. Likewise, you can check your ROM socket: you can know that when you put a program in ROM it will function.

Notice the approach as you develop your circuit. First you design, build, and test just the 68000 and the minimal circuits connected to it. Next you add a module and test it using the Fluke; then add another module and test the same way. All the testing can be done quickly without having to write any 68000 memory test programs or having to single-step through special code.

The troubleshooting functions in Table 8.2 are most useful later in your design when you have a system completed with memory and I/O. Perhaps your 68000 was work-

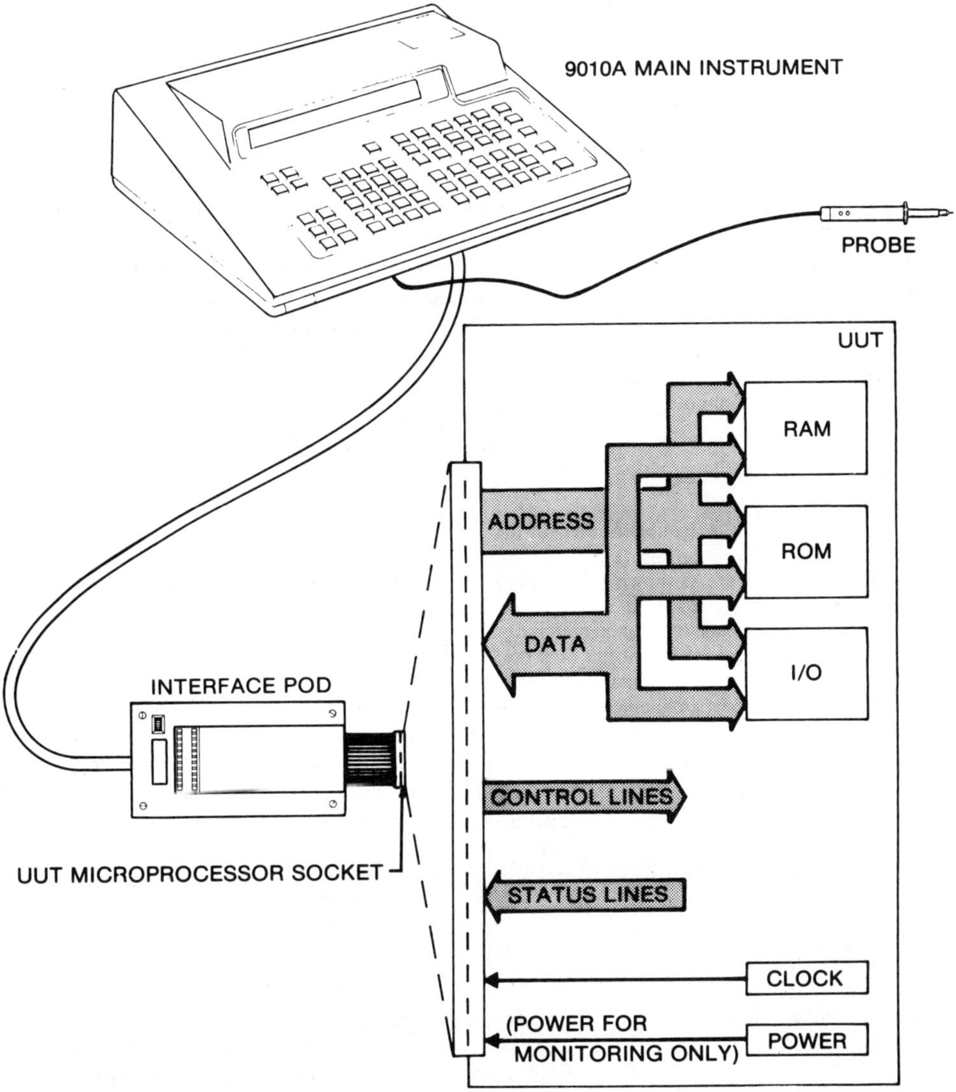

Figure 8.4 Connection of troubleshooter to UUT. (Courtesy John Fluke Mfg. Co., Inc.)

ing without any problems until you added the last 64K of RAM and the system halted. What can you do? You might check RAM to find a defective block, and then try reading and writing to specific addresses. You can write a ramp or a specified bit pattern to a troublesome address and use your oscilloscope to see that the data is being written properly. To resolve address-decoding errors, you can toggle an address bit. Likewise, you can toggle a data bit to help find problems on the data bus.

The probe-troubleshooting modes in Table 8.3 are very useful in tracing a circuit

TABLE 8.1 SUMMARY OF BUILT-IN TESTS.

Function	*Test*	*Summary*
Learn-view	Learn	Generates UUT memory map.
	View	Displays RAM, ROM, and I/O locations found in memory map.
Built-in tests	Bus	Identifies control, address, and data bus lines that are drivable and not shorted.
	I/O	Tests selected bits for read/write capability.
	ROM	Actual ROM signature compared with a specified signature.
	RAM Short	Tests: (1) r/w capability of every data bit at every address, (2) data lines tied together, (3) address-decode errors within the address block.
	RAM Long	Tests (1)–(3) as in RAM Short; (4) pattern sensitivity check.
	Auto	Combination of four tests: Bus, ROM, RAM Short, and I/O.

TABLE 8.2 SUMMARY OF TROUBLESHOOTING FUNCTIONS.

Read	Read data at a specified address or microprocessor status.
Write	Write specified data to an address or to the μp control lines.
Ramp	Performs a series of write-data operations at a specified address. Data written starts with zero and counts upward until all bits are 1.
Walk	Also performs a series of write-data operations at a specified address. A specified bit pattern is written. rotated, written again, until all the bits have been rotated back to their original positions.
Toggle-address	A specified bit in an address is toggled from one logic state to the other.
Toggle-data	A specified data bit at an address is toggled from one logic state to the other.
Toggle-data control	Toggles a specified control line from one logic state to the other.

TABLE 8.3 SUMMARY OF PROBE TROUBLESHOOTING MODES.

Pulse mode	The probe can generate pulses to force microprocessor bus lines high or low. The pulses can be high or low at a freerunning frequency of 1 KHz; also, they can be synchronized to the microprocessor address or data-valid times.
Response mode	Indicates logic high, low, or 3-state. May be freerun or synchronized to μp address or data-valid.
Read-probe mode	Gathers probe response data and creates a signature.

failure. When you troubleshoot a digital circuit you would like to stop the clock a moment while you check logic levels, perhaps tracing through a circuit to find a short or open. In general, you cannot stop a microprocessor unless you have designed in a single-step circuit. However, if you can synchronize the probe so it is enabled only when the data bus or address bus is valid, then you can use the probe effectively.

Consider this example. Set the tester so it writes a certain data pattern to a single RAM address. Synchronize the probe for data and simply probe each of the data lines to see if the data is being written as it should. In addition to verifying that the data is proper at the RAM chip itself, you can also work your way back through all the chip-select circuits to find a possible problem there.

After reading the operator manual for the details on how to use the troubleshooter, you should take special care in setting up the test system. The Fluke should *always* be turned on *before* your UUT is powered up and kept on until after your UUT is powered down. This is because the pod has internal protection circuitry that must be on while your system has power applied.

8.1.6 Logic Analyzer

The Hewlett-Packard HP-1631D shown in Figure 8.5 is an example of a typical modern logic analyzer. Similar to the oscilloscope, it is a passive observer of your system: it is not an active participant and cannot control or stimulate. It can, however, be used in a number of different ways to obtain valuable information about your system. Generally, the nature of the information is most helpful to the design engineer developing the system; as a test and troubleshooting instrument, the logic analyzer is usually an overkill.

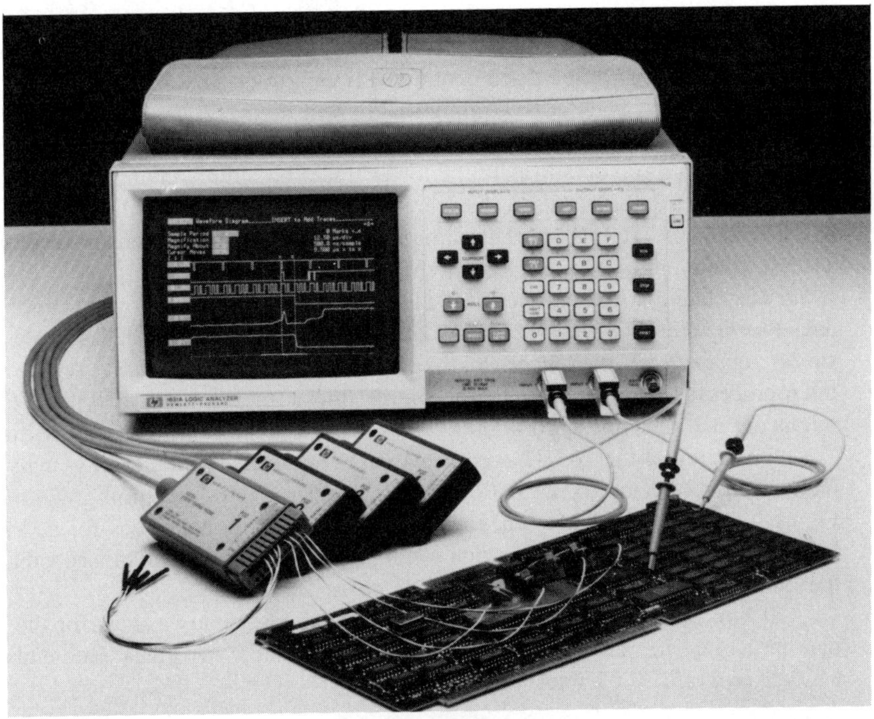

Figure 8.5 The Hewlett-Packard 1631D logic analyzer. (Courtesy Hewlett-Packard)

Think of the logic analyzer as a sophisticated multichannel oscilloscope, but instead of showing perhaps two signals, it can display 16 at once. Another important improvement over the oscilloscope is that the logic analyzer does not have to continuously sweep a repetitive "scope" pattern: it digitizes and stores single events for display and later analysis.

The 1631D features operation in three important domains:

- Analog
- Timing
- State

As an analog analyzer, the 1631D simultaneously acquires data on two channels at a 200 MHz sample rate; it stores this data in a trace memory that is 1024 samples deep for each channel. The data can be acquired repetitively or can be acquired only upon a unique event in your system. For example, recall that in the clock design of Chapter 5 the PWR-DWN* control was kept low until the system power, V_{cc}, was valid; also, PWR-DWN* was asserted 1 μs before V_{cc} was removed. Clearly you cannot use an oscilloscope to display whether your power-down circuit works; you need some way of triggering on a single event and then storing the data. Figure 8.6 shows the traces obtained using the analog feature of the 1631D. The analyzer was set to trigger on a rising V_{cc} in 8.6(a) and set to trigger on a falling PWR-DWN* in 8.6(b).

Functioning as a timing analyzer, the 1631D samples data on up to 16 channels at a 100 MHz rate. For each channel, 1,024 samples of data are stored. As in the analog mode, data capture can be done continuously or can be set to trigger on a unique event. For example, look back at the timing diagram in Figure 7.20. Seven channels of timing data were acquired and stored in memory. Once the data is in memory, you can examine a portion of it in more detail (as in the lower trace) by simply changing the magnification. No qualifying trigger was used in Figure 7.20 because the read I/O just happened to occur at the instant the 1631D started taking data. If you wanted to ensure capturing the I/O access, you might set to trigger on sM1 low.

The state analyzer function of the 1631D involves sampling up to 43 channels of data *synchronously with the clock of the system being tested.* 1024 samples of data are stored for each of the channels. Normally, these channels are used to sample the microprocessor data, address, and control lines; for example, a typical configuration might use 16 data lines, 20 address lines, and several control or status lines.

The setup of the 1631D as a state analyzer is similar to the timing-analysis setup. In fact, when connected to the 68000, the analyzer can produce timing diagrams just like Figure 7.20. The only difference is that there are additional traces for address and data lines as well. You can examine such timing diagrams and see the binary values change as the 68000 goes from one address to the next.

If you take each instant in time and convert the binary values for the address and data buses into hexadecimal, then you can make a table of values. Remember the CLR/MOVE program in Chapter 7?

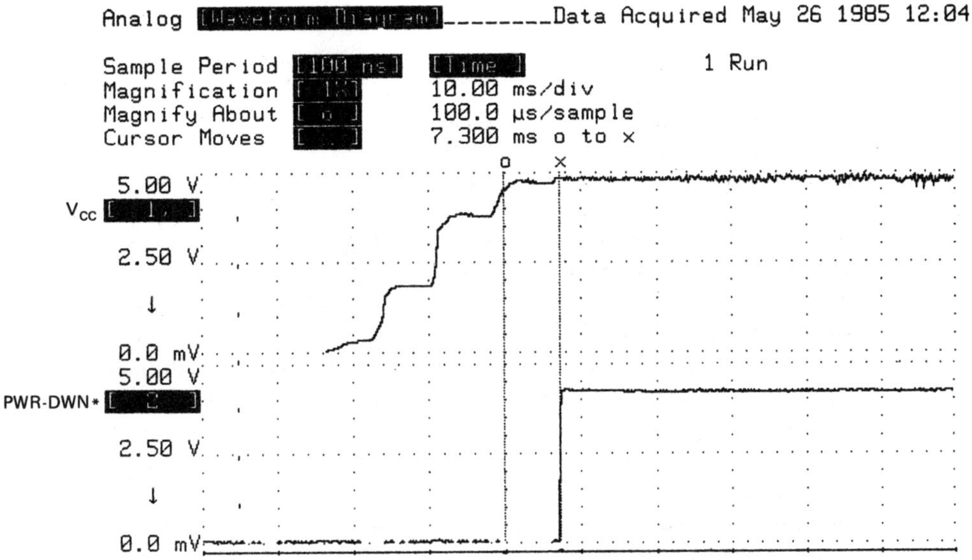

(a)

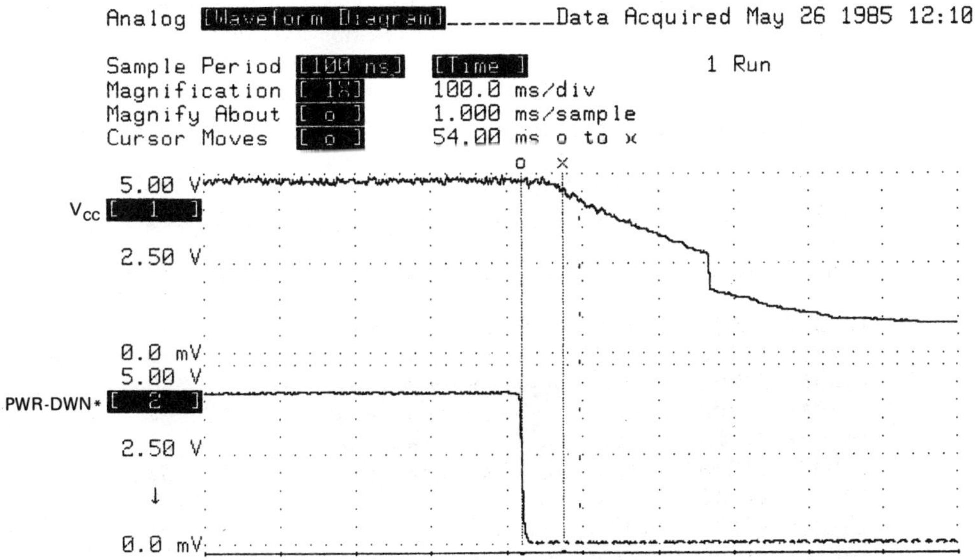

(b)

Figure 8.6 Analog timing diagrams obtained using the HP-1631D. (a) V_{cc} rises above 4.5 V at turn-on; 7.3 ms later PWR-DWN* is negated. (b) At system turn-off, PWR-DWN* is asserted 54 ms before V_{cc} drops below 4.5 V. This data was taken using the clock circuit in Chapter 5.

Program counter	*Machine code*	*Instruction*	*Operand*	*Comments*
1000	4241	CLR.W	D1	Clear register D1
1002	103C0006	MOVE.B	#6,D0	Put 6 in register D0
1006	4E71	NOP		No operation
1008	60F6	BRA.S	$1000	Loop back

This code loads into memory as shown in Figure 7.8. Suppose you set up the 1631D so it captures timing data when this program executes. Figure 8.7 shows the state analyzer display of this data in its hexadecimal form. Look at the first line, address $1000: the 68000 reads the first op-code $4241. Then it reads another op-code at $1002. You can immediately see the state of the 68000 using the analyzer like this.

If you know the op-codes, you can disassemble (inverse-assemble) the code to generate the assembly-language statements of the program. You can do this manually by looking up the op-codes in the 68000 programming manual. The easy way, of course, is to use the disassembler program in the 1631D. Look at the lower half of Figure 8.7: the data was converted into the corresponding 68000 instructions. Notice the unused prefetch of $1234 that the 68000 makes.

Being able to disassemble 68000 code is very useful, especially if you have a problem in which you are not sure what code the processor is executing. You can start at the very beginning (at RESET) and work your way through the steps the processor took when it went astray. Figure 8.8 shows the actual execution sequence of the S-bug monitor upon reset.

```
State Listing_____________________INSERT to inverse-assemble______

Label> ADDR   68000 Mnemonic                            STAT
Base > [HEX]  [               ASM                    ]  [HEX]

[Mark] XXXXX  [           All Cycles                 ]   XX

+0002* 01000     4241 supr program read                  30
+0003* 01002     103C supr program read                  30
+0004* 01004     0006 supr program read                  30
+0005* 01006     4E71 supr program read                  30
+0006* 01008     60F6 supr program read                  30
+0007* 0100A     1234 supr program read                  30
+0008* 01000  CLR.W    D1                                30
+0009* 01002  MOVE.B   #06,D0                            30
+0010* 01004     0006 supr program read                  30
+0011* 01006  NOP                                        30
+0012* 01008  BRA.B    001000                            30
+0013* 0100A     1234 unused prefetch                    30
+0014* 01000  CLR.W    D1                                30
+0015* 01002  MOVE.B   #06,D0                            30
+0016* 01004     0006 supr program read                  30
+0017* 01006  NOP                                        30
```

Figure 8.7 Data obtained during the execution of the program in Figure 7.8.

```
State Listing_____________________INSERT to inverse-assemble______
                                                               <I
Label>         ADDR   68000 Mnemonic                       STAT
Base >         [HEX]  [           ASM                   ]  [HEX]

[Mark]         XXXXX  [         All Cycles              ]   XX

+0000*         00000     0000 supr program read             30
+0001*         00002     0444 supr program read             30
+0002*         00004     00FD supr program read             30
+0003*         00006     0146 supr program read             30
+0004*         D0146  MOVEM.W rm=0001,000406                30
+0005*         D0148     0001 supr program read             30
+0006*         D014A     0406 supr program read             30
+0007*         D014C  MOVE.W   SR,000406                    30
+0008*         00406     FF00 supr data write               29
+0009*         D014E     0406 supr program read             30
+0010*         D0150  MOVEM.L rm=FFFE,-[A7]                 30
+0011*         00406     FF00 supr data read                28
+0012*         D0152     FFFE supr program read             30
+0013*         00406     2704 supr data write               29
+0014*         D0154  LEA.L    000786,A7                    30
+0015*         00442     0540 supr data write               29
```

Figure 8.8 The code executed on booting system with reset. This code is exactly the same as the Figure 7.25 timing diagram. The first four 16-bit reads fetch the SSP and PC; they are *not* disassembled.

If your processor halts after millions of instructions, you cannot reasonably trace starting at RESET. Set an event trigger or some special event, then the 1631D will start capturing data.

A summary of the analog, timing, and state features is shown in Figure 8.9. The specifications of the HP-1631D are in Figure 8.10.

8.2 TESTING THE EDUCATIONAL COMPUTER BOARD (ECB)

Before you try using your test equipment to find a problem in a defective board or to bring up your own processor, take a look at a working system. In general, whenever you begin a new design project, try testing an existing board, even if it is not quite the same as your intended product. Not only will you become familiar with using the test equipment, but you can see better what to expect when your job is done. This preview can help you develop a sense of what ''smells right'' in a circuit or system. Without this experience, you can easily waste hours trying to fix a circuit that is already working properly.

Your purpose in testing is investigative—you want to explore and learn. Treat your effort on the ECB the same as any other lab or design work: write it up in your lab book! Tape program listings and printouts from any equipment into the lab book for future reference. You will want to compare the ECB data with data from your own designs many times during your project.

Analog Performance Features

- 200 MHz sample rate
- 50MHz analog bandwidth
- 2 channel simultaneous acquisition
- 1024 deep acquisition memory per channel
- analog triggering - slope/level on internal or external
- analog waveform displayed in full pixel graphics
- x and o cursor system for waveform time and voltage measurments
- post acquisition processing for auto answers and statistical characterization
- cummulative display mode for infinite persistence applications

Timing Performance Features

- 100 MHz sample rate on up to 16 channels
- 1024 deep acquisition memory per channel
- pattern, edge, and glitch triggering
- waveform or list displays of acquired data
- x and o cursor system for waveform time interval measurements
- post acquisition processing for auto answers and statistical characterization

State Performance Features

- external clock rates to 25 MHz
- two phase demultiplexing
- up to 43 channels (1631D)
- 1024 deep acquisition memory per channel
- pattern, sequence, and occurrence count triggering
- storage qualification
- state and time interval histogramming

Figure 8.9 A brief summary of the analog, timing, and state performance features of the HP-1631D. (Courtesy Hewlett-Packard)

To test the ECB, start with a close examination of its block diagram. You want to get a feel for the big picture and then relate that to the software design. Figure 8.11 shows a condensed block diagram of the ECB. At a glance, you can see that it has ROM and RAM as well as I/O capabilities. Relate this to the memory map on Figure 8.12. You can

Features and Specifications

MEASUREMENT CONFIGURATION/CHANNELS

HP 1631A State	HP 1631A Timing	HP 1631A Analog	HP1631D State	HP1631D Timing	HP1631D Analog
35	—	—	43	—	—
27	8	—	35	8	—
—	8	—	27	16	—
—	—	2	—	16	—
—	8	2	—	—	2
27	8	2	—	16	2
35	—	2	27	16	2
			35	8	2
			43	—	2

MEASUREMENT FUNCTIONS

ANALOG

CHANNEL 1 and 2 (VERTICAL)

Probe Factors: 1:1, 10:1, or 50:1 probe attenuation factors may be entered to scale the HP 1631A/D to input voltages at the probe tip. All vertical specifications relate to a 1:1 probe factor.
Range: 40 mV to 2.5 V full-scale, automatically calibrated internally with two-digit resolution with each change in format specification.
Bandwidth (-3 dB) dc coupled: dc to 50 MHz
Dc gain accuracy: ±2.5% of full-scale
Channel isolation: 55 dB from dc to 50 MHz
Analog-to-digital conversion (ADC) resolution: ±1 LSB, which is ±1.6% of full-scale
Dc offset range/resolution (relative to center of range):

Offset Range	Offset Resolution
1.5V	approximately 1 mV

Transition time: ≤6 ns, 20% to 80% of full-scale.
Input coupling: dc
Input RC: 1 MΩ ±2%, shunted by approximately 14 pF
Maximum safe input voltage: ±40 V (dc + peak ac)

TRIGGER (ANALOG)

Sources: channel 1, channel 2, or external trigger input.
Edge: rising or falling edge may be selected for any source.
Sensitivity: (square wave up to 10 MHz)
.2 of full-scale for channels 1 and 2
50 mV p-to-p for external
(square wave up to 50 MHz)
.3 of full-scale for channels 1 and 2
100 mV p-to-p for external
Level range/resolution:
internal: (within the display window): approximately 1% of full scale
external: ±2 V in 1 mV steps
External trigger input:
Maximum safe input voltage: ±40 V (dc + peak ac)
input coupling: dc
input RC: 1 MΩ±2%, shunted by approximately 14 pF

TIME BASE (HORIZONTAL)

Sample period: 5 ns to 500 ms in a 1-2-5 sequence.
Range 500μs to 500 s full-scale (10 divisions).
Time base accuracy
sample period: ±.01%
time-interval measurement accuracy: (equal rise and fall times)
single-shot: ±1.5 ns for 5 ns sample period ±1 sample period for sample periods of 10 ns or greater
continuous: ±.15 times sample period, based on 100 averages
Delay
tracepoint: equals trigger plus delay; trace point can be delayed from 0 to about 260k sample periods after the trigger.
tracepoint placement accuracy: within ±1 sample period ±.1 times fullscale voltage divided by the slew rate of the input signal.
tracepoint position: can be set approximately 50 sample periods from the start, end, or near the center of the data record. A 1024-sample record can be positioned with about 950 samples before the tracepoint, or with the entire data record beginning up to about 260k samples after the trigger.

Notes: specifications apply after a 30 minute warm up period. Single-shot reconstruction uncertainty = ±1 ns (applies for time ranges of 50 ns thru 2 μs)

ANALOG OPERATING CHARACTERISTICS

Digitizer: two channels are digitized simultaneously.
Digitizing Technique Real-time digitizing: all data points are digitized, at equal selectable increments in time, on each acquisition.
Digitizing Rates: selectable, 2 samples/second to 200 megasamples/sec.
Voltage Resolution: 6 bits; 1 part in 64.
Acquisition Memory: 1024 samples, 6 bits per channel, 2 channels; up to 1000 samples are used for display; magnifier allows full screen display from 1000 samples to 25 samples; the entire 1024 sample record can be accessed via HP-IB and HP-IL.

DISPLAY

WAVEFORM

Straight line: waveforms are displayed by connecting adjacent sample points with a vertical and a horizontal line.
Filtered: a post acquisition interpolation filter provides up to 19 additional points between each sample point; waveforms are displayed by connecting adjacent interpolated points with two lines, as above.
Data Display Formats: one or two analog waveforms can be displayed simultaneously in the analog waveform display or with a combination of timing waveforms in the timing waveform display.
Single: the display retains the previous acquisition until RUN is pressed.
Continuous: the display is updated with each new waveform acquisition.
Cumulative: all successive waveform acquisitions are displayed together until STOP is pressed.
Waveform Trace: allows selected tracepoint conditions to be changed in continuous trace/display mode.
Graticules: full grid

INDICATORS

Memory: the amount of acquisition memory displayed is indicated below the graticule as a solid bar with the remaining memory shown in dots at double the graticule dot density.
Cursors: X and O cursors are shown as solid vertical lines in the display. The X cursor is indicated as a tic on the top of the memory bar; the O cursor is indicated as a tic on the bottom of the memory bar.
Tracepoint: shown as a vertical dashed line in the display.

RUN/REAL-TIME/STOP/RESUME FUNCTIONS

RUN: allows an acquisition when tracepoint conditions are met. Clears all previous traces and statistics.
STOP: immediately halts acquisition; acquisition can be resumed. If in continuous trace mode or single display mode, acquisition is halted after trace is complete.
RESUME: Allows acquisition to continue after STOP for the purpose of continuing to obtain statistics under tracepoint and/or X-O cursor conditions. The waveform display is not cleared if in the cumulative display mode.
STOP/STOP: aborts acquisition; acquisition cannot be resumed.

MEASUREMENT AIDS

Cursors: two cursors (X and O) are provided for making voltage and time measurements on displayed waveforms. Both absolute and differential values are provided for voltage measurements. Dual cursor time measurements can be made between two points on the same waveform or between two points on different waveforms.

POST PROCESSING

Cursor Statistics: X to O cursor statistics are provided for continuous voltage and time measurements: maximum, minimum, mean and standard deviation. Single cursor voltage statistics can be obtained on either waveform. Dual cursor statistics can be obtained between two points on the same waveform or between two points on different waveforms (time only).
Cursor Placement: Both X and O cursors can be uniquely specified with respect to the tracepoint or acquisition start, by selection of channel 1 or 2, rising or falling edge, voltage level, hold or delay time.
Stop Continuous Run: pressing RUN processes waveform acquisitions until the cursor-based RUN-STOP condition is met; RUN-STOP conditions include greater-than/less-than time intervals, or a specific number of acquisitions. The time from the end of an acquisition until the instrument is ready to accept a new acquisition is approximately 40 ms (with statistical measurements OFF).

SETUP AIDS

Presets: scales the vertical range to predetermined values for displaying ECL (0.0 V to −2.0 V) or TTL (−0.5 V to +5.5 V) waveforms.
Activity: aids the scaling of vertical range and offset using a display of signal activity placed with respect to the voltage limits specified. Activity shown while not running.

TIMING

Timing Mode/Clock
Ranges: 10 ns to 500 ms in a 1-2-5 sequence.

Figure 8.10 Features and specifications of the HP 1631D logic analyzer. (Courtesy Hewlett-Packard)

Timebase Accuracy
sample period: ±0.01•
time interval accuracy
single-shot: ±1 sample period.
continuous: ±.15 sample period, based on 100 averages.
Glitch: with glitch detection on, the number of timing channels is halved, with 1k memory depth.
Minimum Detectable Glitch: 5 ns wide at threshold.
Timing Mode/Data Indexing
Asynchronous pattern: 20 ns to 1 ms in a 1-2-5 sequence with an accuracy of ±20% or 15 ns, whichever is greater. Glitch or edge on selected channels ANDed with asynchronous pattern.
Maximum time delay: Approximately 2^{18} times the sample period to a maximum of 9999 seconds.
Timing Mode/Expansion
Times 1 to times 40 in a 1-2-4 sequence. Display is a compressed representation of the 1k memory in times 1 magnification. In times 2 magnification and above, each display sample represents a single sample in memory.
Timing Mode/Overview
Graph: A graph of any user-defined label can be shown. The user can specify the upper and lower bounds of the graph, and all 1024 states of the memory can be simultaneously displayed.

MEASUREMENT AIDS

Cursors: two cursors (X and O) are provided for making time measurements on waveform patterns.
POST PROCESSING
Cursor Statistics: X-to-O cursor statistics are provided for time measurements; maximum, minimum, mean and standard deviation.
Cursor Placement/Data Marks: both X and O cursors and up to four data marks (a,b,c, and d) can be uniquely specified with respect to the tracepoint or acquisition start by selecting up to eight timing patterns (Pn) in conjunction with choices of entering/leaving the pattern (including any glitch) along with greater-than/less-than time intervals.
Stop-Continuous Run: Pressing RUN processes timing data acquisitions until the cursor-based RUN-STOP condition is met. RUN-STOP conditions include greater-than/less-than time intervals or a specific data mark quantity, a specific number of acquisitions, or a sequence of up to four data mark terms. The time from the end of the acquisition until the instrument is ready to accept a new acquisition is approximately 100 ms (with statistical measurements and data marking off).

STATE

Memory
Data acquisition: 1024 words
Compare: 16 words
Search: Memory may be searched for any pattern defined within a label set. All pattern matches in memory may be marked or separately displayed.
State Mode/Clocks: three ORed clocks operate in one-phase or two-phase demultiplexing mode. Clock edge is selectable as positive, negative, or both edges for each clock. Different edge selections may be made on the same clock if it is used in both phases of the multiplexed mode.
State Mode/Data Indexing
Resources: four terms including the Boolean NOT of each term, any pattern or NO pattern; a term is the AND combination of bit patterns in each label. Terms may be used as often as desired.
Trigger: up to four resource terms may be used in sequence to establish the trace parameter. The last term in the sequence may use up to four resource terms in an ORed format.
Restart: one to four resource terms may be used in an ORed condition for a sequence restart condition.
Store qualifiers: one to four resource terms may be used in an ORed format. Store qualification may be separately defined for each term in the trigger sequence.
Occurrence: the number of occurrences of the last event in the sequence may be specified up to n=59999.
Edit compare: trace until compare "equal to" or "not equal to" is provided. The compare file is the width of the analyzer, with a depth of up to 16 words. Each word in the compare buffer can have "don't cares" and can be compared anywhere in the 1024-word memory.
State Mode/Overview
XY chart: a chart of any user-defined label can be shown. The user can specify the upper and lower bounds of the chart, and all 1024 states of the memory can be simultaneously displayed.
Time-interval measurement: A timer can be started on completion of a sequence of up to three resource terms with restart and occurrence capabilities such as state data indexing. The timer can be stopped on an ORed combination of one to four resource terms. A histogram of the start/stop measurement is displayed. The user can specify up to eight time ranges. Minimum time, maximum time, average time, last time, total time, and total samples are also displayed.

Resolution: displayed statistics—250 ns or 1% of reading, whichever is greater, (four digit display).
State label measurement: a histogram of any user-defined label can be shown. The user can specify up to eight labels and ranges.
Maximum count: 2^{63} -1.

INTERACTIVE MEASUREMENTS

ACQUISITION: analog, timing and state data acquisition occur simultaneously.
ARMING: any of the three analyzers can be master while the remaining two are slave.
Master state: the waveform analyzer and the timing analyzer can be simultaneously armed by the full data indexing capability of the state analyzer.
Master timing: the waveform analyzer and the state analyzer can be simultaneously armed by the full data indexing capability of the timing analyzer.
Master analog: the timing analyzer and the state analyzer can be simultaneously armed by the full analog indexing capability of the waveform analyzer.
Arming time: the time required to arm and be armed in a master/slave configuration is as follows:

	State	Timing	Analog
State	N/A	Approximately 12 sample periods* −20 ns	Approximately 8 sample periods* −20 ns
Timing	Approximately 55 ns	N/A	Approximately 8 sample periods* −10 ns
Analog	Approximately 70 ns	Approximately 12 sample periods* +5 ns	N/A

* Of the master

TRACEPOINT ALIGNMENT: analog, timing, and state acquisition data can be correlated in time.
Mixed display: timing channels can be displayed on the same screen with analog channels; the tracepoint and time/div are common to timing and analog in this display mode, and set by the timing analyzer.
Tracepoint alignment: analog waveform data alignment to timing analyzer data is less than 1 analog sample period + timing sample period + 15 ns
Operating modes: to correlate data between analyzers, the slave analyzer must be set up to trigger on a DON'T CARE (timing) or TRIGGER IMMEDIATE (analog) condition. Any other slave trigger condition results in uncorrelated data.
Timing analyzer master: analog slave: trigger immediate.
Analog master: timing analyzer slave: trigger pattern, all DON'T CAREs.
State analyzer master: timing analyzer slave: trigger pattern, all DON'T CAREs; analog slave: trigger immediate.
Insert-to-correlate: provides cursor correlation, between timing and analog data. Cursors in one waveform display can be directly placed at the same time location as those cursors in the other waveform display by pressing insert-to-correlate. The cursor in the MAGNIFY ABOUT [ ] selection is cursor-correlated. Going to a post-processing menu causes the cursors to return to their specified location.

STATE/TIMING INPUT SPECIFICATIONS
PROBES

RC:100kΩ, ±2% shunted by approximately 5 pF at probe body.
Minimum Swing: 600 mV p-p
Minimum Input Overdrive (Above Pod Threshold): 250 mV or 30% of input amplitude, whichever is greater.
Maximum Voltage: ±40 V, peak.
Threshold Voltage: −9.9 V to +9.9 V in 0.1 V increments.
accuracy: 2.5% ±120 mV.
Dynamic Range: ±10 V about threshold.

STATE MODE

Clock Repetition Rate: single phase: 25 MHz with single clock and single edge specified; 20 MHz with any ORed combination of clocks and edges. multiplexed: master-slave clock timing; master clock must follow slave clock by at least 10 ns and precede next slave clock by 50 ns or more.
Clock Pulse Width: ≥20 ns at threshold.
Setup Time: ≥20 ns, the time data must be present prior to clock transition.
Hold Time: 0 ns, the time data must be present after clock transition.

Figure 8.10 (Continued)

Ordering Information

TIME MODE

Glitch: with glitch detection on, number of timing channels is halved. Minimum detectable glitch: 5 ns width at threshold.

GENERAL CHARACTERISTICS

LABELS

Input channel labels: up to eight state, 16 timing, user-defined, five-character labels may be assigned bit patterns in any configuration up to 43 bits per label. Bits may be used in more than one label and need not be contiguous. Primary use is for identifying bits assigned to bus structures such as address, data, and status.
User field: all labels with four bits or less allow mnemonics to be assigned to specific patterns. Primary use is to identify such functions as read, write, opcode, etc.
Relocatable field: any single label may be defined to have relocatable properties to facilitate viewing software modules in the format they were written. Up to sixteen module starting-locations may be specified, allowing trigger parameters to be based on module names, plus an offset value. An onboard calculator that operates in hex, octal, binary, or decimal facilitates generating the offset table.

TIME-OF-DAY-CLOCK: a 24-hour clock prints out the time of data collection on all stored records.

ACTIVITY MARKERS: provided in the format display for identification of active inputs.

HP-IB I/O PORT: an HP-IB connector, along with an eight-position HP-IB switch, is located on the rear panel. Five positions on the switch are used to determine the address, two positions are used to determine the system controller modes. The HP-IB can be used in the following environments.

1. Logic analyzer being controlled from a controller, such as an HP series 200/300 computer.
2. Logic analyzer is the bus controller used for disc and printer operations.
3. Logic analyzer is controlled via HP-IL.

OUTPUTS/REAR-PANEL BNCs: one output BNC is located on the rear panel with TTL output. High is ≥2 V into 50Ωs; low is 0.4 V into 50Ωs. The BNC can be programmed from the keyboard to provide the following signals.

1. Pulse on state tracepoint
2. High until state tracepoint
3. Low until state tracepoint
4. High on last sequence
5. Constant high
6. Constant low
7. High on timing pattern
8. 5 ms burst for oscilloscope probe compensation
9. Positive edge on analog trigger

A second BNC is located on the rear panel to provide +5 V for the HP 10269B probe (preprocessor) interface.

OPERATING ENVIRONMENT
Temperature: 0° to 55° C (32° to 131° F)
Humidity: up to 95% relative humidity at 40° C.
Altitude: to 4600 m (15,000 ft).
Vibration: vibrated in three planes for 15 minutes each with 0.3 mm excursions, 5 to 55 Hz.
Dimensions: refer to outline drawing:
Weight: HP 1631A; 13.2 kg (29 lb) net; 17.7 kg (39 lb) shipping.
HP 1631D; 13.8 kg (30 lb) net; 18.4 kg (40 lb) shipping.
Power: 115/230 Vac, −22% to +10%; 300 W max; 48-66 Hz.
PROGRAMMABILITY:
All instrument configurations and acquisition data may be remotely programmed via HP-IB (IEEE-488 or HP-IL.

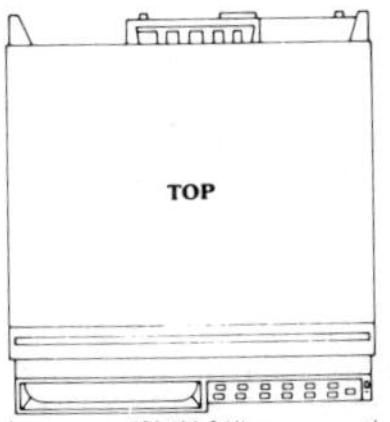

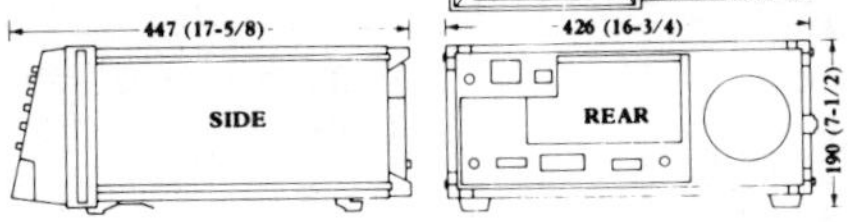

5954-2614 Data Subject To Change Printed in U.S.A.

HP 1631A Logic Analyzer
(35 channels state, 8 timing, 2 analog) **$11 000**
HP 1631D Logic Analyzer
(43) channels state, 16 timing, 2 analog) **$13 000**

INDIVIDUAL ACCESSORIES (supplied with the HP 1631A/D)

HP 10271A: state data probe (quantity: 3)
HP 10272A: state and timing data probe (quantity: 1, 1631A; 2, 1631D)
HP 10017A: 10:1 divider probe (quantity: 2)
HP 10271-63201: lead set for each HP 10271A state data probe
HP 10272-63201: lead set for each HP 10272A state and timing data probe
HP 10230-62101: grabber tip for 10271A and 10272A
HP P/N 1250-1454: BNC-to-mini-probe adapter

SUPPORTING INSTRUMENTS

HP 10269B probe interface (requires a preprocessor) **$450**
HP 10331A HP 1630A/D-to-HP 1631A/D upgrade kit **$3 500**
Preprocessors are available for the following microprocessors:
Z80, Z8001, Z8002, NSC800, 8085, 8086/88, 80186/88, 80286/88, 6800/02, 6809/09E, 68000/10, 68008
See the HP 1631A/D Preprocessor/interface module data sheet

PRODUCT SUPPORT PACKAGE

HP 01631-90904: HP 1631A/D operating and programming manual
HP 01630-90916: HP 1631A/D and HP 1630A/D/G service manual
HP 01630-68705: HP logic analyzer support package including the HP 5957-7306 training (HP 1630A/D/G, HP 1631A/D)
HP 5957-7306: HP logic analyzer service training only (HP 1630A/D/G, HP 1631A/D)

TRAINING COURSES AND SERVICES

HP 50600A: instrumentation consulting service
HP 1631A/D and 24 users seminar

ACCESSORIES AND PERIPHERALS

PROBES AND PROBING ACCESSORIES
HP 10017A: 1 MΩ, 10:1 divider probe (1 m)
HP 10018A: 1 MΩ, 10:1 divider probe (2 m)
HP 10021A: 1:1 miniature probe (1 m)
HP 10022A: 1:1 miniature probe (2 m)
HP 10026A: 50Ω, 1:1 miniature probe (1 m)
HP 10027A: 50Ω, 1:1 miniature probe (2 m)
HP 10002A: 1 MΩ, 50:1 divider probe (1 m)
HP 10032A: 100:1 miniature probe (1 m)
HP 10100C: 50Ω, BNC-male-to-BNC-female feedthrough termination
HP 10024A: 16-pin IC test clip
HP 10211A: 24-pin IC test clip
HP 10240B: BNC-to-BNC ac coupling capacitor

TESTMOBILE
HP 1008A: testmobile for the HP 1631A/D

COVER
HP 10062A: front-panel cover

PERIPHERALS
HP 9121S/D: 3 1/2 inch microfloppy single-sided disc drive
HP 9122S/D: 3 1/2 inch microfloppy double-sided disc drive
HP 2225A: Thinkjet ® printer
HP 2671G: graphics printer
HP 92191A: box of ten blank 3 1/2 inch single-sided discs
HP 92192A: box of ten blank 3 1/2 inch double-sided discs

HP-IB CABLES
HP 10833A: 1 m
HP 10833B: 2 m
HP 10833C: 3 m
HP 10833D: 0.5 m

RACK MOUNTING
HP 5061-9678: Rack mount hardware (rack mount slides are not recommended)

FOR ADDITIONAL INFORMATION and a thorough discussion of the measurements required in modern digital design, refer to the *HP 1631A/D-1 Product Note — "Solving Complex Digital Design Problems with the HP 1631A/D — A Guide to Cross Domain analysis."* Order publication number 5954-2618

For more information, call your local HP sales office listed in the telephone directory white pages. Ask for the Electronic Instruments Department. Or write to **Hewlett-Packard: U.S.A.-P.O. Box 10301, Palo Alto, CA 94303-0890. Europe** -P.O. Box 999, 1180 AZ Amstelveen The Netherlands. **Canada**-6877 Goreway Drive, Mississauga, L4V1M8, Ontario. **Japan**-Yokogawa-Hewlett-Packard Ltd., 3-29-21, Takaido-Higashi, Suginami-ku, Tokyo 168. **Elsewhere in the world,** write to Hewlett-Packard Intercontinental, 3495 Deer Creek Road, Palo Alto, CA 94304.

Figure 8.10 (Continued)

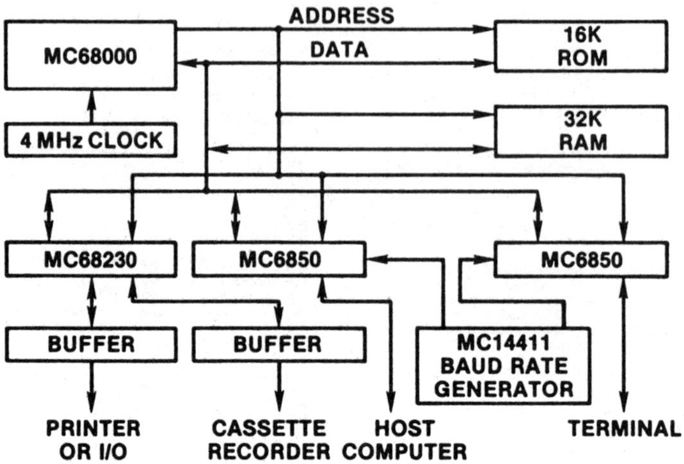

Figure 8.11 ECB block diagram. (Courtesy Motorola Inc.)

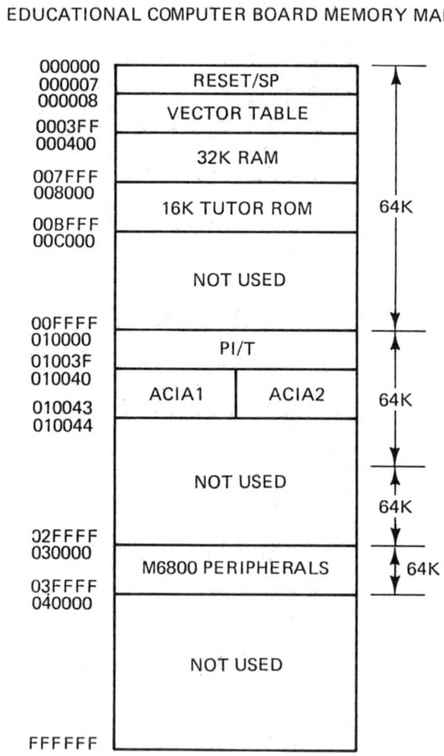

Figure 8.12 ECB memory map. (Courtesy Motorola Inc.)

see that RAM is decoded as the lower 32K with the TUTOR monitor program immediately after it. The parallel interface and timer (PI/T) and the two asynchronous communications interface adapters (ACIA) are decoded in the next 64K page. Decoding is provided for 6800-type peripherals in the fourth 64K page.

8.2.1 Clock and Reset

The block diagram in Figure 8.13 shows enough hardware detail for you to use it directly when testing the ECB. Identify the block marked "clock and reset." It is one of the easiest modules to test, and a good place to start your exploration. Refer to the full schematic diagram of the 68000 ECB in your ECB manual (MEX68KECB/D2) and find the system clock located at U16. Also find the reset circuitry connected to the 68000; it is made up of U42, U43, and U44.

Sometimes working from the full schematic is confusing because of all the detail. If you extract the relevant circuits from the schematic and redraw them,[1] you will have the circuits in Figure 8.14. It is easy to use the modular approach and understand how each circuit works.

How can you test the two modules in Figure 8.14? Use your oscilloscope to see the 8 MHz oscillator and also the 4 and 1 MHz counter outputs. Figure 8.15 shows the output you measure if you use the HP-1631D logic analyzer in its analog mode; the waveform is identical to what you see with any dual-trace oscilloscope.

The test of the power-on reset circuit in Figure 8.14 is a bit more difficult unless you have a storage oscilloscope. Figure 8.16 was done using the 1631D to capture the single event of power being applied; you can see that RESET* is asserted low until about 500 ms after the power was applied. However, a delay of this length can easily be observed using your dual trace scope or just a pair of LEDs (one shows power on, the other shows RESET* high).

8.2.2 Address Decoding and DTACK*

The next module to examine is marked "Decode and Control" in Figure 8.13. This particular circuit decodes the address being generated by the 68000 and, if the address corresponds to a device shown in the memory map (Figure 8.12), it enables the device and also returns DTACK*. It is *most important* for you to understand the functioning of this circuit and how DTACK* is generated. When you grasp this concept, then you can easily design your own simplified DTACK* circuit.

The address decode section is shown in Figure 8.17; find ROMEN, the ROM enable output from U29B. The ROMEN output goes directly into the circuit shown in Figure 8.18. Part of the Figure 8.18 schematic is the ROM pair that is enabled by ROMEN; the other part is the DTACK* generator. You can condense the circuit to its essentials as in Figure 8.19.

[1]Do not waste time redrawing large modules; rather, use a photocopier, clip out the module, and tape it in your lab book.

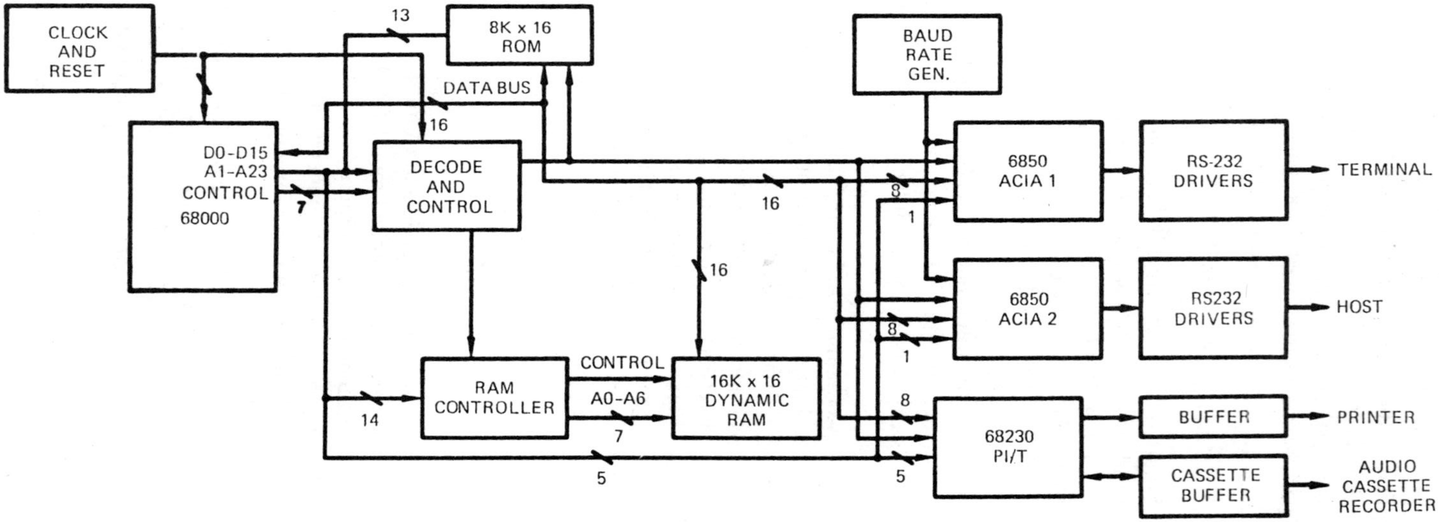

Figure 8.13 M68KECB detailed block diagram. (Courtesy Motorola Inc.)

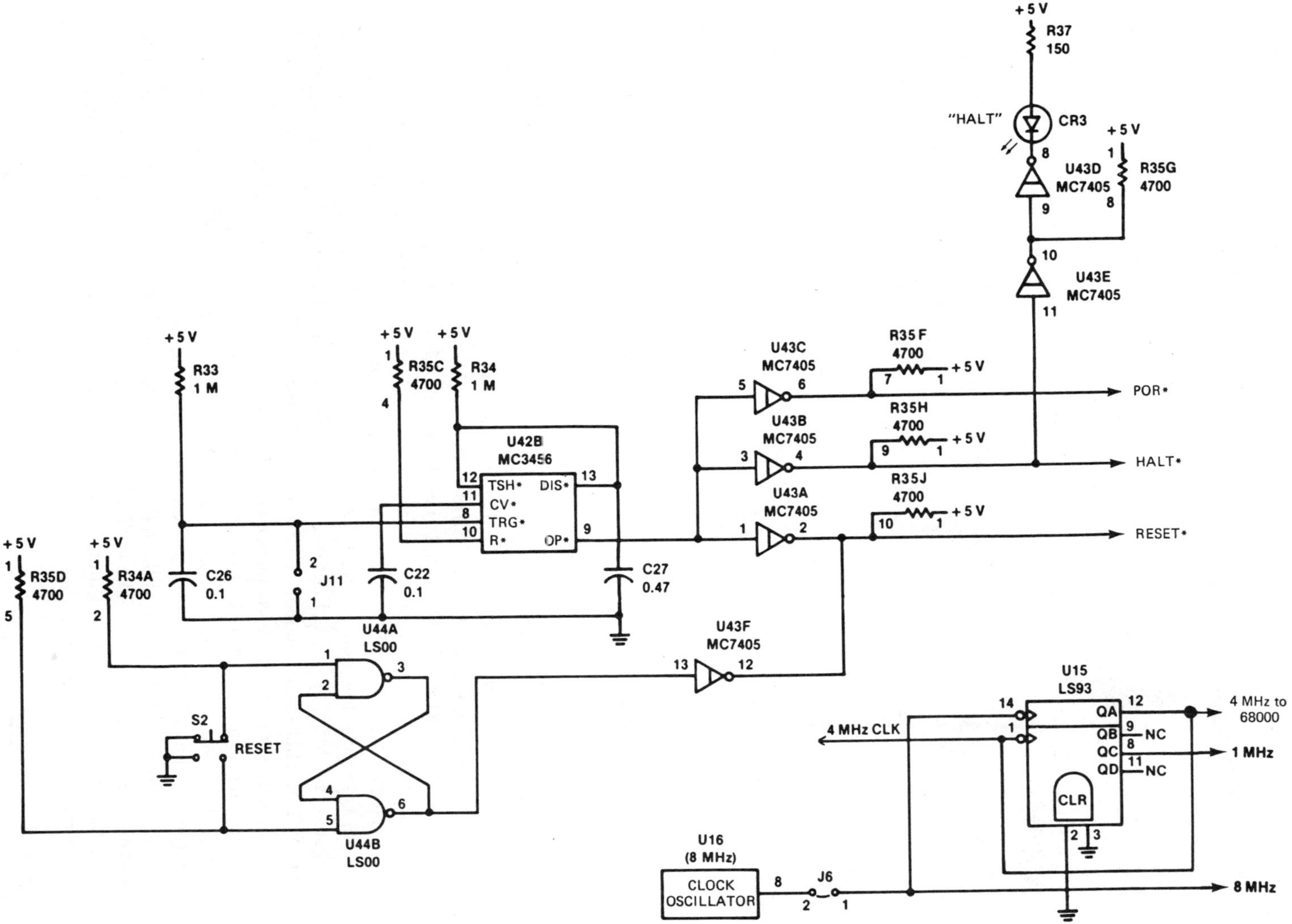

Figure 8.14 Reset circuit and clock generator schematic diagram. (Courtesy Motorola Inc.)

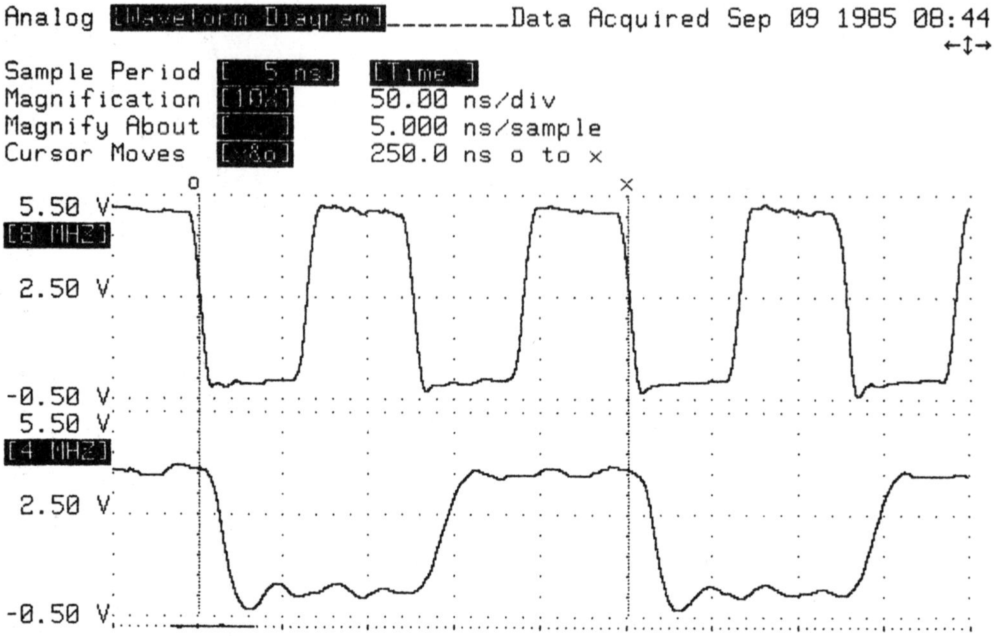

Figure 8.15 Timing diagram of the ECB clock oscillator at 8 MHz and the 4 MHz clock that drives the 68000.

This is how the address decoder and DTACK* work together when ROM is being accessed; you can trace the circuit and see that the RAM follows the same approach. You know from your studies of the 68000 timing diagrams in Chapter 7 that a valid address is put on the address bus during S1 and then AS* is asserted low during S2. In Figure 8.19, if the address is between $8000 and $BFFF, then ROM-RANGE* is true. As soon as AS* is asserted, then ROMEN is asserted to enable the ROMs during S2. Notice that ROMEN was holding the U22 flip-flops in a cleared state until it was asserted. On the next rising 8 MHz clock edge, Q1 in U22 is set; several pulses later, Q4 is set and the complement output Q4* goes low and asserts DTACK*. At the end of the bus cycle when AS* is negated, ROMEN goes back LOW, thereby clearing the U22 flip-flops and negating DTACK*. This timing sequence is shown in Figure 8.20.

Overall, the bus cycle sequence is to decode an address range, wait for the address strobe, and then allow a timer to start; in the ROM case, this timer is simply four flip-flops. As soon as the timer is done, then DTACK* is sent to the 68000. As the 68000 finishes the bus cycle, the timer is held reset until the next cycle.

If you do not present a valid address for ROM or RAM, then there is no way this circuit can return DTACK*. The 68000 is hung up unless you have some way to detect that the processor is caught waiting indefinitely. In such a case a watchdog timer and error-recovery code are required.

```
Analog Trace Specification ________________________________

[  Single   ] Trace Mode
[  Single   ] Display Mode

Post Processing              [Off]
Statistical Measurements     Off

Sample Period [  2 ms]  Acquisition Time: 2.000 s


[Start ] Trace 0000 [ns] After Trigger

   Trigger          [  VCC    ]
   Edge              [ Rising ]
   Trigger Level     [+] 00.50V

Waveform Display Mode:  [Straight Line]
```

(a)

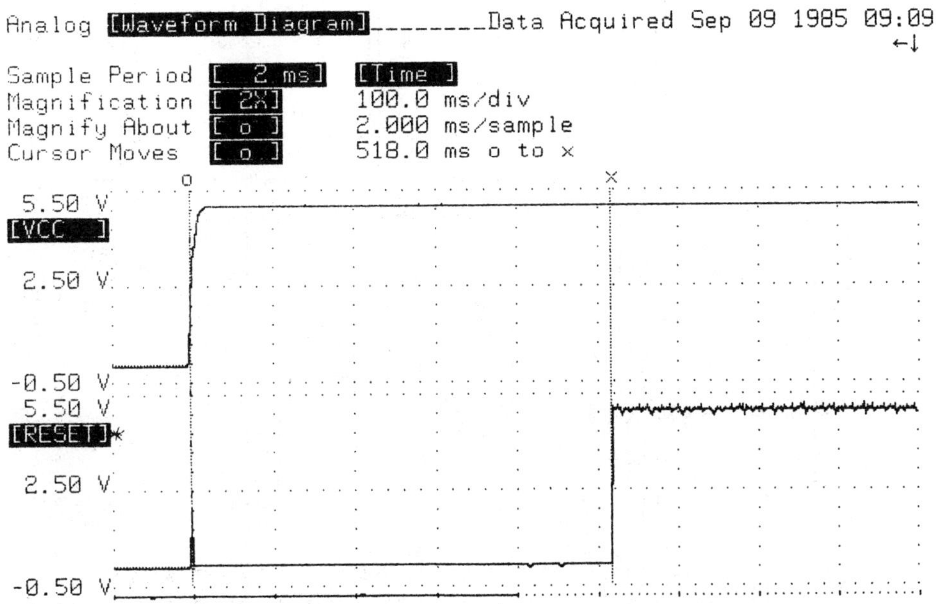

(b)

Figure 8.16 Test of the power-on reset circuit in the ECB. (a) Analog setup using the HP-1631D. (b) Trace of V_{cc} turn-on and RESET* negation about 500 ms later.

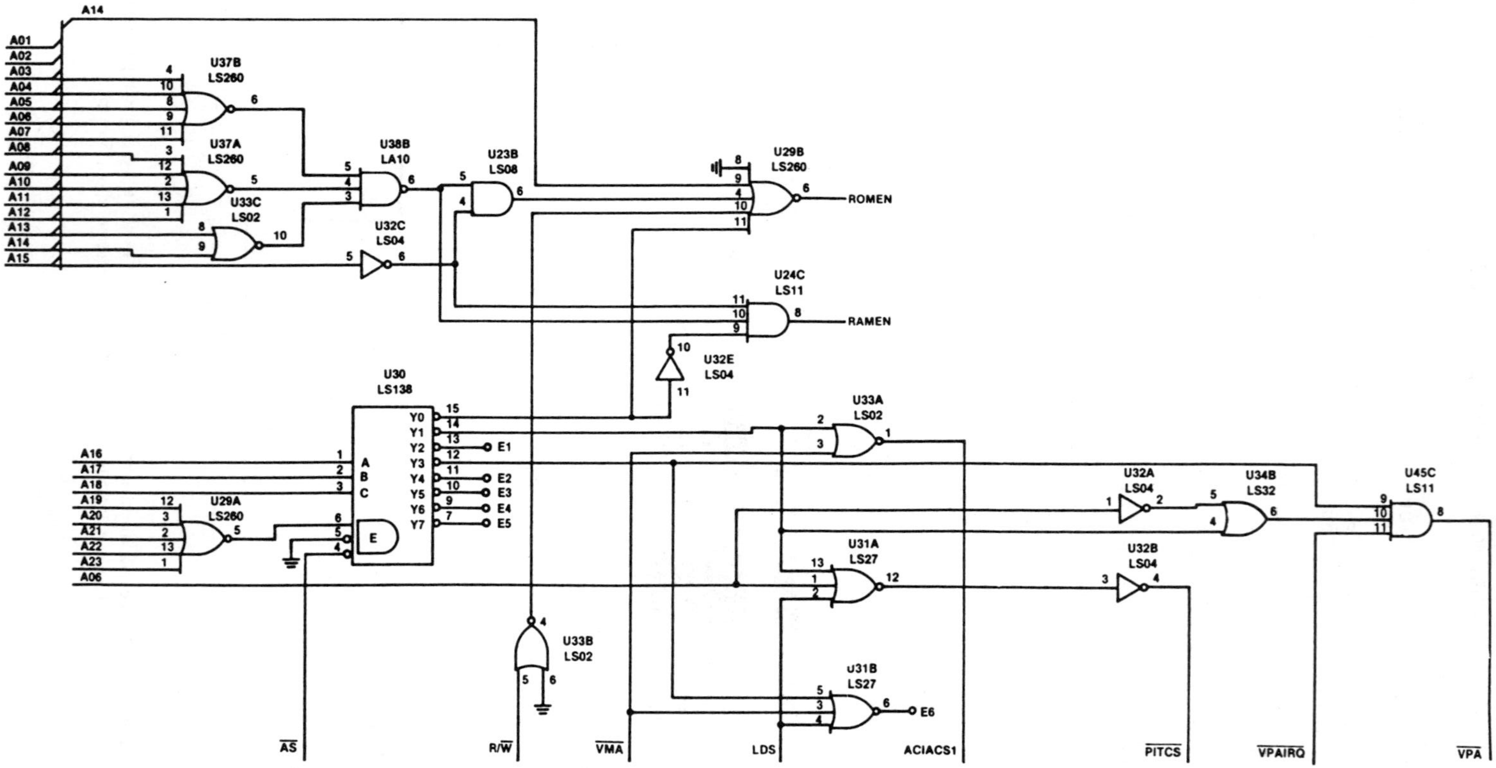

Figure 8.17 ECB decoder schematic. (Courtesy Motorola Inc.)

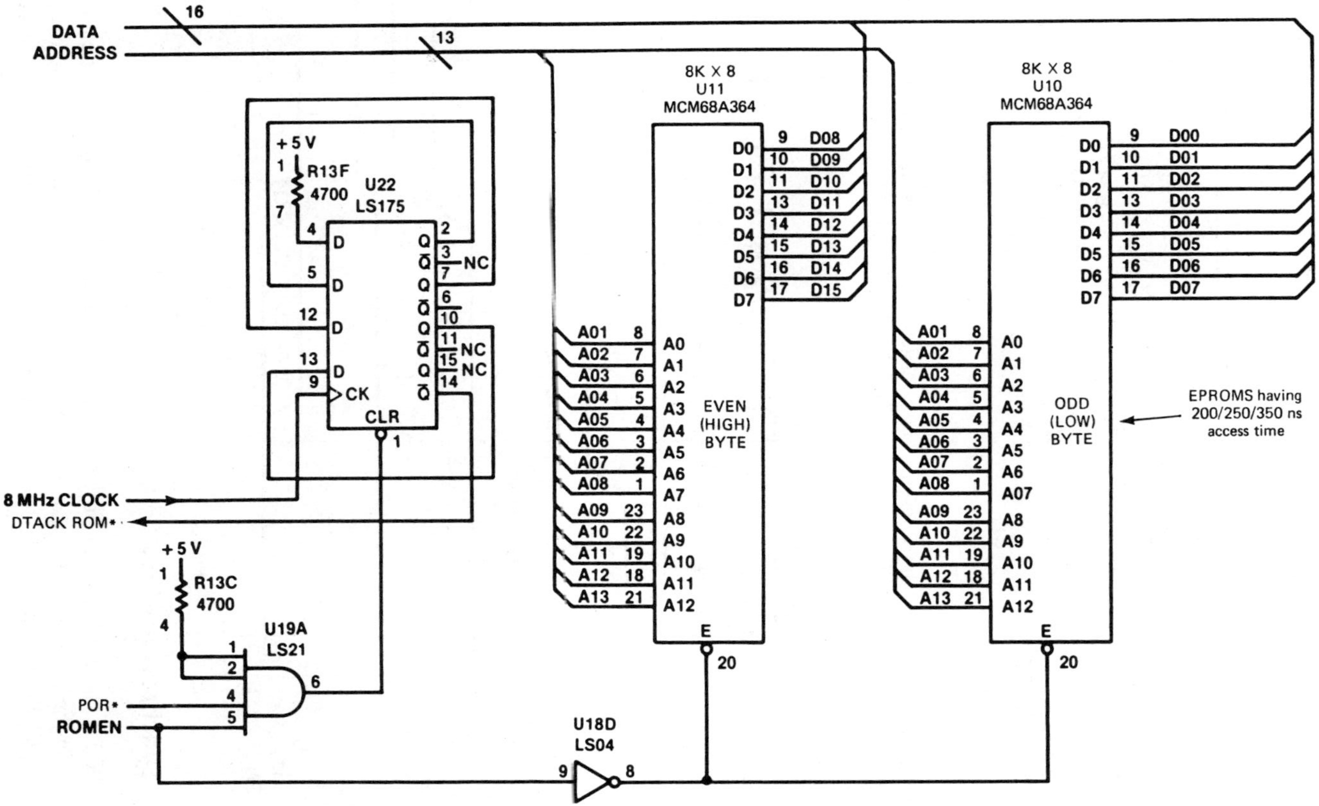

Figure 8.18 ROM DTACK* schematic. (Courtesy Motorola Inc.)

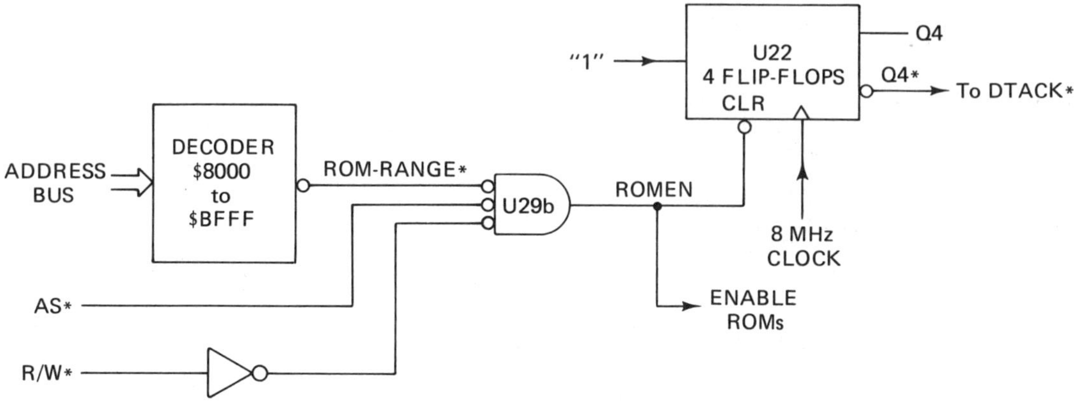

Figure 8.19 Sketch of the functions to generate DTACK* for reading the ECB ROMs.

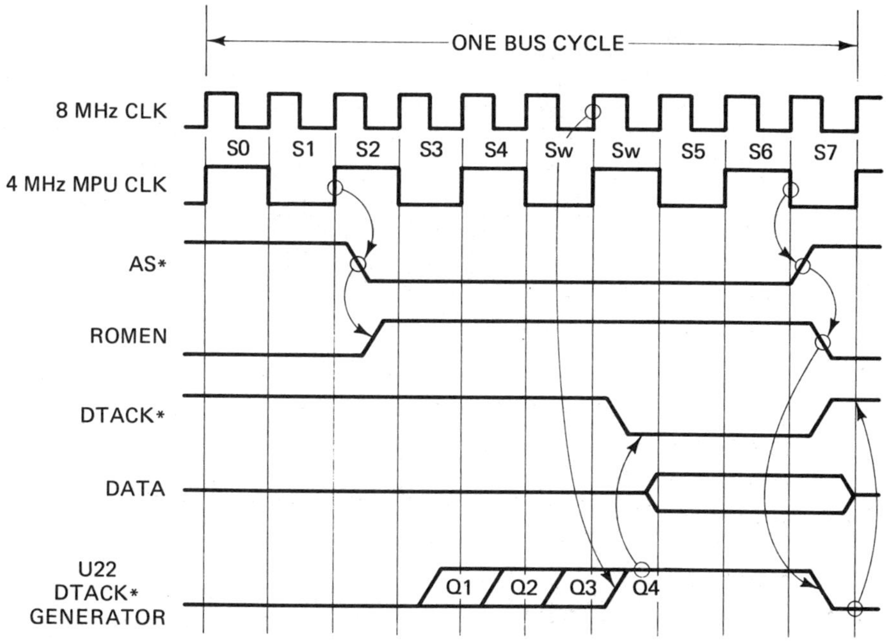

Figure 8.20 ROM and DTACK* timing.

8.2.3 Synchronous Interface

The 68000 is an asynchronous processor, and consequently the duration of each bus cycle depends on the peripheral devices being addressed. If certain memory requires two waits, for example, the DTACK* generator knows to hold for the extra time; if a very slow I/O device needs extra time to respond, then DTACK* can be held back even longer.

The processor can also function synchronously using the three bus-control lines shown in Figure 8.21. Using these controls, it can work with the 6800-family of peripher-

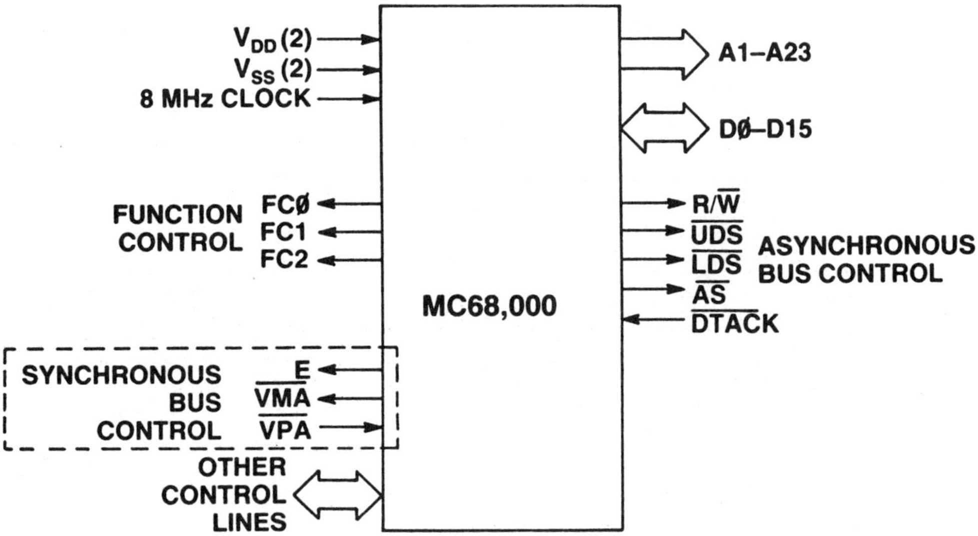

Figure 8.21 Synchronous bus control pins to run the 68000 with 6800-type peripherals. VPA* is Valid Peripheral Address, VMA* is Valid Memory Address, and E is the Enable output running at one-tenth of the 68000 clock. (Courtesy Motorola Inc.)

als. Data transfer does not use DTACK* at all; instead, the 68000 synchronizes using valid peripheral address (VPA*) generated by the decode hardware. Figure 8.22 shows the sequence flowchart for a typical read or write cycle. This sequence is expanded in Figure 8.23, showing the timing relationship between the various signals.

The synchronous bus cycle begins just the same as any other bus cycle as far as the 68000 can tell. The first the 68000 knows that a synchronous bus cycle is required is when VPA* from the peripheral goes low. (Note that DTACK* should not be asserted during a synchronous bus cycle.) The 68000 will then wait (if necessary) until E is low, and then assert VMA* to complete the chip-select for the peripheral. When E goes high, the peripheral puts its data on the bus; when E goes low, the 68000 reads the data on the falling edge of S6. After reading the data, the 68000 concludes the bus cycle by negating VMA* and the data and address strobes.

Figure 8.24 shows how the various controls are connected to the peripheral device to implement the above bus cycle. As the bus cycle begins, the peripheral address conditioned by AS* forms VPA* to initiate the synchronous transfer. Part of this address decode can be used as shown to derive a partial chip-select; note, however, that AS* is *not* used to form chip-select. When the 68000 asserts VMA*, the peripheral selection is completed. The 6800-type devices then read or write on the falling edge of E.

The reason that AS* is not used as part of the chip-select circuit is because of its timing in relation to E. Because 6800-type devices read or write on the falling edge of E, they must remain selected for their required hold time after E (about 10 ns). The timing diagram in Figure 8.25 (bubble 49) shows that AS* can be negated up to 70 ns before the falling edge of E. Consequently, the 6800-peripheral might be deselected before it could complete its read or write operation.

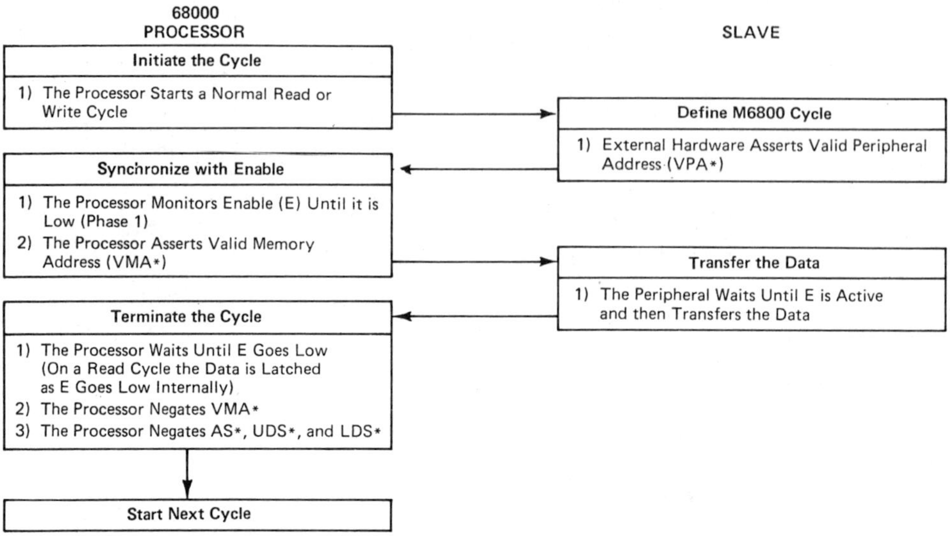

Figure 8.22 M6800 interfacing flowchart. (Courtesy Motorola Inc.)

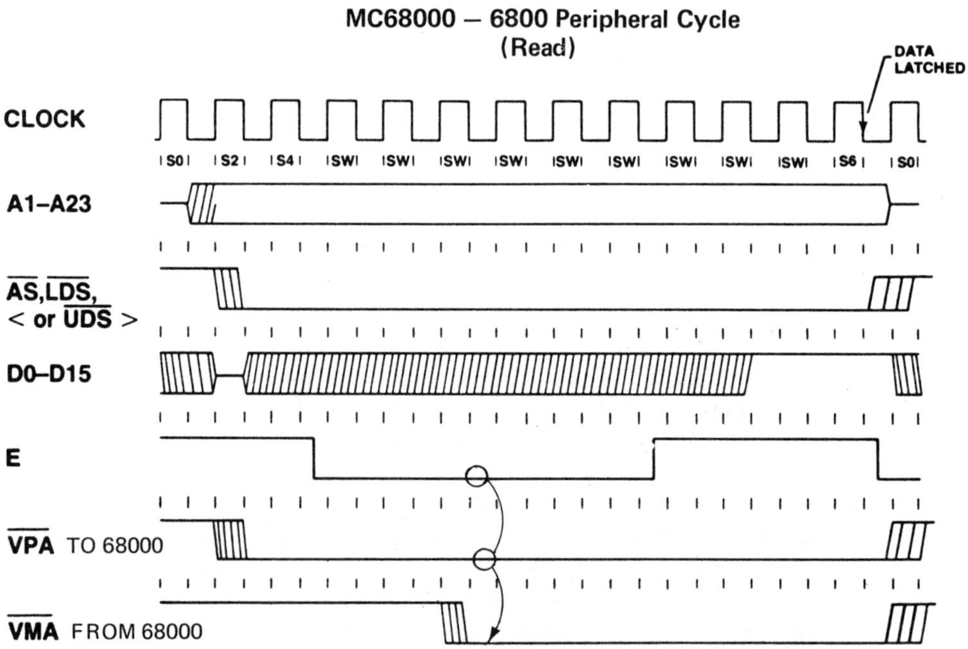

Figure 8.23 Timing diagram for a typical synchronous read of a 6800-type peripheral device. (Courtesy Motorola Inc.)

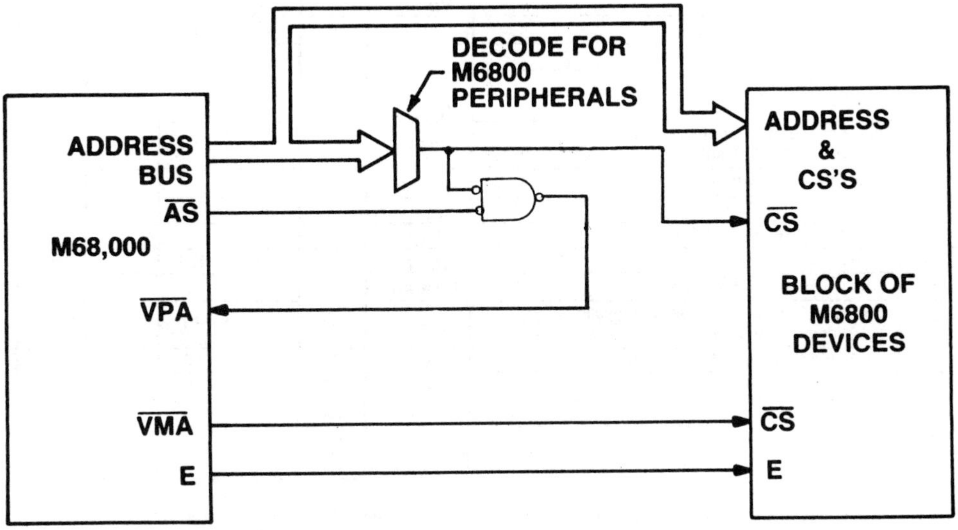

Figure 8.24 Connection of 6800 peripherals to the 68000. Note that AS* is not used to select the chips. (Courtesy Motorola Inc.)

You can easily examine the operation of the synchronous interface between the 68000 and the 6850 ACIAs in the ECB. Figure 8.26 shows the sequence measured using the HP-1631D Logic Analyzer; the TUTOR monitor code being executed at the moment when the data was taken was looping while waiting for a console key-press. However, to observe the sequence using an oscilloscope, the RAM-refresh bus-request circuit must be disabled. This is because the ECB refreshes RAM every 100 μs or so; this activity uses DMA and prevents synchronizing the oscilloscope. The timing obtained after disabling the DMA (by grounding pin 6 on U42) is shown in Figure 8.27; this pattern repeats over and over, so that an oscilloscope trace like Figure 8.28 can be obtained easily. While synchronized with VPA*, the oscilloscope can also be used to check the other control lines shown in Figure 8.27.

8.3 TESTING AND TROUBLESHOOTING TECHNIQUES

Testing and troubleshooting a digital logic circuit is usually fairly straightforward if there is no microprocessor involved. You can easily check voltages and signals with your oscilloscope and find opens or shorts. If you want, you can stop the system and manually clock it from state to state so you can see if a particular component is faulty.

When you add a microprocessor, however, you cannot stop the system and look at voltages; the processor clock must be kept on. If you want to hold the system in a given state, you must provide a hardware single-step circuit to control the microprocessor program execution. When the processor is left on, synchronizing the oscilloscope is difficult because repeating patterns are not found on any of the buses. In fact, the bus architecture

Num.	Characteristic	Symbol	8 MHz		10 MHz		12.5 MHz		Unit
			Min	Max	Min	Max	Min	Max	
12	Clock Low to $\overline{\text{AS}}$, $\overline{\text{DS}}$ High	t_{CLSH}	–	70	–	55	–	50	ns
18	Clock High to R/$\overline{\text{W}}$ High	t_{CHRH}	0	70	0	60	0	60	ns
20	Clock High to R/$\overline{\text{W}}$ Low (Write)	t_{CHRL}	–	70	–	60	–	60	ns
23	Clock Low to Data Out Valid (Write)	t_{CLDO}	–	70	–	55	–	55	ns
27	Data In to Clock Low (Setup Time on Read)	t_{CLDO}	15	–	10	–	10	–	ns
29	$\overline{\text{AS}}$, $\overline{\text{DS}}$ High to Data In Invalid (Hold Time on Read)	t_{SHDII}	0	–	0	–	0	–	ns
40	Clock Low to $\overline{\text{VMA}}$ Low	t_{CLVML}	–	70	–	70	–	70	ns
41	Clock Low to E Transition	t_{CLET}	–	70	–	55	–	45	ns
42	E Output Rise and Fall Time	$t_{Er,f}$	–	25	–	25	–	25	ns
43	$\overline{\text{VMA}}$ Low to E High	t_{VMLEH}	200	–	150	–	90	–	ns
44	$\overline{\text{AS}}$, $\overline{\text{DS}}$ High to $\overline{\text{VPA}}$ High	t_{SHVPH}	0	120	0	90	0	70	ns
45	E Low to Control, Address Bus Invalid (Address Hold Time)	t_{ELCAI}	30	–	10	–	10	–	ns
47	Asynchronous Input Setup Time	t_{ASI}	20	–	20	–	20	–	ns
49[1]	$\overline{\text{AS}}$, $\overline{\text{DS}}$ High to E Low	t_{SHEL}	–70	70	–55	55	–45	45	ns
50	E Width High	t_{EH}	450	–	350	–	280	–	ns
51	E Width Low	t_{EL}	700	–	550	–	440	–	ns
54	E Low to Data Out Invalid	t_{ELDOI}	30	–	20	–	15	–	ns

NOTE:

1. The falling edge of S6 triggers both the negation of the strobes ($\overline{\text{AS}}$ and x$\overline{\text{DS}}$) and the falling edge of E. Either of these events can occur first, depending upon the loading on each signal. Specification #49 indicates the absolute maximum skew that will occur between the rising edge of the strobes and the falling edge of the E clock.

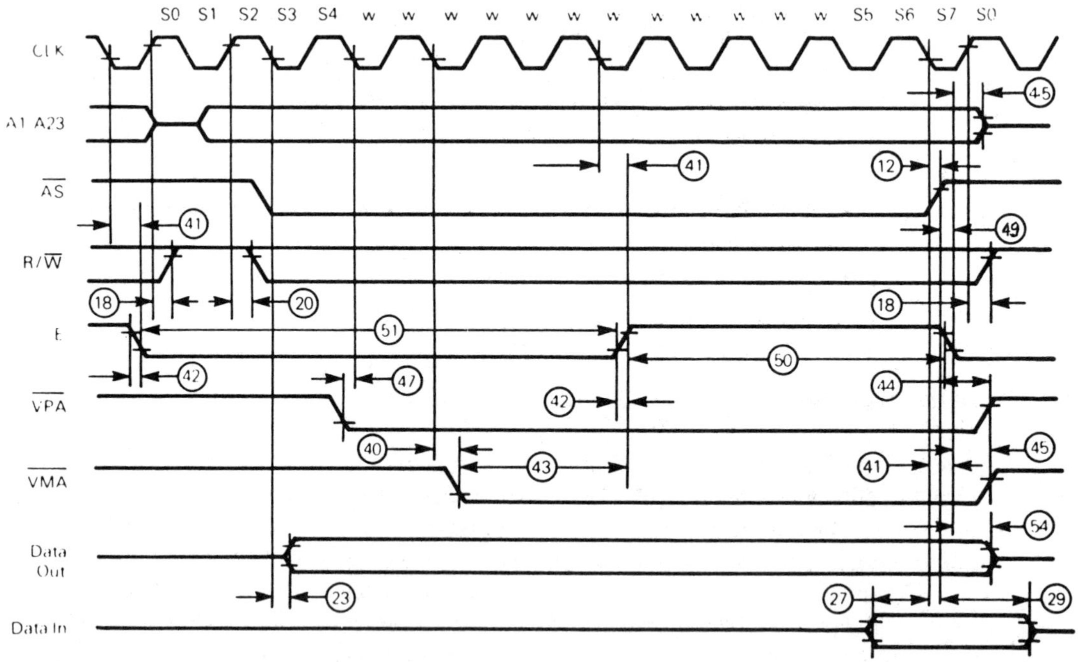

NOTE: This timing diagram is included for those who wish to design their own circuit to generate VMA. It shows the best case possibly attainable

1-80

Figure 8.25 MC68000 to M6800 peripheral specifications and best-case timing diagram. (Courtesy Motorola Inc.)

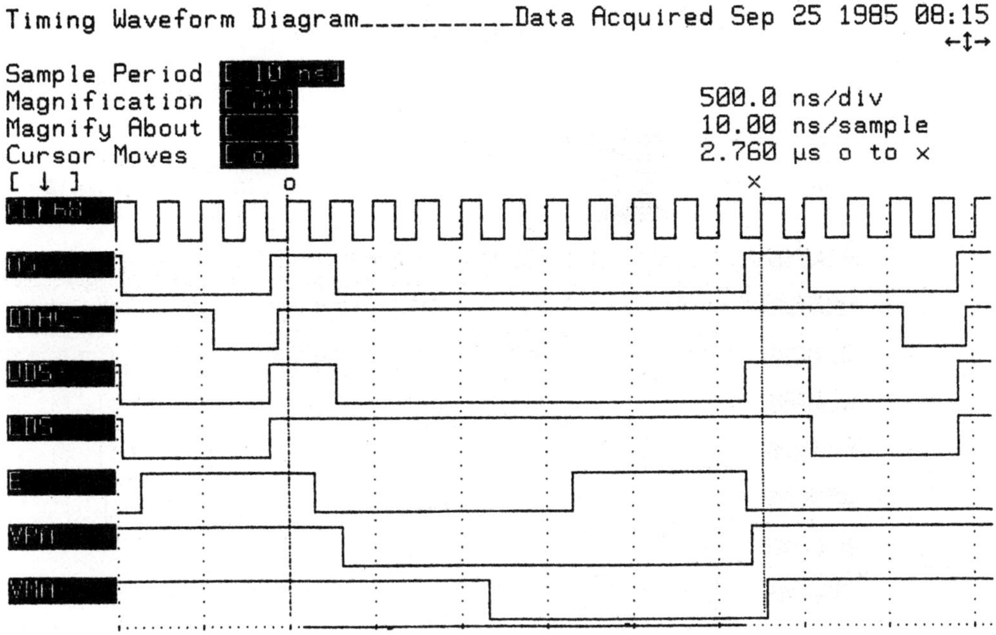

Figure 8.26 Typical synchronous read bus cycle on the ECB.

itself adds to the difficulty because many different devices are connected to the bus; any one bit shorted could cause the whole system to fail.

Testing and troubleshooting a microprocessor system can be quite difficult if a traditional approach is used with common lab test equipment. Problem-solving techniques are always helpful in determining symptoms and in localizing faulty circuits, but an overall strategy is necessary. This overall strategy depends on the system itself and whether it is already built or is a new design.

- Troubleshooting Case: If the system has already worked satisfactorily in the past, then the task at hand is to find and fix the cause of the failure.
- New-System Case: If the system has never run because it is a new design being developed, then the task is to turn on each section systematically so that the entire system will run.

8.3.1 Troubleshooting

Assuming that the microprocessor system once worked, there are a number of different strategies that can be employed to get the defective system back in operation. Depending on the situation, some of these strategies might be directly applicable while others might not be relevant at all. The task is to find and fix the failure.

ECB WITHOUT
RAM REFRESH (U42 pin 6 GND)

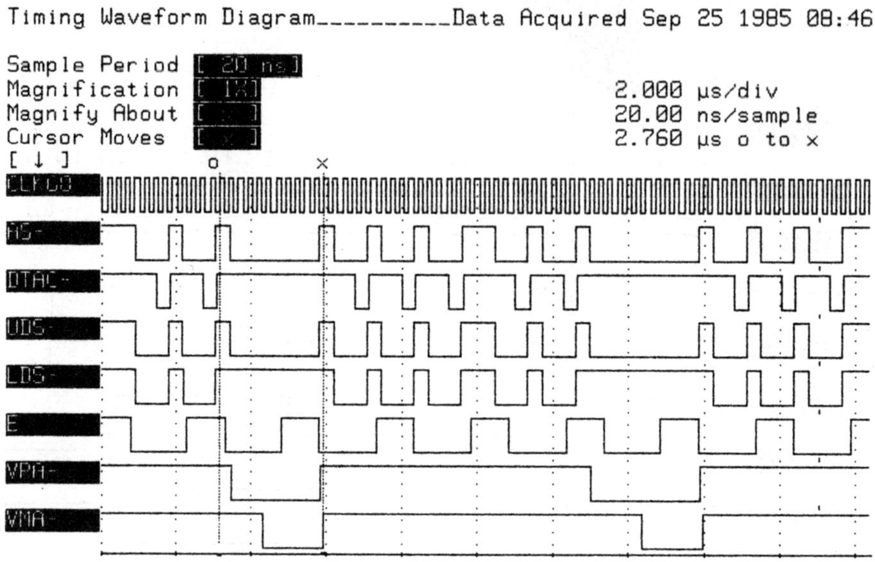

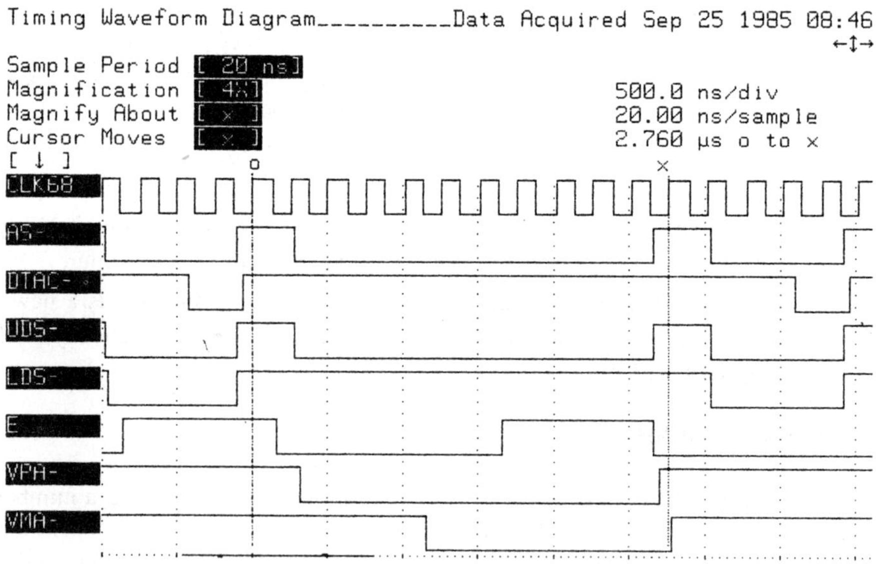

Figure 8.27 ECB synchronous read bus cycles with RAM-refresh disabled.

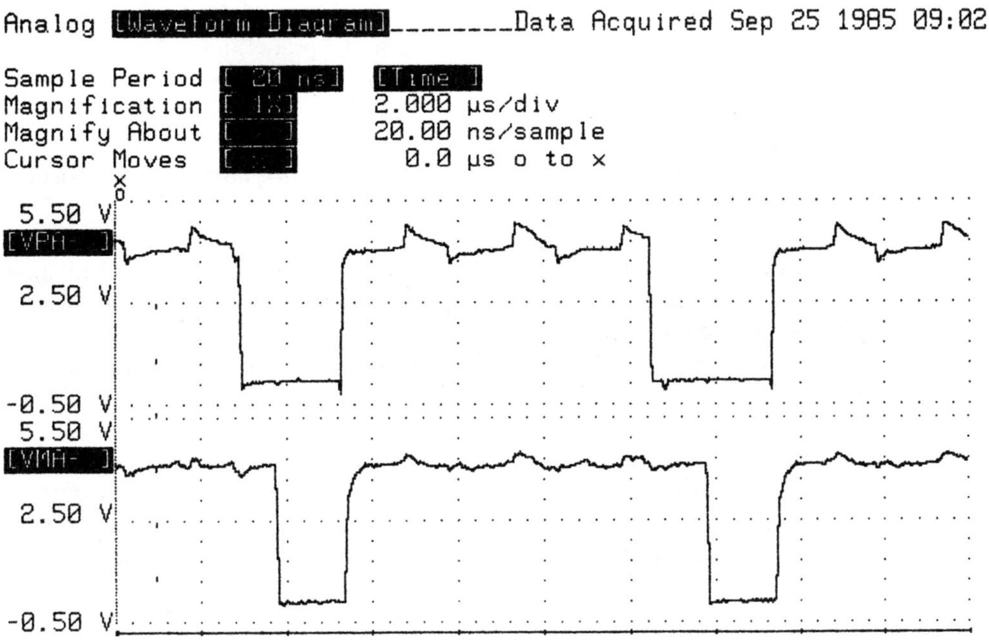

Figure 8.28 ECB oscilloscope data on VPA* and VMA* while RAM refresh is disabled. The oscilloscope can synchronize easily on VPA*.

Board swap. If the system has a number of circuit boards that can be easily removed and replaced, then one strategy to get the system in operation quickly is to swap boards. If replacing one board does not work, replace another (or all) until the system works again.

Known-good system. Another strategy to get a defective system running is to compare it with a known-good system. By comparing inputs and outputs of each of the modules in the system, one might be able to locate a defective board or component and fix it.

Symptom list. If the designer of the system anticipated certain problems, perhaps he prepared a list of symptoms and their causes. If so, then the troubleshooting strategy can be simply a matter of looking up the problem and then fixing its cause.

Troubleshooting tree. This is similar in concept to the symptom list, but has far more detail. Basically, it is a flowchart of various observations and measurements. Depending on how a particular circuit checks out, the tree then indicates to check other parts of the system. After a number of tests are done, some probable failure causes are indicated.

Diagnostic programs. If the system can run at all, then perhaps it can execute diagnostic programs to check various parts of the system. For example, a memory-test program would be useful in finding any defects in memory that might be causing the system to fail. If the system will not run a program, the processor can be forced to freerun.

Half-split the system. To find a system failure, split the system in half and check for proper signals at the midpoint; if the signals are as expected, then the problem is in the following circuits. Half-split again until the defective module or component can be identified.

In-circuit emulation. By removing the microprocessor and connecting an external ICE, it is possible to find a number of system faults. Even if the system will not run, an ICE can be used to check memory, I/O circuits, and buses for problems. The Fluke Troubleshooter or a Static Stimulus Tester (SST) as described by Coffron (see ''Further Reading'') can be used.

When troubleshooting a system that has worked before, it is generally desirable to get it executing software as soon as possible. Once programs can be executed, the various diagnostics can run detailed tests on all the major system components. Even if just one scope-loop program can run, that can be used to test many circuits using just an oscilloscope.

8.3.2 New Systems

Bringing up a new processor system is similar to troubleshooting a once-working system in one point: it is desirable to execute software as soon as possible. Other than that, the normal troubleshooting strategies really do not fit. The best way to bring up a new system is to do it by modules: design, build, and test one module after another until the entire system is complete. The test strategy in bringing up the new system is to allow the 68000 to freerun open-loop as modules are added to the system. In addition to ensuring that the 68000 kernel is always working, the freerunning processor provides most signals necessary to test the various modules being added. When enough modules have been added to run closed-loop (execute a program instead of freerun), there is an excellent probability that the 68000 will run immediately.

The steps involved in bringing up the new system are:

1. Build and test the power-supply module.
2. Build and test the system clock and its drivers for clock distribution throughout the system.
3. Build and test the processor reset and halt circuits. Include a ''Halt'' LED to monitor processor status.
4. Design and build a ''minimum system'' that has just enough circuitry to freerun the processor. For the 68000, this will include power, clock, data bus to EPROM sockets, reset circuit, and a DTACK* generator. When the processor freeruns, the address and control lines can be easily observed with an oscilloscope; in fact, an LED

as in Figure 8.1 can be connected to one of the high-address lines to flash on and off indicating a proper freerun.

5. While the system is still connected to freerun, add address bus circuits to complete all the RAM and EPROM sockets. Check with an oscilloscope: the pulse train at each address pin should appear twice (or half) as fast as its neighbor.
6. Develop the DTACK* generator circuit more completely. At the very start, a simple grounded DTACK* input to the 68000 is sufficient; now build and test a DTACK* generator that will allow for several extra wait cycles. While freerunning, the oscilloscope can easily verify its operation.
7. Up to this point in bringing up the processor, the system has been operating open-loop; that is, there is no feedback path for any of the processor outputs to get back to its inputs and change its behavior. While the processor executes in a freerun mode, there is no RAM or EPROM program code being read. However, after a thorough check of system operation, then it is time to close the loop and allow the processor to read and execute code.

Getting the 68000 to execute a program is not quite as simple as wiring the EPROM sockets and letting the 68000 read a program. When the 68000 is reset (either on power-up or with a switch), it will read memory 0 through 3 for its supervisory stack pointer (SSP) and 4 through 7 for its program counter (PC). This means that the EPROM sockets *must* be decoded for selection when the 68000 reads addresses 0 through 7; it also means that the first eight bytes of the EPROMs are not program bytes, but vectors. Suppose you make EPROMs to do a scope-loop program that is nothing more than JMP 8. The code will be:

Address	*Data in EPROMs*	
0000	00 00	
0002	00 00	SSP to 0
0004	00 00	
0006	00 08	PC vectors to address 8
0008	4E F8	Op-code and
000A	00 08	Operand for JMP 8.

This scope-loop program can be run and checked with an oscilloscope. The data bus lines are probably fault-free if the processor is executing the program, and activity on them can be checked at other sockets to verify that there are no wiring errors.

8. Modify the reset and EPROM-control circuits so that the EPROMs do not have to be decoded at address 0 *except* during reset. Normally, the low memory addresses should be RAM so that exception vectors can be dynamically altered; EPROMs should be elsewhere in memory, such as $8000 in the case of the ECB.
9. After a scope-loop program runs successfully at an address above $8000, add system RAM. Check by writing another simple loop program that will do a read-RAM and a write-RAM over and over. Verify all the timing with an oscilloscope or logic analyzer.

10. If at least 4K of RAM has been decoded starting at 8, and the EPROMs are decoded for 0 to 7 and $8000 to $BFFF, then the TUTOR EPROMs from the ECB can be used in the system. When the system is started, assuming that it does not halt, an oscilloscope can be used to see the activity on the various processor lines while the monitor waits for a key-press.
11. Add a 6850 ACIA decoded at $010040 to serve as a console port and test it with the TUTOR EPROM set. Run various memory testing commands (part of TUTOR code) and scope-loops to check operation of the new system.

8.4 DESIGNING FOR TESTABILITY

When you ran tests on the ECB, you probably had a number of difficulties connecting probes to the circuits being tested. Even finding the circuit itself could have been a problem. Although the ECB was originally designed for evaluation and exploration, it does not have any convenience features to make the tests easy. Consider, for example, where the probe power and ground can be connected. The microclips for the probe are too small to connect to the +5 power for the board, so they have to be connected to an IC; ground and +5 stakes at the edge of the board would be much more convenient and easier to clip onto.

Anytime you have the chance to test a board such as the ECB, jot down your thoughts on what would make the test job easier. As you consider the various modules that go into a new system, ponder how each module can be independently tested as well as how it can be tested when interconnected with other modules. Which circuit functions can be tested by the microprocessor itself? Which circuits are so critical that the kernel will not run without them?

Consider the following list of features for a new design. The idea is to make the design easy to test during the development process and easy to troubleshoot later after the system is complete.

1. Display Lights. Include an LED to indicate the status of the processor. The ''halt'' LED in the ECB is extremely useful, especially when developing new modules. Another LED (a circuit like Figure 8.1) connected to an address pin can indicate that the processor is running; during freerun, an LED connected to A20 flashes on and off every few seconds.
2. Built-In Test Circuits. Reset and abort are two useful circuits in the ECB for test and troubleshooting. The reset switch could have been deleted because the processor is automatically reset when power goes on; however, it was included to allow easy board testing. The abort switch is not absolutely necessary either, but it is extremely useful to recover from programming errors. A single-step circuit would have been a valuable module in the ECB, but was not included.
3. Test Points. Provide stakes for +5 and ground to connect a logic probe. Include stakes for the clock, AS*, DTACK* and any other signals that are generally useful in testing.

4. Test Jumpers. Provide a means of breaking vital circuits by removing jumpers. For example, if you wanted to test the watchdog timer to see how long DTACK* can be missing before the timer signals an error, how can you break the signal path from the DTACK* generator? A test jumper to disable the RAM DMA would be more convenient than using a clip lead to the refresh timer.
5. Test Sockets. If space or cost is at a premium, a test socket should be provided for connection to the circuit board. For example, rather than building in a single-step circuit, put it on an external board and connect it with plug and cable to the test socket. If the tester breaks signal lines, a jumper header can be left plugged into the test socket during normal operation.
6. Board Layout. When laying out the board, be sure to allow room around the 68000 to plug in an ICE cable easily. Likewise, provide clear space at the ends of the 68000 so that the IC can be pried up from its socket without force.
7. Test EPROMs. Sockets should be provided to plug in EPROMs with simple test programs. As with the 68000, allow room around the sockets to facilitate removal of the EPROMs.

8.5 SUMMARY

Knowing the basic facts on the 68000 is not sufficient to design, builid, and test a new CPU board. You also need to be familiar with common test equipment as well as some of the more sophisticated digital test equipment such as in-circuit emulators and logic analyzers. To become familiar with this equipment and also to learn how the 68000 works in an actual system, testing the 68000 ECB is well worth your time and effort.

The simplest test equipment can usually be used to advantage in microprocessor circuits. An LED, a VOM, a logic probe, and a dual-trace oscilloscope can be used to bring up a working 68000 computer system. By freerunning the processor, and also by using scope-loops, the oscilloscope can be used with ease to test and troubleshoot a system; it is easy to hook up quickly to the circuit being tested, but has the disadvantage of displaying only two traces at a time.

The in-circuit emulator (ICE) and logic analyzer are both extremely useful in developing a new system. When using the ICE, for example, it is not even necessary to have a functioning kernel to test the system. The logic analyzer can give timing traces for many signals at once, and does not need to be synchronized like the oscilloscope to get a stable repeating pattern.

When testing the ECB, the easiest modules to check are the clock and reset circuits. DTACK* generation and address decoding are important sections of the ECB to test and understand because similar circuits are required in any new 68000 designs. It is also necessary to understand the synchronous interface so a suitable I/O circuit can be designed.

Testing and troubleshooting techniques depend on whether the system is a new design being brought up the first time, or whether the system worked at one time and has failed for some reason. If the system once worked, then a troubleshooting strategy to find a defective board or component is appropriate: you know that something failed and you need to find it. Bringing up a new system, on the other hand, is a completely different situation: you are not even sure the system can work even if all the parts are good.

The strategy for bringing up the new system is to design, build, and test by modules. The key to testing the system is being able to freerun the processor. While the processor freeruns, stable oscilloscope patterns can be easily checked as more modules are interconnected in the system. Even after the system is built, the 68000 can be freerun as a "test program" to find where a failure is located.

All new designs should provide for testing speed and convenience. It takes very little effort or space to include a simple LED to indicate when the processor halts. Likewise, it is easy to include test points and places to hook logic probe power leads. After the board is built, including these features is difficult, so planning for testing needs to be done early in the design cycle.

Usually, if test points are not included on a board, their absence is only a minor inconvenience: testing is slowed down, but not stopped. If testing requires disabling a certain circuit, however, this might involve cutting a trace on a PC board. It is far more desirable to anticipate the need and provide a jumper block in the circuit: remove the jumper for testing, and replace it for normal operation.

EXERCISES

1. What is a scope-loop? Why would you want to use one?
2. Suppose the 68000 is freerunning. Sketch the pattern for the clock and AS* that might be observed with a dual-trace scope.
3. When using the Fluke 9010A, what power-on sequence is required?
4. Can the Fluke 9010A test RAM? If so, what method is used?
5. Examine Figure 8.6 closely. In the system being measured, V_{cc} is obtained from an 8 V, 25 A linear supply.
   a. Why does the V_{cc} trace go up in steps?
   b. When the system's 110VAC supply is removed, V_{cc} begins to drop exponentially. Why is there a sudden drop in V_{cc} around the 2.5 to 3 V level?
6. The code sequence in Figure 8.8 is only partially disassembled. Why?
7. Disassemble the code segment at $1200. Is it a scope-loop?

```
$1200 31  FC
      00  0A
      11  00
      4E  F8
      12  00
```

8. The 68000 data book specifies an external-reset minimum time. What is it?
9. Do both RESET* and HALT* have to be asserted for a reset? If so, how do you explain the ECB reset circuit given in Figure 8.14?

10. What happens during the initial bus cycles following an external reset if the 68000 fetches PC=0009 at address 4 through 7?
11. What is the period of the upper trace in Figure 8.15? What is its risetime? What is the risetime of the 4MHz trace? Does the 4MHz clock meet the 68000 clock specification?
12. Sketch a DTACK* generator to provide from 0 to 4 wait cycles for the circuit shown in Figure 8.18. Illustrate its timing diagram for a selection of one wait and another timing diagram for three waits.
13. In Section 8.2.3 and in Figure 8.24, AS* is not part of the chip-select circuit. However, a close examination of Figure 8.17 shows that AS* is part of the ACIACS1 signal to the 6850. (On the full schematic, UDS* goes to the 6850 CS2* input as well.)
    a. Is the ECB design on solid ground?
    b. The 6850 requires that CS* be held at least 10 ns after E is low. Is this possible? How does this compare with Figure 8.26?
14. Make a list of test points and test jumpers you would find useful in testing the ECB. Indicate where in the ECB circuit they would be connected.

FURTHER READING

COFFRON, JAMES W. *Practical Troubleshooting Techniques for Microprocessor Systems*. Englewood Cliffs, NJ: Prentice-Hall, 1981.

COFFRON, JAMES W. *Understanding and Troubleshooting the Microprocessor*. Englewood Cliffs, NJ: Prentice-Hall, 1980.

COFFRON, JAMES W. *Using and Troubleshooting the MC68000*. Reston, VA: Reston Publishing Company, 1983.

LENK, JOHN D. *Handbook of Advanced Troubleshooting*. Englewood Cliffs, NJ: Prentice-Hall, 1983.

LENK, JOHN D. *Handbook of Practical Microcomputer Troubleshooting*. Reston, VA: Reston Publishing Company, 1979.

"MC68000 EDUCATIONAL COMPUTER BOARD USER'S MANUAL," MEX68KECB/D2. 2nd Edition. Tempe, AZ: Motorola Literature Distribution Center, 1982.

WILCOX, ALAN D. "Bringing Up the 68000—A First Step." *Doctor Dobb's Journal* 11(1): 60–74. Jan. 1986.

WRAY, BILL, and BILL CRAWFORD. *Microcomputer Systems Design and Debugging*. New York: Marcel Dekker, Inc., 1984.

ZUMCHAK, EUGENE M. *Microcomputer Design and Troubleshooting*. Indianapolis, IN: Howard W. Sams & Co., 1982.

NINE

Bringing Up the Microprocessor

Testing the Educational Computer Board gave you a chance to see how a 68000 runs in a working circuit. With just that brief testing and the hardware overview in Chapter 7, there is no reason why you cannot start building up your own processor board immediately. The sooner you get started, the faster you will learn how design really happens!

This chapter shows you how to create a minimum system and also illustrates some of the design considerations that need attention. This minimum system is the foundation for the total 68000 project and establishes that a modular approach can be applied successfully. Once a minimum system is running, one module after another can be added in building-block fashion until the entire circuit operates and meets project specifications.

There are two ways to bring up a new 68000 microcomputer system: the hard way and the easy way. The hard way is the traditional approach of designing the hardware and then using a development system along with test software and some in-circuit emulation. Given enough hours of testing and correcting problems, the 68000 system has a good chance of running successfully. In contrast, the easy way is to design, build, and test the hardware module by module using the 68000 as a freerunning processor.

The impact of the freerunning technique on hardware development is quite startling. The 68000 kernel shown in Figure 9.1 can be made to run so easily that a logic probe can test it. There is no need for sophisticated digital development tools such as a logic analyzer or a development system with an in-circuit emulator. If troubleshooting is necessary, only a common dual-trace oscilloscope is needed.

Freerunning the 68000 means that the processor is allowed to execute a do-nothing instruction continually. This is accomplished by breaking the normally closed loop between the 68000 and its memory as shown in Figure 9.2. Instead of carrying program instructions from memory, a one-word instruction (call it a "NIL" instruction[1]) can be

[1]The mnemonic NIL is not part of the 68000 instruction set *per se*; the author coined it as a simple expression of the instruction used for freerunning.

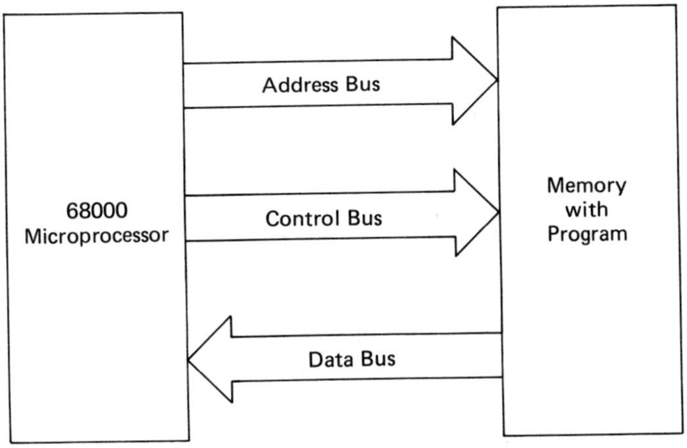

Figure 9.1 The 68000 kernel is the essential minimum hardware needed to allow program execution.

jammed onto the data bus. Thus, when the 68000 reads the data bus for an instruction, it fetches the NIL word, executes it, increments the address, and reads the next NIL. This cycling repeats over the entire 16 Mb address range; when the processor reaches the end of the 16 Mb, it simply starts over again.

The strategy for bringing up the 68000 is this: design, build, and test the 68000 kernel shown in Figure 9.2. Next, design and build one additional module, connect it to the kernel, and test it while the processor is freerunning. Add yet another module and test it while freerunning. The 68000 can be freerun all the way through the entire construction of a complete CPU board. In fact, if a finished processor board fails, it can usually be freerun to help speed troubleshooting. The only part of the system that cannot be easily tested while freerunning is the data bus itself; this is because the NIL instruction is always being forced on the bus.

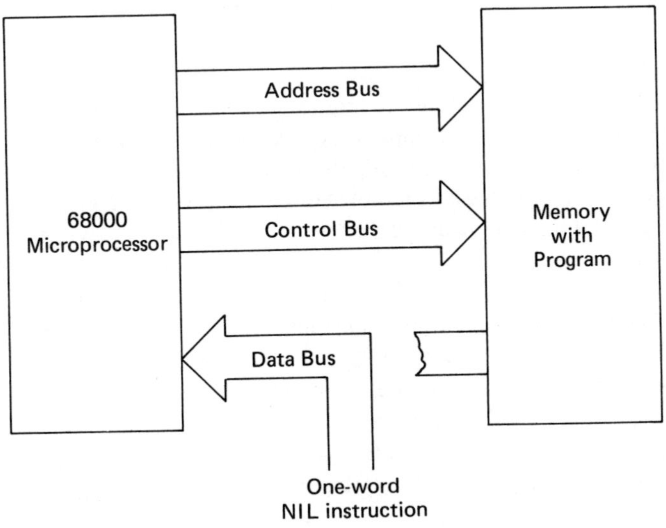

Figure 9.2 To freerun the 68000, the normal feedback path from memory is disconnected and a NIL (do-nothing) instruction is substituted.

9.1 MINIMUM SYSTEM DESIGN

When you begin the design, start with the system block diagram you made in Chapter 6. Using the block diagram in Figure 6.2 as a guide, make a new diagram like Figure 9.3 with some of the first modules highlighted for easy recognition. Make a photocopy of this block diagram and tape it in your lab book as you begin your design work. The idea is to mark the modules you intend to design, build, and test for this minimum system. By marking them, you not only know which modules are necessary, but you also can see how they relate to the total system as you understand it.

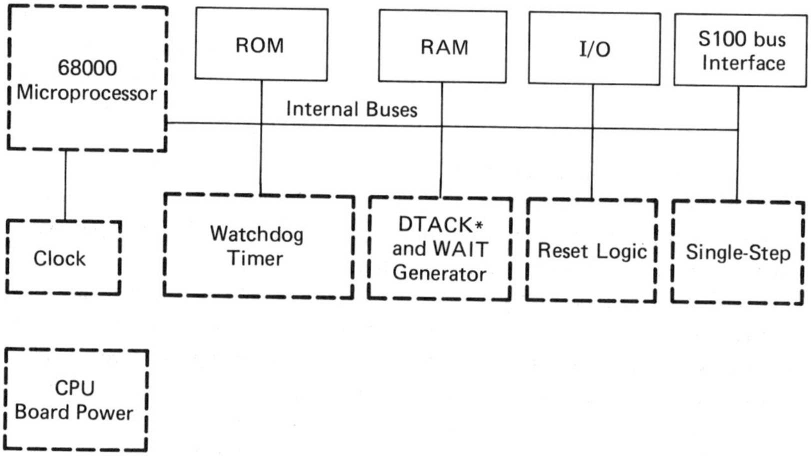

Figure 9.3 The modules on the CPU board as outlined in Chapter 6. The dashed minimum-system functions are designed, built, and tested first.

9.1.1 Power Supply

At this early stage in the design of the 68000 CPU board, it is impossible to make more than just a rough guess of what the actual power supply requirements will be. If you plan on using LS-TTL support logic, you might assume a maximum of about 50 packages at 10 mA each: total about 0.5 A at 5 V. The 68000 maximum dissipation is 1.75 watts maximum, or 350 mA at 5 V. Watch the fine print and footnotes though: the 68000 data book indicates that instantaneous current might peak at 1.5 A. Also, note that the power the 68000 can dissipate becomes lower as the ambient temperature increases.

The footnote on the peak 68000 current should be taken seriously for a sound design. If your supply voltage drops briefly on a surge of current, then you should rethink your design. A simple 7805 1.5 A regulator can be built, but what about voltage drops along the +5V circuit to the 68000? Number 30 wire-wrap connections should not be used; rather, a soldered #24 wire (or two) should connect from each +5V input on the 68000 to the 7805 output. The 68000 ground pins should also use # 24 wire (or heavier) and connect to the system ground bus. Bypass with 0.01 μF capacitors at each of the 68000 power pins.

Given the uncertain power loading of support logic and the possible peak 68000 current requirements, a prototype using two power supplies is appropriate. Two simple +5V regulators with heat sinks can be built easily on an S-100 prototype card. The circuits in Figure 9.4 divide the load between the 68000 and the various support circuits.

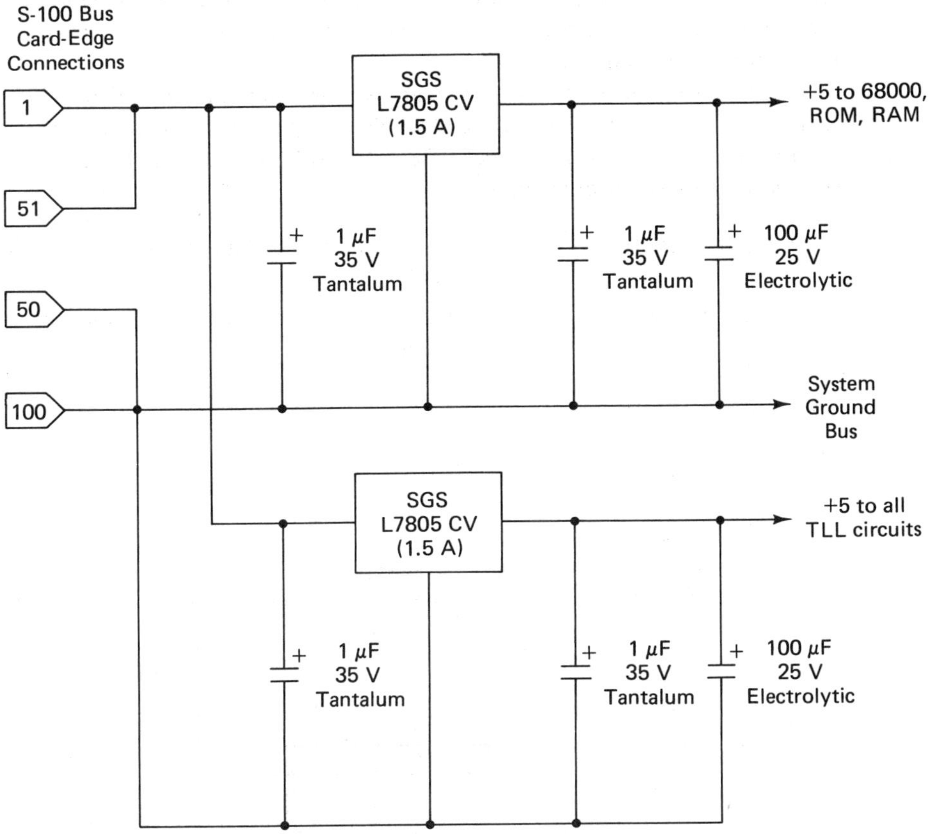

Figure 9.4 The CPU board +5 V supplies. Both are identical except that one powers the 68000 and its EPROM and RAM sockets; the other supply powers all the TTL support logic.

9.1.2 Clock and Driver

Although a clock oscillator can be designed and built using a crystal, some resistors, capacitors, and a 7400 or 7404, it is hardly worth the effort. For prototype work, being able to change the clock frequency easily without redesigning the circuit is a distinct advantage. Consequently, designing with a plug-in DIP oscillator is most appropriate.

Because the 68000 system will use both the clock output and its complement, a minimum-skew driver should be considered. Recall from Chapter 3 that the 74265 quad complementary-output element was used to minimize clock skew; this device and the DIP

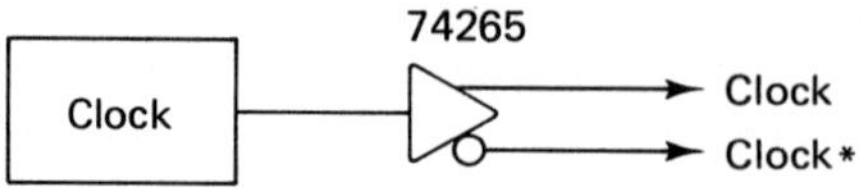

Figure 9.5 Block diagram of the clock module.

oscillator are shown in the Figure 9.5 block diagram. The complement clock could be derived from a 74LS04, but that would introduce a skew between the two clocks of some 10 to 15 ns depending on loading.

A complete clock module schematic is shown in Figure 9.6. The 74265 sections are connected in parallel to increase the clock drive capability. Although there are fewer than ten TTL loads on the system clock, the IEEE Std-696 (Section 3.4.2) requires that bus drivers meet these specifications:

- Low State (V_{OL}): Output voltage less than or equal to +0.5 V at 24 mA sink current.
- High State (V_{OH}): Output voltage greater than or equal to +2.4 V at 2 mA.

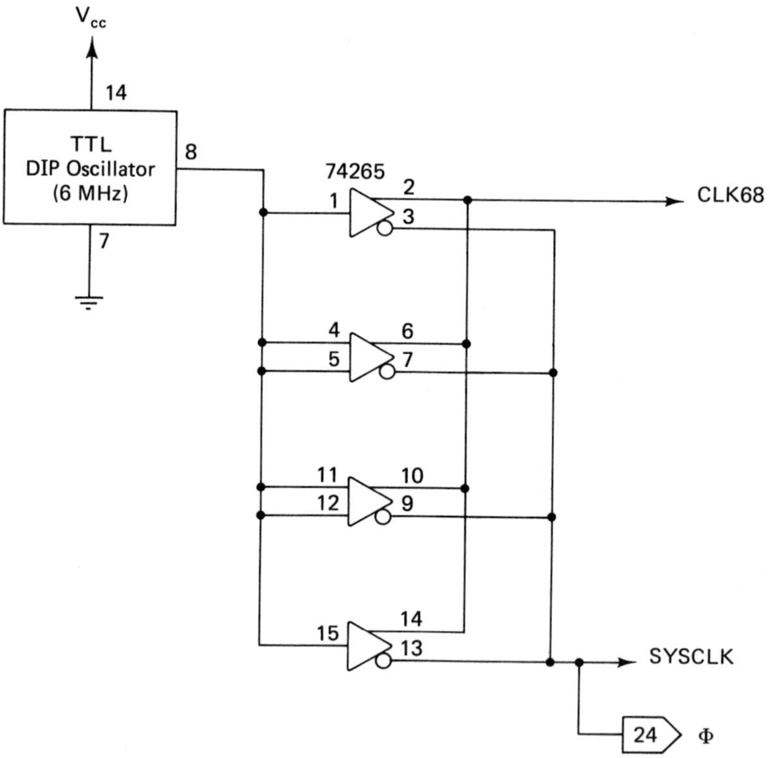

Figure 9.6 Circuit diagram of the clock module. CLK68 and SYSCLK each sink 64 mA (4 × 16 mA) and source 3.2 mA (4 × 0.8 mA).

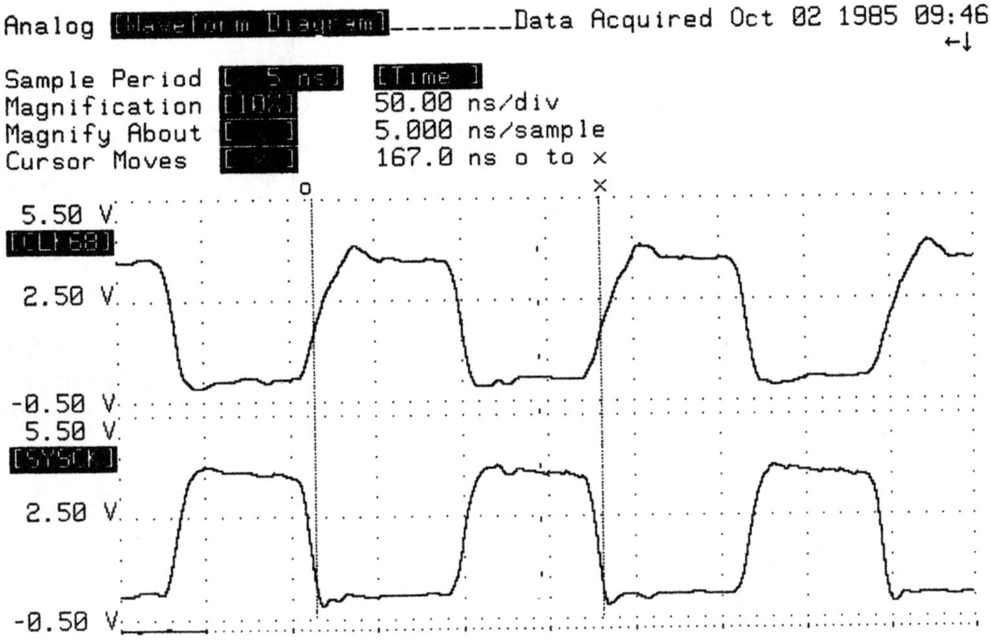

Figure 9.7 68000 clock (CLK68) and the system clock (SYSCLK) running at 6 MHz in the complete S-100 system.

The results of this design are shown in Figure 9.7. It shows the 68000 clock (CLK68) and the system clock (SYSCLK) running in a complete system. The rise and fall times for the system clock at pin 24 on the S-100 bus must be between 5 ns minimum and 50 ns maximum; SYSCLK meets this specification easily. Contrast this with the 68000 clock requirements: the clock risetimes and falltimes must be less than 10 ns maximum. A 10 percent to 90 percent definition of risetime measures about 20 ns. However, the Motorola specification defines the clock risetimes and falltimes between 0.8 and 2.0 V, and the waveform meets this requirement.

9.1.3 Reset Circuit

The reset circuit for the 68000 is fairly straightforward and can be implemented along the lines of the ECB circuit. As drawn in the Figure 9.8 block diagram, the two basic requirements for the module are to:

- reset when power comes on,
- reset when a system external control is asserted.

The ECB power-on circuit provides about 500 ms reset delay as you found when you tested it earlier. The 68000 specifications call for a power-on reset pulse at least 100

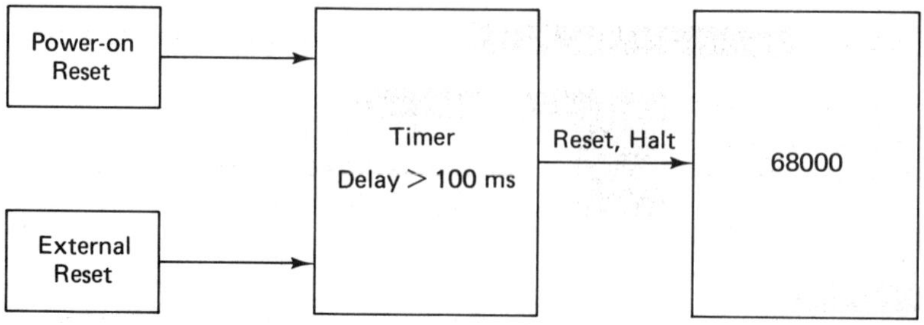

Figure 9.8 Block diagram of the reset module.

ms in duration, and the ECB design meets that easily. The circuit shown in Figure 9.9 is based on the ECB design given in Figure 8.14. Figure 9.10 shows the performance of this circuit as the system reaches normal operating voltage. The timer with the parts given in the schematic provides about 175 ms RESET* to the 68000.

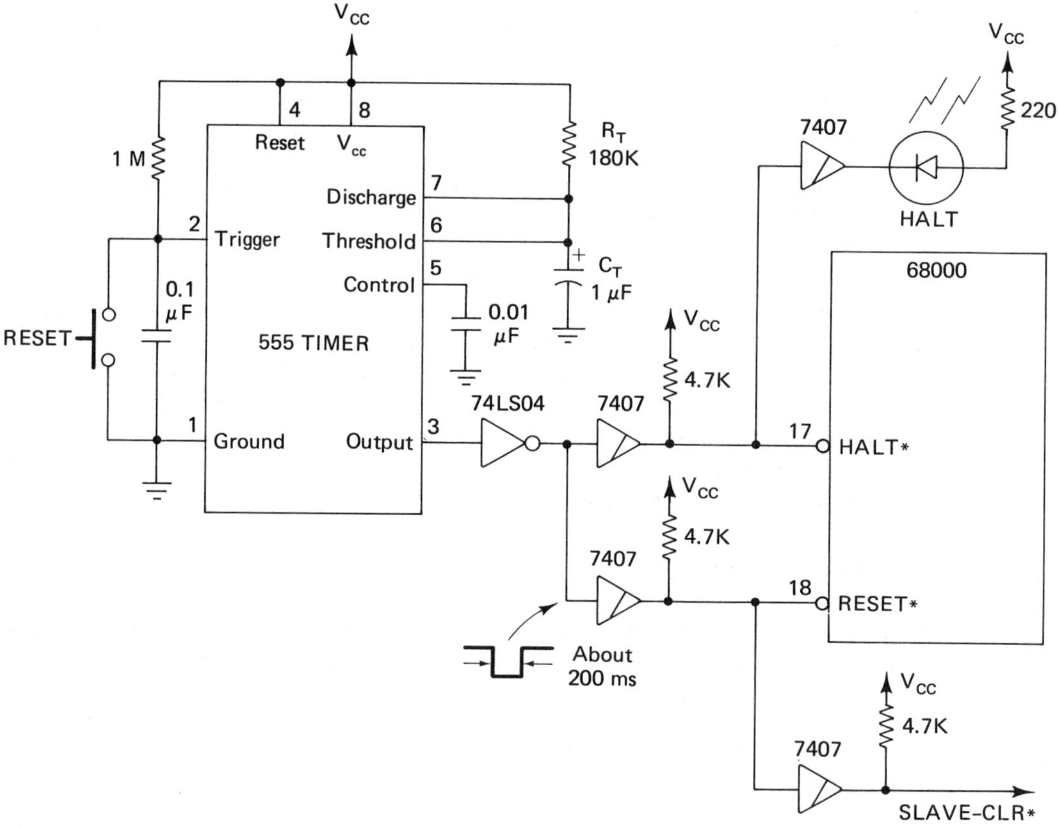

Figure 9.9 Circuit diagram of a simple power-up and reset timer circuit for a 68000 processor. Note the use of open-collector devices on the bidirectional HALT* and RESET* controls of the 68000.

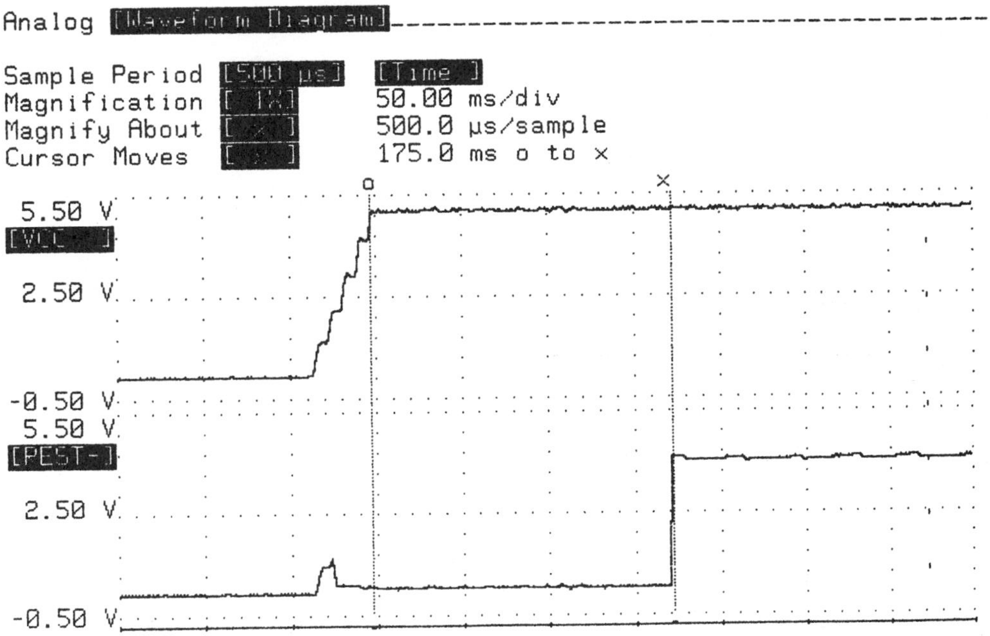

Figure 9.10 Power-up performance of the 555 timer circuit. On power-up, the 555 timer with the parts given in the schematic provides about 175 ms RESET* to the 68000.

9.1.4 Microprocessor Module

All the preceding modules can now be combined with the microprocessor as shown in the block diagram in Figure 9.11. The idea is to freerun the processor so that it continually fetches a one-word NIL instruction, executes it, fetches another one-word instruction at the next even address, and so on through the entire 16 Mb address range. Because each fetch is the same, an oscilloscope can be synchronized easily to view all the control lines and address lines.

Figure 9.12 shows the circuit diagram for the microprocessor module plus all the preceding modules. The data bus is temporarily grounded so that the processor will, upon reset, set SSP=0 and PC=0 and fetch an op-code of 0. The power, clock, and reset modules should have been all checked by now for proper operation and connected ready for the 68000. If the processor is wired as shown, it should immediately begin freerunning. On power-up, the HALT light should flash briefly and then the TEST light will begin flashing on and off.

There is a critical constraint on the op-code that precludes using the NOP instruction in freerunning: whatever is wired to the data bus for the 68000 to read upon reset must be even. The reset sequence in Figure 9.13 is this: the 68000 will do four 16-bit reads to get the initial SSP and PC vectors; then it will fetch its first op-code at the address in the PC. If the PC is not aligned on an even address, the 68000 detects an address error and immediately begins illegal-address exception processing. It tries to push its status on the stack at the beginning of the exception, but the stack is also an illegal address (the same

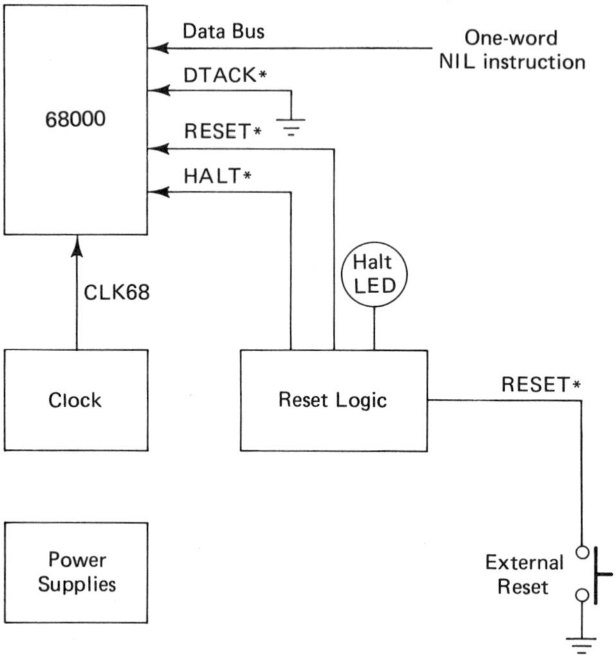

Figure 9.11 Block diagram of the minimum system.

noneven number as in the PC). The result is the fatal "double bus fault" that stops all processing and asserts the HALT* output.

The so-called NIL instruction mentioned earlier corresponds to the temporarily grounded data bus. A logical low on all the data lines when the 68000 does a read operation will be interpreted as an op-code of 0000. In the context of its use in freerunning, it *acts like* a no-operation, or NOP. The 68000 does have a NOP op-code ($4E71) but the NOP will *not* work as a freerunning instruction.

The op-code 0000 does, in fact, correspond to a real instruction in the 68000 set. It is the mnemonic ORI.B #0,D0 and it was selected for freerunning for two reasons: first because the op-code was even, and second because connecting all grounds to the data bus was simpler than making sure one or two data lines had a logic "1" on them. When the instruction is considered in its freerunning environment, the "memory" looks like

Address	Data	Program
00 0000	0000 0000	ORI.B #0,D0
00 0004	0000 0000	ORI.B #0,D0
00 0008	0000 0000	ORI.B #0,D0
00 000C	0000 0000	ORI.B #0,D0
00 0010	0000 0000	ORI.B #0,D0
•		
•		
•		
FF FFFC	0000 0000	ORI.B #0,D0.

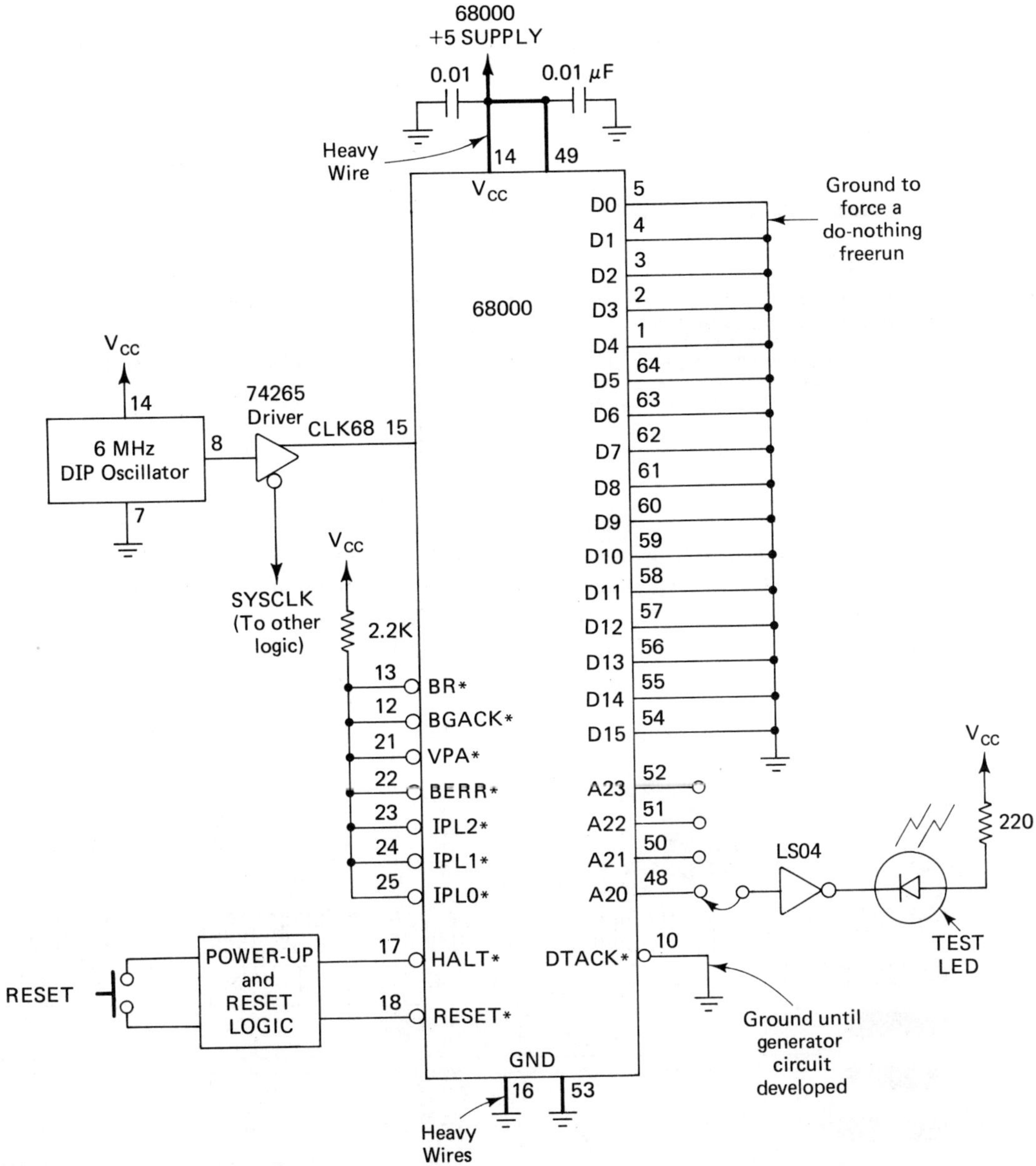

Figure 9.12 Circuit diagram of the minimum 68000 system for freerun test.

The execution time of this "program" can be easily calculated. Each instruction takes eight clock cycles, so for a 6 MHz clock the execution time is 8 × 167 ns or approximately 1.33 μs. A complete sweep through the entire 16 Mb of the 68000 address range takes 1.33 × 4 Mb, or about 5.59 seconds. If you connect the TEST light to the top address bit, A23, it will be on for 2.8 seconds and then off for 2.8 seconds. You can connect the TEST light to A20 permanently: it will stay on for 0.35 seconds and off for

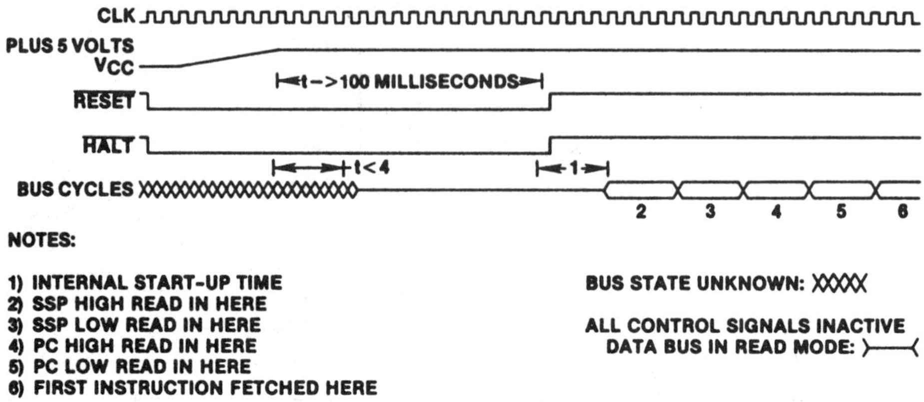

Figure 9.13 Sequence of operations when the 68000 RESET* and HALT* lines are asserted. (Courtesy Motorola Inc.)

0.35 seconds. It provides a rather reassuring flash rate during development work and is not nearly as unsettling as a constant red HALT light.

Figure 9.14 shows the performance of the minimum system with DTACK* grounded. Upon RESET* and HALT*, the 68000 begins reset exception processing and gets its SSP and PC from the data bus. When freerunning, all the processor controls such as UDS* and LDS* are active; R/W* will never go low with the NIL instruction.

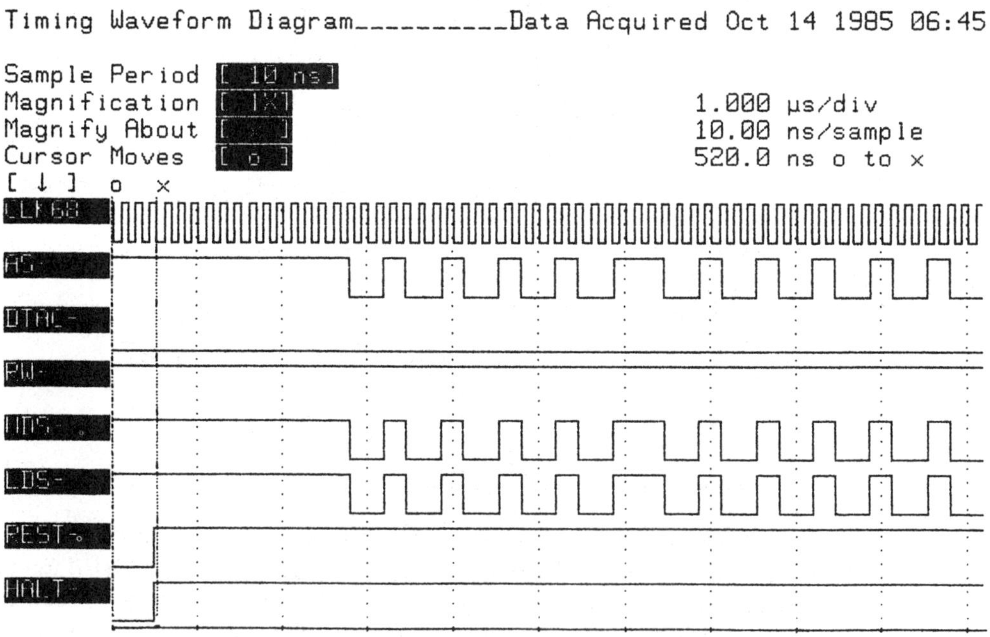

Figure 9.14 Typical freerun starting from RESET* and HALT* asserted low. The clock is running at 6 MHz. DTACK* is grounded in this example.

9.1.5 DTACK* and Wait Generator

For the minimum system, the whole issue of waits and DTACK* can be postponed until after the processor freeruns. Once the processor runs, however, the DTACK* and wait generator module should be connected.

In general, DTACK* must be asserted low at least one setup time before the falling edge of the clock at S4 in each bus cycle; it must be negated sometime after AS* goes high (see data sheet bubble 28). If DTACK* is not present at the end of S4, then the 68000 inserts waits until DTACK* goes low. In the minimum case, grounding DTACK* continuously will allow the processor to run bus cycles without waits.

The circuit diagram of a simple DTACK* and wait generator is shown in Figure 9.15. Its basic function is to provide DTACK* anytime the 68000 executes a bus cycle. Unlike the circuit used in the Motorola ECB, this unit does not detect whether RAM, ROM, or I/O is being addressed: it *always* supplies DTACK*.

The advantage in always getting DTACK* when the 68000 does a bus cycle is that the RAM, ROM, and I/O modules can be added later, and the circuit does not change. If the added module does not work properly, at least the processor does not hang waiting for a DTACK* that never comes. On the other hand, if the 68000 reads an address that has not yet been decoded, there is no way to detect the error and tell the 68000 to begin exception processing. At this early stage in the system development, there is no way to handle exceptions. Thus, the simple generator should be more than adequate.

Notice in the circuit diagram that BCYCLE is a combination of the data strobes as well as AS* and R/W*. The AS* defines the time in the bus cycle when the address bus is valid; it also provides a lock-out mechanism to implement the read-modify-write instruction. Because the read-modify-write (mnemonic TAS for "test and set") instruction requires a read *and* a write bus cycle, there is no way AS* could be used alone to generate two DTACK* signals. However, the UDS* and LDS* controls are asserted for each bus cycle of the TAS, and they can be used to initiate BCYCLE.

If UDS* and LDS* can be used to initiate operation of the DTACK* generator circuit, why include AS* and R/W* at all? The reason is to avoid an extra wait being added to a write bus cycle. If you compare the timing diagrams of the 68000 read cycle and the 68000 write cycle, you notice:

- AS*, UDS*, and LDS* are all asserted at the same time when the 68000 does a read bus cycle, and
- UDS* and LDS* are asserted *one clock cycle* after AS* when the processor does a write bus cycle.

To avoid the extra wait during a write bus cycle, BCYCLE must be asserted at the same time as it is for a read bus cycle. This can be done by ANDing AS* with R/W*. The R/W* line goes low shortly after AS* (bubble 20A) during all write bus cycles, and it can take the place of the data strobes to start BCYCLE.

Either the 68000 clock (CLK68) or the inverted clock (SYSCLK) can be used to drive the 74LS164 wait generator. Examine the timing diagram in Figure 9.15 closely: AS* goes low in S2 about 60 ns after the rising edge of the clock (see bubble 9 in the

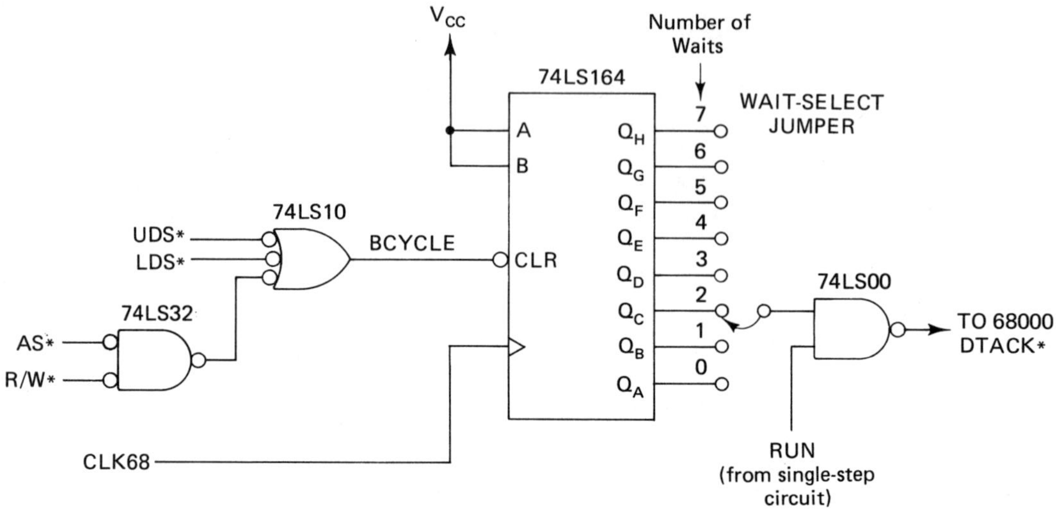

Propagation Delays:	74LS00	t1 = 9–15 ns Average
	74LS10	t2 = 9–15 ns Average
	74LS32	t3 = 14–22 ns Average
	74LS164	t4 = 17-27 ns Q low-to-high from Clock
		t5 = 24-36 ns Q high-to-low from Clear

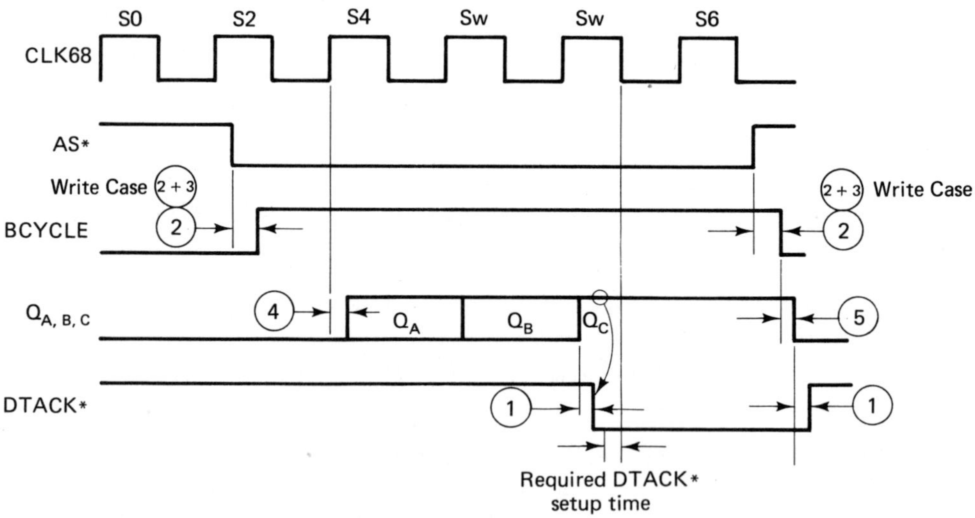

Figure 9.15 Circuit diagram of a simple DTACK* and wait generator (a), and its timing diagram (b).

68000 data manual). Add to that a maximum propagation delay of about 37 ns (15 + 22 ns) through the logic to get BCYCLE. Consequently, BCYCLE might not be asserted until almost 100 ns after the leading edge of the clock in S2. If you allow 36 ns setup for the 74LS164 before the next clock edge, then that total is over 130 ns. If SYSCLK were used to trigger the 74LS164 at the end of S2, then half a period of the clock must be greater than 130 ns: the maximum clock speed would have to be less than 4 MHz. Using CLK68, however, means that the 74LS164 has until the beginning of S4 before it will be clocked. Thus, the worst-case clock speed is almost 8 MHz for this circuit.

An extra input labeled "RUN" is provided in the module to use an optional single-step circuit. By negating RUN (i.e., making RUN a logic low), DTACK* will be held up indefinitely. Design for testability: even if you do not include a single-step circuit on your processor board, you can use a RUN input with an external plug-in circuit.

9.1.6 Testing the Minimum System

Each of the modules (power supplies, clock, and reset logic) could have been designed, built, and tested individually before they were interconnected. If they were not, they are not so complex that they cannot be built and tested as a complete system all at one time. In the interest of not burning out ICs, however, it might be wise to build and test the power supplies separately to make sure that the voltages are in the proper range.

The system test at this point is simple: connect the test LED to one of the high address pins and turn on the power. The halt LED should light briefly while the power-on circuit times out, and then the test LED should begin flashing on and off. Press the external reset button and the halt LED should come on; release the reset and the 68000 will begin freerunning again. Use an oscilloscope to check the clock signal, AS* and other control lines, and each of the address pins; record all of the observations in your lab book for future reference.

If the 68000 does not freerun at this point, go through a troubleshooting sequence to correct the difficulty. Check these connections:

1. Power at both power pins of the 68000; ground at both of the ground pins?
2. Clock at the processor?
3. DTACK* grounded? If the wait generator is installed, disable it temporarily until after the processor freeruns.
4. All the data bus lines grounded?
5. RESET* and HALT* both high after the initial power-on clear?

Troubleshooting the 68000 might be easier if you place a large label on the top of the 68000 package; write the pin numbers and functions on the label as you need them. That way, you can find each of the pins easily for testing and future wiring.

The modular approach to designing a complete system depends on following a sequence of design, build, and test. At this point in the development, the minimum 68000 must work; if it does not, there is no sense in going further. The strategy is to add one module after another to the freerunning system; if the system will not freerun, there is some fatal flaw that *must* be corrected.

9.2 IEEE STD-696 SYSTEM DESIGN

Refer to Figure 9.3 and see how much difference there is between the "minimum system" and the "S-100 system" at this point in the design. All the same highlighted modules are required; the only difference at the block diagram level appears as one module marked "S-100 Bus Interface." Physically, a minimum system would probably be built on a prototyping plug-in wireboard; the prototype S-100 system would be made on a standard-size S-100 card using wire-wrap.

The IEEE Std-696 system will be designed as a "permanent bus master" on the S-100 bus. As described in Section 2.3 of the IEEE standard, the permanent master is capable of generating and timing all bus cycles while it controls the bus; it also transfers messages to and from slaves on the bus. Normally the permanent master controls the bus, but it may relinquish the bus to a temporary master for an arbitrary number of bus cycles. The implementation of the permanent bus master follows a specified state diagram for required synchronous bus cycles.

9.2.1 Power Supply

The power supply module shown in Figure 9.4 can be used with a minimum system or with an S-100 system: the power input and ground lines are shown in the schematic with the bus connector numbers for the S-100 bus. Figure 9.16 shows that the power supply

Figure 9.16 The power supply module wired into the upper-left corner of a standard S-100 wire-wrap board.

module takes up very little room on the standard board. One of the regulators provides power to the 68000 and its memory ICs using two bus rails at the top of the board. The other regulator provides +5V to all the TTL logic using the grid of power and grounds that cover the whole board. Monolithic 0.01 μF capacitors are placed between power and ground every several ICs as the construction continues.

9.2.2 Clock and Driver

The clock and driver circuit in Figure 9.6 can also be used with a minimum system or an S-100 system without special modification. The schematic indicates just one bus connection, pin 24, to provide a "system clock" for synchronous operation on the S-100 bus. This clock signal is a requirement for a permanent master on the bus (Section 2.3.4). Notice that this clock is inverted from the clock used on the 68000. This is because certain events in the S-100 system take place when the 68000 clock (CLK68) is falling at the end of the S4 or S6; these bus events require the clock rising, so an inverted clock (SYSCLK) is provided.

9.2.3 Reset Circuit

The block diagram in Figure 9.8 describes the minimum performance required of the power-up and reset circuit. However, the IEEE Std-696 requires (Section 2.3.4) that the bus master respond to RESET* on the bus rather than a board-mounted pushbutton. A power-on clear (POC*) is also described but not required. Section 2.2.9.4 describes the system reset functions as RESET* (pin 75), SLAVE-CLR* (pin 54), and POC* (pin 99). RESET* and SLAVE-CLR* are both open-collector, and POC* is an active line. Implementation of these three reset functions can be done with only minor modification of the reset circuit described for the minimum system. The S-100 version of the circuit is shown in Figure 9.17.

The 74LS125A buffer is used to obtain the active drive requirement of POC* ($V_{OL} \leq 0.5$ V at 24 mA sink, $V_{OH} \geq 2.4$ V at 2 mA). The standard calls for POC* to assert RESET* and SLAVE-CLR*. It does this by connection through the 7407 to the RESET* input, which then drives the SLAVE-CLR* line. The 7407 is necessary here because the bus RESET* line is bidirectional, and if not prevented, an external reset on the bus could activate POC* unintentionally.

The POC* line must be active for at least 10 ms (Section 2.2.9.4). A simple RC timer with the 74LS125A buffer can be used to accomplish this on power-up. The performance of the circuit is shown in Figure 9.18 as the system power comes on: POC* goes high about 45 ms after the system power is at its operating level.

The 45 ms provided by POC* is not alone sufficient to accomplish the 68000 power-on reset. However, if the POC* signal is used to trigger the 555 timer, then it is possible to obtain adequate 68000 reset time. In the power-on case, shown in Figure 9.19, the 68000 RESET* and HALT* lines are held asserted for approximately 128 ms after POC* is negated. Consequently, on system power-up, the 68000 RESET* and HALT* lines are held low for about 80 ms (Figure 9.18) plus the 128 ms, or about 200+ ms total.

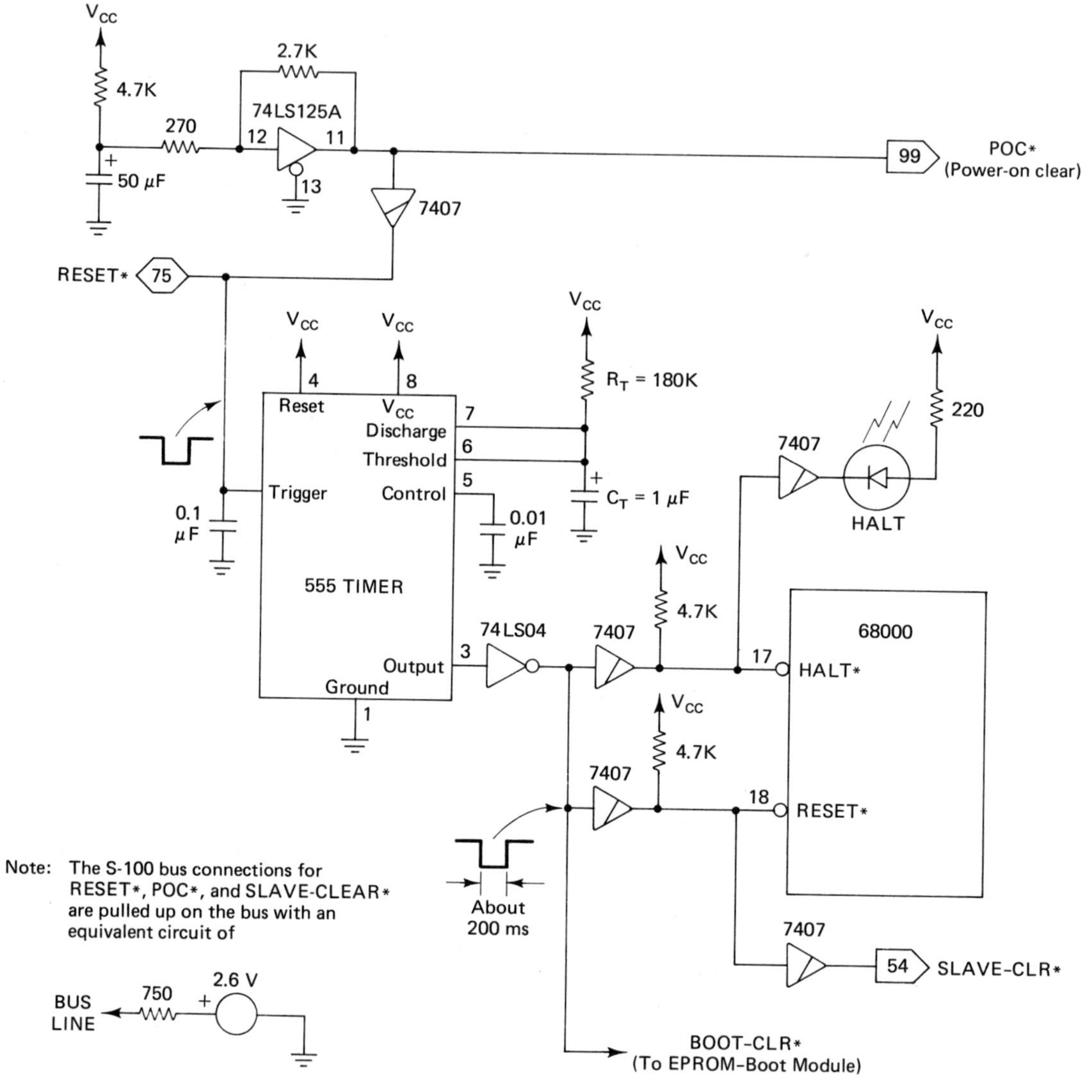

Figure 9.17 Circuit diagram for the reset module.

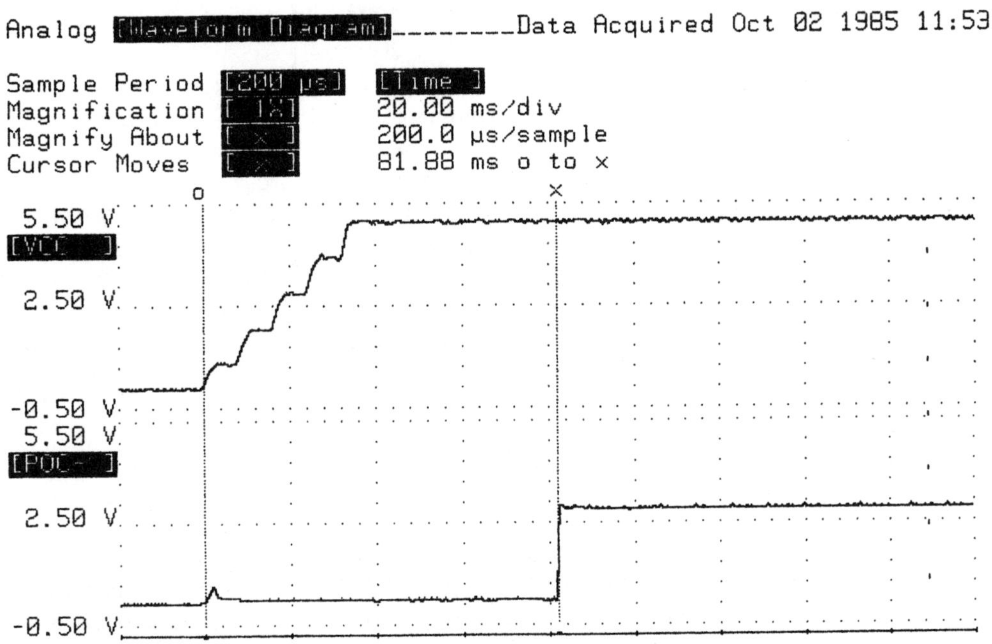

Figure 9.18 System power-on sequence. Top plot is V_{cc} increasing to its operating +5 V. Lower plot shows power-on clear, POC*, held low for about 45 ms after V_{cc} is valid.

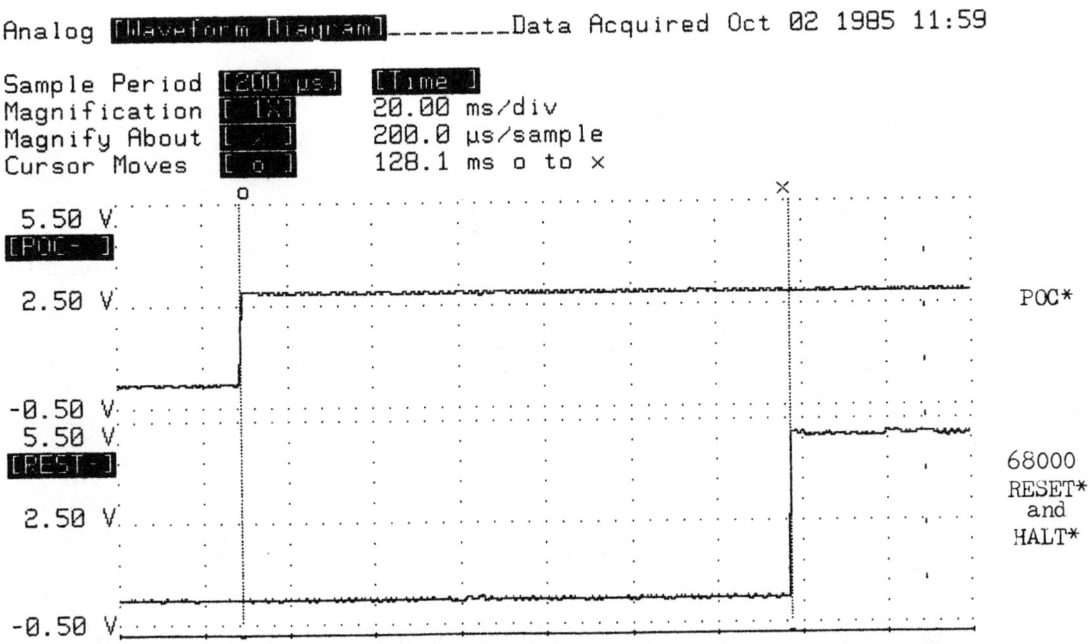

Figure 9.19 Performance of the 555 timer on system power up. About 128 ms after POC* is negated, the 68000 RESET* and HALT* are negated.

Why not simply design the POC* circuit for the whole 200 ms on reset? If that were done, then would it not be possible to eliminate the 555 timer? The answer is yes and no: the power-on design would work fine, but the external reset signal becomes a problem. You cannot assume a clean debounced reset-switch closure coming from the external circuit. Perhaps the last bounce might not be 10 clock cycles long, which is the minimum requirement for resetting the 68000 after the power is already turned on. So, in addition to providing power-on delay, the 555 also acts as a system reset-switch debouncer. Figure 9.20 shows that the 68000 RESET* and HALT* lines are asserted for almost 200 ms as a result of the external reset. The external reset in this case is simply a quick manual press of the system reset button.

9.2.4 Microprocessor Module

Following the same approach as earlier, the various modules in the S-100 system can be combined as shown in the block diagram in Figure 9.21. The only differences from the minimum system are that RESET* comes from a system bus connection, and SLAVE-CLR* and POC* signals are provided to the system bus. The one-word NIL instruction is still on the 68000 data bus for freerunning, and DTACK* may be either grounded or come from a wait generator as described earlier.

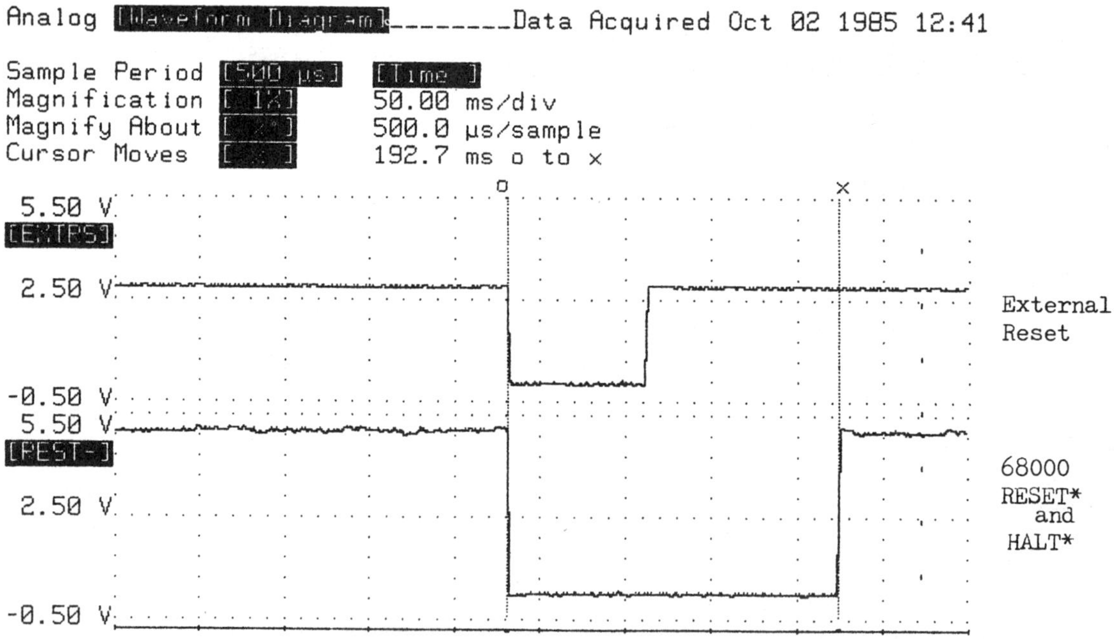

Figure 9.20 Performance of the 555 timer when a brief external reset (top plot) is applied. The timer will assert RESET* and HALT* for about 200 ms.

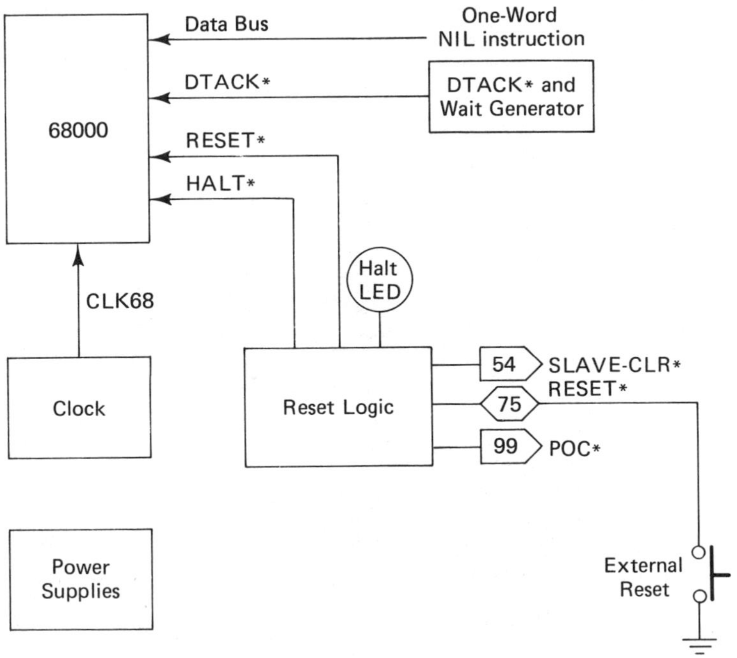

Figure 9.21 Block diagram of the S-100 minimum system.

Compare the S-100 circuit diagram shown in Figure 9.22 with the minimum system circuit in Figure 9.12. There is virtually no difference between them other than the physical bus connections at this point. After wiring the S-100 modules, you should be able to freerun the 68000 as easily as before with DTACK* grounded.

9.2.5 DTACK* and Wait Generator

After the processor freeruns with DTACK* grounded, connect the circuit shown in Figure 9.23 for the S-100 DTACK* and wait generator. The design is based on Figure 9.15 for the minimum system, but has several modifications that are necessary for proper operation with the S-100 bus. The circuit is a final "as built" version, and some of the modifications depend on the form of the final system as well as S-100 requirements.

Notice that the 74LS109A is connected in almost the same way as the 74LS164 in the earlier wait circuit: the data strobes or write pulse form BCYCLE, which is used to hold the flip-flop in a cleared state until a bus cycle starts. Assuming that RUN from the single-step circuit is high, the flip-flop is set on the leading edge of CLK68 just as before. When set, the DT-ENAB line (DTACK* enable) is high, which enables the 74LS164.

Examine the timing diagram in Figure 9.23 closely. The 74LS164 provides waits as before, but it is connected to SYSCLK rather than CLK68. The reason why it must trigger on the falling edge of the 68000 clock (rising edge of SYSCLK) relates to the IEEE Std-696 (Section 3.10) timing requirements for RDY and XRDY. Both RDY and XRDY

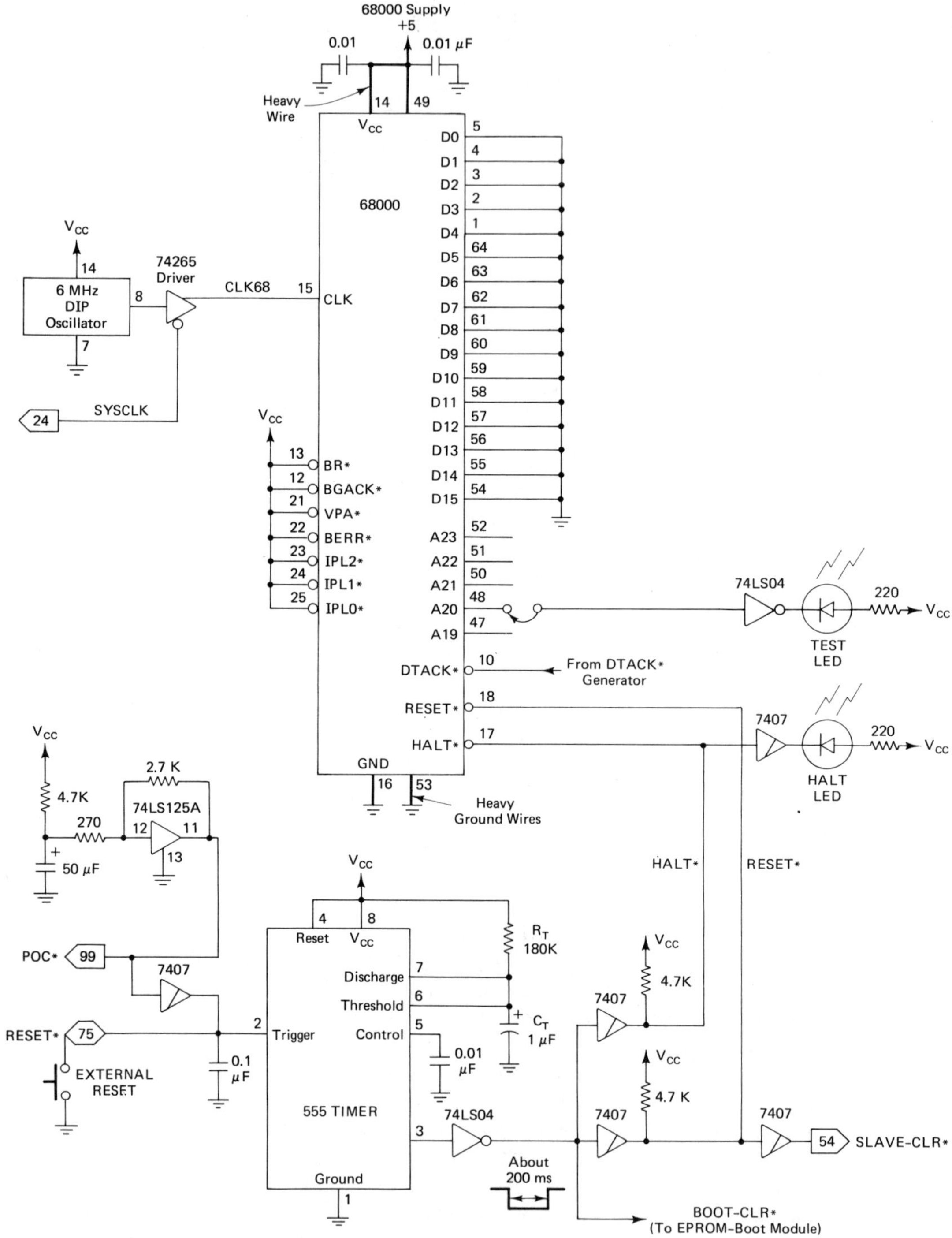

Figure 9.22 Circuit diagram of the complete minimum system as configured for the IEEE-696 bus.

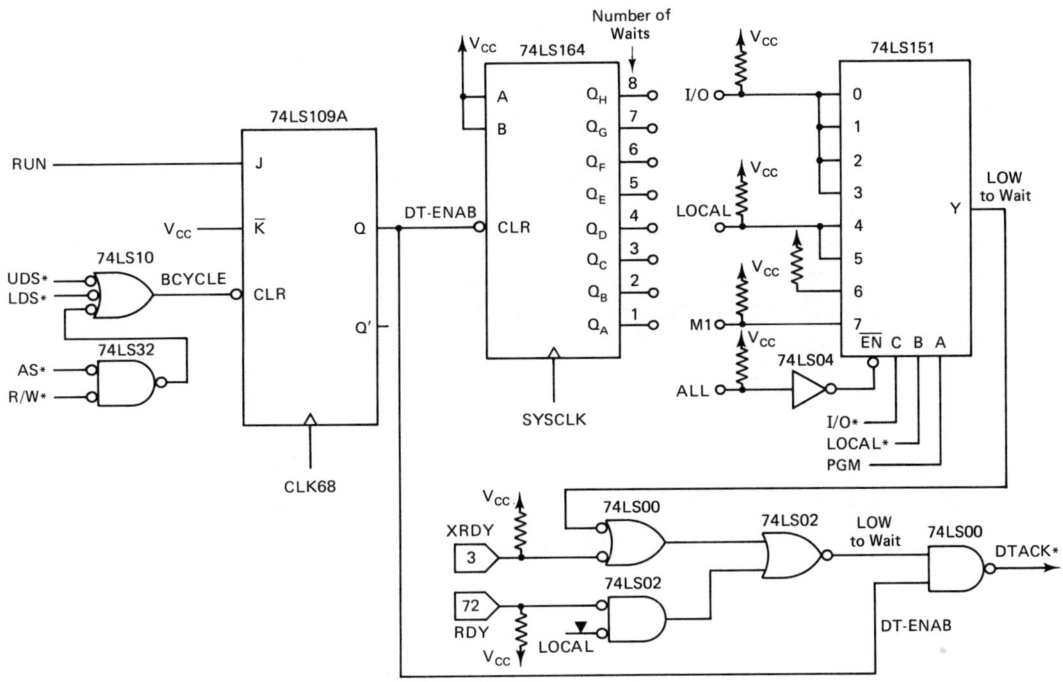

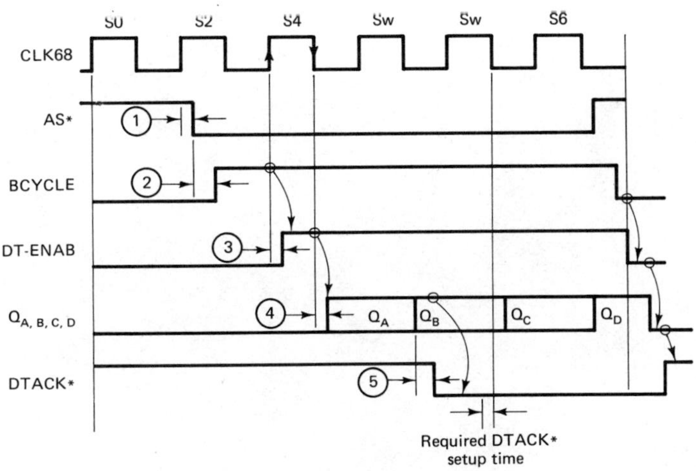

Figure 9.23 Circuit diagram of DTACK* and wait generator for the IEEE Std-696 CPU design. No jumpers are needed between the 74LS164 and the 74SL151 if waits are not required.

will be LOW at least 70 ns before the rising edge of SYSCLK if the addressed peripheral in the system needs wait states; this LOW must be recognized on a 68000 falling clock. Likewise, the 74LS164 output must also be recognized on the 68000 falling clock; in addition, the propagation delay through the 74LS164 and the 74LS151 is too long to use anything but SYSCLK.

The 74LS151 1-of-8 selector is used to allow the choice of different waits for I/O operations, for on-board local bus cycles, for op-code fetches (M1 for machine-cycle 1), or for all bus cycles. Its select inputs marked I/O*, LOCAL*, and PGM will be developed later: connect them in their negated state for now. In contrast to Figure 9.15, note that no jumpers are required unless waits are needed.

DTACK* depends on several different components in this design: the bus cycle, RUN true, waits selected by the 74LS164/151 wait generator, and waits required by the system through RDY and XRDY. Of these, the most time-critical is the RDY/XRDY component from the system. It is necessary to inhibit DTACK* one setup time (20 ns) before the 68000 falling clock edge at S4, and the RDY/XRDY appears just 70 ns in advance. This leaves 50 ns for the signal to propagate through several levels of gates. In the worst case, the timing is very close; in reality, RDY usually goes LOW one clock cycle in advance (167 ns) and goes HIGH one-half clock cycle in advance (83 ns) of the falling clock edge.

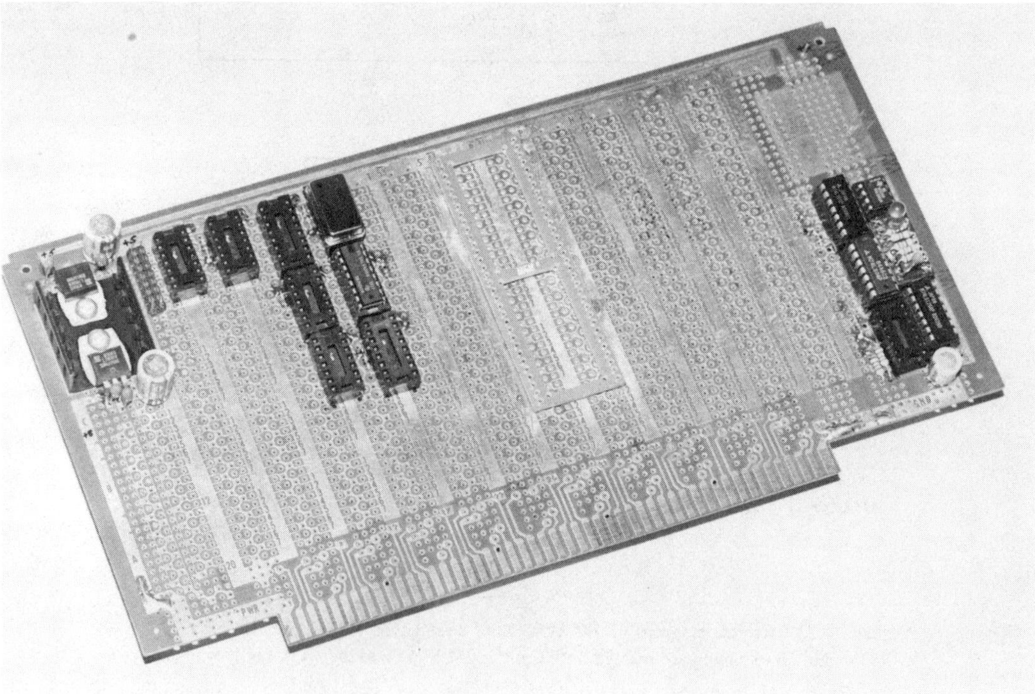

Figure 9.24 Continued construction of the CPU board. The 68000 is in center; clock, DTACK* and wait, and power to the left; reset and halt logic on the right.

9.2.6 Testing the IEEE STD-696 System

By now all the essential modules should have been constructed on an S-100 prototype board; one example layout is shown in Figure 9.24. The 68000 was centered on the board with the idea of putting RAM and EPROM sockets on either side of it. The clock, DTACK* and wait module, and power supply are on the left; the reset and halt logic is in the right corner of the board. Figure 9.25 shows the same board with the two freerunning headers plugged into the EPROM sockets to the left of the 68000; RAM will be on the right of the 68000. The single-step circuit is in the upper-right corner of the board. The four sockets by the RAM will be used later for the data-bus buffers to the S-100 system.

Testing the CPU board is simplified if an empty S-100 frame (card cage) is available. Just plug the CPU board into a bus socket and apply power following the same general procedure as described for the minimum system. To avoid any possible interaction with RDY or XRDY, any other cards plugged into the bus should be removed.

After power-up, the 68000 should freerun as usual. Assuming a 6 MHz clock, the test LED connected to A20 should flash at a rate of 0.35 seconds on, 0.35 seconds off.

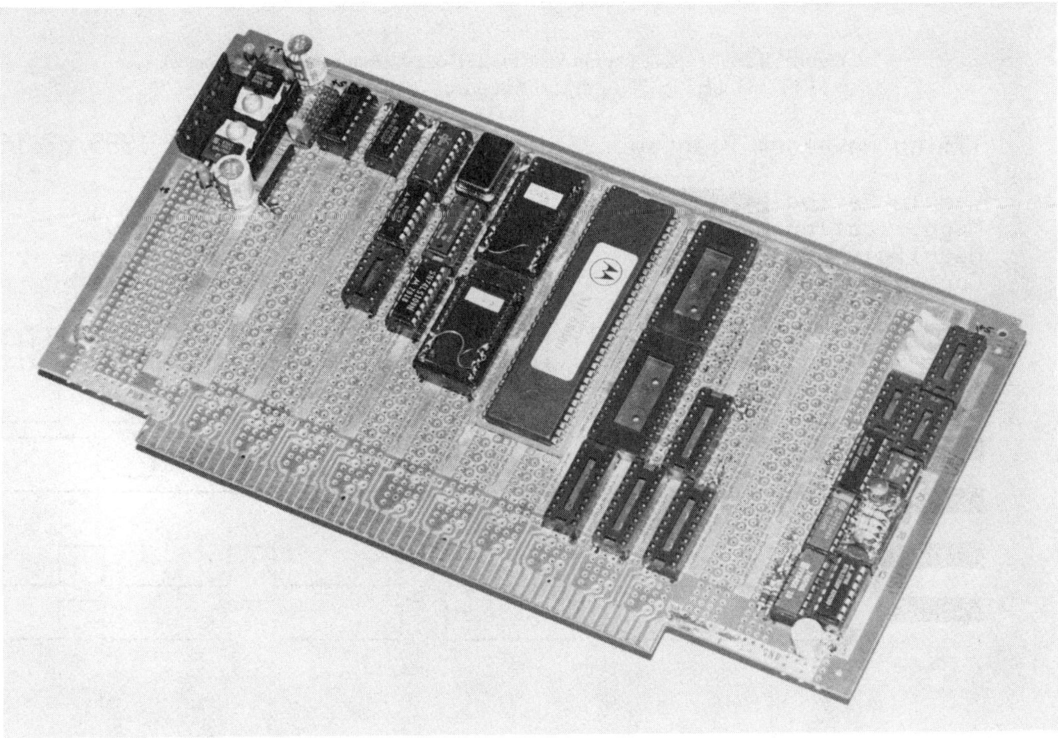

Figure 9.25 The CPU board with added sockets for memory on either side of the 68000. Single-step circuit and step switches are in the right corner. Two 24-pin component carriers are plugged into the EPROM sockets to the left of the 68000 to freerun.

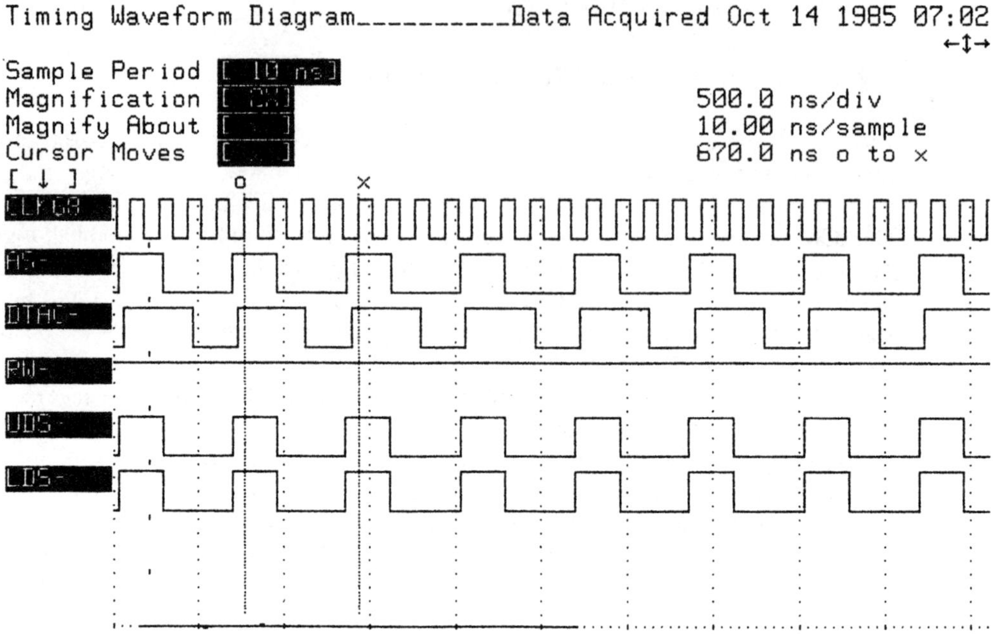

Figure 9.26 Typical freerun with the DTACK* circuit enabled. The clock is 6 MHz, and there are no wait states inserted.

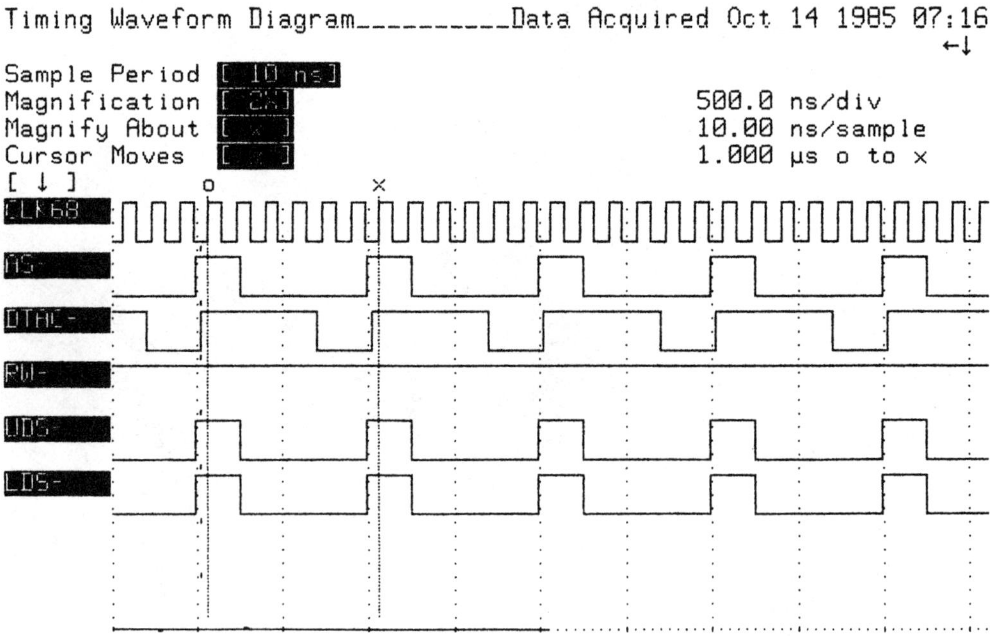

Figure 9.27 Typical freerun with DTACK* enabled. This timing shows DTACK* delayed enough to cause two waits in each bus cycle.

You can test the wait circuit easily either by using an oscilloscope to look at the bus cycles or by simply timing the test LED flashes. For example, a single wait will add 167 ns to each bus cycle, two waits add 333 ns, etc; you can calculate what the slower flash rate should be and verify it by watching the LED.

Figure 9.26 shows the performance of the 68000 freerunning with no waits inserted; Figure 9.27 shows the behavior of the system with two waits. The effect of delaying DTACK* is simply to increase the duration of the bus cycle; all the controls such as UDS* and LDS* remain asserted for the extra time. The "o" and "x" markers indicate the beginning and ending of a typical bus cycle.

9.3 SINGLE-STEP MODULE DESIGN

Either the minimum system or the S-100 version can be used with a hardware single-step module. The purpose of the single-stepper is to execute one *bus cycle* at a time rather than run full-speed through a program (either freerunning or a program in memory). This is different from the typical software single-step command found in software debug programs: the software approach executes a single *instruction,* which might be one or more bus cycles long, and then the processor continues to execute code (in this case, the debug program code.) Although the 68000 might appear "stopped" when the user executes a software single-step instruction, the processor is still very much in action. In contrast, the hardware single-stepper will completely stop the processor and allow execution of only one bus cycle at a time.

Why use a hardware single stepper at all? During the development of the hardware, it is helpful to freeze the system and look at the data, address, and control bus lines to verify that they truly have the expected data present. For example, suppose you freerun the processor and would like to verify that the address bus is counting upward as you expect. When you single-step, check each address line with a logic probe, execute one step, check the addresses again; you should see that the address has incremented upward.

During freerunning, single-stepping is not very useful. However, once you have a simple EPROM program written to do a scope loop, the small number of bus cycles involved in the program can all be stepped through manually and the 68000 bus lines checked for correct values. If the scope-loop program fails to run properly, the single-step capability can quickly locate possible wiring errors or EPROM decoding errors. The trick is to make sure that the test program in the EPROM pair is small enough so that a check of all its bus cycles is not unreasonable. Several instructions are probably the most you would want to single-step through. An effective scope-loop program must be small to synchronize the oscilloscope, so most of these types of programs are quite suitable for single-stepping.

There are two basic approaches to single-stepping the 68000. As outlined in Table 9.1, one method is to use the 68000 HALT* control, and the other technique is to hold up DTACK*. When HALT* is asserted, the processor will complete its current bus cycle and then three-state the data and address buses; the processor controls will not be asserted. While the 68000 is halted like this, it will respond to BR* and allow bus arbitration; thus,

TABLE 9.1 COMPARISON OF 68000 STATUS WHEN SINGLE-STEPPING.

	*Implement SS using HALT**	*Implement SS by holding DTACK**
Data Bus	3-state	Asserted
Address Bus	3-state	Asserted
Controls		
AS*, UDS*, LDS*, R/W*	High	Asserted
FC	3-state (depends on mask set)	Asserted
Behavior	68000 does usual bus arbitration. (3-states controls when bus relinquished.)	68000 will *not* respond to BR*. (No ECB memory refresh.) 68000 will respond to BERR*

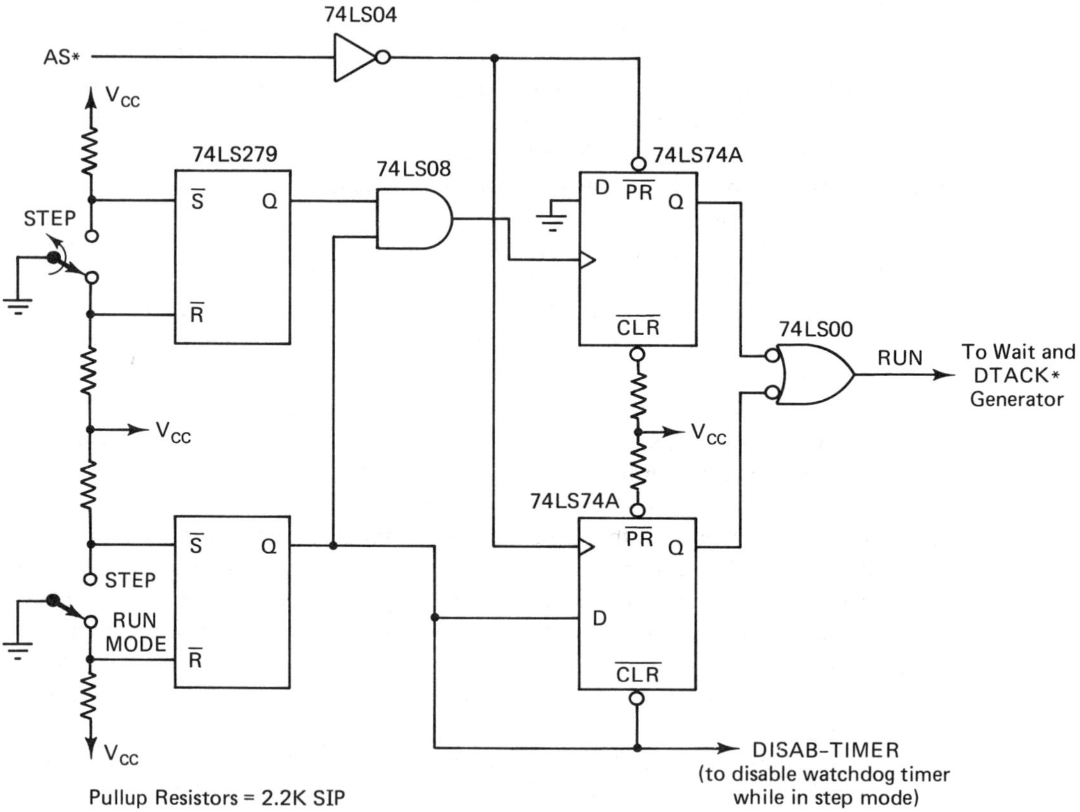

Figure 9.28 Circuit to implement a single-step function by holding DTACK*.

if dynamic memory needs refreshing, it can be done while the processor is running or halted. On the other hand, if DTACK* is held up, the current bus cycle is not completed until a ''step'' is allowed by asserting DTACK*; all data, address, and control bus lines will remain asserted. While the 68000 waits for DTACK* it will not respond to BR* and will not allow bus arbitration; it will, however, respond to BERR* as usual.

Both methods of single-stepping involve a flip-flop circuit that permits control of either HALT* or DTACK* for exactly one bus cycle. The method most useful in bringing up a new 68000 system is the DTACK* approach because the data and address bus values are asserted while stepping. This is the real value of the hardware single-step circuit: being able to hold the 68000 static while you examine the various bus lines.

A circuit that can be used to implement a single-step function by holding DTACK* is shown in Figure 9.28. The RUN output from the stepper goes directly into the DTACK* circuits in Figures 9.15 or 9.23. Its output is always RUN high when not in the step mode; when in the step mode, the RUN output stays low until the step switch is pulsed. When the step switch is pulsed, RUN is asserted for just long enough to finish the current bus cycle. The 68000 then continues onward and begins a new bus cycle, which gets held again waiting for DTACK*.

Recall that the 68000 will respond to BERR* while it waits for DTACK*. In fact, if the processor accidentally addresses a nonexistent peripheral and does not receive a DTACK*, the BERR* is the usual method of breaking the indefinite waiting. A watchdog timer is typically in the system, such as you found in the ECB, to signal an error if a bus cycle takes too long. While single-stepping, this timer must be disabled. The DISAB-TIMER output (HIGH to disable) is provided to accomplish this so the single-stepper does not cause a bus error.

9.4 SUMMARY

After studying the 68000 microprocessor and then testing it in the Educational Computer Board, the idea of building a simple system of your own probably seemed like a major project. Indeed it well could become a difficult situation without following the strategy of designing, building, and testing by modules.

The key to making a first 68000 system is to build a simple freerunning minimum system made up of just the bare essentials. This minimum system, or kernel, can be built easily and tested with nothing more complex than a logic probe. Once this system runs, you can add one module after another as you learn more about the 68000: the system expands as your understanding grows.

Freerunning the kernel involves forcing the 68000 to continually execute a do-nothing NIL instruction. This is done by breaking the normal data path from memory to the 68000. Instead of fetching program instructions from memory, the 68000 receives a single 16-bit word that is actually wired directly onto the data bus. After executing this dummy instruction, the 68000 increments to a new address to fetch another NIL instruction. This fetch-execute sequence repeats over the entire address range of the 68000. Each of the address and control lines from the processor can be tested easily with a logic probe or oscilloscope while freerunning.

Because of the modular nature of the 68000 system development, you can develop either a minimum system on a prototype wireboard or start an IEEE Std-696 CPU board. Either approach requires the same basic modules: power supplies, clock and driver, reset circuit, and the microprocessor. After these modules work together in a successful freerun, a DTACK* and wait generator module can be added. If you want, you can also add a single-step circuit to help in future development of the system.

If you choose to do a minimum system on a proto wireboard, the final result of your work will be a 68000 with one or two serial ports, some RAM, and a system monitor similar to the ECB's TUTOR. In contrast, the IEEE Std-696 approach will result in a wire-wrap CPU board with the 68000, some RAM, a system monitor, and no serial ports; the CPU will have to interface with the S-100 system for I/O. However, the 68000 board will be able to access not only large amounts of RAM, but also be able to access a disk controller and boot a full disk-operating system. Thus, the IEEE Std-696 approach will go far beyond the level of the single-board ECB or minimum system.

EXERCISES

1. What is the kernel of the 68000 system?
2. Why is freerunning the 68000 important?
3. Outline the strategy for bringing up the 68000 system.
4. Sketch the waveform of the clock required by an 8 MHz 68000. Note on the drawing the actual times involved.
5. Characterize the load the 68000 clock input presents to the clock drive circuit.
6. On power-up, how long must the halt and reset pins be asserted on the 68000?
7. If the 68000 is already powered up, how long must halt and reset be asserted to reset the 68000?
8. When the 68000 executes a RESET instruction to clear peripherals, how long does the signal remain asserted? How can you experimentally measure it? Sketch the required load for the measurement.
9. Characterize the RESET* input to the 68000 and calculate maximum and minimum bounds on the pull-up resistor shown in Figure 9.9.
10. Characterize the HALT* input to the 68000 and calculate maximum and minimum bounds on the pull-up resistor shown in Figure 9.9.
11. Sketch a simple test setup that would allow you to check the performance of the 555 timer with an oscilloscope.
12. Calculate the RC combination for a 555 timer that provides a 300 ms reset pulse. Select realistic parts.
13. Sketch a timing diagram with CLK68, AS*, UDS*, LDS*, and HALT* for the first eight bus cycles after RESET* and HALT* go high.
    - **a.** Do the sketch assuming that the data bus has 0000 wired in.
    - **b.** Do the sketch assuming that the data bus has $4E71 (the 68000 NOP instruction) wired in.

14. Assume that the 68000 is freerunning with a clock of 4 MHz.

- **a.** How long will an LED connected to A23 stay on?
- **b.** Suppose your wait generator is set for three waits (three clock cycles). How long will the test LED on A23 stay on?

15. Sketch the timing diagram for the execution of a TAS instruction. Assume that a wait circuit like Figure 9.15 is installed and set for one wait, and that the clock is 4 MHz. Show in the sketch CLK68*, AS*, UDS*, LDS*, R/W*, BCYCLE, and DTACK*. Indicate approximate propagation delays with bubbles and estimate their maximum/minimum values as appropriate.

16. Explain why R/W* is part of the Boolean expression for BCYCLE.

17. How long should it take POC* to go high from a power-up with the parts shown in Figure 9.17?

18. Sketch the timing diagram for a 6 MHz freerunning system using the circuit shown in Figure 9.23. Assume that the wait generator is set for two waits. Include CLK68*, AS*, and DTACK*, and indicate approximate propagation delays. Compare your sketch with Figure 9.27. Do they correlate well?

19. The single-step circuit in Figure 9.28 was implemented using the 74LS279. Why would that particular IC be selected? Suggest an alternative circuit not using the 74LS279. Can you design a circuit with fewer parts?

FURTHER READING

DOBRIN, ANDREJ, and FRANC NOVAK. "Freerunning the M68000." *Electronics Test* (April 1984): 124.

IEEE *Standard 696 Interface Devices*. New York: IEEE, 1983.

"MC68000 16-BIT MICROPROCESSOR DATA MANUAL." Austin, TX: Motorola Semiconductor Products, Inc.

STARNES, THOMAS W. "Handling Exceptions Gracefully Enhances Software Reliability." *Electronics* (Sept. 11, 1980): 153–57.

STOCKTON, JOHN, and VICTOR SCHERER. "Learn the Timing and Interfacing of MC68000 Peripheral Circuits." *Electronic Design* (23): 57–64. Nov. 8, 1979.

WILCOX, ALAN D. "Bringing Up the 68000—A First Step." *Doctor Dobb's Journal* 11(1): 60–74. Jan. 1986.

TEN

Memory Design

Freerunning the 68000 for the first time was probably the high point of your day. When the 68000 first ran, you had something concrete to see and use as a foundation for all your future design. By now, you should have a system that looks something like Figure 10.1: a 68000 with reset logic, a single-step module, and a DTACK* and wait generator. It will start up and freerun at full speed, freerun slowed down with wait states, or run in single-step mode so you can check each address and control line.

The next step is to close the loop between memory and the 68000 so the processor can execute simple programs. The purpose of this chapter is to help you design the memory modules, both ROM and RAM, so that your 68000 can begin performing small tasks. The strategy is to gradually add more capabilities to the 68000 so the processor itself can begin testing each of the new modules you install. For example, if you can execute a program in ROM, then use such a program to test all RAM locations when you build the RAM module.

Throughout all of the development of the ROM and RAM modules, the 68000 should be *able* to freerun. After adding data and address bus lines to the first pair of EPROM sockets, plug in your ''freerun headers'' and be sure that the processor still runs properly. You must *always* be able to fall back to a known good condition. Even though you carefully design a new module and buzz out the circuit before turning on the power, sometimes an oversight can cause problems. Unless the error is directly related to the data bus, putting the 68000 into a freerun can always help you find the difficulty.

10.1 MEMORY DESIGN

When you studied troubleshooting in Chapter 8 and read about how to bring up a new system, you were given a simple scope-loop program that did a JMP 8 over and over. The memory map containing that simple first program is shown in Figure 10.2. You are al-

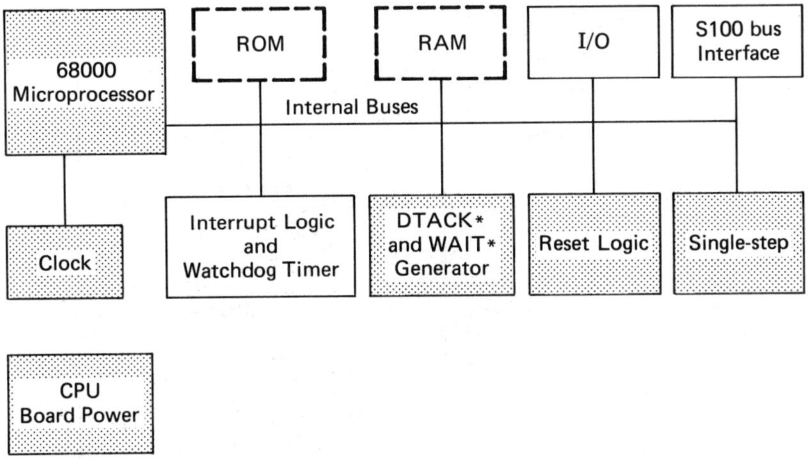

Figure 10.1 The highlighted ROM and RAM modules will be developed in this chapter. The shaded modules have already been designed.

ready familiar with the 68000 reset sequence: first the 68000 reads the SSP at address 0, reads the PC at address 4, and then begins the program with a fetch at the PC location. In this first program, the PC is set to 8, and location 8 contains the jump instruction.

Normally, you do not put a program in low memory except when you first build your ROM circuit and do not have any decoding designed or constructed. The 1,024 lowest bytes of memory are reserved for the exception vectors shown in Table 10.1. The reset vectors, SSP and PC, are the two you have already used; the others you will use as necessary during the development of the 68000 project. All the other vectors can be stored in either EPROMs or RAM decoded for low memory; the only requirement is that the initial SSP and PC vectors be in EPROMs.

The goal in developing your system memory is to get TUTOR running as soon as possible. This is because you can use it as a powerful test and debugging tool as you add more hardware to your system. For example, you can use it to test whole blocks of memory or to execute any number of scope loops. To use TUTOR without making any

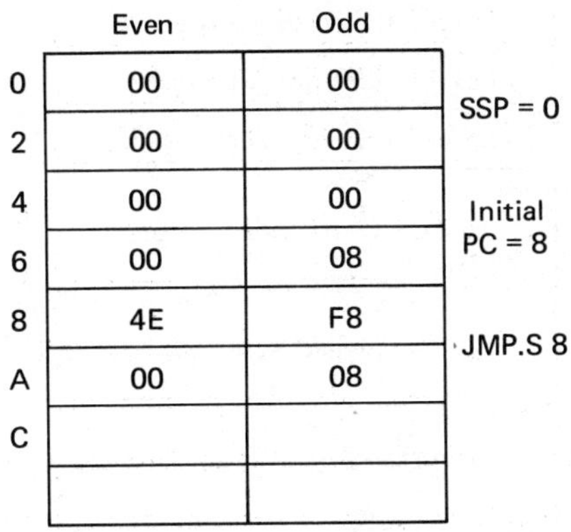

Figure 10.2 Memory map of the simple first program from Chapter 8.

TABLE 10.1 EXCEPTION VECTORS LOCATED IN LOWEST 1024 BYTES OF MEMORY.

Memory Address (Hexadecimal)	
0	Reset: Initial SSP
	Reset: Initial PC
8	Bus Error
C	Address Error
10	Illegal Instruction
14	Zero Divide
18	CHK Instruction
1C	TRAPV Instruction
20	Privilege Violation
24	Trace
28	Line 1010 Emulator
2C	Line 1111 Emulator
30	Unassigned Reserved
3C	Uninitialized Interrupt
40	Unassigned Reserved
60	Spurious Interrupt
64	Level 1 Interrupt Autovector
68	Level 2 Interrupt Autovector
6C	Level 3 Interrupt Autovector
70	Level 4 Interrupt Autovector
74	Level 5 Interrupt Autovector
78	Level 6 Interrupt Autovector
7C	Level 7 Interrupt Autovector
80	16 Trap Instruction Vectors
C0	Unassigned Reserved
100	192 User Interrupt Vectors
3FF	

modifications to it, configure your system so it has RAM and I/O where TUTOR expects it; later, you can modify TUTOR for operation elsewhere if you want.

The strategy you will want to follow in designing your system memory is this: first develop a simple program in low memory as above. Next design a boot circuit plus address decoder and move the simple program so it executes at higher memory (say $8000 like TUTOR in the ECB). Then design a RAM module for 4K of memory decoded at 0 (or 8) and write an EPROM program that executes above $8000 that will do reads and writes to RAM. With a memory map like the ECB's, you should be able to put TUTOR EPROMs into your 68000 board and run. After you develop I/O capabilities, you can use the TUTOR firmware to do more sophisticated memory testing and program development.

You can see the progression of this strategy easily using memory maps. Figure 10.3 shows the system memory when a boot circuit and address decoder have been added. Notice the technique of providing the reset vectors when the system is first booted: the first 8 bytes of EPROM pair are decoded at address 0. When the 68000 jumps to $8008, the EPROMs are selected again and the program begins execution.

After you add 4K (or perhaps 16K) of RAM to your system, your memory map will look like Figure 10.4. Instead of doing just a jump over and over, the program at $8008 is a scope loop that writes 16 bits to a word in RAM. While looping, you can check the timing of the RAM-enable and write control lines as well as the data being written.

Compare this with the ECB memory map in Figure 10.5. In both cases the first 8 bytes of the EPROMs provide the vectors for a jump to EPROM memory space upon reset. Rather than arbitrarily setting the SSP to 0 and then jumping to $8008, however, TUTOR sets the inital SSP at $444 in RAM and then jumps to $8146. Initialization code in TUTOR repositions the stack and also sets up the Table 10.1 exception vectors it uses.

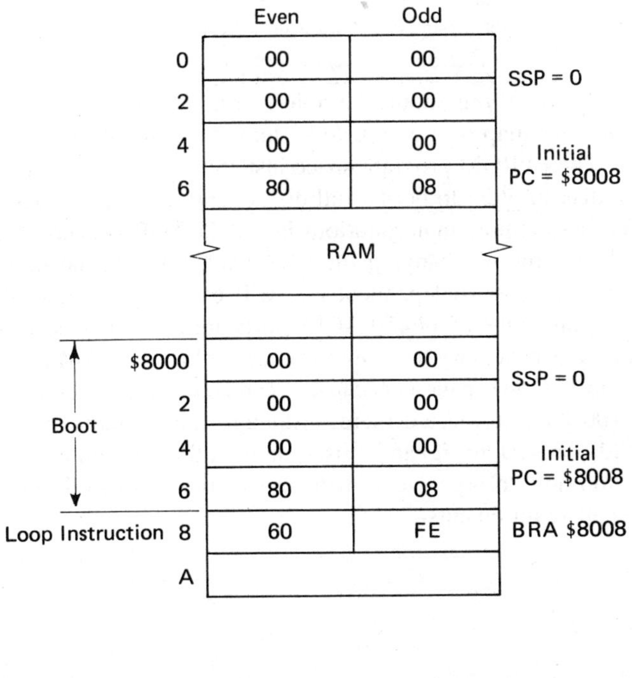

Figure 10.3 Memory map of system using an EPROM normally decoded at $8000. When the 68000 is reset, however, the EPROM code marked "Boot" is enabled starting at address 0. Either the BRA or JMP.L instruction can be used for the scope loop. A JMP.S works, but the 16-bit short address ($8008) is sign-extended by the 68000 so that $FF8008 actually appears on the address bus.

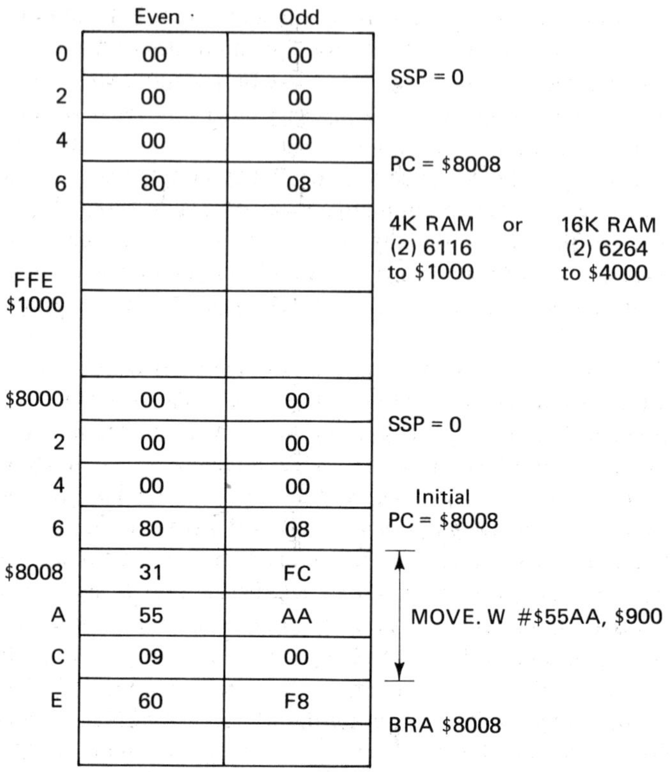

Figure 10.4 Memory map of the next phase of the system after 4K or 16K of RAM is added to low memory. A small scope-loop to write to a RAM address begins at location $8008.

If your system is set up similarly, then you should be able to run TUTOR directly.

Figure 10.6 shows the memory map of a complete system configuration that uses TUTOR as the system monitor. The EPROM program space just above TUTOR contains code to read the first track of a disk in order to boot a full disk operating system (DOS). The only difference from the earlier memory configurations is that TUTOR is decoded at $FD0000 rather than $8000. This requires changing the reset vector: the actual object code contained within TUTOR is position-independent and will execute anywhere the EPROMs are decoded. The location of the two 6850 ACIA ports are also changed from $010040 up to $FF0040; the move is necessary to allow for a large block of RAM at low memory. The selection of the top $FF 64K page is because it can be easily decoded, and most I/O boards using the S-100 bus are located there. Although this memory map is designed for use in an IEEE Std-696 system, it can be used in any other system as well. There are very few constraints on how to organize your memory, and you can design it easily to match your own special requirements.

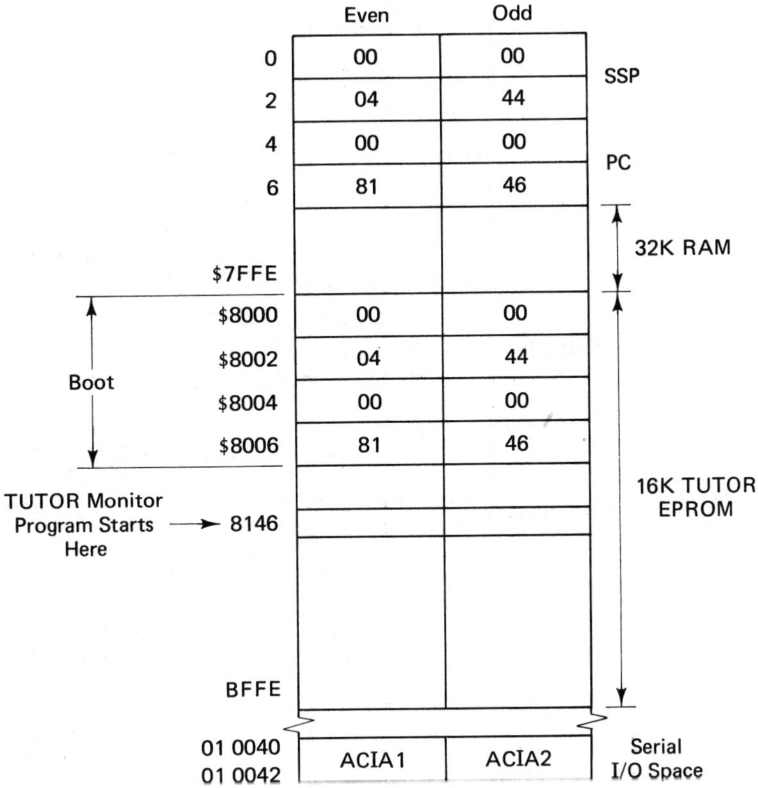

Figure 10.5 Memory map of the ECB with the TUTOR EPROM decoded at $8000. Upon reset, the EPROM code marked "Boot" is also decoded at address 0.

10.2 EPROM CIRCUIT DESIGN

The EPROM design for the first 68000 program can be as simple as the circuit shown in Figure 10.7. This configuration of two EPROMs can run the quick jump-to-location 8 program as shown in the memory map in Figure 10.2. No special decoding is used; the 2 data strobes and the lowest 11 address lines of the EPROMs are sufficient for 4,096 unique addresses.

Without using more address lines, only 4K different addresses are available out of the entire 16 Mb range of the 68000. For simple debugging and testing, however, this will be adequate. Recognize that the data in the lowest 4K is duplicated, or shadowed, into each following 4K because of the incomplete decoding. This means the data that appears at address 0 also appears at 0 + 4096, 0 + 8192, 0 + 12288, 0 + 16384, and so on through memory.

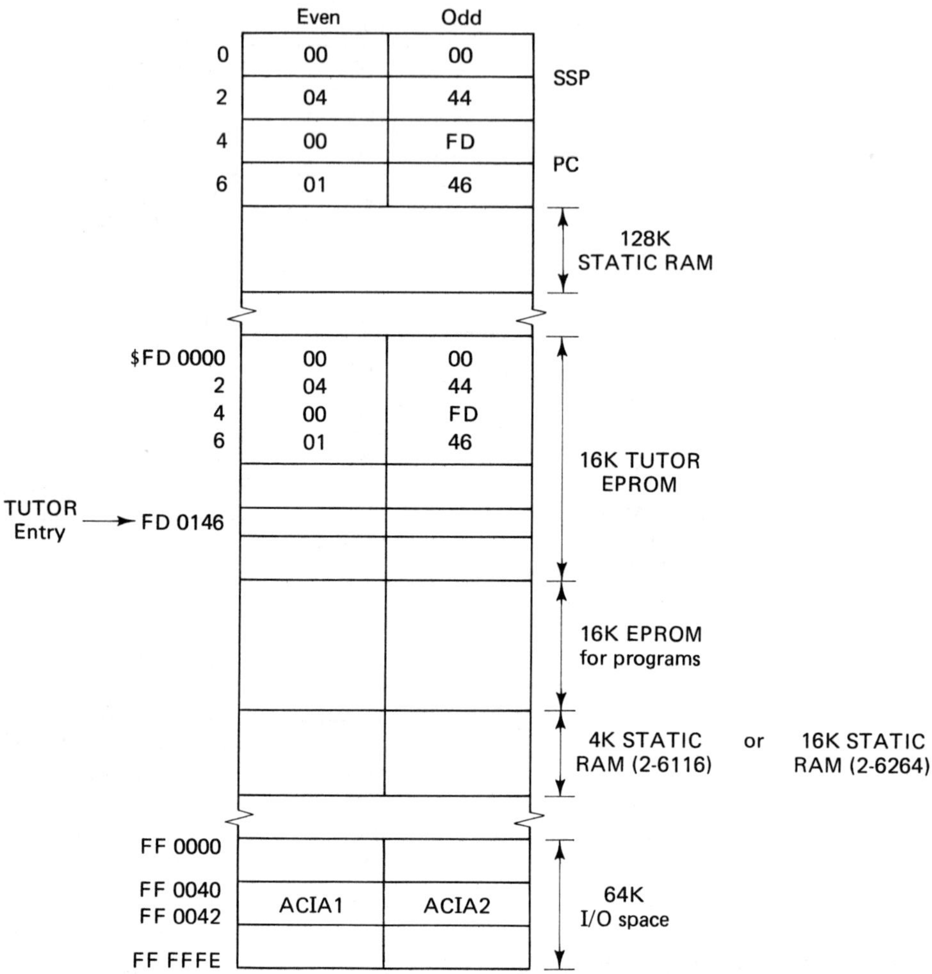

Figure 10.6 Memory map of a complete system using TUTOR as the monitor and having the capability of booting a disk operating system.

10.2.1 EPROM Wait Calculation

One of the most important concerns in designing memory to run with the 68000 is the response time of the memory devices. It takes EPROM and RAM chips a finite time from when they are addressed until when they can present valid data to the processor. If the 68000 ran slowly and the memory could respond quickly, then valid data would always be available. This is not the case, however, and you must provide a way for the 68000 to wait for slow memory devices.

The DTACK* and wait generator you designed in Chapter 9 will provide from 0 to 7 or 8 waits to lengthen the 68000 bus cycle. The sequence of states was S0, S1, S2, S3,

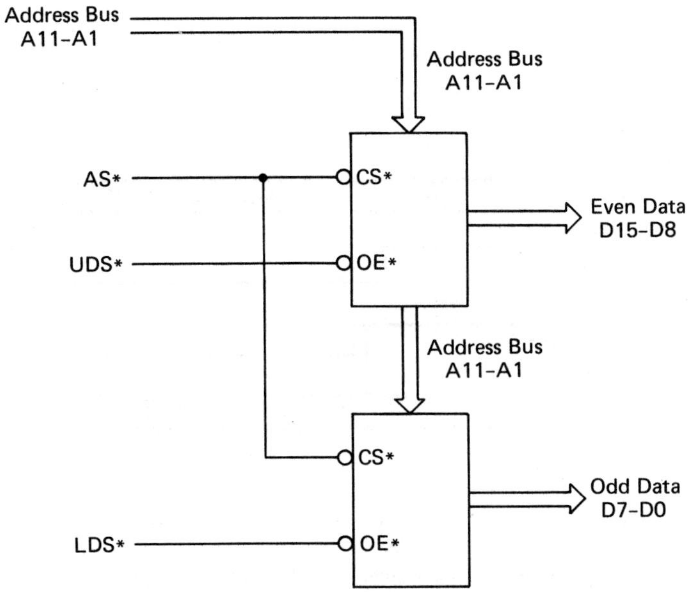

Figure 10.7 A first pair of EPROMs connected without address decoding logic. Using 2716s (2K × 8) without this decoding, the output data will repeat itself every 4K addresses.

S4, Sw, Sw, . . ., S5, S6, S7. You can use this wait generator to run the 68000 with slow memory. For example, if your memory is very slow you might add three waits to the 68000 bus cycle; every time the processor does a memory read or write, its bus cycle will be longer by three waits.

You can arbitrarily add as many waits as you like to the bus cycle, but the penalty is that the overall system performance will be slower. If a normal read bus cycle takes four clock cycles, adding in just one wait increases the bus cycle to five clock cycles; the effect is a 25 percent increase in bus cycle time. The system performance drops quite dramatically as waits are added: just two waits will increase bus cycle time by 50 percent. Consequently, it is necessary to calculate accurately how many waits are required; do not use more waits than absolutely necessary.

If you refer to the 2716 EPROM data sheets in the Appendix, you will find that there are two read modes specified:

- Read with chip-select always asserted, and
- Standby mode with chip-select asserted during the read.

To find how many waits are required for either mode, calculate how long the bus cycle must be. Next, divide this time by the time of one clock cycle to find how many clock cycles are in the bus cycle. Any amount over four clock cycles is the number of waits that must be added.

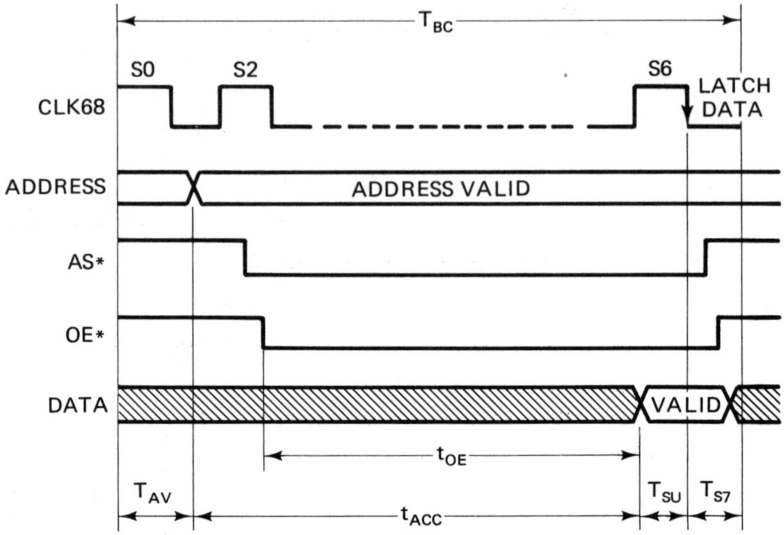

Figure 10.8 Timing diagram of EPROM-read when data-valid depends on the address; the EPROM CS* is held low continuously. The output enable, OE*, is derived from the 68000 data strobes and is assumed asserted at least t_{OE} before the data is valid.

Case I—Read with chip-select always asserted. This mode is even simpler than the circuit in Figure 10.7. The AS* signal is not used at all: ground the CS* inputs to the EPROMs directly. The EPROM outputs are enabled by the UDS* and LDS* signals connected to the OE* controls. The timing diagram for this circuit is shown in Figure 10.8; the various symbols used in the diagram are defined in Table 10.2.

TABLE 10.2 DEFINITION OF THE TIMES USED IN THE EPROM TIMING-DIAGRAM ANALYSIS. THE NUMBERS IN PARENTHESES REFER TO THE 68000 READ-CYCLE TIMING SPECIFICATION BUBBLE NUMBER.

T_{BC}	Time for complete bus cycle: four clock cycles + any waits
T_{CLK}	Period of system clock, CLK68
T_{Sx}	State x time (as T_{S0}, T_{S1}, etc.): half of T_{CLK}
T_{AV}	Time to address valid: $T_{S0} + t_{CLAV}$ (6)
T_{SEL}	Time to select device using ROMSEL* or RAMSEL*. Function of address, AS*, and decode propagation time.
T_{SU}	Setup time: Data-in to clock low at end of S6 (27)
t_{CS}	Chip select to output-valid delay
t_{OE}	Output enable to valid-output delay
t_{ACC}	Address to output delay
t_{CLAV}	Time of clock low to address valid (6)
t_{DICL}	Data in to clock low (27)
t_{CHSL}	Clock high to AS*, DS* low (9)

The analysis requires timing specifications on read and write cycles found in the 68000 technical manual (Section 8, "Electrical Specifications"). Several different columns of data are given depending on the processor actually used in the system. You must know or assume which 68000 you will be using; to complete the following analysis an 8 MHz processor is assumed. Assume also that the 68000 clock, CLK68, is running at 6 MHz.

The relevant time involved in Case I is how long from a valid address it takes the EPROMs to provide valid data. The data must be valid at least one setup time ahead of the end of S6 when the 68000 will latch whatever data is present. The bus cycle time beginning at S0 and continuing through S7 must be greater or equal to the sum of the times indicated in Figure 10.8:

$$T_{BC} > T_{AV} + t_{ACC} + T_{SU} + T_{S7}$$

where T_{AV} = Time from start of bus cycle until address is valid

$= T_{S0} + t_{CLAV}$

$= 167/2 + 70$

$= 153$ ns

t_{ACC} = Access time of the EPROM

= 450 ns (from EPROM data sheet)

$T_{SU} = t_{DICL}$ (68000 setup time for read)

= 15 ns

$T_{S7} = 167/2 = 83$ ns

so that $T_{BC} > 153 + 450 + 15 + 83$

> 701 ns

The total number of clock cycles in the bus cycle then becomes

$$N_{CCBC} = 701/167 = 4.2$$

A normal bus cycle is four clock cycles; therefore one wait must be added to run this system with a 6 MHz clock.

The analysis did not include the time t_{OE} indicated in Figure 10.8. The time t_{OE} = 120 ns maximum in the EPROM data sheet, and it will not be a problem as long as the EPROM OE* controls are connected to UDS* and LDS* from the 68000. The data strobes are asserted during S2, and remain asserted for S3, S4, S5, and S6; this time far exceeds the required 120 ns for the output to become valid.

Case II—Standby mode, chip-select asserted during read. This read mode is implemented by the Figure 10.7 circuit with the 68000 AS* signal connected to the CS* inputs to the EPROMs. As in Case I, the EPROM outputs are enabled by the UDS* and LDS* signals connected to the OE* controls. The timing diagram for this circuit is shown in Figure 10.9; the symbols used in the diagram are defined in Table 10.2 with those for

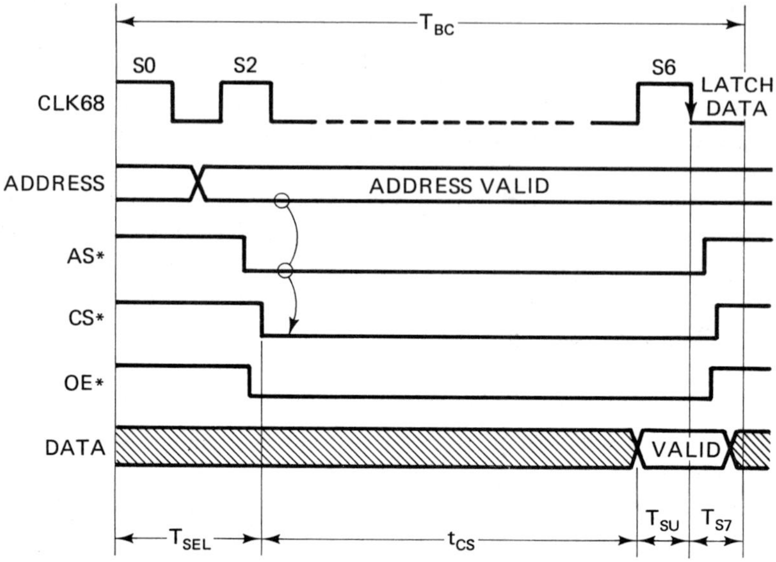

Figure 10.9 Timing diagram of EPROM-read when data-valid depends on the chip select; the chip select is a function of the address and AS*. The output enable, OE*, is derived from the 68000 data strobes as is assumed asserted at least t_{OE} before the data is valid.

Case I. As in Case I, assume an 8 MHz 68000 running with 6 MHz clock. Also, assume that there is no decoding propagation delay to obtain CS*.

The relevant time involved in Case II is how long from an asserted chip-select it takes the EPROMs to provide valid data. As before, the data must be valid at least one setup time ahead of the end of S6 when the 68000 will latch whatever data is present. The bus cycle time beginning at S0 and continuing through S7 must be greater or equal to the sum of the times indicated in Figure 10.9:

$$T_{BC} > T_{SEL} + t_{CS} + T_{SU} + T_{S7}$$

where

$$\begin{aligned} T_{SEL} &= \text{Time from start of bus cycle until CS* asserted} \\ &= T_{S0} + T_{S1} + t_{CHSL} \\ &= 83 + 83 + 60 \\ &= 227 \text{ ns} \end{aligned}$$

$$\begin{aligned} t_{CS} &= \text{Chip-select to output delay} \\ &= 450 \text{ ns (from EPROM data sheet)} \end{aligned}$$

$$\begin{aligned} T_{SU} &= t_{DICL} \text{ (68000 setup time for read)} \\ &= 15 \text{ ns} \end{aligned}$$

$$T_{S7} = 167/2 = 83 \text{ ns}$$

so that

$$T_{BC} > 227 + 450 + 15 + 83$$
$$> 775 \text{ ns}$$

The total number of clock cycles in the bus cycle then becomes

$$N_{CCBC} = 775/167 = 4.6$$

A normal bus cycle is four clock cycles; therefore one wait must be added to run this system with a 6 MHz clock.

10.2.2 Maximum Clock speed

The preceding calculations for the required number of waits can leave one somewhat unsure of the actual margin involved in a design. In Case I, the calculated number of required clock cycles is 4.2, so you add a wait cycle to the system to run the clock at 6 MHz. How fast can the system be run if no waits are provided? How fast can it run with the wait included? Likewise in Case II: how fast can the clock run with no waits and again if a wait is provided?

Case I–Read with chip-select always asserted. The calculation follows the same general form as described earlier and sketeched in Figure 10.8:

$$T_{BC} = T_{AV} + t_{ACC} + T_{SU} + T_{S7}$$

If no waits are provided, there are eight clock states, T_S, in the bus cycle. Substituting in the values used before and assuming an 8 MHz 68000, solve the equation for T_S:

$$8T_S = (T_S + 70) + 450 + 15 + T_S$$
$$6T_S = 535$$
$$T_S = 89 \text{ ns}$$

The clock period is twice the state time (89 × 2) or 178 ns. The maximum clock is therefore 1/178 ns, or 5.6 MHz.

Suppose that one wait is provided so the EPROM can run at 6 MHz. How fast can the system operate? One wait will add two clock states to the bus cycle, so solve the modified equation for T_S:

$$10T_S = (T_S + 70) + 450 + 15 + T_S$$
$$8T_S = 535$$
$$T_S = 67 \text{ ns}$$

The clock period for this state time is 134 ns. With one wait, the maximum clock is therefore about 7.5 MHz.

Case II–Standby mode, chip-select asserted during read. The calculation follows the same general form as described earlier and drawn in Figure 10.9:

$$T_{BC} = T_{SEL} + t_{CS} + T_{SU} + T_{S7}$$

If no waits are provided, there are eight clock states, T_S, in the bus cycle. Substituting in the values used before and assuming an 8 MHz 68000, solve the equation for T_S:

$$\begin{aligned} 8T_S &= (T_S + T_S + 60) + 15 + T_S \\ 5T_S &= 525 \\ T_S &= 105 \text{ ns} \end{aligned}$$

The clock period for this state time is 210 ns. Consequently, with no waits, the EPROM can be run at a maximum frequency of about 4.8 MHz.

Add the one wait required so the 68000 system can run at 6 MHz. How fast can the processor run now? Modify the equation as in Case I to get:

$$\begin{aligned} 10T_S &= (T_S + T_S + 60) + 450 + 15 + T_S \\ 7T_S &= 525 \\ T_S &= 75 \text{ ns} \end{aligned}$$

The clock period for this state time is 150 ns. So one wait will allow the system to operate at about 6.7 MHz maximum.

10.3 ADDRESS DECODER DESIGN

In the first EPROM circuit in Figure 10.7, it was not necessary to include any address decoding because the processor operated just in low memory EPROM space. When you make the transition to the more advanced memory map in Figure 10.3 that locates EPROM memory at $8000, then an address decoder is necessary.

The new EPROM circuit with address decoding is shown in Figure 10.10. It is identical to the earlier circuit in Figure 10.7 except that a ROMSEL* control connects to the CS* inputs to select the EPROMs. Instead of just AS*, now the EPROMs are selected only on a particular address qualified by AS*. Notice that the new diagram indicates all the address lines A23 through A1 connected to the decoder and EPROMs. This implies that the decoded address is unique in the entire 16 Mb of possible addresses.

The EPROM circuit need not be fully decoded like this, however. Instead of using all the 68000 address lines, partial decoding can be used. The first EPROM design used partial decoding (done by the EPROMs' internal circuits) to give 4,096 unique addresses. Because of the partial use of the address bus, the EPROMs were selected for every address that was a multiple of 4,096.

Block decoding is a viable compromise between the full decoding of all addresses and the partial decoding done within the EPROMs or other memory devices. Block decoding means that the high-order, or most significant, bits of the 68000 address bus are used to separate the total 16 Mb into smaller pieces that are unique among themselves. For example, suppose that you build the simple decoder circuit shown in Figure 10.11. This decoder responds to the 8 highest address bits and not to any of the lower bits. When any

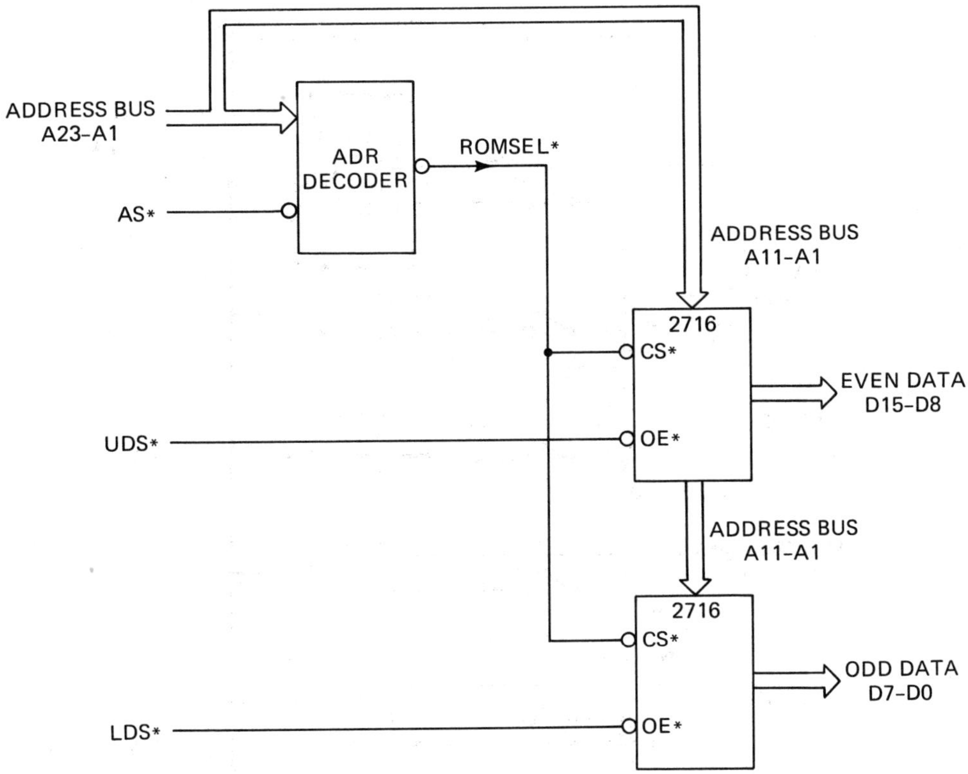

Figure 10.10 Byte-addressable 2716 EPROM pair providing a total of 4K bytes of nonvolatile memory. The 68000 can read the even EPROM, the odd EPROM, or both EPROMs together as a 16-bit word.

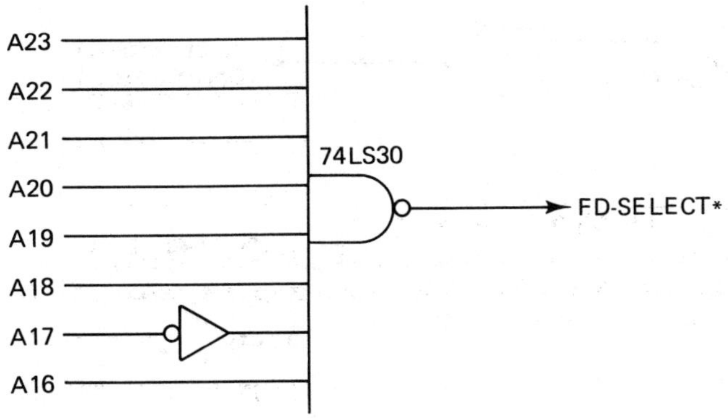

Figure 10.11 A simple address decoder circuit. When the high-address bits select the 64K page starting at address FDxxxx, then the output FD-SELECT* is asserted.

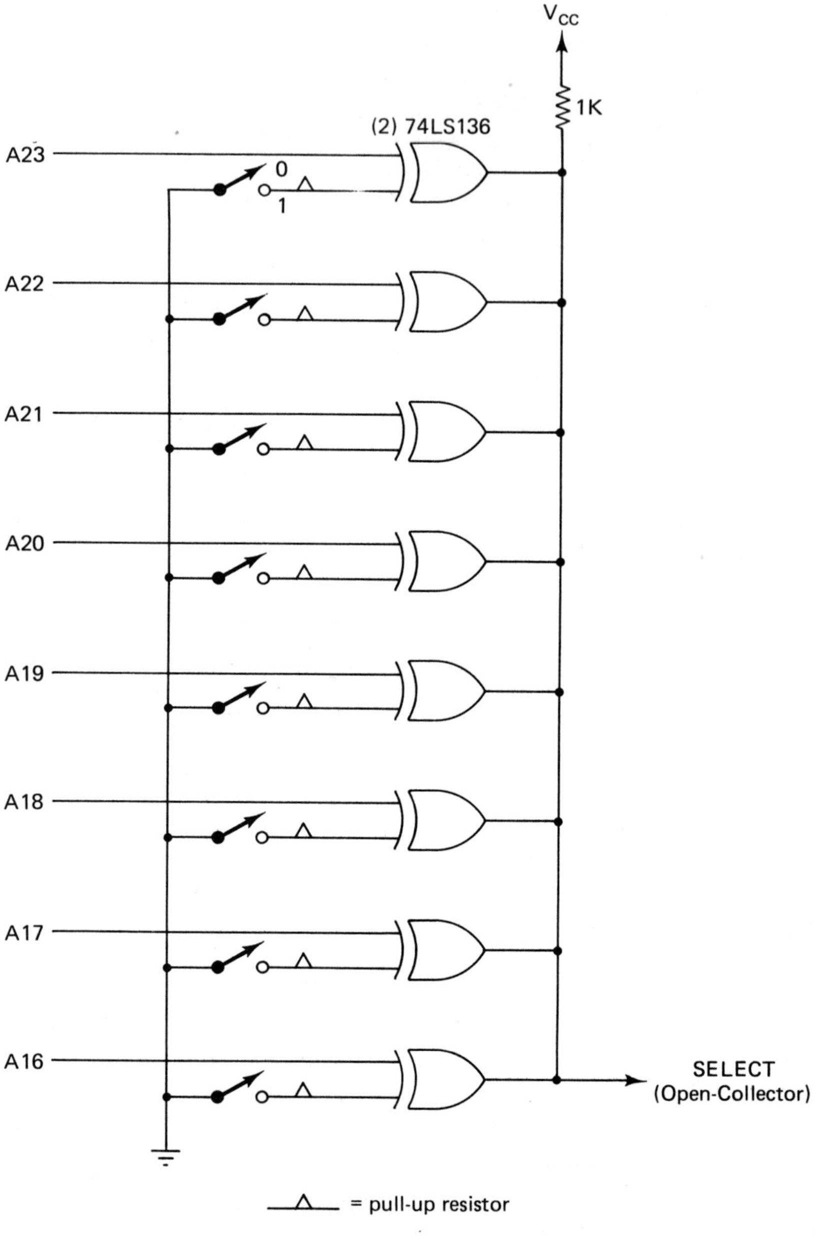

Figure 10.12 An address-decoder circuit that will select any 64K page of memory from the entire 16 Mb range of the 68000. With all the switches open as drawn, this decoder will assert SELECT for the lowest 64K starting at address 0.

address in the range $FD0000 to $FDFFFF appears on the address bus, then FD-SELECT* is asserted. It responds for just one 64K page out of all 256 64K pages that the 68000 can address.

Although this block decoder circuit has very few parts, it is not especially flexible. If you want to configure memory differently, say for selection of block $AB, then you need to recognize the A23-A16 bit pattern of 1010 1011; rather than one inverter, now there are three required.

The circuit shown in Figure 10.12 provides the flexibility of being able to change the block address easily. Two 74LS136 packages, a SIP resistor, and an eight-position DIP switch is all that is required. Following the same approach, but using one IC package, an 8-bit equal-to-comparator can be connected as in Figure 10.13. Finally, Figure 10.14 illustrates a block-address decoder with one IC package having internal pull-up resistors.

Within any 64K block, you can decode into smaller blocks of 8K each using a 74LS138 3- to 8-line decoder. If, for example, you intend to use two 2732 EPROMs (each 4K bytes × 8 bits), then both their CS* controls connected to one 74LS138 output will provide full address decoding. In this case, following Figure 10.10, the decoding is done by

A23–A16	64K block decode (Figures 10.11–10.14)
A15–A13	74LS138 3-to-8 decoders (Each output makes a ROMSEL*)
A12–A1	Both 2732 chips
UDS*, LDS*	Even EPROM, Odd EPROM output enables

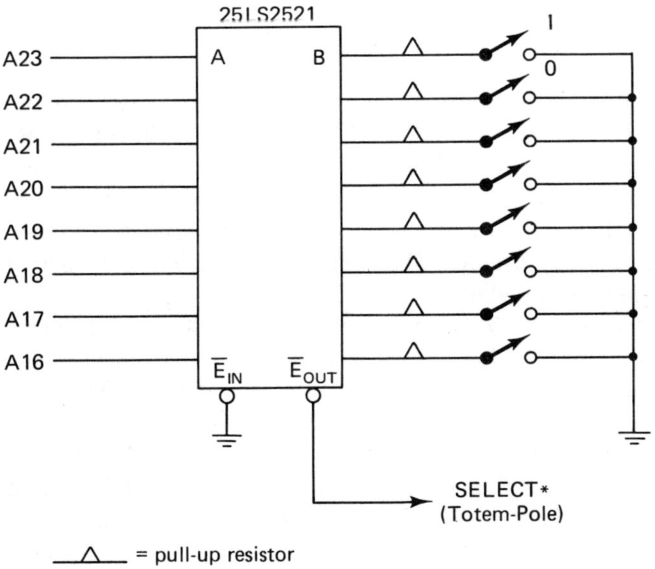

Figure 10.13 An address-decoder circuit using a single IC package; this circuit will select any 64K page of memory from the entire 16 Mb range of the 68000. With all the switches open as drawn, the decoder will assert SELECT* for the top 64K page starting at FF0000. Note that the switch logic is opposite from the previous circuit.

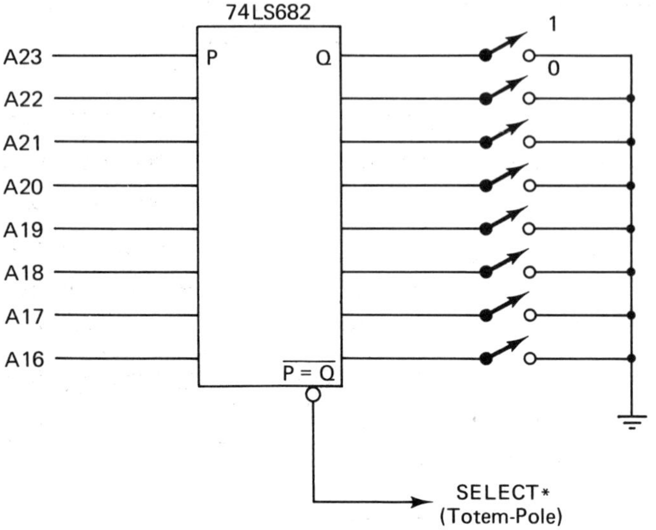

Figure 10.14 An address decoder using an 8-bit magnitude comparator with built-in pullup resistors. The 74LS683 provides the same function but has an open-collector output. The decoder will select any 64K page from memory. With all the switches open, the decoder will assert SELECT* for the top 64K page starting at FF0000.

10.4 RESET VECTOR GENERATION

When you configure the system memory to Figure 10.3 with EPROM located at $8000 (or anywhere but 0), you must still provide some way for the 68000 to read its SSP and PC when reset. A straightforward approach might be to decode at $8000 for programs or a TUTOR monitor and also decode a pair of EPROMs at 0 as well. These EPROMs would contain not only the reset vectors, but also the various other exception vectors outlined in Table 10.1. Unfortunately, this means that you cannot change the exception vector addresses dynamically: any change requires a new pair of EPROMs.

Another way to obtain the reset vectors might be to use the approach taken in the ECB design shown in Figure 10.15. In this technique, the first 8 bytes of the (TUTOR) EPROM pair contain the SSP and PC vectors. When addresses 0 through 7 appear on the address bus, then the EPROMs are selected; when addresses $8000 through $BFFF appear, they are also selected. Examine the memory map in Figure 10.5 again: the contents of the EPROMs appear in two memory locations. The reset PC is $8146 where the 68000 begins executing TUTOR initialization code.

This technique assumes that the EPROMs are in one location, $8000, and they stay there forever. Any changes in the base address of the EPROM set to implement a new system configuration such as Figure 10.6 will require reworking the address decoder. The design in Figure 10.16 avoids this completely: rather than recognize a particular address such as 0 through 7, it responds to the system reset signal and enables the EPROMs only during the first four bus cycles. While enabling the EPROMs, it disables RAM that might be decoded in low memory so that there are no problems with bus contention.

The reset sequence for this circuit is shown in Figure 10.17. The signal BOOT-CLR* from the reset module is low only while the 68000 is being reset: it causes the outputs of the 74LS164 to go low. One of these outputs, Q_D, enables the EPROM pair and deselects RAM. Then, after four positive-going AS* edges, the Q_D output goes high

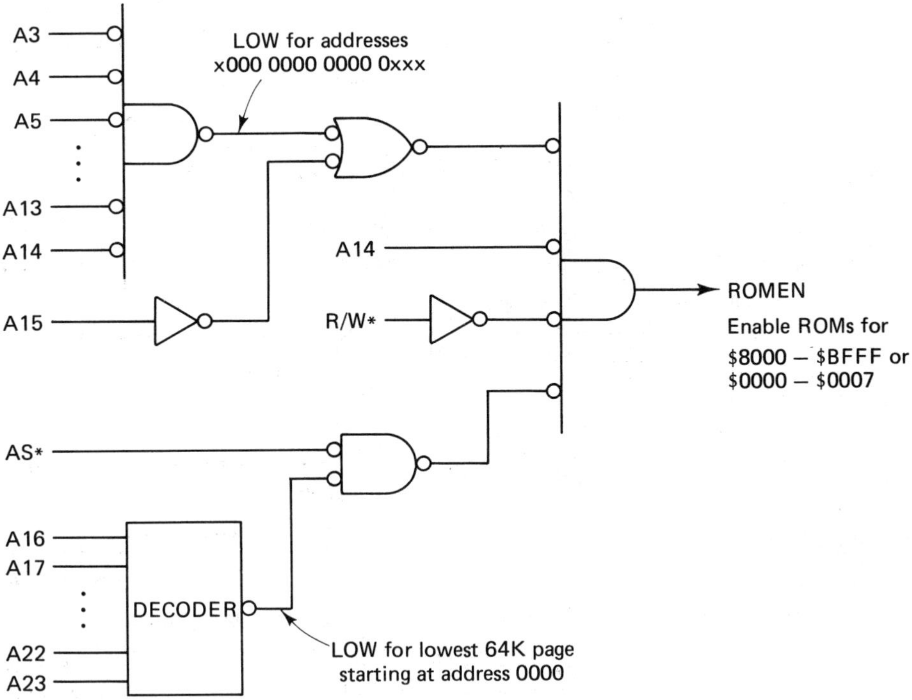

Figure 10.15 Technique used in the Educational Computer Board to provide the reset vectors at address 0. Whatever is stored in the first 8 bytes of the ROM pair appears at address 0 *and* address $8000.

and disables the EPROMs. Note though, that the first bus cycle after the reset is still in EPROM memory space so that the system can get properly initialized; the only difference is that this bus cycle is not addressing low memory anymore.

10.5 AN EXAMPLE RAM DESIGN

One valid way of understanding an unfamiliar area, such as designing the RAM module, is to study an application note from the manufacturer. As part of new product introduction, and current product support, most semiconductor manufacturers publish a number of papers and notes on how to use their products. Motorola's Application Note AN-867 on designing a high-performance MC68000 system operating at 12.5 MHz is useful in considering RAM design.

Figure 10.18 shows an outline of the memory circuit used in the system. No wait states are provided because one of the design objectives was maximum-speed operation. Given this situation, examine the design and evaluate whether the system truly meets worst-case timing at 12.5 MHz and find the time-critical gates. The symbols used in the read and write analysis are shown in Table 10.3 and Table 10.4, respectively.

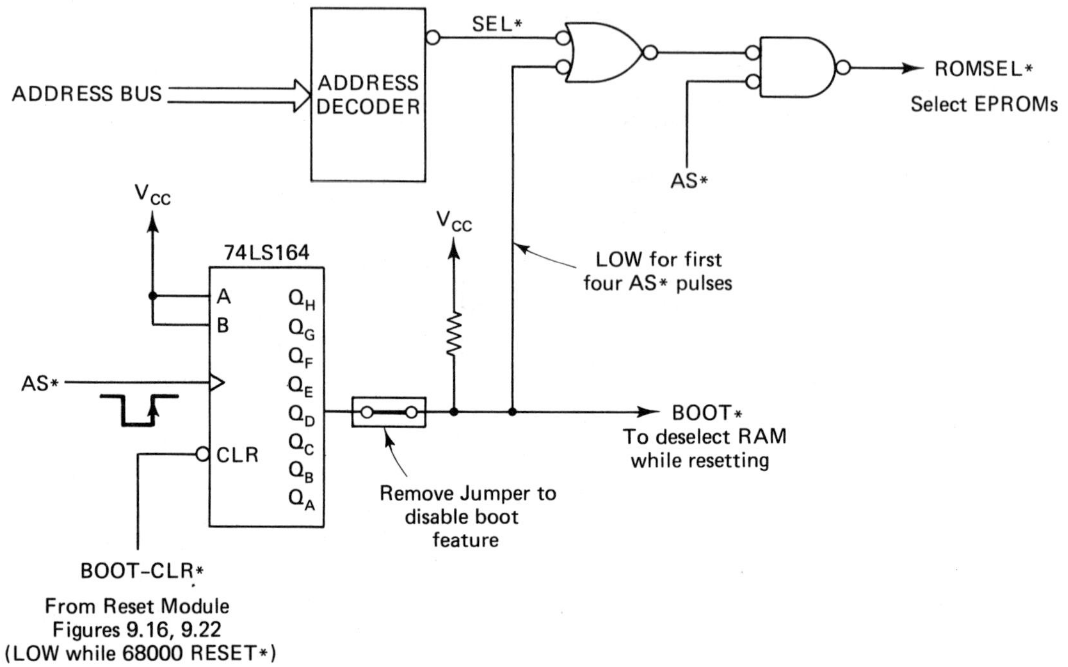

Figure 10.16 One method of obtaining ROMSEL* when the 68000 is first reset. Any RAM that might be decoded at address 0 is deselected during BOOT* to avoid bus contention.

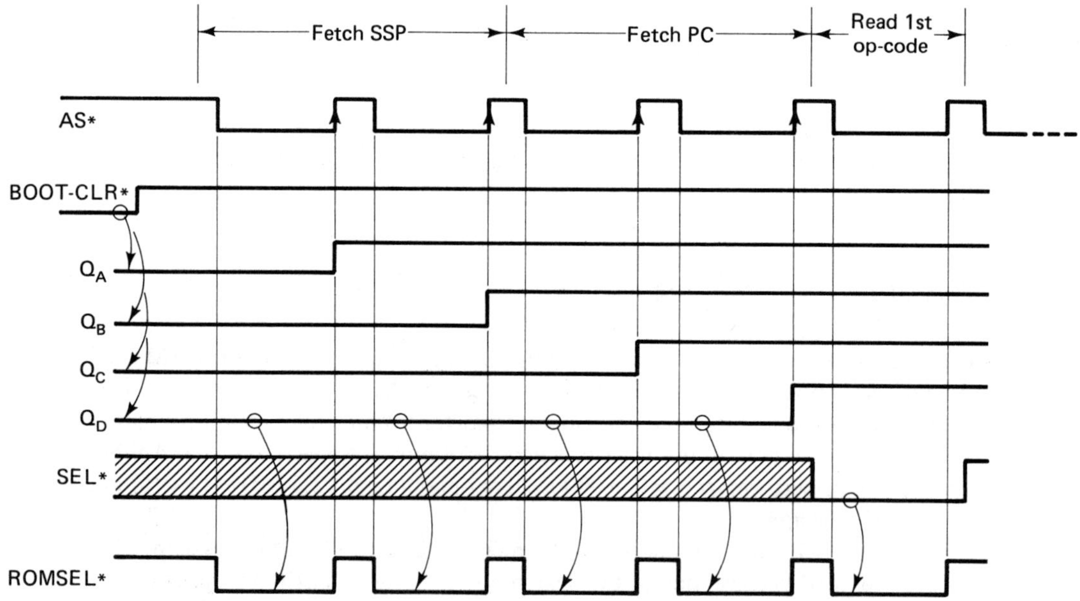

Figure 10.17 Timing diagram of the boot circuit. ROMSEL* is asserted by Q_D during the first four bus cycles; after that, ROM is selected based on the address being decoded.

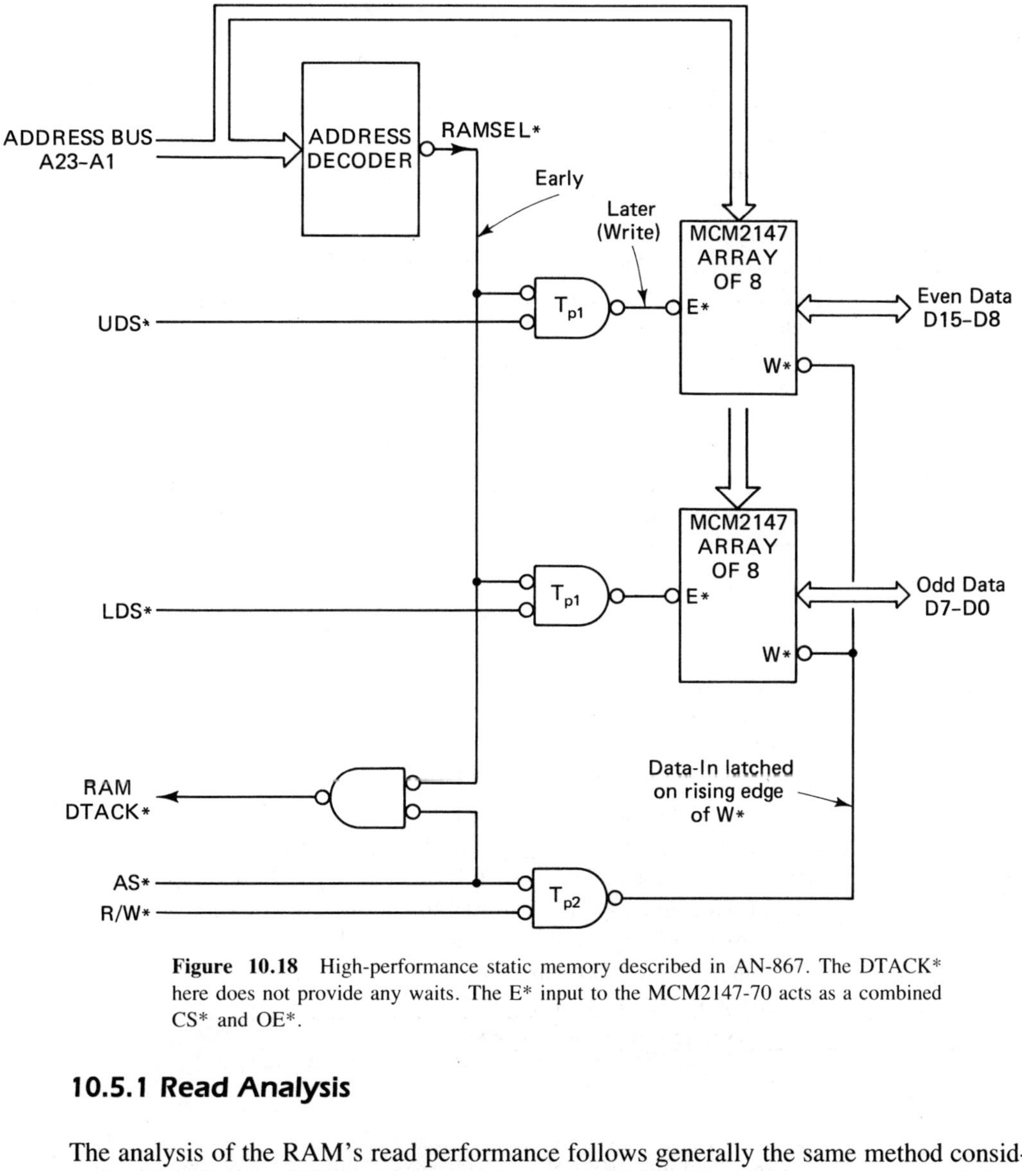

Figure 10.18 High-performance static memory described in AN-867. The DTACK* here does not provide any waits. The E* input to the MCM2147-70 acts as a combined CS* and OE*.

10.5.1 Read Analysis

The analysis of the RAM's read performance follows generally the same method considered earlier for the EPROMs. The E* input to the MCM2147-70 (4K × 1 bit) RAMs functions the same as the EPROM chip-select and output-enable combined: when a valid address is present, asserting E* will get data output. This output data must be valid at least one setup time ahead of the end of S6 when the 68000 will latch whatever data is present. The bus cycle time beginnng at S0 and continuing through S7 must be greater than or equal to the sum of the times indicated in Figure 10.19:

$$T_{BC} > T_{SEL} + T_{ELQV} + T_{SU} + T_{S7}$$

TABLE 10.3 DEFINITION OF THE TIMES USED IN THE MCM2147 RAM-READ TIMING-DIAGRAM ANALYSIS. THE NUMBERS IN PARENTHESES REFER TO THE 68000 READ-CYCLE TIMING SPECIFICATION BUBBLE NUMBER.

T_{BC}	Time for complete bus cycle: four clock cycles + any waits
T_{CLK}	Period of system clock, CLK68
T_{Sx}	State x time (as T_{S0}, T_{S1}, etc.): half of T_{CLK}
T_{AV}	Time to address valid: $T_{S0} + t_{CLAV}$ (6)
T_{DS*}	Time until UDS*, LDS* are valid: $T_{S0} + T_{S1} + t_{CHSL}$ *(9)*
$T_{RAMSEL*}$	Time to decode address and assert RAMSEL*
T_{SEL}	Time to select device using E. Function of address, UDS*, LDS*, and decode propagation time.
T_{P1}	Propagation time through the gate at E* input to RAM
T_{SU}	Setup time: Data-in to clock-low at end of S6: t_{DICL} (27)
t_{ELQV}	Enable-low to output-valid time
t_{CHSL}	Clock-high to AS*, DS* low (9)
t_{CLAV}	Time of clock-low to address valid (6)
t_{DICL}	Data-in to clock-low (27)

TABLE 10.4 DEFINITION OF THE TIMES USED IN THE MCM2147 RAM-WRITE TIMING-DIAGRAM ANALYSIS. THE NUMBERS IN PARENTHESES REFER TO THE 68000 WRITE-CYCLE TIMING SPECIFICATION BUBBLE NUMBER.

T_{BC}	Time for complete bus cycle: four clock cycles + any waits
T_{CLK}	Period of system clock, CLK68
T_{Sx}	State x time (as T_{S0}, T_{S1}, etc.): half of T_{CLK}
T_{DS*}	Time until UDS*, LDS* are valid for write: $T_{S0} + T_{S1} + T_{S2} + T_{S3} + t_{CHSL}$ *(9)*
T_{P1}	Propagation time through the gate at E* input of RAM
T_{P2}	Propagation time through the gate at W* input of RAM
T_{WREN}	Time to write-enable device using E: $T_{DS*} + T_{P1}$
t_{ELWH}	Time from chip enable low to write high
t_{WHDX}	Time from write-high to data-not-valid (RAM hold time)
t_{CHSL}	Clock-high to AS*, DS* low (9)
t_{CLSH}	Clock-low to AS* high (12)
t_{SHDOI}	AS*, DS* high to data-out invalid (25)

where

$$T_{SEL} = \text{Time from start of bus cycle until E* asserted}$$
$$= T_{P1} + \text{The larger of either}$$

$$T_{RAMSEL*} = T_{AV} + T_{\text{decoder}}$$
$$= T_{S0} + t_{CLAV(6)} + T_{\text{decoder}}$$

or

$$T_{DS*} = T_{S0} + T_{S1} + t_{CHSL(9)}$$

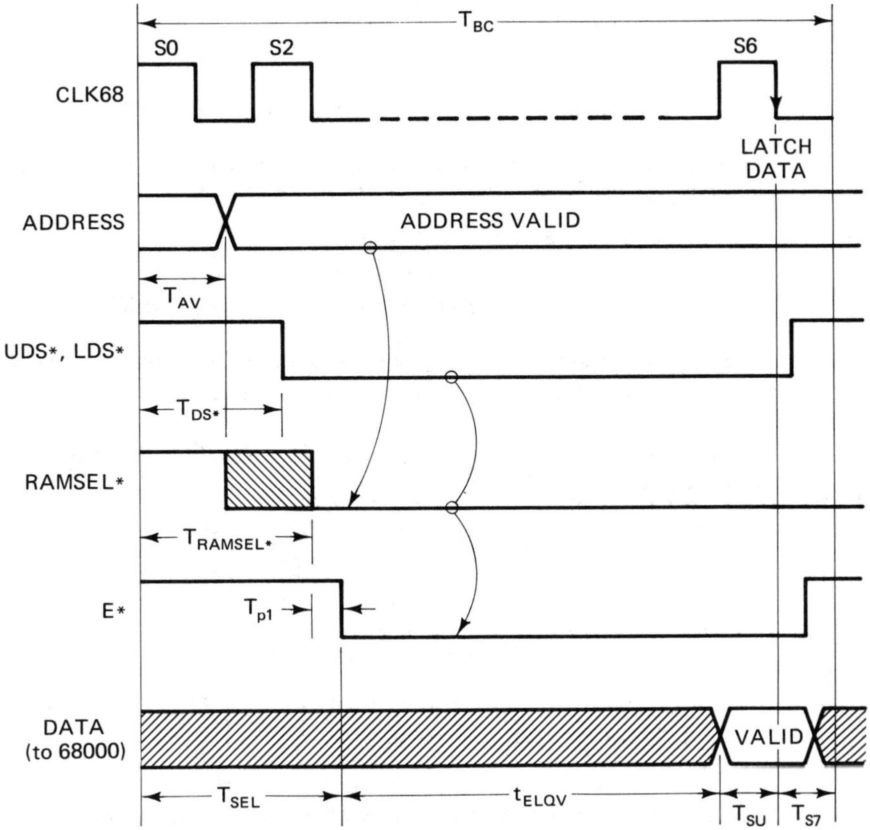

Figure 10.19 Read-timing diagram of MCM2147 RAM circuit in AN-867.

t_{ELQV} = Enable-low to output-valid (from RAM data sheet)

T_{SU} = $t_{\mathrm{DICL}(27)}$ Setup time for 68000 read

Use the above relationships and some of the facts about the system as described in the applicaton note. First, the system clock is 12.5 MHz (T_S = 40 ns), so the 68000 must, of necessity, be rated for that speed: any data from the 68000 data sheet must be for the high-speed processor. There are four levels of gates in the decoder, so the worst-case propagation delay for 74LS-TTL components is 4 × 22 ns, or 88 ns total. The one OR gate marked "T_{P1}" and located at the E* input to the RAM array is a 74LS32 for the initial analysis; it is T_{P1} = 22 ns in the worst case.

First, calculate the time for the RAM-select signal to get to the 74LS32 gate at the E* input. At this point in the analysis, it is not certain whether the slower select signal is from the decoder circuit or from the data strobes. Calculate the time involved in propagating the signal through the address-decoder circuit:

$$\begin{aligned} T_{RAMSEL*} &= T_{AV} + T_{\text{decoder}} \\ &= T_{SO} + t_{CLAV(6)} + T_{\text{decoder}} \\ &= 40 + 55 + 88 \\ &= 183 \text{ ns to get a select to the 74LS32.} \end{aligned}$$

Second, calculate the time to propagate a select signal to the 74LS32 gate from the data strobe controls:

$$\begin{aligned} T_{DS*} &= T_{SO} + T_{S1} + t_{CHSL(9)} \\ &= 40 + 40 + 55 \\ &= 135 \text{ ns to get a select to the 74LS32.} \end{aligned}$$

This signal is earlier than the select signal from the address decoder and will not affect the overall bus-cycle timing. Use the longer time, $T_{RAMSEL*}$, in the following calculations.

Third, calculate the time from the start of the bus cycle until E* is asserted. Base this on the slower select time above.

$$\begin{aligned} T_{SEL} &= T_{P1} + T_{RAMSEL*} \\ &= 22 + 183 \\ &= 205 \text{ ns to assert E*.} \end{aligned}$$

Next, substitute into the bus-cycle relationship to find

$$\begin{aligned} T_{BC} &> T_{SEL} + t_{ELQV} + T_{SU} + T_{S7} \\ &> 205 + 70 + 10 + 40 \\ &> 325 \text{ ns for a complete bus cycle.} \end{aligned}$$

Last, find the total number of clock cycles in the bus cycle:

$$N_{CCBC} = 325/80 = 4.06$$

This value indicates that a wait must be included in the given system. It is only 5 ns too slow in the worst case, and would probably work quite well as is. An easy fix, however, is to substitute a 74S32 for the 74LS32 OR gate at the E* input to RAM. The higher speed Schottky TTL has a maximum propagation time of 7 ns rather than 22 ns; thus, the bus cycle time will be faster by 15 ns and within the 320 ns maximum. With this simple change, the worst-case RAM read will perform as intended.

10.5.2 Write Analysis

The write analysis is based on the timing diagram in Figure 10.20. First, the RAM must be selected as it was earlier for a read by asserting the E* control input. Then, to accomplish the write operation, the W* control must also be asserted. The actual write takes place during the overlap time while E* and W* are both asserted. The data write will be successful as long as E*- low to W*- high (specified as t_{ELWH}) is sufficiently long *and* the data-hold requirements are met. Both conditions must be verified as successfully met when completing the write analysis.

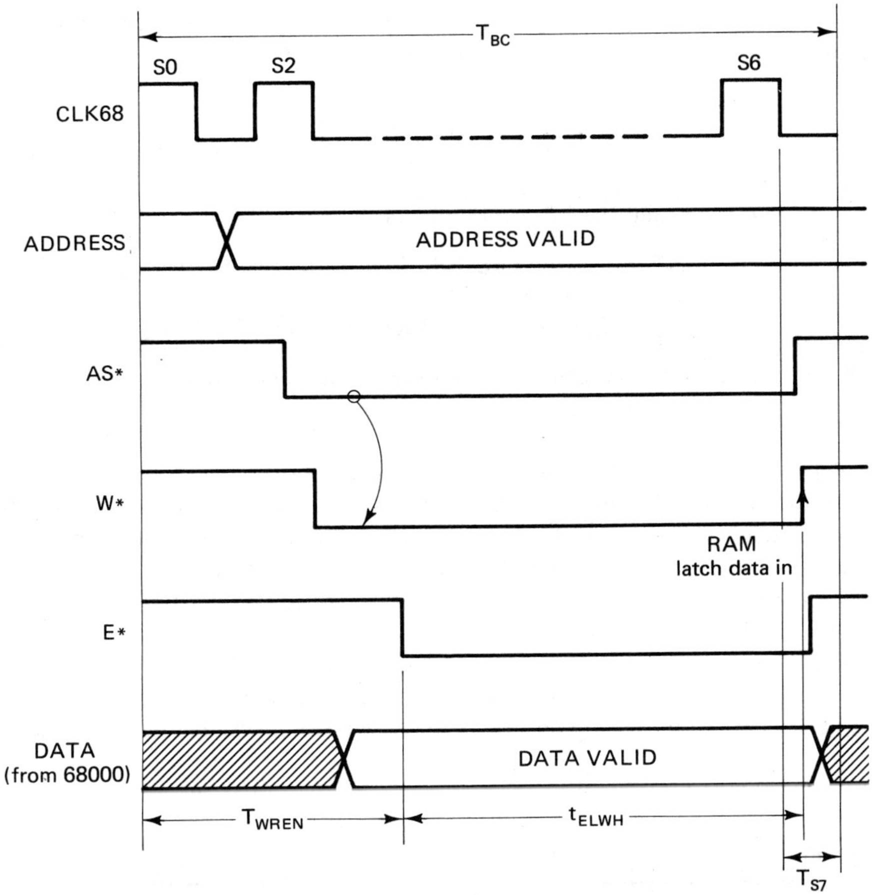

Figure 10.20 Write-timing diagram of the MCM2147 RAM circuit in AN-867. E* is a function of RAMSEL* and the data strobes.

The first condition on the overlap time can be expressed as part of the bus cycle time:

$$T_{BC} > T_{WREN} + t_{ELWH} + T_{S7} \text{ (for the worst case)}$$

where

$$\begin{aligned} T_{WREN} &= \text{Time from the start of bus cycle until E* is asserted} \\ &= T_{P1} + T_{DS^*} \\ &= T_{P1} + T_{S0} + T_{S1} + T_{S2} + T_{S3} + t_{CHSL(9)} \end{aligned}$$

$$t_{ELWH} = \text{Enable E*-low to write W*-high (from RAM data sheet)}$$

Use the same general facts as in the read analysis concerning the 68000 clock at 12.5 MHz and the high-speed 68000 data-sheet information. All the same decoder times are still relevant, except that the propagation delay (183 ns) will not control when E* is asserted; this is because the data strobes are delayed by one clock cycle during a write operation. The time to get E* asserted becomes

$$\begin{aligned} T_{WREN} &= T_{P1} + T_{S0} + T_{S1} + T_{S2} + T_{S3} + T_{CHSL(9)} \\ &= 22 + 40 + 40 + 40 + 40 + 55 \\ &= 237 \text{ ns to assert E*.} \end{aligned}$$

Next, substitute into the bus-cycle relationship to find

$$\begin{aligned} T_{BC} &> T_{WREN} + t_{ELWH} + T_{S7} \text{ (for the worst case)} \\ &> 237 + 55 + 40 \\ &> 332 \text{ ns for a complete bus cycle.} \end{aligned}$$

Last, find the total number of clock cycles in the bus cycle:

$$N_{CCBC} = 332/80 = 4.15$$

This value indicates that a wait is also required for the system to perform at 12.5 MHz. However, this calculation is based on the 74LS32 OR gate at the E* input. It has to be changed to a 74S32 for proper worst-case performance of the read and appears necessary for the write case as well. How does this change affect the analysis? Make $T_{P1} = 7$ ns maximum instead of 22 ns to find that $T_{BC} = 317$ ns. This should be an adequate correction for the write operation.

The second condition on data-hold time must now be verified for the complete write analysis. An expanded view of the write timing diagram is shown in Figure 10.21; refer back to Figure 10.18 for the circuit. The issue of concern is whether the 68000 holds the

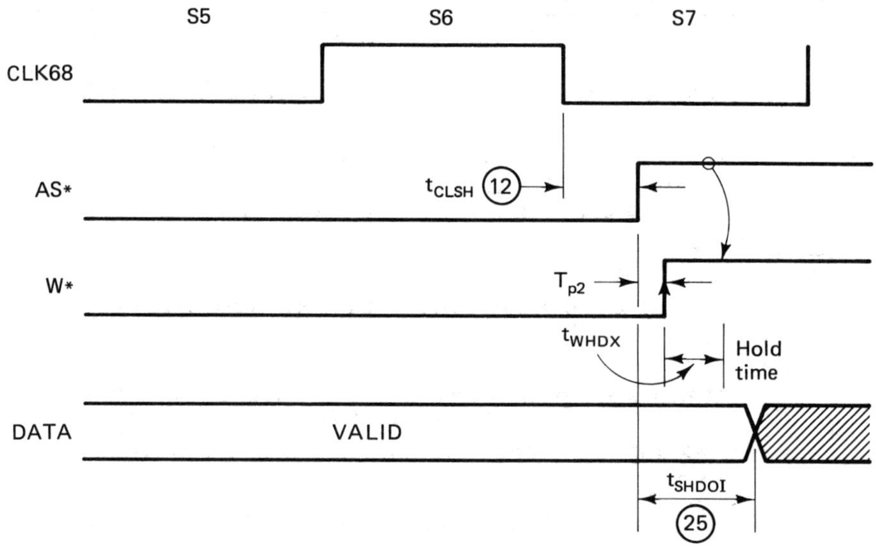

Figure 10.21 Detail sketch of the timing at the end of the MCM2147 write bus cycle.

data bus valid long enough to meet the RAM data-hold requirement. At the end of the write, the sequence of events is this:

- The 68000 negates AS*.
- T_{P2} ns later, W* is negated.
- The t_{WHDX} hold time is fulfilled.
- The data bus becomes invalid after t_{SHDOI} ns.

This indicates that the 68000 *must* hold the data valid for at least t_{WHDX} beyond W* high. This can be expressed as

$$\begin{aligned} T_{P2} &< t_{SHDOI(25)} - t_{WHDX} \\ &< 15 - 10 \\ &< 5 \text{ ns propagation delay through gate at W* input.} \end{aligned}$$

It appears that the OR gate at the W* input is very time-critical and must also be a Schottky device. If the 74S32 is specified, it will have a maximum worst-case propagation time of 7 ns, which is still 2 ns too long. For all practical purposes, however, one can quite safely assume that this will not cause a problem; this is because the bus itself will tend to retain its data somewhat beyond t_{SHDOI}.

10.6 EPROM AND RAM CIRCUIT DESIGN

The complete memory block diagram for a practical operational system is shown in Figure 10.22. It is divided up into several main sections: the address decoder, the memory control logic, and the EPROM and RAM array. The address decoder and EPROM designs are based on the byte-addressable block diagram in Figure 10.10; the RAM design is completely new, but is based on the MCM2147 application in Figure 10.18. The memory control logic is a combination of the data strobes and the 68000 read/write control. The analysis of the complete system developed here will be based on the methods developed earlier to determine the number of waits and maximum clock speed for both reading and writing.

The address decoder circuit for the system is shown in Figure 10.23. The top 64K page address is switch-selectable so that the EPROMs and RAM can be located anywhere in the 16 Mb range of the 68000. Within the selected 64K, ROMSEL* can be jumpered to decode at 0 and RAMSEL* decode at $8000; the jumper can reverse this so ROMSEL* is at $8000 and RAMSEL* decodes at 0. The boot circuit from Figure 10.16 provides ROMSEL* (and negates RAMSEL*) when the system is first reset. The LOCAL output tells the wait generator (Figure 9.23) to provide the proper number of waits for the on-board EPROM and RAM memory.

The idea in being able to jumper-configure EPROM at either 0 or $8000 is flexibility when deveoping the new system. The first programs (like the one in Figure 10.2) require the EPROMS to appear at address 0. However, the goal is to get the system running under the original TUTOR as soon as possible. This requires decoding EPROMs at $8000 and

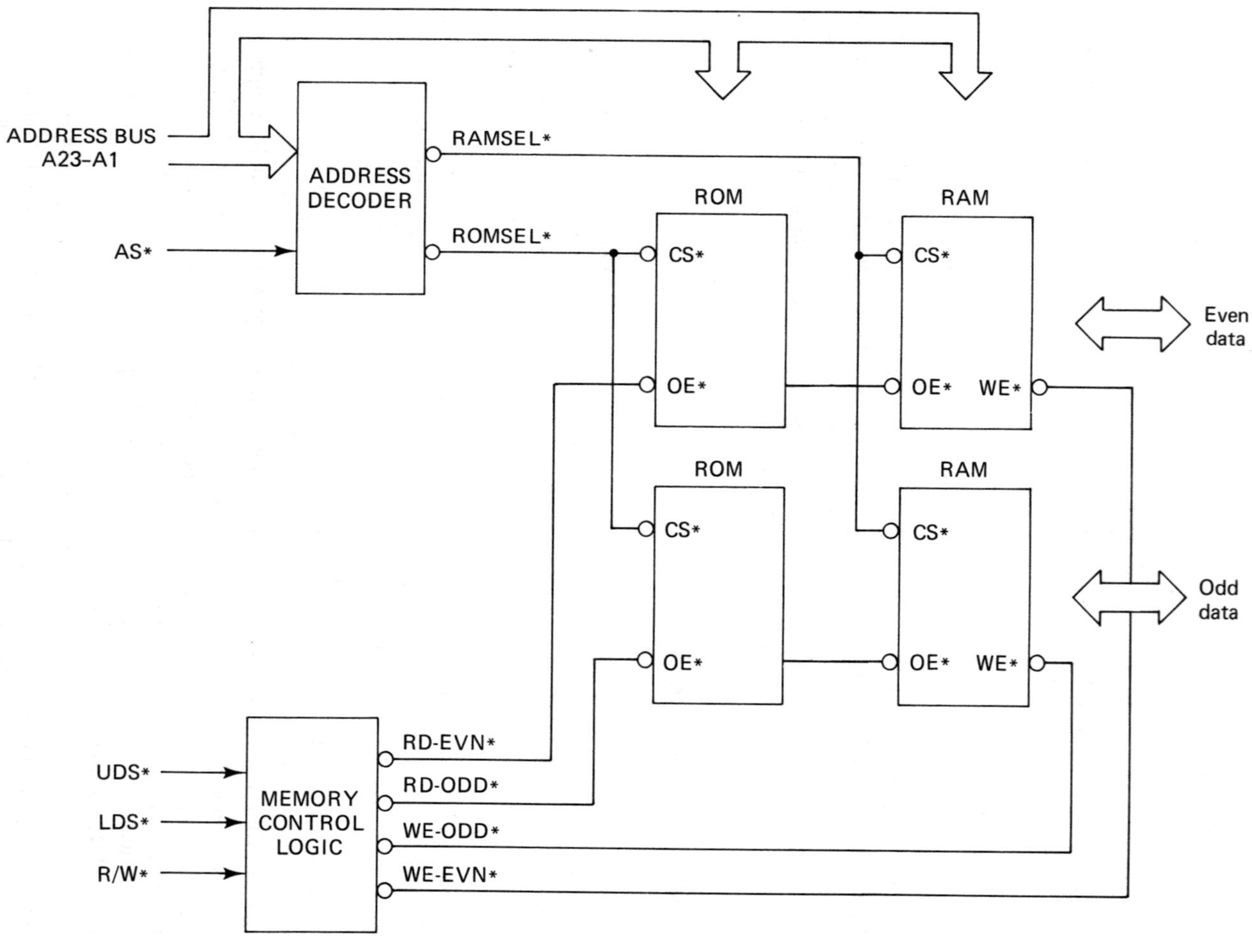

Figure 10.22 Address decoding and control of byte-addressable memory containing both EPROM pairs and RAM pairs.

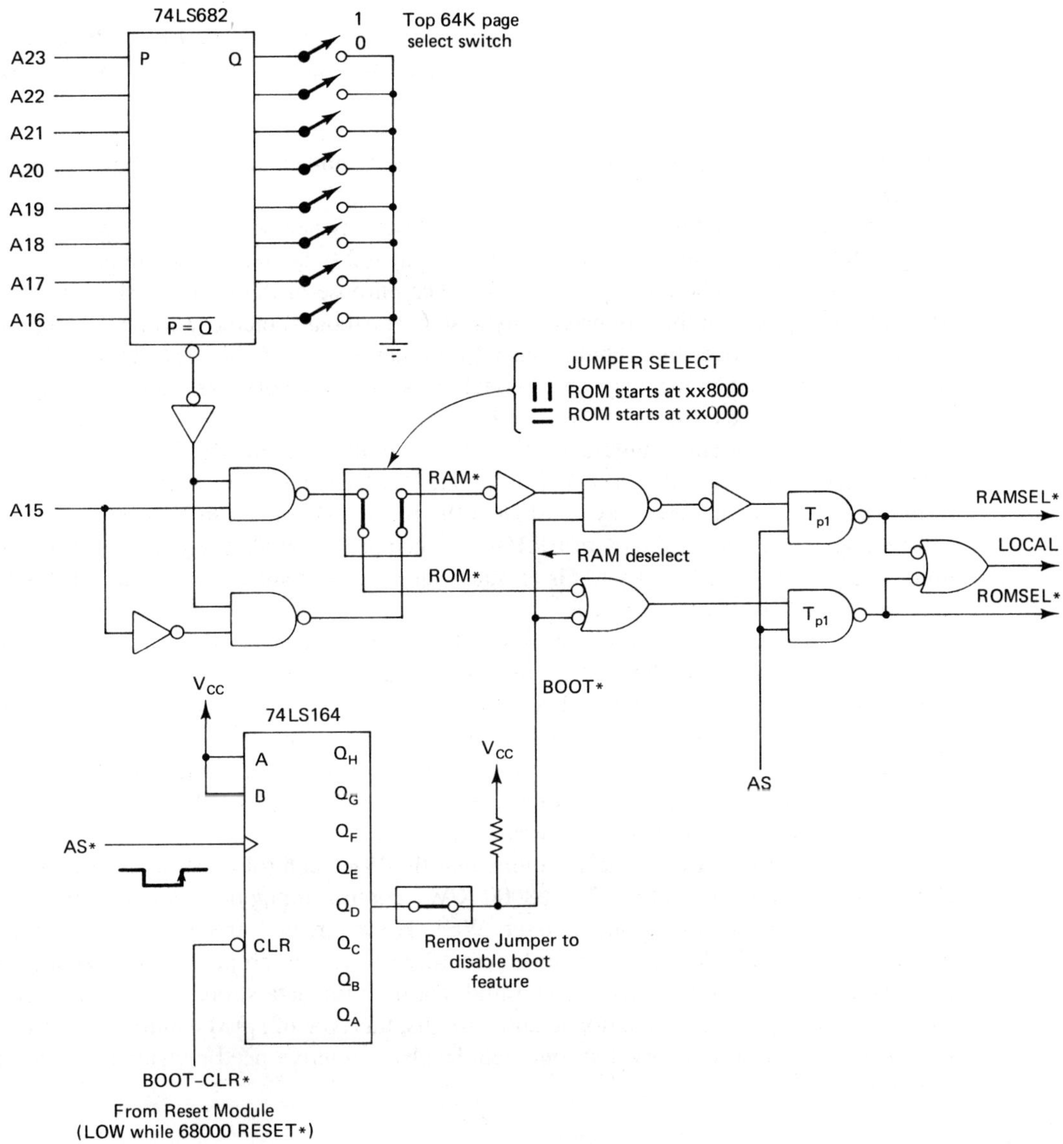

Figure 10.23 Address decoder design that provides EPROM vectors for 68000 reset. The 74LS682 selects the 64K page out of the 16 Mb range; the jumper pair enables ROM or RAM in either half of the selected 64K page.

RAMs at 0. When the memory is first built, and the TUTOR EPROMs first tested, the EPROMs are known good firmware: that is, they have not been modified at all, and any problems will be because of circuit design or construction. Once TUTOR runs at $8000 with local RAM at 0, then the firmware can be changed for a new reset vector and TUTOR decoded to a final address.

In a final configuration like the one mapped in Figure 10.6, the EPROMs are decoded at $FD0000; within the 64K page, this is address 0 rather than address $8000. The swap from $8000 to 0 can be easily done by using the jumpers indicated. Thus, after TUTOR runs successfully at $8000, modify its reset vectors to a final address (say $FD0146), change the jumpers to put the EPROMs at 0, and change the top-page address to $FD.

This simple decoding system provides the flexibility necessary in developing a new design. However, the limitation imposed by this capability is that the maximum "local" on-board memory can be no larger than 64K. The purpose of the local RAM is to allow operation of TUTOR in the absence of any system (off-board) memory while developing the system.[1] In practice, this should cause no problems because the local RAM will not conflict with any system memory: even though the system memory starts at 0 in the Figure 10.6 map and extends upward 128K, 256K, or more, there is plenty of expansion area.

The block diagram in Figure 10.22 and the circuit in Figure 10.23 assume a maximum of 32K EPROM and 32K RAM designated as local memory. After the system is configured in its final form (say at $FD0000), the RAM array can be easily used as EPROM space for a total of 64K of EPROM located at $FD0000. The only constraint on filling the circuit with all EPROMs is to make sure the reset vectors are in the EPROMs that are enabled by the boot circuit.

In the RAM design outlined in Figure 10.22, the chip select CS* comes from the address decoder circuit for both reads and writes; then, in addition to the CS*, the WE* control is asserted when writing to RAM. This RAM design assumes that the OE* controls are high during the write bus cycle. Another design option, called Write Cycle 2, holds OE* low; this timing alternative (not used here) is described in the Appendix data sheets for the 6116 and 6264. As in the case of the EPROMs, RAM may also do byte operations as well as 16-bit word operations.

Note in the RAM data specifications that the WE* control must be asserted *after* CS* for proper RAM operation. The 68000 R/W* control timing does not guarantee this delay, so it cannot be used alone to assert WE*. However, both the data strobes can be combined with the R/W* as shown in Figure 10.24 to ensure proper timing. When you examine the 68000 timing diagram, you find that both the data strobes are delayed by a clock cycle during a write operation to allow for just this type of RAM control. Notice that this memory-control logic involves two gate levels, and *might* need revision after closer analysis.

10.6.1 EPROM Circuit Design

The EPROM portion of the memory design in Figure 10.22 is identical to the EPROM circuit first examined in Figures 10.7 and 10.10. The timing diagram in Figure 10.9 represents not only the previous circuit but also the EPROM design considered here. In both

[1]There is no way to access any system memory on the IEEE Std-696 bus until after the bus interface circuit is complete. Local memory (at 0) must be provided to test the processor using TUTOR.

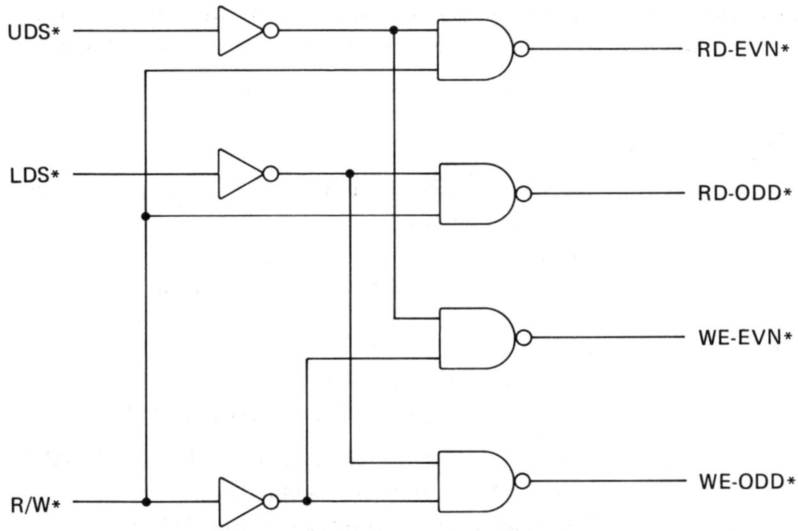

RD-EVN* = UDS* · R/W*
RD-ODD* = LDS* · R/W*
WE-EVN* = UDS* · (R/W*)′
WE-ODD* = LDS* · (R/W*)′

Figure 10.24 Memory-control logic for byte-addressable memory.

cases, the chip-select CS* is derived from the address and AS*; similarly, the output enable OE* comes from the data strobes and is assumed asserted at least t_{OE} before the data is valid.

The design here will involve TUTOR, and consequently at least 16K EPROM space must be provided; at least two 2764 EPROMs are required. They would be sufficient to hold TUTOR, but there would be no room to include extra code for Tiny BASIC or for code to boot a disk operating system. The tradeoff is one of flexibility versus physical space: it would be convenient to have TUTOR in one set of 2764s and application programs in another set of 2764s. However, if space is limited, TUTOR uses only one-half of a pair of 27128s; the other half of such EPROMs can be used for programs. Unfortunately, if some of these programs need to be erased, then TUTOR has to be put in the EPROMs again along with the revised new program code.

Assume for purposes of the current design that 250 ns 27128s are used with an 8 MHz 68000 processor running with a system clock at 6 MHz. Assume that the decoder circuit in Figure 10.23 is used and that it has all 74LS-TTL components. Will the EPROM memory design work at 6 MHz without adding any waits? How fast will it run as a maximum *without* using any waits?

Refer to Figure 10.9 for the EPROM circuit analysis. The relevant time involved here is how long from an asserted chip-select it takes the EPROMs to provide valid data. The data must be valid at least one setup time ahead of the end of S6 when the 68000 will latch whatever data is present. The bus cycle time beginning at S0 and continuing through S7 must be greater or equal to the sum of the times indicated in Figure 10.9:

$$T_{BC} > T_{SEL} + t_{CS} + T_{SU} + T_{S7}$$

where

$$\begin{aligned} T_{SEL} &= \text{Time from start of bus cycle until CS* asserted by } T_{ROMSEL*} \\ &= \text{The larger of either} \\ &\qquad T_{ROMSEL*} = T_{AV} + T_{\text{decoder}} + T_{P1} \\ &\qquad\qquad\qquad = T_{S0} + t_{CLAV(6)} + T_{\text{decoder}} + T_{P1} \end{aligned}$$

or

$$\begin{aligned} T_{ROMSEL*} &= T_{AS*} + T_{P1} \\ &= T_{S0} + T_{S1} + t_{CHSL(9)} + T_{P1} \end{aligned}$$

$$\begin{aligned} t_{CS} &= \text{chip-select to output delay (250 ns from EPROM data sheet)} \\ T_{SU} &= t_{DICL(27)} \text{ Setup time for 68000 read} \\ T_{\text{decoder}} &= \text{Propagation delay in decoder up to last gate} \\ T_{P1} &= \text{Propagation delay through last gate in decoder} \end{aligned}$$

Because the system clock is running at 6 MHz, the state time T_S is 167/2 or 83 ns. Also, there are a number of gates involved in decoding the address: add the worst-case value of the 74LS682 (25 ns) to three levels of ROMSEL* logic (3×15 or 45 ns) for a total of 70 ns propagation delay up to the last gate. The last gate, marked with a delay of T_{P1} in Figure 10.23, is 15 ns, worst case.

First, find the time for the ROM-select signal to get to the last gate in the decoder. It is not certain at this point whether this is the slower signal or whether the AS* comes later; thus, calculate both and use the one arriving later.

$$\begin{aligned} T_{ROMSEL*} &= T_{AV} + T_{\text{decoder}} + T_{P1} \\ &= T_{S0} + t_{CLAV(6)} + T_{\text{decoder}} + T_{P1} \\ &= 83 + 70 + 70 + 15 \\ &= 238 \text{ ns to get a select to the EPROM CS* inputs} \end{aligned}$$

Second, find the time to propagate the ROM-select signal from the last decoder gate by using AS*:

$$\begin{aligned} T_{ROMSEL*} &= T_{AS*} + T_{P1} \\ &= T_{S0} + T_{S1} + t_{CHSL(9)} + T_{P1} \\ &= 83 + 83 + 60 + 15 \\ &= 241 \text{ ns to get a select to the EPROM CS* inputs} \end{aligned}$$

This signal is not much later than the select signal coming through the many gates in the address decoder circuit proper. Use the longer time of 241 ns for T_{SEL} in the rest of the analysis.

Third, substitute all this into the bus-cycle requirement to find

$$\begin{aligned} T_{BC} &> T_{SEL} + t_{CS} + T_{SU} + T_{S7} \\ &> 241 + 250 + 15 + 83 \\ &> 589 \text{ ns for a complete bus cycle.} \end{aligned}$$

The total number of clock cycles in the bus cycle then becomes

$$N_{CCBC} = 589/167 = 3.53$$

A normal bus cycle is four clock cycles, so no waits need be added to run this system with a 6 MHz clock.

To calculate how fast the EPROMs will run without waits, use the bus-cycle equation:

$$T_{BC} = T_{SEL} + t_{CS} + T_{SU} + T_{S7}$$

If no waits are provided, then there are eight clock states, T_S, in each bus cycle. Substituting this in the equation along with the values used in the prior analysis, solve for the state time, T_S.

$$\begin{aligned} 8T_S &= (T_S + 70 + 70 + 15) + 250 + 15 + T_S \\ 6T_S &= 420 \\ T_S &= 70 \text{ ns} \end{aligned}$$

The clock period for this state time is 140 ns. Therefore, with no waits, the 27128 EPROM pair can run at a maximum clock frequency of about 7.1 MHz in the worst case.

10.6.2 RAM Circuit Design

Although the byte-addressable RAM design in Figure 10.22 is different from the MCM2147 circuit in AN-867, the design can be evaluated using the same general approach. In both cases the RAM is selected and then a pulse is applied to write data if necessary. However, there is a significant difference in that the 6116 or the 6264 RAM ICs do not have a single ''E'' input to enable them. Rather, they are selected with a chip-select CS* for either read or write; once selected, the read requires OE* and the write requires WE*.

Read Analysis. A read operation as implemented in Figure 10.22 requires an address selection of both the even and odd RAM chips; either one or both of the RAM output enables are then used to provide the proper data-bus information. Assume that the actual parts are 6116-P3 (150 ns) RAMs with an 8 MHz processor running with a 6 MHz system clock. Assuming the same decoder circuit as in Figure 10.23, will the RAM work at 6 MHz without adding waits? How fast can it run without waits?

The timing diagram for the RAM read analysis is shown in Figure 10.25; the symbols used in the diagram are defined in Table 10.5. The relevant time of concern here is how long from an asserted chip-select (T_{SEL}) it takes the RAMs to provide valid data output. This data must be valid at least one 68000 setup time ahead of the end of S6 when the 68000 will latch the data present on the bus. To analyze, calculate the total bus cycle time from S0 through S7; it must exceed the RAM access time, t_{ACS}, as shown in Figure 10.25:

$$T_{BC} > T_{SEL} + t_{ACS} + T_{SU} + T_{S7}$$

where

$$\begin{aligned} T_{SEL} &= \text{Time from start of bus cycle until CS* asserted by RAMSEL*} \\ &= \text{The larger of either} \\ & T_{RAMSEL*} = T_{AV} + T_{\text{decoder}} + T_{P1} \\ & \qquad\qquad = T_{S0} + t_{CLAV(6)} + T_{\text{decoder}} + T_{P1} \end{aligned}$$

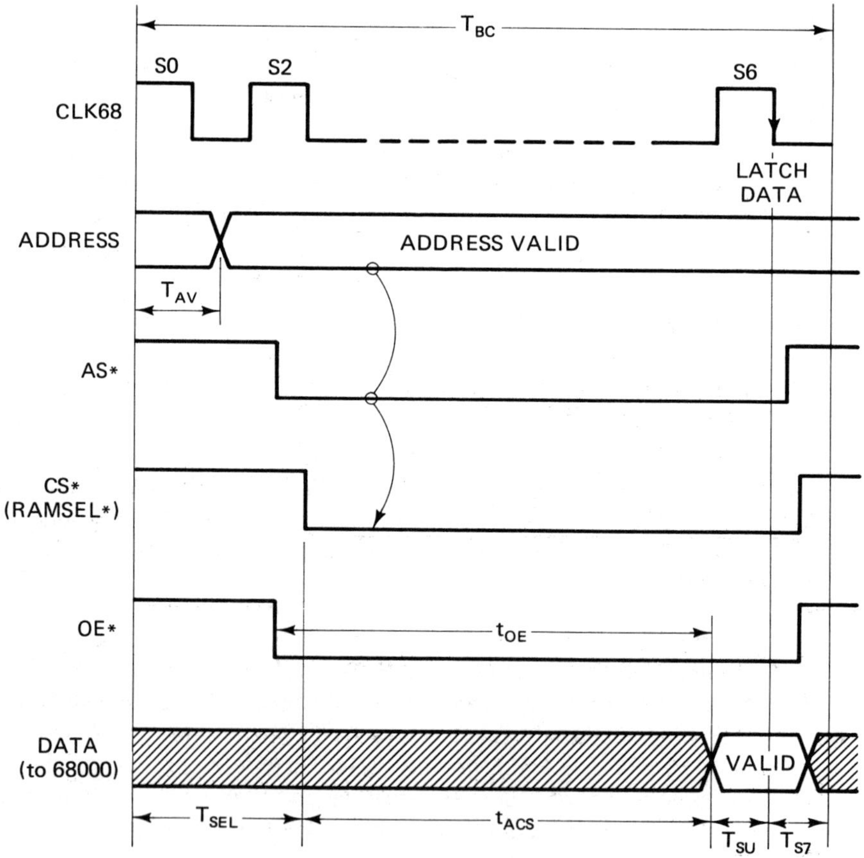

Figure 10.25 Read-timing diagram for byte-addressable RAM pairs.

TABLE 10.5 DEFINITION OF THE TIMES USED IN READ-TIMING ANALYSIS. THE NUMBERS IN PARENTHESES REFER TO THE 68000 READ-CYCLE TIMING SPECIFICATION BUBBLE NUMBER.

T_{BC}	Time for complete bus cycle: four clock cycles + any waits
T_{CLK}	Period of system clock, CLK68
T_{Sx}	State x time (as T_{S0}, T_{S1}, etc.): half of T_{CLK}
T_{AV}	Time to address valid: $T_{S0} + t_{CLAV}$ (6)
T_{AS*}	Time until $AS*$ is valid: $T_{S0} + T_{S1} + t_{CHSL}$ (9)
T_{SEL}	Time to select device using RAMSEL*. Function of address, AS*, and decode propagation time.
T_{SU}	Setup time: Data-in to clock-low at end of S6: t_{DICL} (27)
t_{CS}	Chip select to output-valid delay
t_{OE}	Output enable to valid-output delay
t_{ACS}	Access time from chip select
t_{CHSL}	Clock-high to AS*, DS* low (9)
t_{CLAV}	Time of clock low to address valid (6)
t_{DICL}	Data-in to clock-low (27)

or

$$T_{RAMSEL*} = T_{AS*} + T_{P1}$$
$$= T_{S0} + T_{S1} + t_{CHSL(9)} + T_{P1}$$

t_{ACS} = Access time from chip select (150 ns from RAM data sheet)
T_{SU} = $t_{DICL(27)}$ Setup time for 68000 read
T_{decoder} = Propagation delay in decoder up to last gate
T_{P1} = Propagation delay through last gate in decoder

To begin the analysis, find how long it takes to get the RAM CS* asserted. Because this chip-select signal comes from a combination of the address decoding and AS*, both possibilities must be considered in the complete analysis. The time common to both is T_{P1}; the address-decode time is the sum of

74LS682 worst-case propagation time	=	25 ns
5 levels of logic (15 ns per level)	=	75 ns
T_{decoder} (worst case)	=	100 ns

First, find the time for the RAM-select signal to get through the last gate in the decoder.

$$T_{RAMSEL*} = T_{AV} + T_{\text{decoder}} + T_{P1}$$
$$= T_{S0} + t_{CLAV(6)} + T_{\text{decoder}} + T_{P1}$$
$$= 83 + 70 + 100 + 15$$
$$= 268 \text{ ns to get a select to the RAM CS* inputs}$$

Second, find the time to propagate the RAM select signal using AS*.

$$T_{RAMSEL*} = T_{AS*} + T_{P1}$$
$$= T_{S0} + T_{S1} + t_{CHSL(9)} + T_{P1}$$

$$= 83 + 83 + 60 + 15$$
$$= 241 \text{ ns to get a select to the RAM CS* inputs.}$$

Because this signal is earlier than the select signal coming through the gates of the decoder, it will not affect the total time required to select the RAM. Use the longer time of 268 ns for T_{SEL} in the following analysis.

Third, substitute all the above into the bus-cycle expression:

$$\begin{aligned} T_{BC} &> T_{SEL} + t_{ACS} + T_{SU} + T_{S7} \\ &> 268 + 150 + 15 + 83 \\ &> 516 \text{ ns for a complete bus cycle.} \end{aligned}$$

The total number of clock cycles in the bus cycle then becomes

$$N_{CCBC} = 516/167 = 3.1$$

A normal bus cycle is four clock cycles, so no waits need be added to run this system with a 6 MHz clock.

To find how fast the RAM can run without waits, use the bus-cycle equation:

$$T_{BC} = T_{SEL} + t_{ACS} + T_{SU} + T_{S7}$$

Without waits, there are eight clock states, T_S, in each read bus cycle. Substituting this into the equation with the values just found above, solve for T_S:

$$\begin{aligned} 8T_S &= (T_{AV} + T_{\text{decoder}} + T_{P1}) + t_{ACS} + T_{SU} + T_S \\ &= (T_S + t_{CLAV(6)} + T_{\text{decoder}} + T_{P1}) + t_{ACS} + T_{SU} + T_S \\ 6T_S &= (70 + 100 + 15) + 150 + 15 \\ &= 350 \\ T_S &= 58 \text{ ns} \end{aligned}$$

The clock period for a 58 ns state time is 117 ns. Without using waits, the 150 ns 6116 RAM pair can run at a maximum clock frequency of about 8.6 MHz.

Write analysis. The write operation using the Figure 10.22 RAM is somewhat similar to the read cycle when considering the address selection process; that is, both ROMSEL* and RAMSEL* take about the same amount of time to respond to a valid address from the 68000. However, the RAMSEL* time is not as relevant in the write cycle because of the memory-control logic delay of WE*. This delay, one clock cycle, is necessary so that the RAM WE* is asserted *after* the CS* control. Consequently, the maximum speed calculation depends on the time it takes to assert WE*.

The write analysis is based on the timing diagram in Figure 10.26; the symbols used in the diagram are defined in Table 10.6. Once selected by the CS* signal from RAMSEL*, a successful write requires that WE* be asserted for a stipulated minimum time. The actual write takes place during the overlap time while CS* and WE* are both asserted. The data will write successfully as long as the overlap time is long enough *and* the data-hold requirements are met. Both of these conditions must be verified as properly met when completing the write analysis.

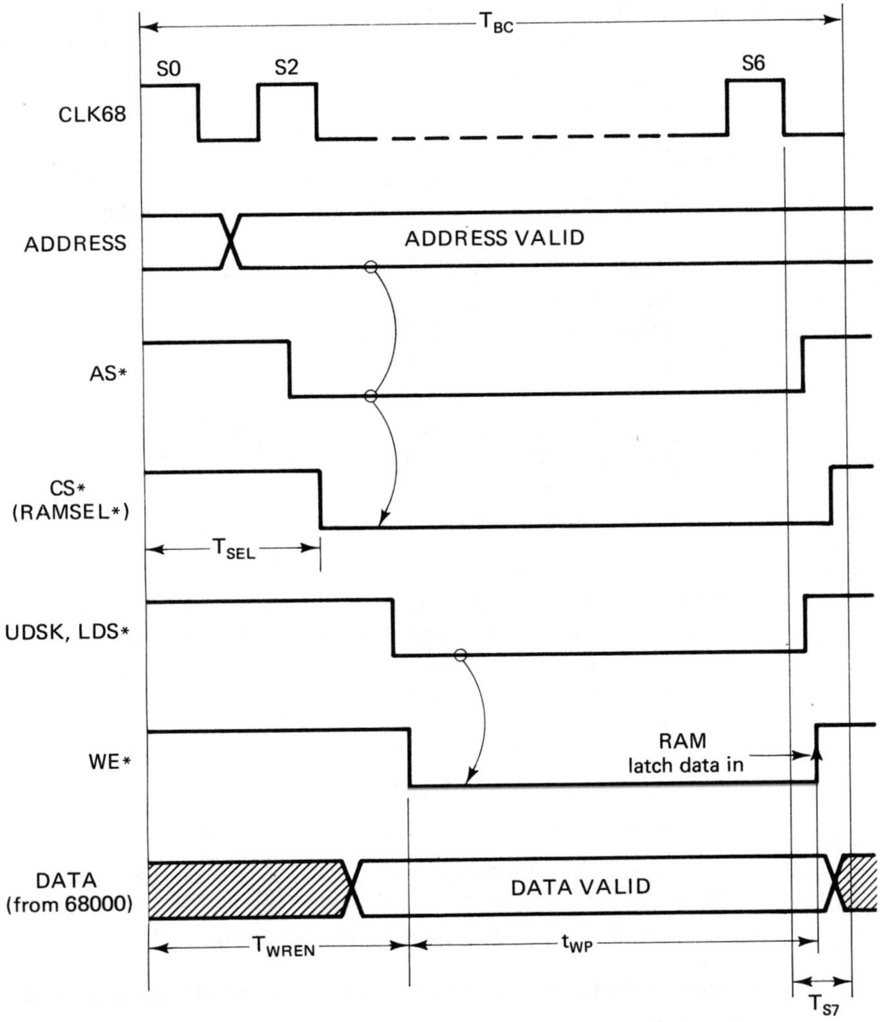

Figure 10.26 Write-timing diagram for byte-addressable RAM pairs.

The first condition, required overlap time, can be expressed as part of the bus cycle time:

$$T_{BC} > T_{WREN} + t_{WP} + T_{S7} \text{ (for the worst case)}$$

where

$$\begin{aligned} T_{WREN} &= \text{Time from the start of bus cycle until WE* is asserted} \\ &= T_{DS*} + T_P \\ &= (T_{S0} + T_{S1} + T_{S2} + T_{S3} + t_{(CHSL(9))}) + T_P \end{aligned}$$

TABLE 10.6 DEFINITION OF THE TIMES USED IN RAM-WRITE TIMING-DIAGRAM ANALYSIS. THE NUMBERS IN PARENTHESES REFER TO THE 68000 WRITE-CYCLE TIMING SPECIFICATION BUBBLE NUMBER.

T_{BC}	Time for complete bus cycle: four clock cycles + any waits
T_{CLK}	Period of system clock, CLK68
T_{Sx}	State x time (as T_{S0}, T_{S1}, etc.): half of T_{CLK}
T_P	Propagation time through the memory-control logic at WE* input of RAM
T_{SEL}	Time to select device using RAMSEL*. Function of address, AS*, and decode propagation time.
T_{DS*}	Time until UDS*, LDS* are valid for write: $T_{S0} + T_{S1} + T_{S2} + T_{S3} + t_{CHSL}$ (9)
T_{WREN}	Time until write-enable: Time to $DS^* + T_p$
t_{CHSL}	Clock high to AS*, DS* low (9)
t_{CLSH}	Clock low to AS* high (12)
t_{SHDOI}	AS*, DS* high to data-out invalid (25)
t_{WP}	Time of write pulse width
t_{DH}	Time from WE* high to data not valid (write hold time)

t_{WP} = Write Pulse. (Overlap time of CS* and WE* must be 90 ns for the 6116 150 ns RAM.)

Examine first how well the overlap requirements are met for the RAM. Use the same clock and parts as in the read analysis. Assume that the memory control logic (Figure 10.24) T_P is two gate levels or about 30 ns, worst case. Substitute the values to calculate the time until WE* is asserted:

$$\begin{aligned} T_{WREN} &= (83 + 83 + 83 + 83 + 60) + 30 \\ &= 422 \text{ ns to assert WE*.} \end{aligned}$$

Now, use this in the bus-cycle equation to find

$$\begin{aligned} T_{BC} &> T_{WREN} + t_{WP} + T_{S7} \text{ (for the worst case)} \\ &> 422 + 90 + 83 \\ &> 595 \text{ ns for a complete bus cycle.} \end{aligned}$$

Last, the total number of clock cycles in the bus cycle becomes

$$N_{CCBC} = 595/167 = 3.6$$

Because a normal bus cycle requires four clock cycles, no waits are required to run the RAM at 6 MHz.

To estimate how fast the RAM can be written without waits, use the bus-cycle equation again:

$$T_{BC} = T_{WREN} + t_{WP} + T_{S7} \text{ (for the worst case)}$$

Substitute T_S as before to obtain

$$\begin{aligned} 8T_S &= (4T_S + t_{CHSL(9)} + T_P) + t_{WP} + T_S \\ 3T_S &= 60 + 30 + 90 \\ T_S &= 180/3 = 60 \text{ ns} \end{aligned}$$

Almost the same as the RAM read, the maximum clock frequency for the 150 ns RAM write is about 8.3 MHz.

The second condition, data-hold time, can be examined easily using Figure 10.27. It is essential that the 68000 hold the data bus valid at least t_{DH} beyond the time WE* is negated. If the data bus becomes invalid before the data-hold time required, then the data might not be successfully written into RAM.

More often than not, an oversight in this aspect of the RAM design might not cause a problem. However, if the timing is off *too* far, then the difficulty will be virtually impossible to track down. The symptom of an improper write to RAM might be an occasional bit or two error during normal use or at temperature extremes. The error might involve a data file and not show up for some time, if ever. On the other hand, if the RAM misses a few bits on a stack pointer, the system crash could be quite spectacular.

Does the 68000 hold the data bus valid long enough to meet the T_{DH} specified for the RAM? As indicated in Figure 10.27, the sequence of events at the end of the write cycle is:

- The 68000 negates DS*.
- T_P ns later, WE* is negated.
- The t_{DH} hold time is fulfilled.
- The data bus becomes invalid after t_{SHDOI} ns.

The timing of these events requires that the propagation time T_P through the memory-control logic be

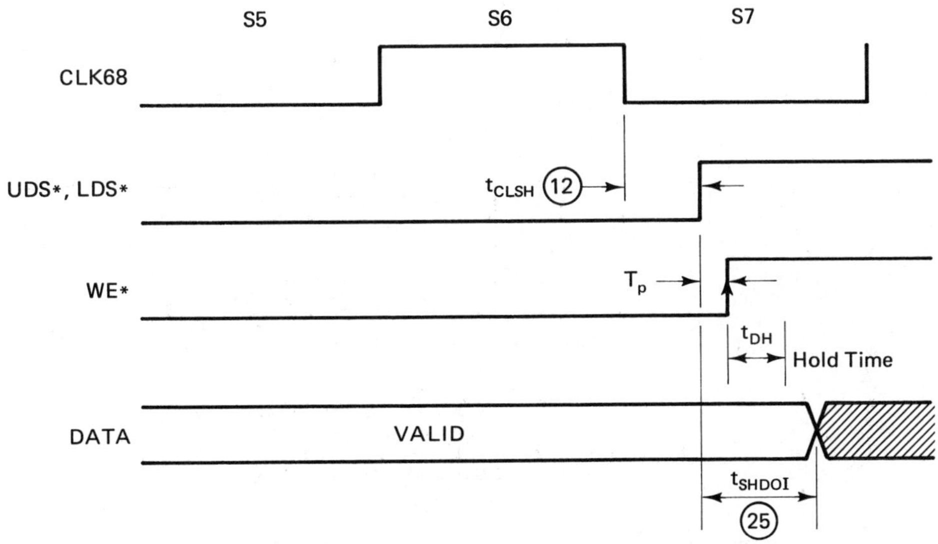

Figure 10.27 Detail of the timing at the end of the write bus cycle for the byte-addressable RAM pairs.

$$\begin{aligned} T_P &< t_{SHDOI(25)} - t_{DH} \\ &< 30 - 10 \\ T_P &< 20 \text{ ns maximum.} \end{aligned}$$

If the maximum propagation time through the memory-control logic must be less than 20 ns to negate WE*, then there is a potential problem here. The circuit in Figure 10.24 was used to provide the WE* control, and it has a worst-case propagation delay of 30 ns. What can be done?

One alternative is to use the same circuit but substitute 74S Schottky devices for the memory-control logic. This is a particularly appealing option if the circuit has already been constructed or if many printed-circit boards are on hand: PCB rework is expensive, and there might not be physical room to change to another circuit.

A second alternative is to change to the circuit shown in Figure 10.28. This design has only one level of gate delay on the write control outputs to WE*. A 74LS32 has a worst-case propagation delay of some 22 ns, so there is almost enough improvement to meet the t_{DH} specification. At the bus speeds used here, this is certainly close enough: the data will tend to stay valid longer due to bus capacitance. For all practical purposes then, Figure 10.28 with a 74LS32 will resolve the hold-time problem.

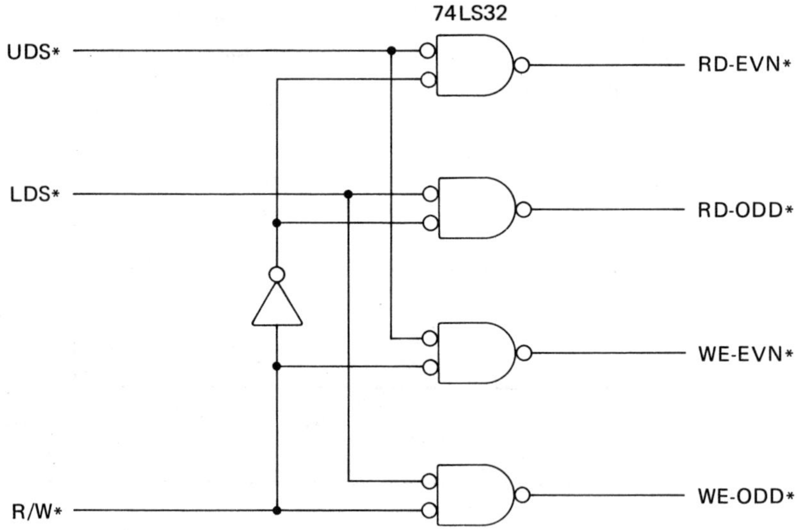

RD-EVN* = UDS* · R/W*
RD-ODD* = LDS* · R/W*
WE-EVN* = UDS* · (R/W*)′
WE-ODD* = LDS* · (R/W*)′

Figure 10.28 A faster memory-control logic circuit for byte-addressable memory.

10.7 IEEE STD-696 SYSTEM DESIGN

The IEEE Std-696 system memory design is based on the memory map shown in Figure 10.6. The actual circuits used to implement this configuration are Figure 10.23 (address decoder) and Figure 10.24 (memory control); both the decoder and control circuits are connected as indicated in Figure 10.22.

The system is developed using the same techniques as the non-IEEE version: freerun the 68000, run an EPROM program at 0, run another EPROM program at $8000, and finally, add RAM at 0. Because the S-100 interface circuits have not been developed yet, it is first necessary to design the circuit according to the memory map in Figure 10.5. Once the 68000 system runs at $8000, then the address decoder can be set so that the EPROMs are addressed at $FD0000 or some other convenient location.

Figure 10.29 shows the CPU board while still half completed. Sockets for the EPROM pair are to the left of the 68000, and RAM is placed to the right. Figure 10.30 shows a closer view of the EPROM and RAM mounted next to the 68000. All four sockets have 28 pins so that easy substitution of parts can be made. Both the EPROM and the RAM sockets have jumpers connected to reconfigure them to take different 24- or 28-pin EPROM or RAM devices.

Figure 10.29 The S-100 CPU board with EPROMs located to the left of the 68000 and RAM to the right. Sockets for address and data bus buffers to the S-100 bus have been added.

Figure 10.30 A closer view of the 68000 and memory. Notice that the pair of 6116 RAMs are mounted in 28-pin sockets; they can be replaced by 6264 RAMS in the same socket.

The EPROM and RAM circuit design in Section 10.6 describes the IEEE Std-696 system shown in the photographs. The performance of this EPROM design is shown in Figure 10.31 for a small scope-loop program:

```
1000    MOVE.W  $FD0000,D0  Read memory over and over again
1006    JMP.S   $1000
```

In the top timing diagram, notice that ROMSEL* (labeled ROM-) has been asserted several times, each assertion indicating a complete loop through the program. Also, one of the address lines is shown (labeled ADR); this is to see generally when the address bus is asserted. The bottom timing diagram is a closer view of an EPROM read cycle.

Compare the calculations in Section 10.6 with the actual data obtained for the 27128 running with a 6 MHz clock. The timing diagram shows that T_{SEL} (time to assert ROMSEL*) is about 200 ns; the expected worst case is about 241 ns. Also, the time between ROMSEL* low and when the 68000 latches the data at the end of S6 is about 380 ns; of this, the 27128s require 250 ns access time (t_{CS}) and the 68000 needs 15 ns T_{SU} for setup time. With no waits, the actual performance is well within specifications.

Figure 10.32 shows the timing of a RAM read while the 68000 executes the scope-loop program:

```
1000    MOVE.W  $FD8000,D0  Read RAM memory over and over again
1006    JMP.S   $1000
```

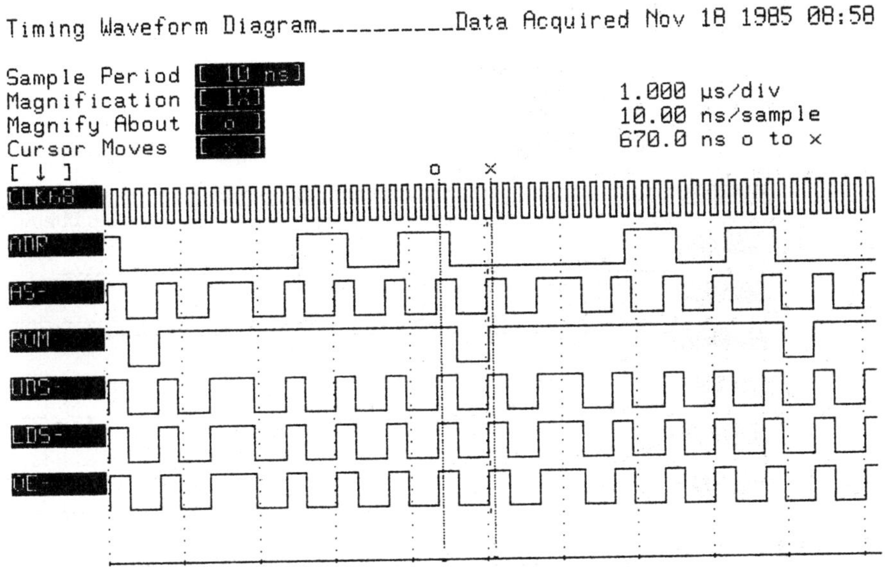

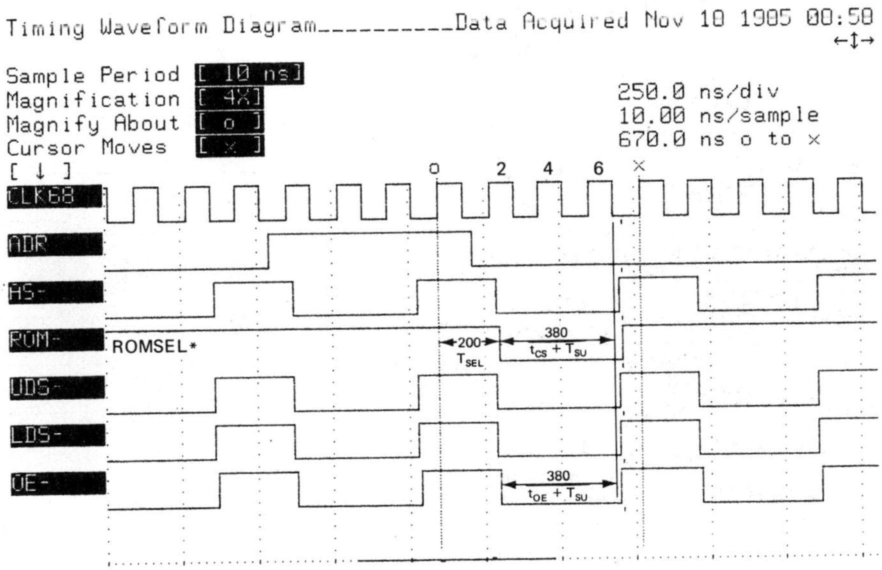

Figure 10.31 Timing of an EPROM read. The 68000 clock is 6 MHz.

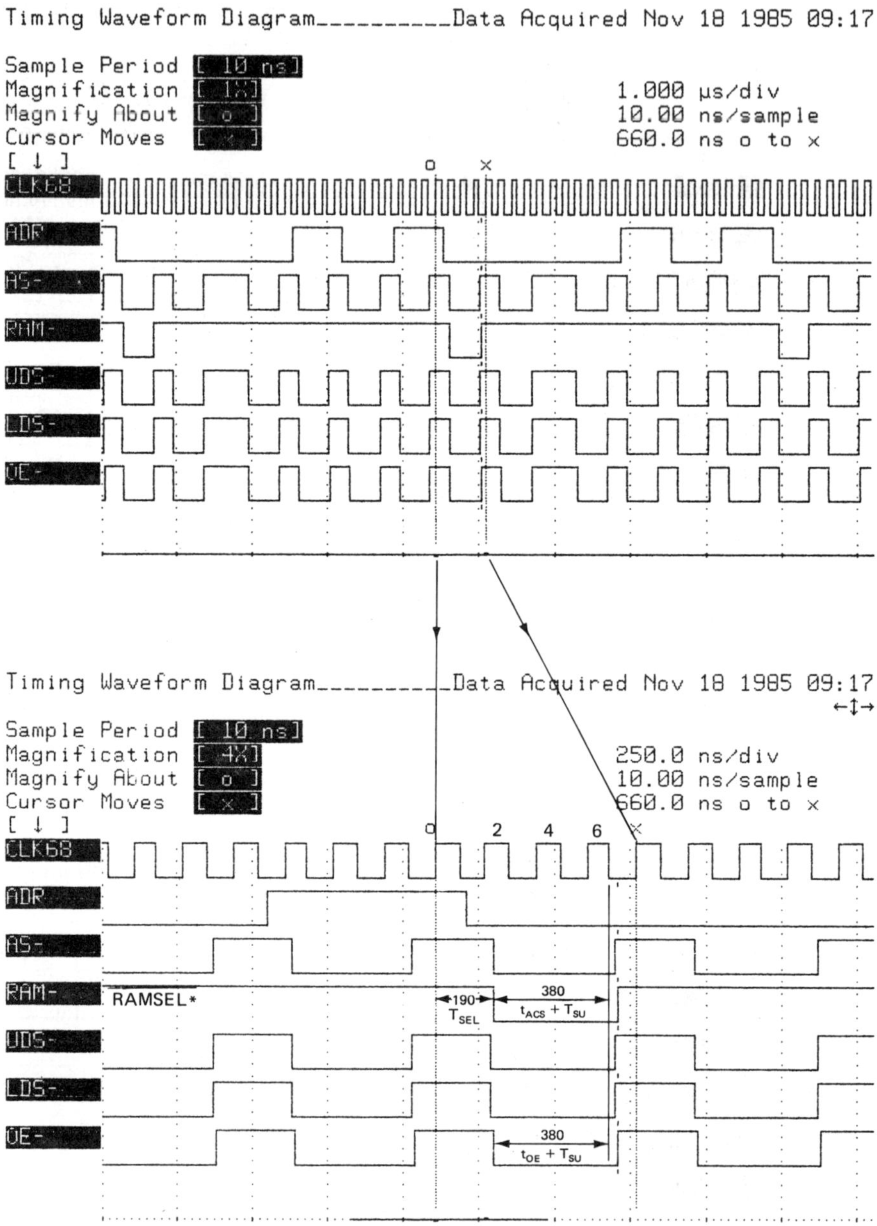

Figure 10.32 Timing of a RAM read operation. The 68000 clock is 6 MHz.

In the top timing diagram, RAMSEL* has been asserted several times indicating several complete loops through the program. The bottom timing diagram gives a closer view of one RAM read cycle.

Look at the RAM calculations in Section 10.6 and compare them with the actual data obtained using 6116 (150 ns) RAMs running with a 6 MHz clock. The timing diagram shows T_{SEL} (time to assert RAMSEL*) is about 190 ns; the expected worst case is about 268 ns. Also, the time between RAMSEL* low and when the 68000 latches the data at the end of S6 is about 380 ns; of this, the 6116s require only 150 ns access time (t_{ACS}) and the 68000 15 ns T_{SU} for setup time. With no waits, the actual RAM read performance is well within specifications.

The RAM write timing is shown in Figure 10.33. As before, the 68000 is executing a scope-loop program:

```
1000    MOVE.W  D0, $FD8000    Write RAM memory over and over again
1006    JMP.S   $1000
```

In the upper timing diagram, the program has gone through several loops during the time interval. The lower timing diagram shows the details of one write bus cycle. Notice that a single wait has been added to the write cycle; this is not necessary for proper write timing, however.

The RAM write diagram in Figure 10.33 is similar to the expected timing shown in Figure 10.26. The worst-case situation in that analysis was T_{WREN} = 422 ns to assert the WE* RAM control; the actual measurement is 360 ns, much better than the worst case. In addition, consider the write pulse time T_{WP}: this overlap time must be at least 90 ns for the 6116, and it is met by a substantial margin.

T_{WP} total with one wait	410 ns
Time of one wait	− 167 ns
T_{WP} without waits	243 ns

As discussed earlier, the write data-hold time should be examined to make sure that the 68000 data stays on the bus long enough. Figure 10.34 shows the measurements; the timing diagram is modeled after the sketch in Figure 10.27. Does the 68000 keep the data valid for t_{DH} (10 ns for the 6116) past WE* high? Examine the data to find that

T_P propagation time to negate WE*	10 ns
t_{DH} hold time required	+ 10 ns
t_{SHDOI} must be at least	20 ns

Assuming that the data out from the 68000 does not become invalid faster than 20 ns after the data strobes go high, then this circuit appears satisfactory.

The circuit in Figure 10.24 with LS-TTL was used to take the data in Figure 10.34. In the worst case, the analysis indicated that the propagation time T_P was 30 ns rather than the actual 10 ns. In this one particular case, the parts installed were fast enough to meet the timing specifications of the RAM. In general, however, the choice of LS-TTL parts in

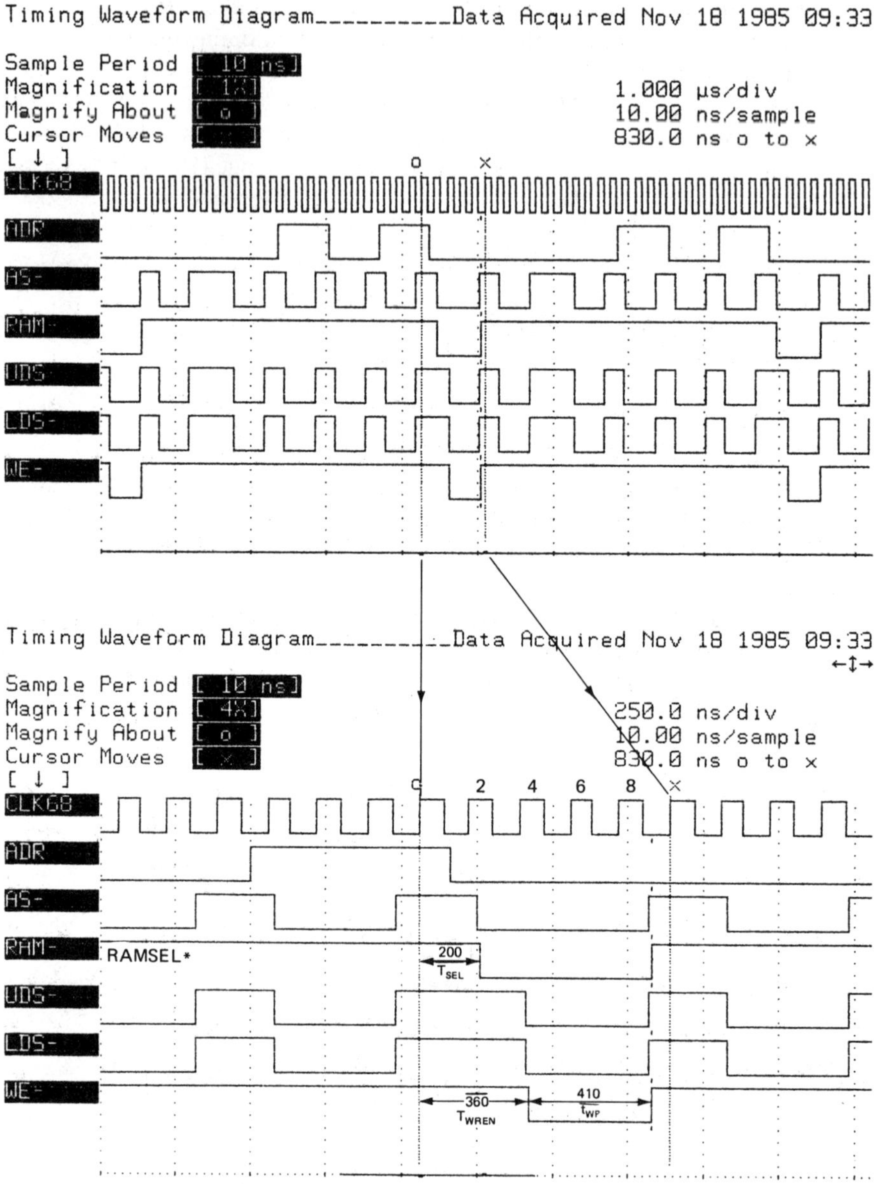

Figure 10.33 Timing of a RAM write operation. The 68000 clock is 6 MHz; a single wait has been included in this write bus cycle.

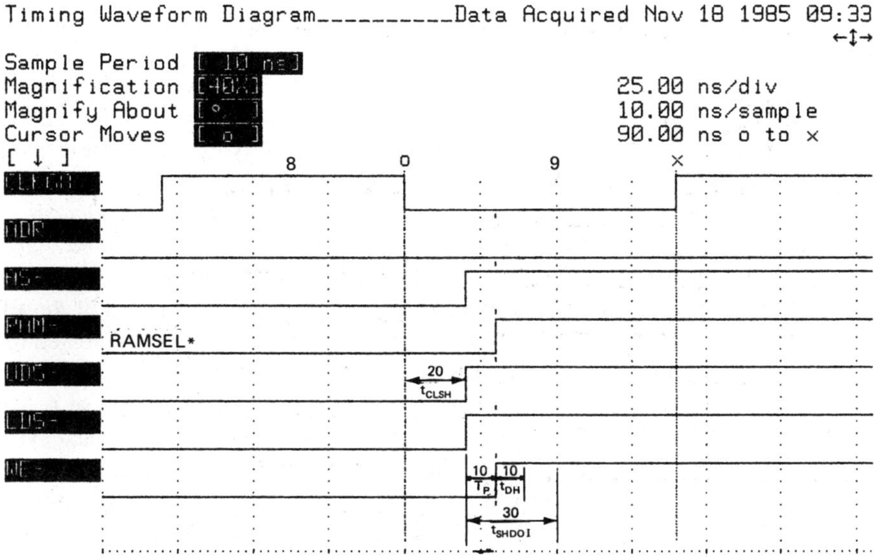

Figure 10.34 Detail at the end of the RAM write operation. The time from the data strobes high until the data bus output from the 68000 is t_{SHDOI}, which is about 30 ns here.

the memory-control logic might lead to marginal performance in some systems. Thus, for quantity production of CPU boards, it would be reasonable to use the faster circuit given in Figure 10.28.

10.8 SUMMARY

Although essential when bringing up the 68000, freerunning cannot execute programs; to do this, the processor requires access to memory where it can read a program for execution. During the development of a total system, a small program can be placed in an EPROM pair and run; some RAM can be added and then tested using another EPROM program. Gradually, the memory can be developed to include complete RAM and EPROM modules that not only support the TUTOR monitor but also allow booting a disk operating system.

The goal when developing the system memory is to get TUTOR running as soon as possible; this is so it can help test the new system as it begins to take shape. The strategy to follow is based on designing, building, and testing each new module being added to the system. First, design a simple EPROM pair to execute a program at address 0; next, add a boot circuit plus decoder so the EPROMs can execute at a higher memory location. After that runs properly, add RAM at low memory and test it with a simple EPROM program. Finally, with the EPROM sockets decoded at $8000, run the TUTOR program.

The first EPROM pair at address 0 is certainly the easiest program possible: it provides the SSP and PC reset vectors and then executes a single instruction to repeatedly jump to location 8. A reset-vector circuit and an address decoder are not required for proper operation. The EPROM circuit, even though simple, must be analyzed for a proper speed match with the 68000. The wait generator already designed with the DTACK* circuit can provide the proper number of waits to match the speed of the EPROMs used in the circuit. The maximum speed of the memory can also be calculated to determine how much margin there is in the overall design. For example, if memory can operate at 10 MHz, then the 68000 should have no problems with operation at 6 MHz.

Although EPROMs could be used in low memory, a practical system should have RAM starting at address 0 and the EPROM located somewhere else in memory. An address decoder is necessary to enable the EPROMs at the higher address, and there are many ways to implement it. A decoder that allows changing the base address of the EPROMs is most desirable; this is because it permits using a variety of EPROM locations depending on the stage of the system development.

When the EPROMs are moved from address 0 to higher memory, the reset vectors must still be provided at addresses 0 through 7. The Educational Computer Board design accomplishes this by enabling the EPROMs at address 0 to 7 and from $8000 to $BFFF. Another approach is to enable the EPROMs for the first four bus cycles after reset; then, regardless of where the EPROMs are decoded, they will always provide the proper reset vectors for the 68000.

Analysis of an example 12.5 MHz RAM design provides valuable insight into possible areas of concern. The circuit did not use any wait states for RAM reads or writes, and some of the timing was critical for proper operation. Examination of this working system showed that a successful read required Schottky TTL in part of the RAM select circuit. Analysis of the write-control circuit indicated Schottky TTL was also required in that area as well.

Based on the analysis of a working memory, and using the memory maps considered early in the chapter, the EPROM and RAM for the prototype system can be designed. No waits are required for operation at 6 MHz, but timing must be closely examined to be sure that the memory will work for the worst-case parts. After analysis of the RAM write circuit, it appeared that a revised control circuit might be appropriate.

Actual timing data for the IEEE Std-696 system indicated that no revision in the circuit was necessary for the typical components used. The measurements showed that the EPROM reads and the RAM reads and writes were all within required specifications. For prototype work, this is sufficient. However, the worst-case analysis indicated that RAM writes needed a faster control circuit. Therefore, for production of CPU boards, it would be best to avoid marginal performance by using the faster circuit.

EXERCISES

1. Why must the 68000 be able to freerun at any point in the design and development of the system?
2. If several data bus lines to the 68000 are accidentally shorted together, will the freerun test run properly? Why or why not?
3. What code must be programmed into the first EPROM pair? Split the code into even and odd parts.
4. What is the value of coding a scope-loop program?
5. Why would you want to get TUTOR running as soon as possible?
6. Outline the strategy you should follow to develop the system memory.
7. In Figure 10.3, the Branch instruction is used rather than a Jump Short to $8008. Under what condition(s) will the Jump Short not work properly?
8. If you write a scope-loop program similar to the one in Figure 10.4, can you tell what data is being written using your oscilloscope? Can you verify the address being written? Describe.
9. Compare the ECB memory map in Figure 10.5 with the system configured as in Figure 10.6. What changes are necessary in TUTOR to implement this new memory map? Is TUTOR code position-independent?
10. If you build the simple EPROM pair in Figure 10.7, why is address decoding not necessary? Is the CS* connection necessary? Are the UDS* and LDS* controls necessary for initial tests?
11. Calculate using a 450 ns 2716 EPROM in the Figure 10.7 circuit.
    - **a.** Assume the clock is 4 MHz. How many waits are required?
    - **b.** Assume the clock is 10 MHz. What 68000 part number must you assume for your analysis? How many waits are required? Sketch one EPROM-read bus cycle to scale; use Figure 10.9 as a model.
12. Use a 300 ns 27128 EPROM pair in the circuit in Figure 10.10.
    - **a.** Assume the decoder propagation delay is 80 ns and the 68000 clock is 6 MHz. How many waits are required? State other assumptions you make in the analysis.
    - **b.** Suppose one wait is provided. How fast can the 68000 clock go and still have reliable EPROM operation?
13. Sketch a circuit to decode the 64K block $FF0000 to $FFFFFF.
14. Describe the requirements of a reset-vector circuit.
15. Two reset-vector circuits are shown in Figures 10.15 and 10.16. Can you devise yet another approach to the reset problem? Describe.
16. Schottky TTL was required in part of the example RAM design in Section 10.5. How fast should the 68000 clock be allowed to run if LS-TTL is used rather than Schottky? Is there a problem with doing this? If so, how can it be resolved?
17. Assume a 12.5 MHz 68000, LS-TTL components, and 250 ns 27128s in the system drawn in Figure 10.22.
    - **a.** If the system clock runs at 10 MHz, how many waits are required for the EPROMs?
    - **b.** How fast can the clock go if no waits are provided?

18. Assume a 12.5 MHz 68000, LS-TTL components, and 250 ns 27128s in the system drawn in Figure 10.22.

   a. Suppose the AS* control is deleted from the decoder circuit. What is the maximum clock speed possible? Sketch the read bus cycle timing to approximate scale.

   b. Are waits required at 10 MHz?

19. Why did you neglect t_{OE} in the above EPROM calculations?

20. Assume a 12.5 MHz 68000, LS-TTL components, Figure 10.24 memory-control logic, and 150 ns 6116 RAMs in the system drawn in Figure 10.22.

   a. If the system clock runs at 10 MHz, how many waits are required for the RAMs when reading?

   b. How fast can the clock go if no waits are provided for read?

21. Do problem 20 for the write case.

22. Given that the 68000 clock will run at 12.5 MHz, design your own memory system to meet the following requirements:

   a. Decode 250 ns 27128 EPROMs at FD0000,

   b. Decode 150 ns 6116 RAMs at either 0 or FE0000, and

   c. Provide 68000 reset vectors.

   Your design should include circuit, timing diagrams, worst-case calculations, and an estmate of how fast the system will run without waits. What steps are necessary to run your design at full clock speed without waits?

23. Ponder the significance of configuring your system with local EPROM and RAM as in Figure 10.6, and then using the RAM as a high-speed cache memory. The system memory (starting at 0) and non-local addresses would be used for I/O and communication with other processors using a system bus separate from the 68000 data, address, and control buses. Assume some sort of bus interface unit to isolate the 68000 from the external system bus.

FURTHER READING

CATES, RON L. "Mapping an Alterable Reset Vector for the MC68000." *Electronics* (July 28, 1982): 111–113.

WEST, TREY. "A High Performance MC68000L12 System with no Wait States." Application Note AN-867. Austin, TX: Motorola Semiconductor Products, Inc.

ELEVEN

Input/Output Design

The critical point in the 68000 design was when you removed the freerun headers and closed the loop with memory. The freerunning was essential to get the system up, but without being able to execute programs in memory, the 68000 could do very little. While freerunning, for example, you could check the control and address lines from the 68000; you could also monitor an address decoder or RAM memory-control circuit for proper operation. Although simple, the first programs were critical because they allowed you to do a number of additional operations not possible by freerunning. These programs could, for example, provide reset vectors and loop, reset and loop in high memory, and finally loop while doing RAM reads and writes.

The concept of modular development is the underlying theme in bringing up the 68000 by freerunning first and then adding programs. Starting with a minimum system with very little more than a 68000, it is possible to build an operating computer board one step at a time by designing, building, and testing each required module. Not only does this modular approach assure a working system, but it also allows you to understand the design fully. In other words, you grow at the same pace your system grows: as you begin your system design, you do not have a complete understanding of the 68000, but you learn more as you develop each module. If you were to try designing the complete system in detail at the beginning, then it might not be a success.

Now that the 68000 runs simple programs from EPROMs, the next step is to add the input/output (I/O) module shown in Figure 11.1. The goal is to run TUTOR EPROMs so that the system can be programmed interactively; that is, rather than making new EPROMs for each new test program, use TUTOR to write the programs for execution out of RAM. This concept is an extension of the modular hardware development: the first simple programs have progressively become more and more sophisticated as the hardware became more complex.

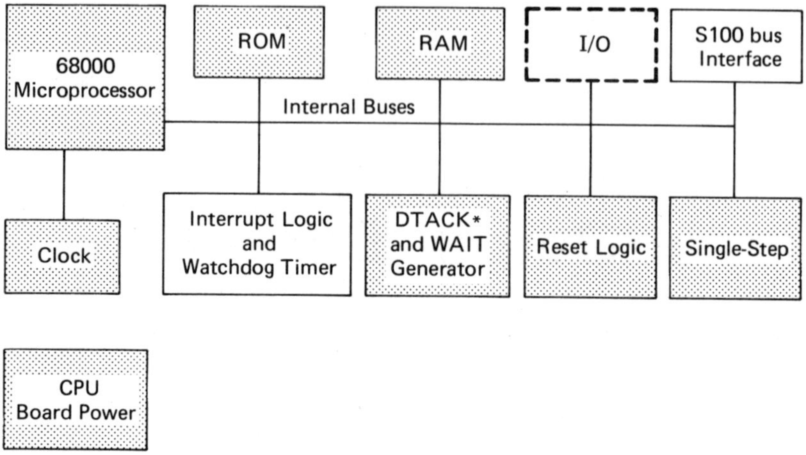

Figure 11.1 The highlighted Input/Output (I/O) section will be developed in this chapter. The shaded modules have already been designed.

In the last chapter, you developed the memory circuits to support the TUTOR firmware. The only difference between TUTOR and the test EPROMs you used in bringing up the 68000 is that TUTOR requires I/O; otherwise, the addressing and control are just like any EPROM. In fact, when TUTOR is running without an I/O module, it continually executes a scope-loop while it waits for keyboard input. This loop can be seen easily with an oscilloscope and is reassuring evidence that the system is ready for the next module.

This chapter shows how to add the necessary I/O to the 68000 system to communicate using the TUTOR firmware. The approach builds on all the past modules and depends on their proper operation. For example, if the TUTOR EPROMs are installed but the 68000 does not appear to be looping while it waits for a key press, then the problem must be corrected before proceeding. Once the I/O has been added to the system, then TUTOR can be used for more thorough testing of RAM as well as testing all future modules as they are integrated into the system.

11.1 SYNCHRONOUS INTERFACE

In Chapter 8 when you studied the Educational Computer Board in some detail, you learned about the 68000's synchronous interface. At that time, without a pressing need for the capability, the synchronous bus information might have appeared useful but somewhat nonessential. I/O can be done with a number of 16-bit 68000-family parts, so why get involved in studying a 6800-family component? The reason is this: to avoid reinventing the wheel. TUTOR is easily available and uses the synchronous 6850.

Although other "better" parts than the 6850 might be used for I/O, they would involve changes in TUTOR. The whole idea in using TUTOR is to get the 68000 up and running easily—not to complicate the process by having to develop new TUTOR code in addition to the new hardware interface. Once I/O using TUTOR is successfully accomplished, then it can be used to develop more advanced I/O if necessary. For example, the MC68681 dual universal receiver transmitter (DUART) described in AN899 can be used for terminal and printer I/O. However, implementing the 68681 interface program requires either an operational TUTOR or a separate development system.

The synchronous interface is quite simple to implement. In Figure 11.2, you can see that there are only three pins on the 68000 that are involved in the interface. The sequence shown in Figure 11.3 outlines how the 68000 and the 6800-family devices synchronize:

- When the bus cycle begins, the 68000 waits for DTACK*.
- If VPA* is asserted (by the 6850 decoder) instead of DTACK*, then the 68000 asserts VMA* when E is low.
- When E goes back high, the 6850 puts data on the bus or prepares to read data from the bus.
- When E goes low at the end of S6, the 68000 latches data coming in or the 6850 latches data from the 68000.
- The bus cycle concludes normally and VPA* and VMA* go high.

This sequence is shown in Figure 11.4 for a typical cycle in which the 68000 reads the data from the 6850. Notice that DTACK* is not shown and *must not be asserted* during the synchronous bus cycle.

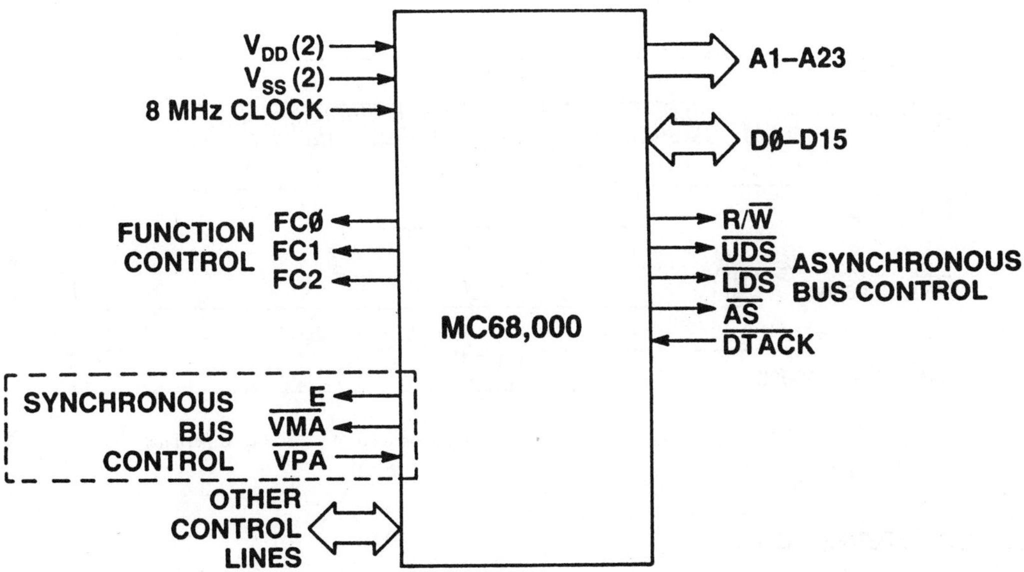

Figure 11.2 Synchronous bus control pins to run the 68000 with 6800-type peripherals. VPA* is Valid Peripheral Address, VMA* is Valid Memory Address, and E is the Enable output running at one-tenth of the 68000 clock. (Courtesy Motorola Inc.)

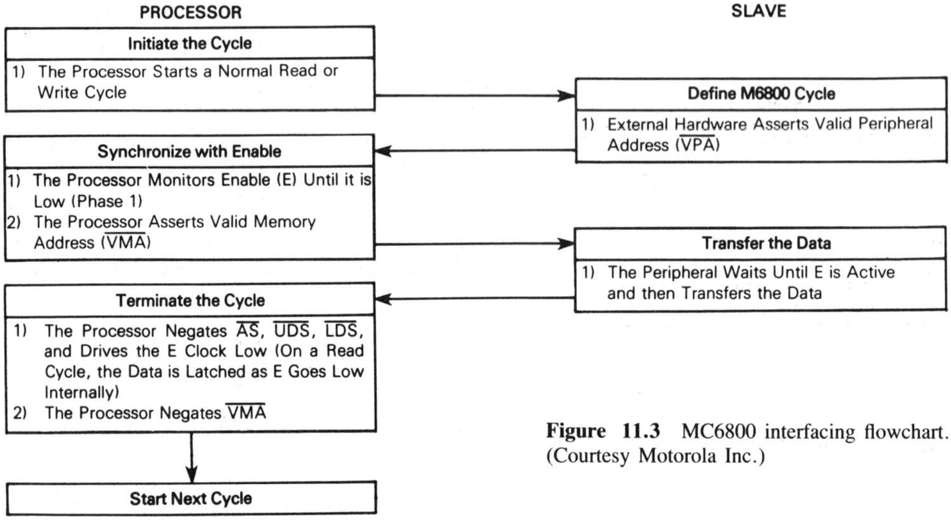

Figure 11.3 MC6800 interfacing flowchart. (Courtesy Motorola Inc.)

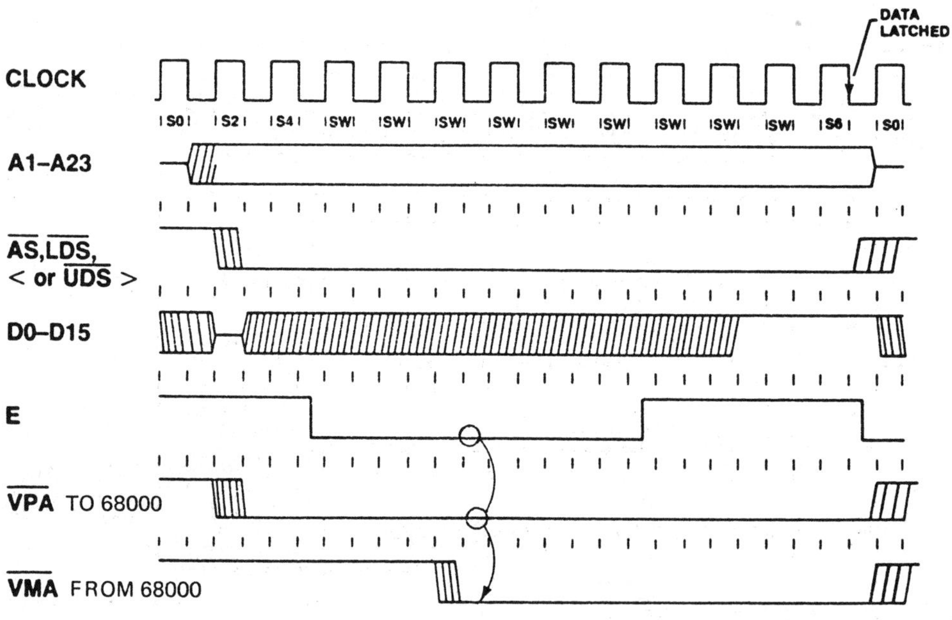

Figure 11.4 Timing diagram for a typical synchronous read of a 6800-type peripheral device. (Courtesy Motorola Inc.)

11.2 ECB INTERFACE

Examine the Educational Computer Board block diagram in Figure 11.5 and compare it with the organization of your system. The ECB uses two 6850 ACIAs for its I/O: one for the system console and the other for connection to a host computer for uploading and downloading programs. Except for exception processing and the two I/O ports, your

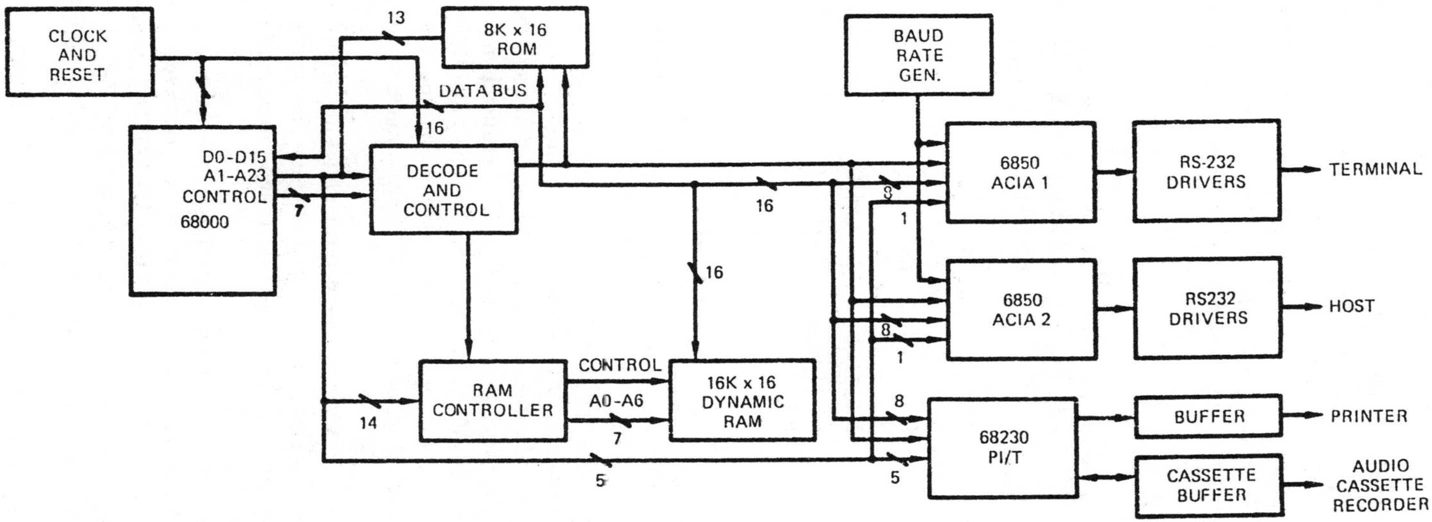

Figure 11.5 MEX68KECB detailed block diagram. (Courtesy Motorola Inc.)

68000 board is now functionally equivalent to the ECB. At this point in your system development, getting your console running is most important; later you can add another 6850 as a host port if you want.

Before going forward in designing your own 6850 I/O, take another look at the performance of the ECB. Figure 11.6 shows the synchronous bus cycles as TUTOR waits for a keypress. Relate this timing diagram to the code being executed by TUTOR:

```
INCHNE      MOVE.B    (A0),D1     Read 6850 status
            AND.B     #$10,D1     Break?
            BNE       BREAK       Process if yes

            MOVE.B    (A0),D1     Read 6850 status
            AND.B     #1,D1       Data ready?
            BEQ.S     INCHNE      Loop back if not

            MOVE.B    2(A0),D0    Read data
            AND.B     #$7F,D0     Remove top bit
            RTS
```

In TUTOR version 1.3, INCHNE is at memory location $9FA6. So, with your own working 68000 system, even without I/O, you can verify that TUTOR is working by single-stepping through this code.

Also, if you disable the ECB RAM-refresh circuit, you can easily examine the bus cycles and get a pattern similar to Figure 11.7. Because the TUTOR software above is in a tight loop waiting for a keypress, any dual-trace oscilloscope can be used to see the signals in the system. By synchronizing on VPA*, you can not only measure VMA* as in the figure, but you can also check the data bus and the 68000 controls for correct values. When you measure the timing of the ACIAs, you find that CS1 is asserted at the same time for each; the selection of the proper ACIA is made by A6, A1, and the two data strobes.

In general, if you have full schematics with all the details of a module you want to understand, it helps to sketch a simplified diagram like Figure 11.8. It shows just an outline of the addressing and 6850 chip-selects and can be used to draw quickly the memory map shown in Figure 11.9.

Because the 6850s are 8-bit devices, it is necessary to connect each to just one-half of the data bus. As shown, ACIA1 for Port 1 is connected to the even data bus lines D15-D8; ACIA2 for Port 2 is on the odd lines D7-D0. This means that an even address is required for access to ACIA1 and an odd address for ACIA2. In hardware, the UDS* and LDS* lines can be used with A6 and A1 for a particularly simple ACIA-select circuit.

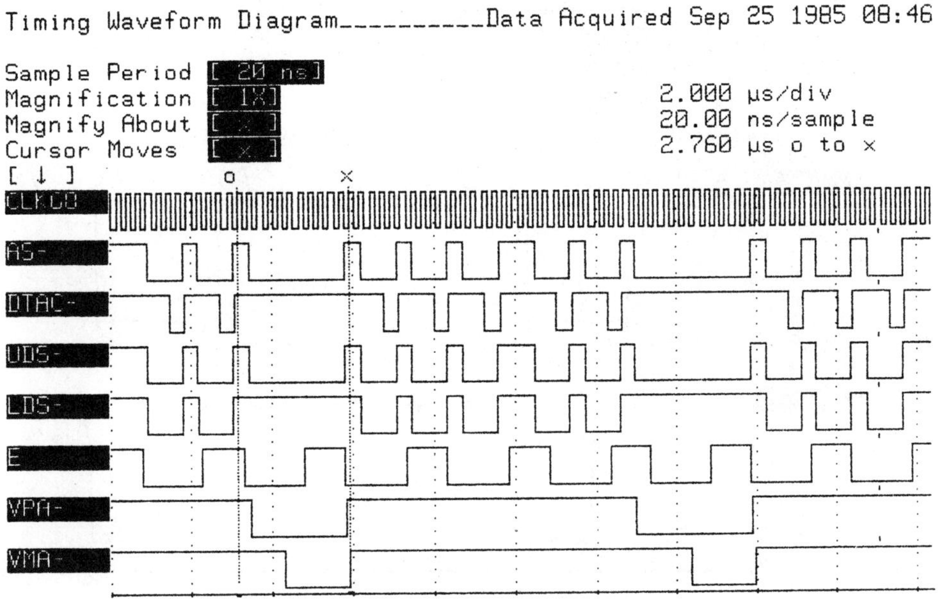

Figure 11.6 ECB synchronous read bus cycles with RAM-refresh disabled.

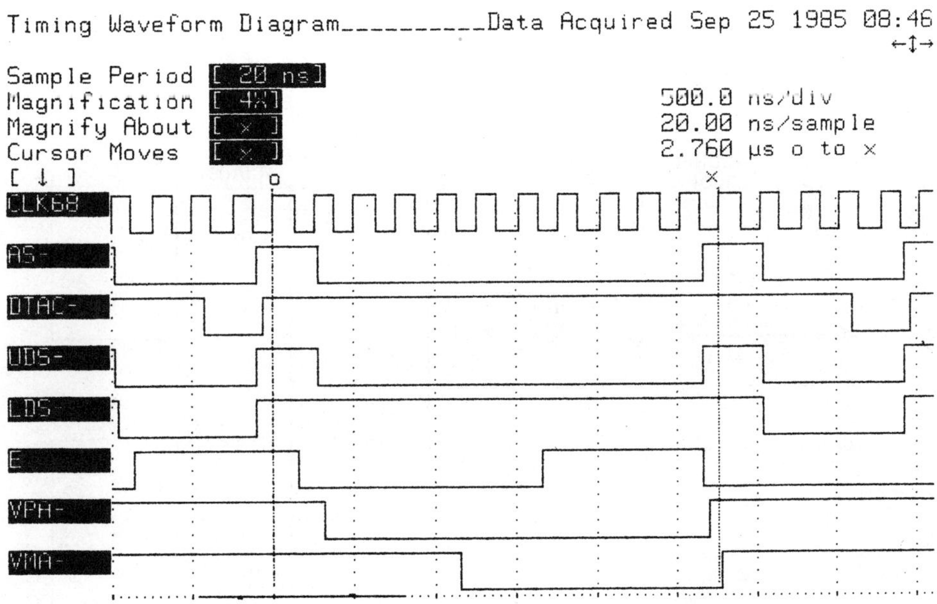

Figure 11.6 continued

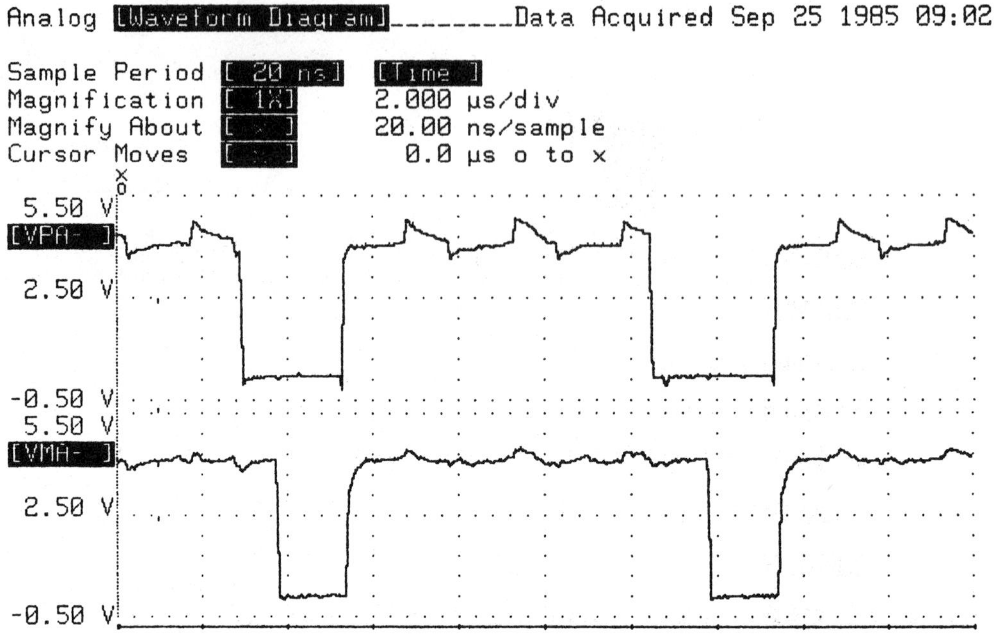

Figure 11.7 ECB oscilloscope data on VPA* and VMA* while RAM refresh is disabled. The oscilloscope can synchronize easily on VPA*.

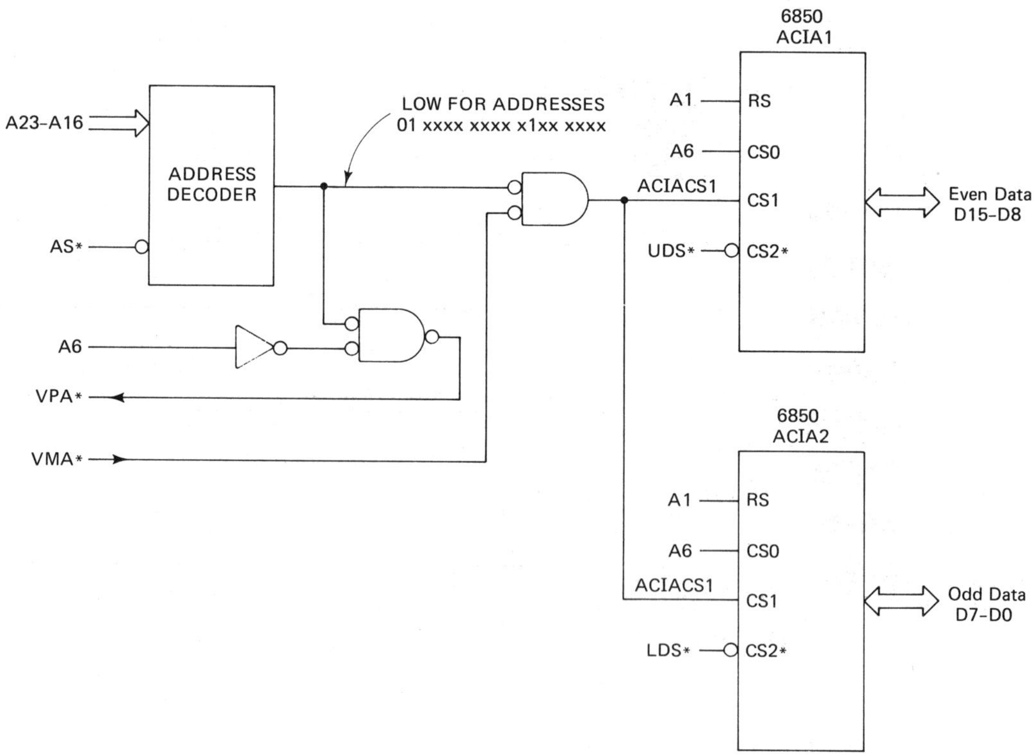

Figure 11.8 Addressing used in the Educational Computer Board to select either ACIA1 or ACIA2; this logic is based on the decoder schematic in Figure 8.15. ACIA1 is at \$010040 and \$010042; ACIA2 is at \$010041 and \$010043.

	Even (UDS*)	Odd (LDS*)
$01 0040	ACIA1 Control/Status	ACIA2 Control/Status
$01 0042	ACIA1 Data	ACIA2 Data

Figure 11.9 Memory map of the TUTOR assignments for I/O using the Educational Computer Board.

11.3 A SINGLE-PORT INTERFACE

The TUTOR firmware requires the memory map in Figure 11.9 for a complete I/O system using two ports. Both of these ports are not necessary initially, and a minimum interface can use just one ACIA. This single port is implemented using ACIA1, and it acts as Port 1 for all the console communications. It should be decoded at $010040 (and $010042) and be connected to the even data bus.

The ACIA need not be fully decoded at $010040. In a small system, it might be entirely reasonable to enable the ACIA when the address is not in ROM or RAM space. The decoding and interface to the 68000, however, will follow the block diagram in Figure 11.10. Also, the ACIA need not be addressed at $010040: this address can be changed

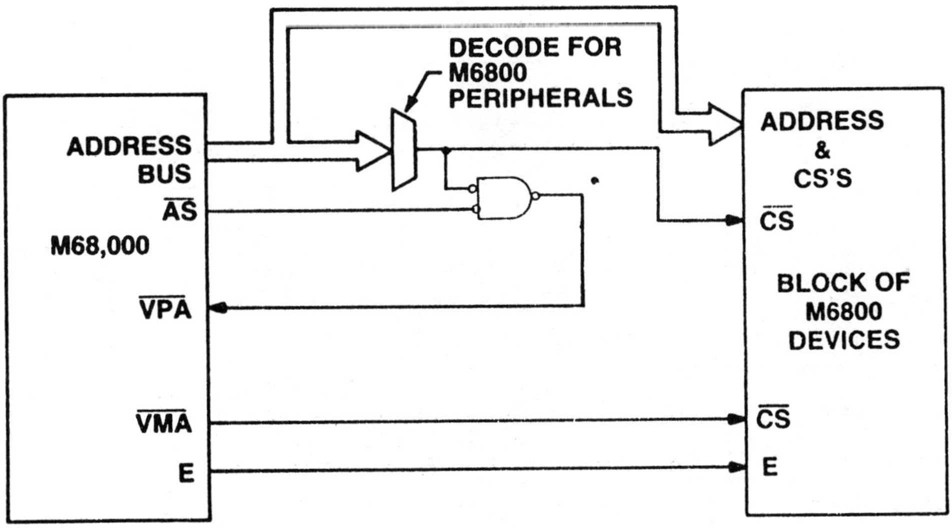

Figure 11.10 Connection of 6800 peripherals to the 68000. Note that AS* is not used to select the chips. (Courtesy Motorola Inc.)

by modifying the TUTOR code slightly in one location. However, at this point in the system development, modifications to TUTOR should be avoided.

A prototype I/O port using the one ACIA can be included on the same board that you use for construction of the 68000. A schematic of a minimum interface is shown in Figure 11.11, and it requires very little board space. If you want, it can be built on a separate protoboard with a ribbon cable interconnection to the 68000 board. On the other hand, if you are designing and building an IEEE Std-696 68000 board, you might not

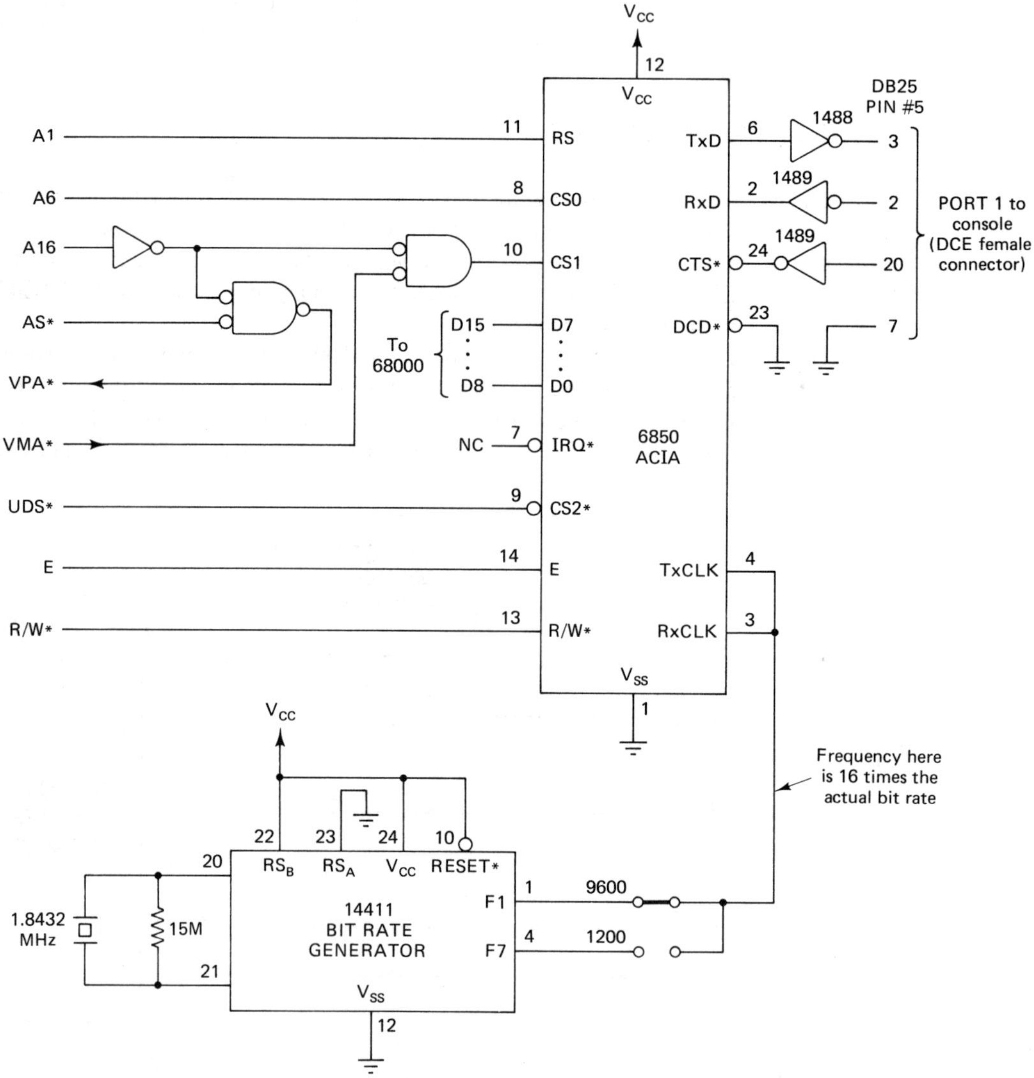

Figure 11.11 Serial Port 1 interfacing the 68000 to the system console. This simple implementation will select the ACIA for any address in the "01" 64K page as well as any other pages having A16 = 1.

even be planning on having I/O on the CPU board. But without the bus-interface circuitry, there is no way to reach external I/O in the full system. In that case, a separate protoboard for test and development is necessary until the bus interface is finished.

11.3.1 Design Overview

The 6850 communication interface in Figure 11.11 depends entirely on the 68000's hardware synchronous bus-control capability. There are no software instructions to force the processor to begin the synchronous bus cycle for I/O; the 68000 is memory-mapped and expects to read and write to memory locations. The synchronous bus cycle begins only by assertion of VPA* rather than DTACK*. Therefore, a part of the interface circuit must recognize the ACIA address and inhibit the normal generation of DTACK* and at the same time assert VPA* instead.

Thus, the address decoder has an additional function in the ACIA circuit: besides recognizing the ACIA address, it must also provide VPA* and inhibit DTACK*. The decoder in Figure 11.11 responds to A16 high by asserting VPA* as soon as AS* goes low; the VPA* signal goes to the 68000 directly and is also used to disable DTACK*. Notice that any address with A16 high will assert VPA*. This incomplete decoding means that there are many addresses in the memory map that will cause this simple I/O port to respond. For a small system, there is no problem with multiple address response because the 68000 will be using only a small portion of its memory. If a more unique address is necessary, then additional address lines can be decoded along with A16.

The 6850 interface designed here does not use AS* as part of the chip select function: it is not necessary. In contrast, the ECB design sketched in Figure 11.8 does use AS* as part of the chip select. Usually this extra qualifier will not cause a problem, but if AS* is negated much before the E clock falling edge, the 6850 could be deselected before the data transfer can take place (see Section 8.2.3 for a more complex discussion of this issue). Rather than blindly copying an existing design, always examine and question the use of each control. In the case of the single-port design, the 68000 interface from the ECB example can be simplified and made more reliable at the same time.

The 6850 requires receive and transmit clocks in addition to the 68000 digital interface. These clocks, both the same for identical data receive and transmit speeds, are standard TTL inputs from a bit-rate generator. As configured by TUTOR, the clock frequency must be 16 times the baud rate (bits per second) of the serial data lines to the system video console. The MC14411 shown in the schematic provides a number of different rates for various console requirements. As drawn, 9600 or 1200 baud communication can be established using a simple jumper for 153.6 kHz or 19.2 kHz, respectively.

The bit-rate generator circuit can be simplified even further by removing the crystal and obtaining the time base from the 68000 clock. In order to do this, however, recognize that this places a constraint on what clock frequency can be used by the 68000: a multiple of the 1.8432 MHz input required by the 14411. For example, suppose you want to run the 68000 at 12.5 MHz; you would only be able to run it at 11.06 MHz so you could divide its clock by 6 for the required 1.8432 MHz to the 14411. Unless you already have the division circuits in place, deriving the 14411 clock from the 68000 clock might not be a simplifying tradeoff.

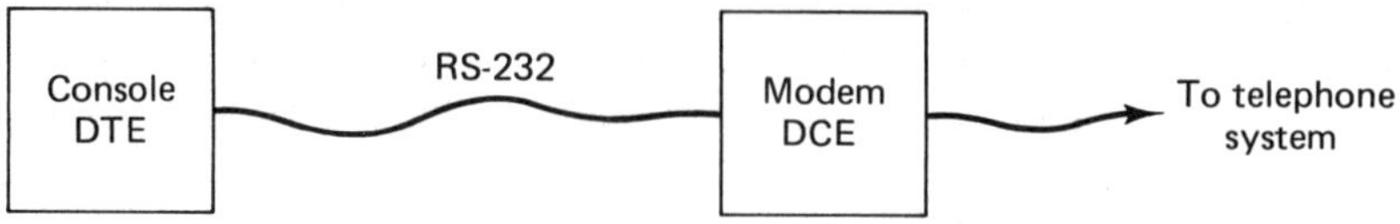

Figure 11.12 RS-232C cable connection between a terminal and a telephone modem.

11.3.2 Serial Interface to the Console

The whole subject of data communication using the EIA Standard RS-232C seems confused and mysterious at first glance. Basically, the idea is to define signal levels and functions at the interface between data terminal equipment (DTE) and data communication equipment (DCE). Using the Standard, electronic equipment can be interconnected and exchange data at up to 20 Kbits/sec. over cables up to 50 feet long. The signal levels are high enough so that there is reasonable noise immunity even if the cables are run in an electrically noisy environment.

In the context of general data communication, a terminal (DTE) might be connected to a phone modem (DCE) as shown in Figure 11.12; the modem would then connect to a dial-up or private-line telephone system. Another modem and terminal at the other end of the telephone system would be able to communicate with the first terminal. As sketched in Figure 11.13, the Standard specifies that the terminal DTE connector should be male; the modem DCE connector should be female. Thus, knowing that a terminal is DTE establishes the gender of its interconnecting cable to the DCE. The Standard also specifies that the DTE transmit data on connector pin 2 and receive on pin 3; the DCE receives on 2 and transmits on 3.

Much of the confusion in the Standard is over the issue of which equipment is DTE and which is DCE. For example, suppose that the terminal connects to a computer, and the computer connects to the modem. The terminal is DTE, and it connects to the computer DCE port; the modem is DCE, and it connects to the computer DTE port. This should establish the gender of all the connectors and which pins are to receive and transmit data. Now add in a printer and call it DTE so it receives data on pin 3. Add in dozens of manufacturers plus misunderstandings on which equipment is used and in what way, and you can see a problem. The usual fix is a null modem to cross-connect lines between

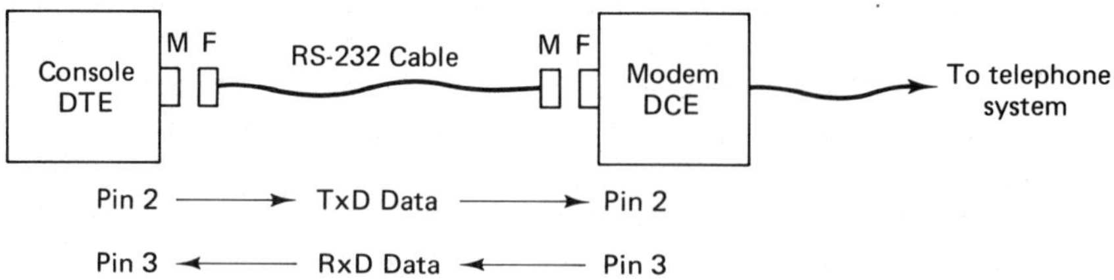

Figure 11.13 Gender and pin numbers for data transfer between DTE and DCE.

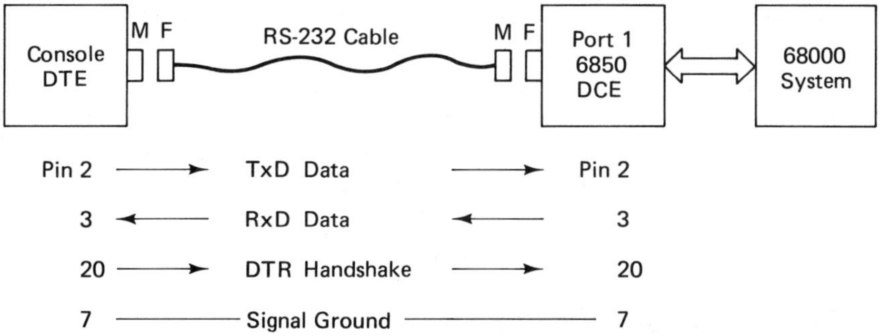

Figure 11.14 The serial data connections between the console and the 6850 communications Port 1.

mismatched equipment; the breakout box is an excellent tool to make such connections quickly.[1]

The serial-data 6850 communication port is configured DCE as shown in Figure 11.14. This means that Port 1 will transmit data on the RS-232C pin 3 and receive data on pin 2; physically, the port will use a standard female 25-pin connector. In addition to the two data lines (and ground), TUTOR requires a third line for handshaking; this line lets TUTOR know that a terminal is connected and ready for data exchange. Other handshaking lines might be required by the console, and they can be easily provided or defeated if necessary.

The voltages appearing on the RS-232C interface are *not* the usual TTL 0 to 5V. The Standard signal voltages, as shown in Figure 11.15, range from + 15 to − 15 V, but typically signals are either + 12 (space) or − 12 V (mark). Because of the difference be-

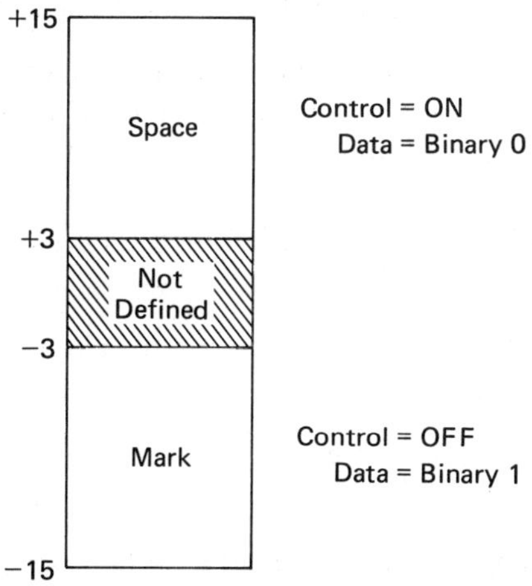

Figure 11.15 Range of voltages on the RS-232C interface cable.

[1]A breakout box is a small breadboard that allows changing the RS-232C interconnections. It is inserted in the serial line between devices.

tween the TTL levels and the RS-232C levels, the 1488 and 1489 interface ICs are used to buffer the connection between the 6850 and the data lines. When no data is being transmitted, the two data lines are in a marking condition; that is, the voltage from signal ground (pin 7) and either pin 2 or 3 is -12 V. A start pulse is $+12$ followed by $+12$ V binary 0 or -12 V binary 1 for the data. The control lines, such as DTR on pin 20, are at -12 V if off and $+12$ V if on. Therefore, to make Port 1 recognize that a terminal is present, $+12$ V must be applied to DTR for an *on* condition. See the Appendix for additional RS-232C information related to the Educational Computer Board.

11.3.3. Bus-Cycle Timing Analysis

Analysis of the single-port interface timing with the 68000 is different from the memory analysis in the last chapter. Instead of calculating how long the 68000 must ''wait'' before completing a bus cycle, the issue here is no more complex than matching the 68000 with a ''fast-enough'' peripheral. When you examine the specifications for the 6850, you find that there are ICs having several different speeds. The 6850, 68A50, and 68B50 have cycle times of 1, 1.5, and 2 MHz, respectively. Which of these is the proper one to use in the serial interface, especially when the 68000 clock is nowhere near 1 or 2 MHz?

The key to the answer here is recognizing that the cycle time of the 6850 refers to the E clock and not the 68000 clock. Even for a high-speed 68000 running at 12.5 MHz, its E output is only 1.25 MHz, or one-tenth of the system clock. Making the appropriate choice of 6850 requires examination of the E-clock pulse width and also verification that data setup and hold times are met. The 6850 chip select initiates the 68000 synchronous bus cycle (by asserting VPA*), so its time does not enter into the calculation at all.

Case I—Read from 6850. Examine the read-cycle timing shown in Figure 11.16. The sequence during the last part of the synchronous cycle is this:

- E goes high — The 6850 responds by putting data on the bus within t_{DDR} maximum. This data must be valid one setup time, t_{CLDO}, before the falling edge of the clock at the end of state S6.
- E stays high for t_{EH} minimum — The 6850 requires E high for PW_{EH} minimum.

These sequences lead to the following requirements that should be met when selecting the appropriate 6800-series devices for the 68000:

- $t_{EH} - t_{CLSH} - t_{SHEL} - t_{DDR} > t_{CLDO}$ Setup time
- $t_{EH} > PW_{EH}$ E pulse-width

The 68000 has no requirement for data hold time beyond the falling edge of the system clock at the end of state S6 when it latches data in. The E clock is always after S6, and the data from the 6850 is always valid until t_{DHR} after E, so data hold is never a problem for a 68000 read.

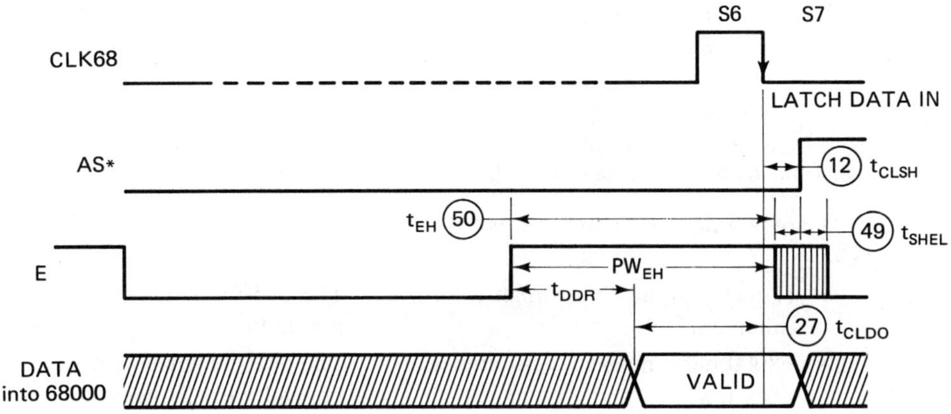

Figure 11.16 Read-cycle timing for synchronous read of a 6850 ACIA. The bubble numbers refer to the 68000 specifications for 6800-type interfacing.

Example 1

Assume a 68000 running with a 12.5 MHz clock. Should you select a 6850, a 68A50, or a 68B50 to read data from a single serial port?

Solution: Check the setup time to see if it meets the requirement

$$t_{EH} - t_{CLSH} - t_{SHEL} - t_{DDR} > t_{CLDO}$$

where

$$\begin{aligned} t_{EH} &= \text{280 ns from the 68000 data sheet, bubble 50.} \\ t_{CLSH} &= \text{50 ns from the 68000 data sheet, bubble 12.} \\ t_{SHEL} &= \text{45 ns from the 68000 data sheet, bubble 49.} \\ t_{CLDO} &= \text{10 ns from the 68000 data sheet, bubble 27.} \end{aligned}$$

$$t_{DDR} = \begin{cases} \text{290 ns for 6850} \\ \text{180 ns for 68A50} \\ \text{150 ns for 68B50} \end{cases}$$

Substituting the values, the 6850 will not work in the worst case; both the 68A50 and the 68B50 will meet the setup time requirement.

Next, check the E-clock pulse-width time to see if it meets

$$t_{EH} > PW_{EH}$$

where

$$t_{EH} = \text{280 ns from the 68000 data sheet, bubble 50.}$$

$$PW_{EH} = \begin{cases} \text{450 ns for 6850} \\ \text{280 ns for 68A50} \\ \text{220 ns for 68B50} \end{cases}$$

Substituting these values, the 6850 is not fast enough; as before, both the 68A50 and the 68B50 will work. Select either one for use as a serial port for reading serial data.

Case II—Write to 6850. The write-cycle timing analysis illustrated in Figure 11.17 could hardly be called more than a quick check of specifications. The sequence at the end of the synchronous cycle is similar to the read case:

• 68000 data-out valid during S3	The 6850 requires data valid for t_{DSW} before E falls at end of S6.
• E goes high and stays high for t_{EH} minimum	The 6850 requires E high for PW_{EH} minimum.
• 68000 data invalid t_{ELDOI} after E goes low	The 6850 requires data valid for t_{DHW} beyond when E goes low.

These sequences lead to the following requirements that should be met when selecting the appropriate 6800-series devices for the 68000:

- $t_{\text{valid data}} > t_{DSW}$ Data setup time
- $t_{EH} > PW_{EH}$ E pulse-width
- $t_{ELDOI} > t_{DHW}$ Data hold time

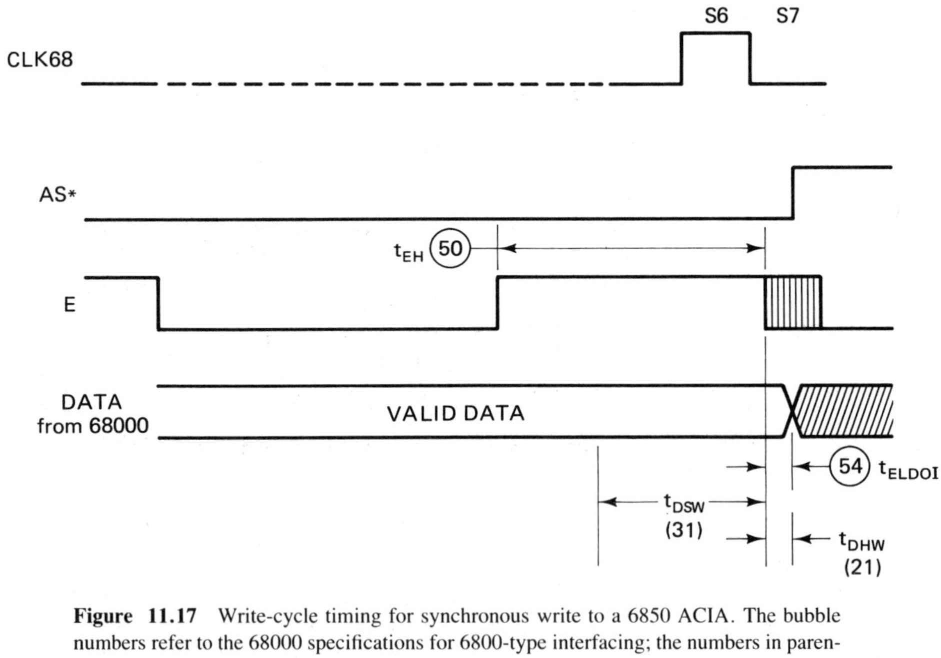

Figure 11.17 Write-cycle timing for synchronous write to a 6850 ACIA. The bubble numbers refer to the 68000 specifications for 6800-type interfacing; the numbers in parentheses refer to specifications on the 6850 data sheet.

Example 2

Assume a 68000 running with a 12.5 MHz clock. Should you select a 6850, a 68A50, or a 68B50 to write a single serial port?

Solution: See if the 68000 provides data at least t_{DSW} before E goes low. The slowest case 6850 requires $t_{DSW} > 165$ ns. Data is valid before the E clock goes high, and the E clock itself is longer than this. Thus, this aspect of timing does not enter into the selection.

Next, check the E clock pulse-width time to see if it meets

$$t_{EH} > PW_{EH}$$

where $t_{EH} =$ 280 ns from the 68000 data sheet, bubble 50.

$$PW_{EH} = \begin{cases} 450 \text{ ns for } 6850 \\ 280 \text{ ns for } 68A50 \\ 220 \text{ ns for } 68B50 \end{cases}$$

Substituting these values, we find that the 6850 is not fast enough; either the 68A50 or the 68B50 will meet the pulse-width time.

Now, see that the data-hold time specifications are met:

$$t_{ELDOI} > t_{DHW}$$

where

$t_{ELDOI} =$ 15 ns from the 68000 data sheet, bubble 54.
$t_{DHW} =$ 10 ns for all 6850,A,B

In all cases, there is no difficulty in meeting this timing specification. The conclusion, then, is to use either a 68A50 or a 68B50 for serial data output.

11.3.4 Testing the Interface

The single serial port in Figure 11.11 can be tested by modules by first checking the bit-rate generator for proper output. Assuming that the console communications will be at 9600 baud, the output from the 14411 should be 16×9600 or 153.6 kHz. The second module to check is the 1488 and 1489 buffer pair to the RS-232C interface: the console should provide about +12 on pin 20 and data on pin 2 of the DB-25 connector. Check pin 20 with a voltmeter; check pin 2 with a logic probe for activity when you press a console key. The +12 V on pin 20 is interpreted as control = ON (Figure 11.15); it forces the 1489 output to about 0.2 V, which asserts CTS*.

The 6850 itself cannot be tested without first initializing it using software: it requires configuration information before it can be used. Figure 11.18 shows a simple program

```
*       Program to send a test character to serial Port 1
*
*       Initialize port to 8 bit words, 1 stop bit, no parity

             LEA          $010040,A0        Put Port 1 adr in A0
             MOVE.B       #$4B,D0           Char 'K' in D0

INIT         MOVE.B       #$43,(A0)         Send RESET cmd to Port 1
             MOVE.B       #$15,(A0)         Program ACIA normally

STAT         MOVE.B       (A0),D1           Check if port ready
             AND.B        #2,D1             Ready when match
             BEQ.S        STAT

             MOVE.B       D0,2(A0)          Send char to data port
             BRA          STAT
```

Figure 11.18 Scope-loop program to send a single test character out of Port 1.

that first resets the 6850 and then sets it to communicate using 8-bit words with 1 stop bit and no parity. This setup is the normal TUTOR configuration. The program then checks to see if the port is ready for data; when it is, a single letter *K* (an arbitrary choice, and easy to recognize) is sent out. Then the program repeats over, and over, checking status and sending another character every time the 6850 transmitter buffer is empty.

The test program is nothing more than a simple scope loop. It can be programmed into a pair of EPROMs and plugged into the EPROM sockets of the 68000 system. After fetching the SSP and PC at power-up, the 68000 should begin executing the program. Because it loops over very few instructions, the data and control buses can be easily checked for proper values using an oscilloscope. For example, synchronize the scope on VMA*, and you should see a pattern similar to Figure 11.6.

Normally, if no signals are being transmitted from Port 1, the DB-25 connector pin 3 will measure about −12 V. When a character is sent, as sketched in Figure 11.19, a start bit of +12 V initiates the bit sequence. Although data transmission is asynchronous character to character, the bits within each character are synchronous; the "start" bit is used to indicate to the receiving ACIA to begin clocking in bits synchronously at a rate of 9600 per second. The bits are sent least-significant first, so the letter *K* (ASCII 4B or 0100 1011) is actually sent in the sequence 1101 0010. After the data bits and one stop bit are sent, the transmit line stays in the marking (−12 V) condition until the next character.

The transmit-data signal on the interface is shown in Figure 11.20 for the scope-loop program. Compare this with the expected pattern in Figure 11.19. You should see the character sequence repeating every 1.04 ms if the bit-rate generator is properly set for 9600 baud communication. If nothing comes out of the ACIA, but the 68000 seems to be looping properly and enabling the 6850, check that CTS* (6850 pin 24) is asserted low.

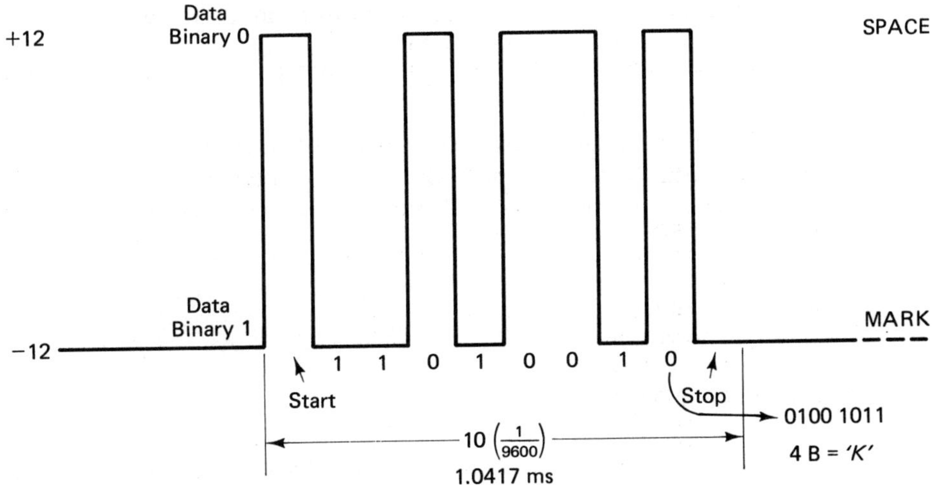

Figure 11.19 A single 8-bit character (the letter K) as it appears on the RS-232C interface. The character is being sent at 9600 baud, 1 stop bit, and no parity.

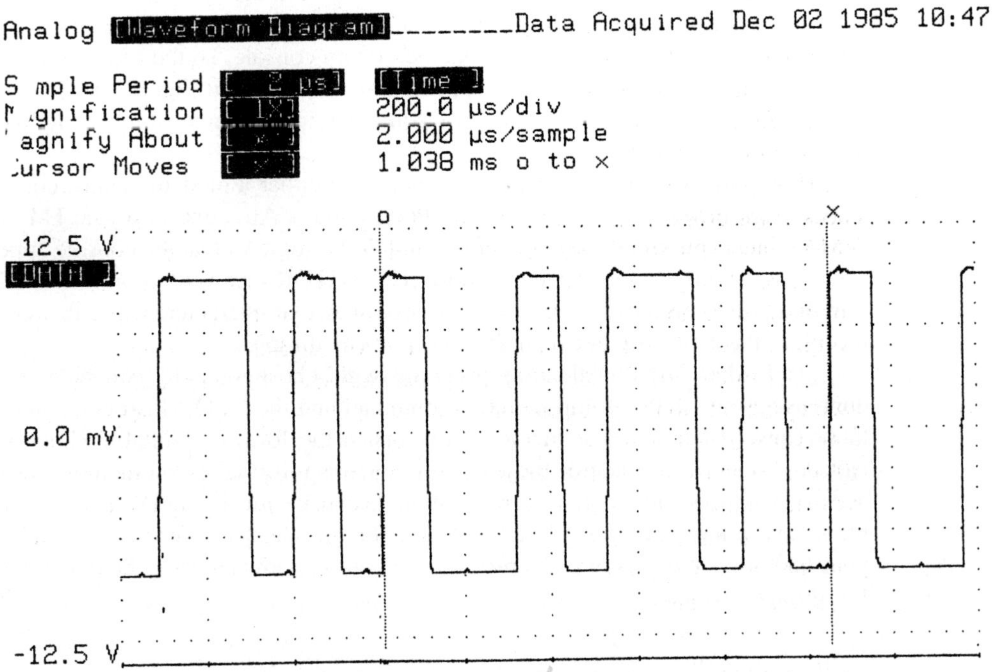

Figure 11.20 Transmit-data signal on the RS-232C interface pin 3 while sending a repeating string of K characters. The "o" and "x" enclose a single K.

At this point, establishing communication with TUTOR is easy. Substitute the TUTOR EPROM set for the test EPROMs and power up the system. The TUTOR prompt should appear on the console; pressing the reset button should get another identical prompt. If you press a "return" on the console, TUTOR should respond with "WHAT" and the prompt again. Next, type "DF" to see if the registers are displayed properly; if some of the display lines overrun each other, check that the handshaking on pin 20 is properly connected to your console. Be sure that the console and Port 1 are set to the same baud rate.

11.4 A TWO-PORT INTERFACE

Once a single-port interface has been established, then you can add a second port similar to the ECB schematic shown in Figure 11.21. Notice the similarities and differences between the single- and dual-port designs. They both use the same bit-rate generator and 1488/89 interfaces to the RS-232C. However, each ACIA has its own address for access to the 68000. The ports are also configured differently: one is DCE and the other is DTE.

The fact that Port 1 is DCE and Port 2 is DTE makes no difference to the 68000. The pin connections and gender of the connectors are the only differences between the two; once the cables are properly connected, then nothing more need be considered. From a software standpoint, Port 1 is always the system console, so the video terminal should be connected to it regardless. The second port, as shown in Figure 11.22, can be connected to either a modem or to a host computer for communication or uploading and downloading programs.

For general interactive communication with either a modem or host computer, the TUTOR command "TM" interconnects Ports 1 and 2. After executing the TM command, console data is passed through the Port 1 and Port 2 logic so that the console appears to be connected directly to the modem or host. The TUTOR firmware monitors the data being sent and will ignore everything but the control-A exit character; when this character is received, then the link between the two ports is disabled.

Uploading and downloading programs with a host computer connected to Port 2 is done using the "DU" dump-memory command and the "LO" load command. Both of these cause the transfer of memory contents in the form of printable character strings called "S-records." Each of these strings contains information on memory location, the actual binary memory contents, and a one-byte check sum. Using DU and LO, it is possible to create large programs in a host computer and then transfer the executable code to your 68000 system. Likewise, a program on your system can easily be uploaded to a host for storage on disk.

11.5 SUMMARY

In the last chapter, you completed a working 68000 board that would not only freerun, but would also execute programs stored in EPROMs. These programs could be used to test various parts of the system and help when debugging new modules. Rather than continually making new EPROMs for system development and testing, you need to get the TUTOR firmware running so that the system can be programmed interactively. However, to use TUTOR, I/O must be added to the system.

A single 6850 ACIA provides the minimum I/O needed to run TUTOR in the 68000 system. This component uses the 68000's synchronous interface for proper operation and involves the use of the E clock. It is not a high-speed device and does not take advantage of the 68000's potential because it was designed much earlier for the 6800 processor. However, because TUTOR supports I/O using the 6850, you can avoid unnecessary design delays by staying with the 6850. After the I/O runs, then other I/O alternatives can be investigated.

The design of the single 6850 port can be modeled after the Educational Computer Board. Unless changes are made in the TUTOR firmware, the port addressing requires ACIA decoding at $010040, which is the same as in the ECB. The ECB also provides an example of using the VPA* and VMA* synchronous controls with the 68000. The only significant design issue that must be considered is the bus timing: you need to select a 6850 fast enough to run with whatever clock speed you use with the 68000. In general, the 68A50 and 68B50 ACIAs are adequate for use with even the fastest 68000 system.

Serial data communication using the EIA Standard RS-232C can be somewhat confusing. You must provide non-TTL signal levels on certain lines of the interface between equipment; which signals go on which lines depends on whether your device is data terminal equipment (DTE) or data communication equipment (DCE). The system console is DTE, so that means your 68000 system Port 1 should be configured as DCE. This determines which signals you need to design for which wire connecting your 6850 to the console.

In addition to developing the I/O interface circuit as a module, the interface can also be tested modularly. After checking for proper bit-rate clocking and proper buffer operation, a small EPROM program can initialize the ACIA port and send out test characters. This program is an ideal scope loop, and can be used to check operation of the 68000 interface with the 6850 as well as the 6850 serial output. After the port operates properly with the test program, the TUTOR firmware can be run. After powering up the system, the TUTOR prompt should appear. Next you can begin using TUTOR's interactive commands to extend and debug additional modules in the system.

The second I/O port is one useful module to add immediately. With an operational first port, the addition is simple and easy to check out. One of its primary uses is commu-

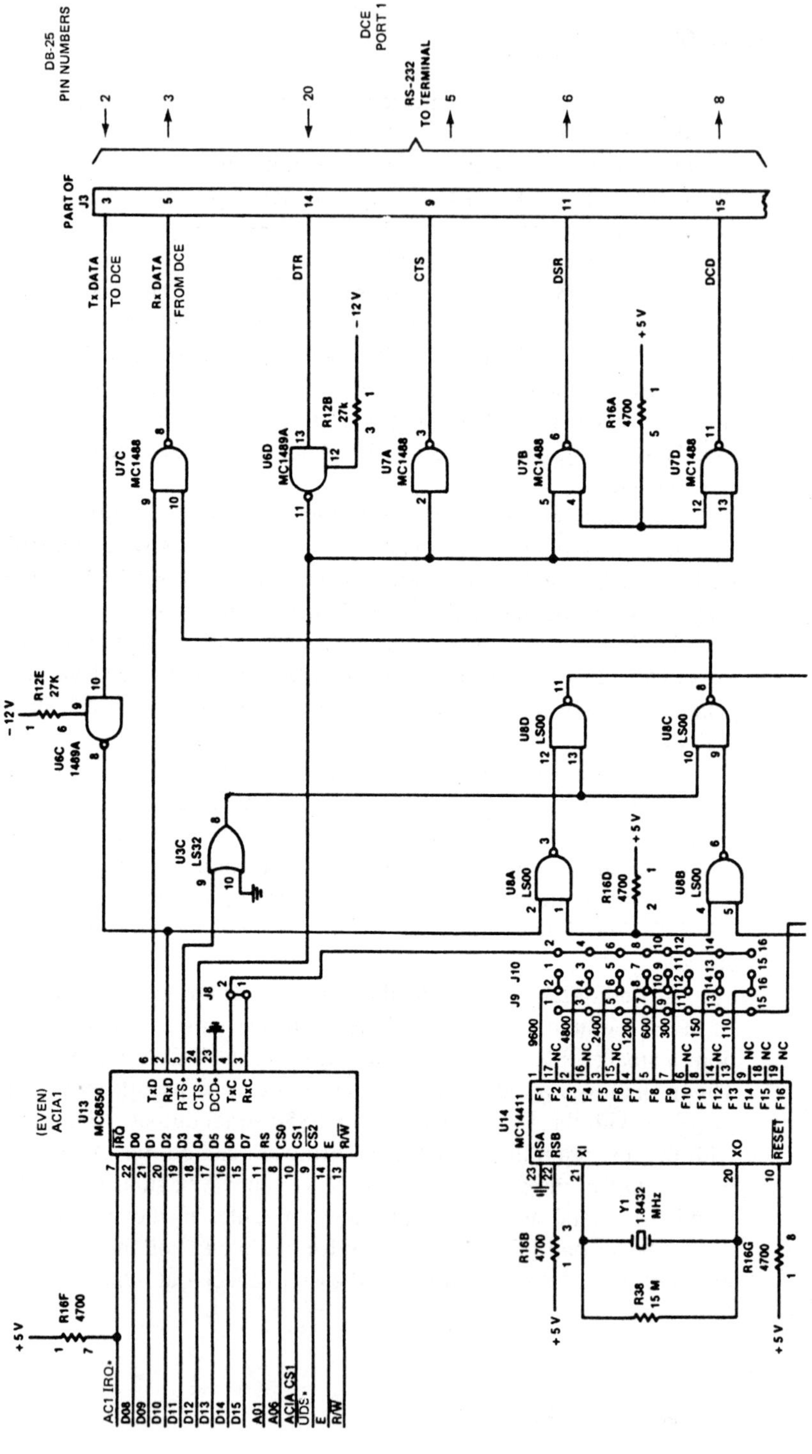
DB-25 PIN NUMBERS
DCE PORT 1
RS-232 TO TERMINAL
PART OF J3
Tx DATA TO DCE
Rx DATA FROM DCE
DTR
CTS
DSR
DCD
U7C MC1488
U6D MC1489A
U7A MC1488
U7B MC1488
U7D MC1488
R12B 27k
R16A 4700
R12E 27K
U6C 1489A
U3C LS32
U8D LS00
U8C LS00
U8A LS00
U8B LS00
R16D 4700
J8
J9
J10
(EVEN) ACIA1
U13 MC6850
U14 MC14411
Y1 1.8432 MHz
R16B 4700
R38 15 M
R16G 4700
R16F 4700
AC1 IRQ*
D08
D09
D10
D11
D12
D13
D14
D15
A01
A06
ACIA CS1
UDS*
E
R/W
9600
4800
2400
1200
600
300
150
110

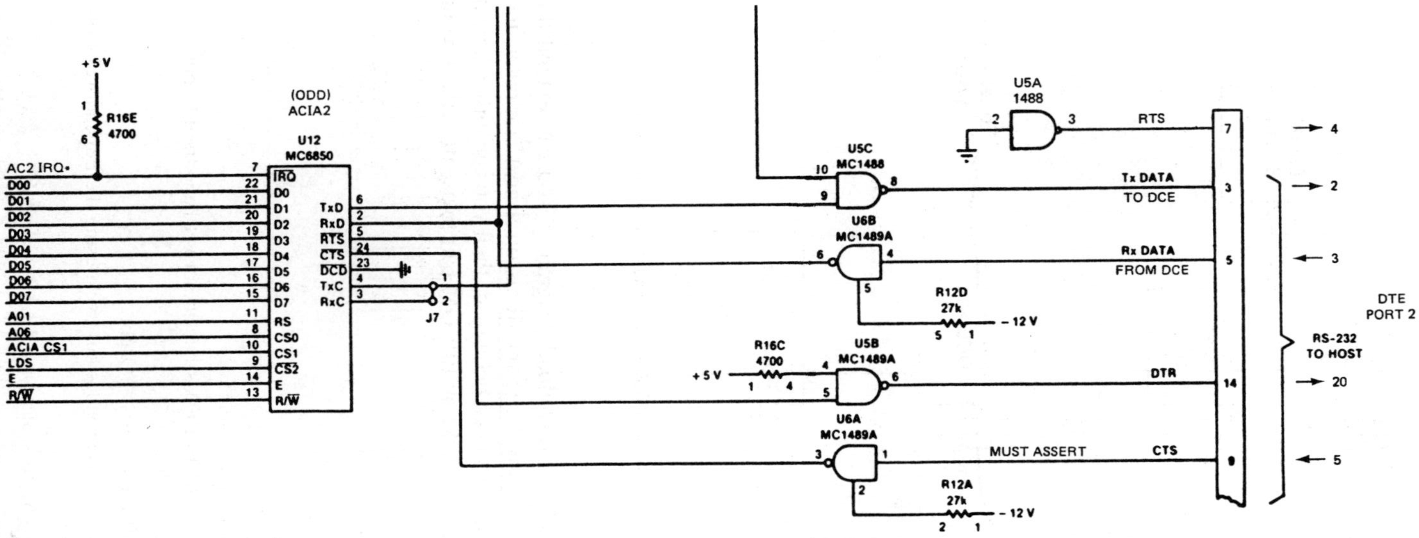

Figure 11.21 Serial Ports 1 and 2 in the Educational Computer board. When TUTOR executes "TM", the ports are interconnected and can directly communiate with each other. (Courtesy Motorola Inc.)

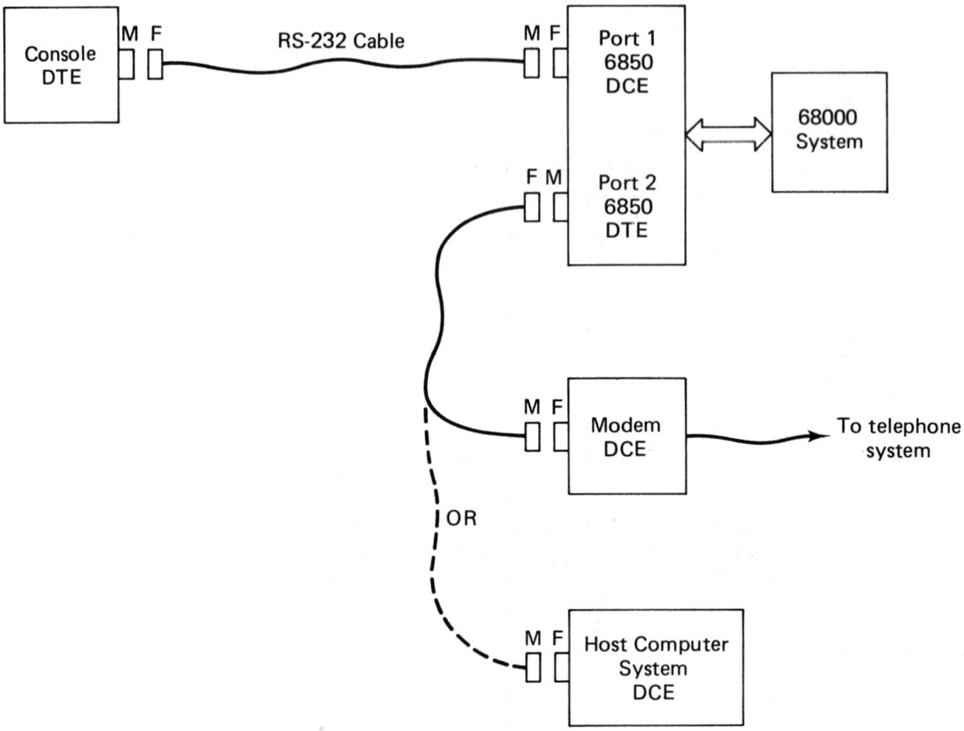

Figure 11.22 Serial data connection between the 68000 system and the console at Port 1 and a modem or host computer at Port 2.

nication with a host computer to upload and download programs. You can extend the power of your system considerably by writing large programs on a host computer and downloading for execution. After the code has been debugged, then you can either save it on a host disk for downloading as needed, or make an EPROM pair to use directly in your system.

EXERCISES

1. Why do you want to run TUTOR as soon as possible?
2. If you set up your 68000 system with TUTOR EPROMs but do not yet have the I/O port constructed, how can you tell if TUTOR is running?
3. Why should you consider using the 6850 for the first I/O port?
4. Why must you disable RAM refresh to see a synchronous bus cycle using the Educational Computer Board?
5. Sketch a typical synchronous read bus cycle to scale for a 10 MHz clock.
6. How long, best and worst case, does a synchronous read bus cycle take using a 10 MHz clock?

7. Suppose you modify TUTOR so that I/O is addressed starting at $FF0040 rather than at $010040. Design the address decoder circuit.
8. Replace the 14411 bit-rate generator with a 555 timer providing the proper bit rate for serial communication at 1200 baud. What are the tradeoffs?
9. Replace the 14411 as in Problem 8, but design for 9600 baud instead. Discuss the tradeoffs and whether you would want to use the 7555 instead of the 555.
10. Suppose that you only have a dual 5-V supply instead of a dual 12-V supply. Can you use the lower voltage to support a serial link between your I/O port and a video console? What are the tradeoffs?
11. Assume you use a 12.5 MHz 68000, but run it with a 10 MHz clock. Should you select a 6850, 68A50, or 68B50 to read data from a serial port? Drop the clock to 8 MHz: what is your selection?
12. Do problem 11 for the case of writing data to the port.
13. Write the program in Figure 11.18 on the Educational Computer Board starting at address $1000. Explain what happens when you run it.
14. Write the program in Figure 11.18 for execution using a pair of EPROMs decoded at address 0. Be sure to include the SSP and PC for the reset vector. Show the actual code that should be in each EPROM when programmed.
15. Sketch the bit pattern you would expect to see if you sent a ")" character instead of a *K* to the serial port. Follow the form of Figure 11.20.
16. Dump the S-records corresponding to the scope-loop program in Problem 13 by using the TUTOR "DU" command. Explain the parts of each line.

FURTHER READING

CURRAN, TIM, and DON FOLKES. "68000 Peripheral Chips Assume I/O Tasks and More." *Electronic Design* (October 13, 1983): 123–28.

ELECTRONIC INDUSTRIES ASSOCIATION. *EIA Standard RS-232C*. Washington, DC: EIA, 1969.

HARPER, KYLE. *A Terminal Interface, Printer Interface, and Background Printing for an MC68000-based System Using the MC68681 DUART*. Application Note AN-899. Austin, TX: Motorola Semiconductor Products, Inc.

MC68000 Educational Computer Board User's Manual, MEX68KECB/D2. 2nd Ed. Tempe, AZ: Motorola Literature Distribution Center, 1982.

MCNAMARA, JOHN E. *Technical Aspects of Data Communication*. 2nd Ed. Bedford, MA: Digital Equipment Corporation Press, 1982. (TK 5105.M4)

MELEAR, CHARLES. *Asynchronous Communications for the MC68000 Using the MC6850*. Application Note AN-817. Austin, TX: Motorola Semiconductor Products, Inc.

MORALES, ARNOLD J. "Interface 6800-μP Peripherals to the 68000." *EDN* (March 4, 1981): 159–61.

NICHOLS, ELIZABETH A., JOSEPH C. NICHOLS, and KEITH R. MUSSON. *Data Communications for Microcomputers*. New York: McGraw-Hill, 1982. (TK5105.N523)

SEYER, MARTIN D. *RS-232 Made Easy*. Englewood Cliffs, NJ: Prentice-Hall, 1984. (TK7887.5.S48)

TWELVE

Exception Processing

After finishing the input/output design in the last chapter, you had an operating 68000 computer board. Finally, all the hardware ran successfully with the TUTOR firmware, and you could write and execute programs. However, unless you design and build the support hardware for exception processing, your system will not effectively take advantage of the 68000's power. For example, suppose you make a programming error, and the 68000 goes into a loop somewhere in memory? Your only recourse so far is to push the reset button (which destroys the stack pointer and program counter contents) and try to guess what went wrong. A better solution is to abort the program gracefully and look at the various registers to find the problem; you can do this with exception processing.

The purpose of this chapter is to examine the 68000's exception processing capabilities and to learn how to use this processing in your system. Besides being able to explain how the 68000 handles exceptions, you should be able to implement the hardware to recover from programming errors. You will also learn how to use and design with interrupts so that your 68000 can respond immediately to real-time events involving data collection or control of equipment. In short, after reading this chapter you will be able to use the full power of the 68000.

The interrupt logic and watchdog timer module in Figure 12.1 provides the hardware support that controls the 68000 exception processing. This module connects to three main groups of signals on the 68000 pins as shown in Figure 12.2.

- Processor Status: Function Code FC2, FC1, FC0.
- Interrupt Control: Interrupt Priority Level IPL2*, IPL1*, IPL0*.
- System Control: Bus Error, Reset, and Halt.

So far, you have experience with the reset and halt signals and have them wired into your system; you will not need to make any modifications to them when you include exception processing.

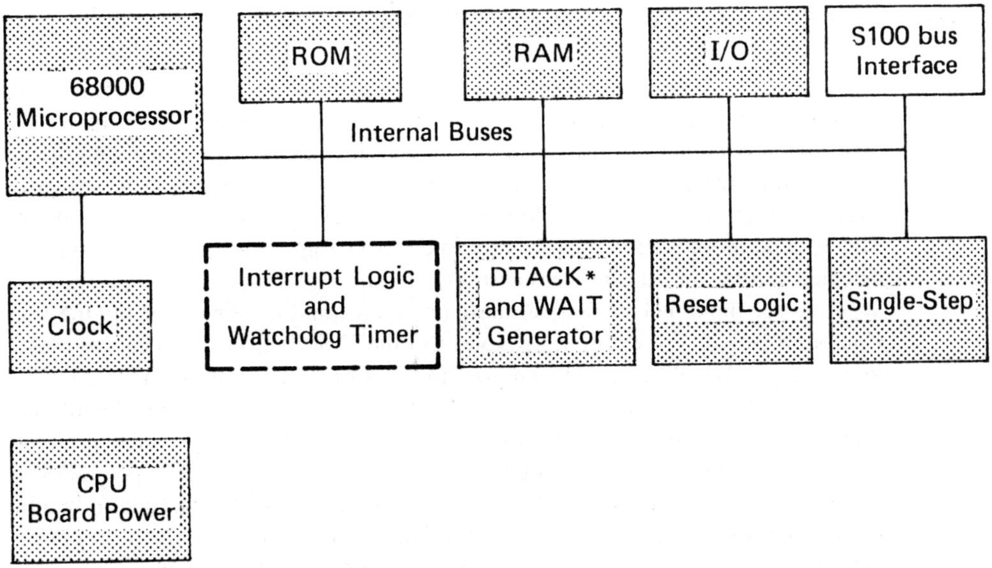

Figure 12.1 The highlighted interrupt logic and watchdog timer module will be developed in this chapter. The shaded modules have already been designed.

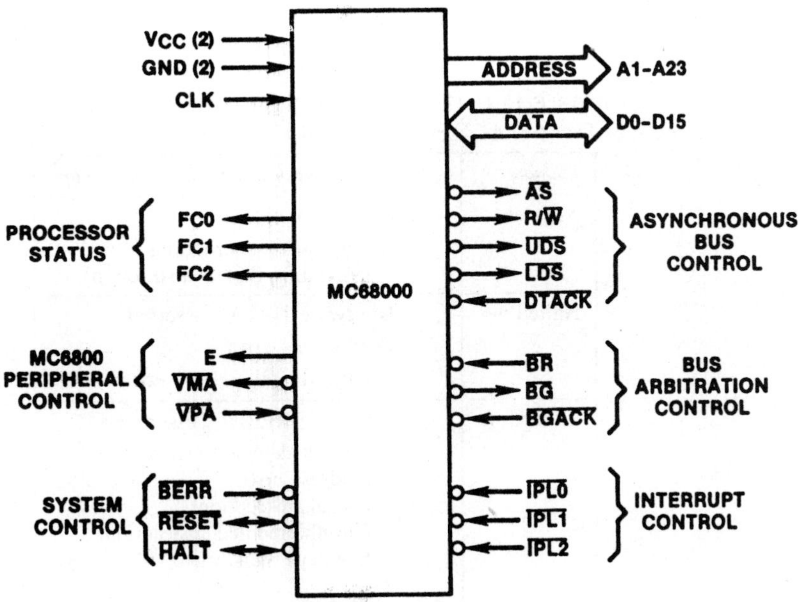

Figure 12.2 Signal lines on the 68000. Processor status, interrupt control, and system control lines implement exception processing. (Courtesy Motorola Inc.)

12.1 PROCESSING STATES AND EXCEPTIONS

The 68000 always operates in one of the three states shown in Table 12.1: normal, halted, or exception. You are already familiar with the normal state in which the 68000 fetches and executes instructions. More than likely, you also have experience with the halted operation from when you first turned on the 68000 and debugged the hardware; a catastrophic failure in the system can prevent normal operation and cause the 68000 to halt. The exception operation deals with interrupts, traps, instruction tracing, internally-detected errors, and the processor reset.

To see the effect of some of these operations on the 68000, test out the Educational Computer Board. For example, if you push the abort button, you cause a non-maskable interrupt or *NMI*. Likewise, when you trace instructions using the TUTOR "TR" command, you are using exception processing. Pushing the reset button is the ultimate exception; in fact, it is the only way to recover when the processor is in the halted state.

An exception is any deviation from normal processing. When the 68000 processes an exception, it executes one of a number of special modules of code to handle the unusual conditions efficiently. This means that, in addition to the main program, the programmer must provide exception-handler code for each expected exception. After the exception code has been written, the 68000 can call it as needed. For example, the exception processing can be initiated by the 68000 *internally* when:

- an address error is detected,
- an illegal or unimplemented op-code is executed,
- a privilege violation has occurred,

TABLE 12.1 PROCESSING STATES OF THE 68000 AND THE TYPICAL OPERATIONS AND THEIR CAUSES.

State	*Typical Operations or Cause of Exception*
Normal	Instruction fetch Execution of instructions (including STOP instruction)
Halted	Hardware HALT* asserted Double bus error Double illegal-address error
Exception	Hardware RESET* asserted Internally detected errors Address error Illegal instruction Unimplemented instruction Privilege violation Trace Interrupts Trap instructions

- tracing mode is active ($T = 1$), and
- instructions (such as TRAP) are executed.

Exception processing can be caused *externally* by:

- a system reset,
- a bus error, and
- an interrupt.

These various exceptions have different levels of priority depending on the nature of the cause. Table 12.2 shows these priorities and the action caused by each. The highest priority exception, of course, is the system reset caused by asserting the 68000 RESET* control. Asserting the bus error control, BERR*, also causes an immediate response: whatever instruction was in process is terminated within two clock cycles. An address error, such as reading an op-code at an odd address, causes an abort of the current bus cycle and also leads to exception processing.

TABLE 12.2 PRIORITIES OF THE VARIOUS EXCEPTION GROUPS AND THE ACTIO N TAKEN BY THE 68000.

Group and Priority	*Type of Exception*	*Exception Processing Action*
0 Highest	Reset (RESET*) Bus Error (BERR*) Address Error	Current bus cycle aborted within 2 clock cycles.
1	Illegal Instruction Unimplemented Instr. Privilege Violation	Finish current bus cycle, then start exception processing.
	Trace Interrupt	Finish current instruction, then start exception processing.
2 Lowest	TRAP, TRAPV, CHK Zero-Divide	Exception processing started by executing the instruction.

The lower priority exceptions in Groups 1 and 2 are noncatastrophic and do not cause such immediate action. There is really nothing "wrong" with the system; that is, there is no reason to think that the bus cycle or current instruction cannot be completed without error. So, rather than interrupt processing immediately, the current bus cycle or instruction is completed before exception processing begins.

The 68000 does exception processing by using a table of vectors located in low memory from address 0 to $3FF. These vectors are memory locations, each two words long, that contain the addresses of routines for handling exceptions.[1] Table 12.3 shows all

[1]The TUTOR firmware initializes the exception vector table. In general, however, it is the programmer's responsibility to make sure the vectors are properly set. The vector address is simply (vector number) $\times 4$. For example, the address of vector #15 is ($F)$\times$4 or $3C.

TABLE 12.3 EXCEPTION VECTORS LOCATED IN LOWEST 1,024 BYTES OF MEMORY. EACH VECTOR IS A 32-BIT LONG WORD.

Memory Address (Hexadecimal)		Vector Number (Decimal)	Vector Number Hexadecimal)
0	Reset: Initial SSP	0	0
	Reset: Inital PC	1	1
8	Bus Error	2	2
C	Address Error	3	3
10	Illegal Instruction	4	4
14	Zero Divide	5	5
18	CHK Instruction	6	6
1C	TRAPV Instruction	7	7
20	Privilege Violation	8	8
24	Trace	9	9
28	Line 1010 Emulator	10	A
2C	Line 1111 Emulator	11	B
30	Unassigned Reserved		
3C	Uninitialized Interrupt	15	F
40	Unassigned Reserved		
60	Spurious Interrupt	24	18
64	Level 1 Interrupt Autovector	25	19
68	Level 2 Interrupt Autovector	26	1A
6C	Level 3 Interrupt Autovector	27	1B
70	Level 4 Interrupt Autovector	28	1C
74	Level 5 Interrupt Autovector	29	1D
78	Level 6 Interrupt Autovector	30	1E
7C	Level 7 Interrupt Autovector	31	1F
80 BC	16 Trap Instruction Vectors	32 47	20 2F
C0 100	Unassigned Reserved		
 3FF	192 User Interrupt Vectors	64 255	40 FF

the vector allocations that are currently assigned to production 68000s. As shown in Figure 12.3, when the 68000 begins processing an exception, it saves its current context (status register and program counter) on the system stack, reads the vector information at one of the table addresses, and then jumps to the vector address. After completing the exception-handling routine, the 68000 then returns to the code it was executing before the exception. Naturally, this pattern is very general and simplified: many more details must be added for a complete picture of what happens when the 68000 begins an exception.

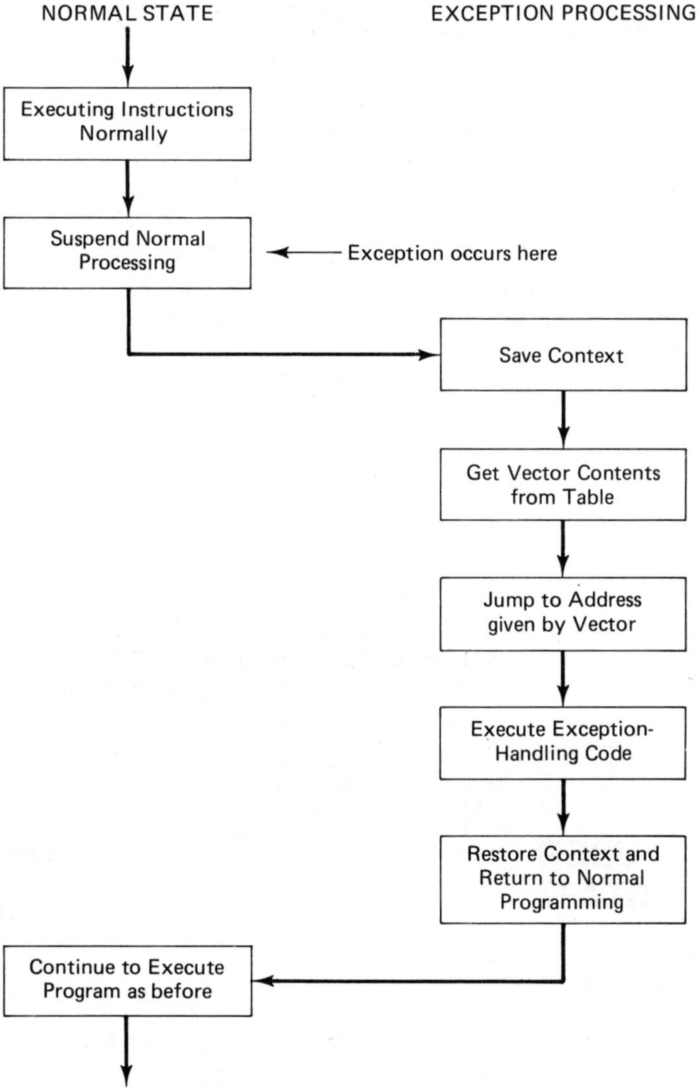

Figure 12.3 General pattern of how exception processing alters the normal pattern of an executing 68000 program.

The reset exception is slightly different: when the 68000 begins this exception, two vectors (SSP and PC) rather than one are accessed. Also, the context is not saved; if the processor had to be reset, whatever was in the registers was most probably not worth saving. This reset exception is the one that you implemented earlier when you first began building your 68000 system. When you asserted the RESET* control, the 68000 fetched the SSP and PC from your EPROM decoded at address 0. Do not confuse the reset exception with the RESET *instruction:* the instruction does not cause an exception and does not reset the 68000. All the instruction does is assert the 68000 reset control as an *output* to reset external devices in the system.

12.2 PRIVILEGE STATES

Although it is not obvious when you first bring up the 68000 and run your first program, you are operating in the ''supervisor'' state. When in the supervisor state, you have access to every instruction that the 68000 can execute. As shown in Figure 12.4, there is also a second state, the ''user'' state, which does not have access to every 68000 instruction. The purpose of this lower-privilege state is to provide security for the operating system: user application programs access their own code and cannot disturb the system.

Whether the 68000 is in the supervisor or user state depends on the setting of the supervisory *S*-bit in the status register shown in Figure 12.5. If $S=1$ (set), then the 68000 is in the supervisor state, and all instructions are allowed. The status register (SR) can be changed while in the supervisor state to get into the user state by making $S=0$. Once in the user state, however, it is impossible to go back, because the instruction to change the *S*-bit is not allowed! Figure 12.6 shows the 68000 privilege states and these restricted instructions. However, because all exception processing is done while in the supervisor

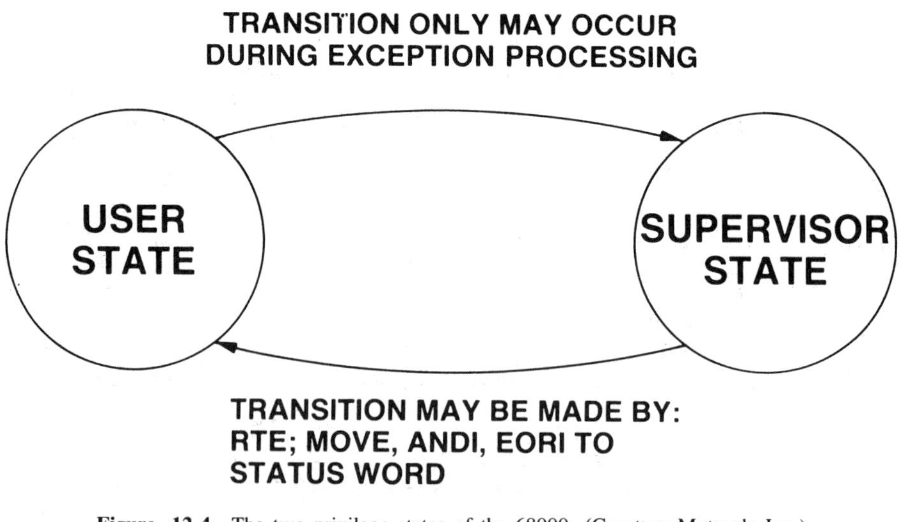

Figure 12.4 The two privilege states of the 68000. (Courtesy Motorola Inc.)

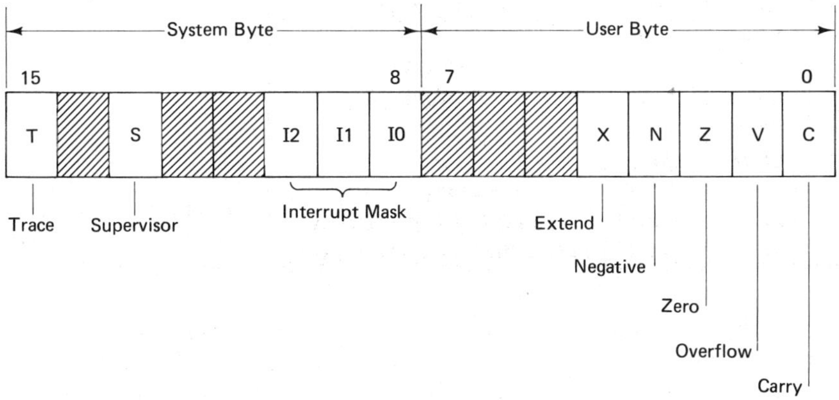

Figure 12.5 Status register of the 68000.

state, you can return via an exception if necessary. If all else fails, asserting the RESET* line brings up the 68000 in the supervisor state.

The concept of supervisor and user states works out quite conveniently for operating system design. User application programs can take advantage of powerful system utilities by calling a TRAP instruction, and yet the system is protected. For example, in TUTOR, the TRAP 14 handler provides a number of data conversion and input/output routines for the user. When the TRAP is executed, the user receives all the *benefit* of the supervisor state, but cannot stay in that state. As soon as the TRAP's RTE (return from exception) instruction is executed, the user state is in force again. The only way to stay in the supervisor state is if the system programmer explicitly provided a means for a user to stay.

STATE	S BIT	OPERATION
USER	0	SOME INSTRUCTIONS ARE NOT ALLOWED: STOP, RESET, MOVE An, USP; RTE; AND to SR; EOR to SR; OR to SR; MOVE TO SR: CAN ONLY BE PLACED IN SUPERVISOR STATE DURING AN EXCEPTION
SUPERVISOR	1	ALL INSTRUCTIONS MAY BE EXECUTED

Figure 12.6 The two privilege states and their instructions. (Courtesy Motorola Inc.)

FC2	FC1	FC0	CYCLE TYPE
LOW	LOW	LOW	
LOW	LOW	HIGH	USER DATA
LOW	HIGH	LOW	USER PROGRAM
LOW	HIGH	HIGH	
HIGH	LOW	LOW	
HIGH	LOW	HIGH	SUPERVISOR DATA
HIGH	HIGH	LOW	SUPERVISOR PROGRAM
HIGH	HIGH	HIGH	INTERRUPT ACKNOWLEDGE

Figure 12.7 Function code outputs indicate the processor state and type of bus cycle. (Courtesy Motorola Inc.)

It would appear that these two privilege states depend on just the *S*-bit being set or reset. Actually, there is hardware to enforce the state of the machine: the function code outputs. As shown in Figure 12.7, the output of these status lines indicates the processor state (supervisor or user) and the type of bus cycle; these outputs are valid whenever AS* is asserted. They can, for example, be used to implement a memory-protection design. Reading memory is not a restricted activity by itself, regardless of whether the 68000 is in the supervisor or user state. There is no way to protect supervisor memory in software: it must be in hardware.

A simple memory-protection circuit is shown in Figure 12.8 . It is intended to protect supervisor memory by using one of the function code outputs. The memory map for the circuit is designed with the low 8 Mb allocated for the supervisor only; the high 8 Mb can be accessed by both the user and the supervisor. The circuit is identical to one you might normally use to control any memory array; the only difference is that FC2 = LOW inhibits a chip select of the low memory bank. Consequently, when the *S*-bit is 0 during the user state, it is physically impossible to enable the lower memory array even though the address decodes properly.

One important point to keep in mind when considering the user and supervisor states: there are two separate stack pointers. When you reset the 68000 and come up in the supervisor state, the A7 register contains the SSP that was found in the lowest four locations in the boot EPROM. If any operation is planned for the user state, the *user* stack pointer *must* be initialized (see the instruction MOVE USP); it does not get set with the SSP on a cold boot. In addition, if memory protection is provided, care must be taken that the USP stays in allowed memory space as the stack grows. Recall that the stack pointer moves from higher to lower addresses as the stack grows; avoid placing the stack too near disallowed memory.

12.3 RESET EXCEPTION PROCESSING

As mentioned earlier, asserting the 68000 RESET* line causes an immediate highest priority exception. In addition to being used for system initialization, it is also used for recovery from catastrophic system faults. All 68000 systems must have boot software and hardware to allow a satisfactory system initial reset: this was done even in the simple

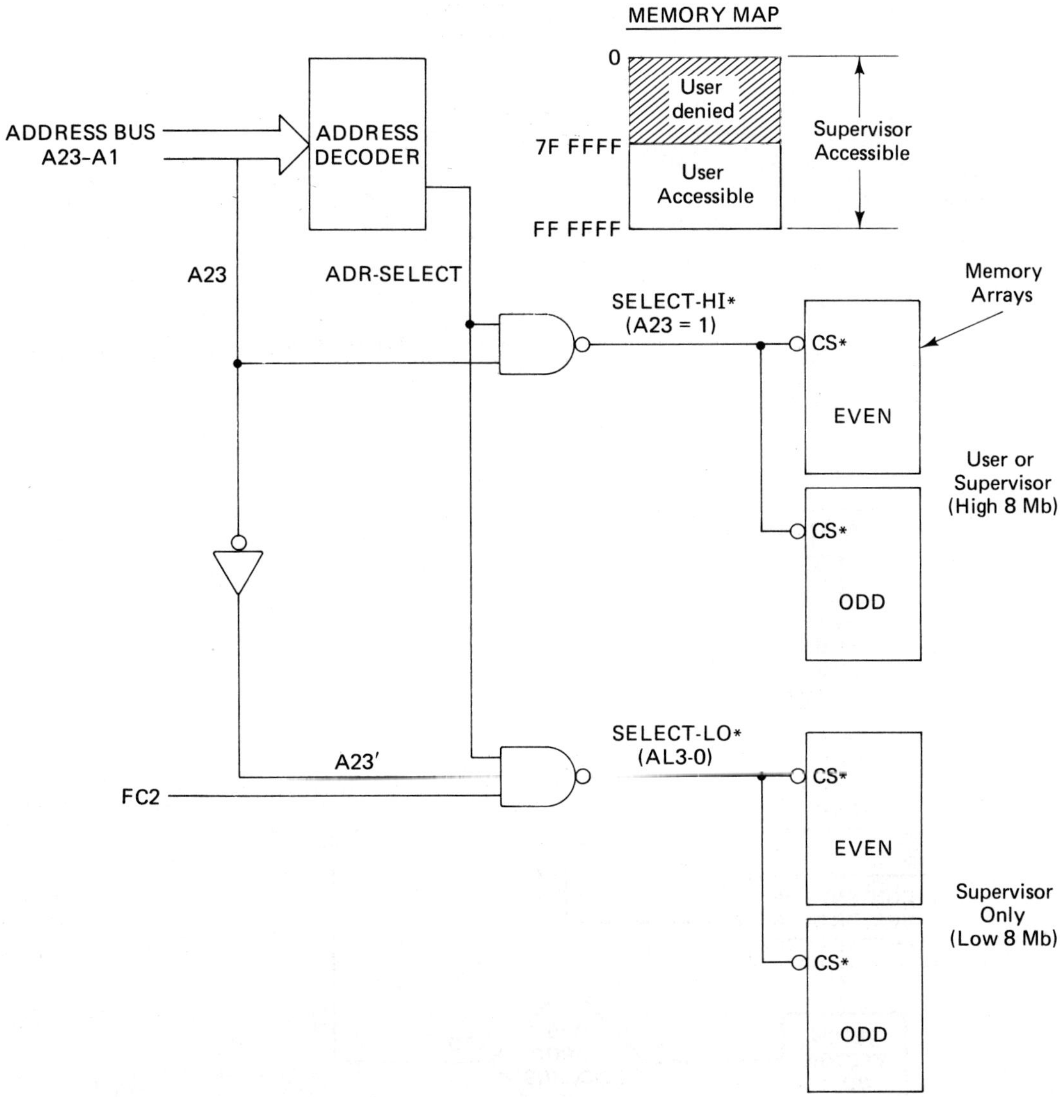

Figure 12.8 An example memory-protection circuit based on the function code output of the 68000.

freerun circuit when the SSP and PC were both initialized to 0 on power-up. Later, after you added EPROMs, you provided the pointers as part of your programming.

As shown in the memory-map detail of Figure 12.9, the supervisor stack pointer (SSP) and the program counter (PC) occupy a total of eight memory locations. The first four addresses (two words) are referred to as Vector 0, and the next 4 locations as Vector 1. In the example shown, the first word ($0020) is most significant; the next word ($0000)

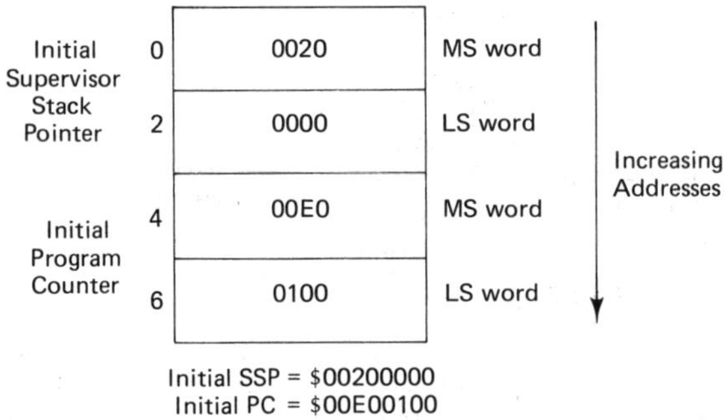

Figure 12.9 The 68000 reset exception vectors.

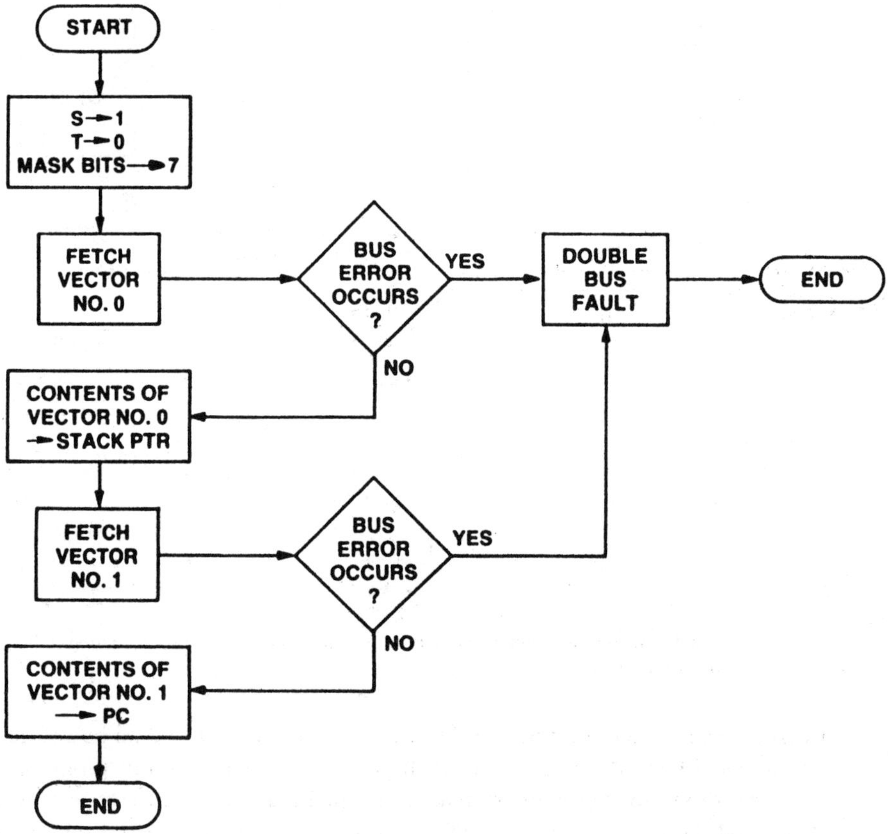

Figure 12.10 The 68000 reset exception-processing sequence. (Courtesy Motorola Inc.)

is least significant; taken together, they set the SSP to $00200000. Similarly, the PC most significant word is first, so that the initial PC gets set to $00E00100.

The reset exception sequence is shown in Figure 12.10. Because of the profound effect it has on the system, the pattern is not quite the same as a normal exception. The exception is processed in this order:

- The supervisor bit is set to 1.
- The trace bit is set to 0 so the processor will not trace.
- The interrupt priority mask is set to 111. This prevents recognition of all interrupts except a level-7 *NMI*.
- The SSP is fetched from address 0.
- The PC is fetched from address 4.
- The 68000 then fetches its next program op-code at the address given by the PC.

If the 68000 cannot read the SSP and PC vectors for some reason, then the error condition is a bus fault; the result is an immediate and final halt. The HALT* control line is asserted by the 68000, and nothing will happen until the hardware is repaired.

12.4 INTERNALLY-GENERATED EXCEPTIONS

Many of the 68000 exceptions are generated internally. These exceptions are caused by internally detected errors (address error, illegal instruction, unimplemented instruction, and privilege violation), by the trace mode, and by the special instructions (such as TRAP and CHK). Except for the address error, which will be treated later, these internally generated exceptions follow the processing flow shown in Figure 12.11. The sequence is this:

- The supervisor bit is set to 1.
- The trace bit is set to 0 so the processor will not trace.
- The vector number corresponding to the required exception is determined internally. This vector number is then used to calculate the address of the exception vector.
- The current program counter and processor status are saved on the supervisory stack.
- The new program counter is set equal to the long word found at the exception vector address.
- The 68000 then fetches its next program op-code at the address given by the PC.

The supervisory stack operation is shown in Figure 12.12. Starting from a stack pointer SSP, the pointer is first predecremented to SSP-2; next the least significant 16 bits of the program counter (PCL) are stored. After predecrementing to SSP-4, the most significant bits of the program counter (PCH) are saved. Last, the 16-bit status register is stored at SSP-6. After the exception-handler code is completed, an RTE instruction will

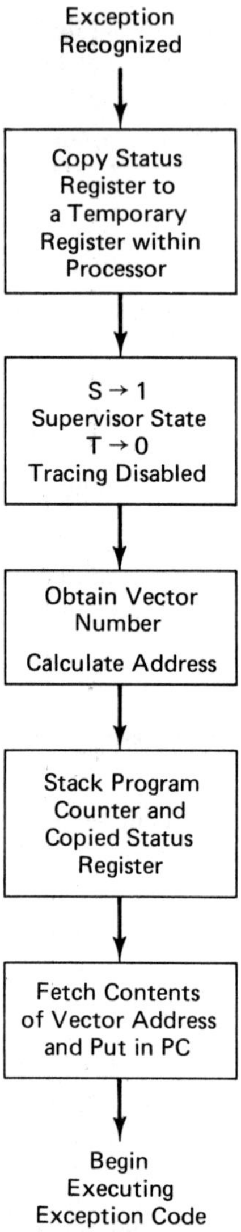

Figure 12.11 The general flow of exception processing.

cause a return to the code that was executing before the exception. The RTE pops the SR and PC off the stack in the reverse order from exception entry.

The program counter value that gets placed on the stack is the next instruction to be executed; that is, the two-word prefetch mechanism in the 68000 is not affected by this exception processing. On the other hand, a bus error or address error will not leave a predictable PC on the stack; these errors, however, have a special stacking sequence that provides context information that might allow processor recovery. In a like manner, interrupt and trace exceptions both discard the two-word prefetch.

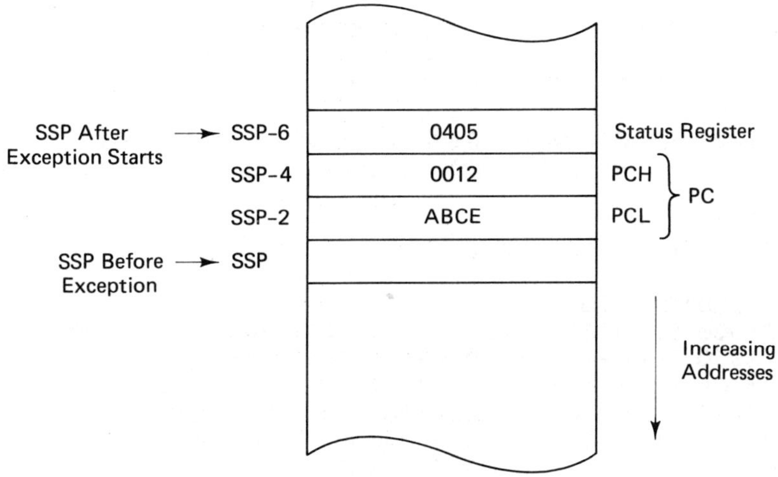

Figure 12.12 Supervisory stack operation at the beginning of an exception. The next instruction to execute after returning from the exception will be at PC = \$0012ABCE with SR = \$0405.

12.4.1 Illegal and Unimplemented Instructions

An illegal instruction is a bit pattern that is not one of the defined op-codes for the 68000. Normally, you would not be able to assemble a program without such an instruction being detected; it might arise, however, if a read bus cycle accesses a defective memory address. When the processor detects the illegal instruction, it begins exception processing using Vector 4 located at address \$10.

Figure 12.13 illustrates how TUTOR handles an illegal instruction located at address \$1000. The illegal instruction is MOVE D0, \$1000, which has a bit pattern 0011 1001 1100 0000 or \$39C0. This bit pattern has to be generated and entered into memory by hand because TUTOR will not assemble it. When TUTOR encounters the instruction (by "TRacing" at address \$1000), it displays "ILLEGAL INSTRUCTION" and the register values. This response is contained in TUTOR's exception-handler code that is associated with Vector 4.

The unimplemented instructions are bit patterns that begin with either 1010 or 1111. The processor does not flag these as errors, but does begin exception processing at either Vector 10 or Vector 11. These patterns can be used by the programmer to emulate an instruction that is not part of the standard 68000 instruction set. For example, you can define a special instruction to do floating-point math or perhaps an FFT butterfly. Only the first 4 bits are used to detect the unimplemented instruction; this means that the remaining 12 bits of the op-code can be used as a pseudo operand for passing immediate data or indicating an option within the exception handler.

```
DF
PC=00001000 SR=2704=.S7..Z.. US=FFFFFFFF SS=00000786
D0=00003930 D1=FFFF3900 D2=FFFF39C0 D3=00000000
D4=00000004 D5=0000002C D6=00000002 D7=00000000
A0=00010040 A1=0000832C A2=00000414 A3=00000554
A4=00001002 A5=00000540 A6=00000540 A7=00000786
---------------------001000     39C0                    DC.W    $39C0

TUTOR  1.3 > TR
PHYSICAL ADDRESS=00001000

ILLEGAL INSTRUCTION
PC=00001000 SR=A704=TS7..Z.. US=FFFFFFFF SS=00000786
D0=00003930 D1=FFFF3900 D2=FFFF39C0 D3=00000000
D4=00000004 D5=0000002C D6=00000002 D7=00000000
A0=00010040 A1=0000832C A2=00000414 A3=00000554
A4=00001002 A5=00000540 A6=00000540 A7=00000786
---------------------001000     39C0                    DC.W    $39C0

TUTOR  1.3 >
```

Figure 12.13 Illustration of how TUTOR handles an illegal instruction stored in memory at $1000. (Courtesy Motorola Inc.)

12.4.2 Privilege Violation

The 68000 will begin privilege-violation exception processing using Vector 8 if $S = 0$ and the user attempts to use a privileged instruction. These restricted instructions, listed in Table 12.4, involve the operations that can affect the system itself. Suppose, as in Figure 12.14, the 68000 is in the user state ($S = 0$) running a program that tries to execute the

TABLE 12.4 A LIST OF THE 68000 PRIVILEGED INSTRUCTIONS. THESE CAN BE EXECUTED ONLY IF THE S-BIT IS SET.

RESET	RESET EXTERNAL DEVICES
RTE	RETURN FROM EXCEPTION
STOP	STOP PROGRAM EXECUTION
ORI to SR	LOGICAL OR TO STATUS REGISTER
MOVE USP	MOVE USER STACK POINTER
ANDI to SR	LOGICAL AND TO STATUS REGISTER
EORI to SR	LOGICAL EOR TO STATUS REGISTER
MOVE EA to SR	LOAD NEW STATUS REGISTER

(Courtesy Motorola Inc.)

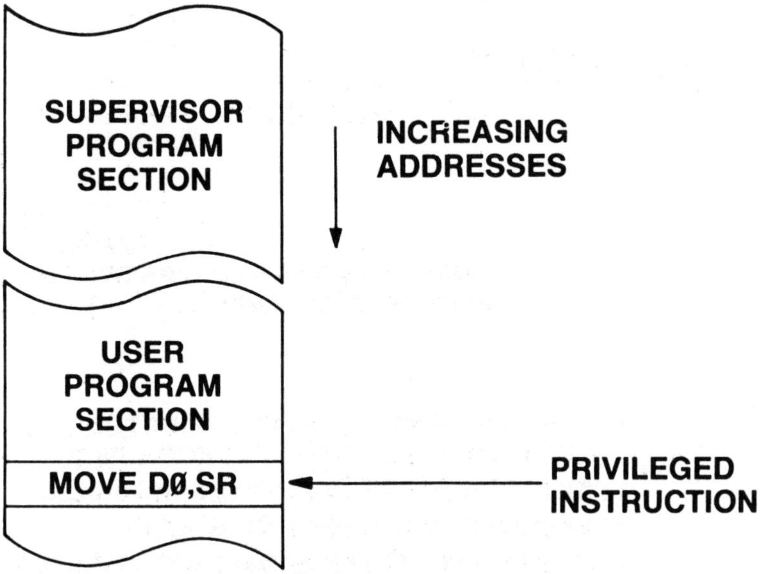

Figure 12.14 An example of a privilege violation. The supervisor status bit $S = 0$ in this case and leads to a privilege-violation exception. (Courtesy Motorola Inc.)

privileged MOVE D0,SR. This generates an internal exception and causes the processor to start exception processing at address $20.

12.4.3 TRACE

Instruction tracing is one of the most convenient tools you can use in developing software. In the case of the 68000, you can use the trace exception by setting $T = 1$ in the system status register. While in the trace state, the processor begins exception processing at Vector 9 after each instruction is executed. This general sequence is shown in Figure 12.15. The exception-processing code should typically include a display of the contents of the 68000 registers (like TUTOR) and provide control of execution. At the end of the exception, the trace routine must execute an RTE to return to the main program.

12.4.4 TRAP Instructions

Certain special instructions are used specifically to cause the 68000 to begin exception processing. For example, the TRAP instruction is one very useful way of making calls to the operating system from the user state ($S = 0$) to take advantage of common system utility programs. Other trap instructions are intended to cause an exception when a runtime error is detected: TRAPV and CHK will flag an arithmetic overflow or a register value out of bounds. Likewise, the DIVS and DIVU instructions cause an exception if a divide by zero is attempted.

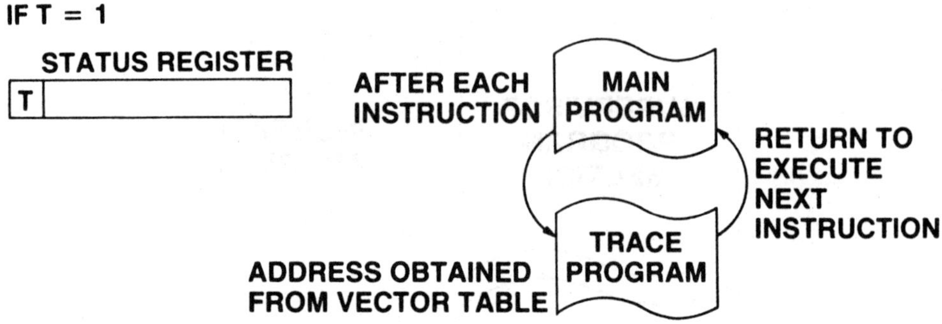

1. IF, UPON COMPLETION OF AN INSTRUCTION, T = 1, GO TO TRACE EXCEPTION PROCESSING.
2. EXECUTE TRACE EXCEPTION SEQUENCE.
3. EXECUTE TRACE SERVICE ROUTINE.
4. AT THE END OF THE SERVICE ROUTINE, EXECUTE RETURN FROM EXCEPTION (RTE).

Figure 12.15 Operation of the trace mode. (Courtesy Motorola Inc.)

There are 16 TRAP instruction vectors available for making system calls. These instructions are programmed as TRAP #0 through TRAP #15; when executed in a program they cause the processor to fetch the contents of addresses $80 through $BC, respectively, for exception processing. Consider TUTOR's TRAP $14, for example: its address is $B8, and the 32-bit contents at $B8 are $0000BE70. When this TRAP is executed, the 68000 will load its program counter with $0000BE70 and process the exception; it exits the exception with an RTE to go back to the calling program.

Up to 255 different system functions can be accessed by the TRAP 14 handler in the TUTOR firmware. The desired function number is passed to the system in the low-order byte of register D7, and then the trap is invoked. The calling sequence is

```
MOVE.B      #<function number>,D7
TRAP        #14
```

in which the <function number> is a number between 0 and 254. Consider the example shown in Figure 12.16 using TUTOR to convert four hex digits into their ASCII equivalents. The conversion function is number 232, and it requires the four hex digits in D0. The last two lines of the program use function 228 to return from the user program back to the TUTOR supervisor. After running the program, notice the result: the ASCII answer is in memory at $900, the buffer area pointed to by A6.

```
MD 1000 B;DI
001000     1E3C00E8              MOVE.B  #232,D7
001004     4E4E                  TRAP    #14
001006     1E3C00E4              MOVE.B  #228,D7
00100A     4E4E                  TRAP    #14

TUTOR  1.3 > DF
PC=00001000 SR=2708=.S7.N... US=FFFFFFFF SS=00000774
D0=0000378C D1=FFFF3900 D2=FFFF39C0 D3=00000000
D4=00000004 D5=0000002C D6=00000002 D7=000000E9
A0=00010040 A1=0000832C A2=00000414 A3=00000554
A4=00001002 A5=00000540 A6=00000900 A7=00000774
--------------------001000     1E3C00E8             MOVE.B  #232,D7

TUTOR  1.3 > GO
PHYSICAL ADDRESS=00001000

TUTOR  1.3 > MD 900
000900     33 37 38 43 00 00 00 00  00 00 00 00 00 00 00 00  378C........

TUTOR  1.3 > DF
PC=00001004 SR=2708=.S7.N... US=FFFFFFFF SS=00000774
D0=0000378C D1=FFFF3900 D2=FFFF39C0 D3=00000000
D4=00000004 D5=0000002C D6=00000002 D7=000000E8
A0=00010040 A1=0000832C A2=00000414 A3=00000554
A4=00001002 A5=00000540 A6=00000900 A7=00000774
--------------------001004     4E4E                 TRAP    #14

TUTOR  1.3 >
```

Figure 12.16 A simple example program using TUTOR's TRAP 14 handler. This program converts 4 hex digits in D0 into ASCII and saves in the buffer at address $900. (Courtesy Motorola Inc.)

12.5 BUS- AND ADDRESS-ERROR PROCESSING

The bus- and address-error exceptions are the next highest priority after the reset exception. Either error requires immediate action by the 68000 to preserve the state of the processor and to avoid destruction of memory contents. The bus-error exception is initiated externally by hardware assertion of the BERR* control; the address error is begun internally when the 68000 attempts to access a word or long word at an odd address. Both bus- and address-error exception processing follow this sequence:

- The Supervisor bit is set to 1.
- The Trace bit is set to 0 so the processor will not trace.
- The vector number corresponding to the required exception is determined inter-

nally. This vector number (2 for bus error, 3 for address error) is then used to calculate the address of the exception vector.

- The current program counter and processor status are saved on the supervisory stack. In addition, the 68000 instruction register, the address being accessed, and a super-status word are saved.
- The new program counter is set equal to the long word found at the exception vector address.
- The 68000 then fetches its next program op-code at the address given by the PC.

The supervisory stack order for the bus- and address-error exceptions is shown in Figure 12.17. The first three words pushed onto the stack follow the same pattern as a normal exception. However, because the exception disrupted the processor mid-

CH12TBLF

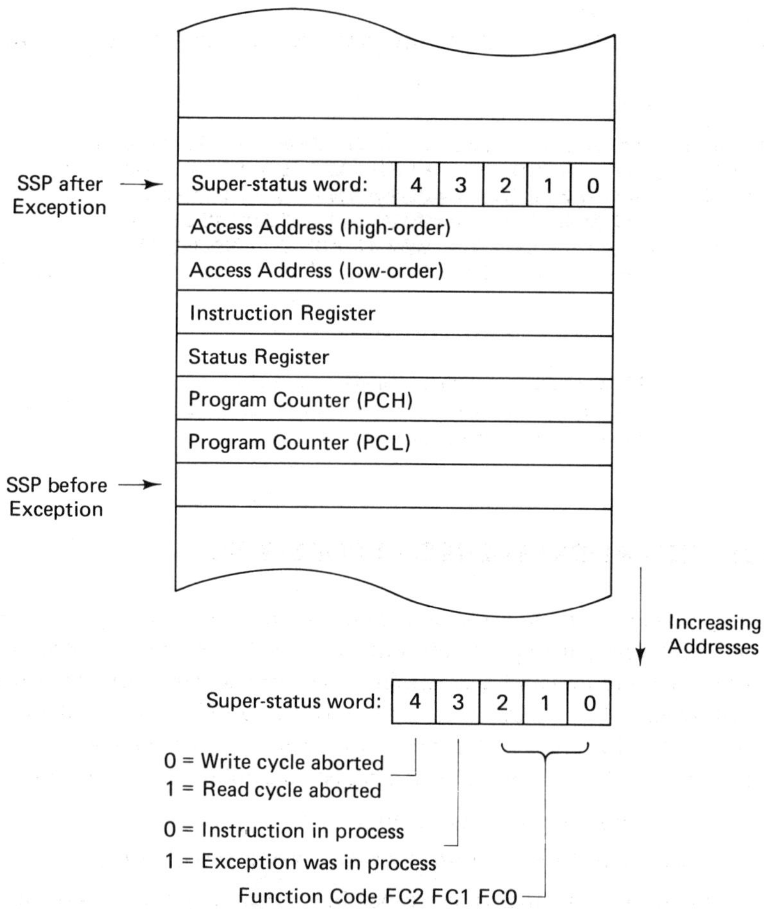

Figure 12.17 Supervisory stack at the beginning of exception processing for a bus or address error.

instruction, more information is saved on the stack than before. After the status register, the 68000 instruction register is stacked: this is the first word of the instruction being processed when the error occurred. The address being accessed comes next on the stack. Last, the stack receives a super-status word containing information telling

- whether the operation was reading or writing;
- whether the 68000 was processing an instruction or processing a Group 0 or Group 1 exception already, and
- the function code outputs.

The program counter that gets placed on the stack is not as predictable as when processing a ''normal'' exception. The PC might be from one to five words beyond the address of the exception that caused the error-processing exception. At best, depending on the nature of the current instruction, the PC will be nearby the error. In general, the bus-error and address-error exceptions allow the system programmer to examine the condition of the processor; usually the processor cannot recover by itself and run without intervention by the operator.

12.5.1 Bus Error

The DTACK* generator was one of the first modules you built into your 68000 system; recall that its purpose was to provide a handshake signal to the processor so the 68000 could finish its bus cycle. One of the features of the 68000 is its asynchronous bus: it allows you to interconnect different-speed peripherals. The drawback, of course, is the question of how long is ''too long'' for the 68000 to wait for a response from a device. Without some intervention from outside the processor, the 68000 could get hung indefinitely waiting for a response that will never arrive.

A watchdog timer like the one in Figure 12.18 can be used to intervene if a bus cycle takes too long. The AS* control from the 68000 is always asserted during a bus cycle, so that it can be used to start a timer at the beginning of every bus cycle. If AS* stays low for several times the response speed of the slowest device on the bus, then the timer can signal a bus error. The error output signal asserts the BERR* input to the 68000.

At this point, the processor can do either of two things: begin bus-error exception processing using Vector 2, or try a re-run of the bus cycle. If the timer asserted only BERR*, then the 68000 will begin the bus-error exception processing. On the other hand, if the timer asserted HALT* and BERR* together, then a re-run is possible: first negate BERR*, then one or more clock cycles later negate HALT*. Recognize that a re-run could repeat many times, so the hardware must provide a means for ultimately reverting to bus-error exception processing.

A double bus fault has occurred if a bus-error exception takes place while the processor is already processing a previous bus error. For example, suppose the 68000 tries to write a word to RAM, but no RAM DTACK* comes back. When the watchdog timer signals BERR*, the 68000 begins bus-error exception processing by stacking the various registers. Suppose that no RAM DTACK* comes back from the stack-writing operation

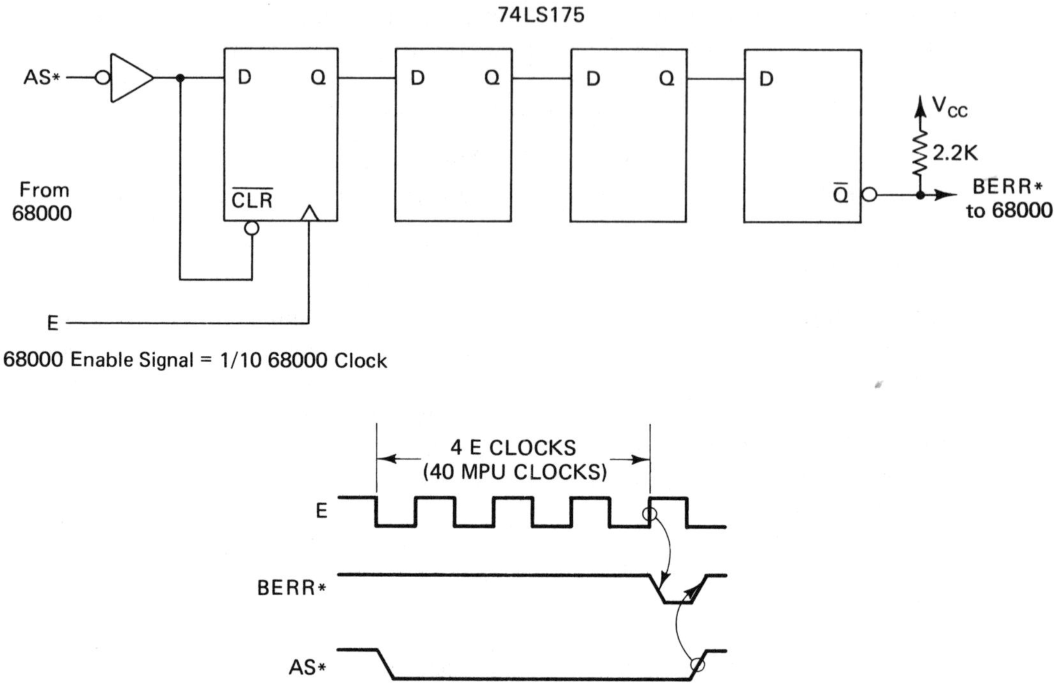

Figure 12.18 Watchdog timer circuit to signal a bus error if AS* stays asserted longer than 40 clock cycles.

either: the timer asserts BERR* again. At this point, the processor has experienced a double bus fault, halts completely, and asserts HALT* as an output.

A double bus fault can also happen during a power-on reset. If there is a bus error while reading the SSP and PC vectors, then the 68000 will respond as if it had a double bus fault. There is no second chance, so to speak. Normally, the exception processing would come first, and then the double bus fault; in the startup, however, exception processing is impossible when the vectors cannot be accessed at all.

12.5.2 Address Error

Address-error exception processing is begun internally by the 68000 if it tries to read or write a word or long word at an odd address. The operation of the exception is the same as the bus-error case, including the information that goes on the stack. The only difference is that the address-error Vector 3 is used to process the exception.

If there is an address-error exception during the processing of a previous bus fault or address error, or during a reset, then the 68000 will halt with a double bus fault. As with any situation in which the 68000 asserts HALT*, the only possible recovery is to assert RESET*.

Address errors can be somewhat difficult to catch, because the assembler will not normally flag them. Consider these examples:

```
MOVE    D0,$2001
MOVE    D0,$06(A0)    * where A0 has an odd number
MOVE    D0,$05(A0)    * where A0 has an even number
```

The first example will always result in an address error exception; the other two may or may not run, depending on the data. Clearly not good program design, but easy enough to slip on nevertheless.

12.6 INTERRUPT EXCEPTIONS

In the last chapter you found that the TUTOR monitor waited for your key press by looping in a small section of code. The fact that the processor continually executed this code made it easy to synchronize an oscilloscope to any of the control lines and do troubleshooting. During each loop, the 68000 polled the status of the port to see if a character was ready; for each character you typed, the 68000 checked thousands of times to see if you were done. Not a very efficient way to spend processor time if there is something better to do.

The alternative to polling an I/O port waiting for a key press is to use interrupts. With an interrupt-driven keyboard, the processor can run a program, control external hardware, or do math operations during the time between keystrokes. To the user, it would seem that the 68000 is doing several things at once, but it is really just switching from one thing to the next very quickly as needed. When you press a key, the hardware signals the 68000 that it wants attention; at the end of the current instruction, the processor will allow itself to be interrupted.[2] This externally caused interrupt is controlled using the 68000 exception-processing mechanism.

Interrupts must have a priority level associated with them. For example, in addition to a keyboard, you might also have an interrupt-driven printer port connected to the 68000. When the printer is ready for another character, it interrupts the processor and causes an interrupt exception handler to send the data. You probably would not want the printer to interrupt your typing at the keyboard though: that would mean a possible lost character while the 68000 was servicing the printer. To avoid this problem, the keyboard should have a higher priority than the printer. Doing this, the higher-priority interrupt request of the keyboard can cause the 68000 to defer processing the printer interrupts.

12.6.1 Processing Interrupts

Interrupt exception processing is initiated by asserting the 68000 interrupt priority level (IPL*) lines. There are seven different interrupt-priority levels in the 68000, as shown in Table 12.5; the priority of a particular interrupt is determined by which three lines are

[2]The interrupt pins are checked at the beginning of some instructions, e.g., MULU and MOVEM.

TABLE 12.5 THE SEVEN INTERRUPT PRIORITY LEVELS AND THE INPUTS REQUIRED TO CAUSE EXCEPTION PROCESSING.

Interrupt Level Requested		*Interrupt Priority Level Inputs Required*		
		*IPL2**	*IPL1**	*IPL0**
7	NMI—Highest Priority	L	L	L
6		L	L	H
5		L	H	L
4		L	H	H
3		H	L	L
2		H	L	H
1		H	H	L
0	No Interrupt Requested	H	H	H

asserted by the external hardware. Normally, these negative-logic inputs are pulled HIGH if interrupts are not implemented or if there are no interrupts pending. In the example above, suppose the keyboard is assigned a priority level 4 and the printer level 3. To cause a level-4 interrupt, the keyboard hardware would have to provide a LOW-HIGH-HIGH logic pattern to IPL2*, IPL1*, and IPL0*. The printer, to initiate a level-3 interrupt exception, would need to assert a logic HIGH-LOW-LOW to the IPL* inputs.

The interrupt mask in the processor's status register determines which interrupts are recognized. This mask, shown in Table 12.6, is set while in the supervisor state: interrupts above a certain priority level are recognized, while remaining lower interrupts are

TABLE 12.6 THE INTERRUPT MASK PROVIDES A MEANS FOR RECOGNIZING ONLY CERTAIN OF THE INTERRUPTS TO THE 68000. THE LEVEL-7 INTERRUPT MAY NOT BE MASKED OUT.

Status Register

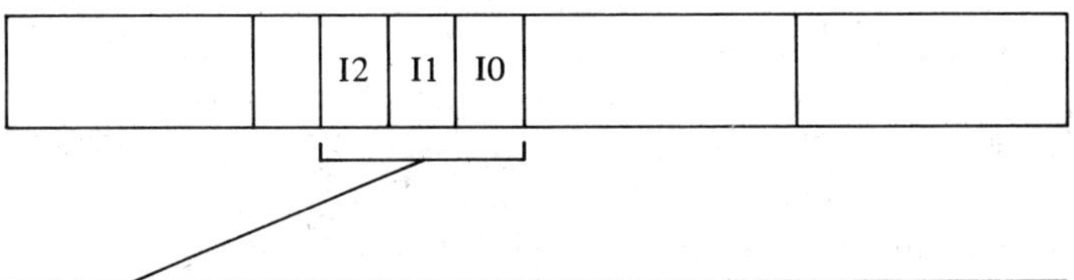

Interrupt Mask	Priority Levels Recognized	Priority Levels Ignored
1 1 1	7 (only NMI)	1–6
1 1 0	7	1–6
1 0 1	6–7	1–5
1 0 0	5–7	1–4
0 1 1	4–7	1–3
0 1 0	3–7	1–2
0 0 1	2–7	1
0 0 0	1–7 (all)	None

ignored even though they might assert the IPL* lines. When the 68000 is reset, the initial mask is set to 111 so that the only interrupt that will be recognized is the non-maskable interrupt (*NMI*): it overrides any code in progress and cannot be turned off (masked off) by software. Notice the way the mask is set up: all interrupts *above* the priority level in the mask will be recognized. For example, if the mask is 011, that means interrupt requests with priority levels 4, 5, 6, and 7 can cause interrupt exception processing; all interrupts with levels 1, 2, and 3 will be ignored.

The general pattern of interrupt exception processing is shown in Figure 12.19. During each instruction the 68000 samples the IPL* inputs and compares them to the interrupt mask; if there is no pending exception whose priority is greater than the mask, then it goes on to the next instruction. If an exception priority exceeds the mask, then the interrupt exception processing begins. This processing, simplified greatly, involves saving the machine's context (PC and SR) and then jumping to the proper interrupt service routine (ISR). After executing the ISR code to read a keyboard character or send a character to the printer, for example, the exception concludes with an RTE instruction. This restores the context, and the 68000 then continues with its normal processing of a program as though nothing had happened.

To use interrupts, the starting addresses of the interrupt service routines must be stored in the exception vector table. Table 12.7 shows an expanded view of the memory allocations for interrupts. When an interrupt-based system is first started up, the hardware will likely assert some interrupts; they cannot be recognized until the service code is in place. Thus, while the vector table and the ISRs are being loaded into memory, the interrupt mask should be set to 111 to disable all interrupts (except the *NMI*). After all the system components are properly initialized, the interrupt mask can be set to the required level.

There are 192 vectored interrupts and 7 autovector interrupts shown in Table 12.7. When one of these interrupt exceptions is requested by asserting the IPL* control lines, the 68000 will acknowledge the interrupt by running a special bus cycle. This interrupt acknowledge (IACK) bus cycle determines which type of interrupt (user-vectored or autovectored) is required and the address of the vector in the vector table. The interrupt selected during IACK is determined by:

- If VPA* is asserted, then autovectoring is assumed. The autovector number corresponds to the priority level that was requested on the IPL* controls.
- If the peripheral places a vector number on the D7-D0 data bus lines, and then asserts DTACK*, then user-vectoring is assumed. The vector number ($40 to $FF) is multiplied by 4 to give the vector address in the table.
- If a vector number had not been programmed into the interrupting peripheral before an interrupt was initiated, then vector number $F is placed on the data bus. After the peripheral asserts DTACK*, the 68000 assumes uninitialized interrupt and uses the vector table entry at address $3C.
- If no response comes back at all from any peripheral, the processor can only assume that a spurious interrupt request was caused by noise on the IPL* lines. In this case,

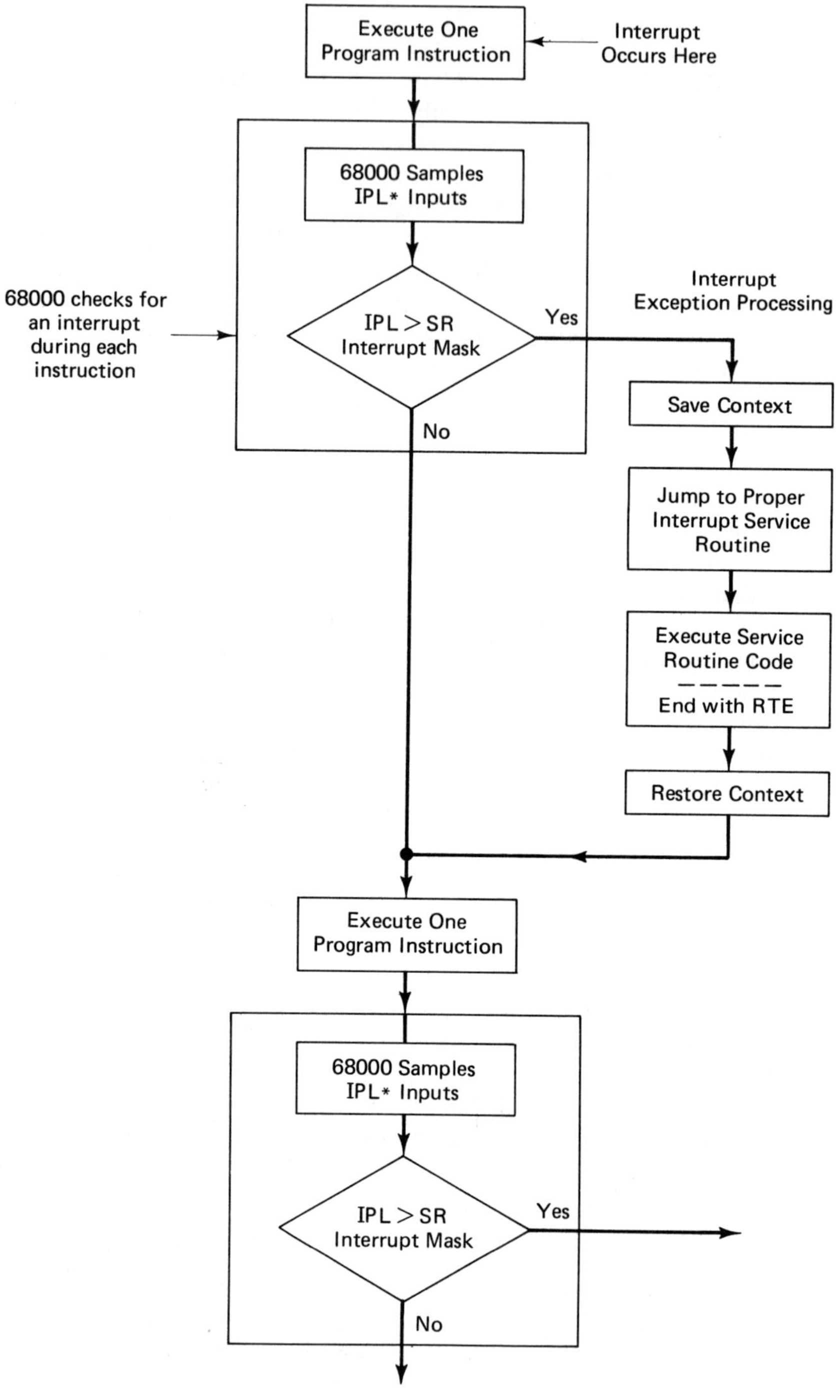

Figure 12.19 General pattern of interrupt exception processing. The 68000 samples the IPL* inputs during each instruction and compares them with the interrupt mask.

TABLE 12.7 AN EXPANDED VIEW OF THE INTERRUPT EXCEPTION VECTOR TABLE. EACH VECTOR IS A 32-BIT LONG WORD POINTING TO A LOCATION IN MEMORY.

Memory Address (Hexadecimal)		Vector Number (Hexadecimal)
3C	Uninitialized Interrupt	F
40	Unassigned Reserved	
60	Spurious Interrupt	18
64	Level 1 Interrupt Autovector	19
68	Level 2 Interrupt Autovector	1A
6C	Level 3 Interrupt Autovector	1B
70	Level 4 Interrupt Autovector	1C
74	Level 5 Interrupt Autovector	1D
78	Level 6 Interrupt Autovector	1E
7C	Level 7 Interrupt Autovector	1F
100	User Interrupt Vector	40
104	User Interrupt Vector	41
	⋮ Total of 192 User Interrupt Vectors ⋮	
	User Interrupt Vector	
3FC	User Interrupt Vector	FF

neither VPA* nor DTACK* will be asserted, so the watchdog timer must signal a bus error. When BERR* is asserted, the 68000 processes the "spurious interrupt" using the vector table entry at address $60.

12.6.2 Acknowledging Interrupts

The overall interrupt exception-processing sequence is shown in Figure 12.20. This sequence starts only if the priority of the interrupt request is greater than the mask in the status register. Before the interrupt is acknowledged by the 68000, it makes a copy of the

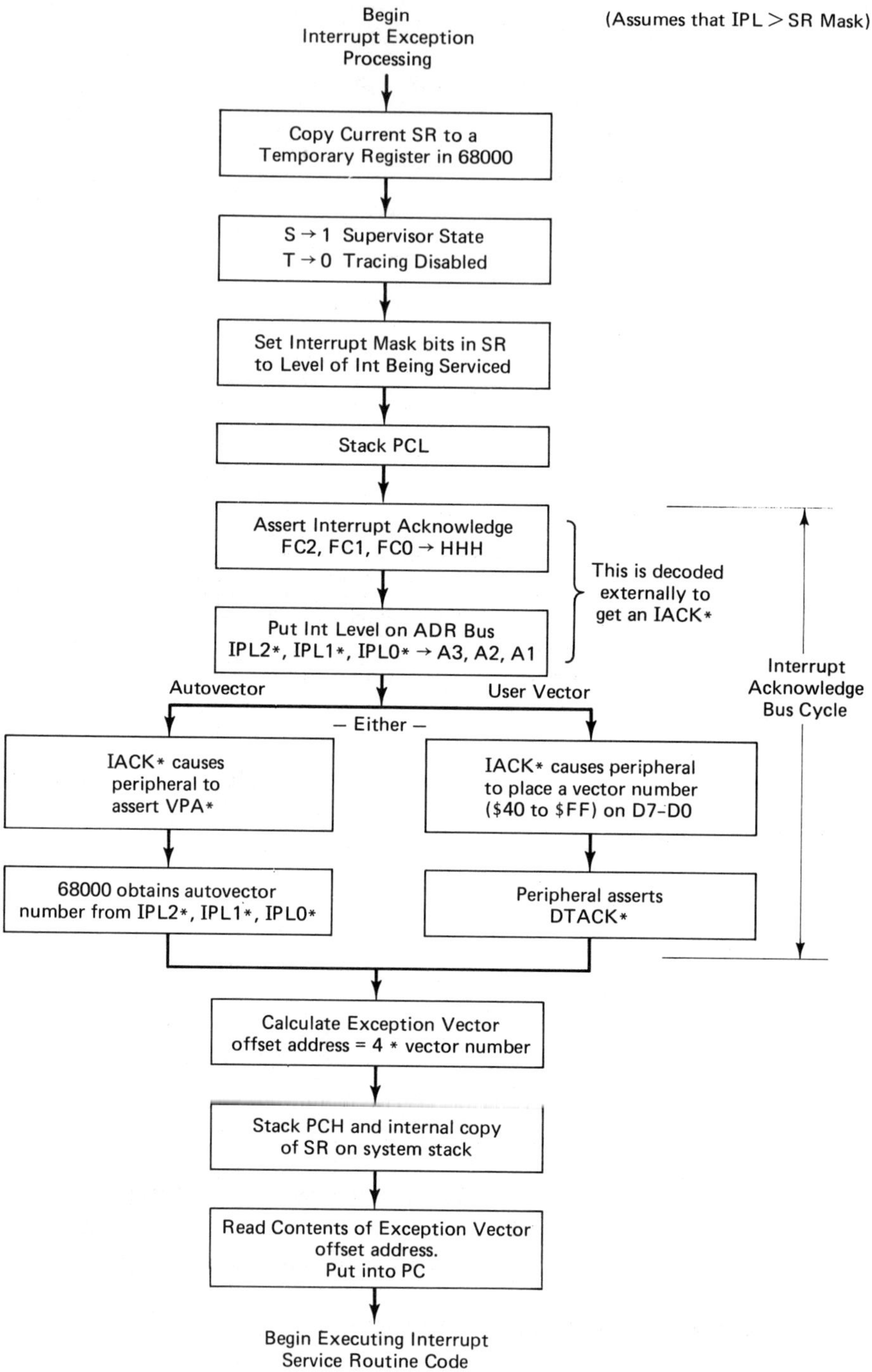

Figure 12.20 Interrupt exception-processing sequence. The diagram assumes that IPL > SR mask.

current SR and then enters the supervisor state with tracing disabled. Next, the interrupt mask bits are set to the level of the interrupt being serviced: this allows only interrupts of higher priority than the current one to become active. Finally, after stacking the low-order word of the program counter (PCL), the 68000 begins its interrupt-acknowledge (IACK) bus cycle. The purpose of the IACK bus cycle is to determine the starting location of the desired interrupt service routine.

To ensure successful recognition of the interrupt, the IPL* lines must remain asserted at least until the IACK bus cycle. This bus cycle begins by setting all function code FC2, FC1, and FC0 outputs HIGH. At the same time, the interrupt level is placed on the A3, A2, and A1 address lines so external logic can determine which interrupt level is being recognized; the other address lines are set high. Note that the interrupt level placed on the A3-A1 lines is positive logic. For example, a level-4 interrupt is initiated by placing LHH on the IPL2*-IPL0* inputs; then during the IACK bus cycle, the A3, A2, and A1 lines are driven HLL or 100 to indicate the level-4 interrupt.

There are two possible IACK bus cycles shown in Figure 12.21. Which one is executed depends on the response from the peripheral that caused the interrupt. At the beginning of the acknowledge bus cycle, the external peripheral logic must decode when the function code outputs go HIGH and the AS* goes low, and then it must respond. In the first case, Figure 12.21(a), if the peripheral can respond with a vector number, then that number is placed on the data bus and DTACK* asserted. The 68000 will read the vector number and conclude the IACK bus cycle. In the second case, Figure 12.21(b), the peripheral can only respond by asserting VPA*. The 68000 interprets that as an autovector request, and generates the autovector number from the IPL* inputs. For example, the level-4 interrupt above would result in a level-4 autovector.

After the IACK bus cycle is finished, the processor calculates the address of the proper exception vector. It does this internally by multiplying the user vector number ($40-$FF) by 4 to get the vector table offset addresses in the range $100 to $3FC. The autovectors are numbers $19 through $1F and result in the vector table addresses $64 to $7C. After placing the program counter (PCH) and the SR on the system stack, the 68000 reads the contents of the vector address in the table and puts it in the program counter. After completing the interrupt service routine, the processor then returns to continue executing the next instruction in its program.

12.6.3 Non-maskable Interrupts (*NMIs*)

The level-7 interrupt cannot be ignored, regardless of the mask level set in the status register. As with any other interrupt, to ensure proper recognition, the IPL* inputs to the 68000 should remain asserted until the IACK bus cycle. The level-7 interrupt is edge-triggered rather than level-sensitive like the other six interrupts. This means that, if the level-7 continues to be asserted, the processor will only recognize the one *NMI* corresponding to when the IPL* inputs were first asserted.

Recall that earlier in the chapter, you tested the Educational Computer Board's abort button and caused an *NMI*. This switch is connected as shown in Figure 12.22(a) to

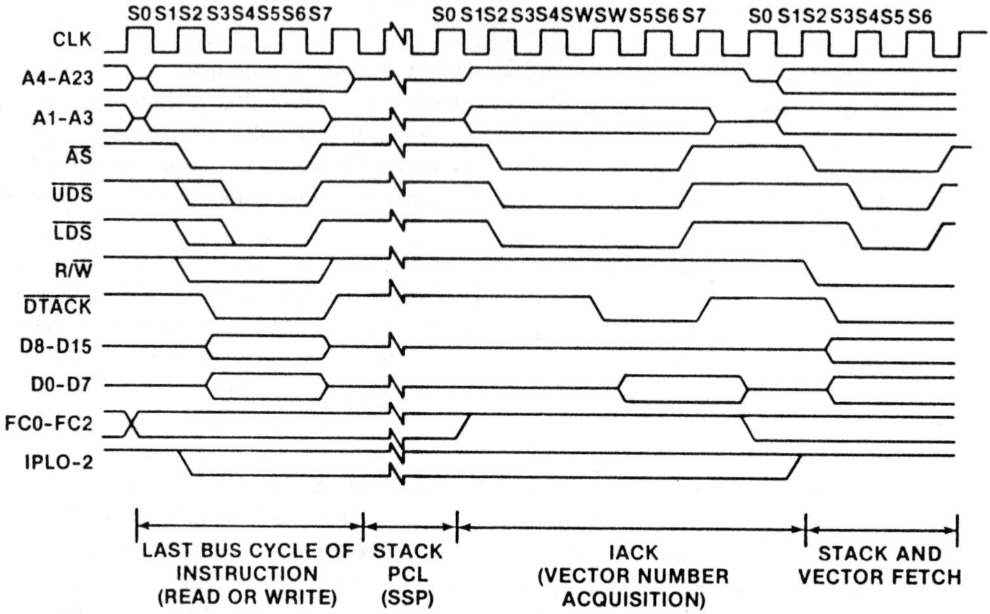

(a)

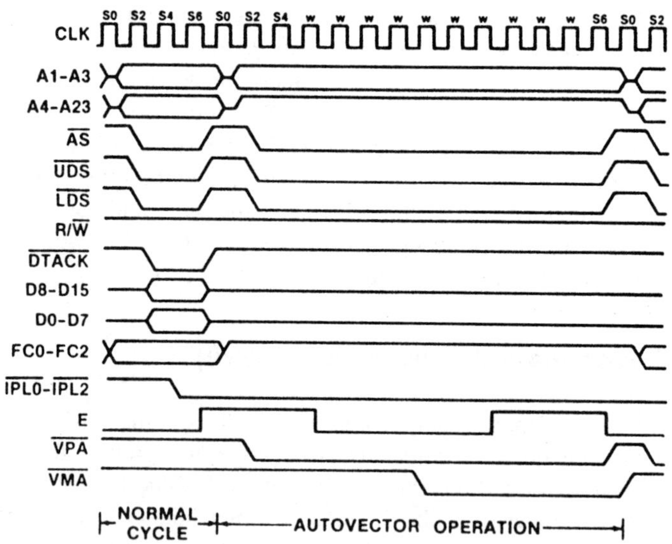

(b)

Figure 12.21 Interrupt acknowledge timing diagrams for (a) user interrupt vectors and (b) autovectors. (Courtesy Motorola Inc.)

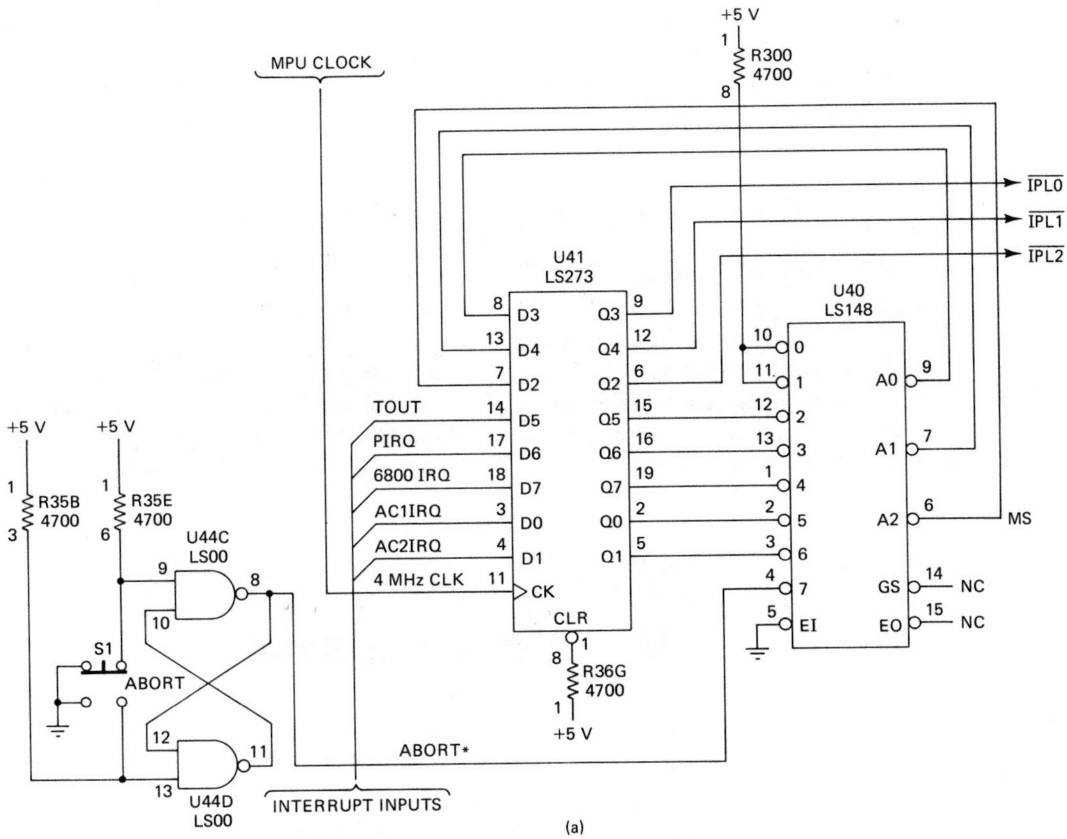

(a)

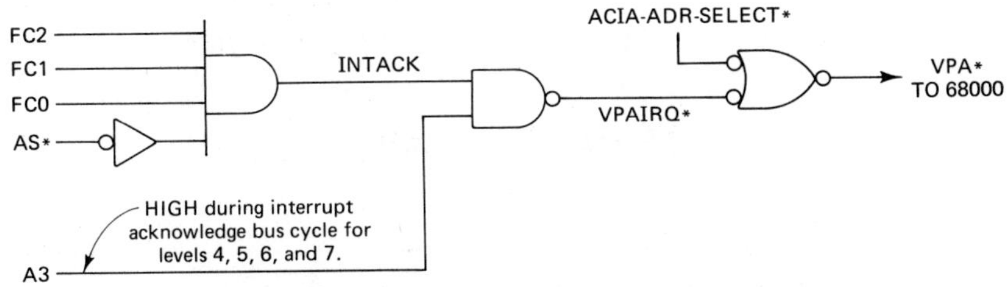

(b)

Figure 12.22 Interrupt synchronizer and level-7 NMI circuit in the Educational Computer Board (a). Interrupt acknowledge circuit for the ACIA portion (b). (Courtesy Motorola Inc.)

a priority encoder 74LS148. The encoder outputs are latched in the 75LS273 to synchronize all incoming interrupts to the system clock.[3] The ABORT* signal from the switch causes the IPL* controls to all go LOW, thus starting the interrupt exception-processing sequence. As soon as the IACK bus cycle begins, the function-code outputs go HIGH, A3-A1 go HIGH, and AS* LOW. These combine as sketched in Figure 12.22(b) to drive VPA* LOW to signal an autovector exception for the level-7 interrupt.

The various other interrupt assignments for the ECB are shown in Table 12.8. Levels 4 through 7 are designated autovector, and 2 to 3 are user vectors generated by the MC68230 parallel interface/timer. The natural distinction between these level assignments is that A3 is always HIGH for levels 4-7 and always LOW for 2-3. Consequently, the basic acknowledge circuit of Figure 12.22(b) can be used for all the autovectored exceptions. INTACK and A3′ are used to signal the 68230 that an IACK bus cycle is in progress: it places a vector number on the data bus and asserts DTACK* instead of VPA*.

TABLE 12.8 INTERRUPT LEVEL ASSIGNMENT IN THE EDUCATIONAL COMPUTER BOARD.

LEVEL	INTERRUPTING DEVICE
1	NOT USED
2	PI/T TIMER
3	PI/T PARALLEL PORTS
4	M6800 INTERFACE*
5	ACIA 1* (TERMINAL)
6	ACIA 2* (HOST)
7	ABORT BUTTON*

*AUTOVECTORED

(Courtesy Motorola Inc.)

12.7 EXAMPLE DESIGNS

After studying the interrupt structure used in the Educational Computer Board, you should be able to adapt some of its features into your own 68000 system. One possibility is to implement interrupts using the 6850 in your I/O module; an extension of that might be a second 6850 to drive a serial printer. In addition to the hardware design, you will also

[3]It is not absolutely necessary to synchronize the IPL* controls to the clock; the 68000 does this internally.

need to design the interrupt service routines and the system initialization code to set up the interrupt vector table. In this section, however, we will consider just the hardware aspects of the design.

12.7.1 Single-Autovector Example

A simple ACIA circuit with a single level-4 autovector is shown in Figure 12.23. This sketch follows the same design as the single I/O port developed in Chapter 11. The only changes from the earlier design are the addition of several gates to recognize the IACK bus cycle and the connection of the 6850's IRQ* back to the 68000.

The circuit is designed for a level-4 interrupt by connecting the IRQ* directly to the IPL2* input; the remaining IPL* inputs should be pulled up to their negated state. Normally the IRQ* output will stay HIGH after resetting the 6850, so no interrupt will be sent to the 68000. Then, after the ACIA is properly initialized, when an incoming character arrives the IRQ* will go LOW. During the IACK bus cycle A3 goes HIGH along with the function codes so that VPA* can be used to indicate an autovector interrupt exception. When the 68000 executes the interrupt service routine, it resets the 6850 IRQ* as it reads the data.

Notice that the IRQ* line is also connected into the interrupt-acknowledge circuit. Because IRQ* stays low until the interrupt is serviced, this line can be used to identify which device requires attention when the 68000 runs the IACK bus cycle. With only one 6850, however, why identify? Consider the possibility of a spurious interrupt in which noise on the IPL* lines causes an interrupt request. During the IACK bus cycle IRQ* will be HIGH, so VPA* does not get asserted. With neither VPA* nor DTACK*, the processor is hung until the BERR* line is asserted by the watchdog timer. When BERR* is asserted during an IACK bus cycle, the 68000 fetches the spurious-interrupt vector rather than the bus-error vector. It can then complete its usual exception processing and recover from the problem.

Testing an interrupt-driven system can be more of a challenge than testing one without interrupts. When there are no interrupts, the program code executes very predictably, one instruction after another, just as it was entered into memory. An interrupt, however, is an asynchronous event that can happen anywhere in the execution of the main program. This means that the processor could be operating properly one moment, and the next moment suddenly crash for no apparent reason. Debugging the interrupt code without being able to single-step the processor requires sophisticated tools.

If you single-step, however, you can step from one bus cycle to the next and check that the logic is properly connected. Do this by putting the 68000 in the step mode and then asserting an interrupt. If the logic tests out correctly, write a simple ISR that just reads the 6850 port into a 68000 register and returns. Naturally, you do not want to develop and test on the same port! Always keep your TUTOR port running normally while you experiment with interrupts using a second 6850 at a different address. Watch the stack closely when you develop your ISR code: if you see the stack getting deeper after each interrupt, then there is a software problem somewhere.

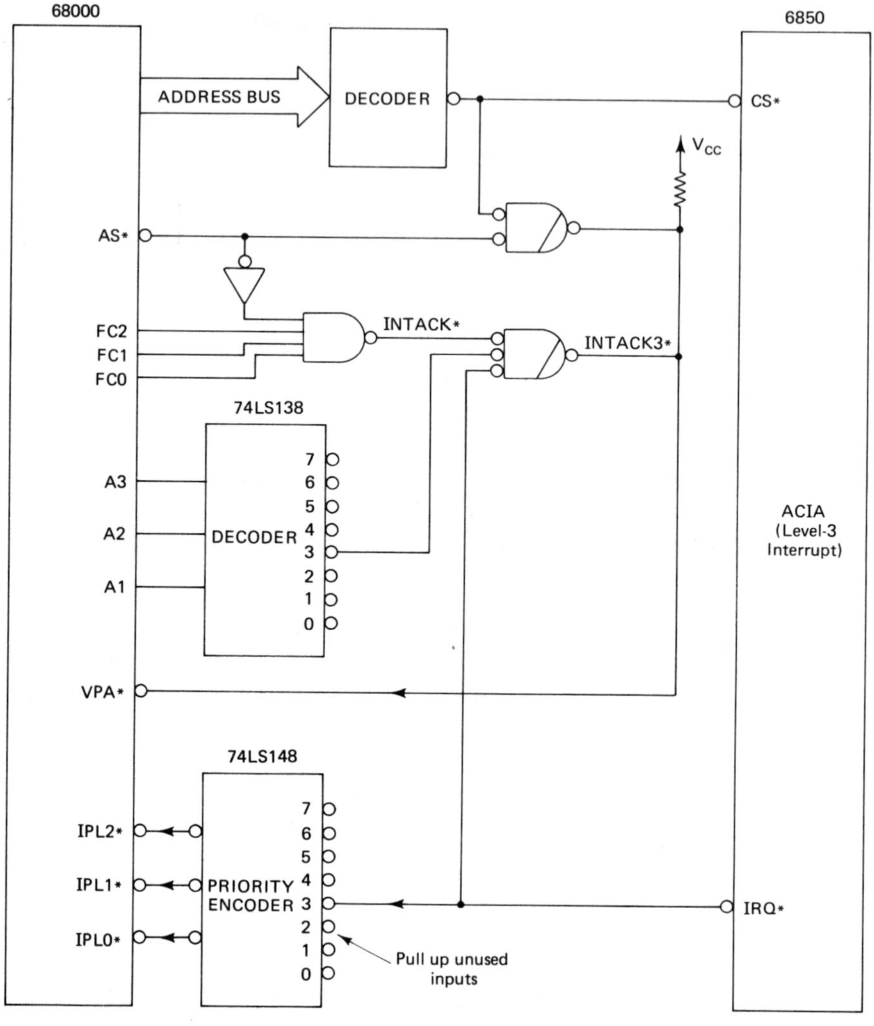

Figure 12.23 A simple ACIA circuit that implements a level-4 autovectored interrupt. During the interrupt-acknowledge bus cycle the level-4 acknowledge results in A3A2A1 = 100; this results in VPA* for the autovector exception. The ACIA is assumed deselected during the IACK bus cycle.

12.7.2 Multiple-Autovector Example

The last example can be easily extended to handle multiple autovectors, as shown in Figure 12.24. The circuit is identical to the last one except that an encoder has been added to the 68000 IPL* inputs and a decoder to the A3-A1 outputs. Each additional device IRQ*

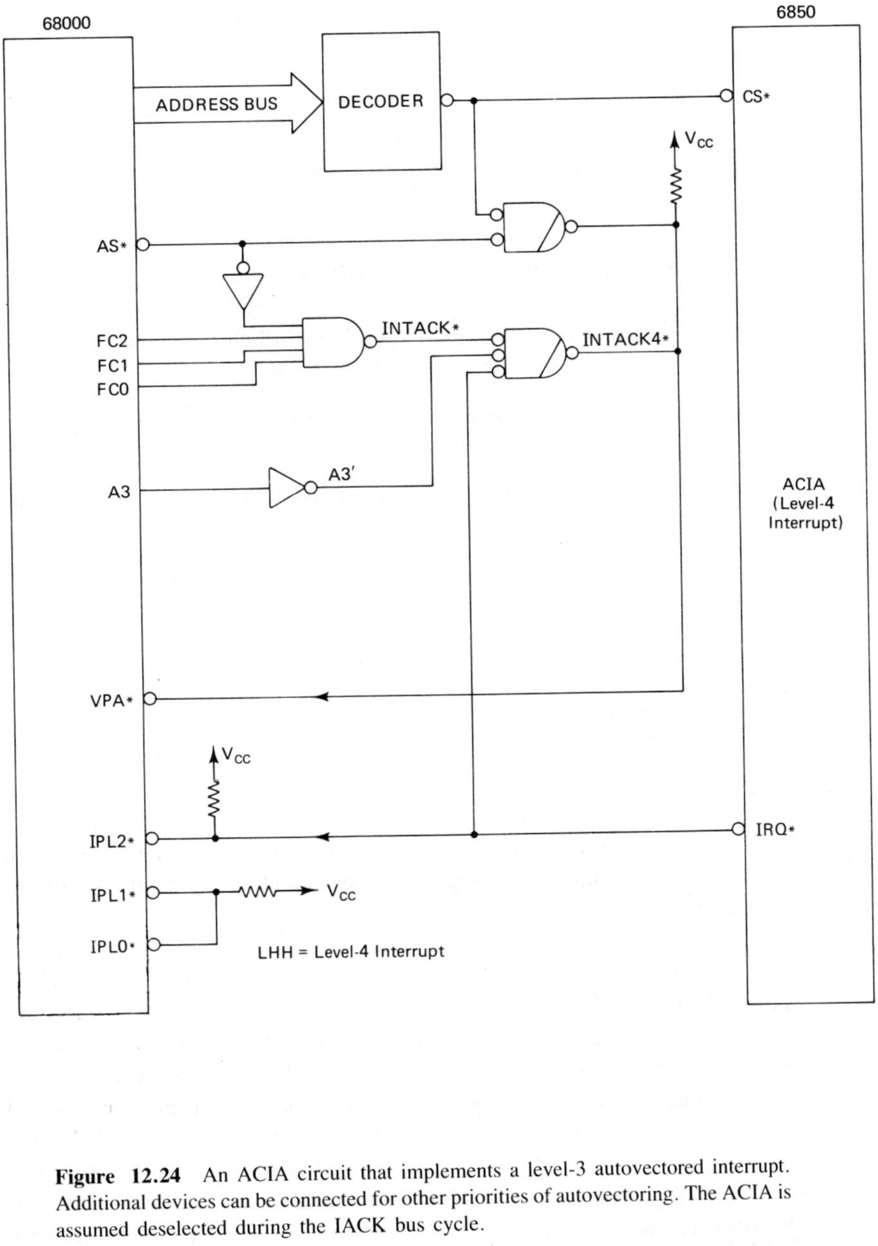

Figure 12.24 An ACIA circuit that implements a level-3 autovectored interrupt. Additional devices can be connected for other priorities of autovectoring. The ACIA is assumed deselected during the IACK bus cycle.

line connects to the encoder and causes the proper level interrupt; when the 68000 responds to each interrupt, the decoder output ANDs with the device IRQ* to obtain an interrupt-acknowledge signal. All these signals are wire-OR'ed together to the VPA* input using open-collector gates.

12.7.3 Vector and Autovectored Example

The basic level-3 autovector circuit in the last example can be expanded to include a vectored controller as shown in Figure 12.25. The new device is connected to the encoder level-5 priority input the same way as the autovectored controller. The difference is in how the unit responds to an IACK bus cycle: rather than assert VPA*, the interrupting device will put its vector number on the data bus and return DTACK*.

12.7.4 IEEE Std-696 Interrupt Example

The IEEE Std-696 bus has a number of control lines that relate to the interrupts. The primary signals that will be considered here are:

INT*	Pin 73	Primary interrupt-request bus signal
NMI*	12	Non-maskable interrupt request line
sINTA	96	Status indicating IACK bus cycle to read the interrupt vector
VI0*	4	Vectored interrupt 0 (highest priority)
.		
.		
.		
VI7*	11	Vectored interrupt 7 (lowest priority)

The primary interrupt control lines, INT* and NMI*, are used to request service from the CPU board acting as the permanent bus master. When INT* is held asserted, the processor responds by starting an interrupt-acknowledge (IACK) bus cycle that asserts sINTA; the slave device in the system then responds by placing vector information on the data bus. On the other hand, the non-maskable interrupt request, NMI*, need not be held: it is asserted as a negative-going edge. The Standard does not require an IACK bus cycle in response to an NMI*.

The vectored lines are used to generate interrupts of eight different priority levels. They may be implemented in a slave interrupt controller that prioritizes the requests and asserts INT* for action by the permanent bus master. Alternatively, the vectored interrupts may be implemented by the bus master itself. In either case, the vectored lines must be held asserted until the interrupt is serviced by the master.

Figure 12.26 shows a circuit to synchronize interrupts from the IEEE Std-696 bus. Depending on how the 68000 CPU board is configured in the system, the INT* input may be disconnected and VI0* used as the highest priority vectored input. Which interrupt gets first service is resolved by the 74LS148 priority controller; its output goes directly to the 68000 IPL* inputs to start exception processing. The two lowest priority vectored inputs are not implemented in the 68000 system.

The NMI* input from the bus will cause an immediate assertion of a level-7 *NMI*. The 68000 will respond on the next instruction by starting exception processing. In addition to the bus NMI* signal, a local on-board abort circuit can be conveniently added to

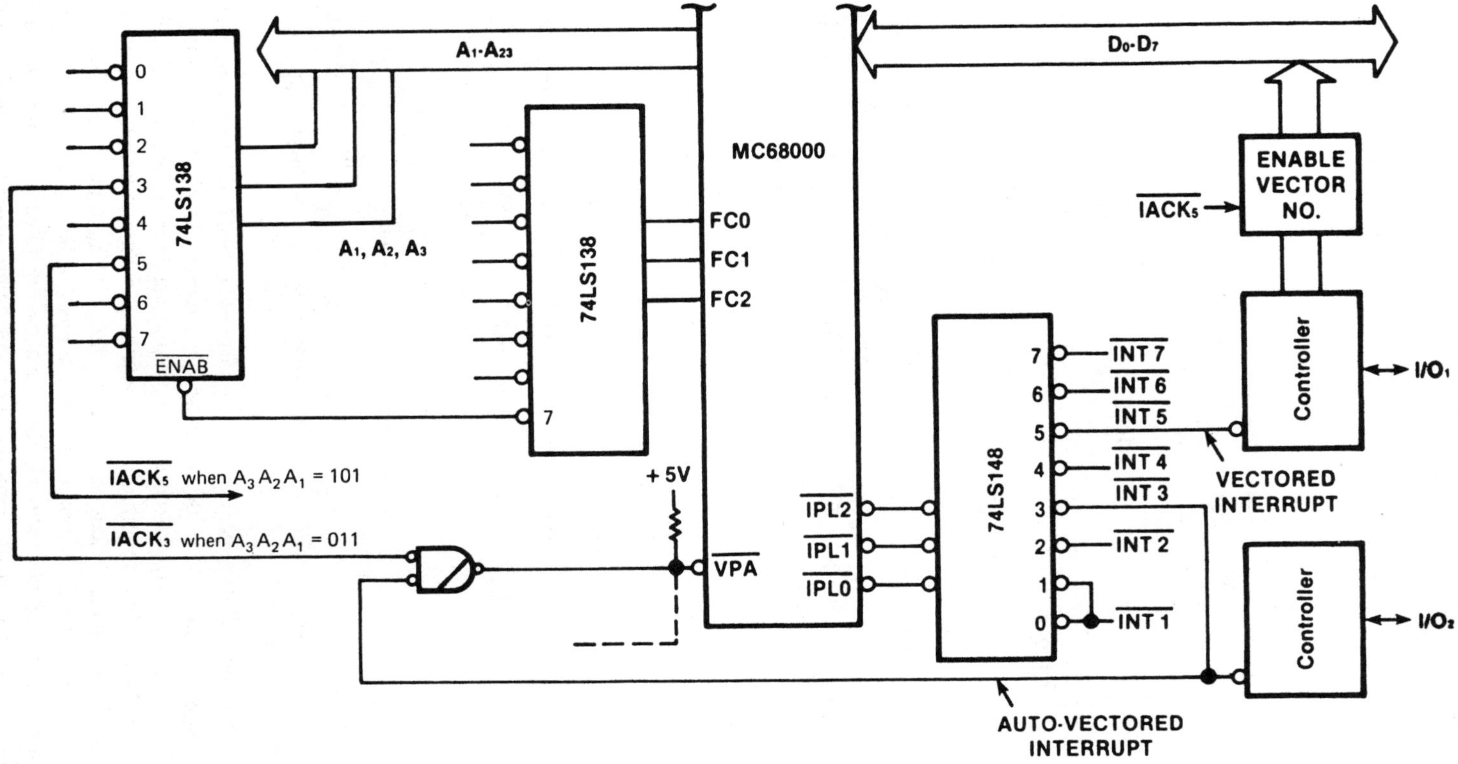

Figure 12.25 An example circuit combining both vectored and autovectored interrupts. (Courtesy Motorola Inc.)

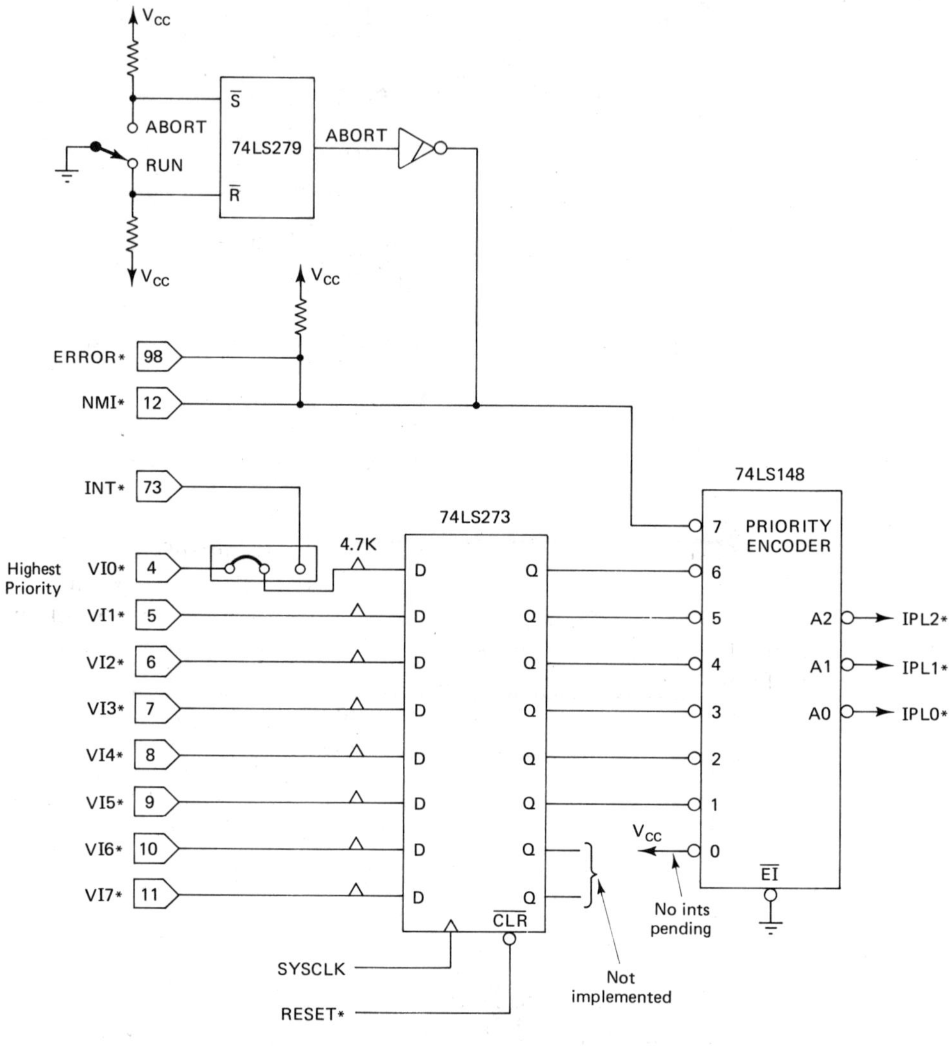

Figure 12.26 Interrupt synchronizer and level-7 interrupt circuit for an IEEE-696 system.

cause the *NMI* exception processing. The TUTOR firmware supports the *NMI* by displaying all the 68000 registers for recovery from programming difficulties.

The interrupt-acknowledge circuit is shown in Figure 12.27. An interrupt acknowledge bus cycle is required in response to a system interrupt, so when the 68000 begins the IACK bus cycle to acquire its vector, the sINTA control is asserted so that the interrupting slave device knows to put data on the bus for the 68000 to read. A jumper is provided to implement autovectoring if the slave cannot place a vector on the bus. Consequently, INT* and any of the vectored interrupt inputs can obtain their vectors directly from the 68000.

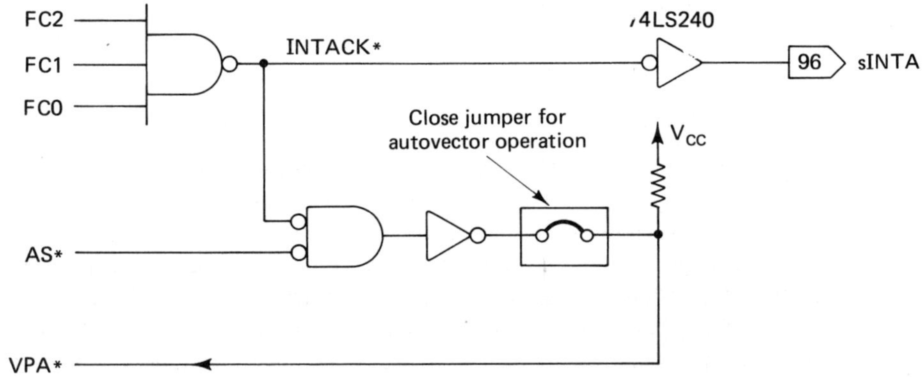

Figure 12.27 Interrupt acknowledge circuit for an IEEE-696 system.

12.8 SUMMARY

This chapter on exception processing covers a wide range of details on how the 68000 handles unusual situations. Any deviation from normal processing can be considered an exception, and each one can be processed differently. Many of the possible exceptions are caused internally when the 68000 detects errors or special instructions; other exceptions come from external sources such as hardware faults or interrupts. Depending on the nature of the cause, the 68000 responds according to priority. A crisis such as a bus or address error causes immediate action, but other exceptions are handled in turn at the end of bus cycles or instructions.

The 68000 can operate in either a supervisor or a user state depending on whether the *S*-bit in the status register is set. While in the supervisor state, the programmer has access to the entire system and can execute any instruction; in the user state, however, certain instructions (and memory locations if the hardware has been so designed) are not allowed. This limited access to system facilities is typically used to protect the system from user errors or tampering. Unless a special exception is provided, it is impossible in software for a user to become supervisor once the *S*-bit is set to user state. However, the user can take advantage of system utility programs by using the TRAP instruction.

The reset exception is the highest priority exception and gets instant attention. When RESET* is asserted, the 68000 begins a complete system initialization that involves reading the SSP and PC vectors from the boot EPROMs. The 68000 is in the supervisory state after reset and begins executing code at the PC location it found in the EPROMs. This code should then initialize ACIAs and other programmable devices necessary to communicate with the rest of the system; it should also initialize the exception vector table in low memory.

The internally generated exceptions are caused by a number of different possible situations:

- internally detected errors
  - address error
  - illegal instruction

unimplemented instruction
privilege violation

- trace mode
- special instructions

Except for the high-priority address error, the exception-processing sequence involves changing to the supervisor state temporarily and then calculating a vector number based on the type of exception. After stacking the current status and PC, the 68000 gets a new PC at the exception's address found in the vector table. Then it executes the exception-handler code, restores the prior status, and returns to where it left off.

Bus and address errors require immediate attention by the 68000 to avoid the destruction of memory contents and to preserve the state of the processor itself. The bus-error exception is initiated externally by the BERR* control; the address error is begun internally when the 68000 attempts to access a word or long word at an odd address. The exception-processing sequence is the same as usual, except that more information is saved on the system stack. This extra information can then be used by the programmer to find the cause of the problem.

The BERR* control is asserted externally by a watchdog timer. When the 68000 starts a bus cycle, AS* goes LOW for only a few clock cycles depending on how many waits are provided for a slow peripheral. If the peripheral fails to respond at all, the 68000 is hung until it either gets a DTACK* (which will never come) or the watchdog timer intervenes. In the latter case, the timer asserts BERR* to signal that bus-error exception processing must begin. If a second bus error occurs while the 68000 is still processing the first bus-error exception, then there is a double bus fault. This stops the 68000 completely, and the processor asserts HALT* as an output.

Interrupts are handled by the 68000 as exceptions and are initiated by asserting the interrupt priority level (IPL*) lines to the processor. There are seven different priority levels of interrupts that are handled according to the setting of the interrupt mask in the status register. The level-7 exception, however, is a non-maskable interrupt (*NMI*) and is processed regardless of the mask pattern. All interrupts, just as with any exception, require that the address of the interrupt service routine (ISR) be stored in the exception vector table.

The interrupts can be either vectored or autovectored. There are 192 vectored interrupt and 7 autovector addresses provided in the vector table. A vectored interrupt is one in which the interrupting device can provide a vector number on the data bus when the 68000 acknowledges it; in contrast, the autovectored interrupt cannot respond with a vector. The usual response sequence during the IACK bus cycle is to provide a vector number and return DTACK* or to simply assert VPA*. When VPA* is asserted, the 68000 goes to the autovector associated with the priority of the interrupt on the IPL* pins.

The complete 68000 exception-processing sequence is shown in Figure 12.28. Aside from reset, the chart summarizes how the processor responds to internally generated exceptions, to error situations, and to both types of interrupts.

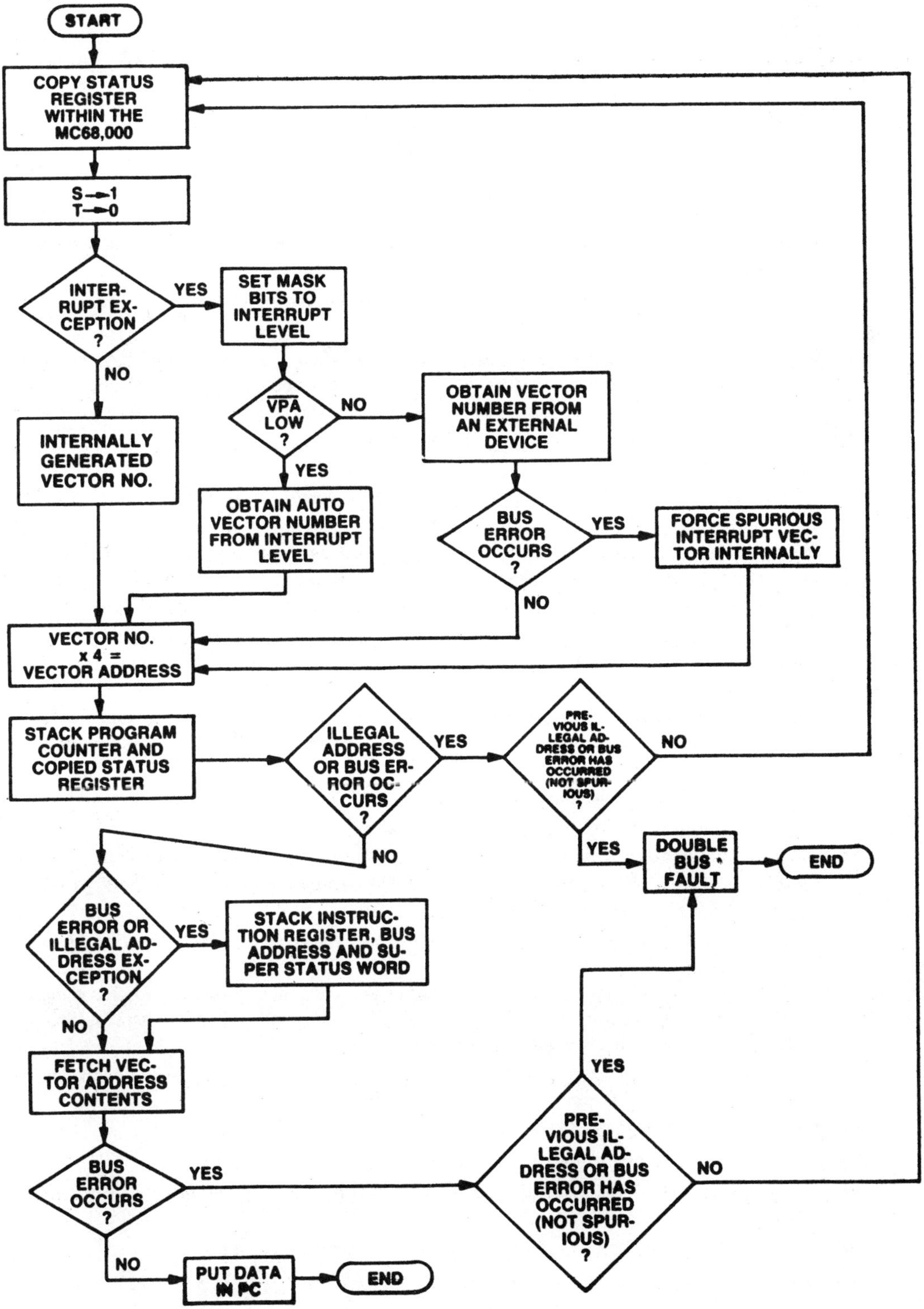

Figure 12.28 Complete exception-processing sequence. Only the reset case follows a different pattern. (Courtesy Motorola Inc.)

EXERCISES

1. What are the three states that the 68000 can operate in?
2. What is an exception?
3. What is the highest priority exception? At what point in the 68000's bus cycle or instruction does it become active?
4. When would you expect to assert BERR*? Why would it be necessary?
5. Where is the exception vector table?
6. While testing a new program, you inadvertently wrote binary zero to memory between $8 and $80. Then you tried to exit the program by pushing the abort button (for an *NMI*), but could not get the processor to respond. What happened? You reset and it came alive again. What happened?
7. If you were writing a boot monitor program like TUTOR, what initial status register setting would you use? Why?
8. What happens when the 68000 tries to read a protected memory array as in Figure 12.8? Predict the results depending on possible error-recovery circuits within a system.
9. Design a protected memory system for a simple 68000 system using a total of 64K starting at address 0. Assume the user has the top 32K and TUTOR and supervisory-only memory the bottom 32K. Show the memory map and circuit.
10. Contrive an illegal instruction and test it using TUTOR. Write a simple exception routine to handle the illegal instruction; remember to store the exception vector in the table and to return with an RTE.
11. Test the TRAP #14 provided in the TUTOR firmware by writing a small program to print the ASCII equivalent of numbers typed at the keyboard. The program should start printing after you enter a carriage return.
12. Assume that you have a watchdog timer like Figure 12.18 and the system clock runs at 6 MHz. How long before a BERR* is asserted?
13. Design an alternative watchdog timer with a different TTL part. Suppose that you have a 68B50 ACIA console port, 150 ns RAM, and 250 ns EPROMs running with a 10 MHz clock. What is the minimum time you *must* provide in the timer to avoid false triggering?
14. Explain a double bus fault. Under what circumstances might you get such a fault? Can you recover by doing an *NMI*?
15. You are developing an interrupt-driven keyboard and have the interrupt service routine in memory and the vector table set correctly. You run the program, but nothing seems to happen. Speculate on possible hardware and software problems.
16. There are 192 vectored interrupts provided in the vector table. The impossible happened: you need one more vectored interrupt. What can you do?
17. What is the purpose of the IACK bus cycle?
18. Are you allowed to assert both VPA* and DTACK* during an IACK?
19. The BERR* line was asserted during the IACK rather than DTACK* or VPA*. What should the 68000 do?
20. Examine Figure 12.20 closely. Why is the PCL stacked when it is?
21. In Figure 12.22, *must* a debounced switch be used for the NMI? Why or why not?

22. In Figure 12.24, the 74LS138 can handle more than just A3-A1. Redesign that section of the logic for fewer parts count.
23. Why should the IRQ* be part of the INTACK circuit?

FURTHER READING

ALEXANDRIDIS, NIKITAS A. *Microprocessor System Design Concepts.* Rockville, MD: Computer Science Press, 1984. (QA6.5.A369)

ANDREWS, MICHAEL. *Self Guided Tour Through the 68000.* Reston, VA: Reston Publishing Co. Inc., 1984.

HARMAN, THOMAS L., and BARBARA LAWSON. *The Motorola MC68000 Microprocessor Family: Assembly Language, Interface Design, and System Design.* Englewood Cliffs, NJ: Prentice-Hall, 1985. (QA76.8.M6895H37)

IEEE Standard 696 Interface Devices. New York: IEEE, 1983.

KANE, GERRY. *68000 Microprocessor Handbook.* Berkeley, CA: Osborne/McGraw-Hill, 1981.

MC68000 16-bit Microprocessor Data Manual. Austin, TX: Motorola Semiconductor Products, Inc.

LIBES, SOL, and GARETZ, MARK. *Interfacing to S-100/IEEE-696 Microcomputers.* Berkeley, CA: Osborne/McGraw-Hill, 1981.

RAFIQUZZAMAN, MOHAMED. *Microprocessors and Microcomputer Development Systems.* New York: Harper & Row, 1984. (QA76.9.S88R33)

STARNES, THOMAS W. "Handling Exceptions Gracefully Enhances Software Reliability." *Electronics* (September 11, 1980): 153–57.

TAYLOR, MITCHELL B. *A Discussion of Interrupts for the MC68000.* Engineering Bulletin EB-97. Austin, TX: Motorola Semiconductor Products, Inc.

WILLIAMS, STEVE. *Programming the 68000.* Berkeley, CA: Sybex, Inc., 1985.

THIRTEEN

Bus Interface Design

At this point in the development of your 68000 board, you should have a working system complete with at least one I/O port. The board already has much of the capability of the Educational Computer Board; in fact, depending on how you designed memory, it might even have more possibilities for extra functions than the ECB. Figure 13.1 shows the general organization of your processor after you added each of the modules discussed earlier, and there is just one left: the interface to the IEEE Std-696 (S-100) bus. The interface module is necessary if you want to expand your board to access more memory, I/O, a disk drive, or special functions such as the clock board in Chapter 5.

In this chapter you will learn how to design and test this interface circuit. After finishing the material here, you should be able to design a bus-state generator circuit that will match the asynchronous 68000 to the synchronous S-100 bus. You will also be able to explain how the 68000 handles bus arbitration and how to interface it properly. There are a number of signals required by the Standard, and you will learn how to generate them on your board. Overall, by the end of the chapter, you will be familiar with the IEEE standard, how to read it, and how to design your circuits to work with it.

The IEEE Std-696 bus, usually called the S-100 bus, is a parallel-backplane bus structure that allows the interconnection of up to 22 individual printed-circuit (PC) boards. It provides the communication between these PC boards using a common set of 100 parallel connecting lines in the backplane or motherboard. Each PC board plugs into a 100-pin connector on the motherboard, where it gets all the signals it needs to perform its function in the system. The maximum switching rate of any signal on the bus is 6 MHz; signals on any individual board, however, are not limited to any maximum.

The PC boards connected together on the bus are classified as either bus masters (permanent or temporary) or bus slaves. The 68000 CPU card, for example, will be designed as a permanent bus master and will be responsible for initiating all the bus signals.

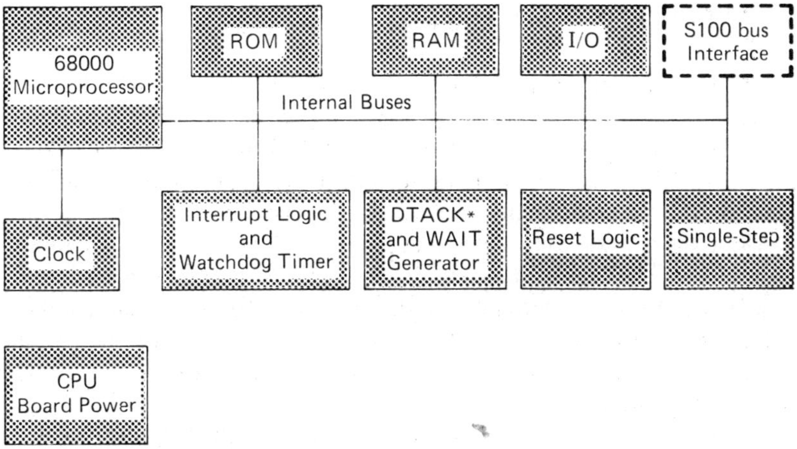

Figure 13.1 The highlighted S-100 bus interface module will be developed in this chapter. All the other modules have been designed and tested.

A temporary master on the bus can request use of the bus and initiate an arbitrary number of bus cycles before returning control to the permanent master. A bus slave, in contrast, does not initiate bus cycles: it responds to requests for information. The clock board in Chapter 5 is an example of a bus slave that provides the time when the CPU asks for it.

The S-100 bus was originally designed in the mid-1970s to interconnect the 8-bit 8080 microprocessor with memory and I/O circuits. Since then, however, the bus connections and signal protocol have been standardized so that PC boards designed by one manufacturer would be able to work (hopefully) with any other S-100 PC boards. During the standardization, the bus was also adapted for use with 16-bit microprocessors. The end result is a bus that can handle both 8- and 16-bit data transfers with 24-bit addressing of 16 Mb. The bus structure is organized into the 8 sets of signals and lines shown in Table 13.1.

TABLE 13.1 ORGANIZATION OF THE S-100 BUS IS DIVIDED INTO EIGHT SETS OF SIGNALS AND ONE SET OF POWER LINES.

Data bus	16 lines
Address bus	16 or 24
Status bus	8
Control output	5
Control input	6
TMA control	8
Vectored interrupts	8
Utility	16
Power	9

13.1 OPERATION OF THE S-100 BUS

To understand the operation of the S-100 bus, compare it with the 68000 when it reads data from memory. First, recall that the 68000 read bus cycle is made up of 8 clock states (4 clock cycles) as shown in Figure 13.2(a). During the bus cycle, the AS* and the UDS* and/or LDS* are asserted to indicate valid address and valid data on the 68000's bus. The address and data strobes are the primary signals indicating to the outside world that a bus cycle is under way. Now, examine Figure 13.2(b) and see the similarity: the S-100 bus also has a bus cycle made up of clock cycles. The normal bus cycle has 3 clock cycles rather than the 4 in the 68000; if desired, an S-100 bus cycle can be extended to 4 by adding BSi (bus-state-idle) at the end of the third bus cycle. Each of the clock cycles are called "bus states"; watch not to confuse this with the 68000 "clock state," which is half the clock period.

Notice also that the S-100 bus has a signal called "pSYNC" that indicates the beginning of a bus cycle. It is similar to the 68000 address or data strobes in the sense that it always starts a bus cycle. It does not, however, convey any information concerning the status of the address or data bus information.

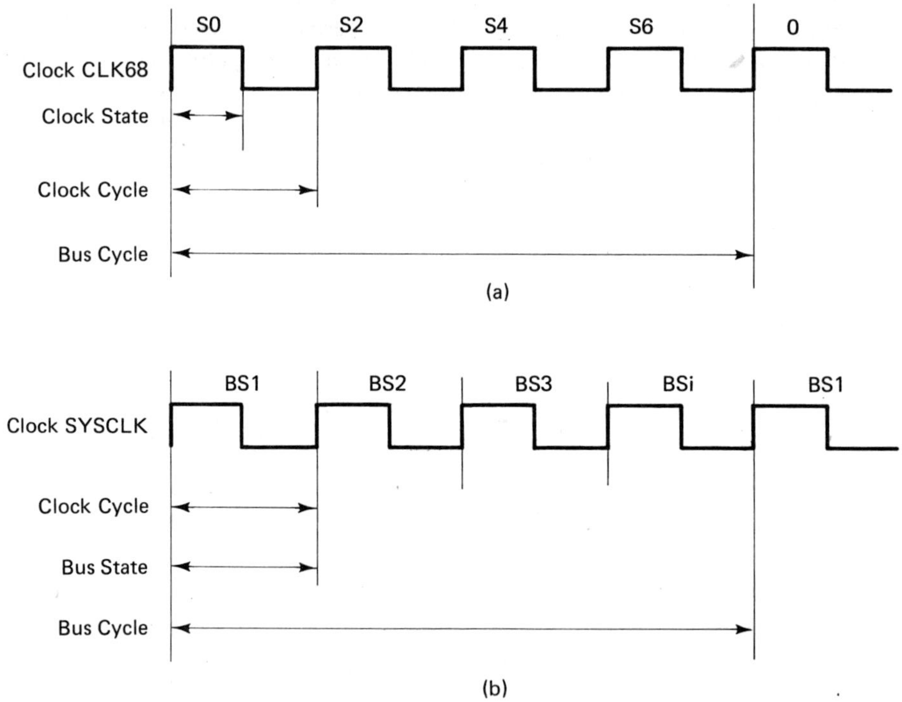

Figure 13.2 Clock and bus cycles. (a) The 68000 bus cycle is composed of four clock cycles, minimum. (b) The S-100 bus cycle has a minimum of three clock cycles. The BSi (bus state idle) is optional.

Figure 13.3(a) shows the 68000 bus cycle with two waits added.[1] These waits are automatically inserted by the 68000 if it fails to detect DTACK* at the falling clock edge in S4. As soon as it receives DTACK* from the peripheral, it concludes the bus cycle with S5, S6, and S7. Figure 13.3(b) shows the operation of the S-100 bus with two added waits. Just as in the 68000 case, the waits lengthen the bus cycle to allow time for the peripheral to respond. All bus signals are held valid during the waits.

There is a fundamental difference between the 68000 and the S-100 bus at this point though. The 68000 inserts waits because it is waiting an unknown time for DTACK*; it is an asynchronous operation (i.e., not necessarily related to the system clock) that is quite flexible and can vary from device to device. The S-100 bus, by comparison, inserts waits synchronously depending on the level of the RDY control input; if RDY is negated (LOW) at the beginning of BS2, then a wait is added. One clock cycle later, if RDY is still LOW, then another wait is added. To operate properly, the RDY control must be synchronized with the system clock.

The operation of the RDY control is illustrated in Figure 13.4 for a typical S-100 bus cycle. As long as RDY is LOW at the rising clock edges shown, then waits will be added to the bus cycle. Some additional S-100 signals are also included in the figure: the

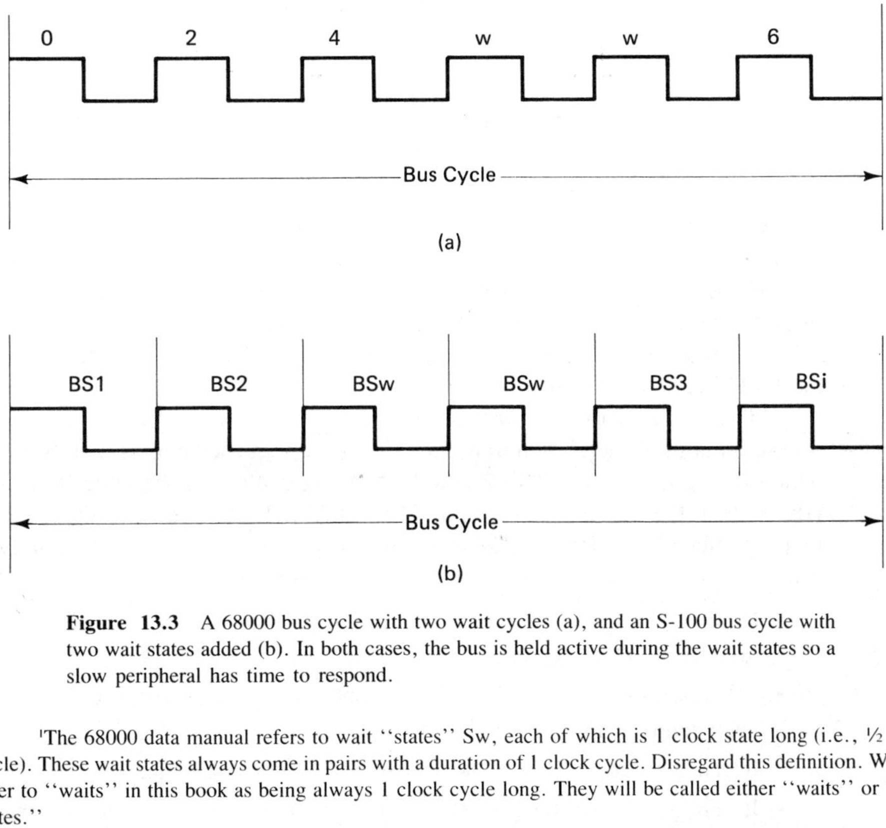

Figure 13.3 A 68000 bus cycle with two wait cycles (a), and an S-100 bus cycle with two wait states added (b). In both cases, the bus is held active during the wait states so a slow peripheral has time to respond.

[1]The 68000 data manual refers to wait "states" Sw, each of which is 1 clock state long (i.e., ½ clock cycle). These wait states always come in pairs with a duration of 1 clock cycle. Disregard this definition. We will refer to "waits" in this book as being always 1 clock cycle long. They will be called either "waits" or "wait states."

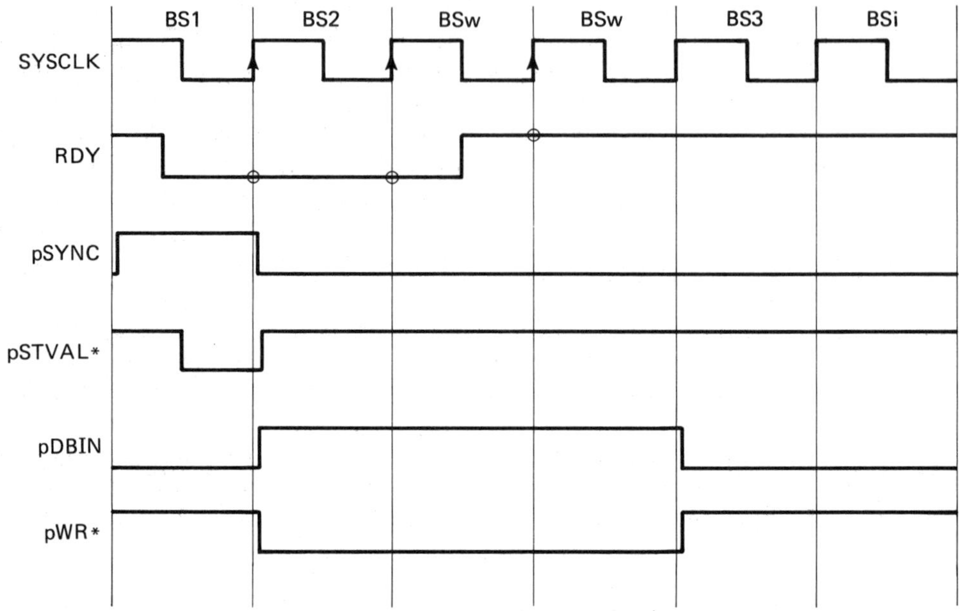

Figure 13.4 The major control signals on the S-100 bus during a typical bus cycle with two waits. pDBIN is asserted HIGH for a read bus cycle; pWR* is asserted LOW for a write bus cycle. RDY negated LOW at the clock rising edge causes the waits to be added.

falling edge of pSTVAL* *during pSYNC HIGH* tells the system that address and data bus values are valid. The control output pDBIN is asserted HIGH to indicate that the bus cycle is to read data; likewise, if pWR* is asserted LOW, then the bus cycle is to write data. All of these control output signals are generated by the "bus master," or CPU board. There may be other masters temporarily in control of the bus, but for the time being, assume that the CPU board is the only master.

The states of the S-100 bus and their relationship to RDY can be represented in state-diagram form as shown in Figure 13.5. The sequence begins with Bus State 1 (BS1), which then goes to Bus State 2 (BS2) on the next clock rising edge. If RDY is asserted HIGH, then Bus State 3 (BS3) is next. If RDY is LOW (i.e., −RDY or RDY′ is true), then Bus State Wait (BSw) is next; the system stays in BSw until RDY finally goes HIGH. There are several possibilities for the system after it enters BS3:

- If the hold request (HOLD*) is asserted, then the master enters BSH and stays there until HOLD* is negated.
- The master can go to BSi if the current instruction is complete and an interrupt has been requested/accepted.
- It can also go to BSi if the instruction is not complete.
- It can go directly back to BS1 if the instruction is complete and there is no hold request or interrupt accept.

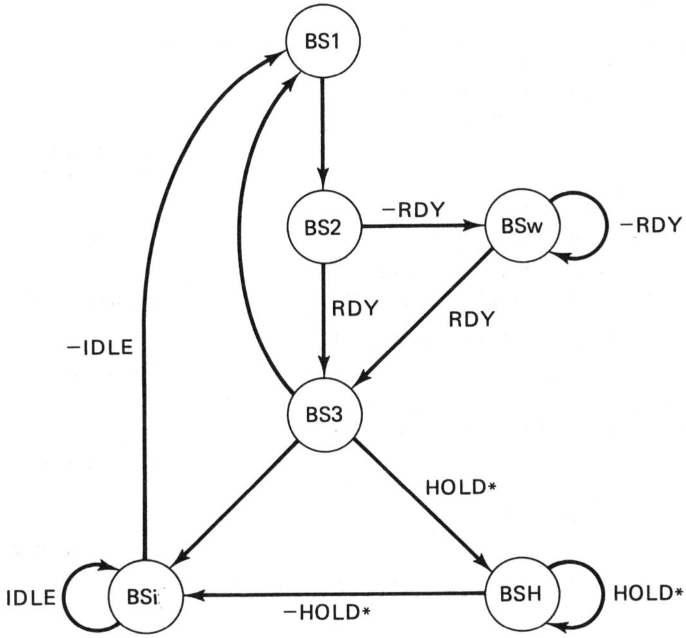

Figure 13.5 State diagram describing the operation of the S-100 bus under control of the permanent master.

Figure 13.6 describes the events that take place during a typical read bus cycle with two wait states; compare this activity with the timing diagram in Figure 13.4. The permanent bus master starts the bus cycle by entering BS1 and asserting pSYNC. Shortly after the beginning of BS1, the master puts the address and status information on the bus; then, as soon as they stabilize, the master brings pSTVAL* LOW to indicate valid status and address. Meanwhile, the slave decodes the address and negates RDY (by making it LOW) before the end of BS1. Shortly after pSTVAL* goes LOW, the master asserts pDBIN to indicate the read bus cycle.

As BS2 starts, the master samples RDY and finds that the slave will need extra time during the bus cycle. The master negates pSYNC and pSTVAL* in BS2 and continues to assert pDBIN. On the next rising edge of the system clock, RDY is still LOW, so another wait state is required. Finally, the slave expects data ready during the following bus state, so it make RDY HIGH. After waiting out the second BSW, the master now goes to BS3.

The master negates pDBIN near the beginning of BS3. The data from the slave must be valid at the falling edge of pDBIN and remain valid for at least 70 ns after pDBIN. Later in BS3, the master removes the address and status information from the bus. The slave is deselected at this point, so its data will be off the bus. During BSi, neither the master nor the slave are transferring information on the bus. The master, however, is still responsible for maintaining control of the bus even though nothing is being done.

State	Master	Slave
BS1	Assert pSYNC. Address and status valid on bus (give time to settle).	
		Decodes address. Negates RDY.
	Assert pSTVAL*. Assert pDBIN or pWR*.	
BS2	Sample RDY (must wait). Negate pSYNC, pSTVAL*.	Recognizes pDBIN and data on the bus.
BSw	Sample RDY (still must wait).	
		Asserts RDY expecting data valid in a clock cycle.
BSw	Sample RDY (continue now).	
		Data must be valid by now.
BS3	Read data. Negate pDBIN.	
		Remove data from bus.
	Remove address and status from bus.	

Figure 13.6 Events during a typical read bus cycle with two waits required by the bus slave.

13.2 BUS-STATE GENERATOR DESIGN

In order to use the asynchronous 68000 on the synchronous S-100 bus, an interface circuit is required. The idea is to match the 68000 bus cycle to the S-100 bus cycle so that all the relevant signals are always properly handled. Figure 13.7(a) shows the essential 68000 signals assuming no waits; Figure 13.7(b) shows the pSYNC and pDBIN S-100 signals assuming no waits.

The first task in the bus-state generator design is matching the length of both bus cycles; that is, the normal 68000 bus cycle and the normal S-100 bus cycle must be the same duration. Therefore, the extra idle state BSi should be added after BS3 in Figure 13.7(b). The idle state has no effect on the bus signals because it is, by definition, a "do-nothing" state.

The next issue to resolve in the design is making sure that the falling edge of the 68000's clock, CLK68, at S6 is lined up properly with the time when the S-100 bus expects to present valid data to the master. This means that the falling edge of pDBIN must occur at the same instant as the falling edge of CLK68 at S6. To do this, redraw the S-100 bus cycle from Figure 13.7 over again, with both these edges lined up at the same time.

Figure 13.8 illustrates the result of shifting the S-100 bus cycle over to the right so S6 and pDBIN line up correctly. One of the first things to notice is that CLK68 is no longer identical to SYSCLK. Part of the bus-interface design, then, requires that

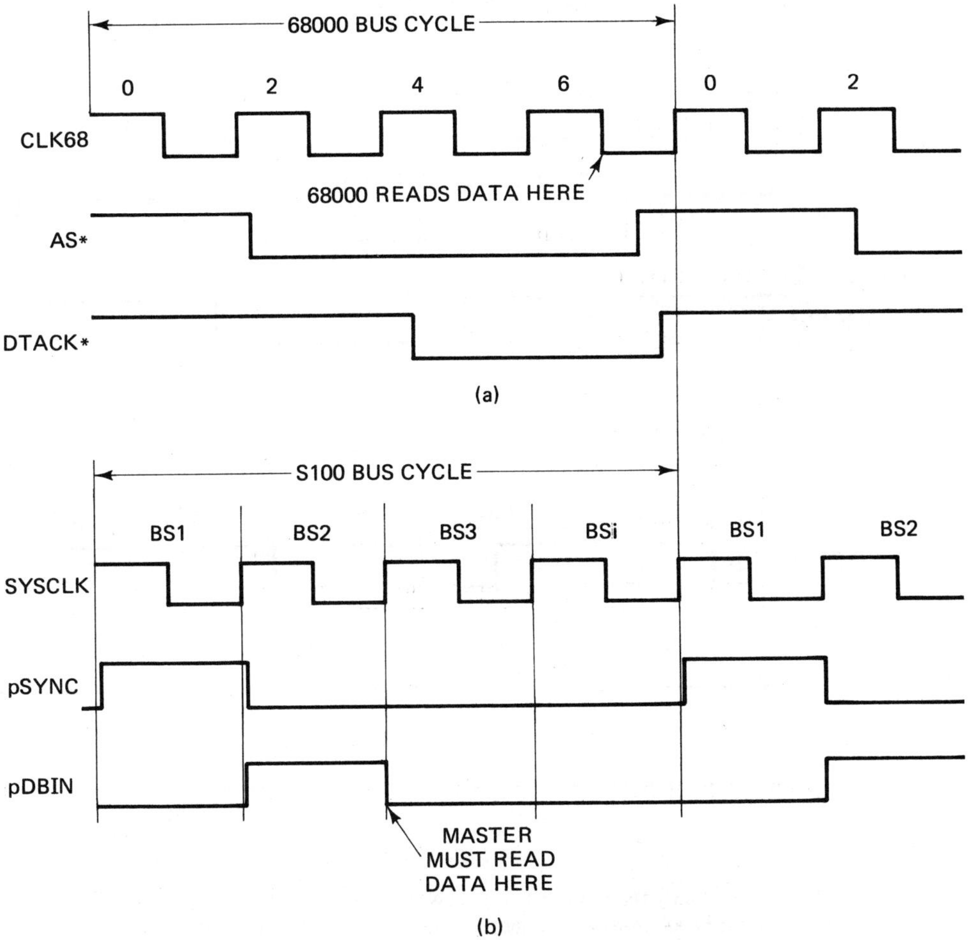

Figure 13.7 The normal 68000 bus cycle (a) and the normal S-100 bus cycle (b). Both timing diagrams assume that no waits are required.

SYSCLK be inverted CLK68. Recognize that this inversion must cause as little skew as possible, so you need to use a device such as the 74265 to provide both clocks to the system.

To always line up the 68000 S6 with pDBIN, a sequential state machine must be designed to make the 68000 look like a synchronous processor. This state machine (the bus-state generator) should always

- start at a certain place in the 68000 bus cycle,
- control when the 68000 will get to S6, and
- provide state outputs matching the S-100 bus cycle.

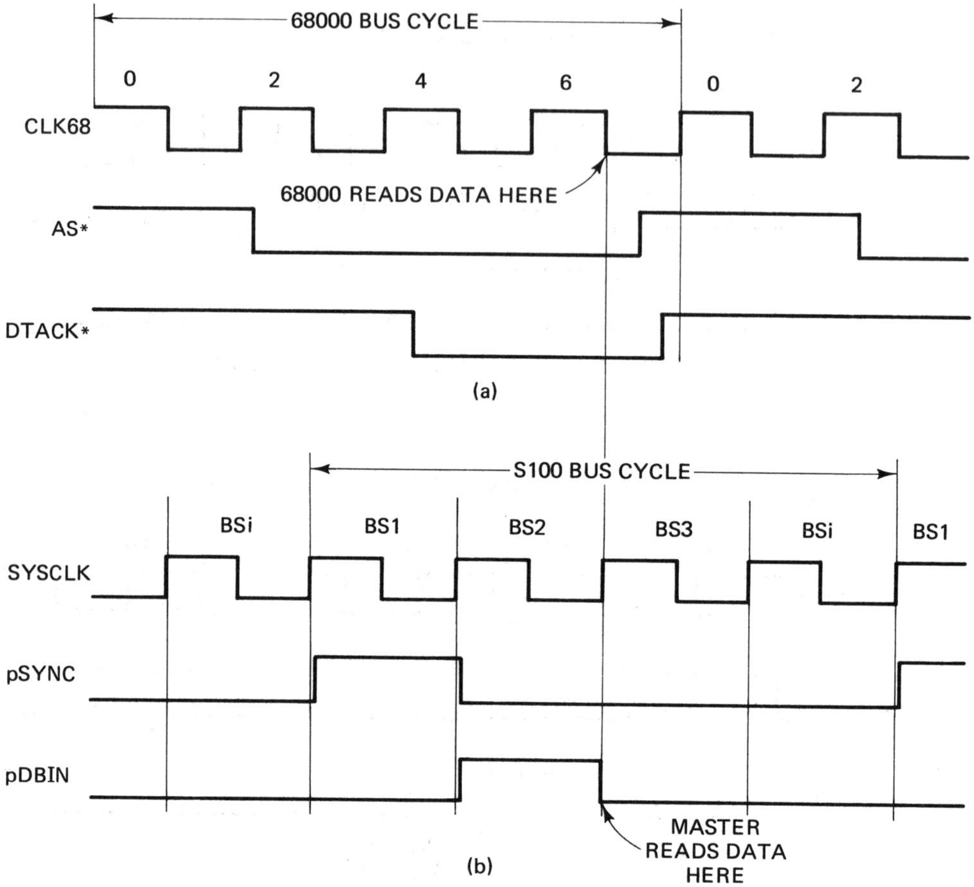

Figure 13.8 The normal 68000 bus cycle (a) and the S-100 bus cycle (b) shifted over so that the 68000 reads data at the same time the data is valid on the S-100 bus.

13.2.1 Starting the Bus-State Generator

The 68000 address strobe is always asserted at the beginning of a bus cycle, and that can be used to start the bus-state generator. Unfortunately, the address strobe stays low during the entire TAS instruction. Recall that the TAS requires two bus cycles: first a read cycle and then a write cycle. So if the address strobe by itself is used to start the bus-state generator, it will not properly start the generator for the last half of the TAS instruction. During the TAS, however, the data strobes are still active, and they can be used to indicate the beginning of the second bus cycle. While not a severe problem, the data strobes are always delayed a clock cycle during a write operation.

Starting the S-100 bus cycle requires a combination of all of the above to work properly. Figure 13.9 shows a simple circuit to create a signal called BCYCLE. You might recall seeing BCYCLE in Chapter 9 when you examined the DTACK* and the wait generator circuit; they are both the same Boolean function. BCYCLE will be asserted HIGH

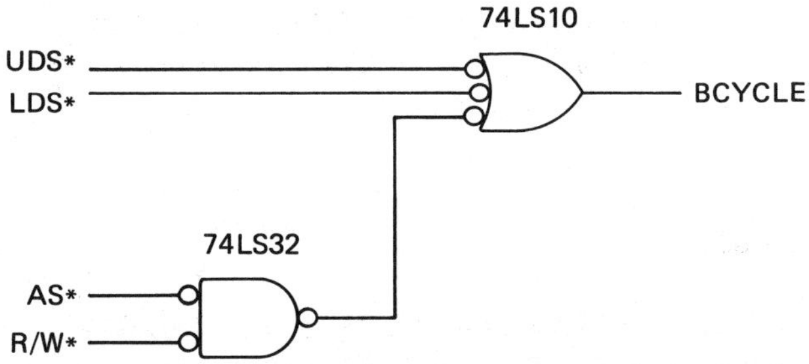

Figure 13.9 A circuit to indicate the start of a 68000 bus cycle. The extra gate with AS* and R/W* is to avoid the one clock-cycle delay when the 68000 does a write operation.

whenever either data strobe goes LOW or whenever the address strobe is asserted during a 68000 write bus cycle. Consequently, BCYCLE will go HIGH during a read, a write (there is no delay because of the late data strobes), or a TAS read and write while AS* stays LOW.

Figure 13.10 illustrates the operation of BCYCLE for the 68000 read and write bus

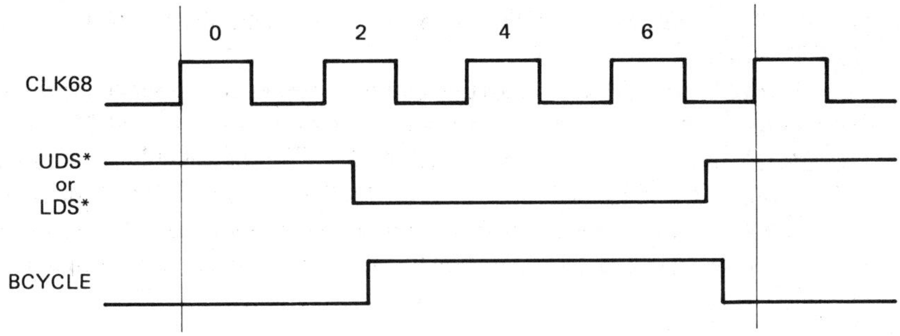

(a)

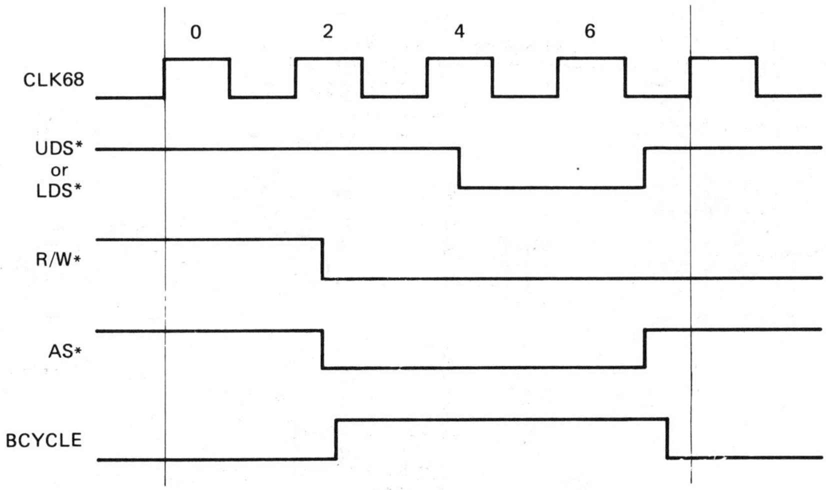

(b)

Figure 13.10 Timing diagram showing BCYCLE derived from the data strobes during a 68000 read bus cycle (a). BCYCLE derived from AS* and R/W* when the data strobes are delayed during a write bus cycle (b).

cycles. Regardless of which bus cycle is being run, the BCYCLE signal always goes HIGH during the 68000 S2. If BCYCLE is HIGH sufficiently before the clock falling edge at the end of S2, then it can be used to start the bus-state generator.

13.2.2 Controlling the 68000

The bus-state generator controls when the 68000 gets to S6 by controlling DTACK*. Examine Figure 13.8(a) again: you see that DTACK* is asserted early in S4 in plenty of time for the falling clock CLK68 at the end of S4. If no waits are required, then the bus-state generator can provide DTACK* during the S-100 bus state BS1. If waits *are* required, then the bus-state generator *must* make sure that DTACK* is HIGH sufficiently before the end of the 68000 S4. The bus-state generator expects the S-100 system to negate RDY before the end of BS1 if waits are needed, and this conveniently happens to coincide with the end of S4. Therefore, RDY can be used to negate the DTACK* signal from the bus-state generator.

Figure 13.11 shows a simplified sketch of the wait control circuit using BCYCLE. (The entire DTACK and wait circuit is shown in Figure 9.23.) The key signal is DT-ENAB, which indicates when DTACK* may be enabled. DT-ENAB is normally LOW while BCYCLE is LOW. After BCYCLE goes HIGH during the 68000 S2, DT-ENAB will go HIGH at the beginning of S4. As long as RDY stays HIGH, DTACK* will be asserted LOW by the end of S4, and the 68000 bus cycle will conclude normally as in Figure 13.8.

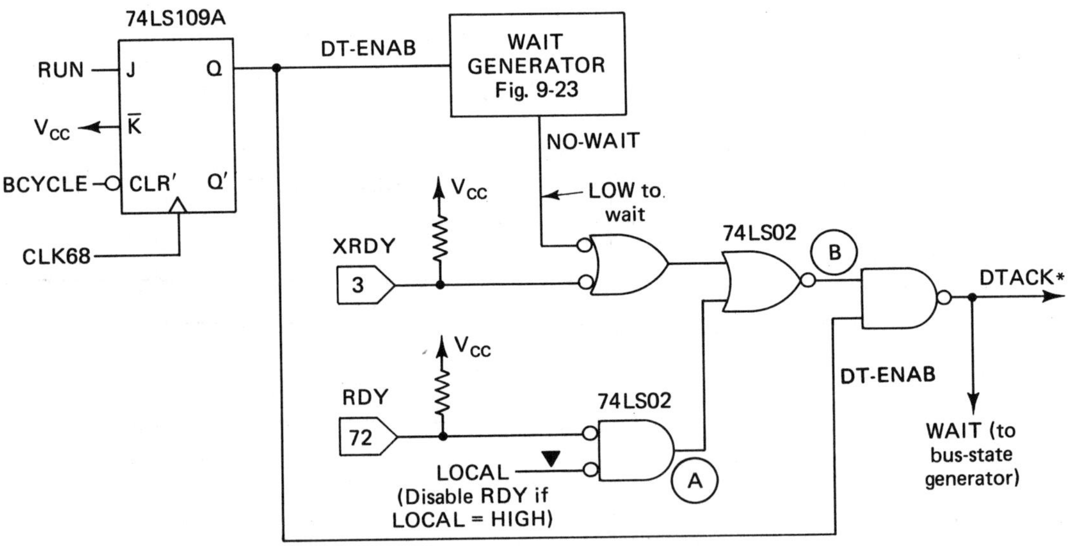

Figure 13.11 Wait-control logic. The Standard specifies an auxiliary-ready or XRDY input that can be used in addition to RDY; its operation is identical to RDY.

If the S-100 bus requires waits, as illustrated in Figure 13.12 for 2 waits, the S-100 bus peripheral will pull RDY to a LOW *before* the end of BS1 (end of 68000 S4). When RDY is LOW, DTACK* stays HIGH even though DT-ENAB is asserted, so the 68000 will insert a wait. One clock cycle later, RDY is still LOW, so the 68000 waits again. Finally, when RDY does go HIGH, DTACK* will go LOW and allow the 68000 to conclude the bus cycle.

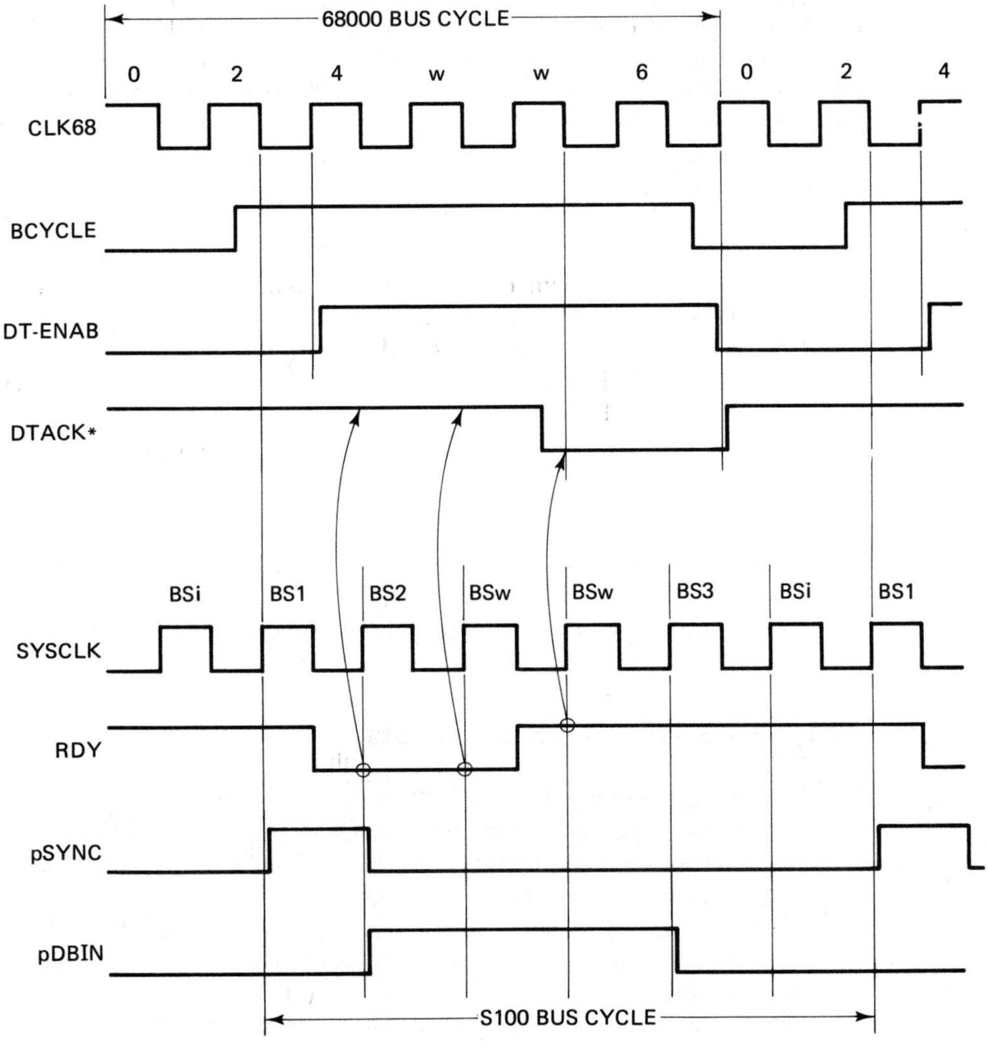

Figure 13.12 Synchronizing the 68000 and the S-100 bus for the case of two waits. The sequence starts when the 68000 causes BCYCLE to go HIGH. That starts the bus-state generator and gets a not-ready response from the peripheral. The 68000 waits until RDY goes HIGH.

Recognize that the timing of RDY is critical. It is important that the source of RDY (some peripheral board, for example) meet the Standard's 70 ns required setup before the end of BS1. If RDY is not negated in time, the 68000 will see DTACK* LOW at the end of S4 and finish the bus cycle. If that happens, the 68000 will read the data bus one or more clock cycles before the peripheral has placed valid data on the bus. The bus-state generator will continue to run properly, but the 68000 will have bad data because it ignored a wait request from the peripheral.

In summary, Figure 13.13 shows the interrelationship between the 68000 signals and the S-100 bus controls. When the 68000 begins a bus cycle, BCYCLE goes high and starts the bus-state generator, a sequential state machine. During its first state, BS1, the generator asserts pSYNC (in addition to address and status signals) on the S-100 bus. The peripheral slave device being addressed negates RDY which causes DTACK* to stay HIGH; the 68000 then inserts waits until the peripheral asserts RDY. As a result, the asynchronous 68000 is locked into a synchronous handshake with the bus.

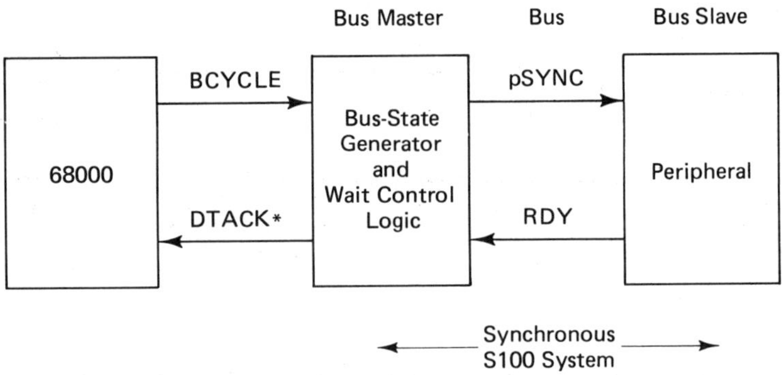

Figure 13.13 Control interrelationship between the 68000 and the synchronous bus.

13.2.3 Bus-State Generator Outputs

Providing the state outputs that match the S-100 bus cycle is fairly straightforward once the bus-state generator can be started at a known point (i.e., S2) in the 68000 bus cycle. The design is based on the state diagram shown in Figure 13.5 for the S-100 bus cycle. To match the 68000 and S-100 bus cycles, an idle state BSi must be included in the design. Then the first rough design can be done with the intention of realizing just the pSYNC and pDBIN signals in Figure 13.12. If these two can be generated, then the others are simple extensions in logic.

Figure 13.14 shows the simplified state diagram of the IEEE Std-696 permanent master during a read operation. The required outputs are included as a function of the state of the machine. When the machine is in BS1, pSYNC is asserted; when in BS2 or BSw, pDBIN is true. Neither BS3 nor BSi require outputs, so for all practical purposes they can be considered equivalent states. If the master is writing to the bus, then the control pWR*

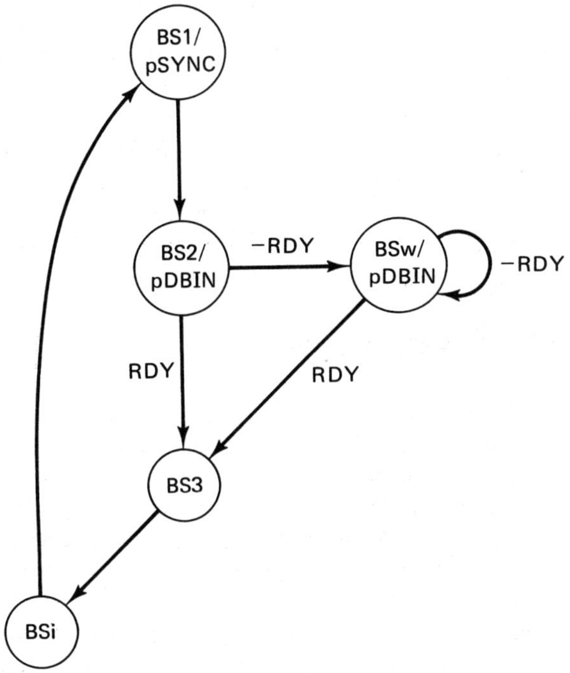

Figure 13.14 State diagram of an IEEE Std-696 permanent master during a read operation. Only the control outputs pSYNC and pDBIN are indicated here; other outputs are also active.

is asserted rather than pDBIN; as far as the state machine is concerned, there is no difference between a read and a write.

The state diagram of the bus-state generator is shown in Figure 13.15. Notice that the sequence is slightly different concerning when BSw is entered: if waits are required, BS2 comes *after* BSw rather than before. Functionally, this makes no difference in the performance of the circuit because the *outputs* of BS2 and BSw are identical. This

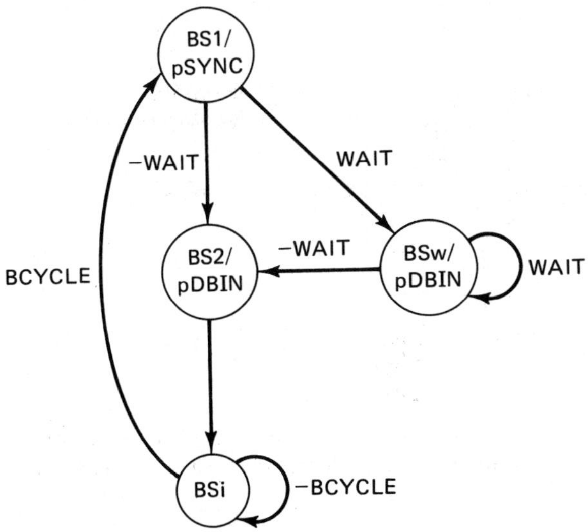

Figure 13.15 State diagram of the bus-state generator. The WAIT signal is derived from the S-100 RDY input:
WAIT = (RDY • DT-ENAB • NO.WAIT)′

configuration of the state diagram is necessary because RDY from the peripheral comes directly at the end of BS1: if waits are needed, then why not enter BSw directly rather than a state later? The only other difference is BS3 and BSi: they are equivalent and there is no reason not to combine them into one state called BSi.

BSi is the normal no-bus-activity state of the bus-state generator: there are no bus outputs asserted by the master. When the processor executes long instructions (like multiply and divide), the 68000 places its many clock cycles at the end of its bus cycle after AS* goes HIGH. During this time, the bus-state generator is in BSi until the 68000 finally finishes executing the instruction.

13.2.4 Bus-State Generator Circuit Design

To design the circuit for the bus-state generator, first sketch an overall block diagram like Figure 13.16. This diagram should show all the required inputs and outputs so that nothing is overlooked during the design. In addition to the signals already mentioned, RESET* is added to make sure that the generator always starts in the proper state. R/W* is used as part of the output function so either pDBIN or pWR* can be selected. VPA* from the 68000 is also provided to inhibit the state machine from doing a bus cycle when the 68000 does autovectoring during an IACK cycle.

The circuit will be designed to perform as in the Figure 13.15 state diagram. The hold state BSH shown in Figure 13.5 and in the S-100 standard will not be implemented as part of the state machine. Entry to BSH involves arbitration and relinquishing the bus to a temporary bus master, and can be more easily accomplished directly by the 68000.

The WAIT input in the state diagram is derived directly from the DTACK* enable signal, the wait-generator output, and the S-100 bus RDY signal. It is

$$\text{WAIT} = (\text{RDY} \bullet \text{DT-ENAB} \bullet \text{NO-WAIT})'$$

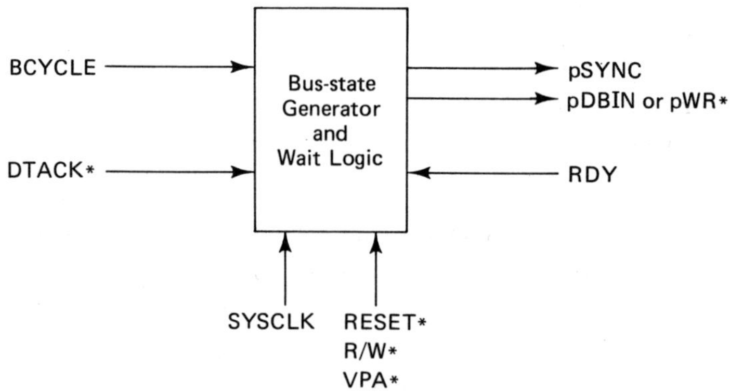

Figure 13.16 Block diagram of the bus state generator showing inputs and outputs. VPA* is used to prevent an S-100 bus cycle when the 68000 autovectors or when the 68000 does a 6800 access.

TABLE 13.2 STATE TABLE FOR BUS-STATE GENERATOR.

Present						*Next*		
Inputs BCYCLE	WAIT	*State*	*A*	*B*	*Output*	*State*	*A*	*B*
0	0	BSi	0	0	None	BSi	0	0
0	1		0	0		BSi	0	0
1	0		0	0		BS1	0	1
1	1		0	0		BS1	0	1
0	0	BS1	0	1	pSYNC	BS2	1	0
0	1		0	1		BSw	1	1
1	0		0	1		BS2	1	0
1	1		0	1		BSw	1	1
0	0	BS2	1	0	pDBIN	BSi	0	0
0	1		1	0		BSi	0	0
1	0		1	0		BSi	0	0
1	1		1	0		BSi	0	0
0	0	BSw	1	1	pDBIN	BS2	1	0
0	1		1	1		BSw	1	1
1	0		1	1		BS2	1	0
1	1		1	1		BSw	1	1

If RDY is LOW, then the peripheral needs more time, and WAIT will go HIGH to force a transition to BSW. DT-ENAB is included to permit WAIT only during a bus cycle. The NO-WAIT signal from the wait generator will go HIGH if there are no required wait states. Notice that the WAIT function is identical to DTACK* itself.

The state table in Table 13.2 describes the bus-state generator present and next states for all combinations of BCYCLE and WAIT inputs. This state table comes directly from the Figure 13.15 state diagram; it should also match the timing diagram in Figure 13.12 except for the BS2, BSw exchange. The binary state assignments are selected carefully:

- BSi = 00 — The idle state is the normal state when the system is reset. Select 00 as BSi because it can be set easily using the flip-flop direct-clear inputs.
- BS2 = 10, BSw = 11 — The output function pDBIN (or pWR*) *must not* have any discontinuity or glitch when the state machine goes from BSw to BS2. If the output is derived only from the most-significant bit, and that single bit is constant when changing from BSw to BS2, then there will be no output glitches.

Assuming that the design will be implemented with D flip-flops, the input equations to the *A* (most significant) and *B* (least significant) flip-flops are the same as the required next states.

Flip-flop *A* input:

D_A = function of inputs and present state
$D_A = f\,(BCYCLE,\ WAIT,$ present $A\ B)$
$D_A = BS1 + BSw$ by inspection

so that

$$\boxed{D_A = B}$$

Flip-flop *B* input:

D_B = function of inputs and present state
$D_B = f\,(BCYCLE,\ WAIT,$ present $A\ B)$
Find D_B using Karnaugh Map:

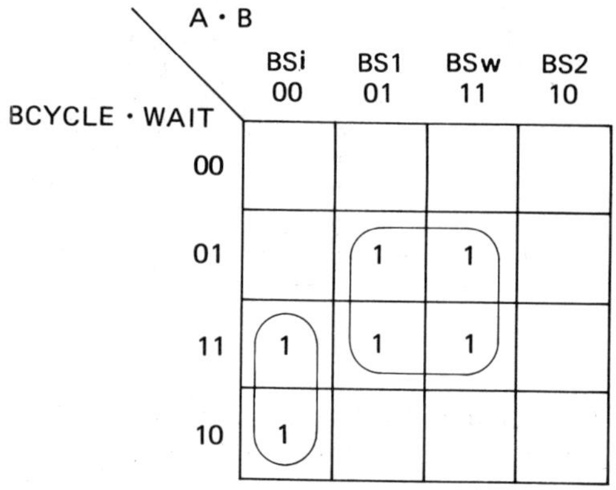

$$D_B = BCYCLE \cdot BSi + WAIT \cdot (BS1 + BSw)$$

so that

$$\boxed{D_B = BCYCLE \cdot A'\,B' + WAIT \cdot B}$$

The output equations are:

$pSYNC = A'\ B$
$pDBIN = A \cdot R/W*$
$pWR* = A \cdot (R/W*)'$

The implementation of these flip-flop input and output equations is shown in Figure 13.17. Notice that the SYSCLK is used for the state machine so it is properly synchronized with the 68000 as in Figure 13.12. Either RESET* or VPA* will reset it to BSI where it will stay until BCYCLE goes HIGH. The processor status-valid signal,

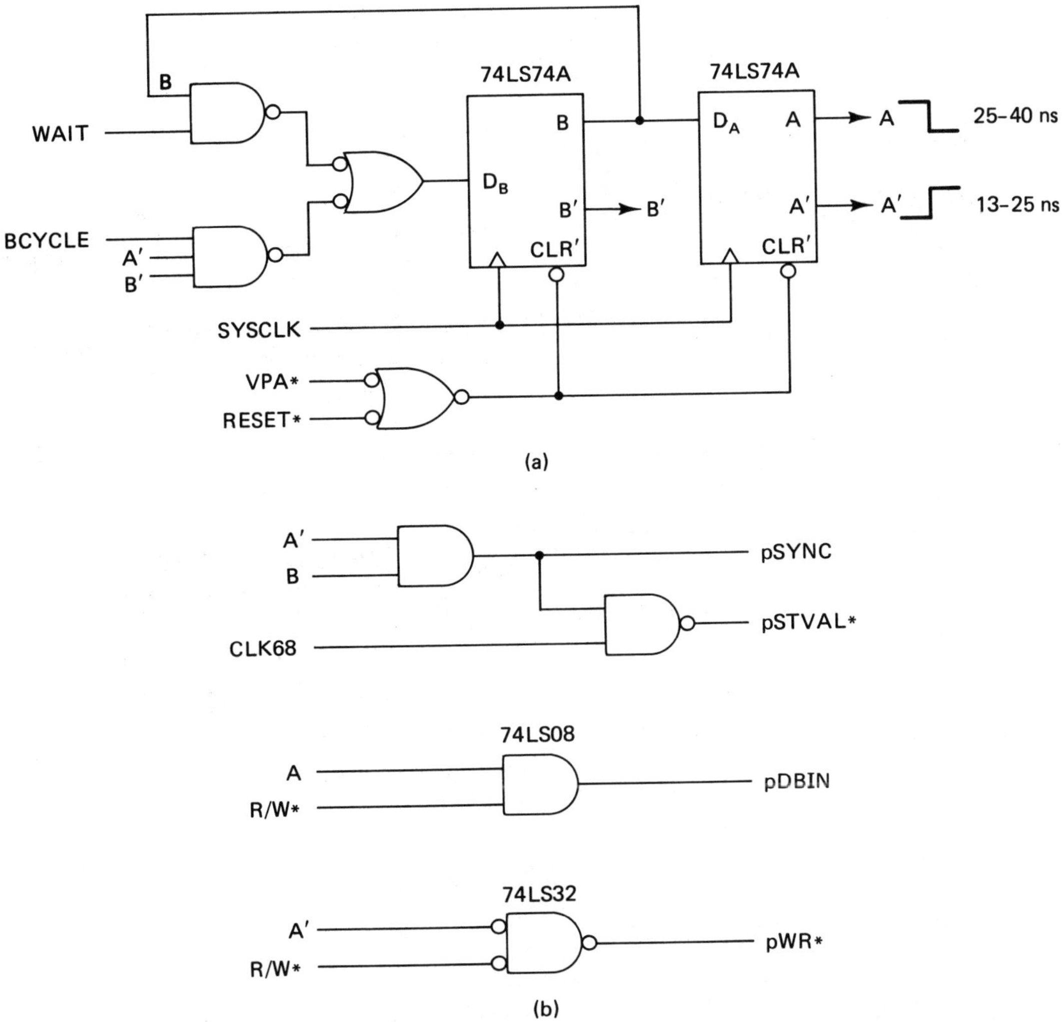

Figure 13.17 Bus-state generator (a) and the output logic (b). Schottky devices should be considered for the bus-state generator and for the pWR* output.

pSTVAL*, can be easily derived from pSYNC and CLK68; it is low for only one clock state in the entire bus cycle. The only difference between pDBIN and pWR* is whether the 68000 is reading or writing, and the R/W* line from the 68000 can be used easily to get both outputs. There will be no glitches in either of these outputs because the "A" flip-flop stays on for both BS2 and BSw. Figure 13.18 shows all these separate circuits combined, forming the complete bus-state and wait generator.

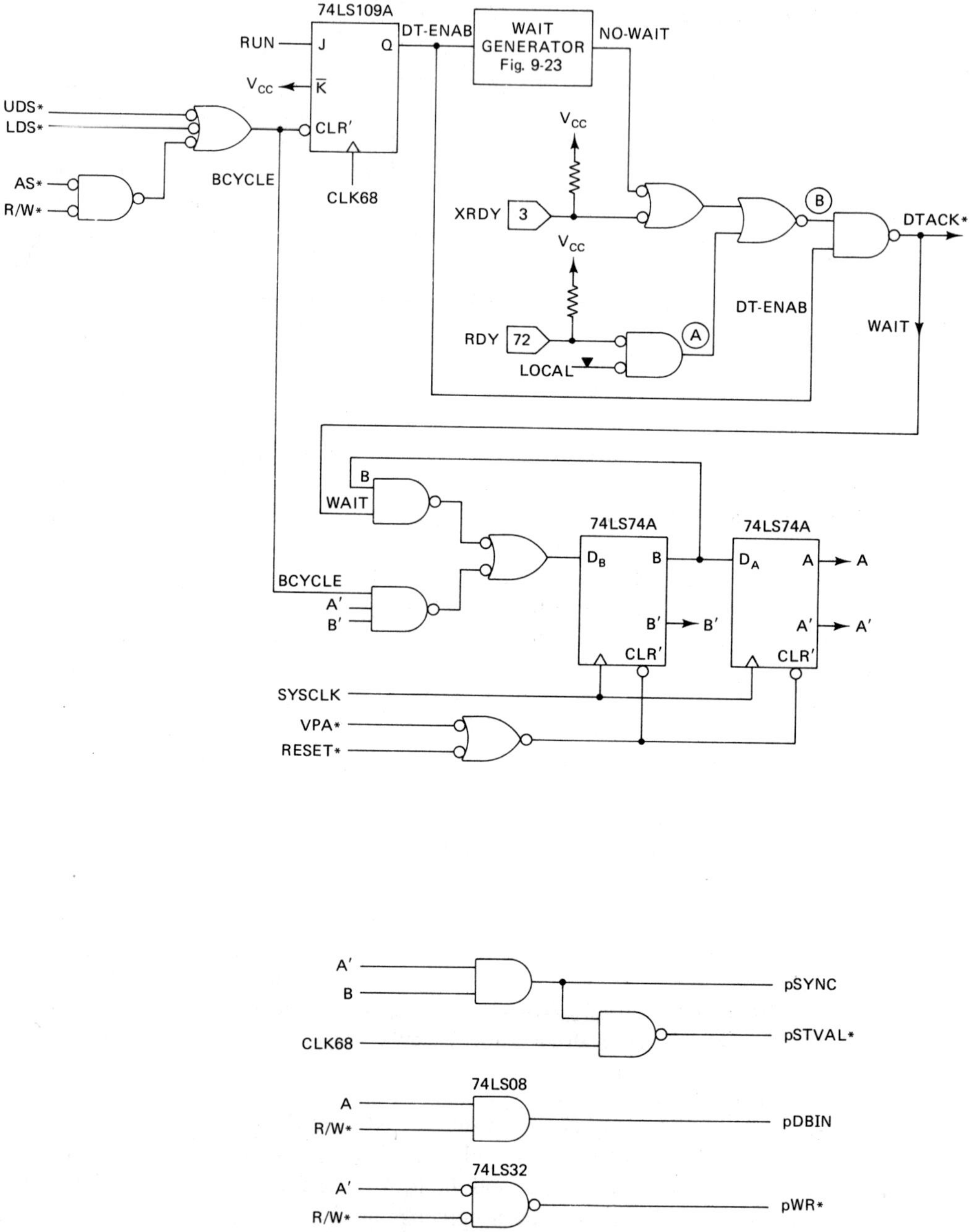

Figure 13.18 Operational bus-state generator with wait control and output logic.

13.2.5 Testing and Specification Checking

The entire bus-state generator can be tested with an oscilloscope and free-running 68000. The development approach throughout the book has been design, build, and test. One of the easiest test methods is to freerun the 68000 so all its bus cycles are identical: this makes it possible to synchronize an oscilloscope to look at all of the data, control, and address buses. It should be possible to freerun the 68000 at any point, regardless of how complex the system has grown; if it fails to freerun, you know that something truly fatal occurred in the system.

Replace the EPROM set on your board with the freerunning headers you made earlier in the system development. If you have not designed in an isolation buffer or a disable-RAM jumper, you might unplug your RAM ICs so their outputs are not driving a short to ground. Once the 68000 is freerunning, check its data, control and address lines and see that all is normal.

The BCYCLE and wait-generator circuit should be already in your system and checked out earlier. Connect the rest of the bus-state generator circuit given in Figure 13.18. There should be no change in the operation of the 68000 as long as you hold RDY asserted HIGH. If you negate RDY, does the 68000 wait for DTACK*? If your watchdog timer is in operation, did the processor halt?

Connect one of the scope traces to BCYCLE and use the other to verify the timing diagram in Figure 13.12. With no waits required (RDY is HIGH), you should be able to see pSYNC, pSTVAL*, and pDBIN every 68000 bus cycle. At this point, the bus-state generator is keeping step with the 68000 and is responsive to it. For example, if the 68000 wait-generator calls for a delay, DTACK* is held HIGH (as usual) and the bus-state generator WAIT stays asserted. Test it: set the 68000 for a wait, and see that pDBIN stretches out by a clock cycle; set two waits, and see pDBIN get longer again.

When the 68000 freeruns, the R/W* control line is always HIGH. This makes pDBIN operational, but pWR* never comes on. You can make a quick check that pWR* is running properly by temporarily providing a LOW instead of R/W* to the output logic.

You can check the timing using your oscilloscope to make sure your design complies with IEEE Std-696. Use the read-cycle and write-cycle timing specifications in Sections 3.8 and 3.9 of the Standard. The SYSCLK clock signal should be used as a reference for all the S-100 bus measurements; its period is t_{CY} = 167 ns for a 6 MHz system. The pSYNC signal should be at least 0.7 t_{CY} or 117 ns wide and start no later than 0.4 t_{CY} or 67 ns after the rising edge of SYSCLK. The pSTVAL* pulse must be at least 50 ns wide. The pDBIN and pWR* outputs must be at least 0.9 t_{CY} or 150 ns wide. These specifications are easy enough to meet because of the state machine design.

Read timing. One critical issue is the alignment of the 68000 data input latch time (end of S6) and the falling edge of pDBIN (end of BS2). Do they line up as shown in Figure 13.8 so that the proper data is on the bus when the 68000 reads it? To answer this question, redraw the 68000 timing diagram as in Figure 13.19(a) to see exactly when the

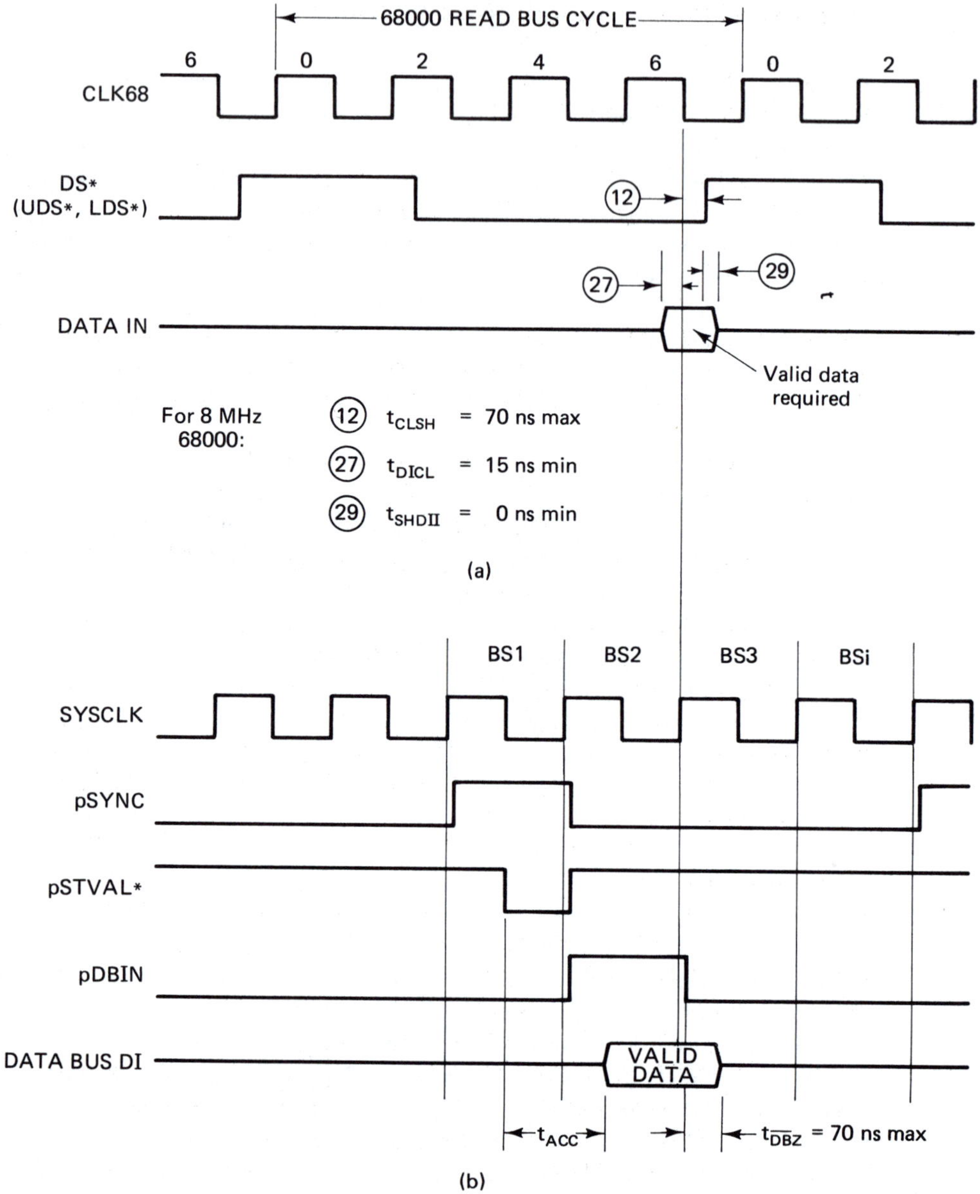

Figure 13.19 Read timing diagram to verify if the 68000 will read valid data. (a) shows when the 68000 will read data, (b) shows when the S-100 bus data will be valid.

68000 requires valid data. According to the diagram, the data must be valid no later than a minimum of 15 ns setup time *before* the end of S6 (Bubble 27). This data should be held constant until the data strobes (DS*) go HIGH, a maximum of 70 ns *after* S6 (Bubble 12). The read hold time (Bubble 29) is zero beyond DS*, so the data need not be kept on the bus any longer than DS* HIGH.

Next, analyze the S-100 read bus cycle shown in Figure 13.19(b). Will the data be valid at least 15 ns ahead of the end of S6? Assuming that the access time t_{ACC} is sufficiently quick, valid data will be on the bus shortly after the slave's bus buffers are turned on by pDBIN. If this is not the case, then the slave *must* negate RDY to put in enough waits so that the data is valid in time for the end of S6. The problem area, though, is at the end of pDBIN: when it goes LOW, the slave buffers go off and the data is gone. If possible in your design, you would prefer to have pDBIN go LOW after some delay. As drawn in Figure 13.18, pDBIN is derived from the *A* output of the 74LS74A; the propagation delay from HIGH to LOW is *slower* than from LOW to HIGH. You can take advantage of this to get the following propagation times:

	Typical	Worst case
Rising SYSCLK at start of BS3 to A = LOW	25	40 ns
A = LOW through 74LS08 to pDBIN = LOW	10	20 ns
	35	60 ns

Keep in mind that the "worst" case is really the "best" in this analysis. Next, assume that the typical slave uses a 74LS10 and a 74LS244 to control and buffer data onto the data bus; they take about 19 (typical) to 40 ns to disable the data out when pDBIN goes LOW. Add all of the above to get 54 to 100 ns delay from the rising SYSCLK until the data is invalid.

What does all this mean? After the falling edge of CLK68 at S6, the data strobes might go HIGH in perhaps 10 or 20 ns to a maximum of 70 ns. The S-100 bus will hold the data valid for typically 54 ns up to a maximum of 100 ns after S6. There is a substantial overlap, but you cannot *absolutely* guarantee that the 68000 will always have data valid until DS* goes HIGH. However, for all practical purposes, there should be no problems reading bus data because production 68000s typically negate the data strobes very soon after S6. The conclusion to accept the design becomes a matter of engineering judgment rather than absolute certainty.

Write timing. A second issue of major importance is the alignment of the 68000 write data with the S-100 write plus pWR*. This write signal is used to provide the write-enable pulse for RAM boards in the system. As such, the end of the pulse provides critical timing to the RAM so that the write can be accomplished successfully. As far as the bus-state generator is concerned, the pWR* output performs the same function for writing data as pDBIN does for reading; the only difference between the two is in the output logic.

Compare the write timing diagram in Figure 13.20 with the previous Figure 13.19 read timing. The clocks, pSYNC, and pSTVAL* are all the same in both cases; the UDS* and LDS* (referred to in general as DS*) are one cycle delayed as usual. In Figure

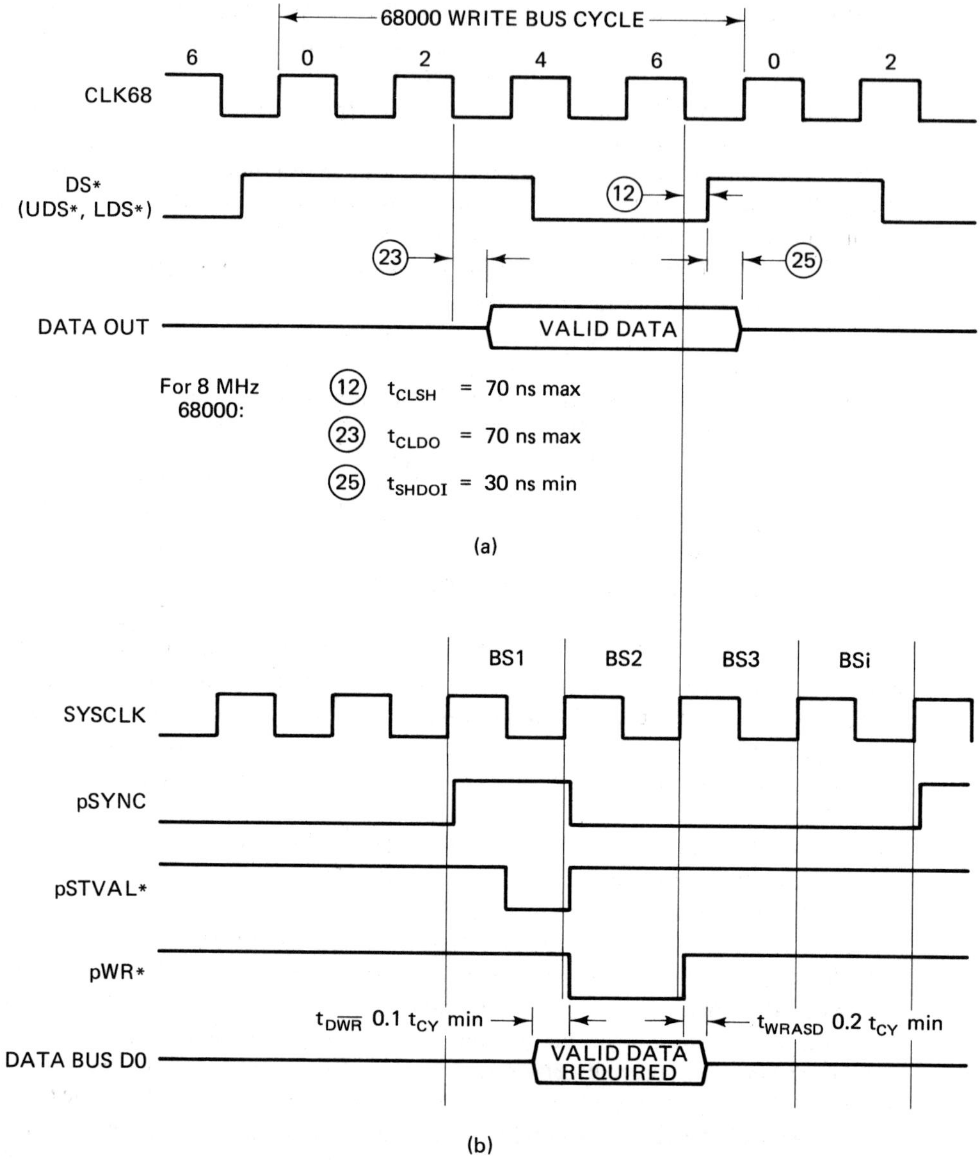

Figure 13.20 Write timing diagram to verify if the 68000 will write valid data to the S-100 system. (a) shows when the 68000 data output is valid, and (b) shows when the S-100 bus requires valid data.

13.20(a), the 68000 places valid data on the bus a maximum of 70 ns after the falling clock at the end of S2 (Bubble 23). In Figure 13.20(b), valid data is required slightly before the start of BS2. There is no problem in meeting this timing requirement.

The difficulty with the write pulse is that the 68000 might remove the data from the bus too quickly at the end of the write sequence. In Figure 13.20(a), valid write data will be on the bus for t_{CLSH} (70 ns maximum, Bubble 12) plus t_{SHDOI} (30 ns minimum, Bubble 25). If DS* goes HIGH in 10 or 20 ns, that means nonvalid data on the bus in 40 to 50 ns. According to Figure 13.20(b), the data should stay valid for 0.2 t_{CY} after pWR* is negated; for a 6 MHz system clock, this is 33 ns after the pWR* goes HIGH. Clearly, pWR* should be negated as fast as possible at the end of BS2 to allow ample time for valid write data.

In Figure 13.18, notice that pWR* is derived from the *A'* output of the 74LS74A. This is done because the propagation delay from LOW to HIGH is less than from HIGH to LOW. Add the delays involved in negating pWR*:

	Typical	Worst case
Rising SYSCLK at start of BS3 to A′ = HIGH	13	25 ns
A′ = HIGH through 74LS32 to pWR* = HIGH	14	22 ns
	27	47 ns

If the S-100 system requires data valid for 33 ns after pWR* HIGH, then the typical to worst times from S6 are 60 to 80 ns. Unfortunately, the 68000 data will be valid 40 to 50 ns typically. The data bus will not suddenly change at the end of 50 ns, but it cannot be guaranteed either.

It appears that the pWR* timing might need more speed than available from the 74LS74A and 74LS32 if the specifications are to be met properly. Consider changing to the Schottky 74S74 and 74S32 to implement pWR*: the propagation delays drop to 6–9 ns and 4–7 ns, respectively. Adding these to the 33 ns data hold time results in a range of 43 to 49 ns from S6. Given that the 68000 will provide valid data for at least 40 to 50 ns, there is no reason to expect a timing problem using the Schottky devices. Naturally, you should verify that the pDBIN timing does not get badly disrupted by the change to Schottky for pWR*.

RDY timing. The last major specification that must be checked is the RDY timing. It is absolutely vital that this part of the design operate properly so that the 68000 and S-100 bus stay synchronized. There should be no difficulties with the 68000 wait-generator circuit (Figure 9.23) at this point: it should be a known-good module in the system. The unknown right now is this: can you put a pSYNC pulse on the bus, get back a not-ready (i.e., RDY = LOW) from the bus, and see the 68000 insert a wait?

Assume that the 68000 is freerunning as before. Connect a simple single-wait generator circuit like the one in Figure 13.21(a). When it detects the beginning of an S-100 bus cycle, it pulls the RDY line LOW so that the bus master will insert a wait state. This

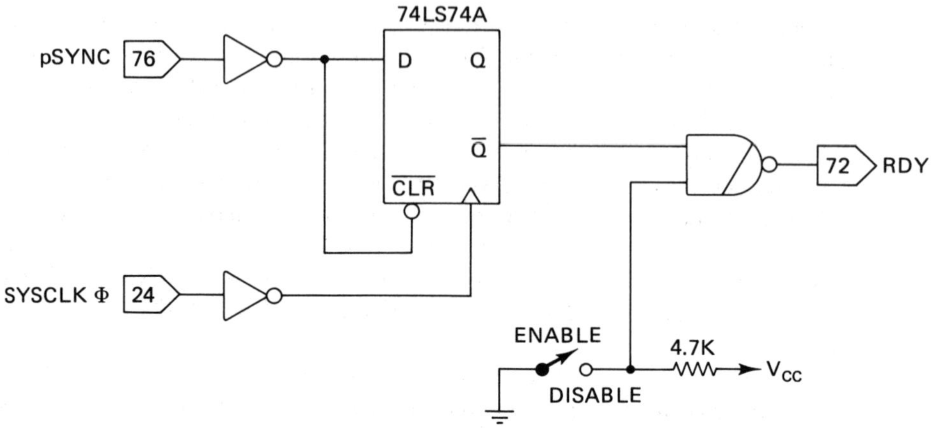

(a)

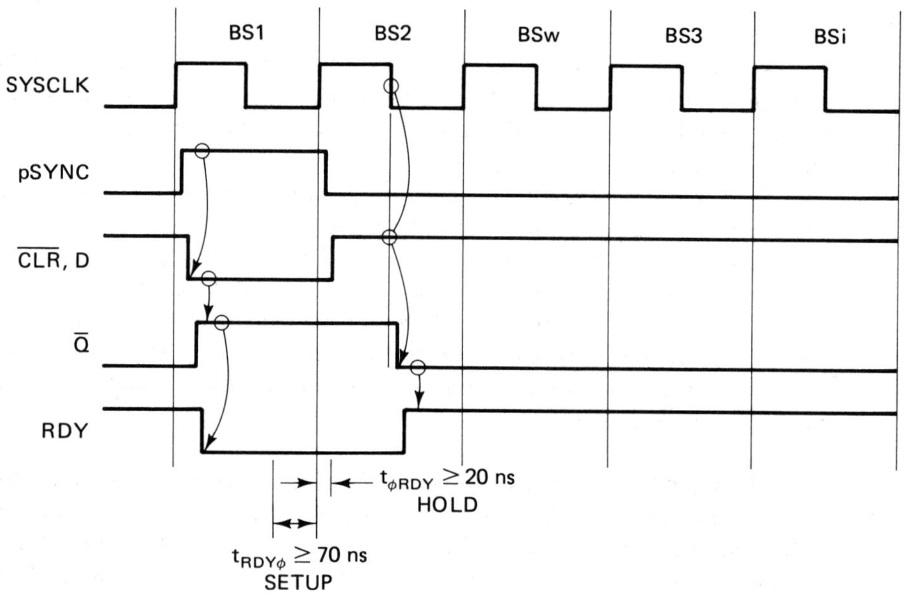

(b)

Figure 13.21 Circuit to generate a single wait state (a), and the timing diagram of its operation on the S-100 bus (b). RDY must be LOW at least 70 ns before the end of BS1 and stay LOW for 20 ns hold time beyond the rising clock at the start of BS2.

particular circuit is typical of most S-100 wait generators and is suitable for testing the bus-state generator. Figure 13.21(b) illustrates the timing sequence during normal operation. The IEEE Std-696 requires the RDY signal LOW at least 70 ns before and 20 ns after the system clock at the end of BS1. With a freerunning 68000, you can check with an oscilloscope that this circuit easily meets the 70 and 20 ns setup and hold times.

The real issue is whether the worst-case RDY (70 setup, 20 hold) will be sufficient to cause the 68000 to insert a wait. Figure 13.22 shows the timing diagram with the minimum RDY signal and its effect on DTACK*. Will RDY = LOW cause DTACK* = HIGH at least 20 ns (t_{ASI}, Bubble 47) *before* the falling edge of CLK68 at S4?

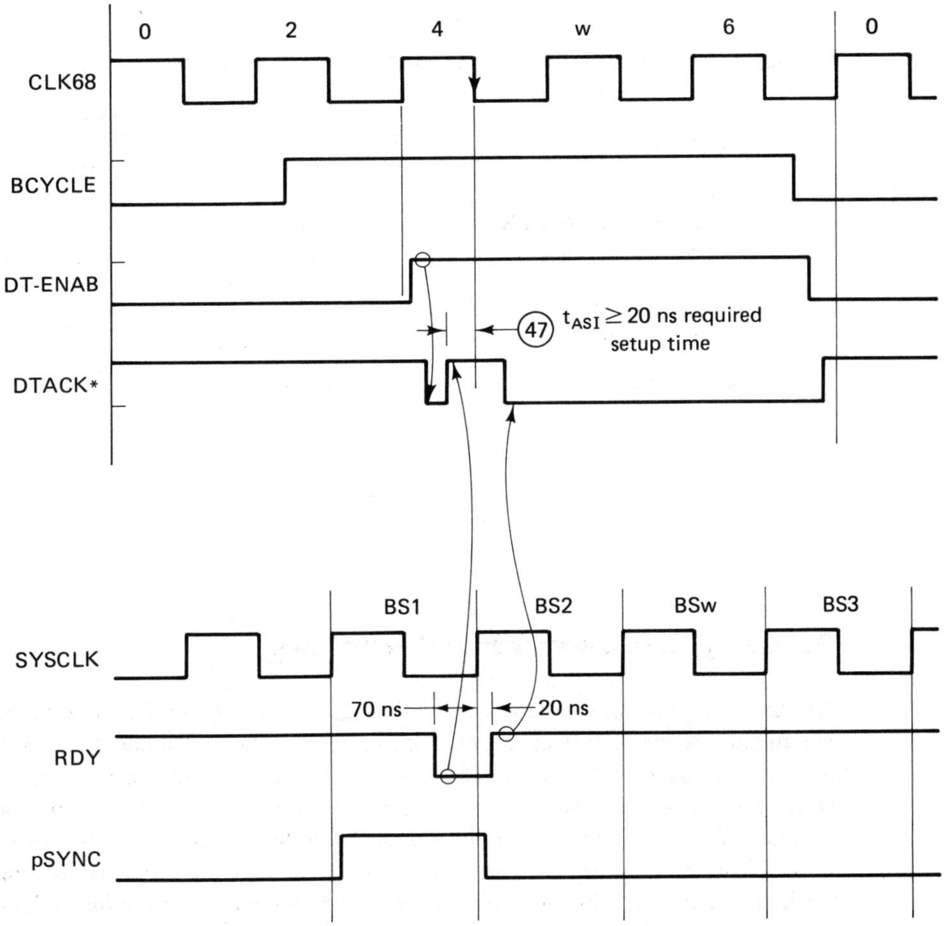

Figure 13.22 Timing diagram showing how a minimum-spec RDY′ signal affects DTACK* and successfully causes the 68000 to wait.

To answer the question, you need to complete a timing analysis of the two main signal paths that control DTACK*. Table 13.3 shows the result of tracing the signals in the circuit shown in Figure 13.18. The first path from DT-ENAB to DTACK* is the one that causes DTACK* to go LOW early in S4. You can see from the table that DTACK* will go LOW 40 ns after DT-ENAB = HIGH. Shortly after that, the RDY = LOW signal through path 2 forces DTACK* back HIGH just in time for the 68000 to recognize it as a HIGH. For success here, 70 ns minus the path-2 time should be greater than the 20 ns setup time for DTACK*. The maximum worst-case time for path 2 is 45 ns, which leaves an adequate 25 ns setup time. When RDY goes HIGH in BS2, DTACK* goes LOW again in ample time to conclude the bus cycle with only the one anticipated wait.

TABLE 13.3 TIMING ANALYSIS OF RDY AND DTACK*. STANDARD TTL LOADING ASSUMED.

		Typical	*Maximum*
Path 1 DT-ENAB = HIGH → DTACK = LOW*			
Clock			
CLK 68 → DT-ENAB	74LS109A t_{PLH}	13	25
DT-ENAB → DTACK*	74LS00 t_{PHL}	10	15
	Total Path 1 =	23	40
Path 2 RDY = LOW → DTACK = LOW*			
RDY → A	74LS02 t_{PLH}	10	15
A → B	74LS02 t_{PHL}	10	15
B → DTACK*	74LS00 t_{PLH}	9	15
	Total Path 2 =	29	45

13.2.6 Bus-State Generator in Perspective

The bus-state generator circuit is certainly the most important design in the S-100 interface module. If the 68000 cannot be synchronized to the S-100 bus, then nothing else in the interface makes much sense. However, the bus-state generator is not the *only* important circuit needed for a complete interface: there are several other sections that need consideration. Figure 13.23 shows a block diagram of the complete interface module with all of these other components. Now that you have had a chance to design using the specifications a little, this block diagram should help put the system into a better perspective.

Table 13.4 lists the subset of the IEEE Std-696 signals that will be implemented in your 68000 board. You can see that the bus-state generator relates to several groups of

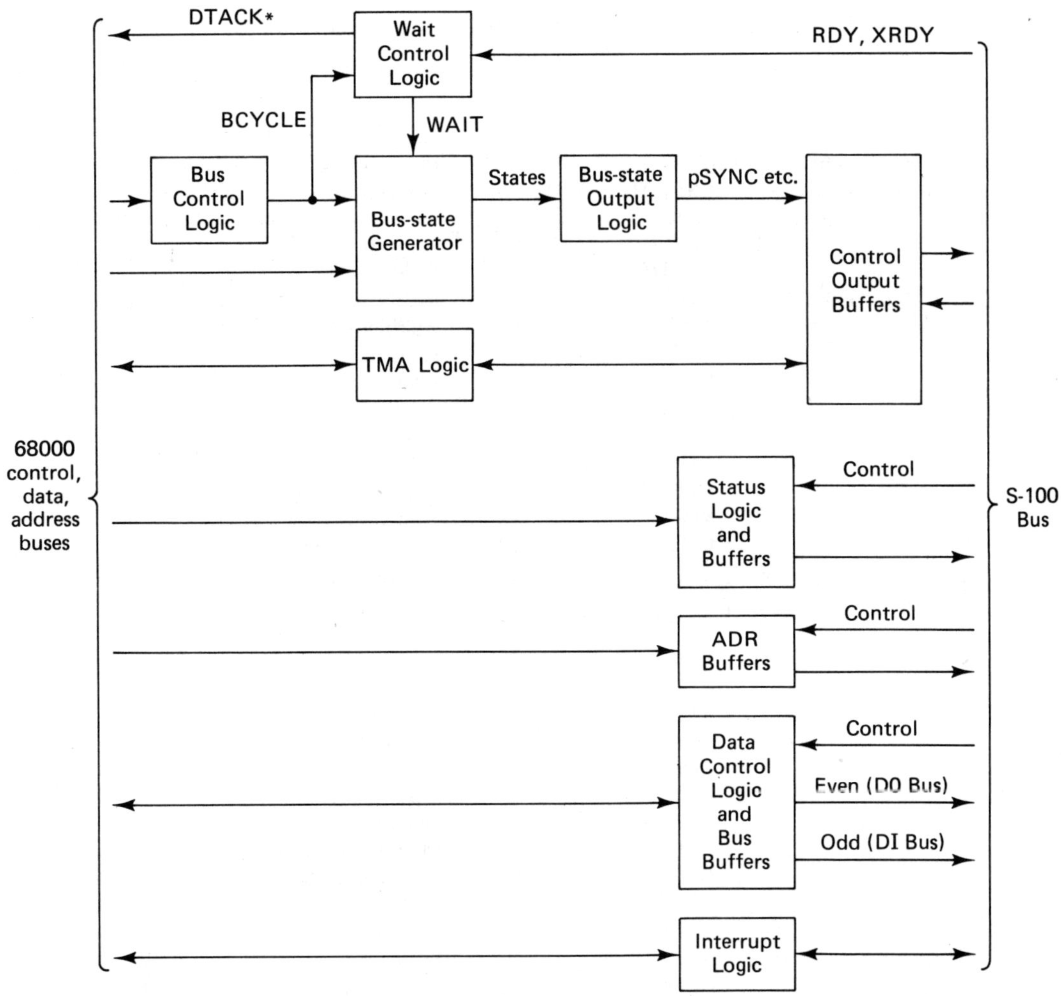

Figure 13.23 Block diagram of complete S-100 bus interface module.

signals on the bus, but mainly the control output. Many of the signals have already been designed into your system, such as the interrupts and the various utility signals. The major areas left that must be designed relate to TMA (temporary master access) and buffering the data, address, and status onto the S-100 bus. The buffering is required not only to provide sufficient drive current to the bus, but also so that the permanent master (the 68000 CPU board) can be removed from the bus by a temporary master.

TABLE 13.4 SUBSET OF THE IEEE STD-696 SIGNALS THAT WILL BE IMPLEMEN TED IN THE FINAL 68000 CPU BOARD.

Group	*Label*	*Pin*	*Function*
Control output	pSYNC	76	Processor synchronize (start bus cycle)
	pSTVAL*	25	Status valid
	pDBIN	78	Data bus in (enable slave bus drivers)
	pWR*	77	Write (data-valid strobe)
	pHLDA	26	Hold acknowledge
Control input	RDY	72	Ready (slave ready for data transfer)
	XRDY	3	Auxiliary ready
	HOLD*	74	Hold request
	SIXTN*	60	Sixteen acknowledge from slave
	INT*	73	Interrupt
	NMI*	12	Non-maskable interrupt
TMA control	ADSB*	22	Address bus buffer disable
	DODSB*	23	Data output buffer disable
	SDSB*	18	Status bus buffer disable
	CDSB*	19	Control output bus buffer disable
Vectored interrupt	VI0*	4	Vectored interrupt 0 (highest priority)
	VI1*	5	Vectored interrupt 1
	VI2*	6	Vectored interrupt 2
	VI3*	7	Vectored interrupt 3
	VI4*	8	Vectored interrupt 4
	VI5*	9	Vectored interrupt 5
Status bus	sMEMR	47	Memory read
	sM1	44	Op-code fetch
	sINP	46	Input data
	sOUT	45	Output data
	sW0*	97	Memory write or output write
	sINTA	96	Interrupt acknowledge (data on DI bus)
	sHLTA	48	Halt acknowledge
	sXTRQ*	58	Sixteen request
Utility bus	Φ	24	System clock, SYSCLK
	CLOCK	49	2 MHz utility clock for peripherals
	RESET*	75	System reset
	SLAVECLR*	54	Slave clear (slave reset)
	MWRT	68	Memory write = pWR* · sOUT'
	ERROR*	98	General error signal
	POC*	99	Power-on clear
Power bus	+8	1,51	
	+16	2	
	−16	52	
	GND	20,50,53,70,100	
Data bus	DI	-	8 bits from bus into CPU board (odd data)
	DO	-	8 bits to bus from CPU board (even data) (both bidirectional when SIXTN*)
Address bus	-	-	24 bits

13.3 BUS ARBITRATION

The system design so far has been concerned with the 68000 acting as a permanent master on the S-100 bus. In addition, there may be up to 16 temporary masters on the bus; one or more of these temporary masters may request the bus from the 68000 CPU board. The process of deciding which temporary master will control the bus, and the sequence of passing bus control to the proper master, is referred to as "bus arbitration." This arbitration is called TMA, or temporary master access.

Figure 13.24 shows the 68000 CPU board connected as a permanent master to the S-100 bus. In its normal system configuration, the CPU will have extensive memory, I/O, and other devices available on the bus for use as required. These system boards are in addition to the "local" memory and I/O functions that have been designed into the 68000 board.[2] The disk controller, one of these system boards, is marked "TMA" to indicate that it can be a temporary master on the bus; when the 68000 is not using the bus, then the disk controller can use it if necessary.

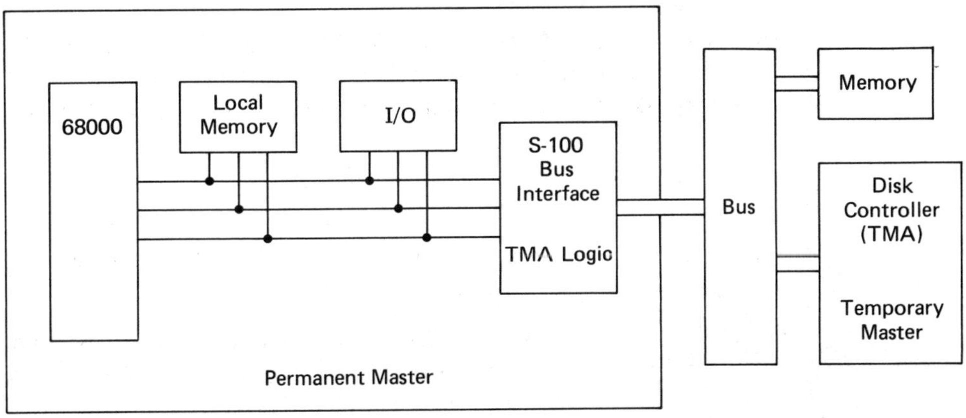

Figure 13.24 The 68000 CPU board as permanent master in an S-100 system.

The rationale behind using TMA is to obtain faster overall system processing speed. Recall that interrupts are used to provide a quick response to an operator at a keyboard: they are an improvement over the processor's constant polling to see if a key is pressed. With TMA, the idea is to allow another device to use the bus while the CPU is doing nonbus computation; however, any overall gain in system speed depends on the 68000 not using the bus extensively. For example, suppose the 68000 is to multiply a series of vectors: while the processor is doing the multiplication of the first set of numbers, the disk controller can move the next set from disk into memory for a subsequent calculation.

[2]The local memory and I/O are absolutely necessary to run the 68000 CPU board "stand-alone" without the S-100 bus. Once the bus interface operates properly, these local functions are not needed.

13.3.1 68000 Bus Arbitration

In order to design the TMA logic to properly interface with the S-100 bus, you must understand how the 68000 handles bus arbitration. As it turns out, the normal 68000 bus arbitration sequence can be used directly with very little external logic. To see how it works, start with the block diagram in Figure 13.25. In this system, the 68000 must read data from the disk and then write it to memory; for permanent storage, the 68000 must read memory and then write the data out to the disk.

A better way of transferring data is to use DMA, or direct memory access, rather than to use the 68000. Figure 13.26 shows a DMA controller (DMAC) connected to the 68000 and to its buses. When data needs to be moved between memory and the disk, the DMA controller requests the bus. Then, when the 68000 finishes its current bus cycle, it three-states its data, address, and control lines so the DMA controller can use the bus: the 68000 is effectively gone and the DMAC alone has the bus. After finishing the reads and writes (while the 68000 does internal calculations), the DMAC signals the 68000 to take the bus back. When it has the bus again, the processor continues with its next bus cycle as though it had never been disturbed.

The transfer of the 68000 bus to a DMAC (or any device capable of being a bus master) requires an orderly procedure so that the bus is always under control of a master. This is accomplished by using the three controls indicated in Figure 13.26 in this sequence:

- BR* is asserted by the DMAC to request the bus,
- The 68000 asserts BG* to say that the bus will be available,
- The DMAC asserts (and holds) BGACK* to indicate mastership.

The details of this bus arbitration are outlined in Figure 13.27.

It is possible to have more than one external device capable of assuming control of the bus. However, the 68000 does not have any means of finding which device has higher priority in case of two or more bus requests, so external arbitration between several external masters should be resolved before the BGACK* control is asserted. The 68000 itself assumes the lowest priority in the system and always relinquishes the bus to any request.

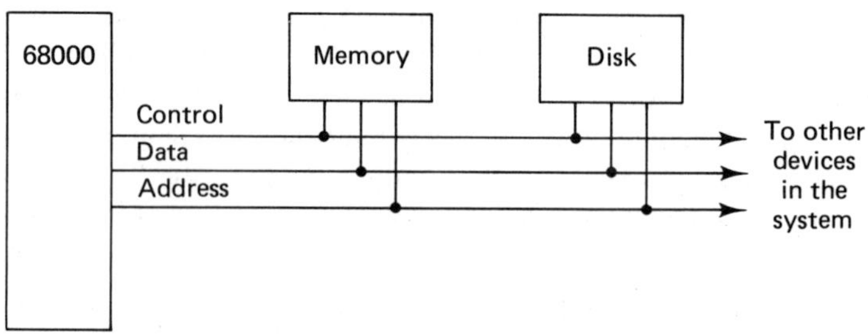

Figure 13.25 Block diagram of a simple 68000 computer system. The 68000 must transfer data between memory and the disk by itself.

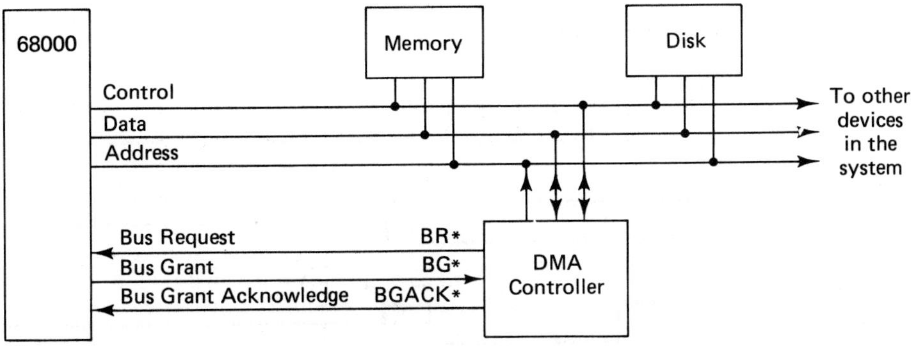

Figure 13.26 68000 computer system using a DMA controller to transfer data between memory and disk. The data need not pass through the 68000 at all.

Processor (68000)	*Requesting Device (DMA Controller)*
	Assert bus request (BR*)
Assert bus grant (BG*) ←	
→	Wait for end of current 68000 bus cycle (i.e., wait for AS* HIGH)
	Assert BGACK*
	Negate BR*
Negate BG* (68000 high-impedance) (and off the bus) ←	
→	Do data transfer or other operations involving use of the 68000 bus lines
	Then when done . . .
	Negate BGACK*
Resume normal operation with next bus cycle ←	

Figure 13.27 Bus arbitration flowchart.

The interface between the 68000 and the S-100 bus will only involve one ''device'' external to the 68000: the TMA logic. Arbitration between TMA devices on the S-100 bus will decide which will be the new temporary master; the 68000 will only have to deal with one of them.

Figure 13.28 shows the 68000 bus arbitration timing diagram. The arbitration cycle begins when the 68000 receives a bus request, BR*, from an external device (as from the TMA logic in Figure 13.24 or the DMAC in Figure 13.26). This bus request can come *anywhere* during the normal bus cycle, yet the 68000 will respond within 1.5 to 3.5 clock

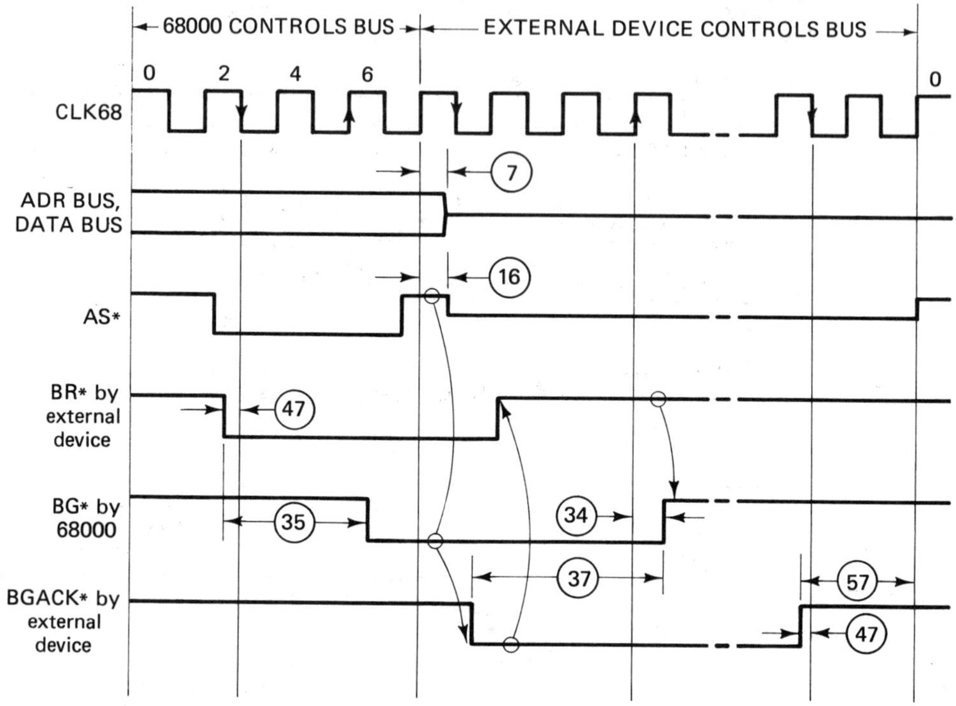

Figure 13.28 68000 bus arbitration timing diagram.

cycles (Bubble 35) by asserting BG*. The processor might not be finished with its current bus cycle when it asserts BG*, so the requesting device must wait until the end of the bus cycle. The AS* always goes HIGH at the end of a bus cycle, and it can be used with BG* to signal the requesting device that the bus is available.

As soon as the new bus master receives AS* HIGH and BG* LOW, it must assert BGACK* to acknowledge its control of the bus. At this point, the 68000 has given up the bus: its address and data buses, function controls, UDS*, LDS*, R/W*, and AS* will go into a high-impedance state. Next, the new master removes its BR* signal so that the 68000 does not expect another new master on the bus; when the processor receives a negated BR*, it negates BG*. As long as the new bus master holds BGACK* LOW, it has the bus for an indefinite time; when it negates BGACK*, however, the 68000 will resume bus control within several clock states (Bubble 57).

13.3.2 TMA Bus Arbitration

The 68000 arbitration is between the processor and a DMA-type device connected directly to the 68000's bus. By contrast, the TMA arbitration is between the permanent bus master (the CPU board) and a temporary master (a disk controller, for example). Rather than using the 68000 bus, they are interconnected by the S-100 bus as shown in Figure 13.24.

The S-100 bus has its own unique arbitration protocol similar to the 68000 bus arbitration. Instead of using three controls, however, the S-100 bus uses only two:

- Bus hold request, HOLD*
- Processor hold acknowledge, pHLDA

As indicated in Figure 13.29, to get control of the bus, the temporary master asserts HOLD* (like BR*); the permanent master responds at the end of its bus cycle by asserting pHLDA (like BG*) to acknowledge the hold request. However, pHLDA is unlike BG* because it indicates that the temporary master has the bus and should transfer control. Also, the HOLD* line must be kept LOW for the entire time that the temporary master needs the bus.

The transfer of the bus to a temporary master involves disabling the permanent master's address, data, and status buses. But to avoid spurious signals on the bus, the control

Permanent Master (68000 CPU Board)	*Temporary Master (Disk Controller Board)*
	Assert bus hold request (HOLD)* →
← Finish current bus cycle	
Assert processor hold acknowledge (pHLDA) →	
	Assert ADSB*, DODSB*, SDSB* to disconnect the address, data, and status buses of the permanent master
	Drive the bus control output lines at the same time as permanent master during transfer (pSYNC, pSTVAL*, pDBIN, pWR*, pHLDA)
	Assert CDSB* to disconnect permanent master control output lines
	Do data transfer or other operations involving use of the S-100 bus
	Then when done . . .
	Negate HOLD* indicating done with bus
	Negate CDSB* to reconnect permanent master control output lines
	Negate ADSB*, DODSB*, SDSB* to reconnect the address, data, and status buses of the permanent master →
← Negate processor hold acknowledge (pHLDA)	
Resume normal operation with next bus cycle	

Figure 13.29 S-100 bus arbitration between the permanent master and a single temporary master.

output lines from the permanent master must not be removed until after the temporary master has enabled its control outputs. During this transfer phase, both masters simultaneously drive pSYNC and pDBIN LOW and pSTVAL*, pWR*, and pHLDA HIGH. Then, after overlapping the controls for a time, the temporary master disconnects the permanent master completely by asserting CDSB*.

Once the temporary master has the bus, it can do its data transfer or other operations without concern for the permanent master: it has complete control of the bus. To do read and write bus cycles, it must follow the usual sequence of starting with pSYNC, pSTVAL*, and then either pDBIN or pWR*. As far as any other boards installed in the system can tell, the temporary master operates just like the CPU board.

When it finishes with the bus, the temporary master returns control to the permanent master by negating the hold request line, HOLD*. Then it negates CDSB* so that permanent master control output lines are reconnected to the bus for a short overlap time. After the transfer of control, the temporary master reconnects the master's address, data, and status buses. Finally, the permanent master negates pHLDA and resumes normal operations with its next bus cycle.

The details of the S-100 bus arbitration sequence are shown in the timing diagram in Figure 13.30. The arbitration cycle begins when the temporary master asserts HOLD*. After the permanent master finishes its current bus cycle, it recognizes the bus request by asserting pHLDA. Because the transfer of control is critical to proper operation of the bus, the IEEE Std-696 defines specific timing requirements for the transfer phase: there must be at least a 0.4 t_{CY} overlap of permanent and temporary control outputs. For a 6 MHz bus, t_{CY} is 167 ns, so the overlap must be at least 67 ns. This timing is done by the temporary master. The timing that must be met by the permanent master, the 68000 CPU board, is the sequence between HOLD* and pHLDA: there must be at least one clock cycle delay from HOLD* LOW to pHLDA HIGH. At the end of the TMA operation, there must be at least another one cycle delay from HOLD* HIGH until when pHLDA goes back low.

13.3.3 TMA Logic Design

To implement the TMA logic module shown in Figure 13.23, the 68000 timing in Figure 13.28 must be reconciled with the S-100 bus timing in Figure 13.30. Consider the initial arbitration request from the temporary master on the S-100 bus when HOLD* is asserted LOW: this request can be used to signal the 68000 by connecting it to the BR* input. Then, when the 68000 is done with its current bus cycle, AS* is HIGH and BG* is LOW: both of them can be used to assert pHLDA back to the S-100 bus temporary master. Figure 13.31 shows the combined timing diagram if this is done. In addition, however, there must be a provision to generate and hold BGACK* as well as remove BR* after BGACK* goes LOW. A flip-flop latch is required to maintain the BGACK* and also pHLDA.

The circuit shown in Figure 13.32 will meet the initial arbitration timing sketched in Figure 13.31. After system reset, the BR* input is negated and the BG* output is HIGH: the flip-flop does not get set. As soon as BG* goes LOW and AS* HIGH (at the end of the current bus cycle), the flip-flop is set on the rising edge of SYSCLK. This asserts pHLDA and BGACK* at the same time as it negates BR*. The circuit meets the S-100

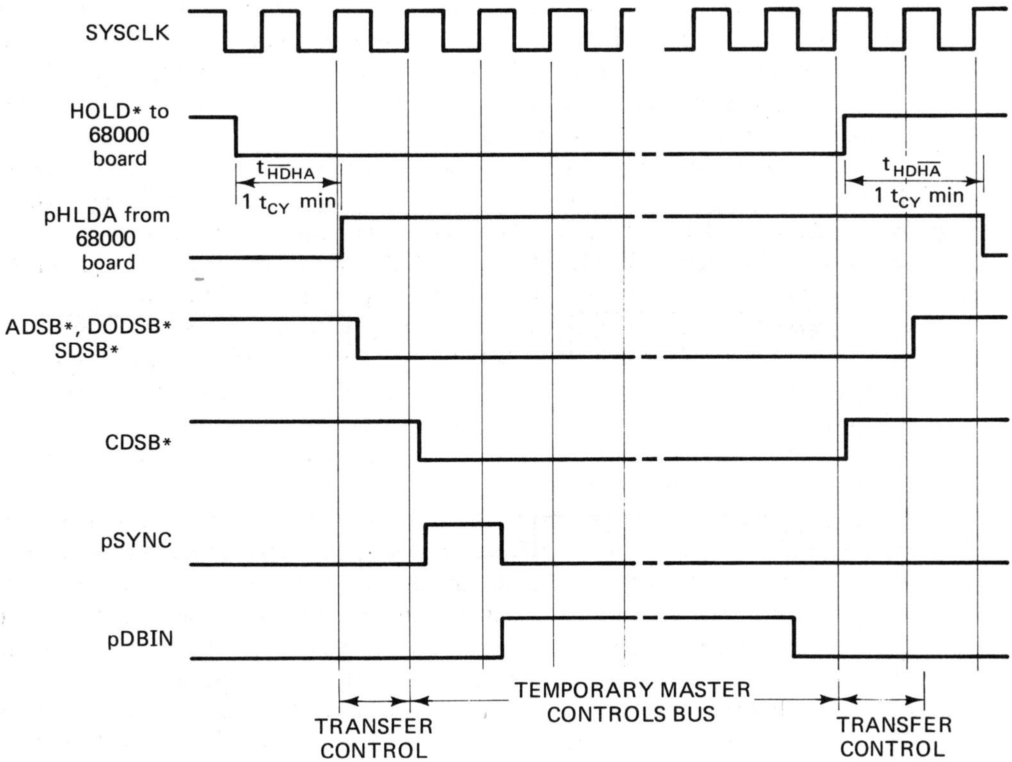

Figure 13.30 S-100 bus arbitration timing diagram.

specification requiring at least a clock cycle delay between HOLD* and pHLDA because BG* goes LOW 1.5 clock cycles (at the soonest) after BR*. At the end of the TMA cycle, this is not the case: after HOLD* is negated, the flip-flop is reset on the next rising edge of SYSCLK. One way around the problem is to OR the HOLD* input with SDSB*; at the worst, pHLDA will never go LOW before the temporary master has returned the bus to the permanent master.

Refer back to the original S-100 state diagram shown in Figure 13.5 for a moment. The bus arbitration circuit just described provides the extra BSH state that was not included when the bus-state generator was designed. The BSH state *could* have been designed as part of the state machine, but it would have made the circuit more complex. Perhaps more importantly, including the arbitration as part of the state machine would have made testing and debugging a much more difficult and time-consuming job; designing the arbitration logic as a separate module avoids the problem completely.

In fact, unless you have a logic analyzer and a temporary master S-100 board conveniently available, proper testing is almost impossible. All the testing so far has been made considerably easier by freerunning: with identical bus cycles, an oscilloscope can synchronize on any bus signal. The bus arbitration is an asynchronous event just by its very nature, and to check its operation you need to capture the event with a logic analyzer.

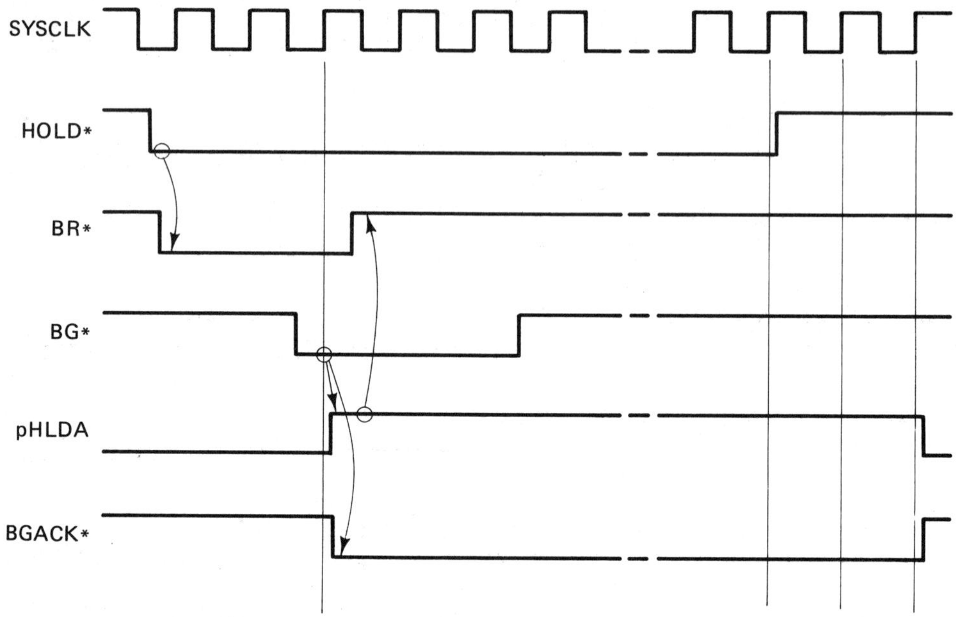

Figure 13.31 Combined timing diagram of the S-100 bus and 68000 arbitration. AS* is assumed HIGH when BG* is LOW; if AS* is delayed, then pHLDA will be later going HIGH. Notice that SYSCLK is used as a reference rather than the 68000's CLK68.

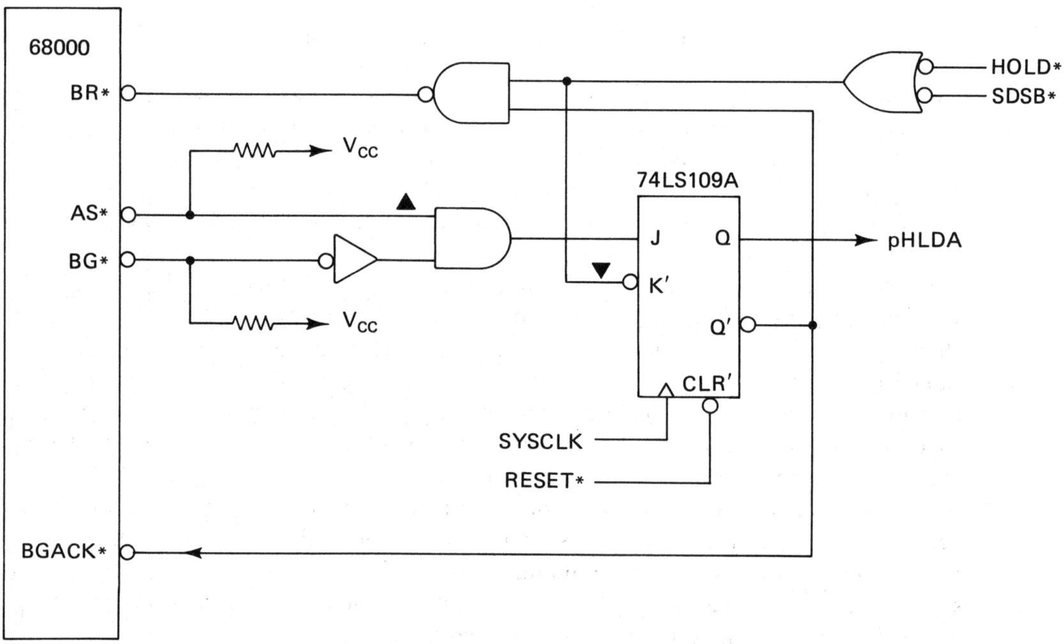

Figure 13.32 Circuit diagram of the TMA logic module.

However, a gross check of the circuit can be done by manually asserting HOLD* and checking if pHLDA goes HIGH and BGACK* LOW. In spite of its operational complexity, this circuit is one of the least troublesome in the entire system.

13.4 DATA BUS CONTROL LOGIC

The S-100 data bus can operate as two unidirectional 8-bit buses or as a single bidirectional 16-bit bus. When transferring byte data from the bus master, the 8-bit DO bus is used; when data is received by the master, the 8-bit DI bus is used. When the bus master calls for 16-bit data transfer, the DO and DI buses are both ganged together and called ED (even data) and OD (odd data), respectively.

There are two control lines that govern whether a 16-bit transfer will take place. The first one, sXTRQ*, is generated by the bus master if it wants to read or write 16-bit data. When the bus slave receives sXTRQ*, it responds by setting its buffers to handle 16 bits and returns an acknowledge signal, SIXTN*, to the master. After receiving the SIXTN* signal, the master gangs the DO and DI buses and does the transfer. If the slave receives sXTRQ*, and *cannot* set its buffers for 16-bit data, it does not assert SIXTN*. Then, when the master sees SIXTN* HIGH, it will not do a 16-bit transfer. At this point, the master must do an 8-bit transfer, even though it originally wanted to do 16 bits. It does this by doing a byte-serial transfer of 8 bits at a time; that is, the master will do two bus cycles instead of one bus cycle. However, if the master cannot do an 8-bit byte-serial transfer, then it must declare a bus error by asserting ERROR*.

The bus-state generator designed earlier will not automatically do byte-serial operations without the addition of extra logic. Consequently, any 16-bit S-100 bus transfers *must* be done with bus slaves (such as memory boards) that can handle 16-bit data. In practice, the restriction to 16-bit memory is no problem, because using 8-bit memory with the 16-bit 68000 essentially halves the processor speed. Note that the byte-serial operation is required *only* when the 68000 wants to transfer 16 bits and the bus slave cannot handle it. Normal 8-bit transfers can be made in all cases.

Figure 13.33 shows the data bus buffers required for the 68000 to properly operate with the S-100 bus. The even-byte (EBXCVR) and the odd-byte (OBXCVR) transceivers are used for 16-bit transfers. If the 68000 is doing a read bus cycle, then both transceivers will be enabled and their direction set for incoming data. For a write bus cycle, each will be enabled and their direction set for data out. For 8-bit transfers, a read bus cycle will require a data path from the DI bus, through the odd-byte transceiver (OBXCVR), to either D7-D0 on the 68000 or through the even-byte buffer (EBRD) to D15-D8 on the 68000. An 8-bit write bus cycle will send data out to the DO bus from either the even-byte transceiver (EBXCVR) or the odd-byte buffer (OBWR).

The summary of these read and write functions is shown in Table 13.5. The 68000 R/W* and data strobes are the primary inputs to the logic to implement the 8- and 16-bit transfers. The outputs from the logic are all the enables and the transceiver direction controls. The 16-bit request, sXTRQ*, is true only when both UDS* and LDS* are both asserted by the 68000.

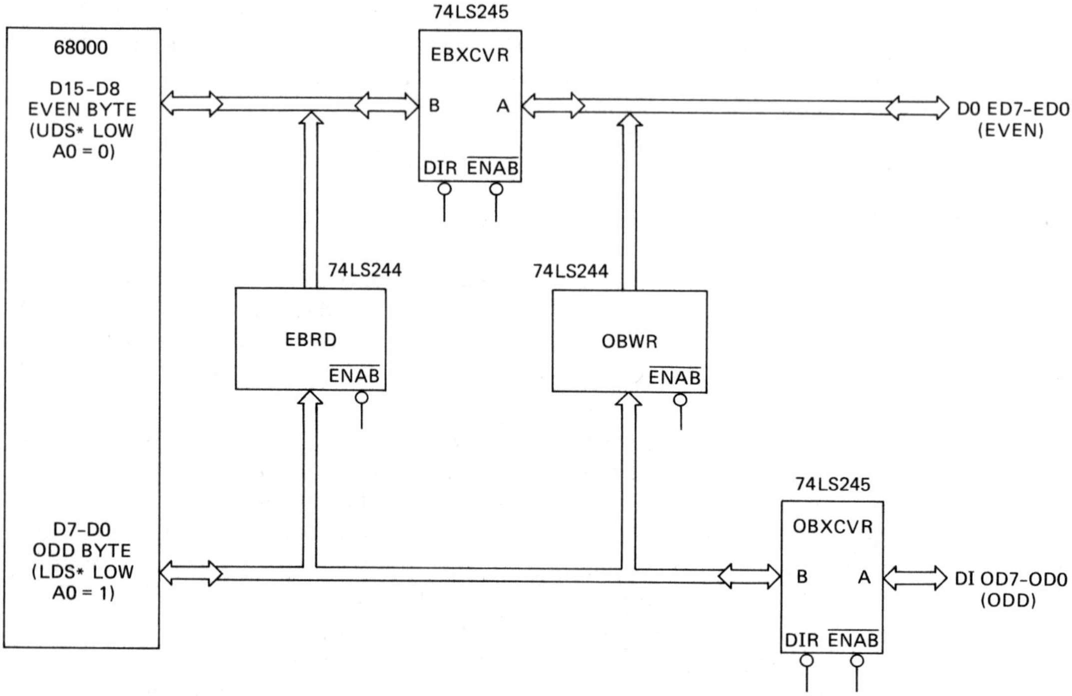

Figure 13.33 Data bus buffers to interface the 68000 to the S-100 bus.

The data bus buffer control logic circuit is shown in Figure 13.34. The control logic in Table 13.5 can be easily implemented using 4-to-1 data selector ICs rather than individual logic gates. The critical factor in favor of this approach is that the data strobe inputs (UDS* and LDS*) are common to all the output functions. The inverted outputs connect directly to each of the data-buffer enable inputs. The enable inputs to the 74LS352s make it easy to implement the data bus disable function required by the TMA logic. The LOCAL* control disables the data bus buffers if the 68000 is accessing memory at an on-board address.

13.5 STATUS AND ADDRESS BUS LOGIC

The status bus consists of eight lines intended to indicate the bus cycle type and the address validity. The logic in Figure 13.35 is sufficient to implement each of the status signals. Most of the outputs are similar in function to the 68000 controls and need no further attention. The sM1 signal indicates an op-code fetch and is derived from the 68000 function controls; when the 68000 is in user or supervisor program space, PGM (for the wait generator) and sM1 are both asserted. The interrupt acknowledge circuit is identical to the design that was developed in Chapter 12.

TABLE 13.5 CONTROL INPUTS AND LOGIC OUTPUTS REQUIRED TO SET THE BUS BUFFERS TO TRANSFER 8- OR 16-BIT DATA.

Type of Transfer to/from bus	*Function*	*Control inputs*				*Control logic outputs*				
		*DODSB** •LOCAL*	R/W*	UDS*	LDS*	sXTRQ*	EBRD	OBWR	EBXCVR	OBXCVR
8-bit	Odd-in	H	H	H	L	H	Off	Off	Off	IN
	Even-in	H	H	L	H	H	ON	Off	Off	IN
	Odd-out	H	L	H	L	H	Off	ON	Off	Off
	Even-out	H	L	L	H	H	Off	Off	OUT	Off
16-bit	16-in	H	H	L	L	L	Off	Off	IN	IN
	16-out	H	L	L	L	L	Off	Off	OUT	OUT
None	LOCAL	L	d	d	d	H	Off	Off	Off	Off
	IDLE	d	H	H	H	H	Off	Off	Off	Off

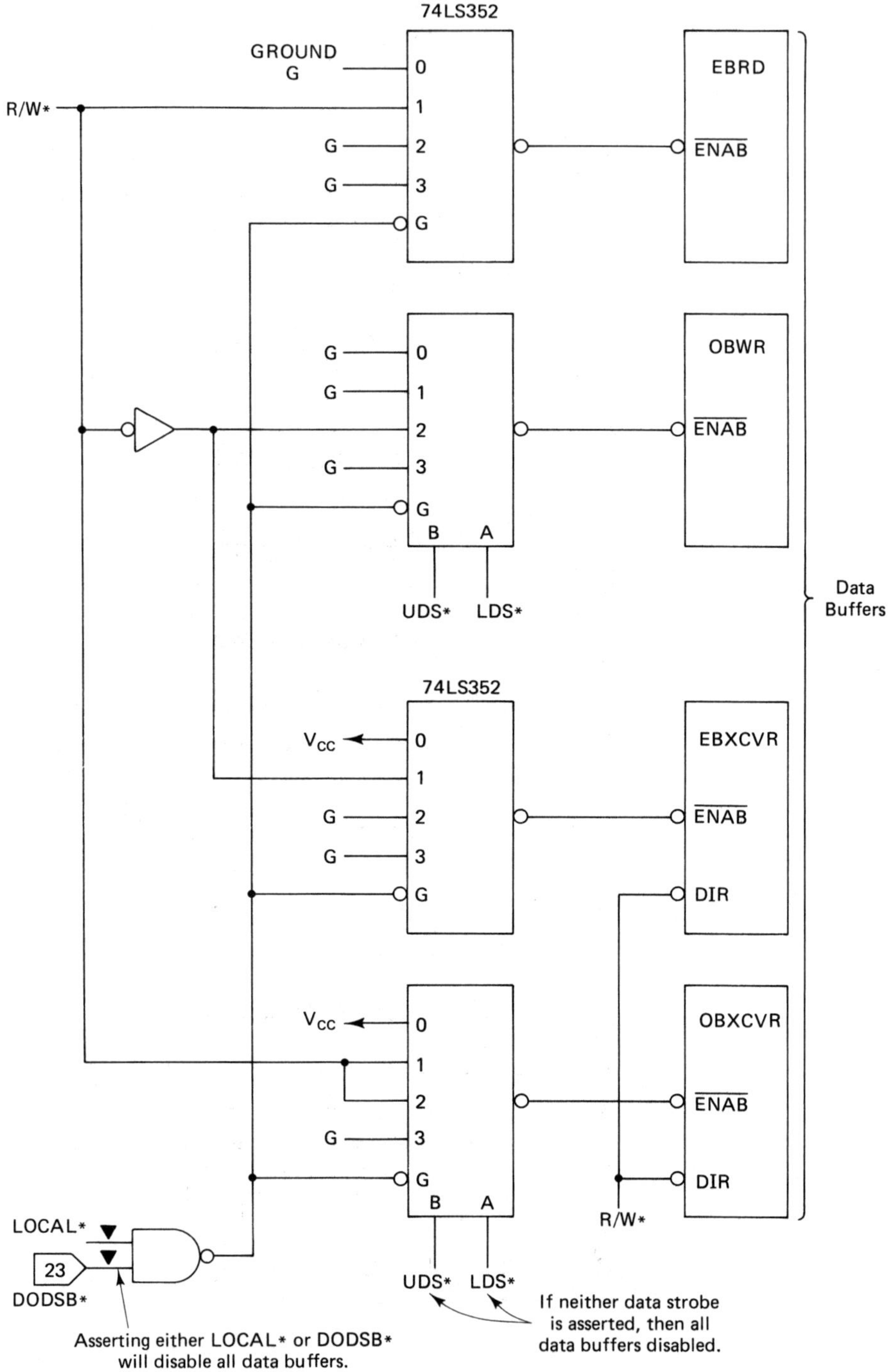

Figure 13.34 Data bus buffer control logic.

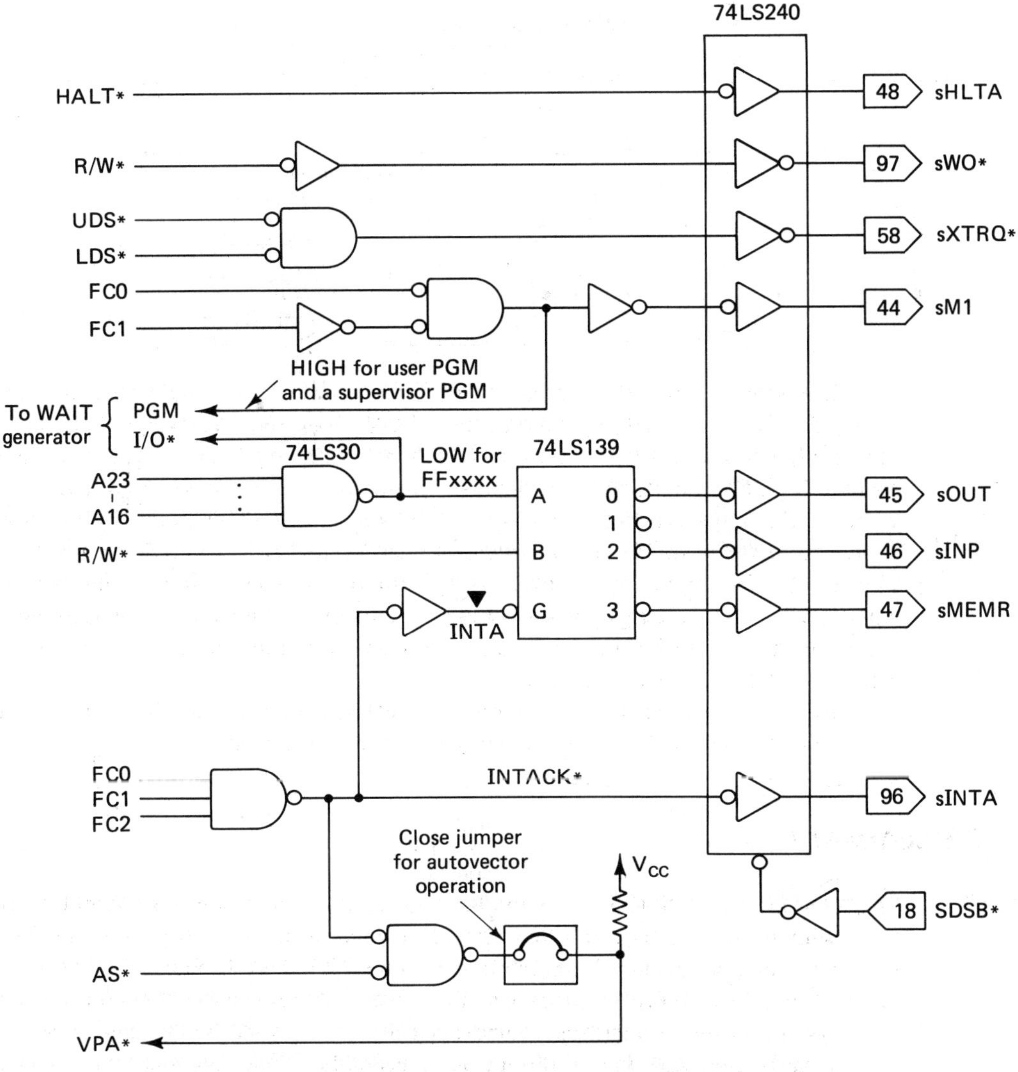

Figure 13.35 Status bus logic circuit.

When not acknowledging an interrupt, the memory and I/O status outputs are asserted according to Table 13.6. The 68000 does all its I/O by memory mapping, but the S-100 bus provides memory mapping and I/O mapping as well. To distinguish between the two, a 64K-byte page of memory can be allocated for I/O and used to control sINP and sOUT. In the circuit shown, I/O space is assumed in the top 64K of the 68000 memory: the 74LS30 decodes $FF xxxx for the wait generator and the I/O status outputs. When memory other than the top 64K is addressed, sMEMR is used.

TABLE 13.6 STATUS OUTPUTS FOR I/O AND MEMORY OPERATIONS. DURING AN INTERRUPT ACKNOWLEDGE, ALL OUTPUTS ARE DISABLED.

		74LS139 Outputs	
*R/W**	*I/O**	*Low output*	*Inverted*
L	L	Y_0	sOUT
L	H	Y_1	
H	L	Y_2	sINP
H	H	Y_3	sMEMR

The address bus buffers are shown in Figure 13.36 along with the circuit to generate A0 for the S-100 bus. A0 equals 0 (a logic LOW) whenever an even data byte is being addressed; it is also LOW whenever a 16-bit word is accessed. This is the same pattern as the 68000 UDS* output, and A0 could be generated by simply connecting UDS* directly to the A0 line at the bus buffer. However, A0 must be held valid on the S-100 bus at least 50 ns after pDBIN; for a write bus cycle, it must be held 0.2 t_{CY} (33 ns for 6 MHz clock) after pWR*. To get the extra delay, an RC circuit provides a simple solution. Keep in mind that the actual delay depends heavily on the components and is not accurate. There is no critical need to be precise though, because the minimum time is 1.5 clock cycles before the data strobe will change.

Both the status bus and the address bus buffers have provision for TMA operations. Each can be disabled by a new temporary master on the bus.

13.6 SUMMARY

The interface to the S-100 bus is the last major hardware module in the 68000 system. Even without the interface, you have powerful processing capability. But with the S-100 interface, you can expand the capabilities of your CPU board to access additional memory, I/O, and disk controller functions. This gives you tremendous flexibility to configure your system so that it matches your exact needs for any particular application.

Boards used with the S-100 bus are classified as either bus masters or bus slaves. The 68000 board will be a permanent bus master and be responsible for initiating all bus signals. It will be responsive to bus requests made by temporary masters that need the bus. One example temporary master access (TMA) operation is to transfer data directly between memory and a disk controller for permanent data storage.

The 68000 bus cycle and the S-100 bus cycle are quite similar in that they are each the same basic duration if one idle state is added to the S-100 bus cycle. Also, each has provisions for wait states to allow for slower peripherals. They differ, however, in the handling of the peripherals: the 68000 is asynchronous and will wait forever until a slow peripheral responds. The S-100 bus is synchronous and waits only if a properly timed ''not ready'' signal requests a delay; if that signal is not present, the S-100 bus will conclude the bus cycle even if the peripheral failed to respond.

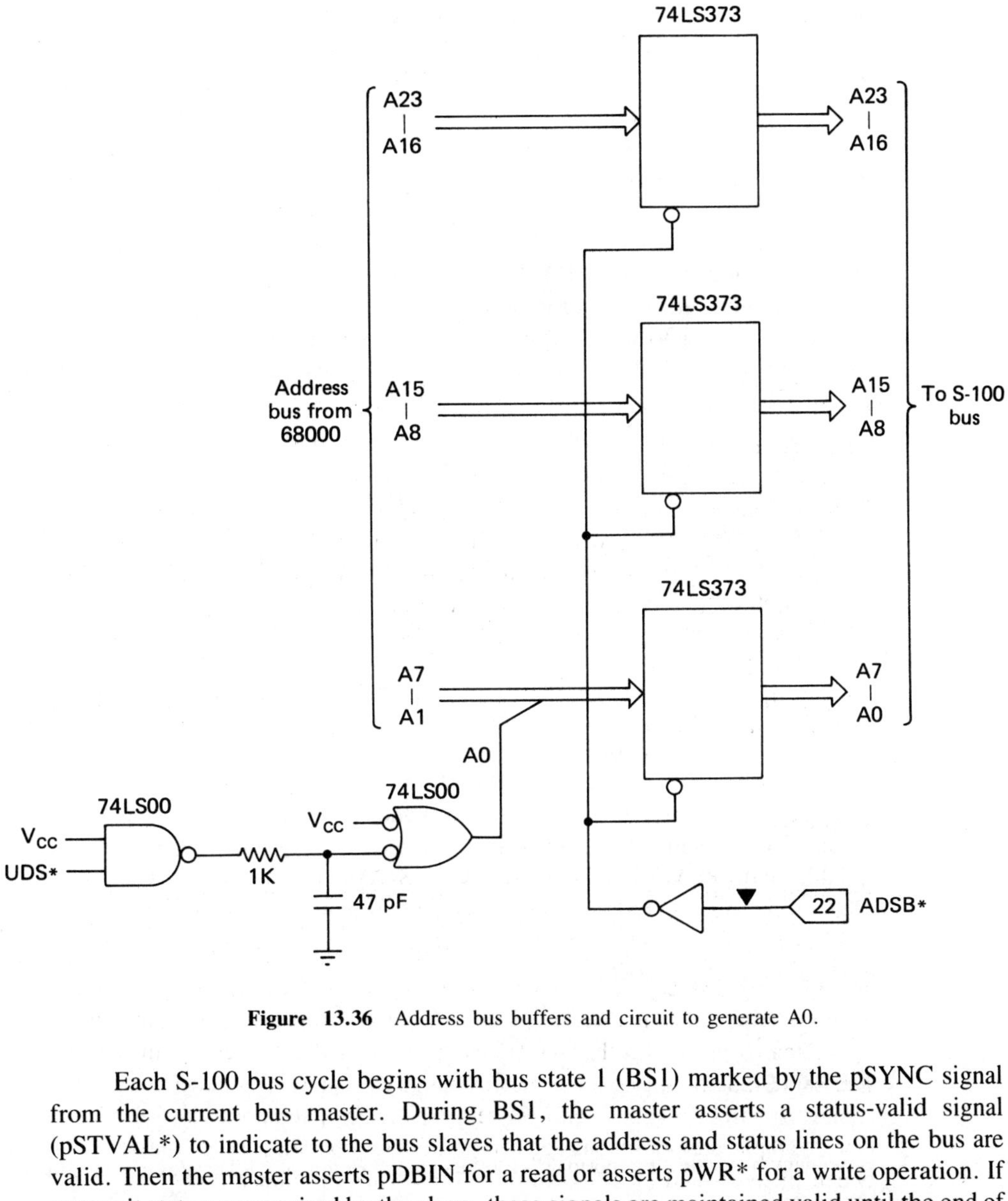

Figure 13.36 Address bus buffers and circuit to generate A0.

Each S-100 bus cycle begins with bus state 1 (BS1) marked by the pSYNC signal from the current bus master. During BS1, the master asserts a status-valid signal (pSTVAL*) to indicate to the bus slaves that the address and status lines on the bus are valid. Then the master asserts pDBIN for a read or asserts pWR* for a write operation. If any wait states are required by the slave, these signals are maintained valid until the end of the bus cycle.

Matching the 68000 to the S-100 bus requires a bus-state generator that will make the 68000 look like a synchronous processor. The state diagram of the S-100 bus can be easily duplicated, but the 68000 bus cycle has to be carefully aligned with the S-100 bus cycle so that the processor will read data at the exact moment the S-100 bus expects valid data. This means that the start of a 68000 bus cycle must always be coordinated with the start of the bus-state generator. Care must also be taken to detect whether the S-100 bus requires any wait states; this also requires coordination with the bus-state generator. The 68000 and the S-100 bus can be synchronized together by using BCYCLE (the start of a 68000 bus cycle), pSYNC, RDY back from a peripheral, and finally DTACK*.

Once the bus-state generator and the wait logic are properly synchronized, the various S-100 control signals can be generated and put on the bus at the proper times. These controls come directly from the bus-state generator circuit and should be checked for conformance with the bus specifications. The most critical signals are pDBIN, pWR*, and the recognition of the RDY line from the peripherals.

Bus arbitration is a major issue in the design of the S-100 interface. In order to allow a temporary master to use the bus, some means of arbitration must be included in the design of the 68000 CPU board. The 68000 already has provision for bus arbitration, and that capability can be used to easily implement the S-100 TMA logic circuit. There are two S-100 controls involved in transferring the bus: HOLD* and pHLDA. If a temporary master needs the bus, it asserts HOLD* and keeps it asserted until it finishes; pHLDA is the hold acknowledge signal to the temporary master that it has the bus.

The S-100 can operate as two unidirectional 8-bit data buses or as a single bidirectional 16-bit bus. Because of this flexibility, control logic must be provided to enable the proper bus configuration as needed. For example, the 68000 might transfer byte data during several bus cycles and then transfer 16-bit data on the next several bus cycles. If a 16-bit transfer is required, sXTRQ* should be generated by the bus master; then, if the slave can set its buffers for a 16-bit transfer, it returns SIXTN* to the master. If SIXTN* is not returned, then the master should do a byte-serial transfer of 8-bits at a time. If the master cannot do this type of transfer, then it must assert ERROR*.

The last major modules in the S-100 interface relate to the status and address buffers. These circuits are fairly straightforward and can be implemented easily. The interrupt portion of the system is the same as the design in the last chapter. One address, A0, is not available on the 68000 but is required by the S-100 bus: it can be derived directly from the UDS* on the 68000. Extra delay is required so that the address stays valid longer than UDS*. This can be done either with a simple RC network or by a more complex latch timed to the system clock.

EXERCISES

1. How many bus states in a normal S-100 bus cycle? How many idle states can be added to a bus cycle?
2. Why must a single idle state always be added to the S-100 bus cycle when using the 68000? Under what circumstances would more than one idle state be added?
3. How does the S-100 bus master know when a peripheral needs more time to respond?
4. What happens if a bus slave negates RDY in the middle of BS3 and holds it LOW for one clock cycle? Why?
5. When does the S-100 bus master read data from the bus?

6. Explain how the bus-state generator detects the start of a 68000 bus cycle.
7. In Figure 13.9, BCYCLE could be generated using only UDS* and LDS*. Explain why this causes an undesirable side effect on the performance of the system. Is it serious?
8. In Figure 13.11, is DT-ENAB necessary? Will the system work with just BCYCLE? Is a simpler alternative design possible?
9. Do you agree or disagree that the state diagrams in Figures 13.14 and 13.15 are functionally equivalent? Why or why not?
10. Redesign the bus-state generator with JK flip-flops. Is there any advantage in using JKs?
11. Suppose Schottky devices are used in the Figure 13.18 bus-state generator and output logic. Analyze the pDBIN signal. Does it meet bus specifications? Redesign as needed.
12. Assume a 12.5 MHz 68000 with a 6 MHz SYSCLK. Verify the read timing along the lines of Figure 13.19.
13. Assume a 12.5 MHz 68000 with a 6 MHz SYSCLK. Verify the write timing along the same lines as Figure 13.20.
14. Design a wait generator like the one in Figure 13.21, but make it for 2 waits. Draw the timing diagram.
15. Rework the timing analysis in Table 13.3 assuming Schottky devices.
16. What is the effect of using CLK68 rather than SYSCLK on the TMA circuit in Figure 13.32? Why must AS* be pulled up?
17. Redesign the TMA circuit in Figure 13.32 so that pHLDA will always go low at least one clock cycle after HOLD* goes HIGH.
18. Redesign the data bus buffer control logic in Figure 13.34 using NAND gates.
19. Redesign the A0 circuit so that it always stays valid until the end of the bus cycle. Does it make a difference which bus cycle is specified? How might that affect your design?
20. Justify the selection of all the bus buffers. Do they meet the requirements of the IEEE Std-696 Sections 3.4–3.7?

FURTHER READING

IEEE Standard 696 Interface Devices. New York: IEEE, 1983.

KANE, GERRY. *68000 Microprocessor Handbook*. Berkeley, CA: Osborne/McGraw-Hill, 1981.

LIBES, SOL, and MARK GARETZ. *Interfacing to S-100/IEEE-696 Microcomputers*. Berkeley, CA: Osborne/McGraw-Hill, 1981.

MC68000 16-bit Microprocessor Data Manual. Austin, TX: Motorola Semiconductor Products, Inc.

FOURTEEN

Software Issues

Throughout the previous chapters, the emphasis has been on hardware design and development: a knowledge of 68000 software has not been required. Aside from a few small test programs that can be placed in EPROMs, the 68000 can be brought up without writing any software. If the processor board has been designed "properly," it can run the TUTOR monitor code immediately. The result, then, is a 68000 CPU board that can respond to simple commands given from a video console: no programming necessary.

The simple commands provided by TUTOR are quite powerful and can be used, for example, to test the 68000 system memory or exchange code with a host computer system. TUTOR's one-line assembler makes writing assembly language programs possible; its disassembler helps the programmer understand code already in memory. For all its capability, however, TUTOR still does not provide the features of a full disk-operating system (DOS).

In this chapter you will learn how to take advantage of TUTOR's programming capabilities and also how to use it for data communication with a host computer. You will learn how to use a cross assembler to develop 68000 programs on a host system for execution on your 68000 board. In addition, you will find how to configure your system so that you can boot the CP/M-68K[1] disk-operating system with your 68000 CPU board.

There are a number of possible software options you might want to consider in the design of your own system. For example, the assumed development sequence presented in the text is:

- Use small test EPROMs to develop hardware modules,
- Get TUTOR running,
- Test memory and other modules using TUTOR,

[1]CP/M-68K is a trademark of Digital Research, Inc.

- Add EPROMs to boot a DOS,
- Upon reset, enter TUTOR; boot DOS by calling boot EPROMs.

One development option might involve bypassing TUTOR completely: upon reset, the 68000 can begin with the DOS-boot code and load CP/M-68K from disk. Another development possibility might involve replacing TUTOR with a public-domain monitor such as VUBUG.[2]

14.1 TUTOR FIRMWARE

TUTOR is the 16Kb monitor program supplied with the Motorola 68000 Educational Computer Board (ECB). It is programmed into a pair of 8K × 8 ROMs (comparable to MCM68764 EPROMs) and provides a complete programming and operating environment. It responds to user commands entered from a console; the command format and syntax are similar to other Motorola 68000 products. These commands fall into four general categories:

1. Display or modify memory.
2. Display or modify 68000 registers.
3. Execute a program.
4. Access I/O resources on the processor board.

The memory allocation assumed when TUTOR runs in the ECB is shown in Figure 14.1. The TUTOR firmware is decoded from $8000 to $BFFF; the ECB RAM is located between 8 and $7FFF. The first ACIA, Port 1 for the operator console, is addressed at $10040 and $10042; the other ACIA, Port 2 for the host computer, is at $10041 and $10043. The ECB also has a 68230 parallel interface/timer (PI/T) that is decoded at $10000. The first eight bytes of the TUTOR firmware provide the initial stack pointer and program counter when the ECB is reset. As long as your processor board is configured with the same port and memory addresses, and your I/O uses the 6850 ACIA, TUTOR will run without any modifications.

14.1.1 Modifying Tutor

In addition to being a valuable monitor for the ECB, the TUTOR firmware can be easily used with other 68000 processor boards. Except for TRAP14, the code is position-independent: it can be decoded anywhere in memory and still function.[3] Consequently, the firmware can be installed in any other 68000 CPU board and used with only a few small modifications. One area to change is the reset vector addresses in the first eight EPROM locations; the other area to change is the addresses of the I/O ports.

The reset vectors in the first memory locations are SP = $0444 and PC = $8146. When the 68000 is reset, the EPROMs are enabled so that the SSP and PC values are both

[2]See *Byte* (January 1984) pp. 403–416.

[3]TRAP14 uses a non-relocatable jump table. If this function is required, a "block move" of TUTOR from its normal EPROM address to $8000 in RAM can solve the problem.

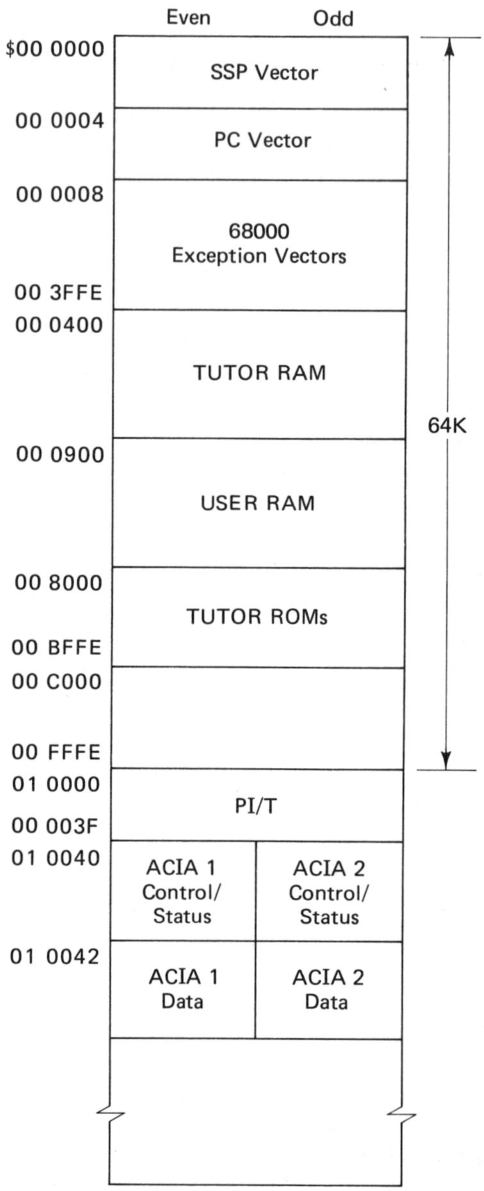

Figure 14.1 Memory map of the Educational Computer Board.

read and the processor begins executing the program at the PC address. If TUTOR is decoded somewhere else in memory, then the initial PC value must be changed to the new location. No change is required for the SSP because TUTOR must have RAM in low memory for the 68000 exception vectors (7 to $3FF) and for its own use ($400 to $8FF). Thus, if your system memory map is not the same as the ECB, you must be sure that RAM is provided at least up to $8FF for TUTOR.

Each of the ACIA addresses appears in only one place in the EPROM set. If you have an ECB running, the location can be found easily by using the block search (BS) command. Otherwise, using the utilities for your EPROM programmer, you can find ACIA 1 about \$1C70 from the start of the EPROM pair; ACIA 2 is \$10 later in memory. The values in TUTOR are ACIA 1 = \$010040 and ACIA 2 = \$010041. Both of these can be changed to some more convenient location in memory. The only constraints are that TUTOR expects the 6850 control and status at the base address (\$010040 for ACIA1) and the 6850 data port at the base address + 2 (\$010042 for ACIA1).

Figure 14.2 shows the memory map of a complete 68000 system using a modified TUTOR as the monitor. There is 128K system memory provided starting at address 0; the memory allocation for I/O is \$FF0000 and up. The changes required to run TUTOR in this configuration are:

	Old Value	*New Value*
Program counter	00 00 81 46	00 FD 01 46
ACIA 1	00 01 00 40	00 FF 00 40
ACIA 2	00 01 00 41	00 FF 00 41
Prompt message	TUTOR 1.3	S-bug 1.3

The new prompt message was used to distinguish the modified version of TUTOR from the original as used in the ECB.

Note that TUTOR is stored in a pair of EPROMs: one even and one odd. This is because the ECB hardware design enables both 8-bit EPROMs together so the 68000 always read 16-bit words. That is, the even EPROM responds to UDS* and the odd EPROM to LDS*. In the complete system using the S-bug code above, both EPROMs are controlled the same way as in the ECB. The code is physically split between the two EPROMs so that even-addressed bytes are in the even EPROM and odd-addressed bytes are in the odd EPROM. For example, the first 8 bytes of the original TUTOR reset vectors appear in memory as:

00 00 04 44 00 00 81 46.

When split into even and odd parts, the code becomes:

```
00    04    00      81         in the even EPROM, and
   00    44    00      46      in the odd EPROM.
```

The modified S-bug reset vectors appear in memory as:

00 00 04 44 00 FD 01 46.

When split into even and odd parts, this code becomes:

```
00    04    00      01         in the even EPROM, and
   00    44    FD      46      in the odd EPROM.
```

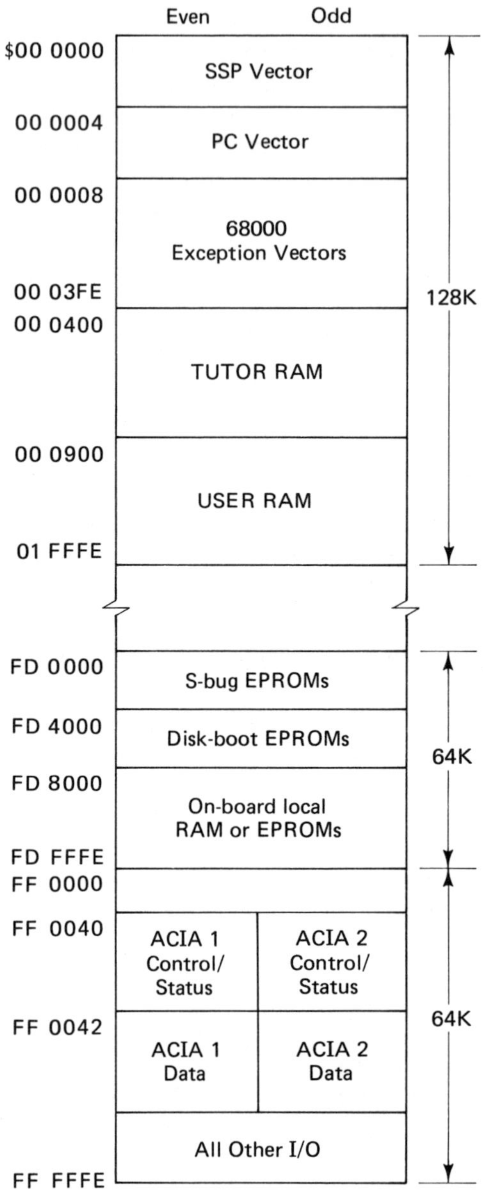

Figure 14.2 Memory map of the author's 10 MHz 68000 computer system using the Motorola TUTOR firmware as the monitor. The modified code is referred to as "S-bug."

14.1.2 Using Tutor

A summary of the TUTOR commands is shown in Table 14.1. Several of the commands are especially useful in bringing up the 68000 and testing it for the first time. For example, "DF" is one of the most frequently used commands; it displays the contents of all the 68000 registers. From a test standpoint, executing DF sends enough data to the console to see if the console handshaking is working properly. The "MD" memory-dump command is also useful during a first check of the system; it displays a line (or more) of memory contents on the console screen in both hex and the ASCII equivalent.

One of the best ways for a hardware designer to learn how to program the 68000 is to use the interactive TUTOR assembler. Try writing some instructions and executing them one by one using the TUTOR single-step trace capability. Figure 14.3 shows a simple program to add register D0 to D1 and then return control to TUTOR by using the TRAP 14 function. After interactively entering the program and setting the PC, D0, and D1 registers, you can use the "DF" command to display the contents of all the registers.

TABLE 14.1 A SUMMARY OF THE TUTOR COMMAND SET.

Command	*Description*
MD	Memory Display in hex, ASCII, or disassembled mnemonics
MM	Memory Modify in hex, ASCII, or interactively assemble
MS	Memory Set
DF	Display Formatted registers
.A0 - .A7	Display and set address registers
.D0 - .D7	Display and set data registers
.PC	Display and set program counter
.SR	Display and set status register
.SS	Display and set supervisory stack pointer
.US	Display and set user stack pointer
BF	Block Fill memory with value
BM	Block Move memory
BT	Block Test segment of memory
BS	Block Search memory for hex or string
DC	Data Conversion for on-screen math
HE	Help with available commands
BR	Breakpoint set
NOBR	Remove breakpoint
GO, G	Go ahead with execution of program
GT	Go until breakpoint
GD	Go Direct; like GO but no initial trace
TR, T	Trace an instruction
TT	Trace with temporary breakpoint
DU	Dump memory to host in S-Record format
LO	Load S-Records from host
VE	Verify memory with S-Records from host
TM	Transparent Mode to pass data between Port 1 and Port 2
*	Send message following "*" to Port 2
PA	Printer Attach
NOPA	Reset printer attach
PF	Port Format: set nulls
OF	Display Offsets for relocating code
.RO - .R6	Display and set relative-offset registers

```
TUTOR   1.3 > MM 1000;DI
001000      00000000                      OR.B        #0,D0 ? ADD D0,D1            <---- Interactive
001002      00000000                      OR.B        #0,D0 ? MOVE.B #228,D7             entry of
001006      00000000                      OR.B        #0,D0 ? TRAP #14                   program
001008      00000000                      OR.B        #0,D0 ?.

TUTOR   1.3 > .PC 1000      <---- Set program counter

TUTOR   1.3 > .D0 1234      <---- Set data register D0

TUTOR   1.3 > .D1 24578     <---- Set data register D1

TUTOR   1.3 > DF
PC=00001000 SR=2708=.S7.N... US=00005000 SS=00000780                       Display the
D0=00001234 D1=00024578 D2=00000000 D3=00000000                             registers
D4=00000000 D5=00000000 D6=00000000 D7=000000E4
A0=00010040 A1=FFFFFFFF A2=00000414 A3=00000554
A4=00009FB2 A5=00000540 A6=00000540 A7=00000780
--------------------001000    D240                       ADD.W    D0,D1

TUTOR   1.3 > GO                                                            Execute the
PHYSICAL ADDRESS=00001000                                                   program at
                                                                              $1000
TUTOR   1.3 > DF
PC=00001002 SR=2700=.S7..... US=00005000 SS=00000780
D0=00001234 D1=000257AC D2=00000000 D3=00000000                             Registers
D4=00000000 D5=00000000 D6=00000000 D7=000000E4                             afterwards
A0=00010040 A1=FFFFFFFF A2=00000414 A3=00000554
A4=00009FB2 A5=00000540 A6=00000540 A7=00000780
--------------------001002    1E3C00E4                   MOVE.B   #228,D7

TUTOR   1.3 > DC $1234+$24578
$257AC=&153516                                                              Check answer
                                                                             using data
TUTOR   1.3 >                                                                conversion
                                                                              command
```

Figure 14.3 A simple ADD-registers program entered interactively. After the addition, the MOVE and TRAP return control to TUTOR. All user entries are underlined. (Courtesy Motorola Inc.)

The "GO" command causes execution of the program at the $1000 set in the program counter; after returning to TUTOR, another DF command shows that the D1 register has a new value. A quick math check with the "DC" command shows that the answer in D1 is correct.

14.1.3 Host Communication

The TUTOR firmware supports communication with a host computer system connected directly to Port 2 as shown in Figure 14.4. All the communication lines utilize the RS-232C standard interface with the 6850 ACIA described in Chapter 11. Typically, a local interconnection will be set to run at 9600 baud at both Port 1 and Port 2. When the operator selects the TUTOR transparent-mode command "TM", the console is connected directly to the host, and the 68000 system can be ignored. However, the 68000 system monitors the data from the console: if it detects the exit character (control-A), then TUTOR disconnects Port 2 and regains control.

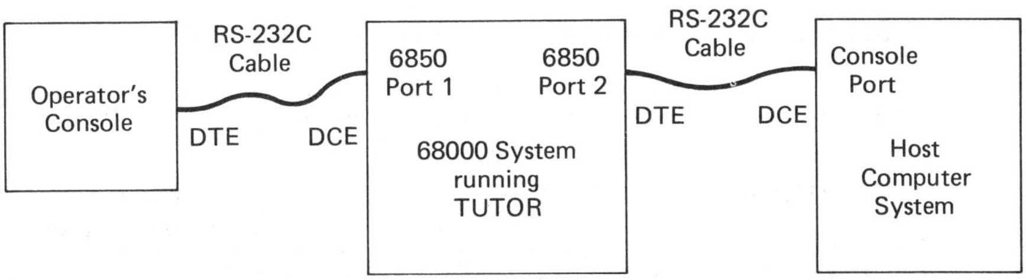

Figure 14.4 The operator's console is connected to Port 1 on the 68000 system; a host computer can be connected to Port 2 if desired. If the operator executes a "TM" command, Port 1 and Port 2 are connected in a transparent mode. While in this transparent mode, the operator can control the host directly.

A 68000 system such as the Educational Computer Board can be left permanently connected into your computer system for convenient programming and testing. For example, the author's installation uses an ECB connected between a Heath H-29 terminal and the console input of a CompuPro S-100 System. When the installation is first powered up, the console communicates only with TUTOR until the TM command connects the console to the main system.[4]

Because the 68000 can be easily programmed with its interactive assembler, it would be convenient if a means of saving programs were available. TUTOR supports a cassette recorder, but this hardware has not been included in the design discussed in this text. An easier way to save programs can be implemented using the connection to the host computer system: TUTOR can send blocks of memory to the host computer using the Figure 14.4 configuration and the dump command. All memory transfers will be made in the form of S-records when using the memory dump "DU" command in Table 14.2.[5] However, unless the host has some means of saving data coming directly in the console port, this method of uploading is not especially useful; a better approach is to use the host's modem port.

Programs that were previously saved on disk can also be downloaded from the host computer system using the connection shown in Figure 14.4. Table 14.2 shows the TUTOR command sequence to make the transfer. All the code intended for 68000 memory must be transmitted in S-record format from the host at a reasonable rate to allow for the slow 68000 in the ECB. This slower data rate is accomplished using the utility program PAGE.COM running under CP/M. The example code to be downloaded is in S-record format and stored on disk under the filename EXAMPLE.HEX.

Usually, the most effective method of using a host computer with a 68000 board is with the configuration shown in Figure 14.5. This approach, using the modem port on the

[4]Rather than use a control-A for the transparent mode exit, the exit character can be changed to a NULL by executing the memory setting command: TUTOR 1.3 > MS 4EA 0 0 <cr>. This change is necessary to avoid a conflict with a common word-processor command.

[5]S-records are ASCII character strings composed of the data plus identifying and checksum information. Because the S-records are ASCII, they can be displayed on a video console.

TABLE 14.2 DATA COMMUNICATION USING THE HOST CONSOLE PORT.

UPLOAD	From 68000 Port 2 to *Console Port*	
	TUTOR 1.3 > DU2 900 1000	Dump S-records of memory between \$900 and \$1000
DOWNLOAD	From Host *Console Port* to 68000 Port 2	
	TUTOR 1.3 > LO ;X=PAGE EXAMPLE.HEX P1	
	Required: Host must use PAGE.COM (or similar) to send the S-record HEX file at a slow rate	

host computer, has the advantage of more flexible host capabilities. For example, data uploaded to the host *console* port usually cannot be saved; however, most modem programs can easily save incoming data. Likewise, modem programs can usually adjust data transmission speed for downloading. The "speed" of transmission is not so much a matter of the baud rate, but more a concern with the processing speed of the 68000 running TUTOR: all the data coming to the 68000 must be converted from S-records, put in memory, and the checksums verified.

Table 14.3 shows the commands necessary to upload and download code using the host modem port. The modem program, MDM727, is one typical public-domain program that provides adequate communication for the data transfers. A second modem program,

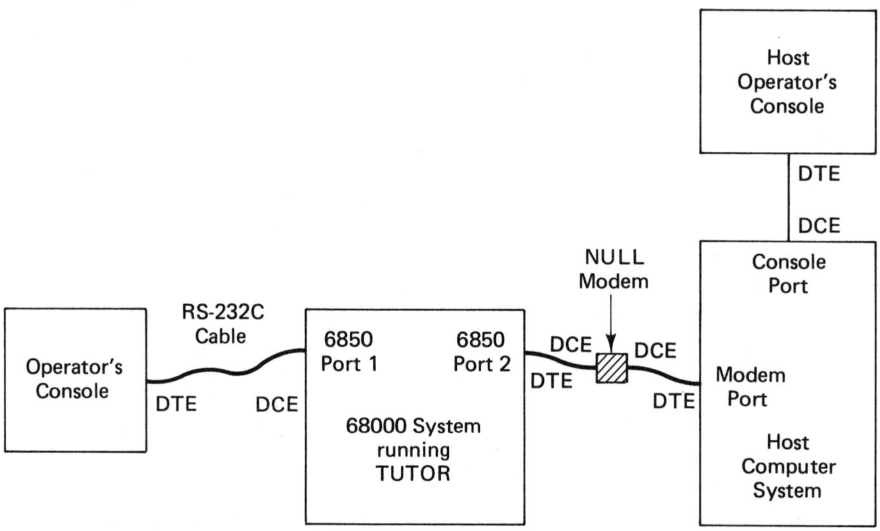

Figure 14.5 An optional connection between the 68000 system and a host computer's modem port. This configuration is useful for uploading S-records to the host or downloading S-records to the 68000 system. The NULL modem swaps RS-232C pins 2 and 3.

TABLE 14.3 DATA COMMUNICATION USING THE HOST MODEM PORT.

UPLOAD From 68000 Port 2 to host *Modem Port*	
At Host	
A > MDM728	Modem program that uses control -W to hold and CR to resume
SET 9600	9600 baud data rate
T NEWFILE.HEX	Open a new file on disk
Control-Y	Begin copying data
At 68000	
TUTOR 1.3 > PF2 FORMAT 15 CHAR NULL 08 C/R NULL 08	Format Port 2 for slower data transmission
TUTOR 1.3 > DU2 900 1000	Dump S-records of memory between \$900 and \$1000
DOWNLOAD From Host *Modem Port* to 68000 Port 2	
At 68000	
TUTOR 1.3 > LO ;X	Load S-records and see echo
At Host	
A > MDM727	Invoke modem program
TLF	Option to send LF at end line
SET 9600	Transfer at 9600 baud
SPD 0, 1	Include 100 ms delay at end of each line
T	Connect
Control-T EXAMPLE.HEX	Send S-record file with delay

MDM728, was assembled that uses control-W/CR instead of control-S/control-Q for handshaking. This is necessary so that the modem program can force TUTOR to pause on uploads.

The upload technique involves formatting TUTOR Port 2 using the "PF2" command, so that it inserts nulls between each character and after each line. Meanwhile, the host modem program is prepared to receive and save all data. The TUTOR dump memory command will send the data up to the host. If the host's buffer fills up, TUTOR must pause until the host writes the data to its disk. However, TUTOR will not respond to any signal other than control-W to pause, which is why the modem program needs modification. TUTOR has provision for changing the handshake option, but this is only good for *downloads* to the 68000 using the load "LO" command.

Downloading from the host modem port to the 68000 can be done using the LO command. There is no pressing need to change the handshake option for downloading as long as the transmission rate is slow enough. As shown in Table 14.3, the modem program is set to send data with 100 ms delay at the end of each line. If errors occur and the host must pause while TUTOR reports the errors, then the PF option bytes can be set. Unfortunately, this handshaking does not regulate the data transfer rate: it only halts the sender while TUTOR reports checksum errors.

14.2 CROSS-ASSEMBLY TECHNIQUES

The interactive assembler is ideal when you want to write a quick test program. Several lines can be easily typed using TUTOR and then executed for immediate results. There is a price for this convenience, however: your program documentation is sketchy and the TUTOR assembler lacks many features that are useful for writing large programs. For example, consider the simple program listing shown in Figure 14.6. Notice that there are no comment lines and no use of labels or symbols; you have to rethink the program every time you look at it. If you want a permanent record of your program design, you need to handwrite marginal notes on the listing to explain each part of the program.

```
TUTOR  1.3 > MM 900;DI
000900    4BF81000           LEA      $1000,A5
000904    4DF81008           LEA      $1008,A6
000908    1E3C00E3           MOVE.B   #227,D7
00090C    4E4E               TRAP     #14
00090E    1E3C00E4           MOVE.B   #228,D7
000912    4E4E               TRAP     #14

TUTOR  1.3 > MM 1000;DI

001000    4869               DC.W     'Hi'
001002    2054               DC.W     ' T'
001004    6865               DC.W     'he'
001006    7265               DC.W     're'

TUTOR  1.3 > GO 900
PHYSICAL ADDRESS=00000900
Hi There

TUTOR  1.3 >
```

Figure 14.6 A simple program written using the TUTOR firmware. Without comment lines, labels, or symbols, it is difficult to see that all this program does is write "Hi There" on the console screen.

One alternative to using the TUTOR assembler is to use a native assembler on a 68000 host computer as shown in Figure 14.7. The host should have a full range of programming and system utilities with a disk operating system. To write a 68000 program that can be downloaded and run on the target 68000 system (e.g., the ECB), the development sequence is:

- Write the assembly language program using the system editor,
- Assemble the program using the 68000 assembler,
- Link the program into an executable file using the linker,
- Test and debug the program on the host if possible,
- Download the code to the target system,
- Test and debug the program on the target system.

In addition to being able to program using labels and symbols, using a host computer provides many other programming conveniences. One useful feature is being able to save programs on disk. However, unless you already have a host 68000 system for program development, this approach to developing a program might not be practical.

As an alternative to the 68000 host computer, program development can be done on any available computer system. There is no reason why programs must be written on a 68000. For example, a Z-80 host can be a very effective development tool to create 68000 code to download to a 68000 target computer. In Figure 14.8, notice that the physical connections are all the same: the only difference is that a cross-assembler rather than an assembler generates the 68000 code. The development sequence using a cross-assembler is:

- Write the assembly language program using the system editor,
- Assemble the program using the cross-assembler,
- Link the program into an executable file using the linker,
- Download the code to the target system,
- Test and debug the program on the target system.

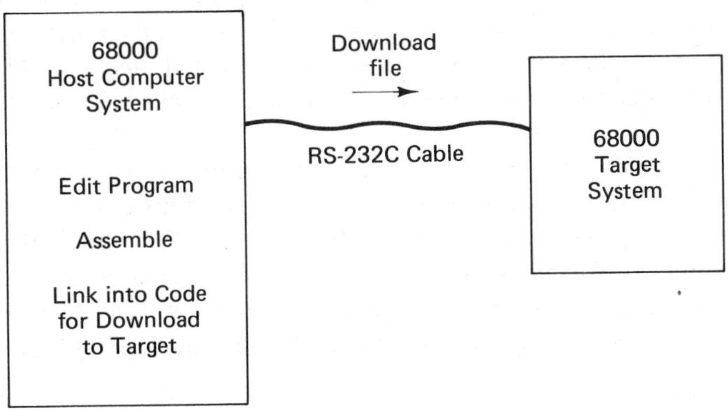

Figure 14.7 Connection between a 68000 host computer and a smaller target computer. Large programs can be written on the host and downloaded for execution on the target.

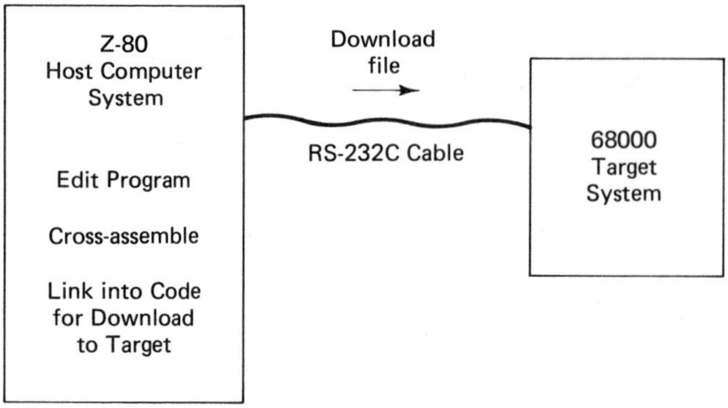

Figure 14.8 Connection between a Z-80 host computer and a smaller target computer. Large programs can be written on the host and downloaded for execution on the target.

Because the host uses a Z-80 rather than a 68000, testing and debugging the program must be deferred until the code is actually downloaded to the target 68000.

Figure 14.9 shows the same program discussed earlier, but written with an editor on a Z-80 CP/M microcomputer system. The format of the program follows Motorola conventions for assembly language programs and can be cross-assembled using the public-domain Quelo Version 1.9 Cross-Assembler.[6] Notice how much easier it is to quickly understand the purpose of the program when proper documentation can be added to the source code.

To cross-assemble the Figure 14.9 source code, the Quelo program can be invoked from the operating system:

A> A68K DEMO

This command runs the cross-assembler to produce the two output files shown in Figure 14.10. The first of these files, DEMO.PRN in Figure 14.10(a), is a listing of the source code and the equivalent object code. The second file, DEMO.HEX in Figure 14.10(b), is the object code in S-record format ready for downloading to the target 68000.

Compare the listing file with the TUTOR program in Figure 14.6 and note some of the differences. Aside from the extra documentation, there is only a slight difference in the generated object code for the LEA (load effective address) instruction. The one-line TUTOR assembler will default to a word-length operand unless the operand entered is larger than 16 bits. In contrast, the cross-assembler defaults to a long-word operand; this can be easily remedied by changing the source code to force a word-length operand. Although there is no effect on the function of the program, the resulting object code is larger than necessary.

The DEMO program in Figures 14.9 and 14.10 is an example of a nonrelocatable program; that is, once it has been assembled, there is no way to relocate it from $900 to any other address unless the whole program is assembled all over again. When the ORG (origin) directive to the assembler is used in the program, it forces the generation of code starting at a specific address. For example, the ORG PROGRAM statement starts the program code at $900, and then the ORG DATA starts the code for the data at $1000. To

[6] See Preface for sources to obtain software.

```
*        DEMO program to display message
*             'Hi There' on console. Uses
*             TUTOR TRAP #14 routines.
*

PROGRAM  EQU      $900     * Start of program
DATA     EQU      $1000    * Start data area

OUT1CR   EQU      227      * String out + CR/LF
TUTOR    EQU      228      * Return to TUTOR

         ORG      PROGRAM

START    LEA      MSG,A5             * Msg adr -->A5
         LEA      ENDMSG,A6          * End+1   -->A6
         MOVE.B   #OUT1CR,D7
         TRAP     #14                * Send message

FINISH   MOVE.B   #TUTOR,D7
         TRAP     #14                * Go to TUTOR

         ORG      DATA

MSG      DC.B     'Hi There'
ENDMSG   *

         END
```

Figure 14.9 A simple demonstration program for use by a cross assembler. This program takes advantage of the TUTOR firmware TRAP #14 functions and writes "Hi There" on the console screen.

relocate the code to any other addresses requires changing either or both of the ORG statements. Deleting the ORG statements will not automatically make the program relocatable: the cross-assembler must be able to generate relocatable code. Unfortunately, the Quelo v1.9 assembler can only create code for specific addresses.

Figure 14.11(a) shows the DEMO program rewritten for the Quelo Version 4.2 Cross-Assembler. This assembler generates relocatable code that can be positioned anywhere in memory without having to reassemble the source if addresses are changed. All addresses are specified in the linking code shown in Figure 14.11(b). In the case of the nonrelocatable cross-assembler, this linking operation was not necessary. However, in exchange for the flexibility of being able to relocate the source program modules, it is necessary to add a linking step to generate executable code for downloading to the 68000.

The source code in Figure 14.11(a) is somewhat different from the original DEMO program. The essence of the program remains, of course, but all the symbol definitions (as MSG, OUT1CR, etc.) have been removed and defined as external symbols by the XREF directive. The advantage of referring to external symbols is that a set of general symbols can be written into one common module and used by all segments of a large program. The XDEF directive tags START as a public symbol, and the PROC directive

```
A68K   1.9   11/08/82 -- Run on 03/08/86
                          *       DEMO program to display message
                          *            'Hi There' on console. Uses
                          *            TUTOR TRAP #14 routines.
                          *

      00000900            PROGRAM EQU     $900     * Start of program
      00001000            DATA    EQU     $1000    * Start data area

      000000E3            OUT1CR  EQU     227      * String out + CR/LF
      000000E4            TUTOR   EQU     228      * Return to TUTOR

000900                            ORG     PROGRAM

000900  4BF9 00001000     START   LEA     MSG,A5            * Msg adr  -->A5
000906  4DF9 00001008             LEA     ENDMSG,A6         * End+1    -->A6
00090C  1E3C 00E3                 MOVE.B  #OUT1CR,D7
000910  4E4E                      TRAP    #14               * Send message

000912  1E3C 00E4         FINISH  MOVE.B  #TUTOR,D7
000916  4E4E                      TRAP    #14               * Go to TUTOR

001000                            ORG     DATA

001000  48 69 20 54       MSG     DC.B    'Hi There'
        68 65 72 65
                          ENDMSG  *

    0 Errors detected
                                  END
```

(a)

```
S00300000FC
S11B09004BF9000010004DF9000010081E3C00E34E4E1E3C00E44E4E76
S10B10004869205468657265 1B
S9030000FC
```

(b)

Figure 14.10 The output from the Quelo Version 1.9 Cross-Assembler. The listing file in (a) shows the object code; the output in (b) is the S-record equivalent of the object code. (Courtesy Quelo, Inc.)

tags it as a procedure entry point; using START this way makes it available for use by the linker after assembly.

The linking code (DEMOLINK) in Figure 14.11(b) defines the external symbols that the program needs. It also establishes the origin of each module of the program. In the example case, just the one module (DEMO1) will be linked at the PROGRAM address \$900. After that, the data module is linked at the DATA address \$1000. If more than one

```
*       DEMO program to display message
*            'Hi There' on console. Uses
*            TUTOR TRAP #14 routines.
*
        XDEF     START

        XREF     MSG
        XREF     ENDMSG
        XREF     OUT1CR
        XREF     TUTOR

START   PROC
        LEA      MSG,A5           * Msg adr --)A5
        LEA      ENDMSG,A6        * End+1   --)A6
        MOVE.B   #OUT1CR,D7
        TRAP     #14              * Send message

FINISH  MOVE.B   #TUTOR,D7
        TRAP     #14              * Go to TUTOR

        END
```

(a)

```
*       Link the DEMO program
*

PROGRAM EQU      $900    * Start of program
DATA    EQU      $1000   * Start data area

OUT1CR  EQU      227     * String out + CR/LF
TUTOR   EQU      228     * Return to TUTOR

        ORG      PROGRAM
        SECTION  0
        LINK     DEMO1

        ORG      DATA
        SECTION  1
MSG     DC.B     'Hi There'
ENDMSG  *

        END      START
```

(b)

Figure 14.11 The DEMO program rewritten for use by a cross-assembler that generates relocatable code. (a) is the source program DEMO1 and (b) is the link-specification file DEMOLINK. (Courtesy Quelo, Inc.)

program module is needed in the final program, then each additional module would be listed in the link specifications.

To cross-assemble the DEMO1 code in Figure 14.11, and then to link using DEMOLINK, several steps are necessary. The commands for the Quelo Version 4.2 cross-assembly are:

A>	A68K	DEMO1	−SX	(Assemble with symbol table and cross-reference table.)
A>	L68K	DEMOLINK	−SXI	(Link with symbol table, cross-reference table, identify modules used in link.)
A>	S68K	DEMOLINK	−MBI	(Generate symbol report with cross-references, memory map, and module revision summary.)

These commands produce a number of output files. The cross-assembly of DEMO1 produces the print file shown in Figure 14.12; notice that all the address and symbol values are incomplete until the linker fills them in. Then, during the link operation, L68K produces the listing files in Figure 14.13 and creates the final S-record file DEMOLINK.HEX in Figure 14.14(a).

The DEMOLINK.HEX code in Figure 14.14(a) can be downloaded to the target 68000 system in exactly the same way as earlier. The S-records are slightly different from the S-records in Figure 14.10(b) because of added linker information, but the result is the same: the program can be successfully executed using TUTOR. The S-records can also be split into two halves as in Figure 14.14(b) and (c); each half can be used by an EPROM programmer to make the even and odd EPROMs used in hardware designs covered in prior chapters.

```
Quelo    ...A68K A4.2  05/10/84    ...Run on Mar 8, 1986  hh:mm:ss
M:DEMO1.R68 , M:DEMO1.PRN , M:DEMO1.S68 = M:DEMO1.A68
...
                                   *       DEMO program to display message
                                   *            'Hi There' on console. Uses
                                   *            TUTOR TRAP #14 routines.
                                   *
                                           XDEF     START

                                           XREF     MSG
                                           XREF     ENDMSG
                                           XREF     OUT1CR
                                           XREF     TUTOR


                        -- -- -- -- -- -- -- -- -- -- -- -- -- --

0'000000                           START   PROC
0'000000  4BF9'00000000                    LEA      MSG,A5        * Msg adr -->A5
0'000006  4DF9'00000000                    LEA      ENDMSG,A6     * End+1   -->A6
0'00000C  1E3C 00'00                       MOVE.B   #OUT1CR,D7
0'000010  4E4E                             TRAP     #14           * Send message

0'000012  1E3C 00'00               FINISH  MOVE.B   #TUTOR,D7
0'000016  4E4E                             TRAP     #14           * Go to TUTOR

0'000018                                   END
    0 Errors
```

Figure 14.12 The output from the Quelo Version 4.2 Cross-Assembler. (Courtesy Quelo, Inc.)

```
Quelo    ...L68K A1.2  05/09/84    ...Run on Mar 8, 1986  hh:mm:ss
I  /EMOLINK.HEX , M:DEMOLINK.LST , M:DEMOLINK.S68 = M:DEMOLINK.L68
 ...
                                   1.  *        Link the DEMO program
                                   2.  *
                                   3.
        00000900                   4.  PROGRAM EQU      $900     * Start of program
        00001000                   5.  DATA    EQU      $1000    * Start data area
                                   6.
        000000E3                   7.  OUT1CR  EQU      227      * String out + CR/LF
        000000E4                   8.  TUTOR   EQU      228      * Return to TUTOR
                                   9.
00000900                          10.          ORG      PROGRAM
00000900                          11.          SECTION  0
                                  12.          LINK     DEMO1
                                  13.
00001000                          14.          ORG      DATA
00001000                          15.          SECTION  1
00001000   48 69 20 54 68         16.  MSG     DC.B     'Hi There'
           65 72 65
00001008                          17.  ENDMSG  *
                                  18.
00001008                          19.          END      START
      0 Errors
```

Figure 14.13 The listing file created by the Quelo linking operation. (Courtesy Quelo, Inc.)

The last part of the cross-assembly is generation of the symbol reports shown in Figure 14.15. For the simple one-module DEMO1 program, this step is clearly optional; for more complex programs, the information contained in it is valuable documentation. The reports shown in the figure relate to the entire program after linking the modules together. If the S68K symbol report generator were run on each individual source module, then output reports would contain details on the line numbers where each symbol appeared.

```
S01100004D3A44454D4F4C494E4B2E48455801
S10B1000486920546865726518
S11B09004BF9000010004DF9000010081E3C00E34E4E1E3C00E44E4E76
S9030900F3
```

(a)

```
:0C0000004B00104D00101E004E1E004E64
:00000000000
```

(b)

```
:0C000000F90000F900083CE34E3CE44E1F
:00000000000
```

(c)

Figure 14.14 The S-record object code generated by the Quelo linker (a). This code can be split into an even half (b) and an odd half (c); the split halves are in Intel hex format. (Courtesy Quelo, Inc.)

```
Page     1 -- DEMOLINK.RPT

Quelo    ...S68K A1.2  05/10/84    ...Run on Mar 8, 1986  hh:mm:ss     ...Page  1
M:DEMOLINK.RPT = M:DEMOLINK.S68
  ...

  ...68000 Linker       ...Module Summary

Module  Ver  Rev Name          Description
------ ---- ---- ------------ ----------------------------------------
    0.    0    0 M:DEMOLINK.H
    1.    1    0 DEMO1
```

(a)

```
Page     2 -- DEMOLINK.RPT

Quelo    ...S68K A1.2  05/10/84    ...Run on Mar 8, 1986  hh:mm:ss     ...Page  2
M:DEMOLINK.RPT = M:DEMOLINK.S68
  ...

  ...68000 Linker       ...Symbol Table  and  Cross Reference

   Value Atr Symbol                        Module number reference/definition(=)
-------- --- --------------------          ------------------------------------------
00000900 a-I <<<<<<<<                            0=
00001000 # E DATA                                0      0=
00001008 @ L ENDMSG                              0=     1
00001000 @ L MSG                                 0=     1
000000E3 # E OUT1CR                              0=     1
00000900 # E PROGRAM                             0      0=
00000900 0 P START                               0      1=
000000E4 # E TUTOR                               0=     1

Attribute Legend

Value Type              Def/Ref Flag   By   S,E,L = public
---------------------   ------------   --------------------
   # - constant            - def/ref    s - SET directive
   @ - abs address       - - def only   e - EQU directive
0..F - reloc address     ? - ref only   r - REG directive
   M - register mask                    l - label
   U - unspecified                      x - XREF directive
   a - address                          i - internally def
   % - error             % - error      % - error
```

(b)

```
Page     3 -- DEMOLINK.RPT

Quelo    ...S68K A1.2  05/10/84    ...Run on Mar 8, 1986  hh:mm:ss     ...Page  3
M:DEMOLINK.RPT = M:DEMOLINK.S68
  ...

  ...68000 Linker       ...Absolute Address Load Map

Section  Address          Module name   Symbol
------- -------- ----- ------------ ----------------------------------------

0 Start 00000900
0       00000900     1. DEMO1
a       00000900                     <<<<<<<<
0       00000900                     START
0 End   00000917
        --------
0 Size        18

@       00001000                     MSG
@       00001008                     ENDMSG
```

(c)

Figure 14.15 Output information from the Quelo S68K symbol report generator. (a) shows the module revision summary, (b) the cross-referenced symbols, and (c) the memory map. (Courtesy Quelo, Inc.)

14.3 BRINGING UP CP/M-68K

The overall development sequence throughout this book has led to an operational 68000 CPU board that runs with the TUTOR EPROM set. The hardware design you use for your CPU depends on the various tradeoffs related to your intended application; the TUTOR code can be easily modified to suit whatever addresses you want for RAM and I/O. The most inflexible constraint using TUTOR is that I/O must be done using the 6850 ACIA. Overall, the CPU design is your own creation.

Running a full disk-operating system (DOS) such as CP/M-68K can make your 68000 board much more useful for program development and application programs. There are, however, more design constraints on the CPU board than before: when you go to a DOS, you also have to include one or more disk drives, a disk-controller board, and much more RAM. Designing and building each of these system components is far beyond the scope of this book and would require substantial time and expense. Consequently, a viable approach to a full DOS requires that the CPU board conform to a standard interface; doing this allows using a standard bus and off-the-shelf disk-controller and memory boards.

The IEEE Std-696 (S-100) bus was selected for the DOS implementation. Figure 14.16 shows the system hardware configured for running CP/M-68K. The bus plus enclosure are the CompuPro Model 8/16. The CompuPro RAM-23 128Kb memory board is capable of 8- and 16-bit transfers and will run with a 10 MHz system clock. The disk controller, a CompuPro Disk-1A, will handle either 5 ¼″ or 8″ disk drives; the author's installation uses a pair of Qume-842 8″ drives. Serial I/O is done with the CompuPro Interfacer-4. A 6850 ACIA board is also connected to the bus.

The overall strategy for bringing up CP/M-68K on the 68000 involves using an IEEE Std-696 CPU board that functions like the CompuPro CPU-68K.[7] Then, rather than spend substantial time modifying plain-vanilla CP/M from Digital Research, simply purchase CompuPro's CP/M-68K off the shelf complete with their CPU-68K CBIOS (Custom Basic I/O System) and "C" compiler. The only drawback in this strategy is that you need the CompuPro Disk-1A (or Disk-1) and the Interfacer-3 or -4 to boot the system. Once the system boots, however, you can modify the CBIOS so the system can use any disk controller or I/O boards you want. For example, the CBIOS can be modified to add the 6850 I/O board so TUTOR and CP/M-68K both use the 6850 port for the system console.

If at all possible, the TUTOR monitor should be used in the early development of the system. Even before attempting the DOS boot, TUTOR should be run to verify operational system components and good RAM. In the event that TUTOR is not installed, however, the 68000 system can still be booted directly from EPROMs. The 6850 I/O board (or a 6850 on the CPU board) is required only if TUTOR is used; without TUTOR, it can be deleted entirely.

You must install the boards indicated in Figure 14.16 in order to get the system running. A minimum memory of 128K is required to boot CP/M-68K; this memory board

[7]Making a functional equivalent to the CompuPro board involves nothing more exotic than designing an S-100 68000 board addressing RAM starting at address 0 and I/O at address $FF0000.

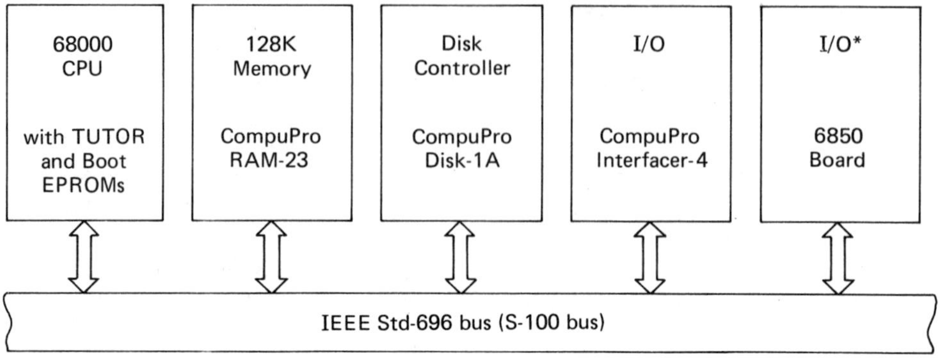

*The 6850 I/O may be located on the 68000 CPU board rather than on a separate card.

Figure 14.16 System configuration for bringing up CP/M-68K on a 68000 processor.

must be able to handle 16-bit transfers if the S-100 68000 CPU board in the Appendix is used. A 6850 I/O board for use with TUTOR is shown in the figure; the 6850 ACIA may optionally be part of the 68000 CPU board instead. Each of the boards should be addressed as shown in Table 14.4. Any address in the range \$FF0000 through \$FFFFFF will be interpreted as I/O, and the 68000 CPU board must run an I/O bus cycle rather than a memory bus cycle.

In order to load CP/M-68K from disk, the 68000 must begin executing code to instruct the disk-controller card to read the first track of the disk. Figure 14.17 shows the boot code necessary to accomplish this. The program is written specifically for the Intel 8272 floppy-disk controller IC in the CompuPro Disk-1A board. Although this code is assembled starting at \$FD4000 using a cross-assembler, the program can be interactively entered into RAM using TUTOR and executed. If a different program execution address is used, it must not be at 0 because the disk data will load there.

TABLE 14.4 ADDRESSES ASSIGNED TO THE BOARDS IN THE CP/M-68K SYSTEM.

Board	*Base Address*
CPU: TUTOR EPROMs	\$FD0000
Boot EPROMs	\$FD4000
Memory: RAM-23	0
Disk controller: Disk-1A	\$FF00C0
I/O: Interfacer-4	\$FF0010
I/O: 6850 board	\$FF0040

14.3.1 CP/M-68K Without TUTOR

The steps you follow in bringing up the DOS without TUTOR are shown in Table 14.5. The code necessary to initialize the 68000 and start the disk controller must be in a boot EPROM pair; these EPROMs will likely be located directly on your CPU board. The addresses you use in the program depend entirely on your CPU board decoding. If you built your CPU based on the hardware designs in the earlier chapters, then all you need do is provide the 68000 reset vectors in the first eight EPROM addresses and follow them with executable code. The reset PC should point to the physical address where the code begins. When you cross-assemble the boot code in Figure 14.17, include the ''DC'' assembler directives for the vectors at the beginning of the program. Allowing 8 bytes for these vectors, your executable code will actually begin at $FD4008.

After powering up the system, the 68000 will reset and begin executing the disk-boot code. The drive-activity light should begin flashing: this indicates that the disk controller is attempting to read the first track of the disk. If the light does not flash, then there is a problem somewhere in the system; it will be impossible to boot the DOS until the difficulty is resolved. Check that all the disk-controller jumpers, Interfacer-4 jumpers, and all addresses are set according to the CompuPro instructions that come with CP/M-68K. When the drive light flashes, insert the CP/M system disk into the drive: soon the CP/M system prompt will appear.

TABLE 14.5 STEPS INVOLVED IN BOOTING CP/M-68K WITHOUT TUTOR.

1. Install the proper boards as shown in Figure 14.16.
2. Set all the addresses according to Table 14.4.
3. Connect the system console to the Interfacer-4 console port.
4. Install an EPROM set with 68000 reset vectors plus the disk boot code given in Figure 14.17.
5. Power up the system. When the 68000 resets, it should begin executing the disk-boot code and cause the drive-activity light to flash.
6. Insert the CP/M-68K system disk into the drive. The CP/M prompt should appear shortly.

14.3.2 CP/M-68K Using TUTOR

The steps you follow in bringing up the DOS using TUTOR are shown in Table 14.6. TUTOR will provide the necessary vectors to initialize the 68000; it will begin operation with the console connected to the usual 6850 Port 1. It is essential that TUTOR perform properly with all the boards connected to the system as shown in Figure 14.16. If it does not run, then troubleshoot the system before going further. Once TUTOR runs, however, use the memory-test ''BT'' function in TUTOR to verify that RAM is good; use some of the other functions to convince yourself that TUTOR is running normally.

As configured in the author's system, TUTOR is located from $FD0000 to $FD3FFF; the next available address is $FD4000 where the boot code is located. TUTOR

```
A68K   1.9   11/08/82 -- Run on 03/08/86
                         *       Boot loader to read from Disk-1A for
                         *       CP/M-68K using 68000 board.
                         *       8/13/85

                         *       Locate just past S-bug Monitor code
FD4000                           ORG     $FD4000

     00FF00C0            DRIADR  EQU     $FF00C0         * In I/O space

     00FF00C0            FDCSTAT EQU     DRIADR          * FDC stat / dr select
     00FF00C1            FDATA   EQU     DRIADR+1        * Data in / out
     00FF00C2            DRSTAT  EQU     DRIADR+2        * Drive stat / DMA adr
     00FF00C3            MOTREG  EQU     DRIADR+3        * Motor register


     00000007            INTFLG  EQU     7
     0000C000            DELAY   EQU     $C000

                         BOOTER:
FD4000  41F9 00FF00C0            LEA     FDCSTAT,A0
FD4006  43F9 00FF00C1            LEA     FDATA,A1
FD400C  45F9 00FF00C2            LEA     DRSTAT,A2

FD4012  7807                     MOVEQ   #INTFLG,D4

FD4014  303C C000        LOOP:   MOVE    #DELAY,D0

FD4018  51C8 FFFE        TIMER1: DBF     D0,TIMER1

                         *  Set DMA address
FD401C  14BC 0000                MOVE.B  #0,(A2)
FD4020  14BC 0000                MOVE.B  #0,(A2)
FD4024  14BC 0000                MOVE.B  #0,(A2)

                         *  Do SPECIFY (3 bytes), RECALIBRATE (2 bytes)
FD4028  49F9 00FD40AE            LEA     CMD1,A4
FD402E  7204                     MOVEQ   #4,D1           * Sending 5 bytes
FD4030  0910             RDY:    BTST    D4,(A0)         * FDC ready?
FD4032  67FC                     BEQ.S   RDY
FD4034  129C                     MOVE.B  (A4)+,(A1)      * Send cmd bytes
FD4036  51C9 FFF8                DBF     D1,RDY

FD403A  0912             RDY1:   BTST    D4,(A2)         * Drive rdy?
FD403C  67FC                     BEQ     RDY1
FD403E  0910             RDY2:   BTST    D4,(A0)         * FDC rdy?
FD4040  67FC                     BEQ     RDY2

                         *  Do SENSE-INTERRUPT-STATUS (1 byte)
FD4042  129C                     MOVE.B  (A4)+,(A1)      * Next cmd in line

FD4044  303C C000                MOVE    #DELAY,D0
FD4048  51C8 FFFE        TIMER2: DBF     D0,TIMER2

FD404C  0910             RDY3:   BTST    D4,(A0)         * FDC rdy?
FD404E  67FC                     BEQ     RDY3
FD4050  1E11                     MOVE.B  (A1),D7         * Read Status Reg 0
```

Figure 14.17 The 68000 boot code used to read the first track of the CP/M-68K system disk. The Intel 8272 floppy-disk controller is used to read the disk.

```
FD4052  0910                RDY4:    BTST     D4,(A0)          * FDC rdy?
FD4054  67FC                         BEQ      RDY4
FD4056  1C11                         MOVE.B   (A1),D6          * Read Pres Cyl Number

FD4058  0407 0020                    SUB.B    #$20,D7          * d5=1 when seek done
FD405C  8E06                         OR.B     D6,D7
FD405E  66B4                         BNE.S    LOOP             * Waiting for disk

                            *  Do READ-DATA (9 bytes)
FD4060  7607                READIT:  MOVEQ    #7,D3
FD4062  49F9 00FD40B4                LEA      CMD2,A4
FD4068  7008                         MOVEQ    #8,D0            * Sending 9 bytes
FD406A  0910                RDY5:    BTST     D4,(A0)          * FDC rdy?
FD406C  67FC                         BEQ      RDY5
FD406E  129C                         MOVE.B   (A4)+,(A1)       * Send cmds
FD4070  51C8 FFF8                    DBF      D0,RDY5

FD4074  0912                RDY6:    BTST     D4,(A2)          * Drive rdy?
FD4076  67FC                         BEQ      RDY6
FD4078  0910                RDY7:    BTST     D4,(A0)          * FDC rdy?
FD407A  67FC                         BEQ      RDY7

FD407C  1E11                         MOVE.B   (A1),D7          * Read Status Reg 0
FD407E  0910                RDY8:    BTST     D4,(A0)
FD4080  67FC                         BEQ      RDY8
FD4082  1C11                         MOVE.B   (A1),D6          * Read Status Reg 1
FD4084  7004                         MOVEQ    #4,D0
FD4086  0910                RDY9:    BTST     D4,(A0)
FD4088  67FC                         BEQ      RDY9
FD408A  1A11                         MOVE.B   (A1),D5          * Read Status Reg 2
FD408C  51C8 FFF8                    DBF      D0,RDY9

FD4090  0207 00BF                    AND.B    #$BF,D7          * Reg 0
FD4094  0206 007F                    AND.B    #$7F,D6          * Reg 1
FD4098  8E06                         OR.B     D6,D7
FD409A  57CB FFC4                    DBEQ     D3,READIT

FD409E  6600 FF60                    BNE      BOOTER           * Around again

FD40A2  41F8 0000                    LEA      $00000000,A0     * 68000 at new code
FD40A6  4239 00FF00C3                CLR.B    MOTREG           * Disable boot rom &
                                                               *  turn motor off
FD40AC  4ED0                         JMP      (A0)

FD40AE  03 8F 22 07         CMD1:    DC.B     03,$8F,$22,07,00
        00
FD40B3  08                           DC.B     08
FD40B4  06 00 00 00         CMD2:    DC.B     06,00,00,00,01,00
        01 00
FD40BA  1A 07 80 00                  DC.B     $1A,07,$80,00

    0 Errors detected
                                     END      BOOTER
```

Figure 14.17 (Continued)

TABLE 14.6 STEPS INVOLVED IN BOOTING CP/M-68K USING TUTOR.

1.	Install the proper boards as shown in Figure 14.16.
2.	Set all the addresses according to Table 14.4.
3.	Connect the system console to the 6850 Port 1.
4.	Install the pair of boot EPROMs given in Figure 14.17.
5.	Power up the system; TUTOR should operate normally.
6.	Using TUTOR, check the operation of the overall system; RAM can be checked easily using the TUTOR "BT" function.
7.	If the boot EPROMs (Step 4) were not available, type in the Figure 14.17 program using TUTOR.
8.	Begin program execution by typing "GO FD4000"; this should cause the drive-activity light to flash.
9.	Reconnect the system console to the Interfacer-4 port.
10.	Insert the CP/M-68K system disk into the drive. The CP/M prompt should appear shortly.

may be programmed by itself into a pair of 2764s and a second pair of 2764s used for the boot code; an alternative is to put both TUTOR and the boot code together in a pair of 27128s. If the boot EPROMs are not used, TUTOR can be used to enter the program line by line into memory and then execute just as if it were in EPROM.

Using the code in Figure 14.17, the disk-read operation can be started by the command:

TUTOR 1.3> GO FD4000

When the program runs, the disk drive-activity light will flash on and off indicating that the controller is trying to read a disk. If the light does not flash, then there is a problem in the system that must be resolved before continuing. Assuming that the light is flashing, disconnect the console from the 6850 port and reconnect it to the Interfacer-4 console port. Next, insert the system disk into the drive. After reading the disk, the CP/M prompt should appear on the console screen.

14.4 SUMMARY

The main emphasis throughout all the previous chapters has been on hardware design and development. Software issues have generally been deferred until the hardware can run a monitor program such as TUTOR. The underlying thought has been to get TUTOR running as soon as possible, and then use it to help test the rest of the hardware as it gets designed into a completed system. After the hardware is fairly complete, however, TUTOR does not provide enough capability to fully utilize the 68000.

During the development of the system hardware, the TUTOR firmware can be used to display or modify the 68000 memory and registers. This is especially important during the early stages of the hardware design because each hardware module must be individually tested. TUTOR can also execute a program by either single-stepping or running continuously. This allows extensive hardware testing and debugging because scope-loop programs and other small test programs can be executed.

The TUTOR firmware, by itself with no modifications, is a valuable part of the system development. However, the TUTOR addresses might not match the system requirements and thus make it unusable unless some changes are made. The most important modification that can be made is to change the reset stack pointer and program counter vectors. These vectors, located at the beginning of the TUTOR EPROMs, can be changed to anyplace in the 16 Mb addressing range of the 68000. In a like manner, the ACIA addresses can be changed to match the needs of a particular system. The author's system, for example, decodes the TUTOR EPROM pair at $FD0000 and the ACIAs starting at $FF0040.

The TUTOR code is programmed into two separate EPROMs: one even and one odd. This is because the 68000 reads 16-bit words and the EPROMs are 8-bit devices. When the processor reads the EPROMs, it enables both of them simultaneously to get even-address and odd-address information on data lines D15-D8 and D7-D0, respectively. Consequently, when new EPROMs are programmed for modified system addresses, the code must be split into even and odd parts.

Using TUTOR is fairly simple, and the commands can be learned quickly by trial and error. Each command can be tested and the results checked by displaying the 68000 registers or the system memory. The 68000 programming language can also be learned by experimentation: the TUTOR one-line assembler provides immediate feedback about programming errors and the effect of each instruction on the state of the machine. There are also a number of functions available in TUTOR so that complex programs can be written using very little code.

The host-communication support provided by TUTOR makes it possible to save programs on another computer system. In fact, the 68000 system can be permanently connected to a host so that either computer can be used. To save programs, TUTOR can send the data to the host where the data is saved on a disk; then to recover the program at some later time, the host can download the code back to TUTOR. The upload/download sequence requires that both computer systems communicate at the same speed and respond to the same handshaking protocol.

The easiest way to write small programs is to use TUTOR; for large programs, however, an assembler on a host computer can provide features not available on TUTOR. The host computer may also use a 68000, but it is not required; its only real advantage is that programs can be tested before downloading. When the host uses something other than a 68000, a cross-assembler is used to generate 68000 code. These programs can be tested and debugged after downloading to the 68000 target computer.

The cross-assembler program on the host computer can generate either absolute or relocatable code. Absolute code is the binary 68000 program intended for execution at only one place in memory; it cannot be loaded into another place in memory without reassembly. Relocatable code, in contrast, can be put anywhere in memory by using a linking program after assembly; the program need not be reassembled for a new load address. Programs that are only several pages long can be easily reassembled, and an absolute assembler is quite satisfactory. Longer programs that are composed of several smaller program modules will benefit from using a relocatable assembler. This is especially true when many common program modules are available in libraries and can be linked into a program as needed.

If you designed your 68000 board to IEEE Std-696 along the lines of the author's board described in the Appendix, then you can bring up the CP/M-68K disk operating system. Rather than spend substantial time modifying the DOS to a new 68000 system, CP/M-68K can be purchased already configured to run on the CompuPro CPU-68K 68000 board. Thus, bringing up the DOS becomes a matter of simply using the CompuPro I/O board and disk-controller board along with your new 68000 CPU. The new 68000 board only needs to address 128K of RAM starting at 0 and to be able to run I/O bus cycles at addresses $FF0000 to $FFFFFF.

Assuming that your 68000 board meets the IEEE Standard, and can handle the proper addresses, then CP/M-68K can be booted either with or without TUTOR. If TUTOR is not available, a pair of boot EPROMs can be prepared that will cause the 68000 to read the first track of the system disk. If TUTOR is available though, the overall system can be checked out easily before booting the DOS. After checking the system, the disk-boot code can be entered interactively and run. Once the boot code is known to work, it can be programmed into an EPROM pair and invoked by TUTOR to bring up the DOS.

EXERCISES

1. Describe the approach to hardware development used in the preceding chapters. Compare this approach to software development and programming.
2. Describe what tasks TUTOR can handle. Of all that it can do, what features do you consider absolutely necessary? Is TUTOR itself necessary at all?
3. Describe how to relocate the TUTOR EPROM pair.
4. Suppose you want to put TUTOR at $080000 and the 6850 ACIAs at $090000. What bytes must be programmed into each of the TUTOR EPROMs?
5. Sketch the cable connections between a 68000 system running TUTOR and a host you plan to use for program development.
6. Make two tables like Tables 14.2 and 14.3 for your system. Describe potential difficulties you might have transferring code.
7. Obtain a cross-assembler for your host system. Write a program like Figure 14.10 and compare its object code with yours. Are the S-records the same? Explain any differences.
8. If your cross-assembler can generate relocatable code, convert your program from Exercise 7 into modules along the lines of Figure 14.11. Assemble and link the code; compare results.
9. Why would you want a disk-operating system on your 68000?
10. Describe how to boot CP/M-68K on your own 68000 system.

FURTHER READING

ANDREWS, MICHAEL. *Self Guided Tour Through the 68000*. Reston, VA: Reston Publishing Co., Inc., 1984.

BACON, JEAN, *The Motorola 68000*. Englewood Cliffs, NJ: Prentice-Hall, Inc., 1986. (QA 76.8.M6895)

BRANDLY, GORDON. "Tiny Basic for the 68000." *Dr. Dobb's Journal* (February 1985): 42–46.

CARTER, EDWARD M., and A. B. BONDS. "The VU68K Single-Board Computer." *Byte* (January 1984): 403–16.

HARMAN, THOMAS L., and BARBARA LAWSON. *The Motorola MC68000 Microprocessor Family: Assembly Language, Interface Design, and System Design*. Englewood Cliffs, NJ: Prentice-Hall, 1985. (QA 76.8.M6895H37)

KANE, GERRY. *68000 Microprocessor Handbook*. Berkeley, CA: Osborne/McGraw-Hill, 1981.

KANE, GERRY, DOUG HAWKINS, and LANCE LEVENTHAL. *68000 Assembly Language Programming*. Berkeley, CA: Osborne/McGraw-Hill, 1981.

KELLY-BOOTLE, STAN and BOB FOWLER, *68000, 68010 and 68020 Primer*. Indianapolis, IN: Howard W. Sams & Co., 1985.

KING, TIM, and BRIAN KNIGHT. *Programming the M68000*. Reading, MA: Addison-Wesley Publishing Co., 1983.

Mc68000 Educational Computer Board User's Manual, MEX68KECB/D2. 2nd Ed. Tempe, AZ: Motorola Literature Distribution Center, 1982.

ROBINSON, PHILLIP R. *Mastering the 68000 Microprocessor*. Blue Ridge Summit, PA: Tab Books, Inc., 1985. (QA76.8.M6895R63)

SCANLON, LEO J. *The 68000: Principles and Programming*. Indianapolis, IN: Howard W. Sams & Co., 1981.

TRIEBEL, WALTER A., and AVTAR SINGH. *The 68000 Microprocessor—Architecture, Software, and Interfacing Techniques*. Englewood Cliffs, NJ: Prentice-Hall, 1986. (QA76.8.M67T75)

WILCOX, ALAN D. "Using and Modifying the 68000 TUTOR Firmware." *Computer Smyth* (July 1986):17–20.

WILLIAMS, STEVE. *Programming the 68000*. Berkeley, CA: Sybex, Inc., 1985.

APPENDIX A

Standards for Schematic Diagrams

A.1 PAPER

Use the same size paper for all the schematics related to the documentation for a single project. Use either

"A" size, 8 ½ × 11 inches, or

"B" size, 11 × 17 inches.

The paper should have zonal coordinates along the borders so that each sector of the drawing can be located in much the same manner as on a roadmap. For example, you might refer to location "A1" in the lower right of the sheet or perhaps location "B2," which is up and to the left of A1.

The paper should be lightly lined with 10 × 10 squares to the inch to assist in drawing. It should not be necessary to use anything more than a straight-edge and a logic-symbol template to do an acceptable drawing.

Put a title block in the lower-right corner of the drawing. Minimum information in the block should be:

Title of the circuit,

Drawing and sheet number,

Revision level of drawing,

Name of draftsman or designer and date.

Use a pencil for all drawings. A dry cleaning pad is helpful to keep the drawing from smudging.

A.2 DIGITAL-LOGIC DRAWING CONVENTIONS

A.2.1

Label all integrated circuits and LSI devices with ''U'' numbers written inside the symbol for the device. For example, write U2 inside the symbol for one of your logic gates. If there are multiple gates within a single IC, append an a, b, c, etc. to the U number. Put the part number of the device above the symbol for quick part identification. Write the circuit pin numbers outside the symbol. Example:

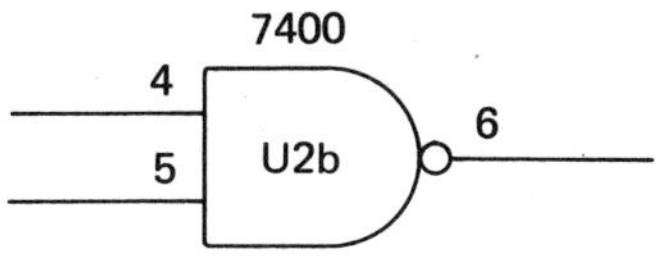

A.2.2

Use mixed-logic symbols to represent the logical functions in the circuit. A NAND gate is identical to an INVERT-OR, and a NOR gate is the same as an INVERT-AND. Use the symbol that indicates how the circuit is intended to perform. Examples:

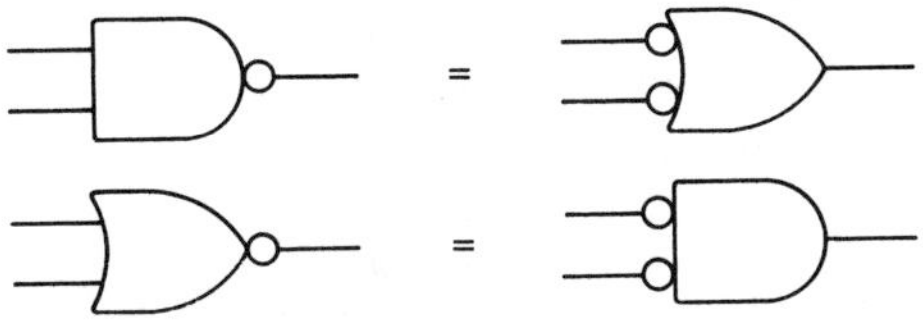

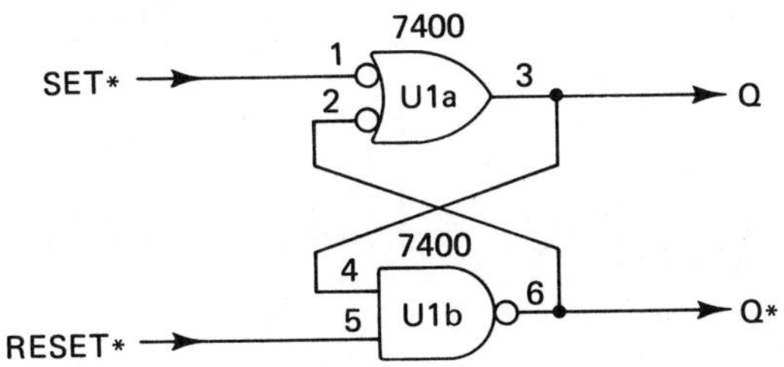

A.2.3

Draw all schematics with the flow of data running left to right or top to bottom. Indicate circuit inputs on left or top and outputs on right or bottom. Show the direction of signals with arrows.

A.2.4

Put function labels *inside* the symbol for logic devices. For example, if a device has inputs A, B, and ENABLE, then show those labels inside the symbol. Example:

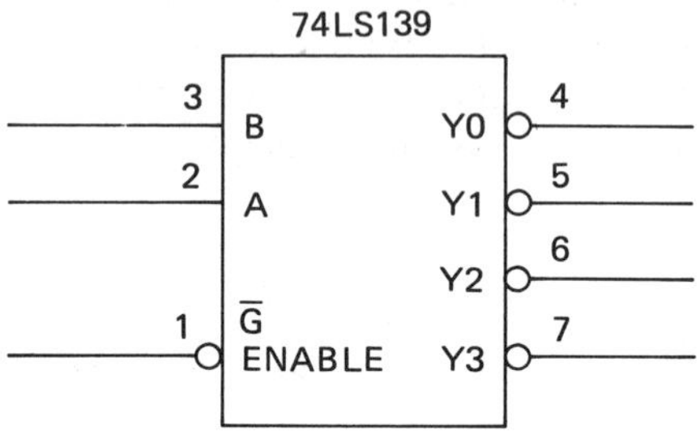

A.2.5

Put bubbles at inputs and outputs as indicated on manufacturer data sheets. For example, if an output is understood to be low when asserted, then a bubble will be indicated at the output; see 74LS139 outputs in A.2.4.

If the manufacturer indicates a function label with an overbar (negative logic), indicate the asserted-low nature of the input or output line by appending a "star." Example:

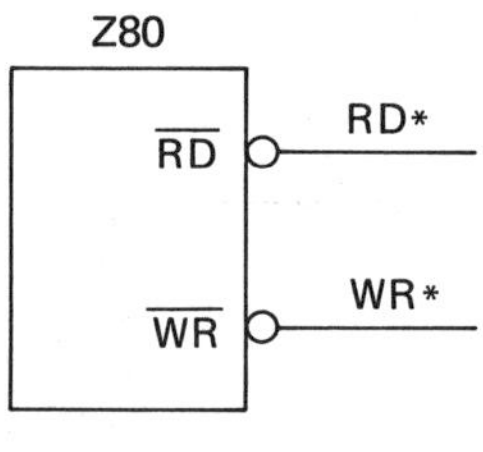

A.2.6

Provide page-to-page connections by using the zonal coordinates of the source signal and the destination. Indicate the name of the signal line on both ends and show the "to" and "from" coordinates. The example below shows a signal named RAS* leaving sheet 1 at location A1 and going to sheet 3 location B2. Be sure to draw arrows indicating the direction of the signals.

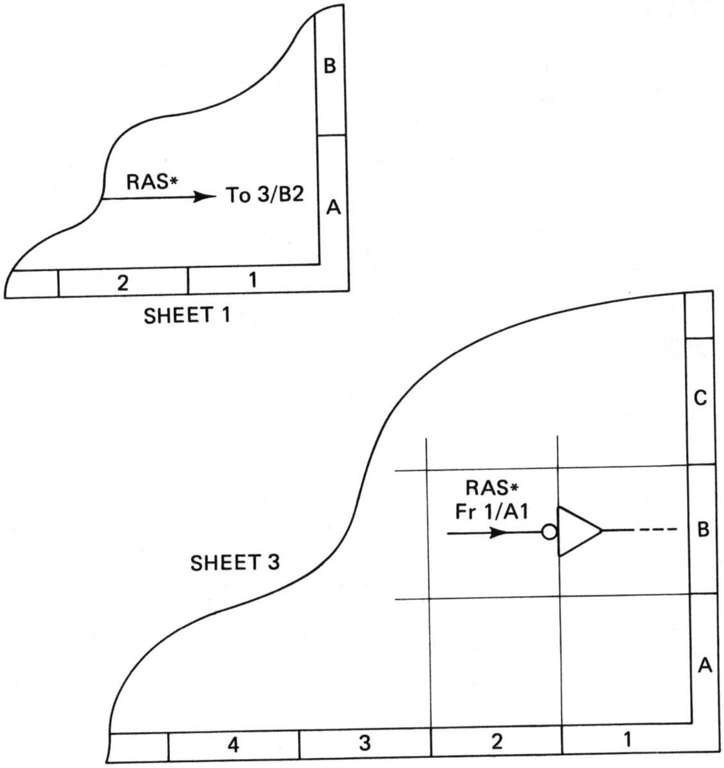

A.2.7

Draw any unused spare gates at the corner of the schematic. Tie all TTL inputs high with a 1K resistor. Example:

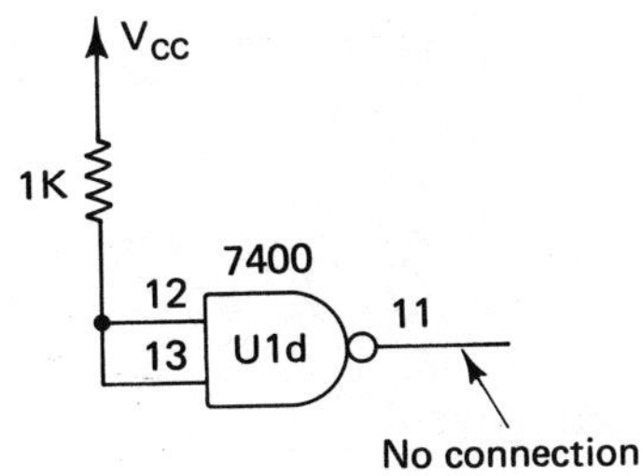

A.2.8

Provide a power table with the schematic diagram to account for power and grounds to all devices. Example:

Part	*Type*	*Ground*	*+Vcc*
U1	7400	7	14
U2	7404	7	14
U3	74LS139	8	16

A.2.9

Draw crossing wires as shown below:

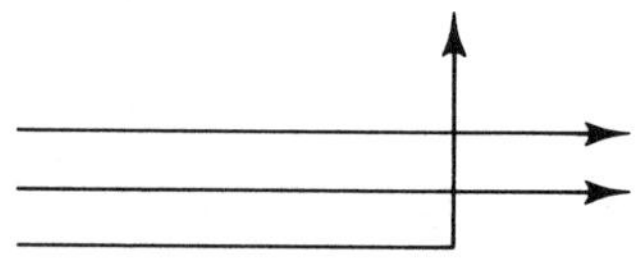

When several wires connect to a common line, connect with a dot and draw the connections slightly offset so they are not mistaken for crossing wires. Example:

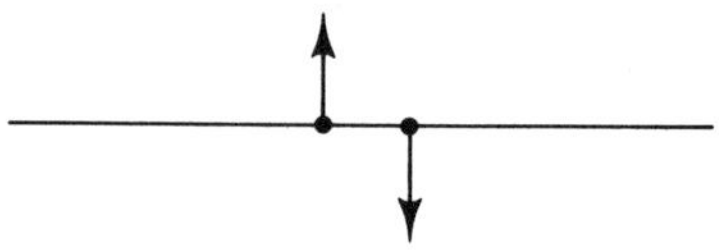

A.2.10

Draw multiwire buses as a heavy line with a slash across it and a number to indicate the wire count. Show the signal name for any wires breaking from the bus. Example:

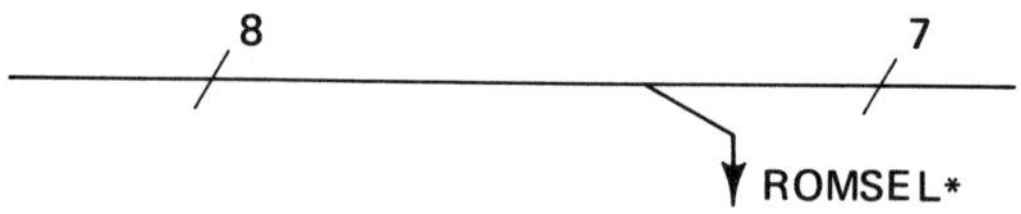

A.2.11

Draw grounds with the symbol: ⏚

Show connection to +5 V supply:

Indicate pullup resistors either as shown in A.2.7 or use the symbol: △

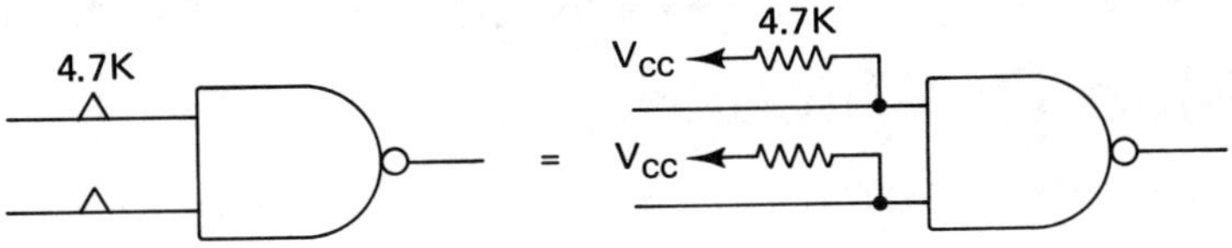

A.3 TYPICAL DRAWING

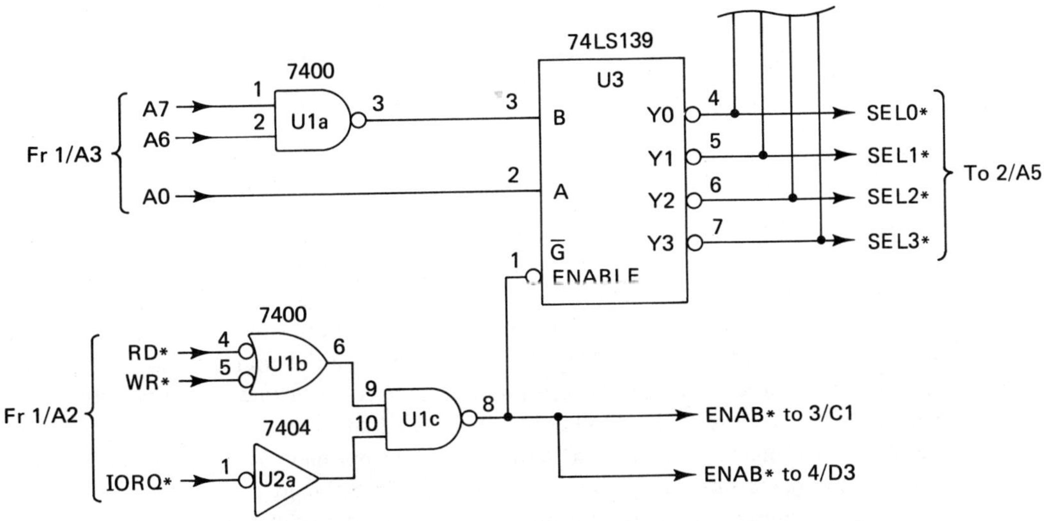

APPENDIX B

Temperature Monitor Technical Manual: Hot-Spot Oil Company

Alan D. Wilcox

March 1987

INTRODUCTION

The purpose of the temperature monitor is to measure and record outside air temperature every hour each day and then calculate heating degree-days over a 24-hour period.

During the heating season it is necessary to know how cold the weather has been each day so that timely oil deliveries can be made. Deliveries made too frequently result in extra driver time and truck mileage as well as extra administrative billing costs. On the other hand, a late delivery can result in delivery driver overtime and in possible loss of customers. If the heating degree-days can be totaled since the last oil delivery, then it is possible to estimate when the next delivery should be made. The temperature monitor provides the basic information needed to make this estimate.

The temperature monitor is a small self-contained unit that can be placed on a desk or other convenient location in the office. A single wire with a temperature sensor on the end is put outside and connected to the monitor. The monitor runs on standard house current, but has an internal battery to retain data in case of power failure. The temperature and degree-days are displayed on the front panel; the time and latest 24-hour cumulative degree-days are printed each hour on a paper tape in the unit.

After setting up the monitor, the paper tape can be checked each morning to see how many heating degree-days were needed during the last 24 hours. This reading can be added to the total degree-days accumulated for each customer since fillup. When the customer total reaches a certain threshold, say 1100 degree-days, it is time to make an oil delivery to that customer.

INSTALLATION

As shown in Figure B-1, place the temperature monitor in a convenient location where it will be used during normal daily operation. Plug the power cord into a wall socket.

Install the temperature sensor outside in a shaded spot and run the wire into the building to the monitor. Attach it to the connector on the rear of the unit.

Press the button marked "test" on the front panel. The monitor will check itself and the sensor you just connected. It will display "OK" in several seconds at the end of the test and you can begin normal operation. If you do not get the "OK" display, refer to the Troubleshooting section in this manual.

OPERATION

To begin operation, push the "start" button on the front panel. You will see a display of the present outside temperature. No data will be recorded on the paper tape until after an hour has elapsed. The correct present outside temperature will be displayed continuously.

To set the time, push the "set time" button on the front panel. Press four numbers on the keyboard for the correct time. All time is maintained in 24-hour format; that is, 1 PM is 1300, 11 PM is 2300, etc. Example entries:

Time is →	7:00 A.M.	Press →	0700
	11:35 A.M.		1135
	8:40 P.M.		2040

To set the time at which the data logging is done, press the "start log" button on the front panel. This should be done on the hour if you want your time and degree-day prints recorded on the hour. If you prefer the prints recorded hourly on the half-hour, then press the "start log" button when the time is half-past the hour.

Note that the first day's reading of degree-days will not be correct until 24 hours have past. After that, the display always shows the correct heating degree-days regardless of when the data log is printed. Every hourly printout will correctly represent the degree-days during the most recent 24 hours.

CIRCUIT DESCRIPTION

The temperature monitor measures the current temperature and continuously displays the temperature and the latest 24-hour heating degree-day summary. Every hour the time and degree-days are printed on a paper tape in the unit. The monitor uses a microcomputer to perform the control of the system and do the various calculations.

The temperature monitor is composed of a number of subsystems as shown in Figure B-2. The temperature sensor is connected to the analog-to-digital (A/D) converter; the output of the A/D converter is interfaced to the microcomputer itself. The operation of the keypad, display, and paper-tape printer are all controlled by the microcomputer.

The temperature sensor, the analog circuits, and the digital interface control for the A/D are shown in the schematic diagram of the unit.

SOFTWARE DESCRIPTION

The temperature monitor software is contained in permanent memory in the microcomputer section. The programs handle all the operations necessary to initialize the unit, to test for proper performance, to set the time, to set the logging time, to read and display temperature, to calculate and display heating degree-days, and to print temperature and degree-days.

The software functions are shown in the structure chart in Figure B-3. The temperature monitor software is divided into four main modules: SELF-TEST, SET-TIME, SET-LOG-TIME, and RUN. When the computer is first turned on, the SELF-TEST code should be executed to verify the system operation and to initialize data memory. The SET-TIME module is used to set the system internal time clock. The SET-LOG-TIME module is used to set when each hour the temperature data is printed on the paper tape. The last module, RUN, is used to control the normal system operation.

When the RUN module is executed, the outside temperature is read once each second, averaged over the last 16 seconds, and the average saved in memory. Each hour all these averages are averaged again and used to calculate the hourly degree-days using the formula "degree-days = 65 − average hourly temperature." The most recent hourly degree-days are saved in memory and averaged together to display and record on the paper tape.

TROUBLESHOOTING

The temperature monitor has an internal self-test feature that will indicate the possible cause of various problems. To use, press the "test" button on the front panel; the display will either indicate "OK" if the system is ready or indicate an error number if there is a problem. Some of the symptoms and their causes are listed in the chart below:

Condition	*Possible Cause/Defect*
Nothing happens at turn-on	Not plugged in Fuse blown Power supply
Fuse blows when plugged in	Short in power supply
Display shows random digits at turn-on	Microprocessor Main memory

Condition	Possible Cause/Defect
When "test" button pressed, the display shows . . .	
blank or random digits	Microprocessor Main memory
01 (Memory error)	Data memory
02 (No temperature)	Temperature sensor Analog amplifier A/D converter
03 (Printer)	Printer out of paper

REFERENCES

This manual contains the technical information on the temperature monitor analog and interface circuits. The circuit diagram and parts layouts for both of these subsystems are provided in the appendix to this manual. Information on the microcomputer subsystem and the computer program listings are not provided; they may be obtained from the factory on special order.

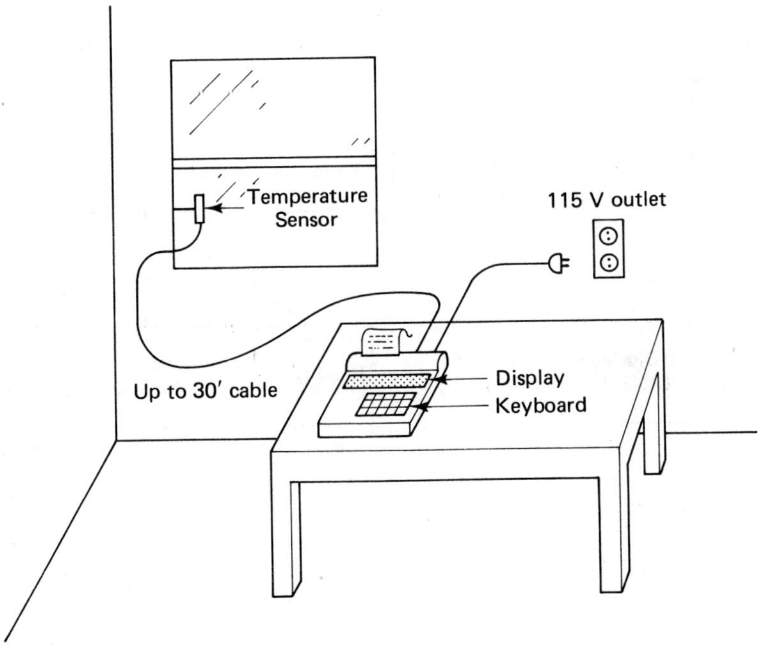

Figure B-1 Temperature monitor setup for normal operation.

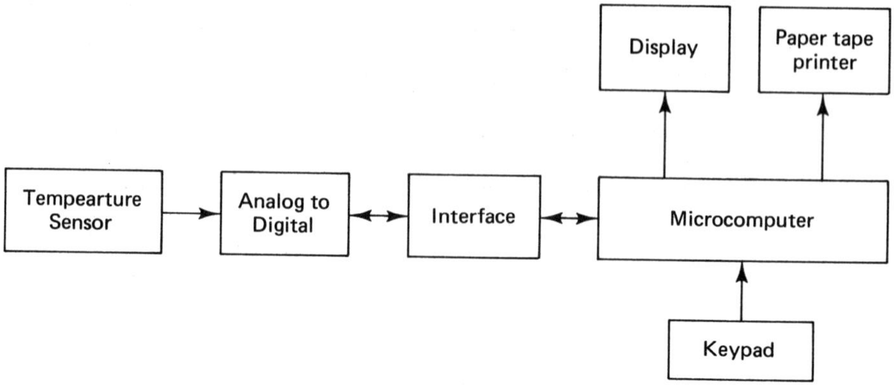

Figure B-2 Block diagram of temperature monitor.

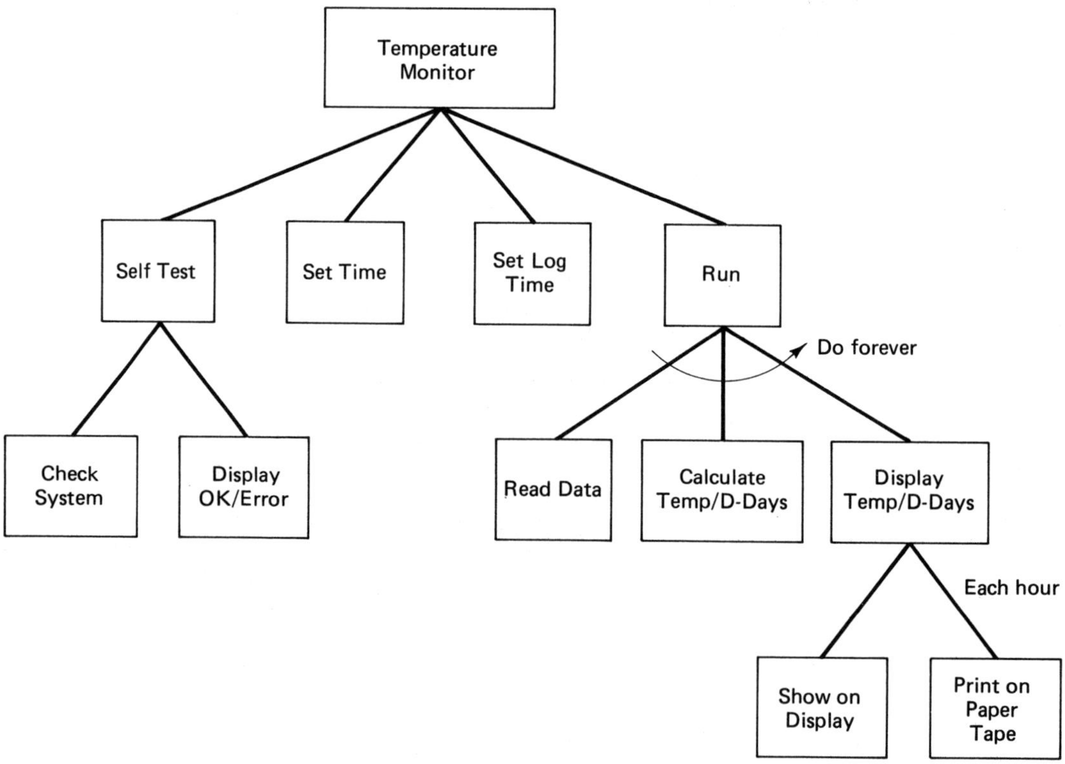

Figure B-3 Temperature monitor system-software structure chart.

SPECIFICATIONS—TEMPERATURE MONITOR

Measures and displays temperature over range −40 to +120°F
Temperature accuracy within 1°F
Displays most recent 24-hour degree-days over the range 0 to 99
Printout on paper tape:
  time each hour
  most-recent 24-hour degree days
Power supply: 115 Vac with backup battery for 3 days' data retention
Display: 6 digit, 0.5″ red LEDs
Keyboard: 36 keys
Printer: Thermal, 5 × 7 matrix characters, prints 20 characters/line
Size: 17″ wide, 10″ deep, 2″ high
Weight: 3 lbs.

WILCOX Engineering		LEWISBURG, PENNSYLVANIA 17837
REVISIONS	TITLE Temperature Monitor	
DRAWN	CHECKED	SCALE	DRAWING NO 1 of 3
APPROVED		

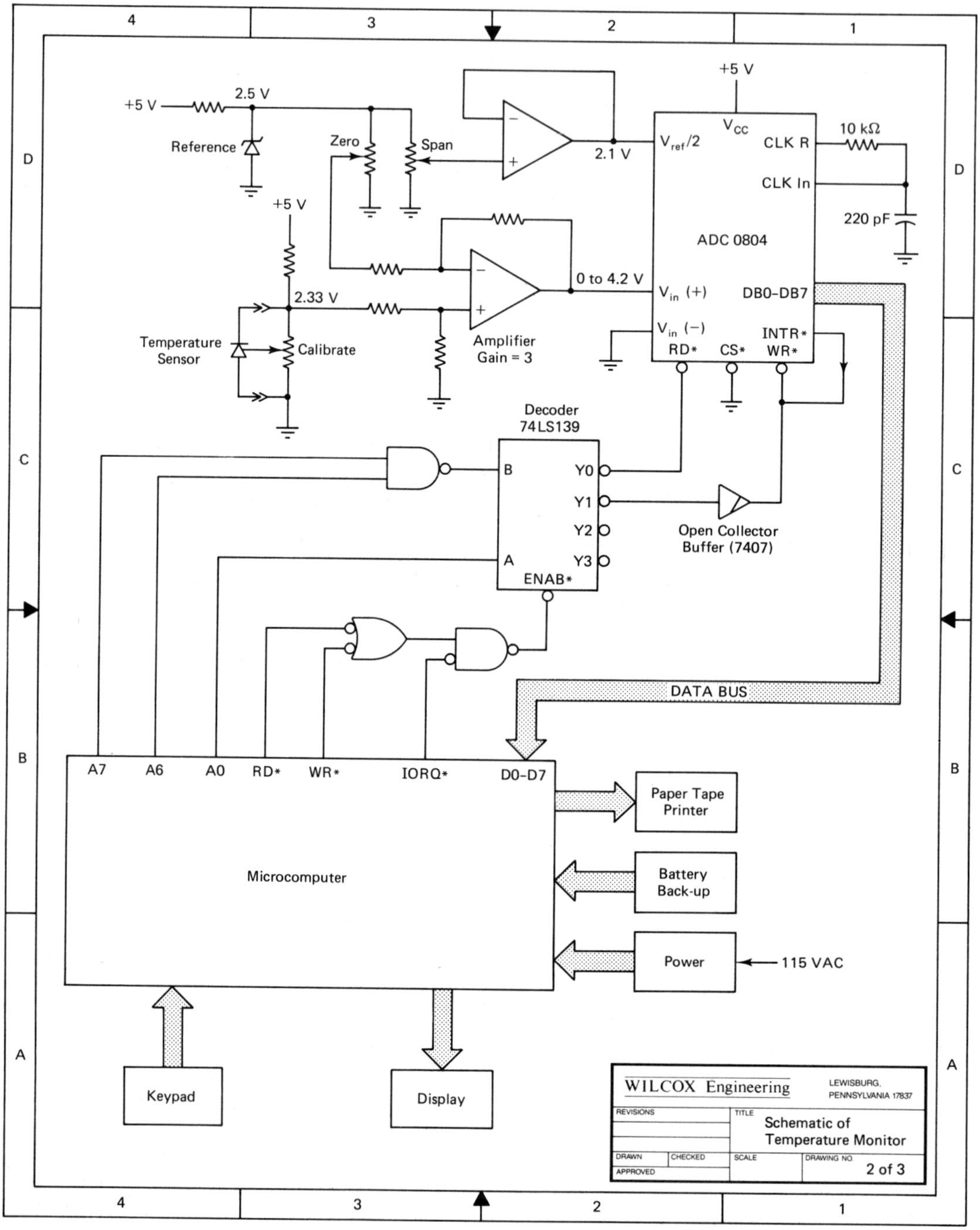
+5 V
2.5 V
Reference
Zero
Span
+5 V
2.1 V
$V_{ref}/2$
V_{CC}
CLK R
10 kΩ
CLK In
220 pF
ADC 0804
+5 V
2.33 V
0 to 4.2 V
V_{in} (+)
DB0–DB7
V_{in} (−)
INTR*
RD*
CS*
WR*
Temperature Sensor
Calibrate
Amplifier Gain = 3
Decoder 74LS139
B
Y0
Y1
Y2
A
Y3
ENAB*
Open Collector Buffer (7407)
DATA BUS
A7
A6
A0
RD*
WR*
IORQ*
D0–D7
Microcomputer
Paper Tape Printer
Battery Back-up
Power
115 VAC
Keypad
Display
WILCOX Engineering
LEWISBURG, PENNSYLVANIA 17837
REVISIONS
TITLE
Schematic of Temperature Monitor
DRAWN
CHECKED
SCALE
DRAWING NO.
2 of 3
APPROVED

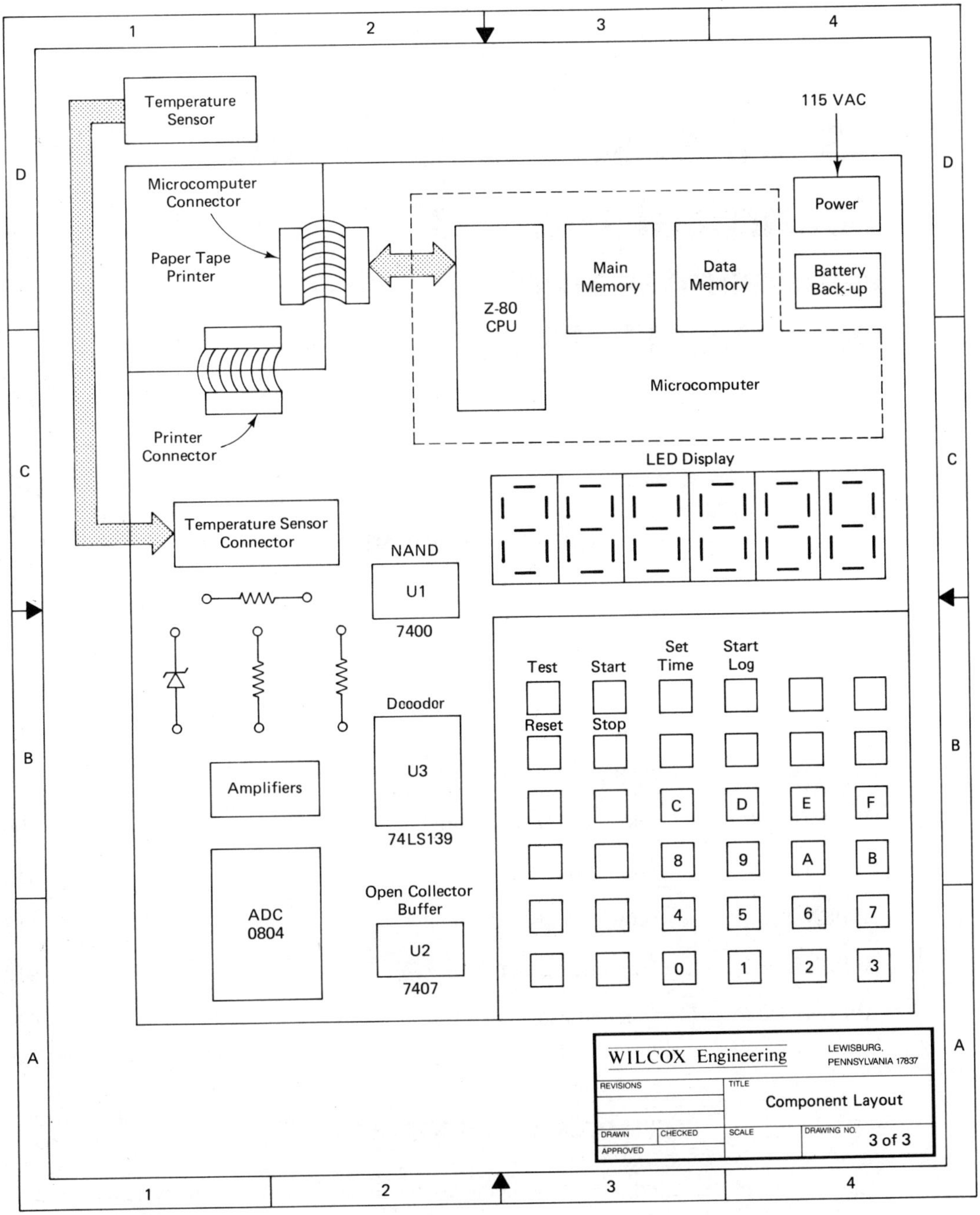
1
2
3
4
D
C
B
A
Temperature Sensor
115 VAC
Microcomputer Connector
Paper Tape Printer
Power
Battery Back-up
Z-80 CPU
Main Memory
Data Memory
Microcomputer
Printer Connector
LED Display
Temperature Sensor Connector
NAND
U1
7400
Test
Start
Set Time
Start Log
Reset
Stop
Dcoodor
U3
74LS139
Amplifiers
C
D
E
F
8
9
A
B
4
5
6
7
0
1
2
3
ADC 0804
Open Collector Buffer
U2
7407
WILCOX Engineering
LEWISBURG, PENNSYLVANIA 17837
REVISIONS
TITLE
Component Layout
DRAWN
CHECKED
SCALE
DRAWING NO.
3 of 3
APPROVED

APPENDIX C

68000-Based CPU Board Technical Manual

Kanwalinder Singh

December 16, 1986

TABLE OF CONTENTS

CHAPTER 1 INTRODUCTION

The purpose of the KS68 is to provide the user with an introducti on to systems based on the Motorola 68000 family of microprocessors. Located on a single protoboard, a complete microprocessor system is provided, including an MC68000 16- bit microprocessor, memory, and a serial communication I/O, besides on-board troubleshooting aids. The user has to connect an RS-232C compatible "dumb" terminal and the power supplies to have a functional system.

For easy use, the board has a resident firmware package that provides a self-contained programming and operating environment. The firmware provides the user with monitor/debug, assembly/disassembly, program entry, and I/O control functions. Utilizing the capabilities provided by the system, the user can investigate and learn the computing power and the architectural features of the 68000. Being a working example of the 68000 external bus structure and interface to memory and peripherals, the KS68 also provides the user with a reference for similar design and/or expansion.

The KS68 features include:

a. 4 MHz (MC68000) 16-bit MPU.
b. Clock speed—8 MHz (max.)
c. 4K bytes of static RAM (6116) arranged as 2K × 16.
d. 16K bytes firmware EPROM (27128) arranged as 8K × 16.
e. 4K bytes of user EPROM (2716) arranged as 2K × 16.
f. One serial, RS-232C compatible, baud rate selectable communication port provided for a terminal.
g. Self-contained operating firmware that provides monitor, debug, and disassembly/assembly functions.
h. RESET and SINGLE-STEP function switches.

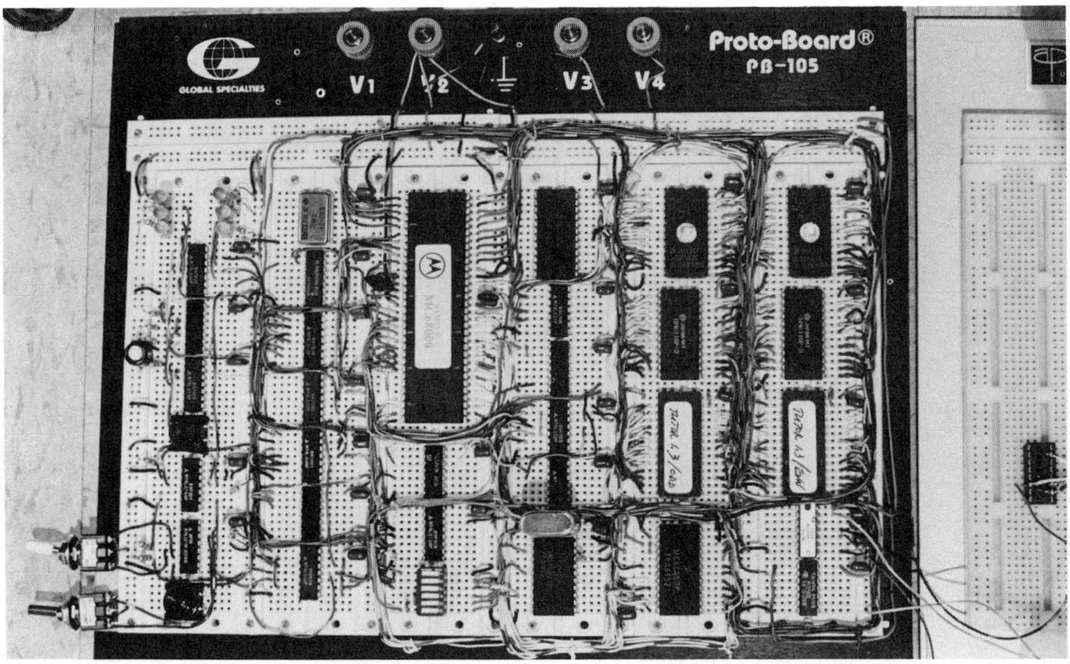

SPECIFICATIONS

Microprocessor	MC68000
Input/output	One serial, RS-232C compatible, baud rate selectable (300, 1200, and 9600 baud) communication port provided for a terminal.
System clock	4 MHz
Memory	4 Kb RAM arranged as 2K × 16, accessible on a byte or word basis. 4Kb EPROM arranged as 2K × 16, accessible on byte or word basis.
Software	16 Kb TUTOR provides monitor, debug, assembly/ disassembly, program entry, and I/O control functions.
Waits	Jumper selectable 0 to 7 waits on all memory operations.
Reset	Boot-up circuitry selects the TUTOR EPROM during the first eight bus cycles, after reset or on power-up, providing the 68000 with the stack pointer and the program counter. During normal operation, RAM is available in lower memory.
Displays	Individual LEDs indicate: 68000 halted condition, freerun, DTACK* status, RAM chip enable, and TUTOR EPROM chip enable.
Control	Switches are provided to single-step the 68000 by delaying DTACK*; all bus signals remain valid and can be easily checked during troubleshooting.
Power requirements (typical)	+5.0 V/750 mA, +12 V/50 mA, −12 V/50 mA.
Operating temp.	0 to 50°C.
Board dimensions	9.2″ × 11.4″ × 1.5″ (L × W × H).

CHAPTER 2 INSTALLATION AND POWER-UP INSTRUCTIONS

2.1 Preparing the Board for Use

Figure 2.1 shows the layout of the KS68. Board preparation involves the following steps:

a. Make the power connections by connecting V2(+5V), V3(+12V), V4(−12V), and GND(GND).
b. Set the single-step switch (SW6) to RUN.
c. Check that jumpers J1 and J2 are in place.
d. Set switches SW2, SW3, and SW4 to OFF.
e. Select communication baud rate using SW7(9600), SW8(1200), or SW9(300).

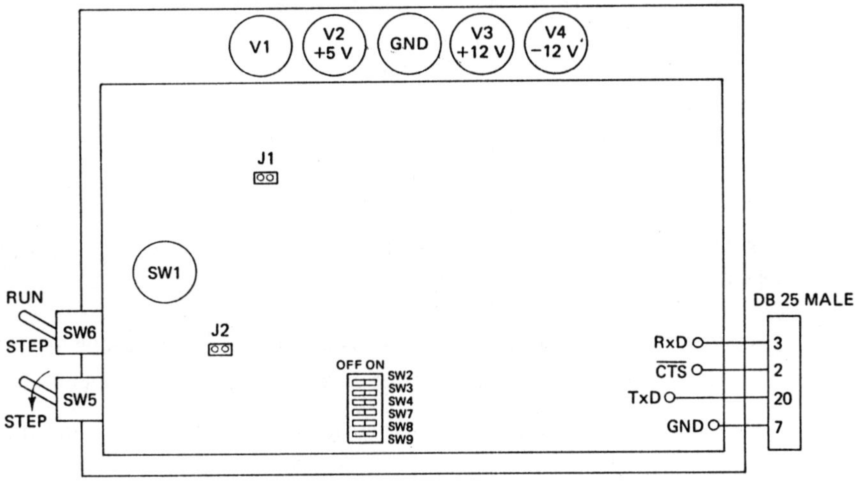

Figure 2.1 KS68 board layout.

2.2 System Hook-Up Instructions

Connect the board to the terminal via the connector provided as shown in Figure 2.2. Check that the terminal and the board are set to the same baud rate.

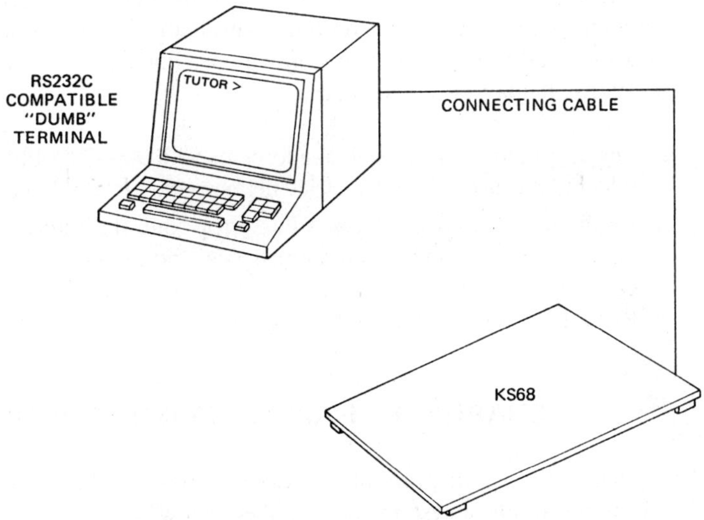

Figure 2.2 System hookup.

2.3 System Turn-On and Initial Operation

a. Be sure all voltages are connected to the board prior to power-up.
b. Turn the power ON.

On power-up, the system should initialize itself and print on the terminal:

TUTOR 1.3>

It is now ready for operation under the control of the firmware. If this response does not appear, perform the following system checks:

a. Press the reset switch (SW1) to ensure that the board has been initialized properly.
b. Check that the terminal and the board are set for the same baud rates.

If the baud rates are set properly and terminal is still not responding properly, the board may require some detailed system checks. Refer to Chapter 5 for details.

CHAPTER 3 OPERATING INSTRUCTIONS

3.1 System Operation

After system initialization or return of control to TUTOR, the terminal will print

TUTOR 1.3 >

and wait for a response.

The user can call any of the commands supported by the firmware. (Refer to Chapters 3, 4, and 5 of MC68000 Educational Computer Board User's Manual for detailed information.) A standard input routine controls the system while the user types a line of input. Command processing begins only after a line has been entered, followed by a carriage return. It may be noted that:

a. The user memory is located at addresses \$000900–\$000FFF. When first learning the system, the user should restrict his activities to this area of the memory map.
b. As the board does not have a bus error control circuit, if a command causes the system to access an unused address (i.e., no memory or peripheral devices are located at that address), the system will just "hang" and do nothing. Press the RESET switch to recover from such a situation.

CHAPTER 4 HARDWARE DESCRIPTION

The functional block diagram of the KS68 is shown in Figure 4.1. The various modules that form the complete system are described below. Before proceeding further, the user is

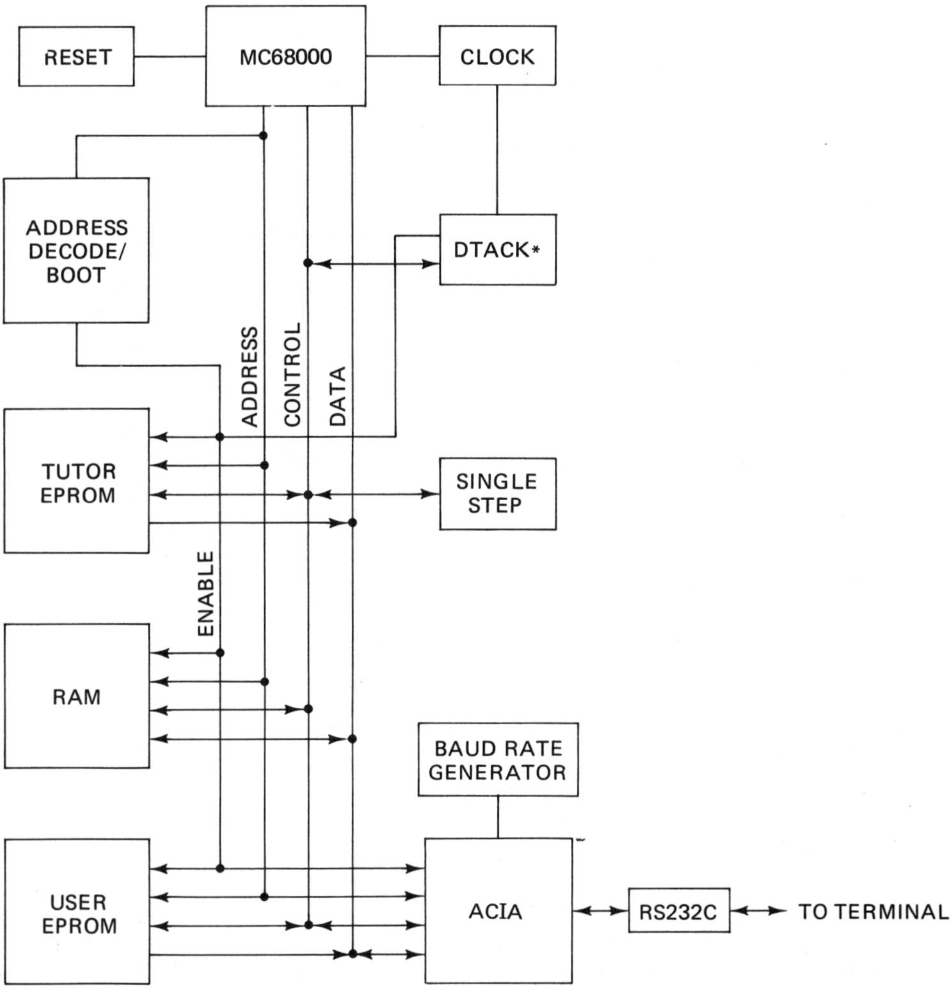

Figure 4.1 Functional block diagram.

advised to go through the 68000 signal and bus operation description given in Section 4 of MC68000 Information Manual.

4.1 Test Module

Reference: Drawing number S-02.

This module monitors the state of some important signals on the board, as shown in Table 4.1.

TABLE 4.1 TEST MODULE CONFIGURATION.

LED #	*Signal name*	*Signal description*	*State when LED will glow*
1.	HALT*	Halt line	Low
2.	A20	Address bit 20	High
3.	DTACK*	Data transfer acknowledge	Low
4.	CETR*	TUTOR EPROM chip enable	Low
5.	CER*	RAM chip enable	Low

4.2 Clock Module

Reference: Drawing number S-03.
This module provides the 68000 clock (CLK68) and an inverted clock (SYSCLK) with a typical skew of 0.5 ns. Both the outputs sink 32 mA (2 × 16 mA) and source 1.6 mA (2 × 0.8 mA).

4.3 Reset Module

Reference: Drawing number S-04.
This module keeps the RESET* and HALT* asserted for about 300 ms, both on power-up and on switch reset. Pressing the RESET switch (SW1) causes all processes to terminate, resets the MC68000 processor and restarts the TUTOR firmware. Pressing this switch should be the appropriate action if all else fails.

4.4 Freerun Module

Reference: Drawing number S-05.
The MC68000 can be made to freerun at any stage by plugging in the 24-pin headers (provided with the board) into the TEST EPROM sockets, by disabling J1 and by putting switches SW2 and SW3 to ON. A steadily blinking LED2 will indicate proper freerun.

4.5 DTACK* Module

Reference: Drawing number S-06.
This module returns DTACK* to the 68000 every time it performs a data operation on the board's memory devices. The module is set up to return DTACK* before the falling edge of state 4 (0 waits) but it can be configured to provide up to 7 waits using jumper J2.

4.6 Address Decode/Boot Module

Reference: Drawing numbers S-07 and S-09.
The memory map of the KS68 is shown in Table 4.2. The RAM is addressed at the bottom of the map ($000000–$000FFF) except during the initialization sequence when the

TABLE 4.2 MEMORY MAP.

Function			Address
System memory	Exception vector table	EPROM	\$000000–\$000007(*)
		RAM	\$000000–\$0003FF
	TUTOR scratchpad	RAM	\$000400–\$0008FF
User memory		RAM	\$000900–\$000FFF
Not used(**)			\$001000–\$007FFF
TUTOR firmware		EPROM	\$008000–\$00BFFF
User memory		EPROM	\$00C000–\$00CFFF
Not used(**)			\$00D000–\$00FFFF
I/O		ACIA	\$010040&\$010042
	Redundant mapping		↓ \$01FFFF
Not used(**)			\$020000–\$07FFFF
Not used(***)			\$080000–\$FFFFFF

* Only during the initialization sequence.
** Decoded on the board—available for future expansion.
***Not decoded on the board.

TUTOR EPROM is decoded at locations \$000000–\$000007. The RAM is divided into two areas: addresses \$000000–\$0008FF are the system area reserved for use by the system firmware, and addresses \$000900–\$000FFF are the user area. Within the system area, addresses \$000000–\$0003FF are used for the MC68000 exception vector table. The remaining 1,280 bytes (addresses \$000400–\$0008FF) are used as scratchpad memory by the TUTOR firmware for data buffers, pointers, temporary storage, etc.

The firmware EPROM is located at addresses \$008000–\$00BFFF. Moreover, a user EPROM is provided at addresses \$00C000–\$00CFFF to hold user-generated code.

The 6850 ACIA is mapped at addresses \$010040 and \$010042. An additional ACIA for a host can be put at addresses \$010041 and \$010043. The ACIA address decode is redundant within the page \$01XXXX. The ACIA can be accessed any time address line A6 = 1 within this page.

Additional areas, as shown in Table 4.2, are decoded on the board for future expansion.

4.7 RAM Module

Reference: Drawing number S-11.

This consists of two 6116 static RAMs arranged as 2K × 16. These can be accessed either on a byte or word basis, using asynchronous data transfer.

4.8 TUTOR EPROM Module

Reference: Drawing number S-12.

The system firmware (TUTOR) is stored in two 27128 EPROMs, half of which are empty. The system EPROM can be read on a byte or word basis. Attempting to write into the EPROM will result in a bus timeout error.

4.9 User EPROM Module

Reference: Drawing number S-08.

The user-generated code can be stored in two 2716 EPROMs provided on the board. These EPROMs are also used for on-board troubleshooting. The user EPROMs can also be read on a byte or word basis.

4.10 Single-Step Module

Reference: Drawing number S-10.

The MC68000 can be stepped through the program space one bus cycle at a time by putting the single-step switch SW6 in the STEP position. The 68000 executes a bus cycle every time SW5 is toggled. This circuit is very useful for on-board troubleshooting.

4.11 I/O Module

Reference: Drawing number S-13.

A single 6850 ACIA connected to the data bits D08-D15 provides serial communication (with handshake) with an RS-232C compatible terminal. The 68000 accesses the ACIA (which is a synchronous device) using a synchronous type of bus transfer involving VPA*, VMA*, and the E clock (E = 400 kHz). A 14411 baud rate generator provides transmit and receive clocks for the ACIA. A pair of 1488 and 1489 line drivers is used to translate the ACIA voltage levels to RS-232C interface levels.

CHAPTER 5 TROUBLESHOOTING

The KS68 uses the freerun and the single-step technique to check all the modules, as described in Table 5.1. The user may use a single test or a group of tests described below to isolate a malfunctioning module. The particular module can then be diagnosed using the module schematics.

TABLE 5.1 TROUBLESHOOTING CHART.

Module name	*Operator function*	*Expected Results*
Clock module	1. Check CLK68 and SYSCLK.	1. See Fig. T-01.
Reset module	1. Check RESET* vs. VCC and SW1.	1. See Figs. T-02 and T-03.
Freerun module	1. Plug in the 24-pin headers into the TEST EPROM sockets.	
	2. Disable J1.	
	3. Enable SW2 and SW3.	
	4. Check all address and data pins, on freerun, with a logic probe.	4. All address pins should be pulsing, and all data pins should be low.
	5. Check AS* vs. CLK68.	5. See Figs. T-04 and T-05.
DTACK* module	1. Disable SW2.	
	2. Put J2 to 0 waits.	2. See Fig. T-05.
	3. Put J2 to 7 waits.	3. See Fig. T-06.
Decode module	1. Check CSR*, CSTR*, CST* and CSIO*.	1. See Fig. T-07.
Test EPROM module	1. Disable SW3 and enable J1.	
	2. Remove freerun headers.	
	3. Put CSTR* into TEST EPROM chip select (pin number 18).	
	4. Plug in TEST EPROMs with scoop-loop 1.*	
	5. Check various address and data pins on run.	5. See Table A-1 for address and data pins status.
Boot module	1. Check BOOT* vs. RESET.*	1. See Fig. T-08.
	2. Check CSR*, CSTR*, BOOT*, CER* and CETR* vs. RESET*.	2. See Fig. T-09.
	3. Put CETR* into TEST EPROM chip select (pin number 18).	
	4. Plug in TEST EPROMs with scope loop2.*	
	5. Check various address and data pins on run.	5. See Table A-2 for address and data pins status.
Single-step module	1. Put SW6 on STEP.	
	2. Single-step scope-loop2* from power-up.	2. See Table A-2 for address and data pins status.

*See Appendix A.

TABLE 5.1 (*Cont'd.*) TROUBLESHOOTING CHART.

RAM module	1. Plug in TEST EPROMs with scope loop3.*	
	2. Single-step scope-loop3 from power-up.	
	3. Check data being written and read from RAM at step 9 and 12 respectively.	3. The data should be $FEDC.
TUTOR module	1. Put CETR* to TUTOR EPROMs chip select (pin number 20).	
	2. Check TUTOR startup sequence.	2. See Fig. T-10.
I/O module	1. Check E, VPA* and VMA* on TUTOR run.	1. See Fig. T-11.
	2. Check RTCLK and T_XD vs. RESET*.	2. See Fig. T-12.
	3. Check R_XD with a logic probe while pressing the BREAK key on the terminal.	3. R_XD should change state from high to low on key depression.

*See Appendix A.

REFERENCES

MC68000 Educational Computer Board User's Manual, MEX68KECB/D2, 2nd Edition, Tempe, AZ: Motorola Literature Distribution Center, 1982.

MC68000 16-bit Microprocessor Data Manual, Austin, TX: Motorola Semiconductor Products, Inc.

The TTL Data Book, Vol. 2, Dallas, TX; Texas Instruments, Inc., 1985.

WILCOX, ALAN D. *68000 Microcomputer Systems; Designing and Troubleshooting*. Englewood Cliffs, NJ; Prentice-Hall, Inc., 1987.

APPENDIX A SCOPE LOOPS

TABLE A-1 SCOPE LOOP1.

	Even	*Odd*	
000000	00	00	SSP to 000444
000002	04	44	
000004	00	00	PC to 000008
000006	00	08	
000008	4E	F8	JMP.S $000008
00000A	00	08	

Data Lines

D15	14	13	12	11	10	9	8	7	6	5	4	3	2	1	0	
0	1	0	0	1	1	1	0	1	1	1	1	1	0	0	0	000008
0	0	0	0	0	0	0	0	0	0	0	0	1	0	0	0	00000A

Address Lines

A15	14	13	12	11	10	9	8	7	6	5	4	3	2	1	0	
0	0	0	0	0	0	0	0	0	0	0	0	1	0	0	0	000008
0	0	0	0	0	0	0	0	0	0	0	0	1	0	1	0	00000A

TABLE A-2 SCOPE LOOP2.

	Even	*Odd*	
000000	00	00	SSP to 000444
000002	04	44	
000004	00	00	PC to 008008
000006	80	08	
008008	4E	F9	
00800A	00	00	JMP.L $008008
00800C	80	08	

Data Lines

D15	14	13	12	11	10	9	8	7	6	5	4	3	2	1	0	
0	1	0	0	1	1	1	0	1	1	1	1	1	0	0	1	008008
0	0	0	0	0	0	0	0	0	0	0	0	0	0	0	0	00800A
1	0	0	0	0	0	0	0	0	0	0	0	1	0	0	0	00800C

Address Lines

A15	14	13	12	11	10	9	8	7	6	5	4	3	2	1	0	
1	0	0	0	0	0	0	0	0	0	0	0	1	0	0	0	008008
1	0	0	0	0	0	0	0	0	0	0	0	1	0	1	0	00800A
1	0	0	0	0	0	0	0	0	0	0	0	1	1	0	0	00800C

TABLE A-3 SCOPE LOOP3.

	Even	*Odd*	
000000	00	00	SSP to 000444
000002	04	44	
000004	00	00	PC to 008008
000006	80	08	
008008	31	FC	MOVE.W#$FEDC,$0408
00800A	FE	DC	
00800C	04	48	
00800E	30	38	MOVE.W $0448,D0
008010	04	48	
008012	4E	F9	JMP.L $008008
008014	00	00	
008016	80	08	

APPENDIX B TIMING DIAGRAMS

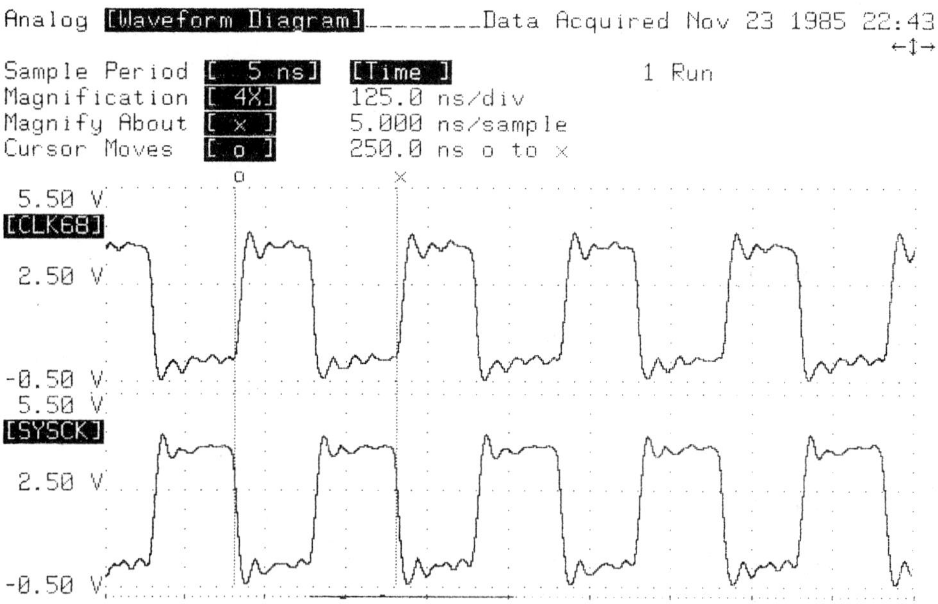

Figure T-01 CLK68 and SYSCLK running at 4 Mhz.

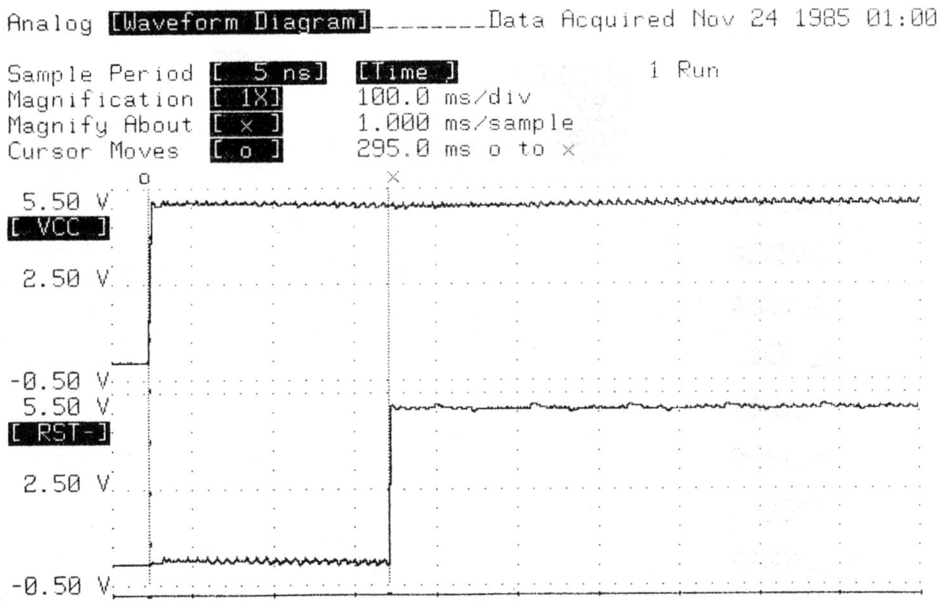

Figure T-02 Power-up reset sequence.

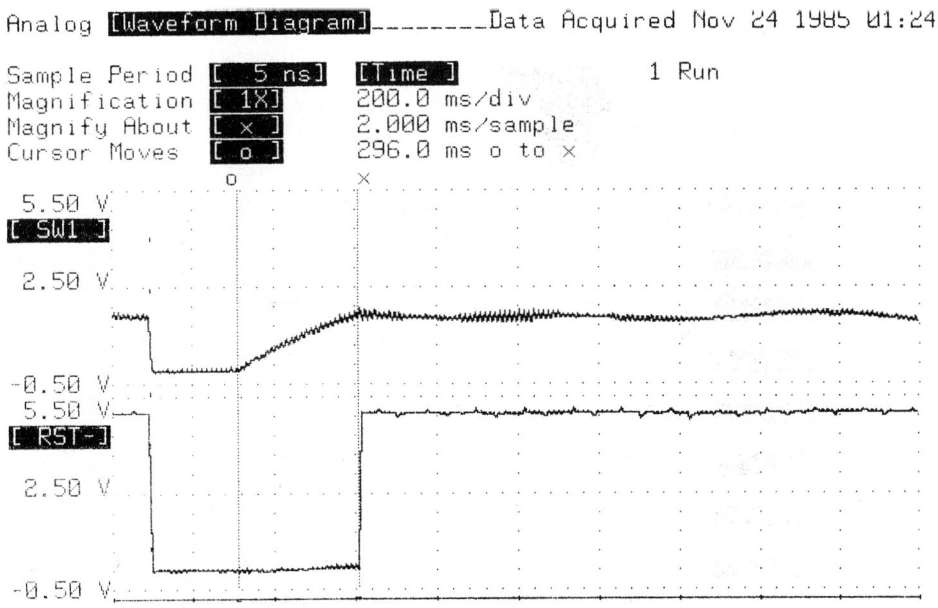

Figure T-03 Switch reset sequence.

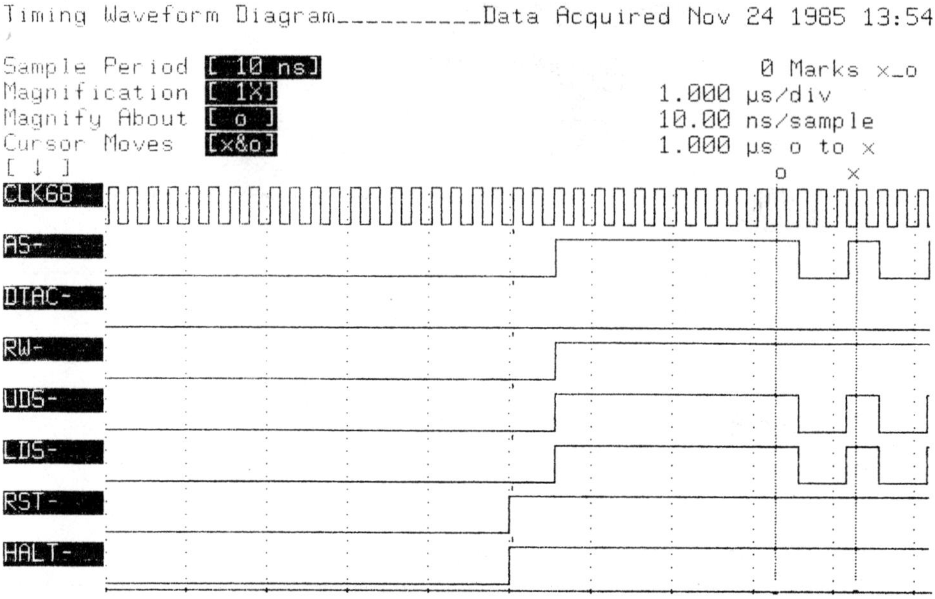

Figure T-04 Power-up sequence on freerun.

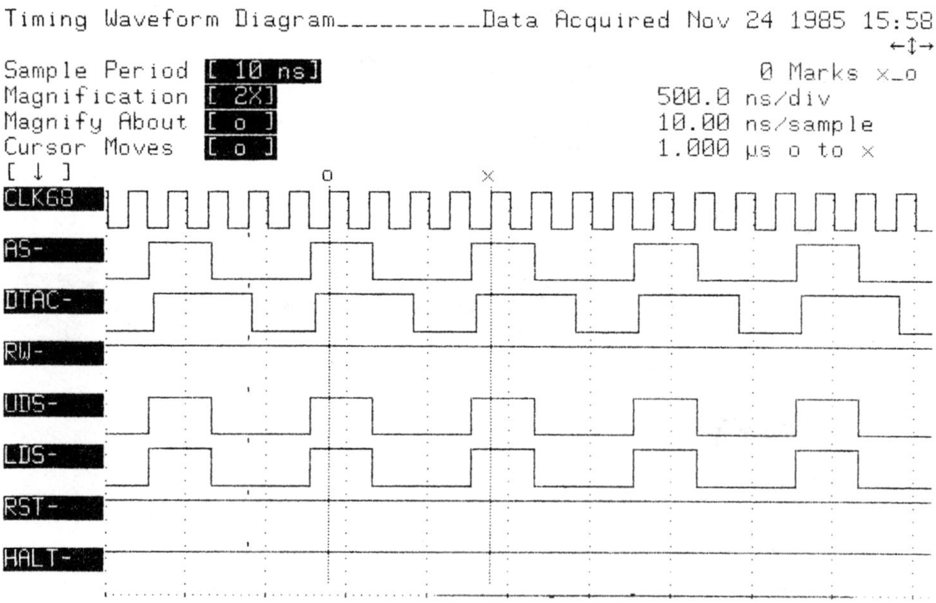

Figure T-05 Freerun with 0 waits.

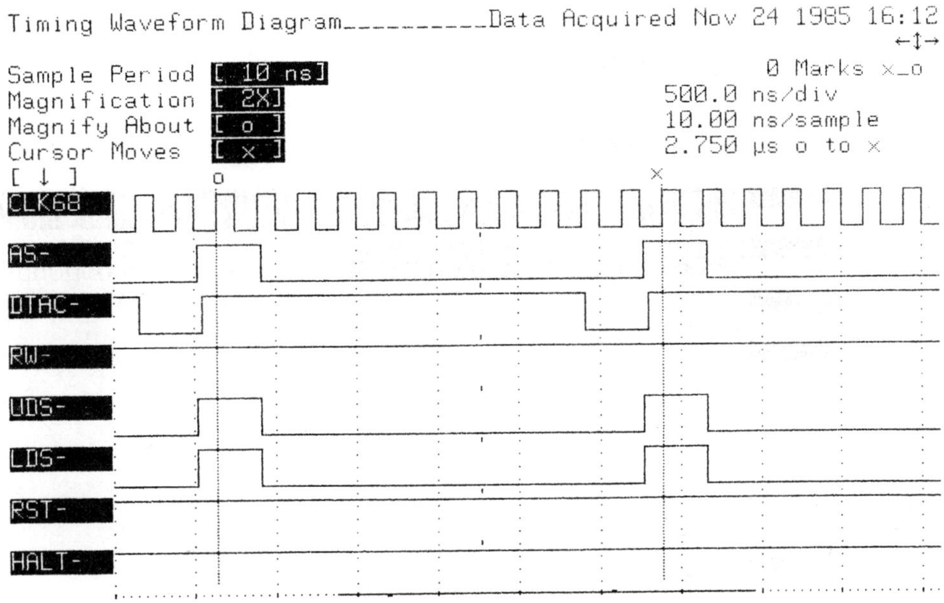

Figure T-06 Freerun with 7 waits.

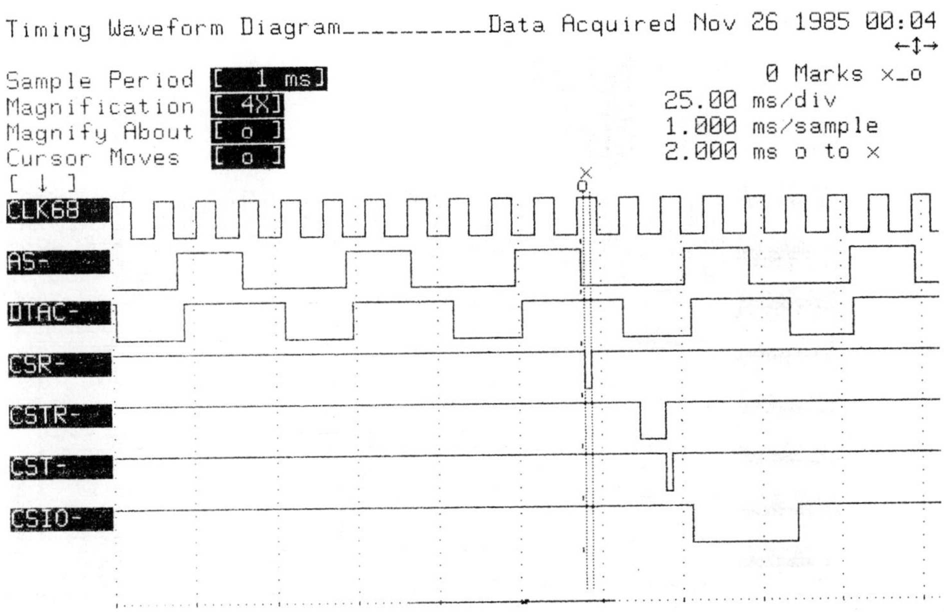

Figure T-07 Decoder module outputs on freerun.

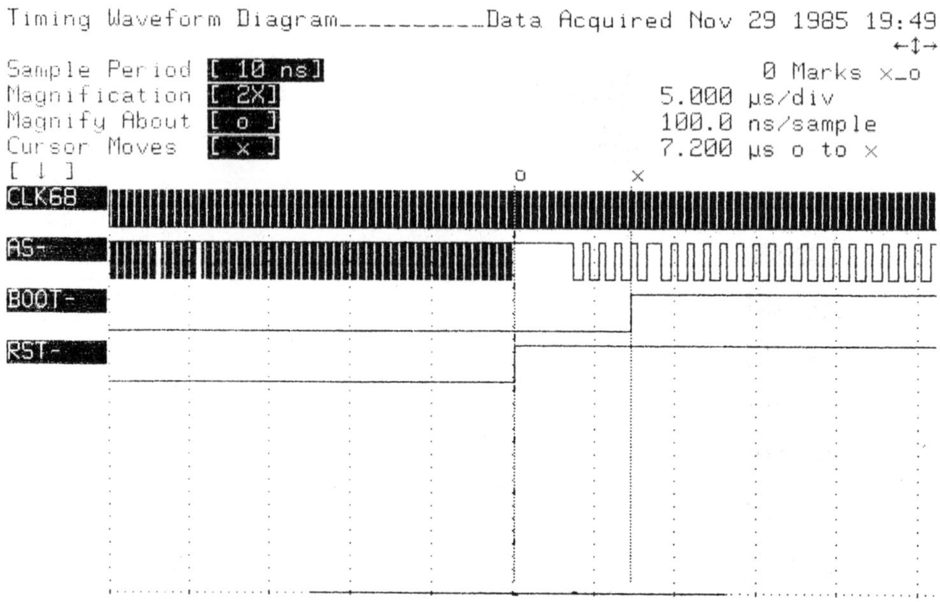

Figure T-08 BOOT* vs RESET* on power-up.

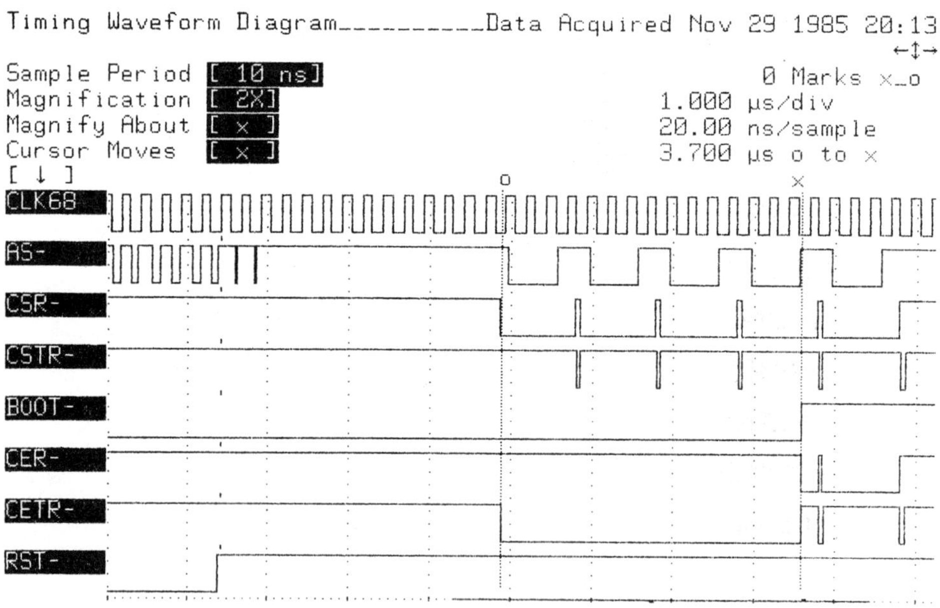

Figure T-09 Chip enables on power-up.

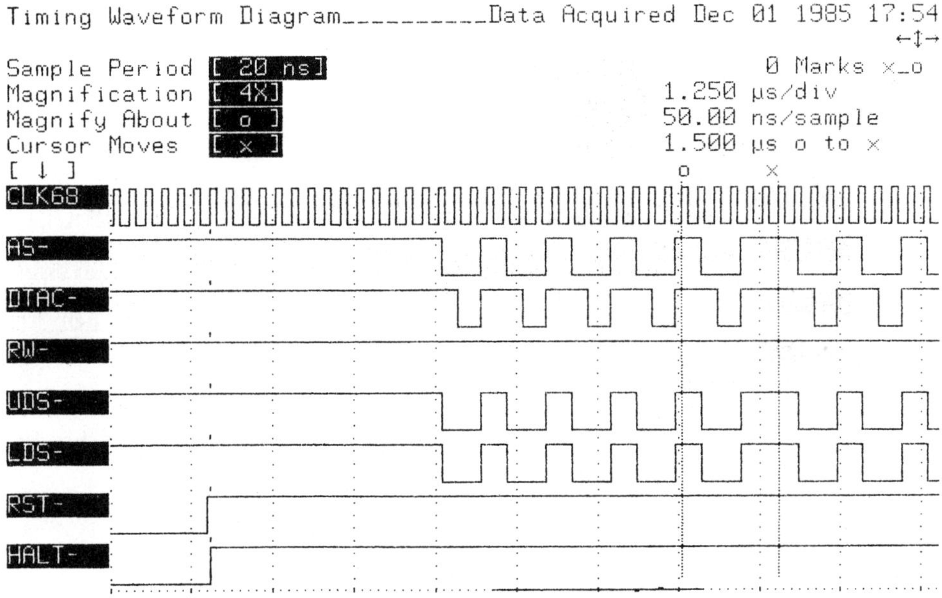

Figure T-10 TUTOR start-up sequence.

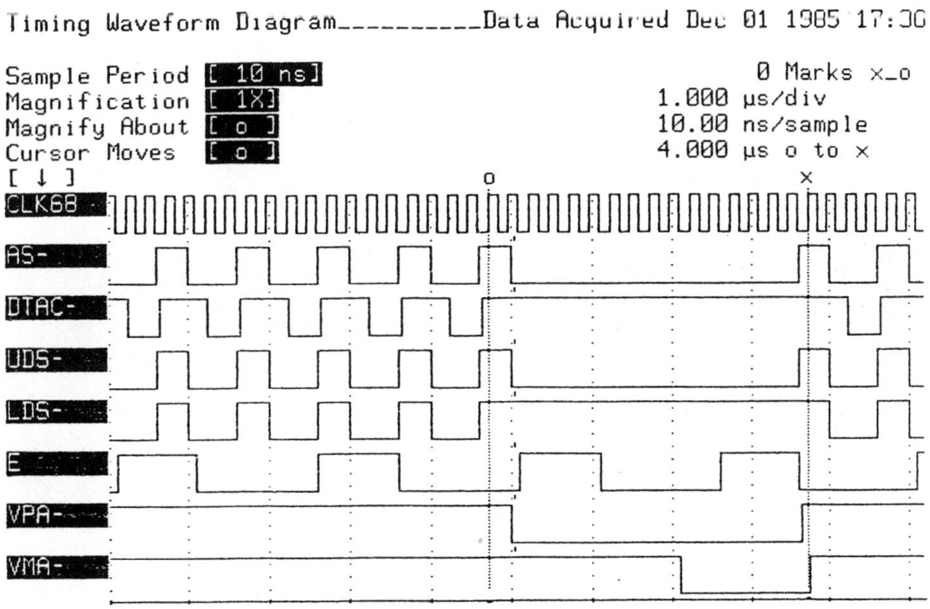

Figure T-11 Synchronous read bus cycle during TUTOR run.

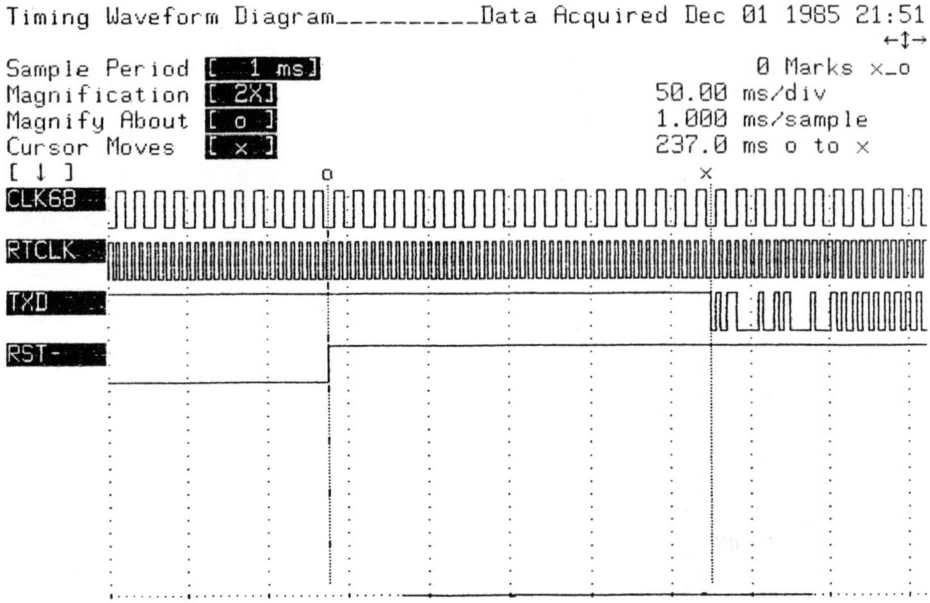

Figure T-12 T_XD vs RESET* on power-up.

APPENDIX C SCHEMATICS

Drawing Index

REFERENCE	TYPE		GND	+5 V	+12 V	−12 V
U1	74LS04		7	14		
U2	7407		7	14		
U3	74LS14		7	14		
U4	74LS74		7	14		
U5	74LS279		7	14		
U6	DIP Oscillator		2	4		
U7	74LS265		8	16		
U8	74LS10		7	14		
U9	74LS32		7	14		
U10	74LS08		7	14		
U11	74LS164		7	14		
U12	74LS00		7	14		
U13	MC68000		16, 53	14, 49		
U14	74LS260		7	14		
U15	74LS138		8	16		
U16	74154		12	24		
U17	74LS21		7	14		
U18	74LS164		7	14		
U19	74LS32		7	14		
U20	74LS02		7	14		
U21	Crystal					
U22	MC14411		12	24		
U23	AM2716		12	24		
U24	HM6116		12	24		
U25	27128		14	28		
U26	MC6850		1	12		
U27	AM2716		12	24		
U28	HM6116		12	24		
U29	27128		14	28		
U30	1488		7		14	1
U31	1489		7	14		

WILCOX Engineering LEWISBURG, PENNSYLVANIA 17837

REVISIONS

TITLE Power/Ground Table.

DRAWN CHECKED SCALE DRAWING NO. S-00

APPROVED

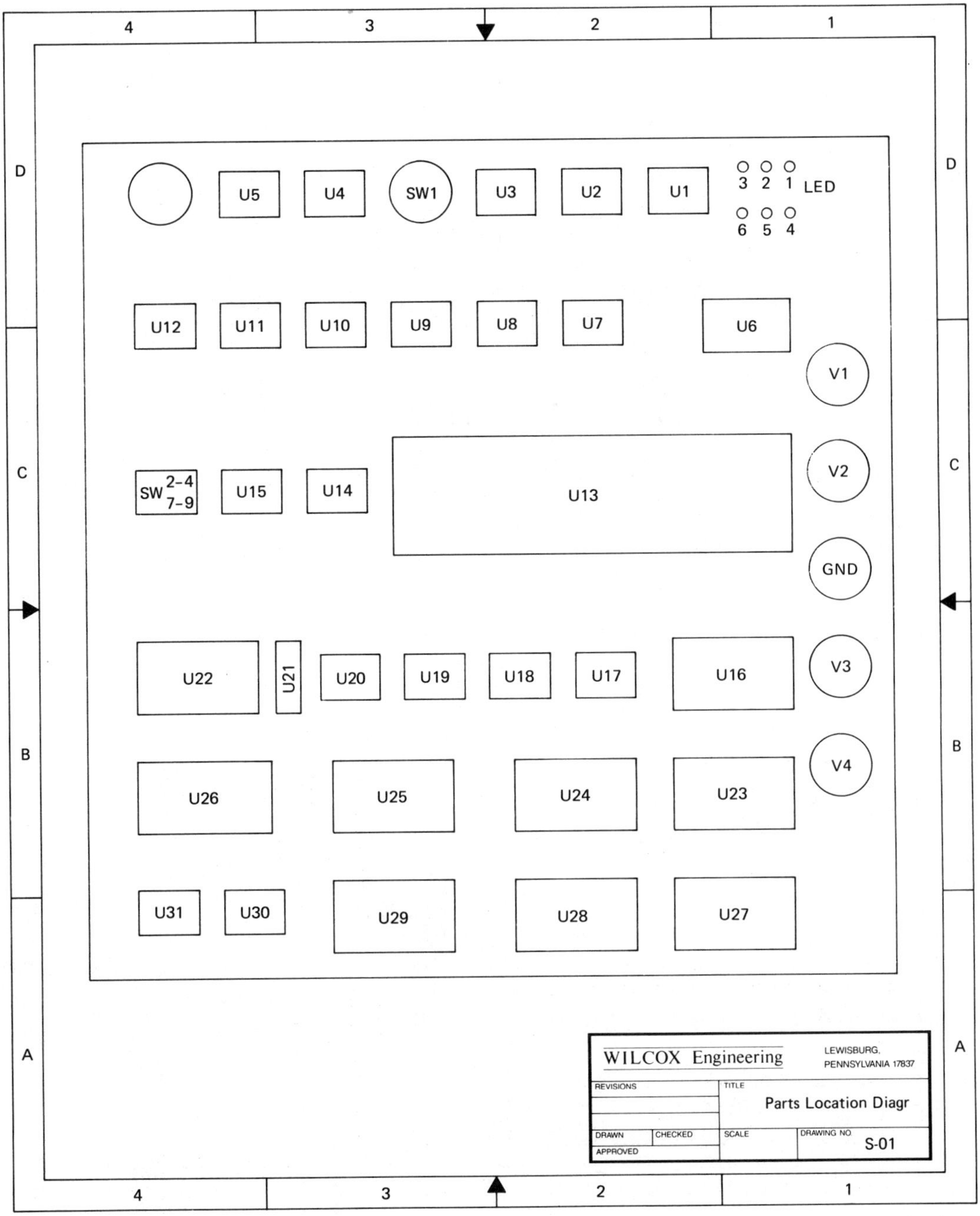
4
3
2
1
D
C
B
A
U5
U4
SW1
U3
U2
U1
3 2 1 LED
6 5 4
U12
U11
U10
U9
U8
U7
U6
V1
SW 2-4 7-9
U15
U14
U13
V2
GND
U22
U21
U20
U19
U18
U17
U16
V3
U26
U25
U24
U23
V4
U31
U30
U29
U28
U27
WILCOX Engineering
LEWISBURG, PENNSYLVANIA 17837
REVISIONS
TITLE
Parts Location Diagr
DRAWN
CHECKED
SCALE
DRAWING NO.
S-01
APPROVED

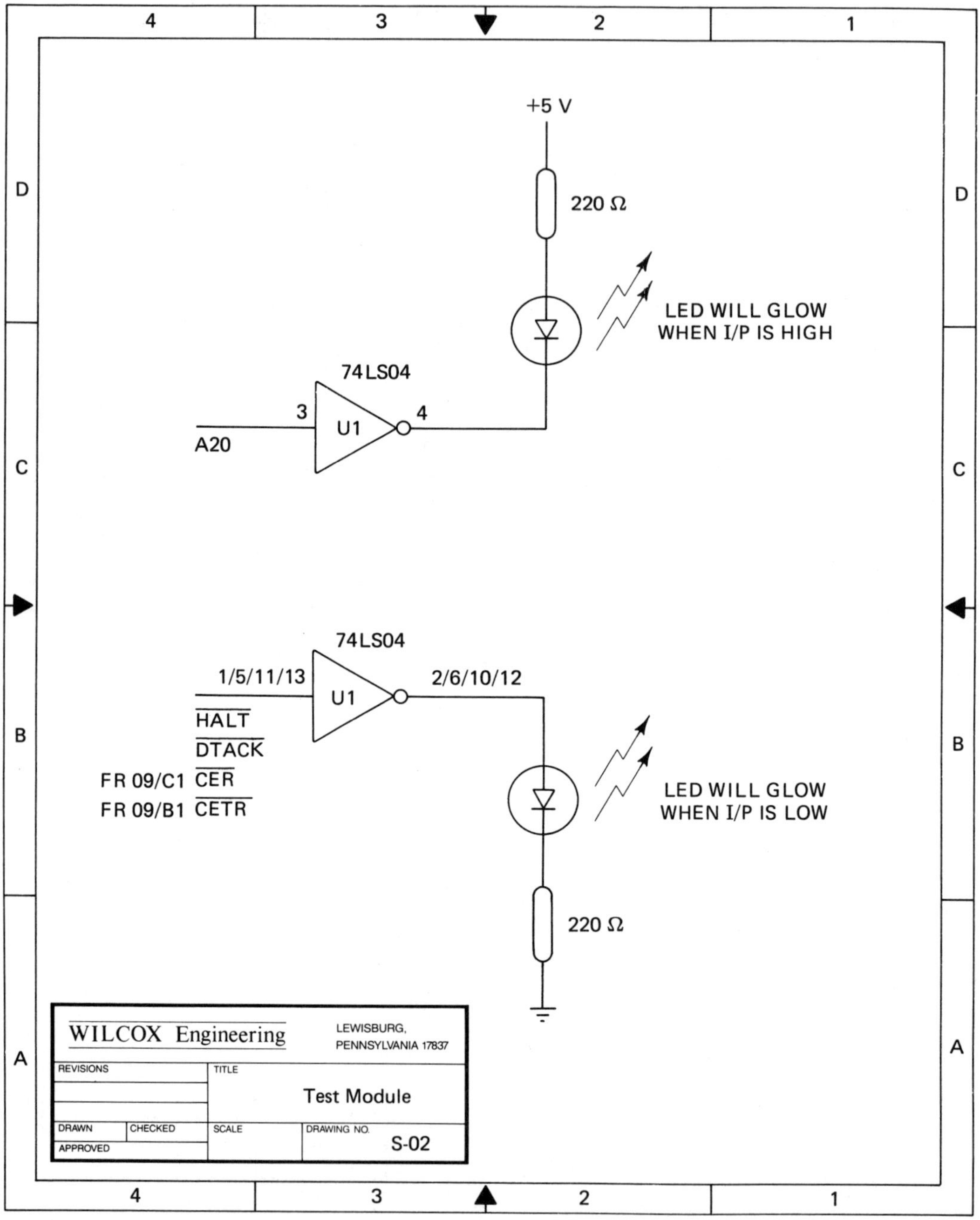
4
3
2
1
D
C
B
A
+5 V
220 Ω
LED WILL GLOW
WHEN I/P IS HIGH
74LS04
3
U1
4
A20
74LS04
1/5/11/13
U1
2/6/10/12
HALT
DTACK
FR 09/C1 CER
FR 09/B1 CETR
LED WILL GLOW
WHEN I/P IS LOW
220 Ω
WILCOX Engineering
LEWISBURG,
PENNSYLVANIA 17837
REVISIONS
TITLE
Test Module
DRAWN
CHECKED
SCALE
DRAWING NO.
S-02
APPROVED

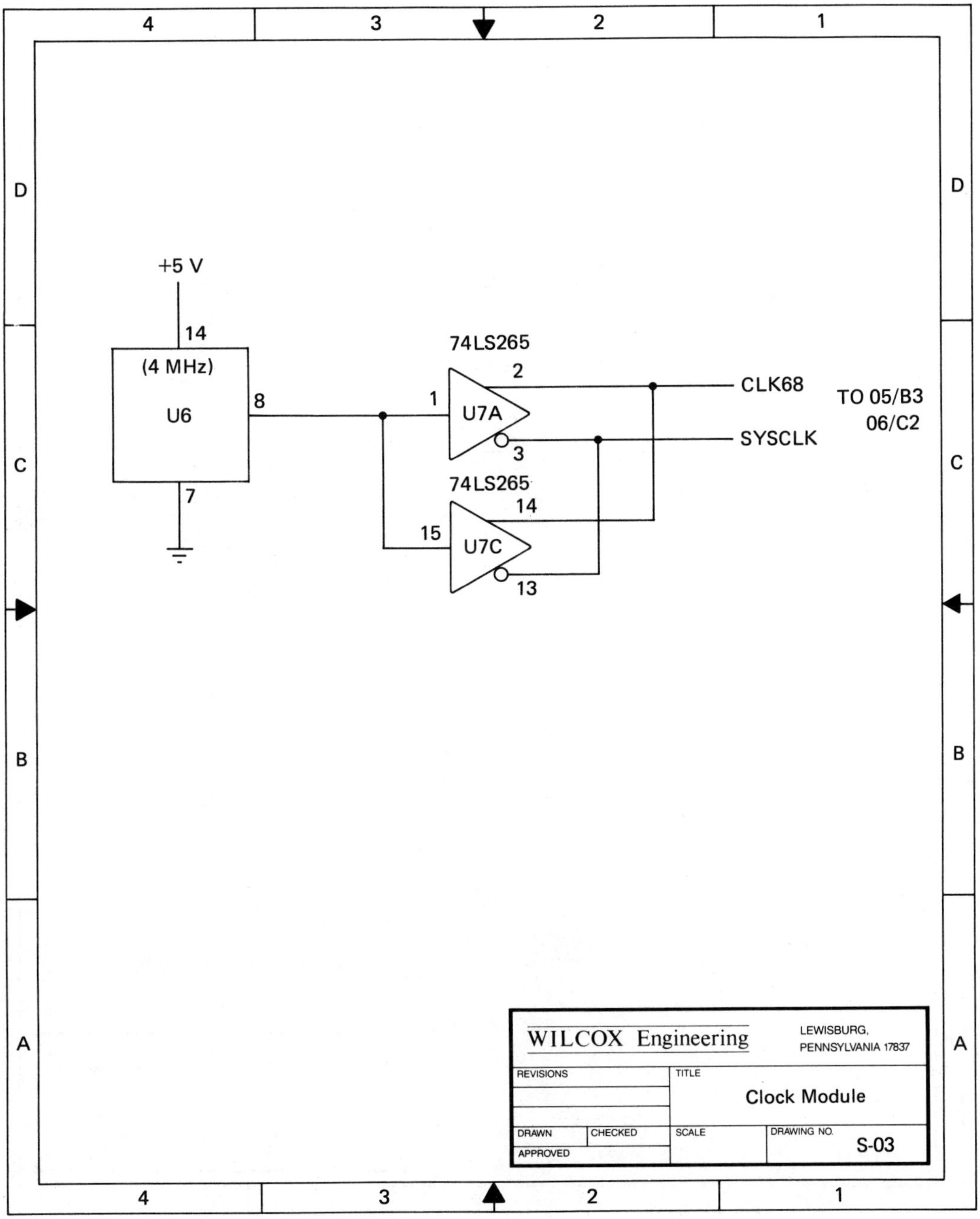
4
3
2
1
D
C
B
A
+5 V
14
(4 MHz)
U6
8
7
74LS265
2
1
U7A
3
74LS265
14
15
U7C
13
CLK68
SYSCLK
TO 05/B3
06/C2
WILCOX Engineering
LEWISBURG,
PENNSYLVANIA 17837
REVISIONS
TITLE
Clock Module
DRAWN
CHECKED
SCALE
DRAWING NO.
S-03
APPROVED

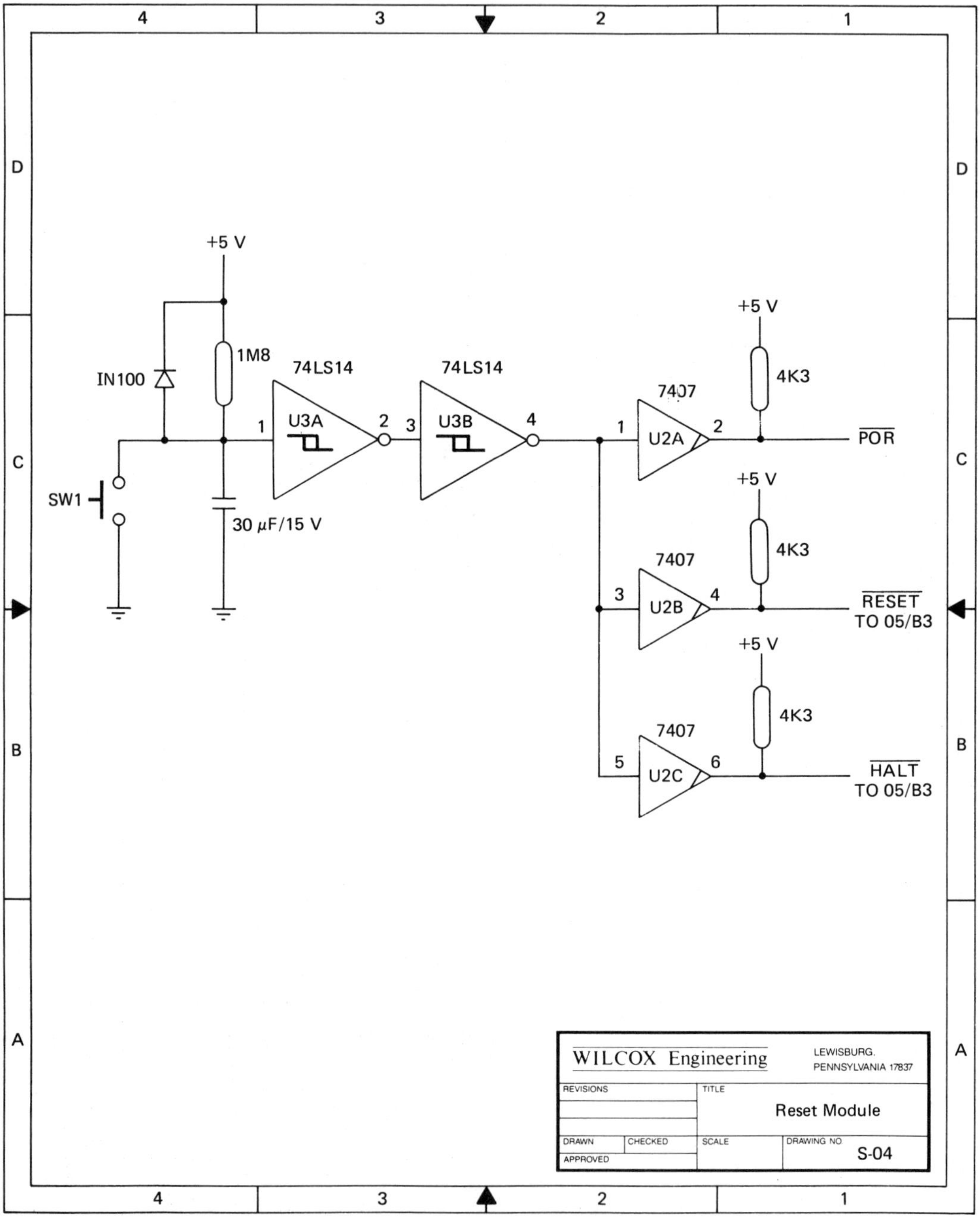
+5 V
1M8
IN100
74LS14
74LS14
U3A
U3B
SW1
30 μF/15 V
7407
U2A
+5 V
4K3
POR
7407
U2B
+5 V
4K3
RESET
TO 05/B3
7407
U2C
+5 V
4K3
HALT
TO 05/B3
WILCOX Engineering
LEWISBURG.
PENNSYLVANIA 17837
REVISIONS
TITLE
Reset Module
DRAWN
CHECKED
SCALE
DRAWING NO.
S-04
APPROVED

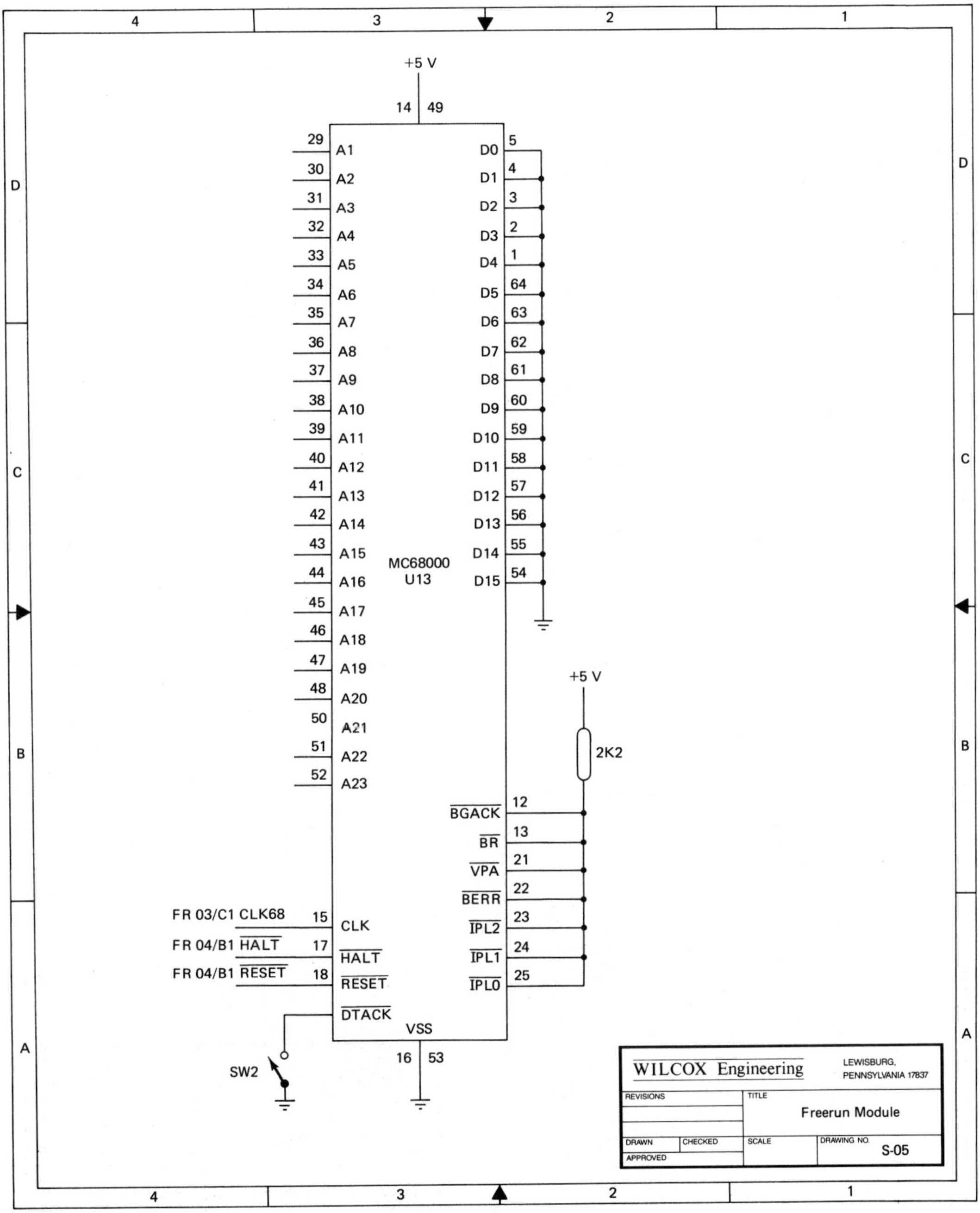

+5 V
14 49
MC68000
U13
29 A1
30 A2
31 A3
32 A4
33 A5
34 A6
35 A7
36 A8
37 A9
38 A10
39 A11
40 A12
41 A13
42 A14
43 A15
44 A16
45 A17
46 A18
47 A19
48 A20
50 A21
51 A22
52 A23
D0 5
D1 4
D2 3
D3 2
D4 1
D5 64
D6 63
D7 62
D8 61
D9 60
D10 59
D11 58
D12 57
D13 56
D14 55
D15 54
+5 V
2K2
BGACK 12
BR 13
VPA 21
BERR 22
IPL2 23
IPL1 24
IPL0 25
FR 03/C1 CLK68 15 CLK
FR 04/B1 HALT 17 HALT
FR 04/B1 RESET 18 RESET
DTACK
VSS
16 53
SW2
WILCOX Engineering
LEWISBURG, PENNSYLVANIA 17837
REVISIONS
TITLE
Freerun Module
DRAWN
CHECKED
SCALE
DRAWING NO.
S-05
APPROVED

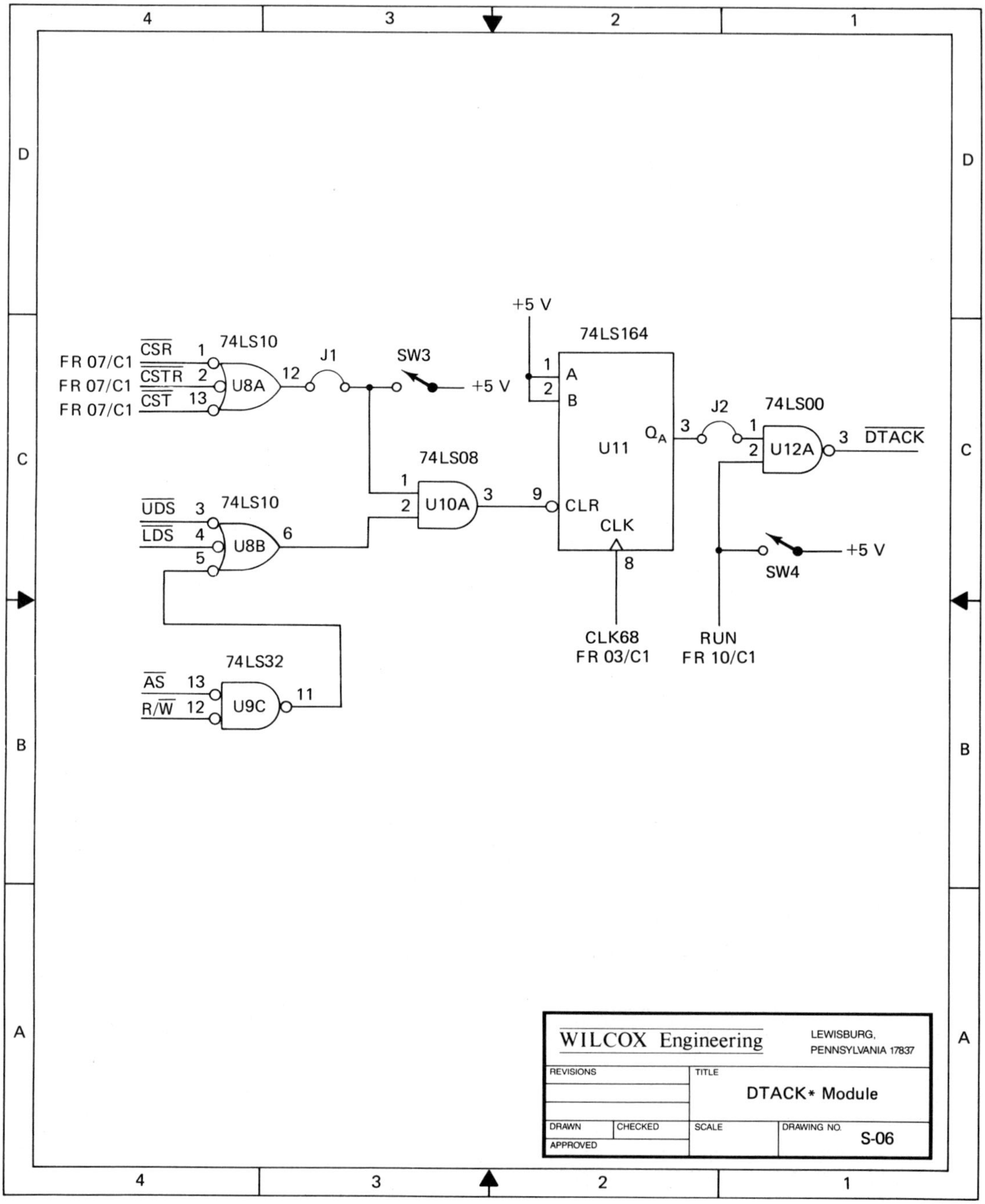

4
3
2
1
D
C
B
A
74LS10
CSR
CSTR
CST
FR 07/C1
FR 07/C1
FR 07/C1
U8A
12
J1
SW3
+5 V
+5 V
74LS164
A
B
U11
Q_A
CLR
CLK
J2
74LS00
U12A
DTACK
74LS08
U10A
UDS
LDS
U8B
74LS32
AS
R/W
U9C
SW4
CLK68
FR 03/C1
RUN
FR 10/C1
WILCOX Engineering
LEWISBURG, PENNSYLVANIA 17837
REVISIONS
TITLE
DTACK* Module
DRAWN
CHECKED
SCALE
DRAWING NO.
S-06
APPROVED

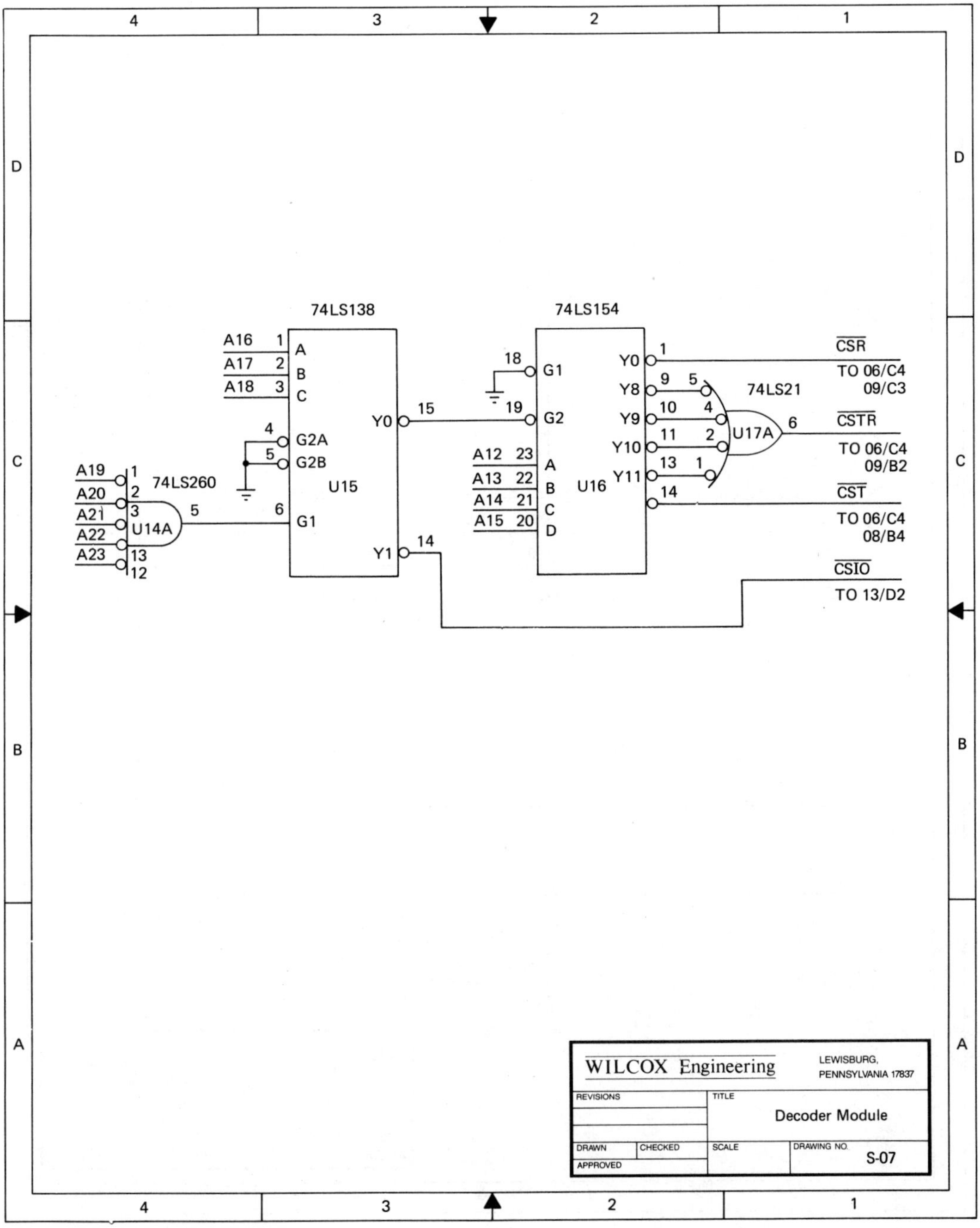
74LS138
74LS154
A16
A17
A18
A
B
C
Y0
Y1
G2A
G2B
G1
U15
G1
G2
Y0
Y8
Y9
Y10
Y11
A12
A13
A14
A15
D
U16
74LS21
U17A
74LS260
U14A
A19
A20
A21
A22
A23
CSR
TO 06/C4
09/C3
CSTR
TO 06/C4
09/B2
CST
TO 06/C4
08/B4
CSIO
TO 13/D2
WILCOX Engineering
LEWISBURG, PENNSYLVANIA 17837
REVISIONS
TITLE
Decoder Module
DRAWN
CHECKED
SCALE
DRAWING NO.
S-07
APPROVED

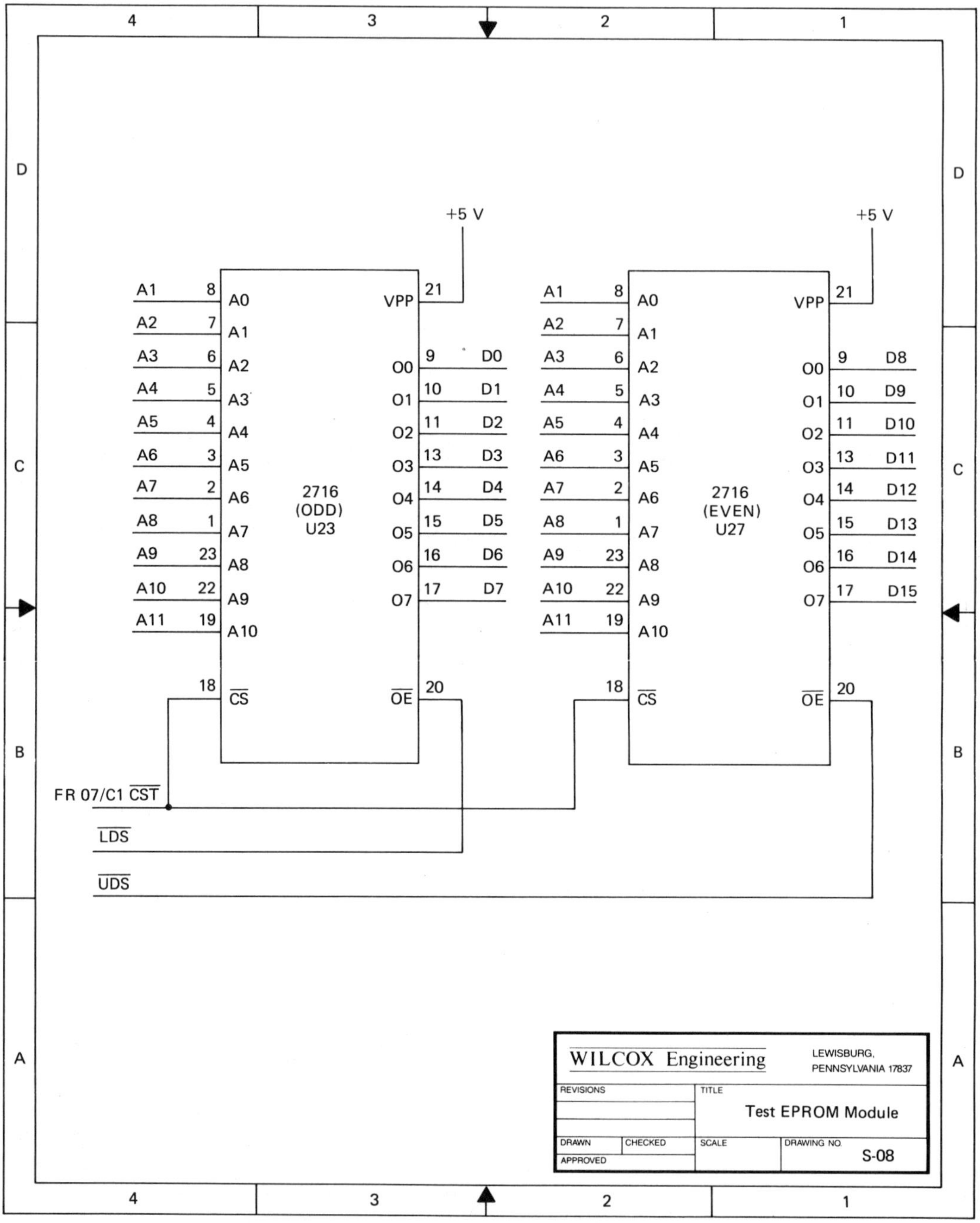
+5 V
A1 8 A0
A2 7 A1
A3 6 A2
A4 5 A3
A5 4 A4
A6 3 A5
A7 2 A6
A8 1 A7
A9 23 A8
A10 22 A9
A11 19 A10
VPP 21
O0 9 D0
O1 10 D1
O2 11 D2
O3 13 D3
O4 14 D4
O5 15 D5
O6 16 D6
O7 17 D7
2716 (ODD) U23
18 CS
OE 20
O0 9 D8
O1 10 D9
O2 11 D10
O3 13 D11
O4 14 D12
O5 15 D13
O6 16 D14
O7 17 D15
2716 (EVEN) U27
FR 07/C1 CST
LDS
UDS
WILCOX Engineering
LEWISBURG, PENNSYLVANIA 17837
REVISIONS
TITLE
Test EPROM Module
DRAWN
CHECKED
SCALE
DRAWING NO.
S-08
APPROVED

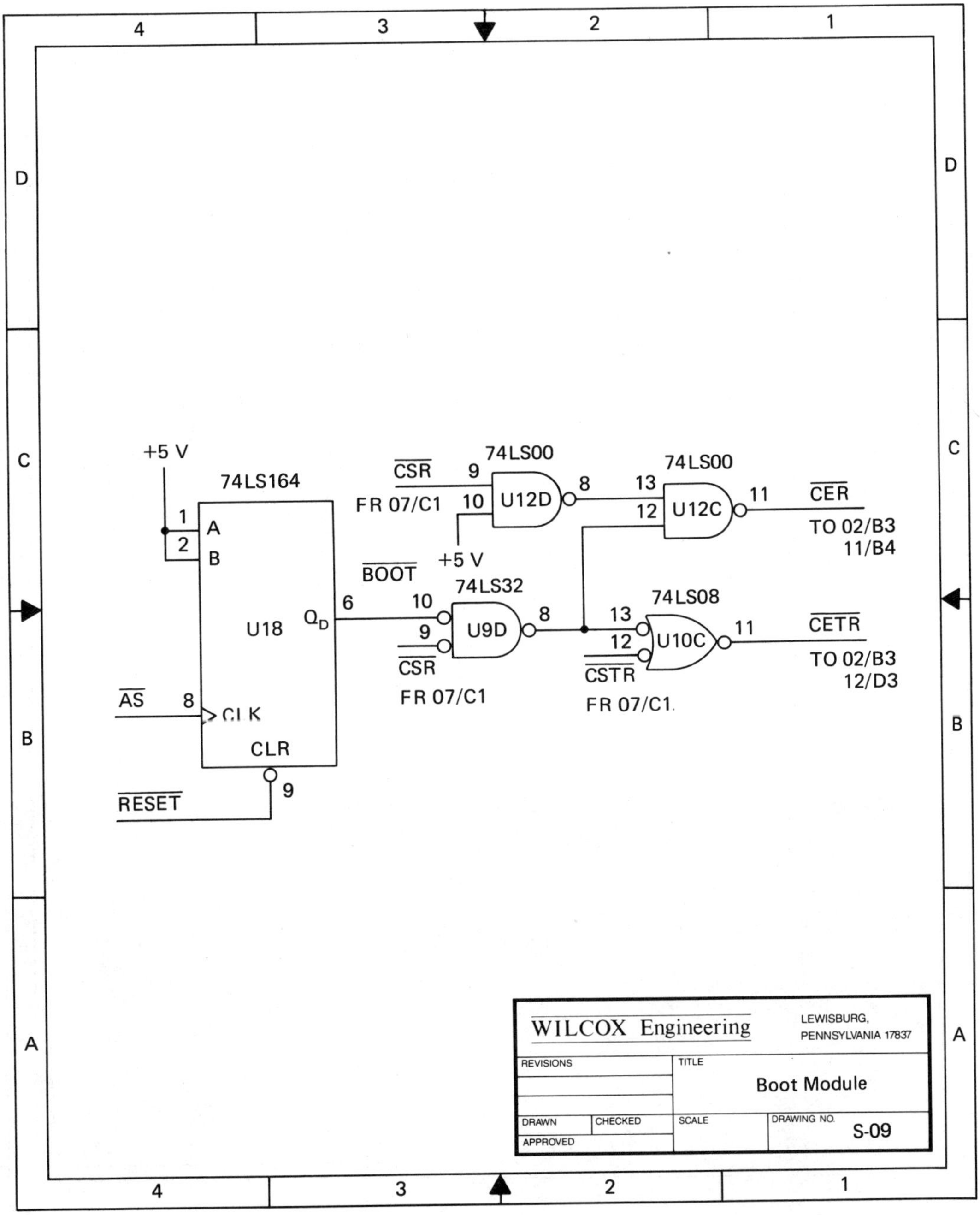
4
3
2
1
D
C
B
A
+5 V
74LS164
1
A
2
B
U18
Q_D
6
$\overline{AS}$
8
CLK
CLR
9
$\overline{RESET}$
$\overline{CSR}$
9
74LS00
FR 07/C1
10
U12D
8
+5 V
$\overline{BOOT}$
74LS32
10
9
U9D
8
$\overline{CSR}$
FR 07/C1
74LS00
13
12
U12C
11
$\overline{CER}$
TO 02/B3
11/B4
74LS08
13
12
U10C
11
$\overline{CSTR}$
FR 07/C1
$\overline{CETR}$
TO 02/B3
12/D3
WILCOX Engineering
LEWISBURG, PENNSYLVANIA 17837
REVISIONS
TITLE
Boot Module
DRAWN
CHECKED
SCALE
DRAWING NO.
S-09
APPROVED

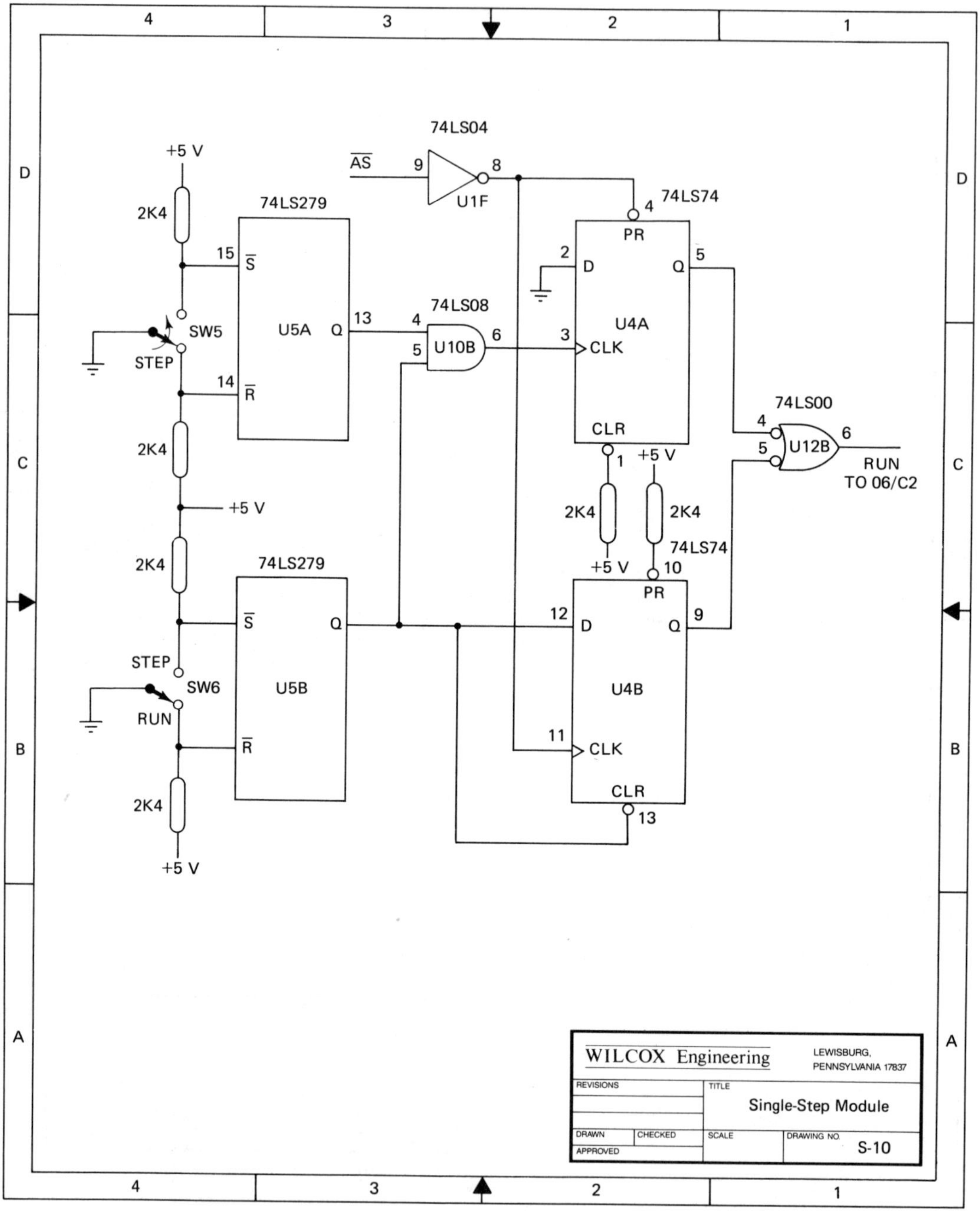

74LS04
AS
9
8
U1F
+5 V
2K4
74LS279
15
S
U5A
Q
13
SW5
STEP
14
R
74LS08
4
5
U10B
6
74LS74
4
PR
2
D
Q
5
3
CLK
U4A
CLR
1
+5 V
74LS00
4
5
U12B
6
RUN
TO 06/C2
2K4
2K4
+5 V
74LS74
10
PR
12
D
Q
9
U4B
11
CLK
CLR
13
74LS279
S
Q
U5B
STEP
SW6
RUN
R
2K4
+5 V
WILCOX Engineering
LEWISBURG, PENNSYLVANIA 17837
REVISIONS
TITLE
Single-Step Module
DRAWN
CHECKED
SCALE
DRAWING NO.
S-10
APPROVED

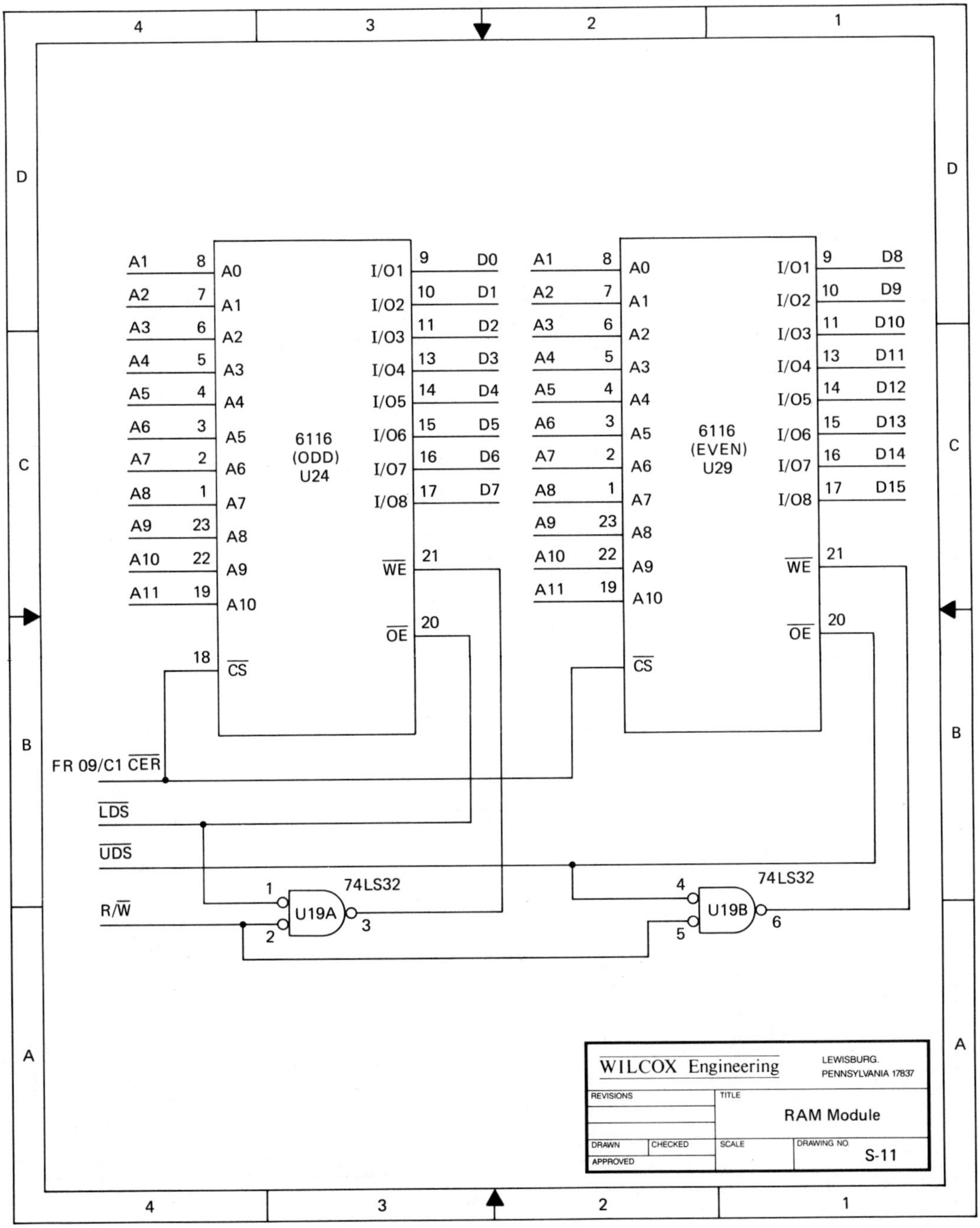
A1 8 A0
A2 7 A1
A3 6 A2
A4 5 A3
A5 4 A4
A6 3 A5
A7 2 A6
A8 1 A7
A9 23 A8
A10 22 A9
A11 19 A10
18 CS
6116
(ODD)
U24
I/O1 9 D0
I/O2 10 D1
I/O3 11 D2
I/O4 13 D3
I/O5 14 D4
I/O6 15 D5
I/O7 16 D6
I/O8 17 D7
WE 21
OE 20
6116
(EVEN)
U29
I/O1 9 D8
I/O2 10 D9
I/O3 11 D10
I/O4 13 D11
I/O5 14 D12
I/O6 15 D13
I/O7 16 D14
I/O8 17 D15
FR 09/C1 CER
LDS
UDS
R/W
74LS32
U19A
74LS32
U19B
WILCOX Engineering
LEWISBURG, PENNSYLVANIA 17837
REVISIONS
TITLE
RAM Module
DRAWN
CHECKED
SCALE
DRAWING NO.
S-11
APPROVED

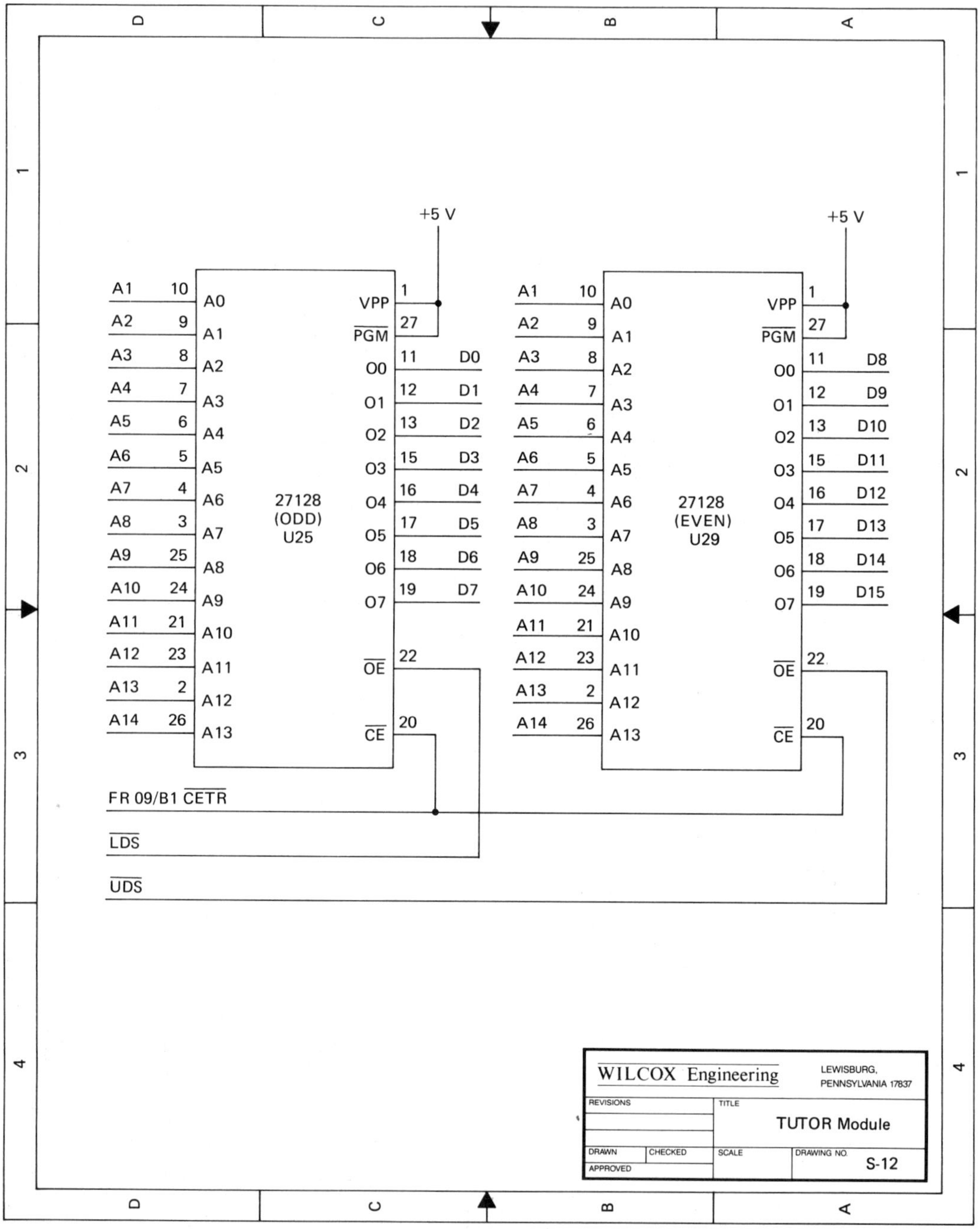
+5 V
A1 10 A0
A2 9 A1
A3 8 A2
A4 7 A3
A5 6 A4
A6 5 A5
A7 4 A6
A8 3 A7
A9 25 A8
A10 24 A9
A11 21 A10
A12 23 A11
A13 2 A12
A14 26 A13
27128
(ODD)
U25
VPP 1
PGM 27
O0 11 D0
O1 12 D1
O2 13 D2
O3 15 D3
O4 16 D4
O5 17 D5
O6 18 D6
O7 19 D7
OE 22
CE 20
27128
(EVEN)
U29
O0 11 D8
O1 12 D9
O2 13 D10
O3 15 D11
O4 16 D12
O5 17 D13
O6 18 D14
O7 19 D15
FR 09/B1 CETR
LDS
UDS
WILCOX Engineering
LEWISBURG,
PENNSYLVANIA 17837
REVISIONS
TITLE
TUTOR Module
DRAWN
CHECKED
SCALE
DRAWING NO.
S-12
APPROVED

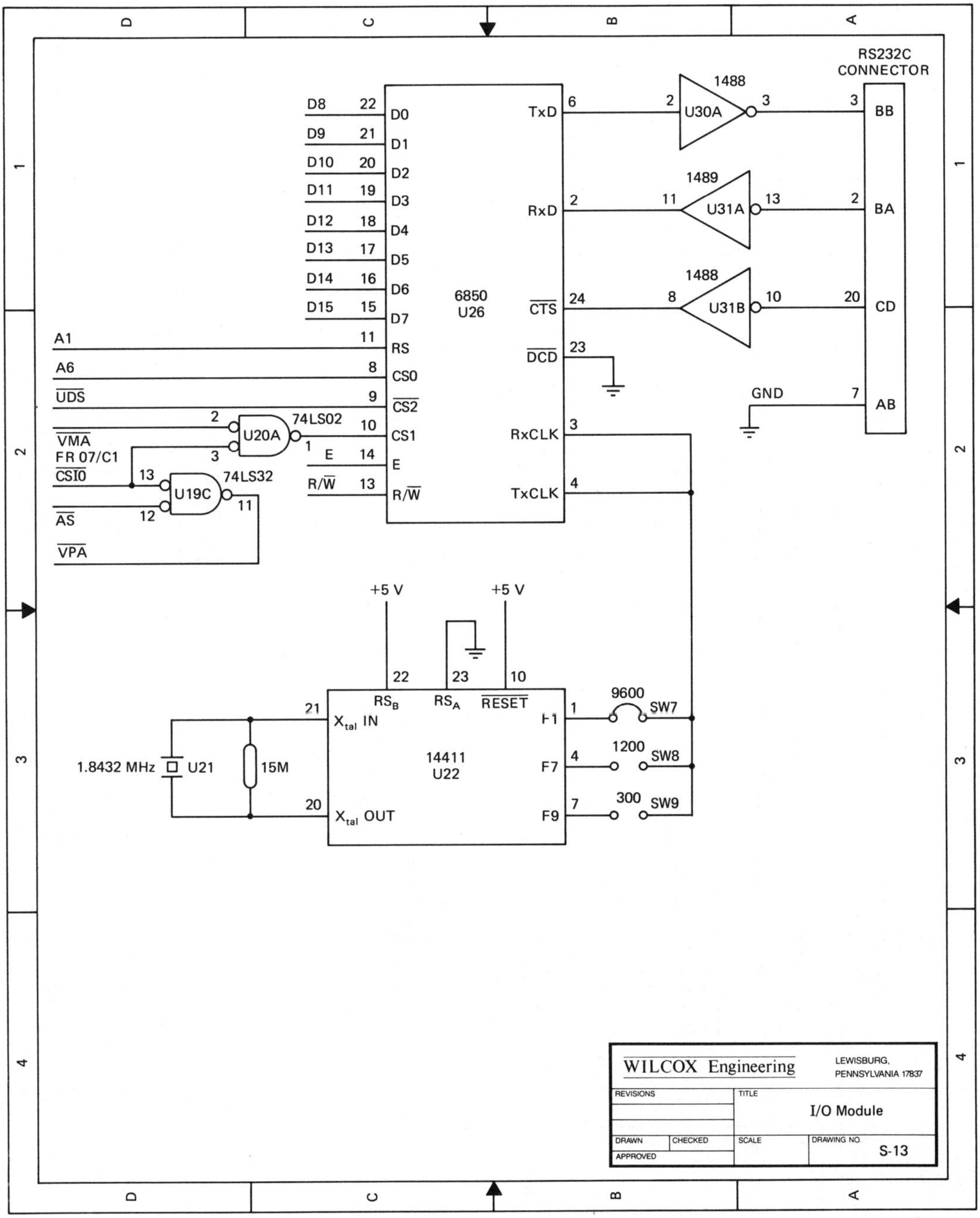
RS232C
CONNECTOR
1488
U30A
1489
U31A
1488
U31B
BB
BA
CD
AB
GND
TxD
RxD
CTS
DCD
RxCLK
TxCLK
6850
U26
D8
D9
D10
D11
D12
D13
D14
D15
D0
D1
D2
D3
D4
D5
D6
D7
RS
CS0
CS2
CS1
E
R/W
A1
A6
UDS
VMA
FR 07/C1
CSI0
AS
VPA
74LS02
U20A
74LS32
U19C
+5 V
+5 V
RSB
RSA
RESET
Xtal IN
Xtal OUT
14411
U22
F1
F7
F9
9600
SW7
1200
SW8
300
SW9
1.8432 MHz
U21
15M
WILCOX Engineering
LEWISBURG,
PENNSYLVANIA 17837
REVISIONS
TITLE
I/O Module
DRAWN
CHECKED
SCALE
DRAWING NO.
S-13
APPROVED

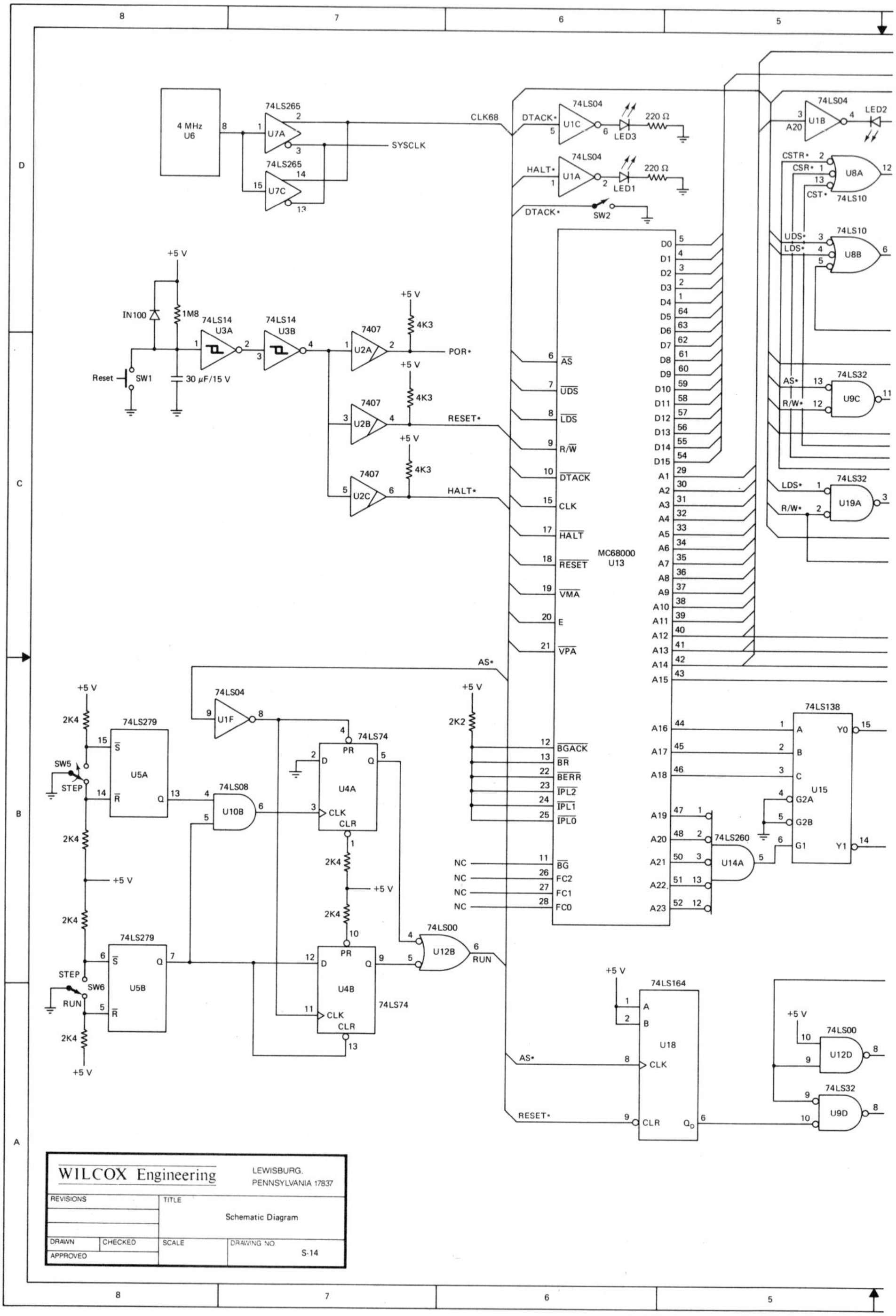
4 MHz
U6
74LS265
U7A
U7C
SYSCLK
CLK68
DTACK*
74LS04
U1C
LED3
220 Ω
HALT*
U1A
LED1
SW2
+5 V
IN100
1M8
74LS14
U3A
U3B
Reset
SW1
30 μF/15 V
7407
U2A
U2B
U2C
4K3
POR*
RESET*
HALT*
MC68000
U13
AS
UDS
LDS
R/W
DTACK
CLK
HALT
RESET
VMA
E
VPA
BGACK
BR
BERR
IPL2
IPL1
IPL0
BG
FC2
FC1
FC0
NC
AS*
2K2
2K4
74LS279
U5A
U5B
SW5
STEP
SW6
RUN
74LS08
U10B
U1F
74LS74
U4A
U4B
PR
CLR
74LS00
U12B
RUN
U1B
LED2
A20
CSTR*
CSR*
CST*
U8A
74LS10
UDS*
LDS*
U8B
74LS32
U9C
R/W*
U19A
74LS138
U15
G2A
G2B
G1
74LS260
U14A
74LS164
U18
U12D
U9D
WILCOX Engineering
LEWISBURG, PENNSYLVANIA 17837
REVISIONS
TITLE
Schematic Diagram
DRAWN
CHECKED
SCALE
DRAWING NO
S-14
APPROVED

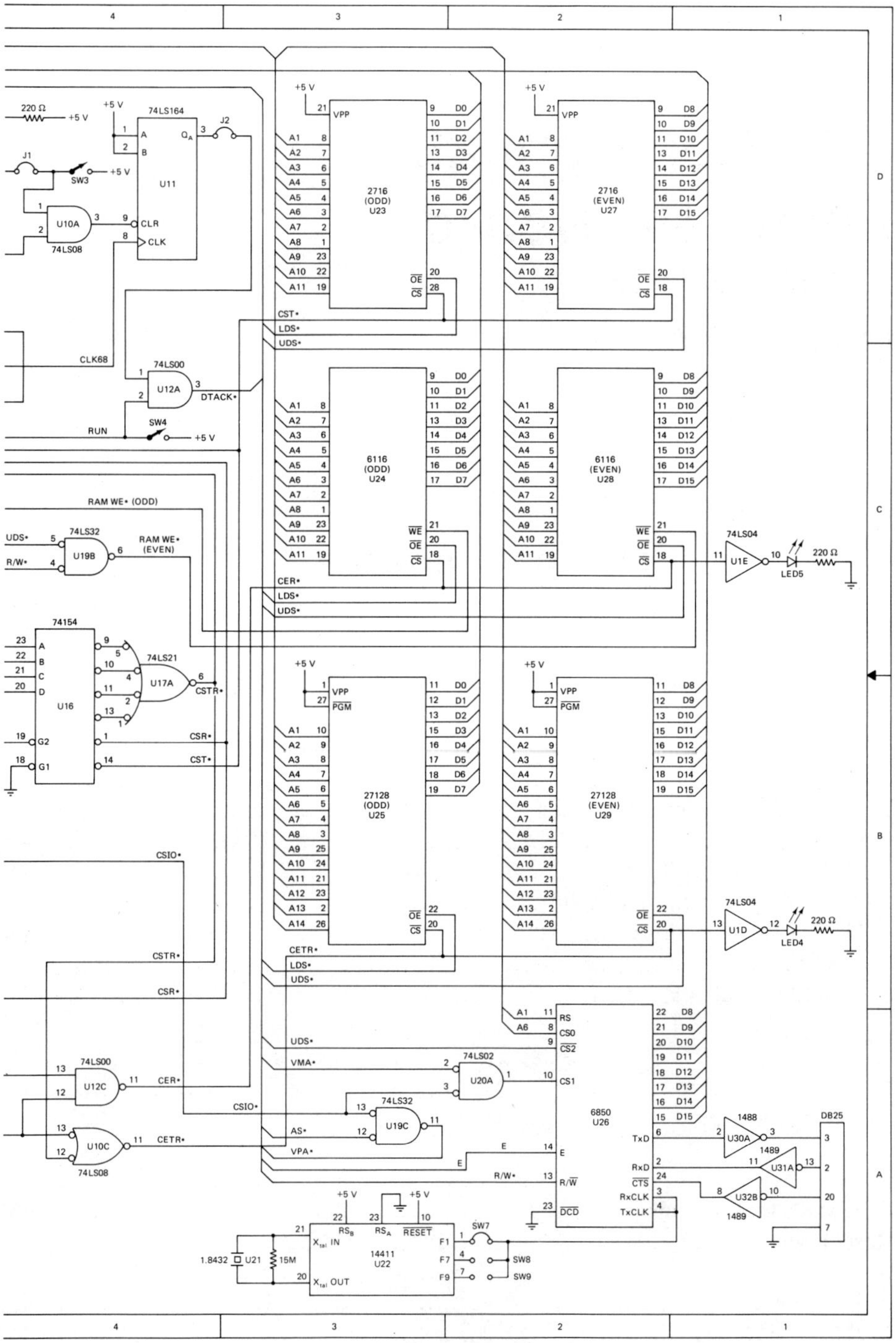

74LS164
U11
J1
J2
SW3
SW4
U10A
74LS08
CLK68
74LS00
U12A
DTACK•
RUN
RAM WE• (ODD)
RAM WE• (EVEN)
74LS32
U19B
UDS•
R/W•
74154
U16
74LS21
U17A
CSTR•
CSR•
CST•
CSIO•
2716 (ODD) U23
2716 (EVEN) U27
6116 (ODD) U24
6116 (EVEN) U28
27128 (ODD) U25
27128 (EVEN) U29
CER•
CETR•
LDS•
74LS04
U1E
U1D
LED5
LED4
220 Ω
6850 U26
74LS02
U20A
U19C
U12C
U10C
VMA•
AS•
VPA•
1488
U30A
1489
U31A
U32B
DB25
14411 U22
1.8432
U21
15M
SW7
SW8
SW9

APPENDIX D

Technical Manual: 68000 CPU Board

Alan D. Wilcox

March 1987

TABLE OF CONTENTS

INTRODUCTION

The 68K-CPU is a 16-bit central processing unit using the 68000 or 68010 microprocessor. Its purpose is to provide computer system control and computational capability while meeting the IEEE Std-696 specifications for a bus master within an S-100 environment. The prototype model shown in Figures D-1 and D-2 was designed in modules for easy service and was constructed on a wire-wrap board for simple modification. When used in an S-100 system, it can run using its own on-board monitor or boot the CP/M-68K disk operating system.

While operating with a 6 MHz system clock, the CPU board fully meets the IEEE Std-696. It may also be operated with an 8- or 10-MHz system clock by replacing the oscillator module; however, it might not work properly with other system components above the Standard's 6 MHz maximum specified clock. It has been tested and runs normally at 10 MHz using the system configuration described in this technical manual.

Figure D-1 Top view of the 68K-CPU board.

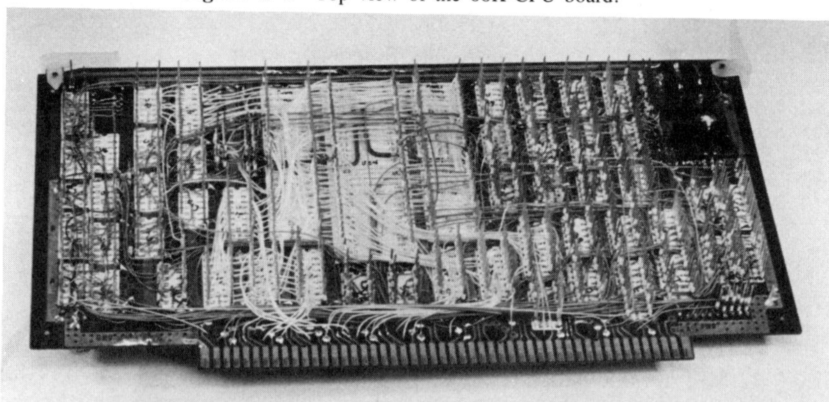

Figure D-2 Bottom view of the 68K-CPU board.

Features

The 68K-CPU has two pairs of 28-pin sockets that allow up to 64K of nonvolatile memory using 27128 EPROMs or 32K of RAM using 6264s. Either or both socket pairs may hold EPROM or RAM. Each pair of sockets is jumpered to allow 2716, 2732, 2764, and 27128 EPROMs or pairs of 6116 and 6264 RAM devices. The on-board local memory space is fully decoded as a 64K block and is switch-selectable anywhere in the full 16 Mb address range of the 68000. One pair of sockets is located in the lower 32K, the other pair in the upper 32K; this mapping can be jumper-reversed. During local memory operations, the CPU data-bus buffers are disabled.

External memory is addressed using the full 24-bit extended address on the bus. Memory transfers are either 8 or 16 bits, and external memory must respond to sXTRQ*. Byte-serial transfers are not supported; a jumper is provided to cause a non-maskable interrupt if a 16-bit operation is attempted to 8-bit memory. Extended I/O-mapped port transfers are implemented in the 64K memory range $FF0000 to $FFFFFF; any I/O below this range is memory-mapped. Standard I/O addressing is also supported for 256 devices.

A mapping circuit enables one pair of EPROMs for the first eight bus cycles after either a reset or power-on. Thus, when the 68000 is reset and reads addresses 0 through 7 for its stack pointer and program counter, it will read the EPROMs regardless of their normal location in memory. This allows system RAM in low memory so that exception vectors can be dynamically altered.

A wait generator jumper selects 0 to 8 wait states on all bus cycles. The jumper can also be set up so that waits are enabled for just I/O operations, program reads, or local EPROM or RAM accesses.

The S-100 bus lines NMI* and ERROR* are implemented as a non-maskable (level-7) interrupt to the 68000. Either the S-100 bus INT* or VI0* line may be jumpered for a 68000 level-6 interrupt. The vectored interrupts VI1* through VI5* are wired for level-5 through level-1 interrupts, respectively. A jumper enables 68000 auto-vector generation.

A watchdog timer can be jumper-enabled to signal a bus error condition if the processor remains frozen for approximately 7 μs; this error causes the 68000 halt LED to light. A second LED is connected to indicate a normal running program.

Switches are provided to single-step the 68000 by delaying DTACK*; all bus signals remain valid and can be easily checked during troubleshooting if necessary. Another switch generates a non-maskable interrupt. Using the Motorola TUTOR monitor, this causes a software abort that preserves all registers for inspection.

A number of jumpers are provided on the 68K-CPU board to allow for various options depending on the system configuration:

Wait select 0 to 8 for I/O, program, or local operation

Watchdog timer enable

Auto-vector enable

Enable NMI*/ERROR* if 16-bit operation to 8-bit board

MWRT enable

Select INT* or VI0* as 68000 level-6 interrupt

EPROM/RAM select for 2716, 2732, 2764, 27128 or 6116, 6264

Memory Pair-1 low, Pair-2 high, or reverse mapping

Reset/power-on jump

The total current required of the +8 V bus is under 1 A typical, 1.5 A maximum. One regulator provides +5 V to the 68000 and memory; a second regulator powers the rest of the board. Two heat sinks are used to allow maximum transistor cooling.

System Configuration

The system configuration depends on the software that will be used with the 68K-CPU. For example, for simple assembly-language programs and experiments, the Motorola TUTOR monitor should be installed. For a more powerful system, firmware can be included on the CPU board to allow booting the CP/M-68K disk operating system (DOS).

The Motorola TUTOR monitor is a 16 Kb program that was originally written for the Motorola Educational Computer Board (ECB). TUTOR EPROMs can be easily installed in the 68K-CPU and perform as the system monitor. TUTOR allows the user to handle memory and register display and modification, memory test, move, fill, and search for strings. In addition, the monitor supports a modem port to upload and download S-records and the console port. An interactive assembler allows the user to write programs easily; an interactive disassembler displays code already in memory.

There are several possibilities for configuration of the processor board within an IEEE Std-696 system:

- Use the CPU card with local on-board memory only,
- Use the CPU with only system memory,
- Use the CPU with both local and system memory.

All of these options require an I/O board for the system console. If the Motorola TUTOR monitor is used, this I/O board should use 6850 ACIAs for each of two serial ports. If a DOS is used, the the I/O board should match the requirements of the operating system.

A minimum system configuration requires the Motorola TUTOR monitor in one pair of memory sockets and a pair of 6116 RAMs (total 4K × 8) in the other pair. Because the monitor uses RAM up to $900, a pair of 6264 RAMs (total 16K × 8) allows for larger programs. Using this configuration with local on-board memory, system memory is not necessary. However, there is no need to use on-board memory in the minimum system: external system memory can be used instead as long as it can do 16-bit bus operations.

Both local and system memory are appropriate when a DOS will be used. The local on-board memory contains the monitor (if desired) and the code to boot the operating system; the system memory is used for the DOS after it boots up. A typical configuration includes the CompuPro Disk-1A controller with a pair of 8″ disk drives, disk-boot EPROM pair, 128 Kb or more of 8/16-bit memory, an I/O board, and CP/M-68K.

CPU SPECIFICATIONS

Processor	MC68000 or MC68010
Clock	6, 8, or 10 MHz using replaceable DIP oscillator
Memory (on-board)	16 to 64K EPROM (2716, 2732, 2764; 27128 pairs) 8 to 32K static RAM (6116, 6264 pairs) Maximum EPROM and RAM combination: 64 Kb Addressable on any 64K block
Waits	0 to 8 waits: On all bus cycles, on I/O, program reads, or local memory bus cycles
I/O	S-100 I/O-mapped port transfers implemented in address range $FF0000 to $FFFFFF
Interrupts	NMI* and ERROR* cause non-maskable interrupt INT* or VI0* jumper selection for a level-6 interrupt Vectored interrupts VI1* through VI5* implemented Autovector enable jumper
Watchdog timer	Signals bus error wthin 7 μs
Displays	LED 68000-Halt light LED test light jumper-connected to indicate running processor
Switches	Single-step/wait or run Software abort (if using TUTOR monitor) Selection of on-board memory base address
Jumpers	Wait selection: 0–8 wait states Watchdog timer enable Autovector enable Memory-access error enable MWRT enable INT* or VI0* as 68000 level-6 interrupt EPROM/RAM device type selection EPROM/RAM address swap Power-on jump enable
Power requirements	+8 V; 1 A typical, 1.5 A maximum
Size	IEEE Std-696 single-height wire-wrap card
Operating temperature	10°C to 35°C

INSTALLATION

The 68K-CPU is designed for installation in an IEEE Std-696 bus enclosure along with other system boards such as memory and I/O. In addition, a console is required equipment. If the CPU will be running with a DOS, then one or two disk drives are also necessary.

Hardware Requirements and Setup

The system configuration for operation with the TUTOR monitor and CP/M-68K operating system is shown in Figure D-3. The hardware required for this configuration is:

68K-CPU board with TUTOR and boot EPROMs,

128 Kb of system memory,

CompuPro Disk-1A disk controller board,

CompuPro Interfacer-4 I/O board,

6850 I/O board for TUTOR.

Because the 68K-CPU will operate as a permanent bus master, there should not be any other permanent bus masters in the system. As shown in Figure D-4, the disk controller board is a temporary bus master and can request the bus when it transfers information between memory and the disk using TMA.

The memory map of the system with the TUTOR monitor and the DOS is shown in Figure D-5. The system memory begins at address 0 and provides a minimum of 128 Kb for proper operation of CP/M-68K. (Additional RAM can be added, but CP/M-68K must be reconfigured to use the extra capability.) The TUTOR EPROMs are located at \$FD0000; when the 68000 is reset, however, these EPROMs are briefly enabled regardless of their location. Local RAM may be installed on the CPU board; its base address will be \$FD8000. All I/O port transfers are implemented in the 64 Kb memory range beginning with \$FF0000; any I/O below this point is memory-mapped.

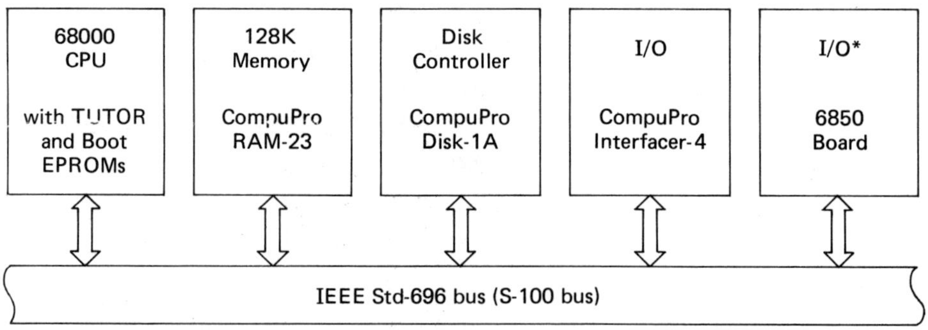

Figure D-3 System configuration for bringing up CP/M-68K on a 68000 processor. (*The 6850 I/O may be located on the 68000 CPU board rather than on a separate card.)

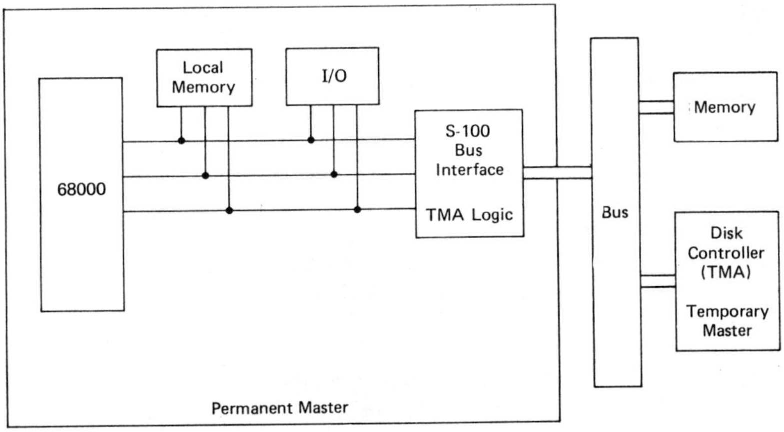

Figure D-4 The 68000 CPU board as permanent master in an S-100 system.

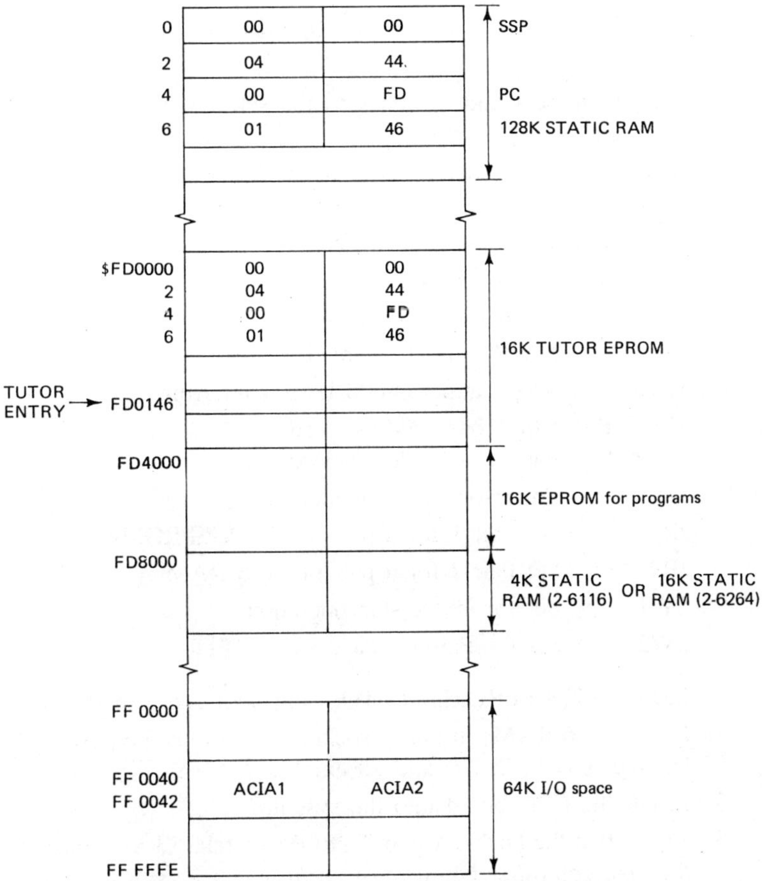

Figure D-5 Memory map of a complete system using TUTOR as the monitor and having the capability of booting a disk operating system.

Settings

1. Assuming the previous memory map, each of the boards in the system should be set according to Table D-1.

TABLE D-1 ADDRESSES ASSIGNED TO THE BOARDS IN THE CP/M-68K SYSTEM.

Board	*Base Address*
CPU: TUTOR EPROMs	$FD0000
Boot EPROMs	$FD4000
Memory: RAM-23	0
Disk Controller: Disk-1A	$FF00C0
I/O: Interfacer-4	$FF0010
I/O: 6850 board	$FF0040

2. Set all jumpers and switches to the settings shown in the Appendix examples. They are:

J1-J8	3 wait states on local bus cycles 8 wait states on I/O operations
J9	Watchdog timer enabled
J10	Autovector enabled
J11	Abort if system memory-access error
J12	MWRT signal enabled
J13 A-C	VI0* causes 68000 level-6 interrupt
J14 A-B C-D	Pair-1 base address $xx0000 Pair-2 base address $xx8000
J15	Power-on jump enabled
JB1	Set Pair-1 for a pair of 27128 EPROMs
JB2	Set Pair-2 for a pair of 6116 RAMs
SW1	Set for single-step operation
SW2	Set for Pair-1/2 base xx = $FD

3. Install 27128 EPROMs (TUTOR and boot code) in Pair-1 sockets.
4. Install 6116 RAMs in Pair-2 sockets. They must be positioned low in the sockets, leaving pins 1, 2, 27, and 28 empty.
5. Install the CPU board into the system.
6. Verify that the Disk-1A boot EPROM switch (S3-8) is turned off. The EPROM on the disk controller board must be disabled.

I/O board with 6850. The TUTOR firmware requires a 6850 port for console I/O. This can be provided by a 6850 located on the CPU board itself (not done in the case of the 68K-CPU because of lack of room) or by a separate 6850 I/O board. Figure D-6 shows an S-100 board with two 6850 ACIAs: one acts as TUTOR Port 1 and the other as Port 2. The addresses are set to $FF0040 as shown in Table D-1.

When the 68K-CPU board is reset, the TUTOR monitor is active and will send its normal prompt message to the 6850 Port 1. The CompuPro Interfacer-4 I/O board is not used at all with TUTOR: it is used only with CP/M-68K.

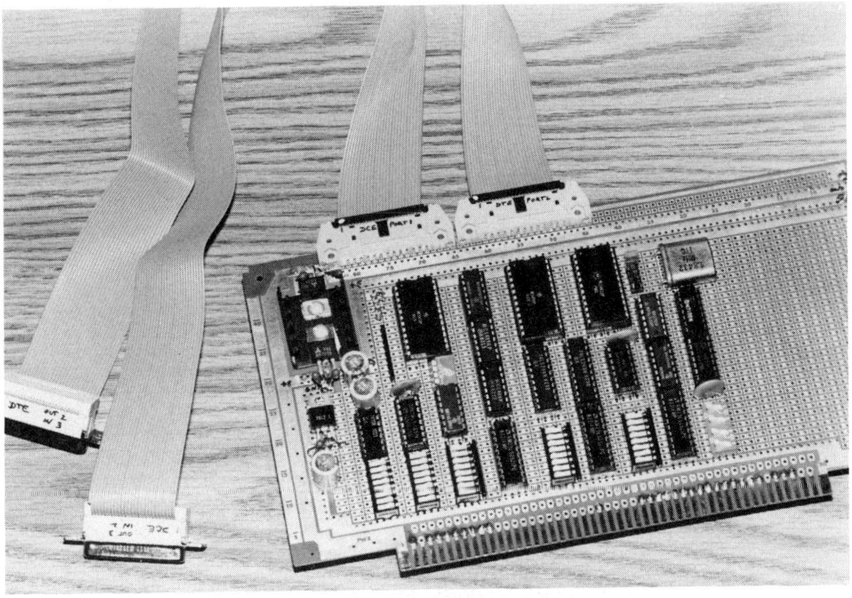

Figure D-6 An S-100 I/O board that provides two 6850 ACIA ports.

Software Requirements and Setup

The normal software required by the 68K-CPU for full system capability includes:

- TUTOR in two 27128 EPROMs (taking half the total space),
- Disk boot code in the upper half of the 27128s,
- CP/M-68K on 8″ disk as configured for the CompuPro CPU-68K.

In order to boot CP/M-68K as purchased stock from CompuPro, an Interfacer-4 is required. After booting the DOS, the BIOS (Basic I/O System) code can be modified to include the 6850 I/O board if desired. By doing this, TUTOR (which *must* use a 6850) and CP/M-68K can both use the same 6850 I/O board.

TUTOR modifications. The TUTOR firmware as purchased from Motorola or duplicated from the ECB assumes RAM from 0 to $7FFF maximum and the TUTOR ROMs from $8000 to $BFFF as shown in Figure D-7. There is *no* modification necessary if the TUTOR firmware is installed in a system with the same memory map. In fact, the 68K-CPU can be run using only local on-board memory in this configuration; however, it cannot boot an operating system. To take full advantage of TUTOR, it must be modified slightly so that it operates above the memory space needed by a DOS.

The TUTOR code can be easily modified for operation at $FD0000 as indicated earlier in Figure D-5. This is because the code is position-independent: it can be decoded anywhere in memory and still be functional. Consequently, the firmware can be installed in the 68K-CPU board and used with only two minor modifications:

1. Change the first 8 ROM locatons for the supervisory stack and initial program counter vectors,
2. Change the memory location of the I/O ports.

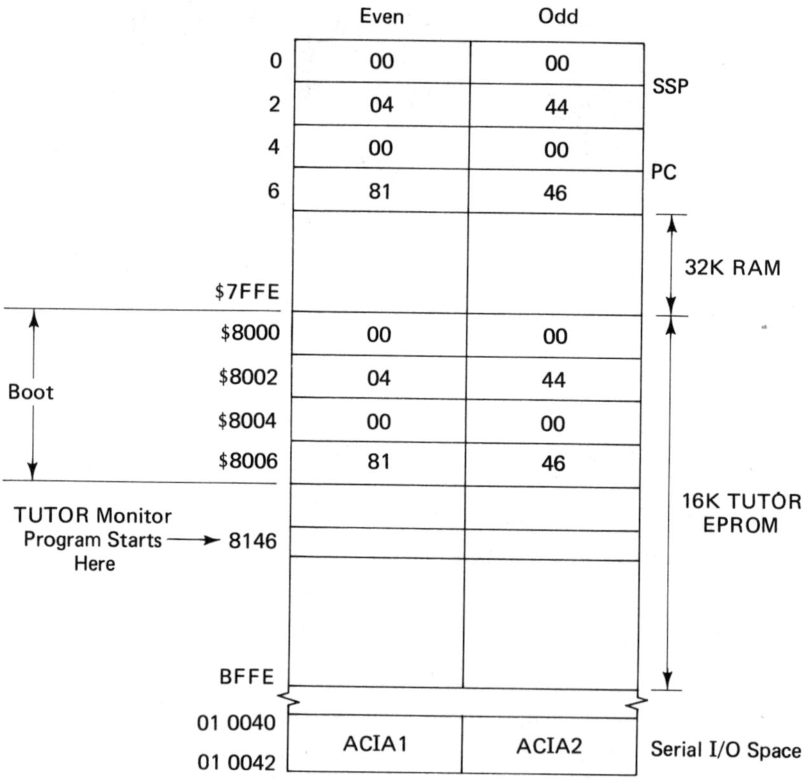

Figure D-7 Memory map of the ECB with the TUTOR EPROM decoded at $8000. Upon reset, the EPROM code marked "Boot" is also decoded at address 0.

These are the changes to TUTOR so it runs as a monitor for the 68K-CPU board with the Figure D-5 memory map:

	Old Value	*New Value*
Program Counter	00 00 81 46	00 FD 01 46
ACIA#1	00 01 00 40	00 FF 00 40
ACIA#2	00 01 00 41	00 FF 00 41
Prompt Message	TUTOR 1.3	S-bug 1.3

All the other TUTOR RAM locations are left just as in the ECB. For example, although the 68K-CPU system has a 128 Kb RAM starting at address 0, there is absolutely no difficulty in letting TUTOR use the lower 2 Kb for scratch RAM. Besides, the low memory area is used for 68000 exception vectors anyway, so there is really no point in modifying anything at all in low memory.

Disk boot code. In order to load CP/M-68K from disk, the 68000 must begin executing code to instruct the disk-controller card that it should read the first track of the disk. Figure D-8 shows the boot code necessary to accomplish this. The program is written specifically for the Intel 8272 floppy-disk controller IC in the CompuPro Disk-1A board. Although this code is assembled starting at $FD4000 for a pair of boot EPROMs, the program can be interactively entered into RAM using TUTOR and executed. If a different load address is used, it must not be at 0 because the disk data will load there.

As configured in the 68K-CPU system, TUTOR is located from $FD0000 to $FD3FFF; the next available address is $FD4000 where the boot code is located. TUTOR alone may be programmed into a pair of 2764s and then a second pair of 2764s used for the boot code; an alternative is to put both TUTOR and the boot code together in a pair of 27128s. If the boot EPROMs are not used, the program can be entered line by line into memory and then executed just as if it were in EPROM.

System Checkout

The required steps in bringing up the DOS using TUTOR are shown in Table D-2. TUTOR will provide the necessary vectors to initialize the 68000 and the code to begin operation with the console connected to the usual 6850 Port 1. It is essential that TUTOR perform properly with all the boards connected in the system as shown in Figure D-3. If it does not run, then troubleshoot the system before going further. Once TUTOR runs, however, use the memory-test ''BT'' function in TUTOR to verify that RAM is good; use some of the other functions to be sure that TUTOR is running normally. The TUTOR command set is shown in Table D-3.

```
*       Boot loader to read from Disk-1A for
*       CP/M-68K using 68000 board.
*       8/13/85

*       Locate just past S-bug Monitor code
        ORG     $FD4000

DRIADR  EQU     $FF00C0         * In I/O space

FDCSTAT EQU     DRIADR          * FDC stat / dr select
FDATA   EQU     DRIADR+1        * Data in / out
DRSTAT  EQU     DRIADR+2        * Drive stat / DMA adr
MOTREG  EQU     DRIADR+3        * Motor register

INTFLG  EQU     7
DELAY   EQU     $C000

BOOTER:
        LEA     FDCSTAT,A0
        LEA     FDATA,A1
        LEA     DRSTAT,A2

        MOVEQ   #INTFLG,D4

LOOP:   MOVE    #DELAY,D0

TIMER1: DBF     D0,TIMER1

*   Set DMA address
        MOVE.B  #0,(A2)
        MOVE.B  #0,(A2)
        MOVE.B  #0,(A2)

*   Do SPECIFY (3 bytes), RECALIBRATE (2 bytes)
        LEA     CMD1,A4
        MOVEQ   #4,D1           * Sending 5 bytes
RDY:    BTST    D4,(A0)         * FDC ready?
        BEQ.S   RDY
        MOVE.B  (A4)+,(A1)      * Send cmd bytes
        DBF     D1,RDY

RDY1:   BTST    D4,(A2)         * Drive rdy?
        BEQ     RDY1
RDY2:   BTST    D4,(A0)         * FDC rdy?
        BEQ     RDY2

*   Do SENSE-INTERRUPT-STATUS (1 byte)
        MOVE.B  (A4)+,(A1)      * Next cmd in line

        MOVE    #DELAY,D0
TIMER2: DBF     D0,TIMER2

RDY3:   BTST    D4,(A0)         * FDC rdy?
```

Figure D-8 The 68000 boot code used to read the first track of the CP/M-68K system disk. The Intel 8272 floppy-disk controller is used to read the disk.

```
         BEQ       RDY3
         MOVE.B    (A1),D7          * Read Status Reg 0

RDY4:    BTST      D4,(A0)          * FDC rdy?
         BEQ       RDY4
         MOVE.B    (A1),D6          * Read Pres Cyl Number

         SUB.B     #$20,D7          * d5=1 when seek done
         OR.B      D6,D7
         BNE.S     LOOP             * Waiting for disk

*  Do READ-DATA (9 bytes)
READIT:  MOVEQ     #7,D3
         LEA       CMD2,A4
         MOVEQ     #8,D0            * Sending 9 bytes
RDY5:    BTST      D4,(A0)          * FDC rdy?
         BEQ       RDY5
         MOVE.B    (A4)+,(A1)       * Send cmds
         DBF       D0,RDY5

RDY6:    BTST      D4,(A2)          * Drive rdy?
         BEQ       RDY6
RDY7:    BTST      D4,(A0)          * FDC rdy?
         BEQ       RDY7

         MOVE.B    (A1),D7          * Read Status Reg 0
RDY8:    BTST      D4,(A0)
         BEQ       RDY8
         MOVE.B    (A1),D6          * Read Status Reg 1
         MOVEQ     #4,D0
RDY9:    BTST      D4,(A0)
         BEQ       RDY9
         MOVE.B    (A1),D5          * Read Status Reg 2
         DBF       D0,RDY9

         AND.B     #$BF,D7          * Reg 0
         AND.B     #$7F,D6          * Reg 1
         OR.B      D6,D7
         DBEQ      D3,READIT

         BNE       BOOTER           * Around again

         LEA       $00000000,A0     * 68000 at new code
         CLR.B     MOTREG           * Disable boot rom &
                                    *  turn motor off
         JMP       (A0)

CMD1:    DC.B      03,$8F,$22,07,00
         DC.B      08
CMD2:    DC.B      06,00,00,00,01,00
         DC.B      $1A,07,$80,00

         END       BOOTER
```

Figure D-8 (*Cont.*)

TABLE D-2 STEPS INVOLVED IN BOOTING CP/M-68K USING TUTOR.

1. Install the proper boards as shown in Figure D-3.
2. Set all the addresses according to Table D-1.
3. Connect the system console to the 6850 Port 1.
4. Install the pair of boot EPROMs given in Figure D-8.
5. Power up the system; TUTOR should operate normally.
6. Using TUTOR, check the operation of the overall system; RAM can be checked easily using the TUTOR "BT" function.
7. If the boot EPROMs (Step 4) were not available, type in the Figure D-8 program using TUTOR.
8. Begin disk boot program execution by typing "GO FD4000"; this should cause the drive-activity light to flash.
9. Reconnect the system console to the Interfacer-4 port.
10. Insert the CP/M-68K system disk into the drive. The CP/M prompt should appear shortly.

TABLE D-3 A SUMMARY OF THE TUTOR COMMAND SET.

Command	*Description*
MD	Memory Display in hex, ASCII, or disassembled mnemonics
MM	Memory Modify in hex, ASCII, or interactively assemble
MS	Memory Set
DF	Display Formatted registers
.A0 - .A7	Display and set address registers
.D0 - .D7	Display and set data registers
.PC	Display and set program counter
.SR	Display and set status register
.SS	Display and set supervisory stack pointer
.US	Display and set user stack pointer
BF	Block Fill memory with value
BM	Block Move memory
BT	Block Test segment of memory
BS	Block Search memory for hex or string
DC	Data Conversion for on-screen math
HE	Help with available commands
BR	Breakpoint set
NOBR	Remove breakpoint
GO, G	Go ahead with execution of program
GT	Go until breakpoint
GD	Go Direct; like GO but no initial trace
TR, T	Trace an instruction
TT	Trace with temporary breakpoint
DU	Dump memory to host in S-Record format
LO	Load S-Records from host
VE	Verify memory with S-Records from host
TM	Transparent Mode to pass data between Port 1 and Port 2
*	Send message following "*" to Port 2
PA	Printer Attach
NOPA	Reset printer attach
PF	Port Format: set nulls
OF	Display Offsets for relocating code
.R0 - .R6	Display and set relative-offset registers

Using the code in Figure D-8, the disk-read operation can be started by the command:

S-bug 1.3> GO FD4000

When the program runs, the disk drive activity light will flash on and off indicating that the controller is trying to read a disk. If the light does not flash, then there is a problem in the system that must be resolved before continuing. Assuming that the light is flashing, disconnect the console from the 6850 port and reconnect it to the Interface-4 console port. Next, insert the system disk into the drive. After reading the disk, the CP/M prompt should appear on the console screen.

After CP/M-68K is running, a number of programs can be executed to make sure the system is satisfactory. A benchmark program such as the Sieve of Erastosthenes can demonstrate how fast the 68K-CPU runs relative to other CPU boards. A C-language version of the sieve program is shown in Figure D-9. The program uses a real-time clock board (Text Chapter 5) to print the program start time and finish times. Running at a 10 MHz clock, the 68K-CPU typically completes the program in 3.6 seconds as shown in Figure D-10.

```
/* ERAST      Prime number generator benchmark program.
              Sieve of Erastosthenes algorithm courtesy of
              Jim Gilbreath. Ref: Byte, Jan 1983, p.284.      */

#include <stdio.h>

#define CLOCK   0xA0   /* port address */
#define  SIZE   8190

char        flags[SIZE+1];

main()
    {
    int i, prime, k, count, iter;

    printf("\n Start  ");
    timeprn();
    printf("\n Doing 10 iterations.\n");

    for (iter = 1; iter <= 10; iter++ )
        {
        count = 0;
        for (i = 0; i <= SIZE; i++)
            flags[i] = TRUE;
        for (i = 0; i <= SIZE; i++)
            {
            if (flags[i])
                {
                prime = i + i + 3;
                for (k = i + prime; k <= SIZE; k += prime)
                    flags[k] = FALSE;
                count++;
                }
            }
        }
```

Figure D-9 Listing of the Sieve of Erastosthenes.

```
   printf("\n %d %d\n", prime, count);
   printf("\n Finish ");
   timeprn();
   }

timeprn()
   {
   int hours, minutes, seconds, hundred;

   hours   = inp(CLOCK+4) & 0xff;
   minutes = inp(CLOCK+3) & 0xff;     /* results read are in hex */
   seconds = inp(CLOCK+2) & 0xff;
   hundred = inp(CLOCK+1) & 0xff;

   printf("Time = %x:%x:%x.%x", hours,minutes,seconds,hundred);
   }
```

Figure D-9 (*Cont.*)

```
S-bug  1.3 > GO FD4000
PHYSICAL ADDRESS=00FD4000


CP/M-68K(tm) Version 1.1
Copyright (c) 1982 Digital Research, Inc.

CompuPro CP/M-68K version 1.1L
Copyright (c) 1983 CompuPro

A>MFORM M X

A>USER 1

1A>DIR
A: HELLO    68K : HELLO    C  : ERAST    68K : TIMER    C : INOUT    C
A: ERAST    C   : TIMEPRN  C  : MISCLIB  O   : MISCLIB  S : TIMEPRN  68K
A: ERASTIME 68K : ERASTIME C

1A>ERASTIME

 Start  Time = 9:49:15.52
 Doing 10 iterations.

 16381 1899

 Finish Time = 9:49:19.16
1A>                                    <-------- RESET 68000 to
                                                 restart TUTOR monitor
S-bug  1.3 >
```

Figure D-10 CP/M-68K boot sequence and execution of the Sieve benchmark program.

OPERATION

The 68K-CPU board can be operated either with the TUTOR monitor program or with the CP/M-68K disk operating system. When the system is first powered up, the 68000 reset vectors in the EPROM set cause the CPU to begin executing the monitor program. Using the TUTOR monitor, the set of commands in Table D-3 can be executed for testing the 68000 or debugging assembly language programs. By executing the disk boot code in Figure D-8, the CPU can read the system tracks on a disk to boot up CP/M-68K. After the DOS is running, all of the normal CP/M-68K operating system commands can be used.

Monitor

To begin monitor operation:

1. Turn on the system power; TUTOR should run immediately.
2. Check 128 Kb system memory by executing "BT 900 01FFFE".

Operating System

To boot the operating system:

1. Start the monitor as above.
2. Execute the disk boot code by typing "GO FD4000".
3. Insert the CP/M-68K system disk into the drive.
4. The DOS sign-on message will appear as in Figure D-10.

CIRCUIT DESCRIPTION

The 68K-CPU was planned for use with either the TUTOR monitor or the CP/M-68K operating system. The processor hardware was designed to meet several important criteria:

- The parts used in the CPU board must be easy to obtain and easy to replace if repair is necessary.
- The CPU board must be highly modular so that each portion of the CPU can be easily designed and developed.
- All the CPU modules must be easy to integrate into a final operational processor board.
- Troubleshooting should be easily accomplished with the modular design of the CPU board.

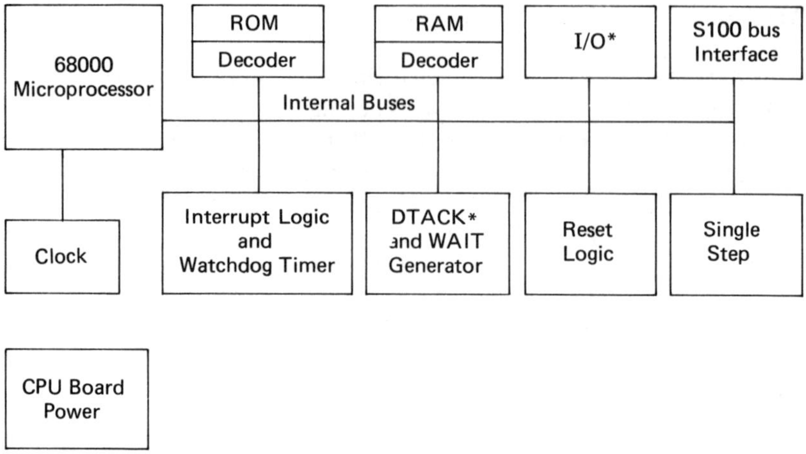

Figure D-11 The major functions on the CPU board. (*The I/O module was not included on the CPU board; a circuit like Figure 11.11 in the text may be added if desired.)

The major modules in the processor board are shown in Figure D-11. They are all interconnected by the address, data, and control buses of the 68000 microprocessor. Each module appears in the schematic diagrams at the end of the technical manual and will be referred to in the following explanations by drawing number.

CPU and Clock Module—Drawing 1

The 68000 microprocessor is the heart of the system; a 68010 can be substituted directly for the 68000 if desired. Either MPU can run with a system clock of up to 12 MHz, although care must be taken that system memory does not require extra wait states. For example, a 10 MHz system with no waits is faster than a 12 MHz system with 1 wait; in such a case, the 10 MHz clock is preferable. If the 68010 is substituted for the 68000, certain exception-handling code in the TUTOR monitor will not return proper results. In general, however, there are no severe problems using TUTOR with the 68010.

Two clock signals are provided for the processor and the S-100 system through the 74265 clock driver. The CLK68 signal goes to the 68000 and several circuits on the CPU board; the inverted clock, SYSCLK, is used on the CPU board and is also the S-100 system clock.

Reset Logic—Drawing 1

The reset logic provides an automatic reset for the 68000 and for the S-100 system upon power-up. Both the RESET* and HALT* controls of the 68000 are held low for approximately 200 ms during this power-up reset of the system. The timer also provides a similar reset pulse when the S-100 RESET* control is asserted. The HALT LED is turned on during this reset time.

In the event of a 68000 error that causes the processor to stop, the 68000 energizes the HALT* control. This also turns on the HALT LED to indicate an abnormal condition.

Single-Step Module—Drawing 1

The hardware single-step module on the 68K-CPU operates by delaying DTACK* so that one bus cycle at a time can be executed. While in the single-step mode, the watchdog timer is disabled so that the timer does not halt the processor. When the 68000 single-steps using a delayed DTACK*, all of the bus signals are asserted. This means that the single-step module can be used to troubleshoot the hardware by checking each bus cycle individually. This is an advantage over the typical software single-step in which a complete instruction is executed for each step.

TMA Module—Drawing 1

The S-100 bus arbitration can be accomplished using the 68000 bus arbitration sequence with very little external logic. The 68000, acting as permanent bus master, will always relinquish the bus to a TMA device requesting it. Thus, when HOLD* is asserted by the system device (such as a disk controller board), the TMA module logic asserts the 68000 BR* control, and the 68000 begins its bus arbitration. After the 68000 finishes its current bus cycle, it asserts BG*, which then signals the TMA device (using pHLDA) that it has the bus. When the TMA device is done with the bus, it negates HOLD* and control returns to thc 68000.

ROM/RAM Decode—Drawing 1

The local on-board ROM and RAM sockets (Pair-1 and Pair-2) are addressed at any 64K boundary in the entire 16 Mb range of the 68000. Switch SW2 allows selection of the base address of this 64K page of local memory. As configured, local memory is set at $FD0000; the $FD page address is set by SW2. Within the 64K page, Pair-1 or Pair-2 sockets can be set at 0 or $8000 base. This means that EPROMs in the Pair-1 sockets can be at $FD0000 and RAM in the Pair-2 sockets can be $FD8000; if jumper J14 is reversed, then Pair-1 is at $FD8000 and Pair-2 at $FD0000.

The boot jumper J15 enables the Pair-1 sockets during the first four bus cycles after a 68000 reset. If EPROMs (such as the TUTOR set) are in the Pair-1 sockets, the 68000 will fetch the SSP and PC vectors from the first eight locations in the EPROMs. Either ROM or RAM can be in either or both pairs of sockets, but for the proper operation of a system reset, the on-board EPROMs *must* be installed in the Pair-1 sockets. Naturally, if some external EPROM board responds to the 68000 SSP and PC fetch upon reset, then J15 must be open; in this case, all four sockets may be RAM, EPROM, or unused.

If J15 is jumpered to enable booting from the 68K-CPU board, then any external EPROMs must be disabled. For example, the CompuPro Disk-1A board has a single boot

EPROM that is enabled by turning on SW3-8; this switch *must* be turned off so as not to conflict with the boot EPROMs on the 68K-CPU board.

The Disk-1A single EPROM cannot be used to boot the 68K-CPU board even if J15 is open. The code contained in the EPROM is suitable for booting, but it can only be read 8 bits at a time. The 68K-CPU board does 16-bit program reads only, and there is no provision for byte-serial reads from the system bus. If the system memory responds to sXTRQ* by placing 16 bits on the data bus and asserting SIXTN* there is no problem; unfortunately, the Disk-1A board can only respond with 8 bits.

When the 68000 reads or writes to an address in the 64K page selected for the on-board ROM and RAM sockets, then LOCAL is asserted. If LOCAL or LOCAL* is asserted, then no data will be transferred to external boards even if they happen to have the same address. The RDY bus signal is also ignored at this time. If a system board responds because of an address overlap (accidental) and asserts RDY, it will have no effect on the 68K-CPU. Note that LOCAL does not disconnect the system control output bus: doing so will cause system failure.

I/O Decode—Drawing 1

The address range from $FF0000 to $FFFFFF is designated as I/O space for the 68K-CPU board. Although the 68000 itself does only memory-mapped I/O, an S-100 I/O bus cycle can be initiated if an address in the top range of memory is used in a program. The I/O* signal from the I/O decoder sets the proper status levels on the bus.

ROM and RAM Module—Drawing 2

The ROM and RAM sockets are enabled by the ROMSEL* and RAMSEL* controls from the ROM/RAM Decoder. The sockets are always selected in pairs (high and low 8-bits) so that the 68000 can do 16-bit read or write operations. When the 68000 does 8-bit operations, either UDS* or LDS* is asserted; the single data strobe along with the ROMSEL* or RAMSEL* control will determine which socket is used.

Both Pair-1 and Pair-2 sockets are identical. Pair-1 is taken as ROM only because this pair will be enabled during a 68000 reset. Either or both pairs of sockets can be used for EPROMs or RAM as long as the 68000 can successfully get the SSP and PC vectors when reset.

Two jumper blocks are provided for the socket pairs so that EPROM or RAM selections can be changed. Both devices in Pair-1 must be identical, and both in Pair-2 must be identical. However, the devices in Pair-1 do not have to match those in Pair-2. The EPROM selection can be made among the 2716, 2732, 2764, and 27128; the RAM can be either the 6116 or 6264. The TUTOR firmware requires a pair of 2764 EPROMs; any disk-booter code must be programmed into additional devices. In the present system, the TUTOR firmware is in a 27128 pair along with the disk-booter code; the Pair-2 sockets use 6116 RAMs.

DTACK* and WAIT Generator—Drawing 3

This module is an integral part of the S-100 interface as shown in Figure D-12 and Figure D-13. Two gates form the bus-control logic and indicate the beginning of every 68000 bus cycle by asserting BCYCLE. This signal is used to return DTACK* to the 68000 so it can complete each bus cycle; if extra wait states are needed, then DTACK* can be delayed by 0 to 8 clock cycles depending on the J1-J8 jumper selection. The S-100 system can also request the 68000 to wait by negating RDY (i.e., pull the RDY line LOW) for as long as needed.

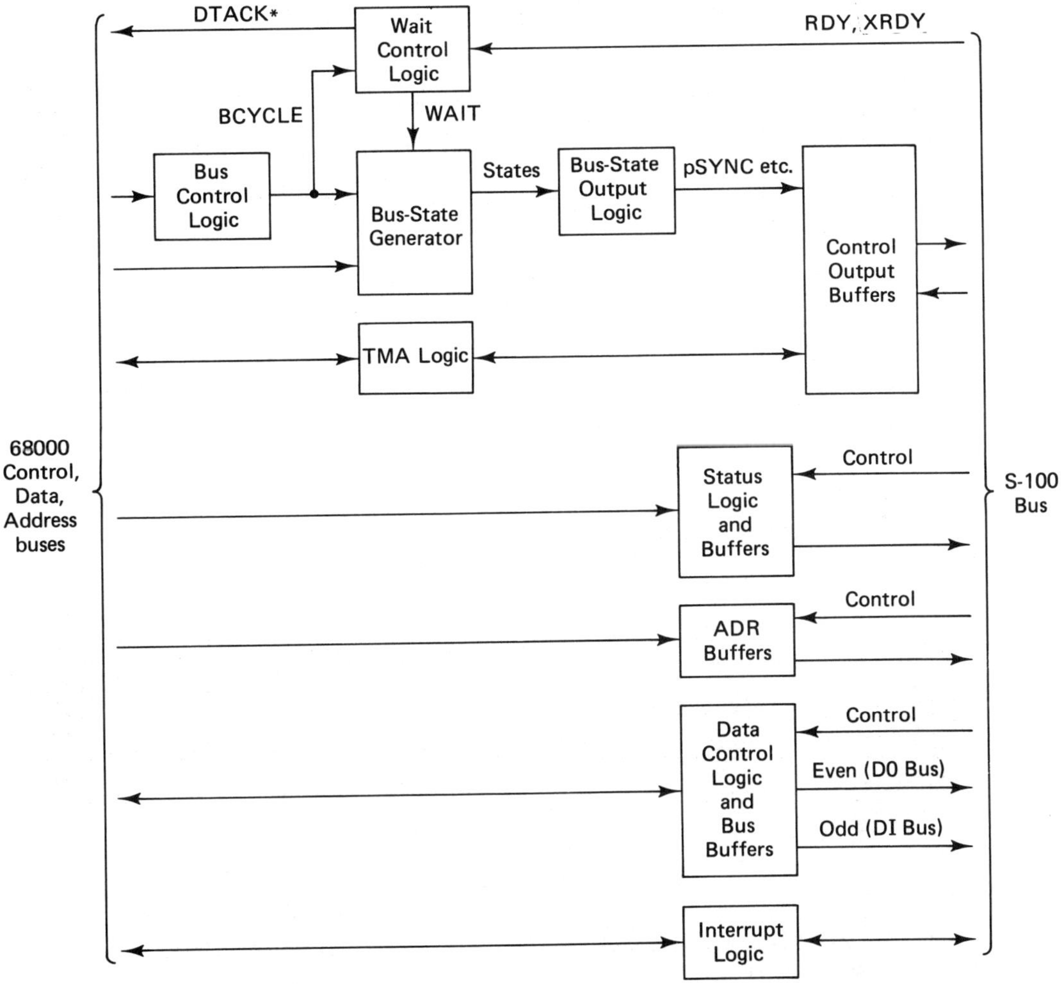

Figure D-12 Block diagram of complete S-100 bus interface module.

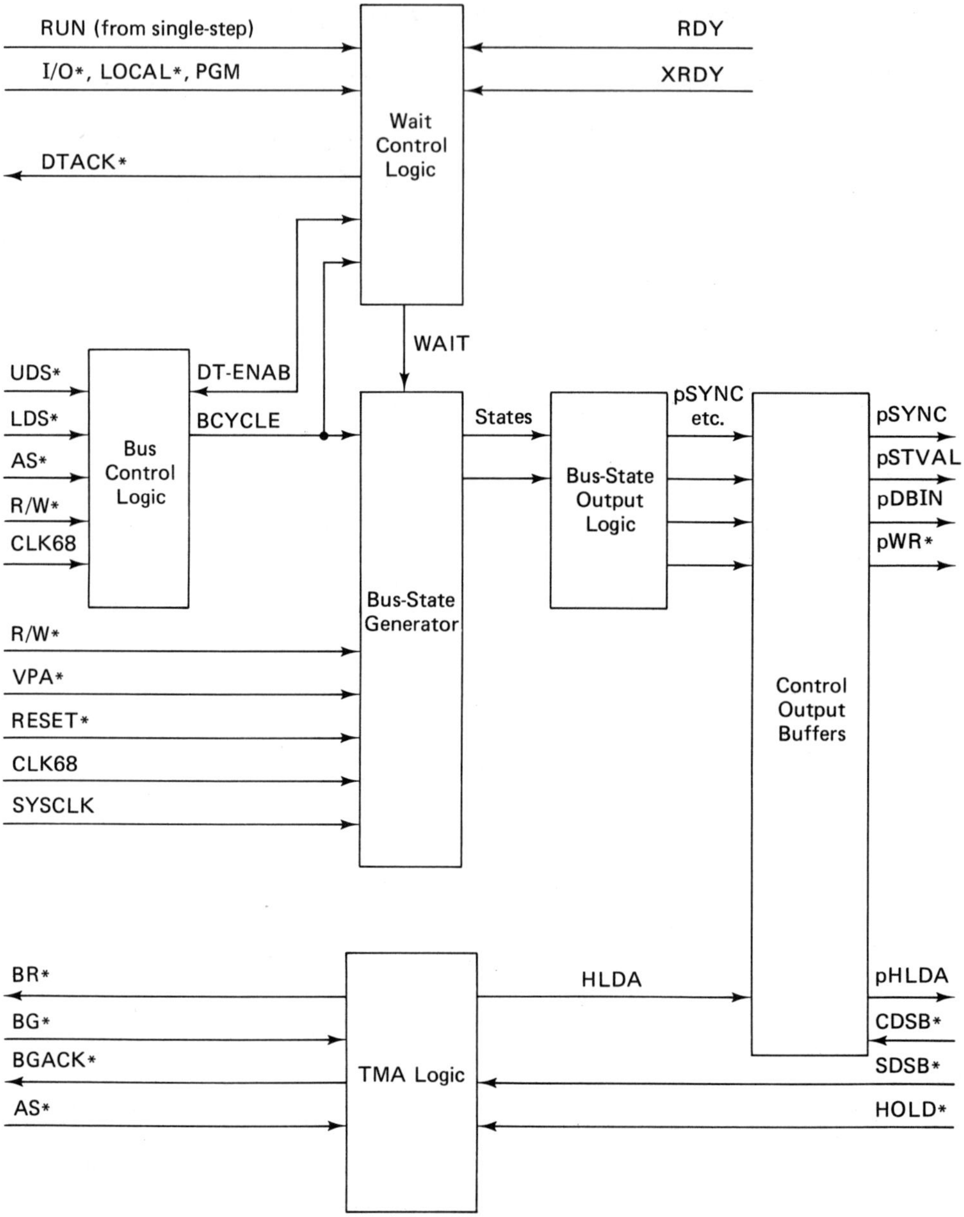

Figure D-13 Detailed block diagram of DTACK* and WAIT generator plus bus-state generator modules.

Bus-State Generator—Drawing 3

As shown in the Figure D-14 state diagram, the bus-state generator is a sequential state machine that stays in the IDLE state, BSi, until BCYCLE is asserted. Once started, it goes to the first state, BS1, and provides the S-100 pSYNC control to the system. Next, if no internal or external waits have been requested, it goes into the second state, BS2, to output either pDBIN (to read) or pWR* (to write). One clock cycle later, it returns to the IDLE state until the next 68000 bus cycle begins. If waits have been requested, the bus-state generator will enter the BSw wait state until WAIT is negated; then it goes into BS2 and finally BSi.

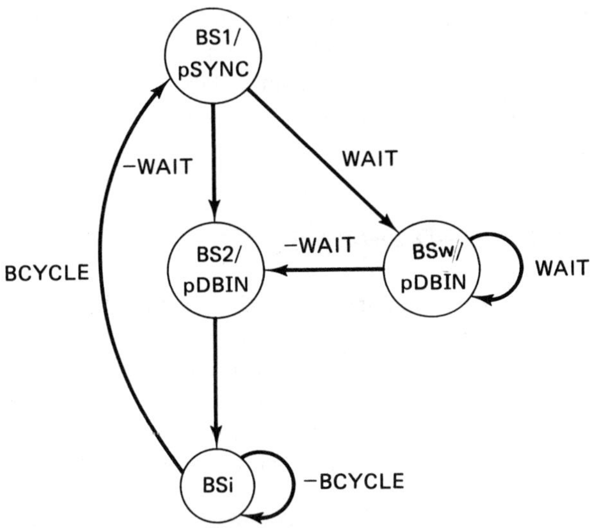

Figure D-14 State diagram of the bus-state generator. The WAIT signal is derived from the S-100 RDY input and the output of the on-board wait generator.

Bus-State Output Logic—Drawing 3

The bus-state output logic drives the S-100 control output bus so that the system always has the proper pSYNC, pSTVAL*, pDBIN, and pWR* signals. The output at any point in time depends only on the state of the bus-state generator. The control output bus buffer can be disabled by the S-100 signal CDSB* so that a TMA device can take over the bus.

Interrupt Logic—Drawing 4

The S-100 bus lines NMI* and ERROR* are implemented as a level-7 non-maskable interrupt (NMI) to the 68000. In addition, a local on-board abort circuit can initiate a level-7 interrupt; the TUTOR firmware supports this NMI by displaying all the 68000 registers for recovery from a program error. For example, if a program appears dead, toggling SW1-3 to ''abort'' will restore control to TUTOR as long as the errant program has not destroyed the level-7 vector in low memory.

The 68K-CPU board requires system memory that responds to the sXTRQ* line with a 16-bit transfer. If only 8-bit memory is present in the system, it will not return SIXTN* in response to the sXTRQ* request for 16 bits; this combination is a memory error that can be flagged by a 68000 interrupt. Jumper J11 can be connected to result in a level-7 NMI if SIXTN* is asserted, sXTRQ* is negated, an interrupt is not being acknowledged, and the processor is not addressing local memory. Note, however, that 8-bit memory can be present in the system so long as the 68000 does only 8-bit operations on it.

Either the S-100 bus INT* or VI0* line may be jumpered for a 68000 level-6 interrupt. The vectored interrupts VI1* through VI5* are wired for level-5 through level-1 interrupts, respectively. The J10 jumper enables 68000 autovector generation for cases when the interrupting slave device cannot place a vector on the bus. When J10 is enabled, INT* and any of the vectored interrupt inputs can obtain their vectors directly from the 68000.

Watchdog Timer—Drawing 4

A watchdog timer can be jumper-enabled to signal a bus error condition if the processor remains frozen for approximately 7 μs; this error causes the 68000 halt LED to light. The timer is automatically disabled when in the troubleshooting single-step mode.

The timer must be disabled by removing the jumper if an external system bus single-step board is used. Unless disabled, the watchdog timer will signal a bus error that halts the 68000 if the Jade ''Bus Probe'' causes an extended wait (by negating XRDY to a LOW level).

Status Logic and Buffers—Drawing 4

The status module provides the required signals to the S-100 bus concerning the bus cycle being executed. The buffer is disabled when the SDSB* is asserted by a TMA device taking over the system bus. The 74LS139 decoder that generates the interrupt acknowledge is used to form the Boolean function INTACK* = FC0 • FC1 • FC2.

Data-Bus Logic—Drawing 5

The data-bus logic is implemented using 74LS352 multiplexers to generate the four buffer-enable signals to properly transfer 8- or 16-bit data from the 68000 to the system. The S-100 bus can do either byte or word transfers: the two 8-bit unidirectional buses for byte operations are ganged together into one 16-bit bidirectional bus for word transfers. The control inputs and the logic outputs are shown in Table D-4.

TABLE D-4 CONTROL INPUTS AND LOGIC OUTPUTS REQUIRED TO SET THE BUS BUFFERS TO TRANSFER 8- OR 16-BIT DATA.

Type of Transfer to/from Bus	*Function*	*Control inputs*				*Control logic outputs*				
		*DODSB** •LOCAL*	R/W*	UDS*	LDS*	sXTRQ*	EBRD	OBWR	EBXCVR	OBXCVR
8-bit	Odd-in	H	H	H	L	H	Off	Off	Off	IN
	Even-in	H	H	L	H	H	ON	Off	Off	IN
	Odd-out	H	L	H	L	H	Off	ON	Off	Off
	Even-out	H	L	L	H	H	Off	Off	OUT	Off
16-bit	16-in	H	H	L	L	L	Off	Off	IN	IN
	16-out	H	L	L	L	L	Off	Off	OUT	OUT
None	LOCAL	L	d	d	d	H	Off	Off	Off	Off
	IDLE	d	H	H	H	H	Off	Off	Off	Off

Data-Bus Buffers—Drawing 5

The four buffers between the 68000 and the S-100 bus are connected as shown in Figure D-15. Using this configuration, the 68000 can read or write 8-bit even-byte or odd-byte data as well as do full 16-bit word transfers. The buffers to the S-100 system are disabled if the 68000 is operating in local on-board memory space.

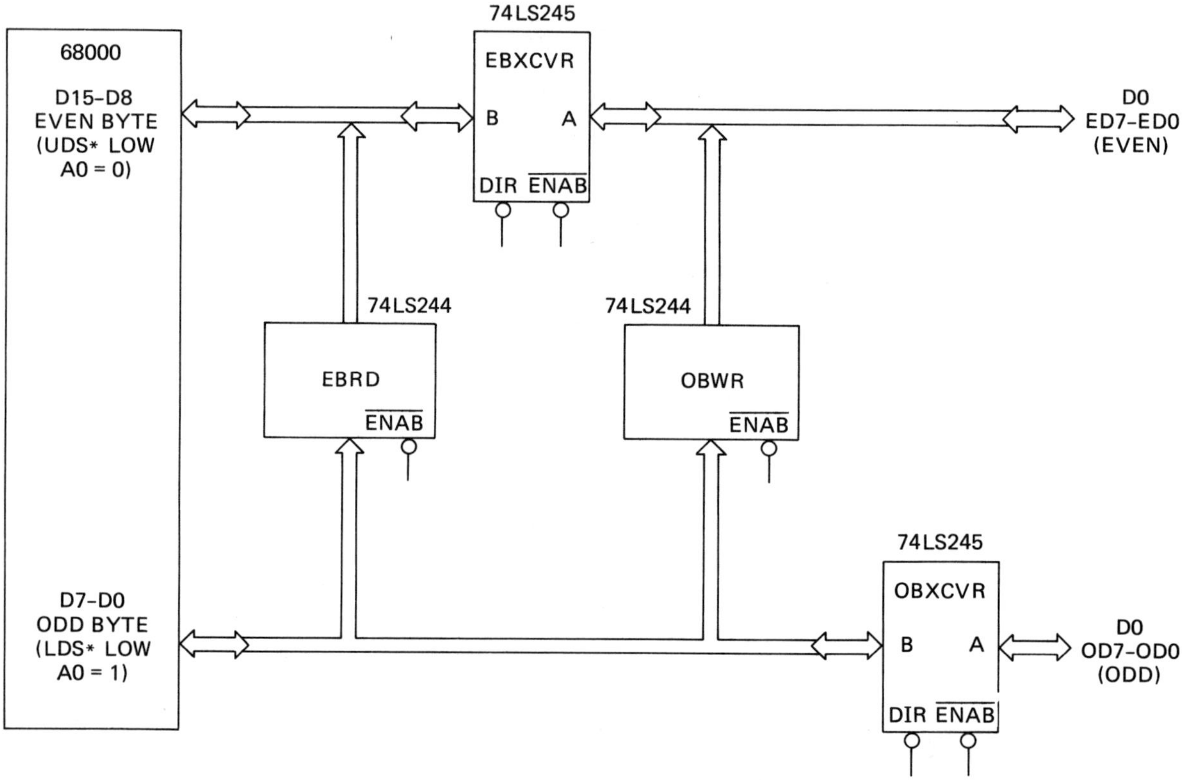

Figure D-15 Data bus buffers to interface the 68000 to the S-100 bus.

Address-Bus Buffers—Drawing 6

The 68K-CPU provides 24 address lines to the S-100 bus. The least-significant address bit, A0, is equal to UDS*. The UDS* signal is lengthened by approximately 100 ns so that A0 stays valid on the system bus until the end of the current bus cycle.

Power—Drawing 7

Two regulated supplies with heat sinks are used for power to the 68K-CPU board. One of the supplies powers the 68000 plus the four ROM/RAM sockets; the other powers all the TTL ICs on the board.

MWRT and 2 MHz Clock—Drawing 7

The memory-write strobe, MWRT, must be provided by the 68K-CPU for proper operation of the system; it can be disabled if necessary. The 2 MHz clock is provided for general system use; it is not synchronized with the SYSCLK.

TROUBLESHOOTING

Because of the highly modular design of the 68K-CPU board, troubleshooting can quickly localize a problem and correct it. Of the many general troubleshooting techniques that can be used to repair a system, the two most powerful are:

1. Freerunning the processor,
2. In-circuit emulation.

These involve removing the 68K-CPU card from the system, setting up test connections, installing an extension card, and taking a number of measurements.

Initial Troubleshooting Tests

Before starting full-scale troubleshooting, do a number of simple checks first:

1. Has one of the single-step or abort switches been accidentally changed to step or halt the processor?
2. Check both the power supplies for $+5$ V $\pm$ 5 percent.
3. Look at the HALT light. Is it on? If not, press the system reset button: the HALT light should go on during the time the button is pressed. If the light stays on all the time, disable the watchdog timer; does it go off?
4. Check the RUN light. It should be partially lit while the 68000 runs the TUTOR monitor. It should never be fully off or on unless the 68000 has stopped somewhere.
5. Plug in a Jade ''Bus Probe'' as shown in Figure D-16. Set it to single-step; reset the 68000, then begin stepping. Does the 68000 properly step through the SSP and PC vector fetches?

Figure D-16 The Jade Bus Probe installed in the S-100 frame for troubleshooting. It is used to display address and data-bus bits for each bus cycle. (Courtesy Jade Computer Products)

6. Remove the other boards from the S-100 system, especially any memory boards. Does the 68000 appear to single-step properly? Has some other board caused the 68000 to halt?
7. Reseat the 68K-CPU in its socket. Be sure the card-edge connections are clean.

If none of the above simple checks gives a clue as to the nature of the system failure, remove the 68K-CPU and install an extension card between it and the S-100 bus. Use a logic probe or an oscilloscope to check quickly some vital points in the system:

8. Check CLK68 and SYSCLK at the outputs of the clock drivers.
9. Is there some activity at the 68000 controls for AS*, UDS*, LDS*, R/W*, and DTACK*?
10. If DTACK* is HIGH and does not appear to change at all, check the DTACK* and WAIT module (Drawing 3). Is RUN set HIGH? Are RDY and XRDY from the S-100 bus HIGH?
11. Use a logic probe with pulse memory connected to DTACK* while holding the system reset. Release the reset: was there any DTACK* activity at all? If so, the 68000 likely ran for a few bus cycles and halted because of bad local memory. Figure D-17 shows the bus activity that takes place on reset.

0000 = 00 00 04 44 00 FD 01 46
FD0146 = 48B8 0001 0406 MOVE.W DØ, $406
FD014C = 40F8 0406 MOVE.W SR, $406

BOOT SYSTEM
RESET S-bug MONITOR

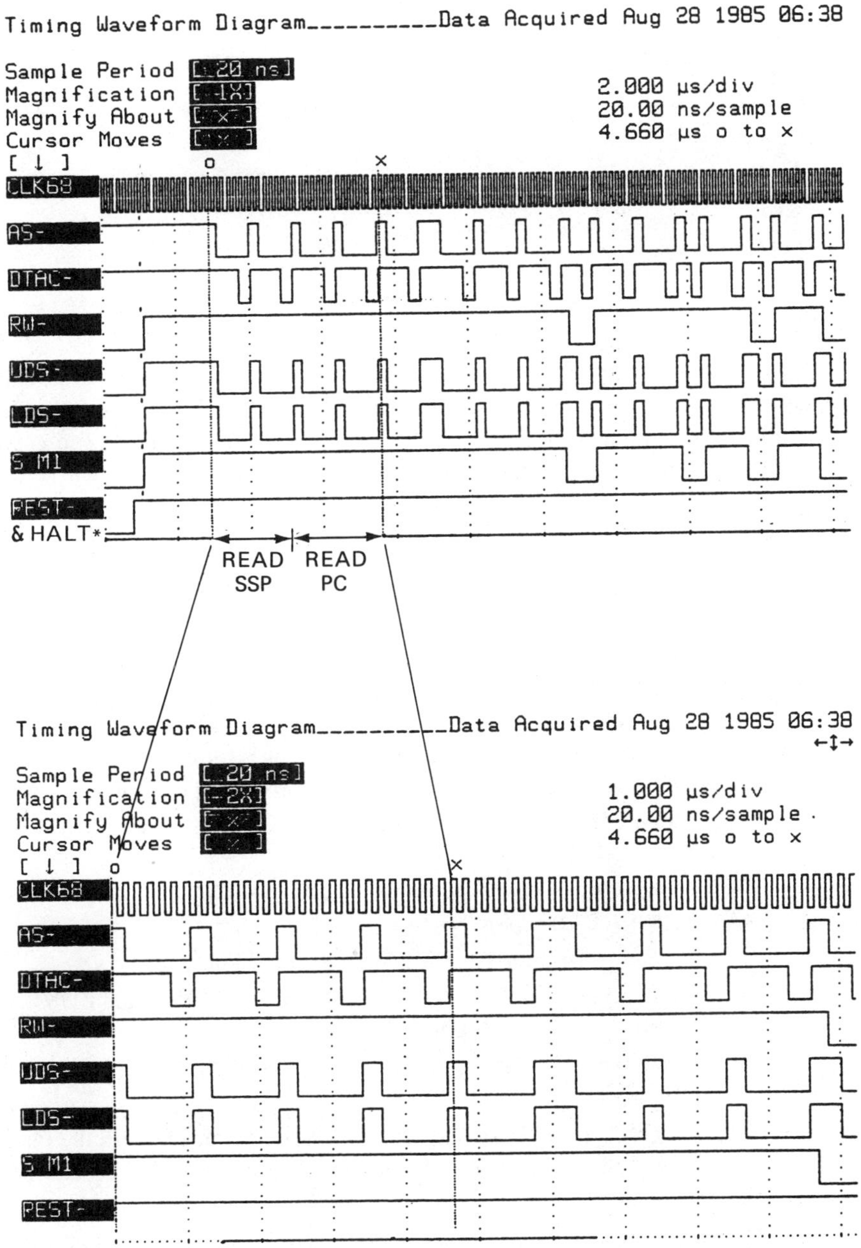

Figure D-17 Typical bus activity when the 68000 is reset.

TABLE D-5 USES FOR VARIOUS COMMON TEST EQUIPMENT.

Equipment	*Check for*
HALT LED on 68K-CPU board	Lights when 68000 halts
	Lights when Reset pressed
RUN LED on 68K-CPU board	Usually partially lit; never fully on or off.
Voltmeter	Proper +5 V supplies and +5 V at all ICs on board
Logic probe	CLK68 and SYSCLK running 68000 address and data strobes DTACK* activity
Oscilloscope	All the above

Table D-5 shows the tools used to check for proper operation of the 68K-CPU. There is no necessity for more complex test equipment when making the initial checks on the processor. If it is not apparent where the problem is by this time, then the 68000 should be put into a freerunning mode. Unless something very drastic is wrong with the 68000 itself and its immediate circuits, the freerun will indicate where the problem is.

Freerunning the Processor

To freerun the 68000, remove the EPROM and RAM ICs from their sockets. Plug two Freerun Headers into the two EPROM sockets; each Freerun Header is a 24- or 28-pin component carrier with the pins corresponding to the data bus connected to ground. Apply power to the 68K-CPU and observe the HALT light flash briefly; next see the RUN light flashing on and off.

1. The RUN light should flash on and off about 3 times a second for a 6 MHz clock. A logic probe connected to A23 will show HIGH for 2.8 seconds and LOW for 2.8 seconds.
2. Set up a dual-trace oscilloscope (bandwidth > 40 MHz) with one trace connected to AS* on the 68000's pin 6:
   a. Use AS* as trigger and synchronize the display.
   b. With the other scope probe, check DTACK*, UDS*, and LDS*. Do they match the traces shown in Figure D-18?
   c. Change the wait-state jumper and see if the bus cycles become longer as shown in Figure D-19.
3. Check each of the address outputs of the 68000, starting with the fastest, A1. Go to A2 and see that it runs half as slowly; go from A3 to A23 and see that each is slower.

While the 68000 freeruns, it is possible to examine the entire system for proper control and address bus operation. If the system freeruns with no problems, the only area

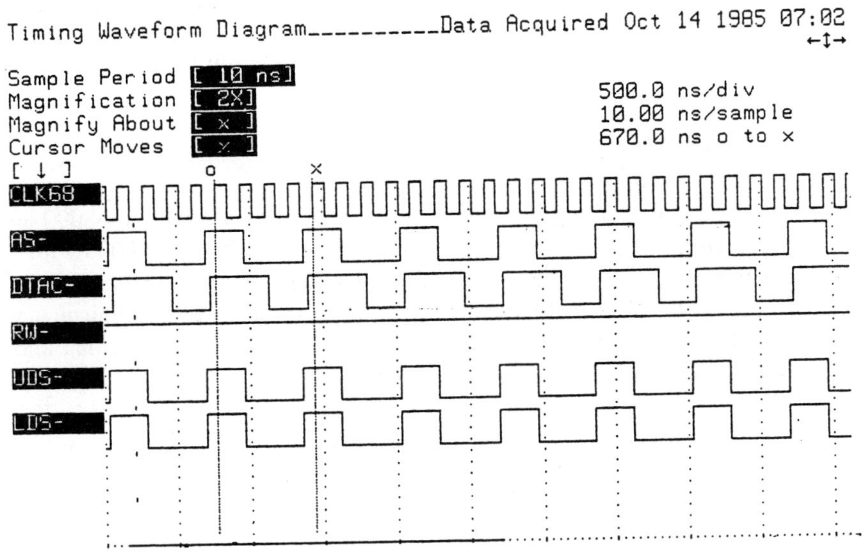

Figure D-18 Typical freerun with the DTACK* circuit enabled. The clock is 6 MHz and there are no wait states inserted.

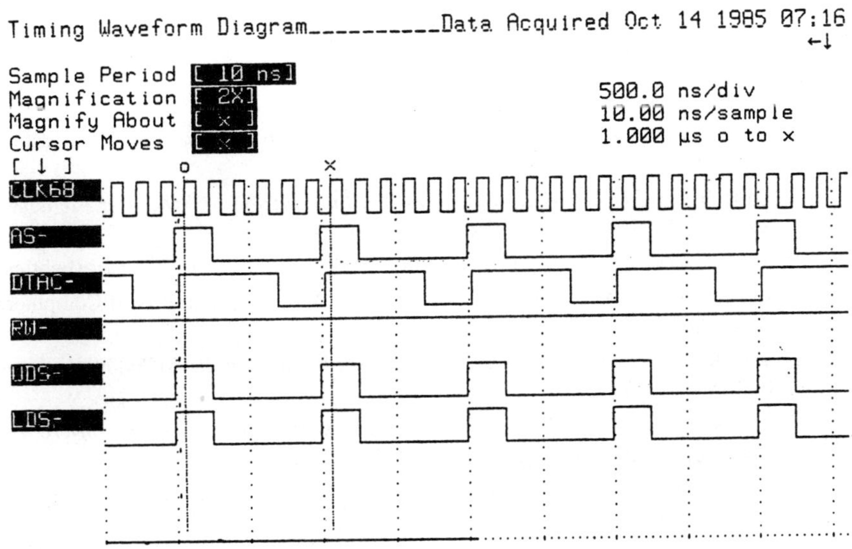

Figure D-19 Typical freerun with DTACK* enabled. This timing shows DTACK* delayed enough to cause two waits in each bus cycle.

left not checked is the data bus. Because the data bus was grounded for freerunning, there was no way to verify its integrity. In-circuit emulation is appropriate at this point in the troubleshooting.

In-Circuit Emulation

The idea behind in-circuit emulation, or ICE, is to remove the 68000 and plug in a test instrument in its place. The test instrument contains its own 68000 with isolation circuits so that it can run regardless of how defective the 68K-CPU board might be at the moment. Details on the ICE methods are beyond the scope of this technical manual.

The Fluke 9010A Troubleshooter is an in-circuit emulator that allows a number of tests that cannot be made in other ways:

1. Bus test—identifies control, address, data bus lines that are drivable and not shorted.
2. RAM test—tests the R/W capability of every data bit at every address, shorted data lines, address-decoder errors.
3. ROM test—acquires a ROM signature to compare against other known-good ROMs.

REFERENCES

ANDREWS, MICHAEL. *Self-Guided Tour Through the 68000*. Reston, VA: Reston Publishing Co., Inc., 1984.

BACON, JEAN. *The Motorola MC68000: An Introduction to Processor Memory and Interfacing*. Englewood Cliffs, NJ: Prentice-Hall, 1986.

BRANDLY, GORDON. "Tiny Basic for the 68000." *Dr. Dobb's Journal* (February 1985): 42–46.

CARTER, EDWARD M., and A.B. BONDS. "The VU68K Single-Board Computer." *Byte* (January 1984): 403–416.

CATES, RON L. "Mapping an Alterable Reset Vector for the MC68000." *Electronics* (July 28, 1982): 111–113.

COFFRON, JAMES W. *Practical Troubleshooting Techniques for Microprocessor Systems*. Englewood Cliffs, NJ: Prentice-Hall, 1981.

COFFRON, JAMES W. *Understanding and Troubleshooting the Microprocessor*. Englewood Cliffs, NJ: Prentice-Hall, 1980.

COFFRON, JAMES W. *Using and Troubleshooting the MC68000*. Reston, VA; Reston Publishing Company, 1983.

DOBRIN, ANDREJ, and FRANC NOVAK. "Freerunning the MC68000." *Electronics Test* (April 1984): 124.

HARMAN, THOMAS L., and BARBARA LAWSON. *The Motorola MC68000 Microprocessor Family: Assembly Language, Interface Design, and System Design*. Englewood Cliffs, NJ: Prentice-Hall, 1985.

IEEE Standard 696 Interface Devices. New York: IEEE, 1983.

KANE, GERRY. *68000 Microprocessor Handbook*. Berkeley, CA: Osborne/McGraw-Hill, 1981.

KANE, GERRY, DOUG HAWKINS, and LANCE LEVENTHAL. *68000 Assembly Language Programming*. Berkeley, CA: Osborne/McGraw-Hill, 1981.

KING, TIM, and BRIAN KNIGHT. *Programming the MC68000*. Reading, MA: Addison-Wesley Publishing Co., 1983.

LENK, JOHN D. *Handbook of Advanced Troubleshooting*. Englewood Cliffs, NJ: Prentice-Hall, 1983.

LENK, JOHN D. *Handbook of Practical Microcomputer Troubleshooting*. Reston, VA: Reston Publishing Company, 1979.

LIBES, SOL, and MARK GARETZ. *Interfacing to S-100/IEEE-696 Microcomputers*. Berkeley, CA: Osborne/McGraw-Hill, 1981.

MC68000 16-Bit Microprocessor Data Manual. Austin, TX: Motorola Semiconductor Products, Inc.

MC68000 Educational Computer Board User's Manual, MEX68KECB/D2. 2nd Ed. Tempe, AZ: Motorola Literature Distribution Center, 1982.

MELEAR, CHARLES. *Asynchronous Communications for the MC68000 Using the MC6850*. Application Note AN-817. Austin, TX: Motorola Semiconductor Products, Inc.

MORALES, ARNOLD J. "Interface 6800-μP Peripherals to the 68000." *EDN* (March 4, 1981): 159–161.

POE, ELMER C., and JAMES C. GOODWIN. The S-100 and Other Micro Buses. Indianapolis, IN: Howard W. Sams & Co., 1981.

ROBINSON, PHILLIP R. *Mastering the 68000 Microprocessor*. Blue Ridge Summit, PA: Tab Books, Inc., 1985.

SCANLON, LEO J. *The 68000: Principles and Programming*. Indianapolis, IN: Howard W. Sams & Co., 1981.

STARNES, THOMAS W. "Handling Exceptions Gracefully Enhances Software Reliability." *Electronics* (Sept. 11, 1980): 153–157.

STOCKTON, JOHN, and VICTOR SCHERER. "Learn the Timing and Interfacing of MC68000 Peripheral Circuits." *Electronic Design* (Nov. 8, 1979) 27(23): 57–64.

TAYLOR, MITCHELL B. *A Discussion of Interrupts for the MC68000*. Engineering Bulletin EB-97. Austin, TX: Motorola Semiconductor Products, Inc.

TRIEBEL, WALTER A., and AVTAR SINGH. *The 68000 Microprocessor—Architecture, Software, and Interfacing Techniques*. Englewood Cliffs, NJ: Prentice-Hall, 1986.

WILCOX, ALAN D. "Bringing Up the 68000—A First Step." *Doctor Dobb's Journal* (Jan. 1986) 11(1): 60–74.

WILLIAMS, STEVE. *Programming the 68000*. Berkeley, CA: Sybex, Inc., 1985.

ZUMCHAK, EUGENE M. *Microcomputer Design and Troubleshooting*. Indianapolis, IN: Howard W. Sams & Co., 1982.

CONTENTS OF APPENDIX

MODULE INDEX

Module	*IC part number*	*DWG number*	*Text figure reference*
Address-Bus Buffers	U27, U28, U32, U35, U56	6	13.36
Bus Control Logic	U31, U34, U36	3	13.9, 13.18
Bus-State Generator	U35, U36, U37, U42	3	13.17, 13.18
Bus-State Output	U38, U40, U42, U56	3	13.17, 13.18
Clock	U29, U30	1	9.6
CPU	U24	1	9.22
Data-Bus Buffers	U18, U19, U20, U23	5	13.33
Data-Bus Logic	U14, U55, U56	5	13.34
I/O Decode	U10	1	10.11
Interrupt Logic	U1, U42, U48, U49, U51	4	12.26
MWRT Logic	U5, U46	7	—
Power		7	9.4
RAM Module (Pair-2)	U7, U13, U21, U22	2	10.24
Reset Logic	U3, U5, U8, U9	1	9.17, 9.22
ROM Module (Pair-1)	U7, U13, U25, U26	2	10.24
ROM/RAM Decode	U11, U12, U15, U16, U17	1	10.23
Single-Step	U1, U2, U6, U8	1	9.28
Status Logic and Buffers	U39, U44, U45, U47, U56, U57	4	12.27, 13.35
TMA Logic	U31, U39, U44	1	13.32
2 MHz Clock	U5, U43	7	—
Wait and DTACK* Control	U33, U34, U41, U46	3	9.23, 13.11
Watchdog Timer	U50, U57	4	12.18

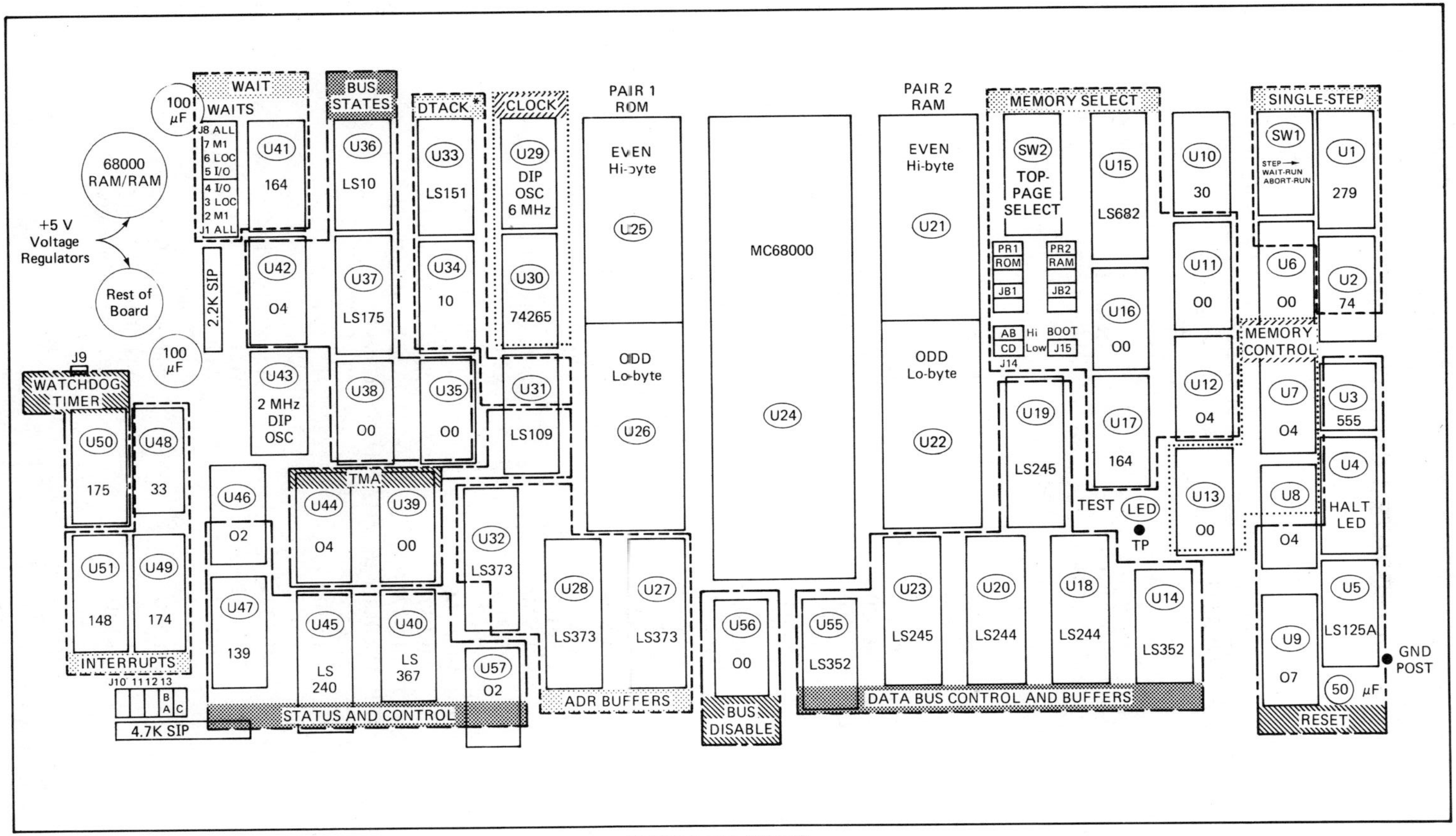

MODULE LOCATIONS

INTEGRATED CIRCUITS INDEX

Part number		*Type*	*Module(s) using*	*DWG number*
U1		74LS279	Interrupt Logic	4
			Single-step	1
2		74LS74A	Single-step	1
3		NE555	Reset Logic	1
4	Halt	LED Circuit	Reset Logic	1
5		74LS125A	MWRT Logic	7
			2 MHz Clock	7
			Reset Logic	1
6		74LS00	Single-step	1
7		74LS04	Memory Control	2
8		74LS04	Single-step	1
			Reset Logic	1
9		7407	Reset Logic	1
10		74LS30	I/O Decode	1
11		74LS00	ROM/RAM Decode	1
12		74LS04	ROM/RAM Decode	1
13		74LS00	Memory Control	2
14		74LS352	Data-Bus Logic	5
15		74LS682	ROM/RAM Decode	1
16		74LS00	ROM/RAM Decode	1
17		74LS164	ROM/RAM Decode	1
18		74LS244	Data-Bus Buffer	5
19		74LS245	Data-Bus Buffer	5
20		74LS244	Data-Bus Buffer	5
21	Even	RAM	Pair-2	2
22	Odd	RAM	Pair-2	2
23		74LS245	Data-Bus Buffer	5
24		68000	CPU	1
25	Even	EPROM	Pair-1	2
26	Odd	EPROM	Pair-1	2
27		74LS373	Address-Bus Buffer	6
28		74LS373	Address-Bus Buffer	6
29	DIP	Oscillator (6 MHz)	Clock	1
30		74265	Clock	1
31		74LS109	Bus Control	3
			TMA	1
32		74LS373	Address-Bus Buffer	6
33		74LS151	Wait Control	3
34		74LS10	Wait Control and DTACK*	3
			Bus Control	3
35		74LS00	Address-Bus Buffer	6
			Bus-State Generator	3
36		74LS10	Bus-State Generator	3
			Bus Control	3

37	74LS175	Bus-State Generator	3
38	74LS00	Bus-State Output	3
39	74LS00	Status Logic	4
		TMA Logic	1
40	74LS367	Bus-State Output	3
41	74LS164	Wait Control	3
42	74LS04	Interrupt Logic	4
		Bus-State Output	3
		Bus-State Generator	3
43	DIP Oscillator (2 MHz)	2 MHz Clock	7
44	74LS04	Status Logic	4
		TMA Logic	1
45	74LS240	Status Buffer	4
46	74LS02	MWRT Logic	7
		Wait Control	3
47	74LS139	Status Logic	4
48	74LS33	Interrupt Logic	4
49	74LS174	Interrupt Logic	4
50	74LS175	Watchdog Logic	4
51	74LS148	Interrupt Logic	4
55	74LS352	Data-Bus Logic	5
56	74LS00	Data-Bus Logic	5
		Status Bus Buffer	4
		Address-Bus Buffer	6
		Bus-State Output	3
57	74LS02	Status Logic	4
		Watchdog Timer	4

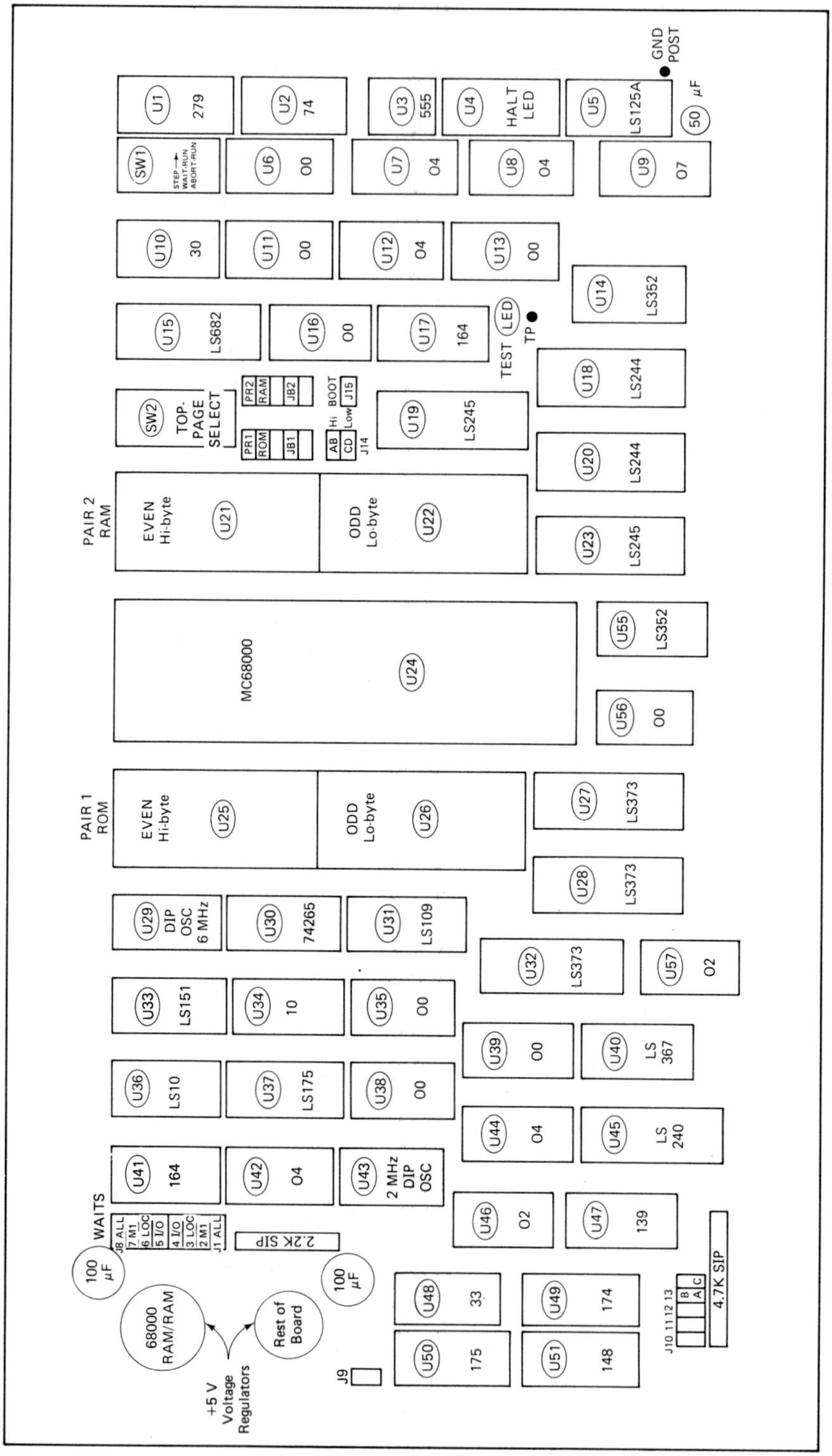

IC LOCATIONS

SPARE ICs

Part Number	Type	Pins	
U1	74LS279	1, 2, 3, 4	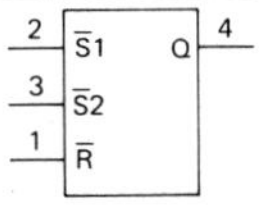
U5	74LS125A	1, 2, 3	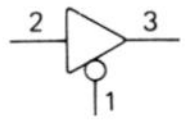
U6	74LS00	1-6	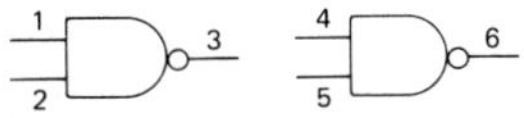
U7	74LS04	8-13	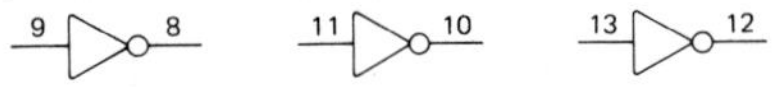
U8	74LS04	1, 2, 3, 4	
U9	7407	1, 2	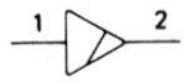
U11	74LS00	11, 12, 13	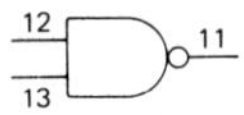
U12	74LS04	8, 9	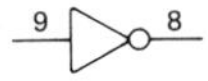
U37	74LS175	2, 3, 4, 13, 14, 15	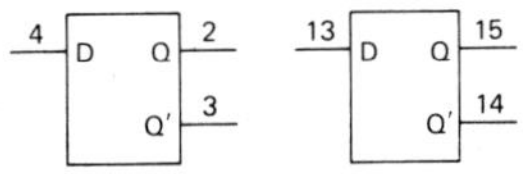
U46	74LS02	1, 2, 3	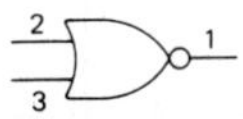

JUMPER SUMMARY

J1 - J8	Wait-state selection
J9	Watchdog timer
J10	Autovector
J11	Memory error
J12	MWRT
J13	Interrupt selection
JB1, JB2	Selection of ROM/RAM type
J14	Address swap
J15	Power-on jump

SWITCH SUMMARY

SW1	Single-step, abort
SW2	On-board address select

LOCATION OF JUMPERS AND SWITCHES

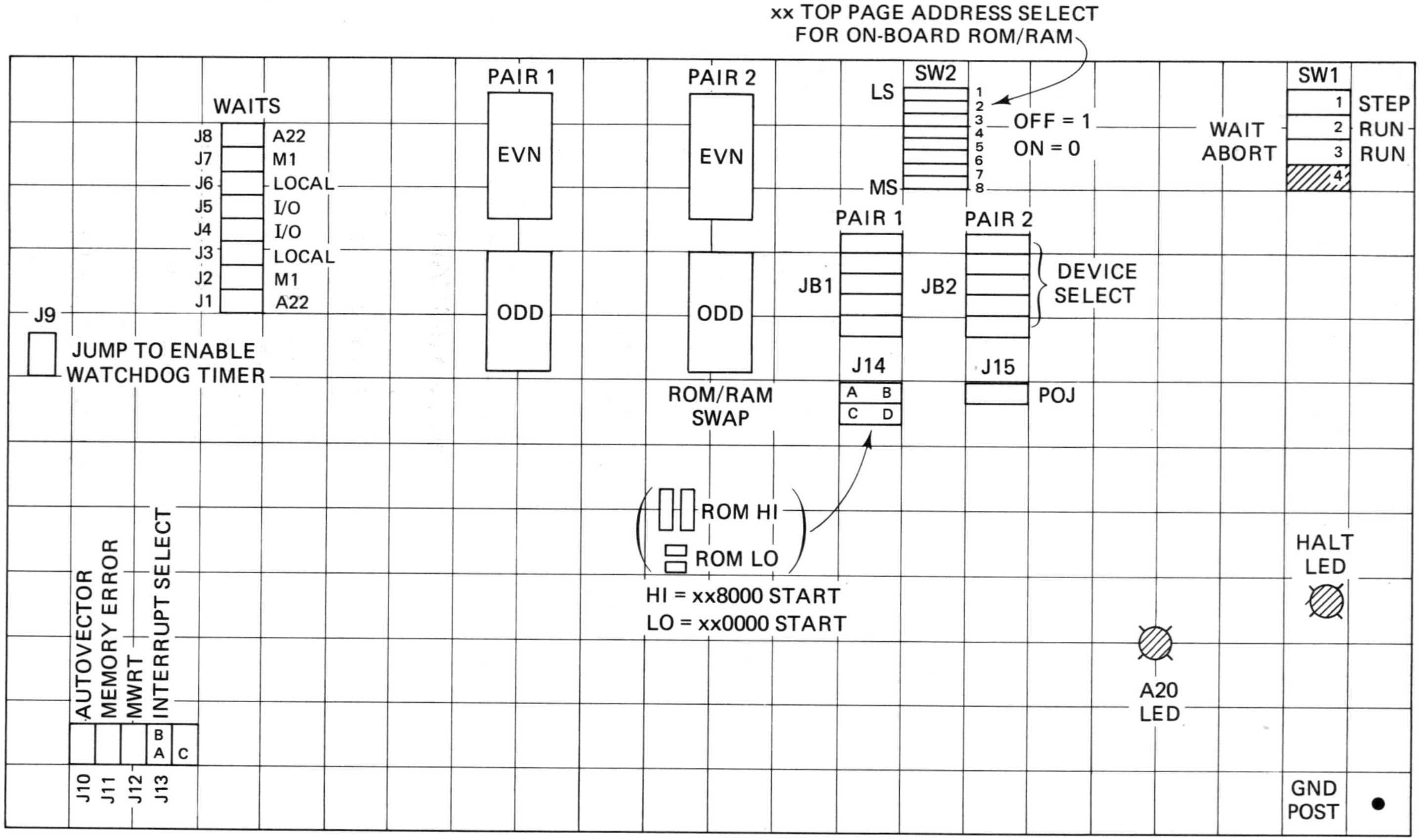

JUMPERS—WAITS

Jumper	*Function*
J1	1 wait
J2	2 waits
J3	3 waits
J4	4 waits
J5	5 waits
J6	6 waits
J7	7 waits
J8	8 waits

Connect any one of these to all, M1, Local, and/or I/O. Use either shorting jumper or wire-wrap. For zero waits, do not connect any jumper.

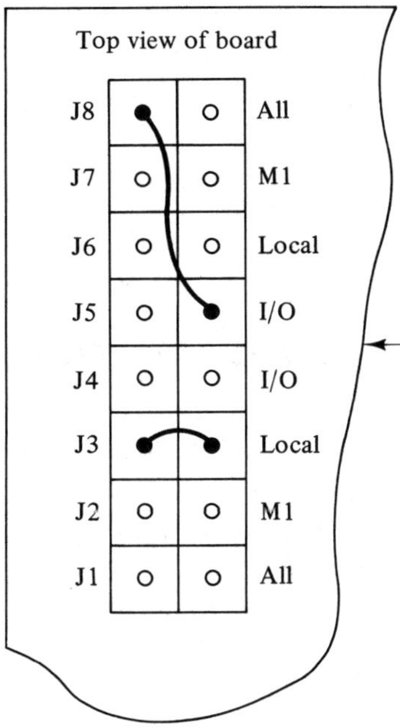

EXAMPLE:
Setting for 10 MHz system clock

3 waits for "Local" on-board bus cycles

8 waits on "I/O" accesses to addresses $FF 0000 to $FF FFFF

JUMPERS—TIMER, MEMORY AND INTERRUPT

Jumper	*Function*
J9	Jump to enable watchdog timer
J10	Jump to enable autovectoring
J11	Abort if system memory-access error
J12	Jump to enable MWRT bus signal
J13	A-B Bus INT* to 68000 level-6 interrupt A-C Bus VI0* to 68000 level-6 interrupt (see sketch on page 480)

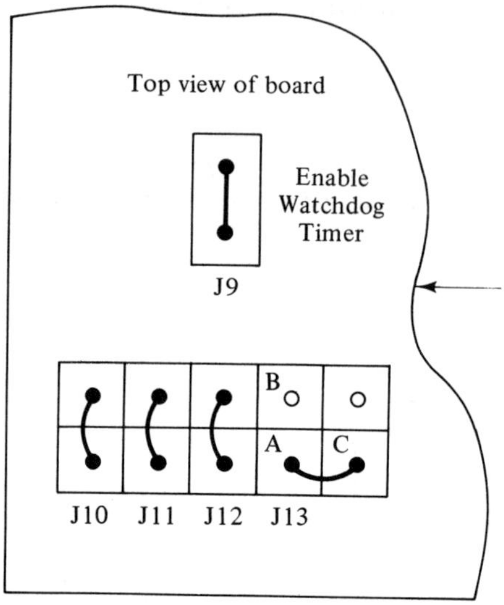

JUMPERS—EPROM/RAM ADDRESS SWAP AND POWER-ON JUMP

Jumper		*Function*
J14	A-B, C-D	Pair 1 base address $XX0000, Pair 2 base address $XX8000
	A-C, B-D	Pair 2 base address $XX0000, Pair 1 base address $XX8000
J15		Power-on Jump: Jump to enable boot feature in which *PAIR-1* sockets are selected during 1st 4 bus cycles after reset or power-on.

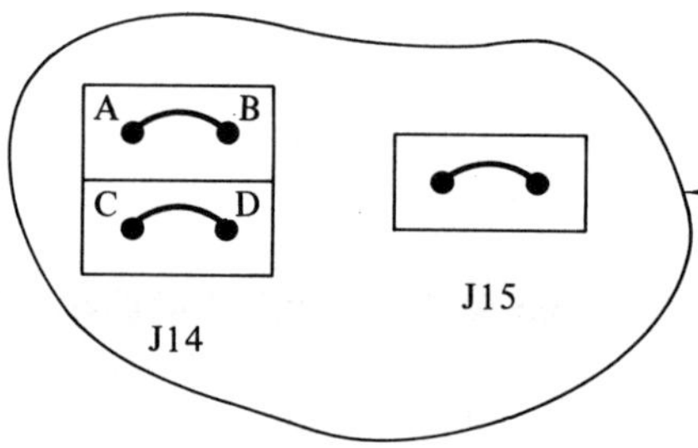

JUMPERS—EPROM AND RAM SELECTION

Jumper Block	*Function*
JB1	Selection Jumper Block for PAIR-1 sockets
JB2	Selection Jumper Block for PAIR-2 sockets

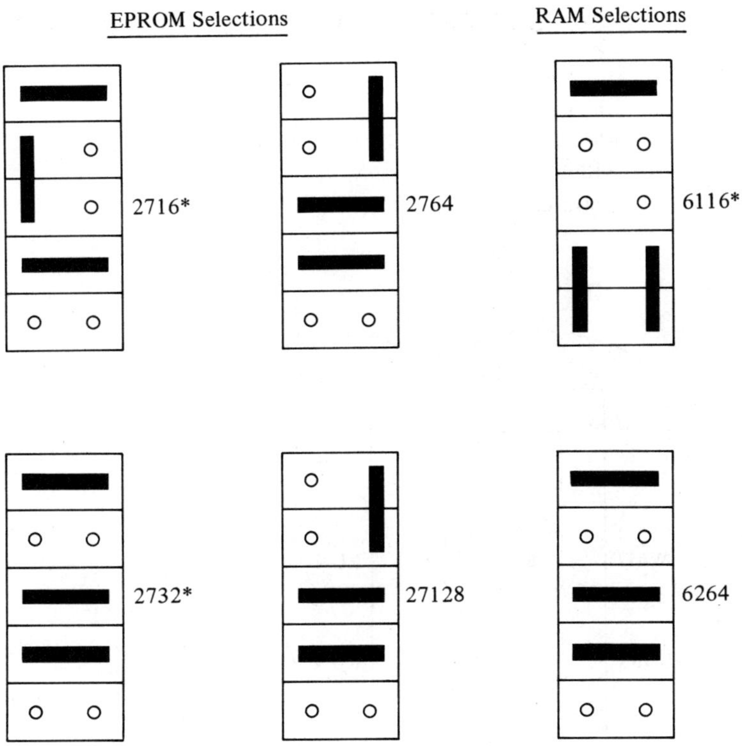

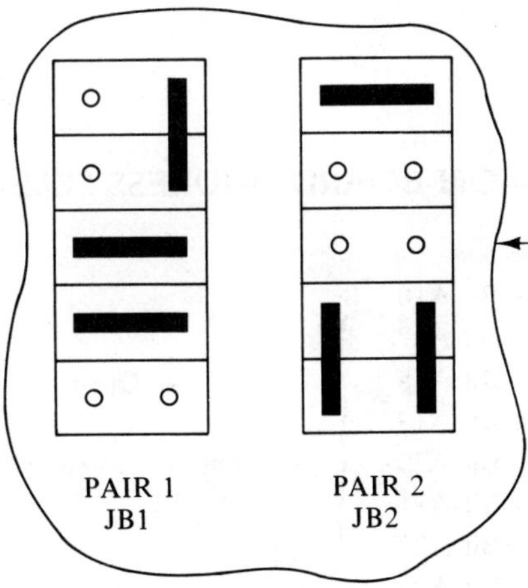

EXAMPLE:
JB1 set for an Even and Odd 27128 pair

JB2 set for an Even and Odd 6116 pair

*Install 24-pin EPROMs or RAMs low in the 28-pin sockets. Socket pins 1, 2, 27, 28 will be empty when using the smaller 24-pin devices.

SWITCHES—SINGLE-STEP AND ABORT

SW1 Position	*Function*
1	Single-step
2	MODE: Wait for STEP or RUN normally
3	ABORT or RUN normally
4	Not used

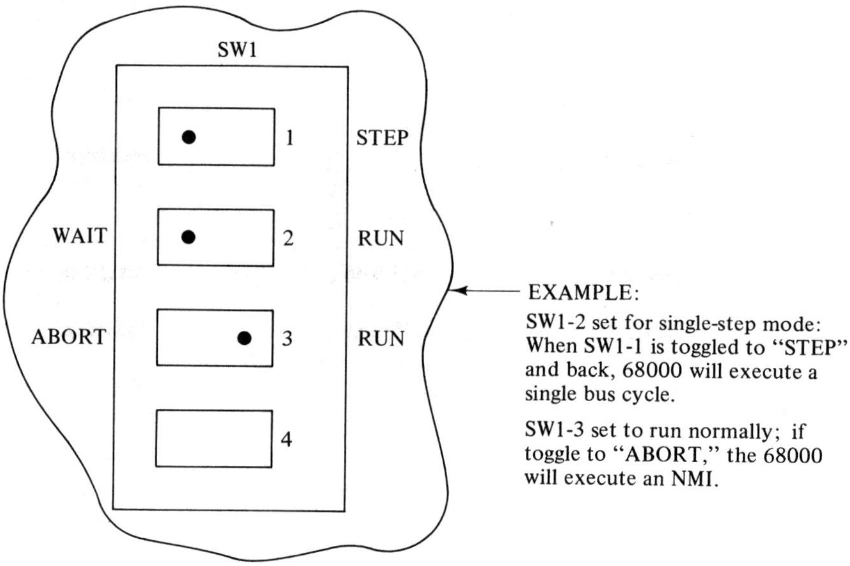

SWITCHES—ON-BOARD ADDRESS SELECT

SW1 Position		*Function*
1	LS	Address Bit A16
2		Address Bit A17
3		Address Bit A18
4		Address Bit A19
5		Address Bit A20
6		Address Bit A21
7		Address Bit A22
8	MS	Address Bit A23

Off = Open = "1"

On = Closed = "0"

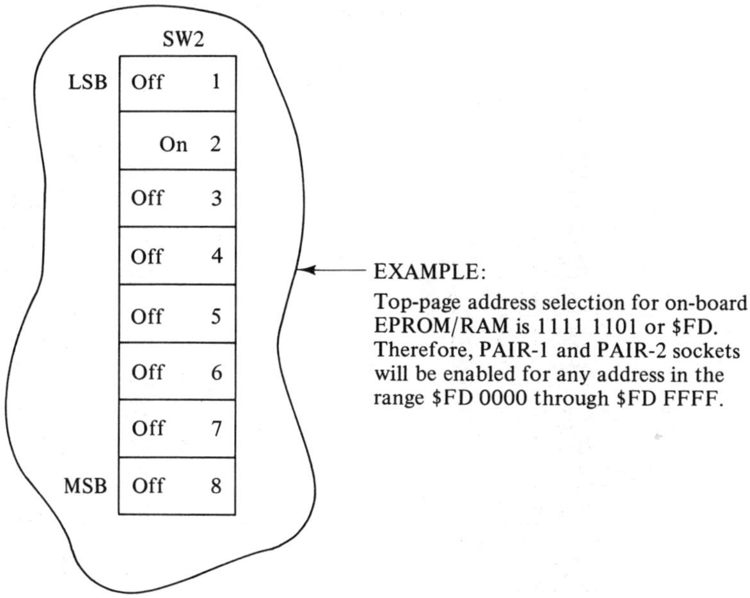

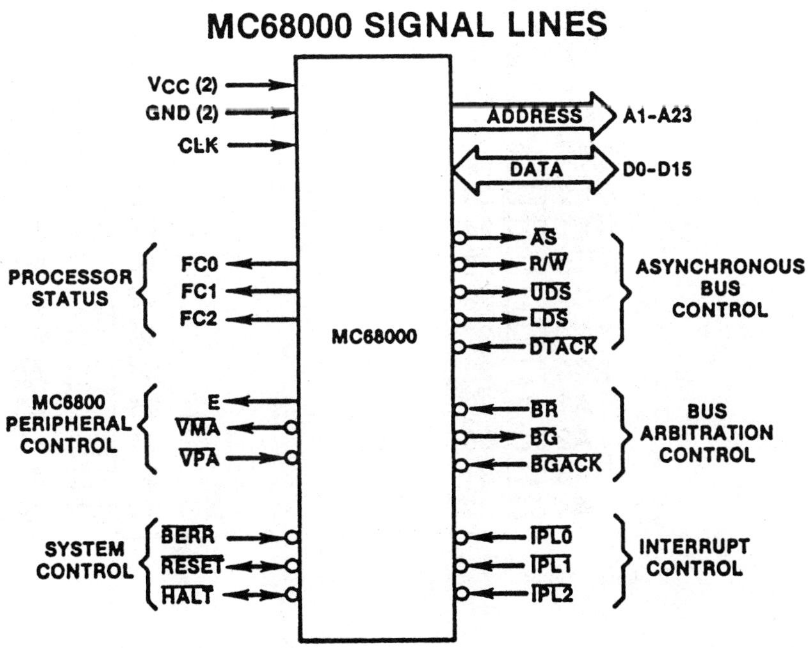

Input and output signals divided by function.
(Courtesy Motorola Inc.)

MC68,000—FOOTPRINT

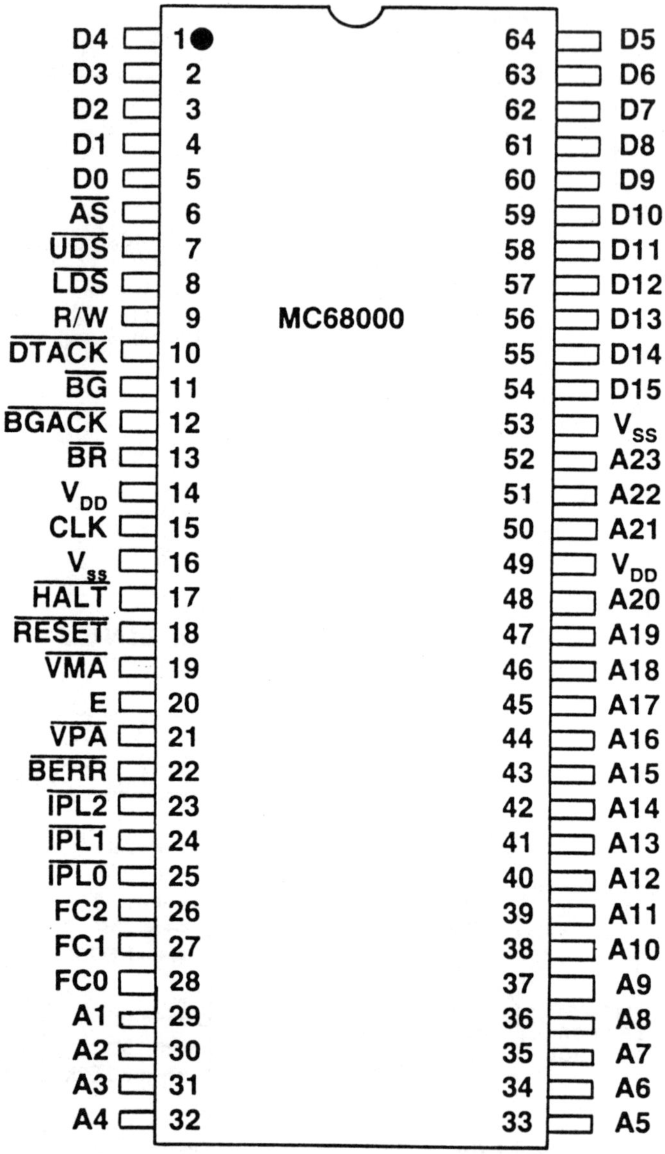

(Courtesy Motorola Inc.)

S-100 BUS CARD-EDGE PINOUTS

Group	*Label*	*Pin*	*Function*
Control Output	pSYNC	76	Processor synchronize (start bus cycle)
	pSTVAL*	25	Status valid
	pDBIN	78	Data bus in (enable slave bus drivers)
	pWR*	77	Write (data-valid strobe)
	pHLDA	26	Hold acknowledge
Control Input	RDY	72	Ready (slave ready for data transfer)
	XRDY	3	Auxiliary ready
	HOLD*	74	Hold request
	SIXTN*	60	Sixteen acknowledge from slave
	INT*	73	Interrupt
	NMI*	12	Non-maskable interrupt
TMA Control	ADSB*	22	Address bus buffer disable
	DODSB*	23	Data output bus buffer disable
	SDSB*	18	Status bus buffer disable
	CDSB*	19	Control output bus buffer disable
Vectored Interrupt	VI0*	4	Vectored interrupt 0 (highest priority)
	VI1*	5	Vectored interrupt 1
	VI2*	6	Vectored interrupt 2
	VI3*	7	Vectored interrupt 3
	VI4*	8	Vectored interrupt 4
	VI5*	9	Vectored interrupt 5
Status Bus	sMEMR	47	Memory read
	sM1	44	Op-code fetch
	sINP	46	Input data
	sOUT	45	Output data
	sW0*	97	Memory write or output write
	sINTA	96	Interrupt acknowledge (data on DI bus)
	sHLTA	48	Halt acknowledge
	sXTRQ*	58	Sixteen request
Utility bus	Φ	24	System clock, SYSCLK
	CLOCK	49	2 MHz utility clock for peripherals
	RESET*	75	System reset
	SLAVECLR*	54	Slave clear (slave reset)
	MWRT	68	Memory write = pWR* · sOUT′
	ERROR*	98	General error signal
	POC*	99	Power-on clear
Power Bus	+8	1,51	
	+16	2	
	−16	52	
	GND	20,50,53,70,100	

Group	Label	Pin	Function
Address Bus	A23	64	Most significant address bit
	A22	63	
	A21	62	
	A20	61	
	A19	59	
	A18	15	
	A17	17	
	A16	16	
	A15	32	
	A14	86	
	A13	85	
	A12	33	
	A11	87	
	A10	37	
	A9	34	
	A8	84	
	A7	83	
	A6	82	
	A5	29	
	A4	30	
	A3	31	
	A2	81	
	A1	80	
	A0	79	Least significant address bit
Data Bus	ED7	90	D15 Even data (DO Bus)
	ED6	40	D14
	ED5	39	D13
	ED4	38	D12
	ED3	89	D11
	ED2	88	D10
	ED1	35	D9
	ED0	36	D8
	OD7	43	D7 Odd data (DI Bus)
	OD6	93	D6
	OD5	92	D5
	OD4	91	D4
	OD3	42	D3
	OD2	41	D2
	OD1	94	D1
	OD0	95	D0

TOP VIEW OF CPU BOARD

BOTTOM VIEW OF CPU BOARD

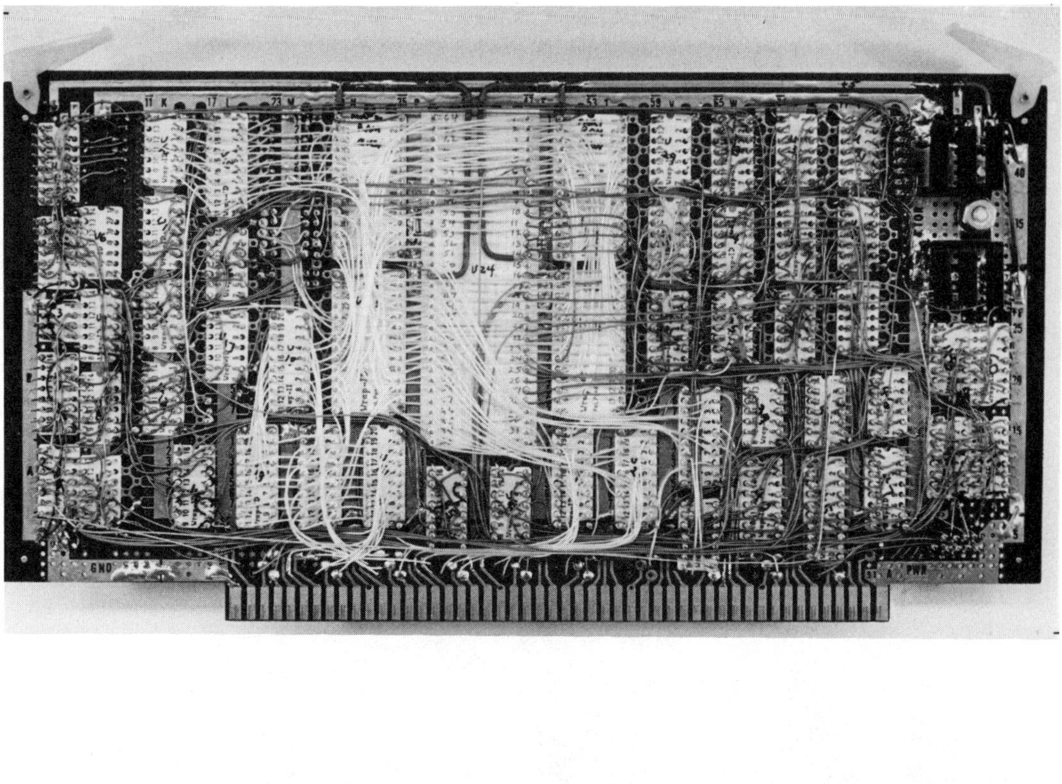

POWER/GND TABLE

Part		*Type*	*Pin GND*	*Pin +5*
U1		74LS279	8	16
2		74LS74A	7	14
3		NE555	1	8
4	Halt	LED Circuit		
5		74LS125A	7	14
6		74LS00	7	14
7		74LS04	7	14
8		74LS04	7	14
9		7407	7	14
10		74LS30	7	14
11		74LS00	7	14
12		74LS04	7	14
13		74LS00	7	14
14		74LS352	8	16
15		74LS682	10	20
16		74LS00	7	14
17		74LS164	7	14
18		74LS244	10	20
19		74LS245	10	20
20		74LS244	10	20
21	Even	RAM	14	28
22	Odd	RAM	14	28
23		74LS245	10	20
24		68000	16,53	14,49
25	Even	EPROM	14	28
26	Odd	EPROM	14	28
27		74LS373	10	20
28		74LS373	10	20
29	DIP	Oscillator (6 MHz)	7	14
30		74265	8	16
31		74LS109	8	16
32		74LS373	10	20
33		74LS151	8	16
34		74LS10	7	14
35		74LS00	7	14
36		74LS10	7	14
37		74LS175	8	16
38		74LS00	7	14
39		74LS00	7	14
40		74LS367	8	16
41		74LS164	7	14
42		74LS04	7	14

Part		Type	Pin GND	Pin +5
43	DIP	Oscillator (2 MHz)	7	14
44		74LS04	7	14
45		74LS240	10	20
46		74LS02	7	14
47		74LS139	8	16
48		74LS33	7	14
49		74LS174	8	16
50		74LS175	8	16
51		74LS148	8	16
55		74LS352	8	16
56		74LS00	7	14
57		74LS02	7	14

LIST OF SCHEMATICS

DWG #	Modules
1	CPU, Reset Logic, Single-step, Clock, ROM/RAM decode, I/O decode, TMA Logic
2	ROM and RAM modules
3	DTACK* and WAIT generator, Bus-state generator and logic
4	Interrupt logic, Status logic and buffer, Watchdog timer
5	Data-bus logic and buffer
6	Address-bus buffer
7	MWRT Logic, 2 MHz clock, power supply

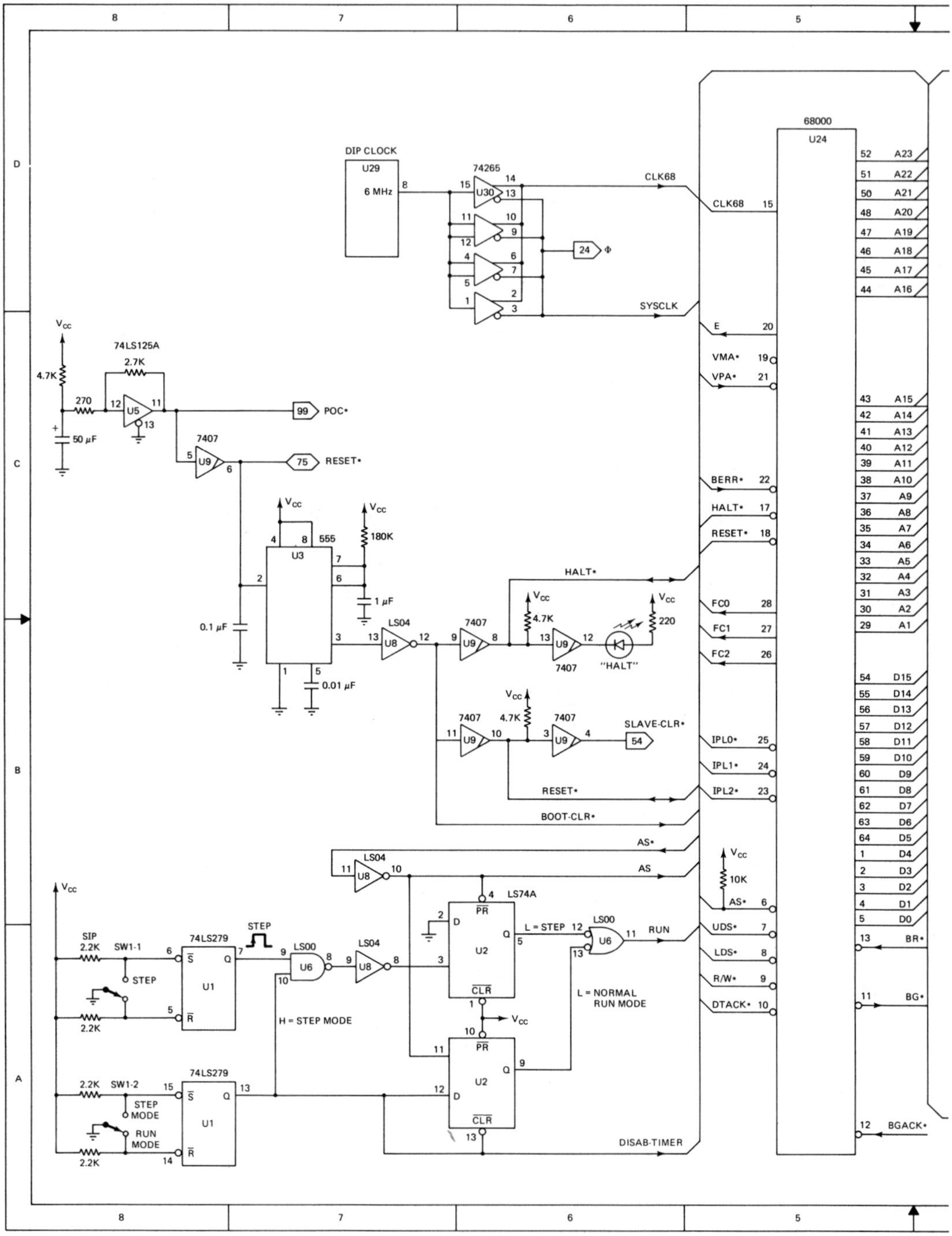
DIP CLOCK
U29
6 MHz
74265
U30
CLK68
SYSCLK
Φ
68000
U24
CLK68
E
VMA•
VPA•
BERR•
HALT•
RESET•
FC0
FC1
FC2
IPL0•
IPL1•
IPL2•
AS•
UDS•
LDS•
R/W•
DTACK•
BR•
BG•
BGACK•
A23
A22
A21
A20
A19
A18
A17
A16
A15
A14
A13
A12
A11
A10
A9
A8
A7
A6
A5
A4
A3
A2
A1
D15
D14
D13
D12
D11
D10
D9
D8
D7
D6
D5
D4
D3
D2
D1
D0
74LS125A
2.7K
4.7K
270
50 μF
U5
POC•
7407
U9
RESET•
555
U3
180K
1 μF
0.1 μF
0.01 μF
LS04
U8
HALT•
4.7K
220
"HALT"
SLAVE-CLR•
RESET•
BOOT-CLR•
AS•
AS
10K
LS74A
U2
L = STEP
LS00
U6
RUN
L = NORMAL RUN MODE
H = STEP MODE
DISAB-TIMER
SIP
2.2K
SW1-1
STEP
74LS279
U1
SW1-2
STEP MODE
RUN MODE

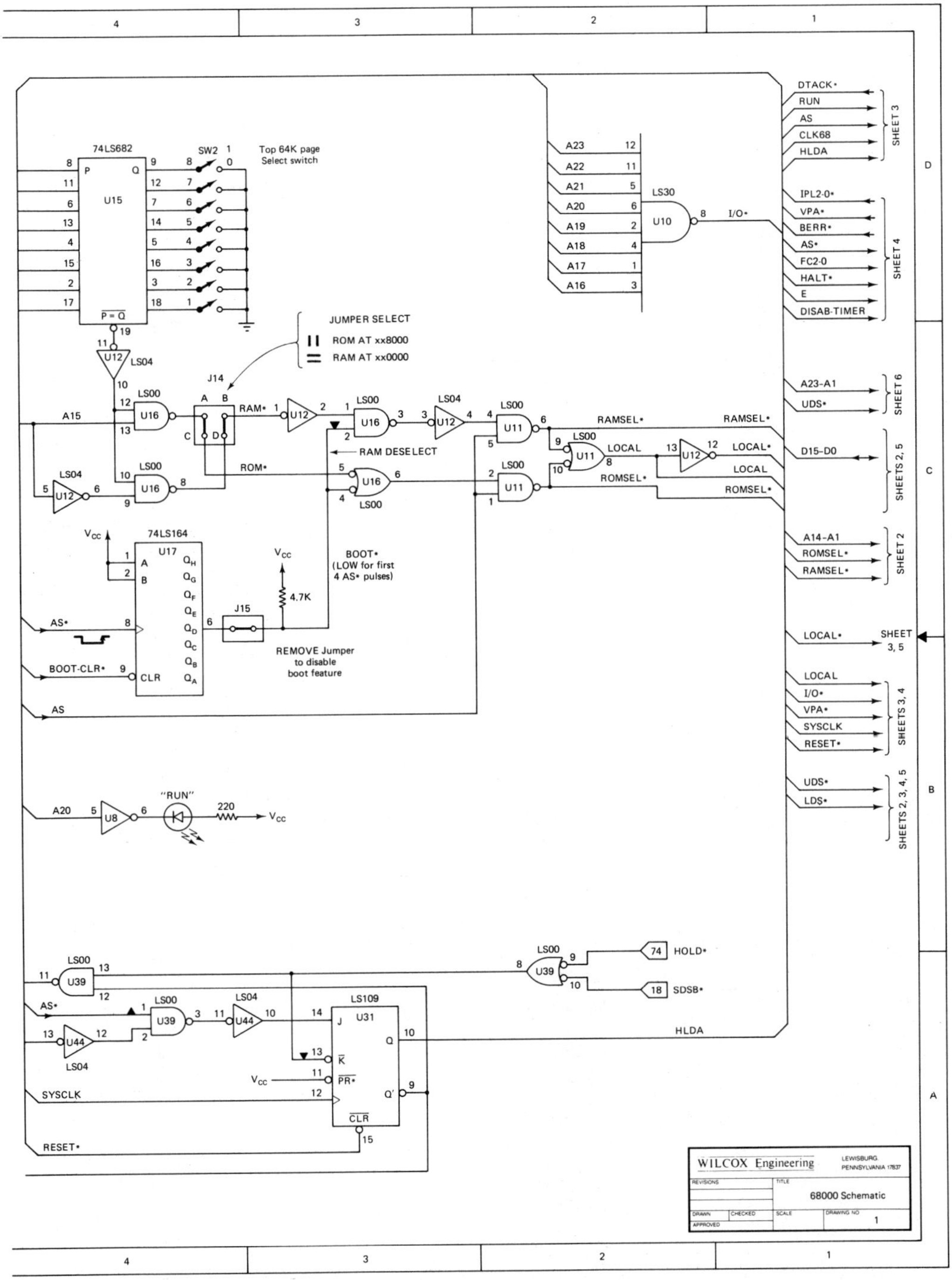
74LS682
U15
SW2
Top 64K page
Select switch
JUMPER SELECT
ROM AT xx8000
RAM AT xx0000
J14
A15
RAM•
ROM•
RAM DESELECT
LS00
LS04
U16
U12
U11
U10
LS30
I/O•
A23
A22
A21
A20
A19
A18
A17
A16
RAMSEL•
LOCAL•
LOCAL
ROMSEL•
74LS164
U17
BOOT•
(LOW for first
4 AS• pulses)
4.7K
J15
REMOVE Jumper
to disable
boot feature
AS•
BOOT-CLR•
CLR
AS
A20
U8
"RUN"
220
V_{CC}
DTACK•
RUN
CLK68
HLDA
SHEET 3
IPL2-0•
VPA•
BERR•
FC2-0
HALT•
E
DISAB-TIMER
SHEET 4
A23-A1
UDS•
SHEET 6
D15-D0
SHEETS 2, 5
A14-A1
SHEET 2
SHEET 3, 5
SYSCLK
RESET•
SHEETS 3, 4
LDS•
SHEETS 2, 3, 4, 5
U39
U44
LS109
U31
HOLD•
SDSB•
WILCOX Engineering
LEWISBURG PENNSYLVANIA 17837
REVISIONS
TITLE
68000 Schematic
DRAWN
CHECKED
SCALE
DRAWING NO
APPROVED
1

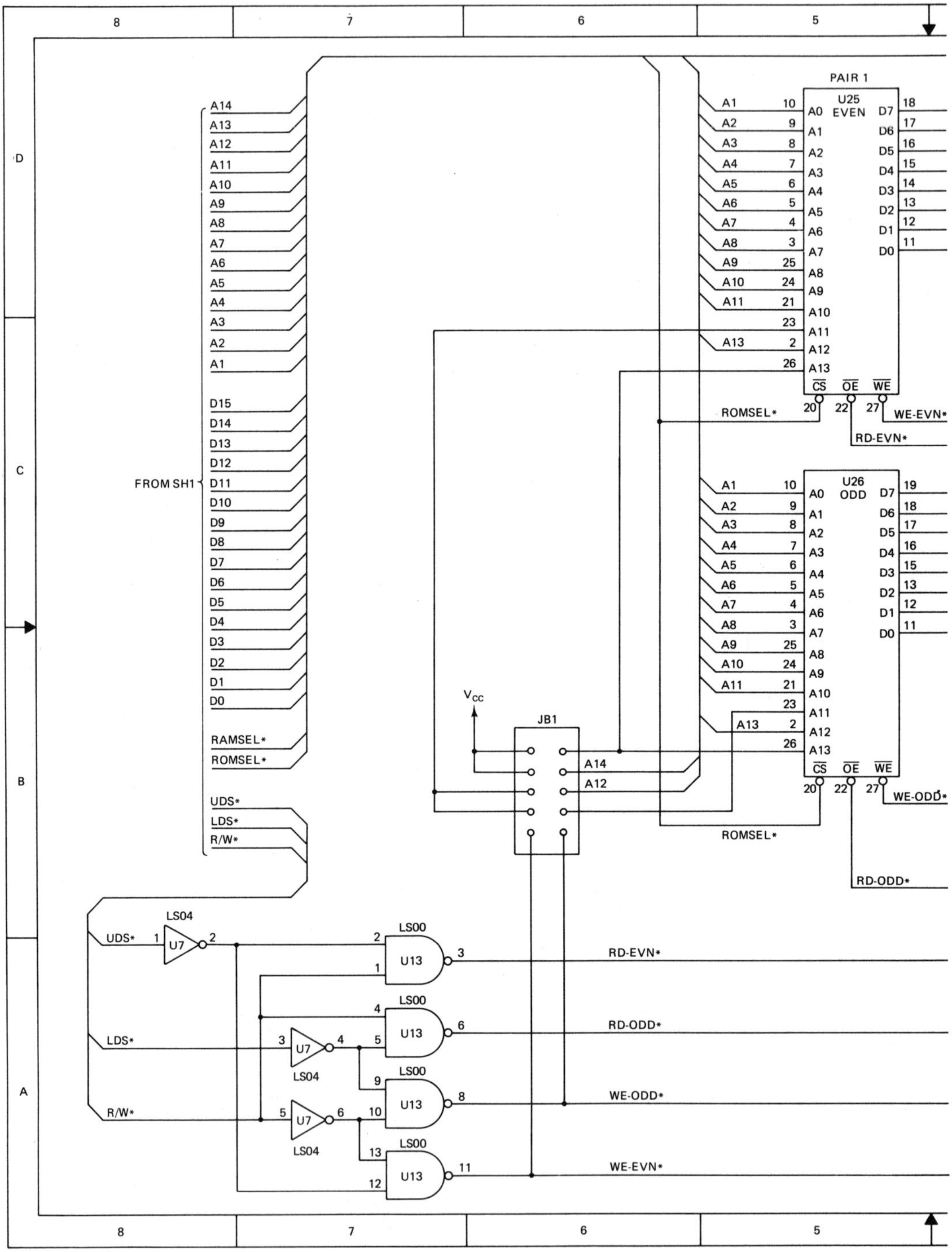
PAIR 1
U25 EVEN
U26 ODD
FROM SH1
A14
A13
A12
A11
A10
A9
A8
A7
A6
A5
A4
A3
A2
A1
D15
D14
D13
D12
D11
D10
D9
D8
D7
D6
D5
D4
D3
D2
D1
D0
RAMSEL*
ROMSEL*
UDS*
LDS*
R/W*
ROMSEL*
RD-EVN*
WE-EVN*
WE-ODD*
RD-ODD*
JB1
Vcc
LS04
LS00
U7
U13
RD-EVN*
RD-ODD*
WE-ODD*
WE-EVN*

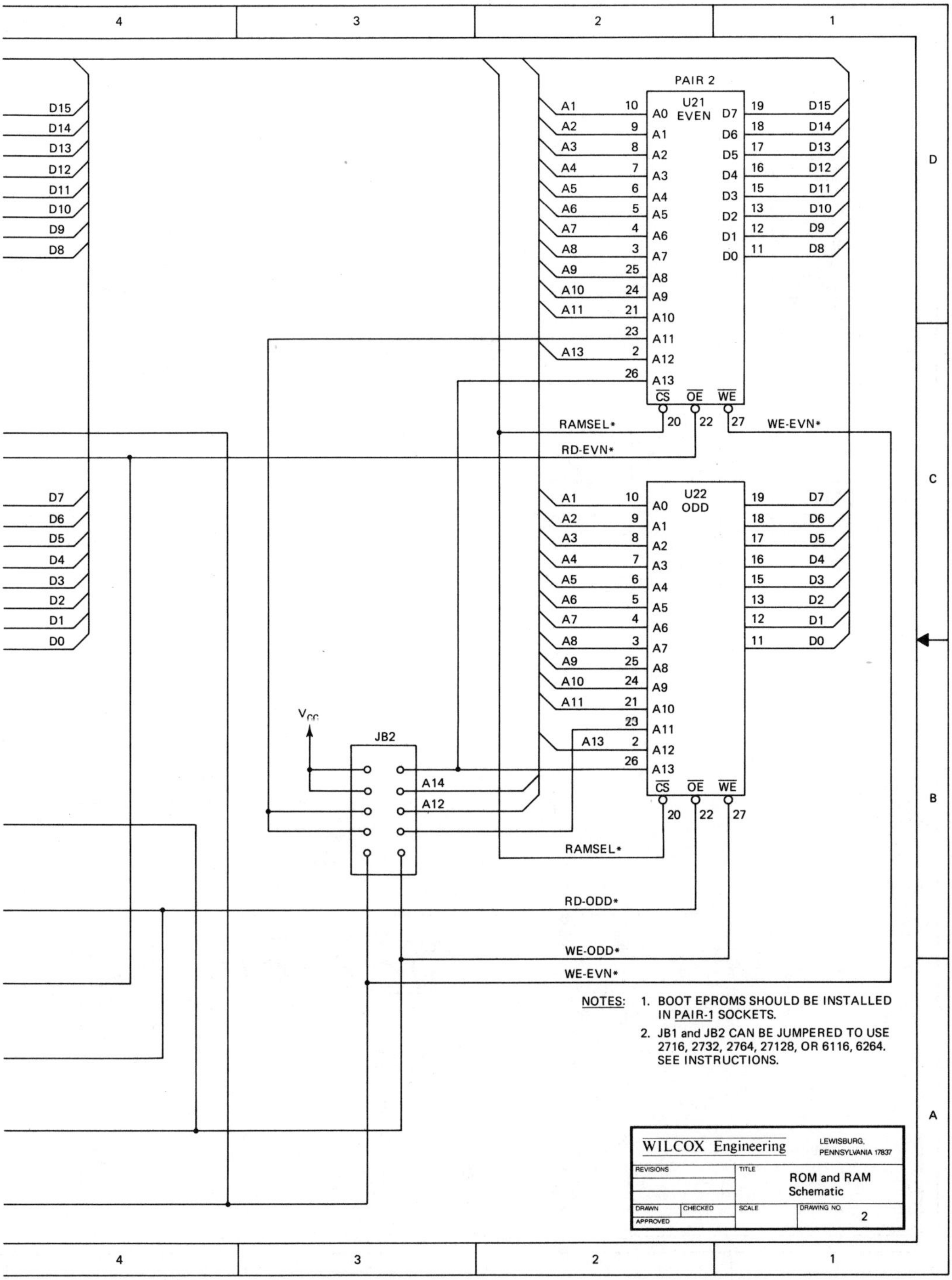
4
3
2
1
D
C
B
A
PAIR 2
U21
EVEN
U22
ODD
A0
A1
A2
A3
A4
A5
A6
A7
A8
A9
A10
A11
A12
A13
D0
D1
D2
D3
D4
D5
D6
D7
D8
D9
D10
D11
D12
D13
D14
D15
CS
OE
WE
RAMSEL*
RD-EVN*
WE-EVN*
RD-ODD*
WE-ODD*
JB2
Vcc
A14
A12
NOTES:
1. BOOT EPROMS SHOULD BE INSTALLED IN PAIR-1 SOCKETS.
2. JB1 and JB2 CAN BE JUMPERED TO USE 2716, 2732, 2764, 27128, OR 6116, 6264. SEE INSTRUCTIONS.
WILCOX Engineering
LEWISBURG, PENNSYLVANIA 17837
REVISIONS
TITLE
ROM and RAM Schematic
DRAWN
CHECKED
SCALE
DRAWING NO.
2
APPROVED

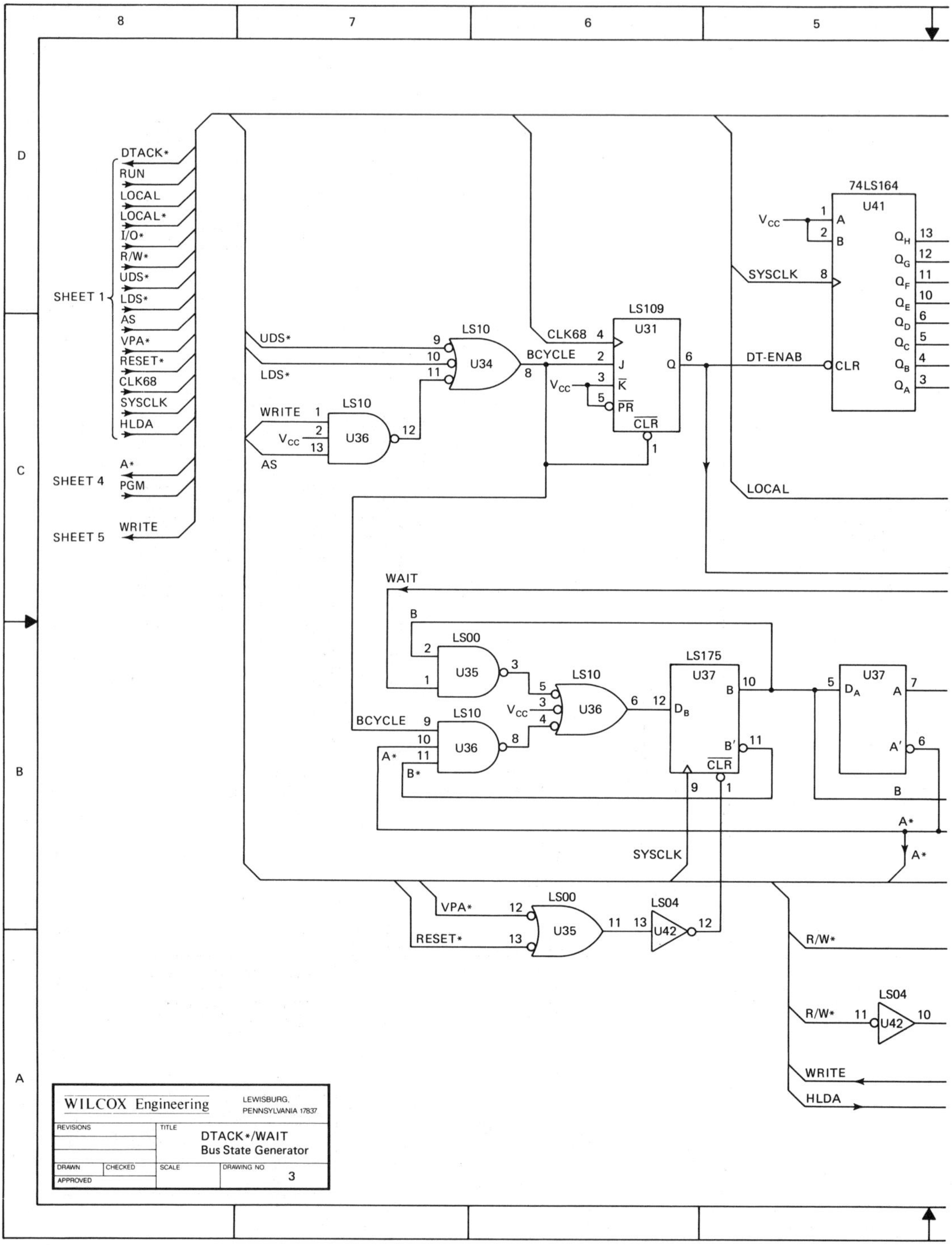

8
7
6
5
D
C
B
A
DTACK*
RUN
LOCAL
LOCAL*
I/O*
R/W*
UDS*
LDS*
AS
VPA*
RESET*
CLK68
SYSCLK
HLDA
SHEET 1
A*
PGM
SHEET 4
WRITE
SHEET 5
UDS*
LDS*
WRITE
AS
LS10
U34
LS10
U36
V_{CC}
BCYCLE
CLK68
LS109
U31
J
$\overline{K}$
$\overline{PR}$
$\overline{CLR}$
Q
DT-ENAB
74LS164
U41
A
B
CLR
SYSCLK
Q_H
Q_G
Q_F
Q_E
Q_D
Q_C
Q_B
Q_A
LOCAL
WAIT
B
LS00
U35
LS10
U36
BCYCLE
A*
B*
LS10
U36
LS175
U37
D_B
B
B′
$\overline{CLR}$
U37
D_A
A
A′
B
A*
SYSCLK
VPA*
RESET*
LS00
U35
LS04
U42
R/W*
R/W*
LS04
U42
WRITE
HLDA
WILCOX Engineering
LEWISBURG, PENNSYLVANIA 17837
REVISIONS
TITLE
DTACK*/WAIT
Bus State Generator
DRAWN
CHECKED
SCALE
DRAWING NO
3
APPROVED

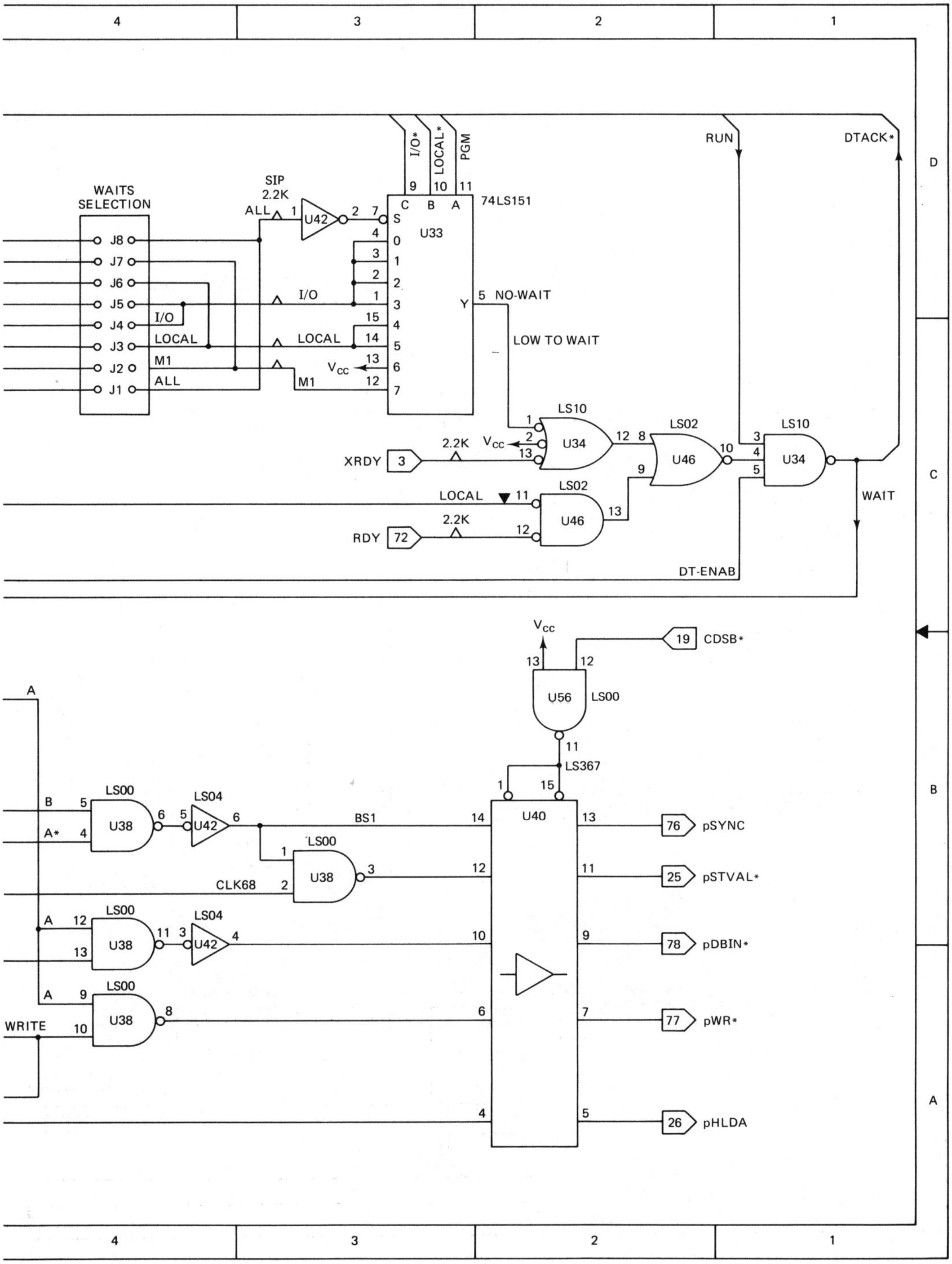

WAITS SELECTION
J8 J7 J6 J5 J4 J3 J2 J1
I/O
LOCAL
M1
ALL
SIP 2.2K
U42
74LS151
U33
I/O*
LOCAL*
PGM
NO-WAIT
LOW TO WAIT
RUN
DTACK*
LS10
U34
LS02
U46
XRDY
RDY
2.2K
WAIT
DT-ENAB
CDSB*
U56 LS00
LS367
U40
LS00
U38
LS04
BS1
CLK68
WRITE
pSYNC
pSTVAL*
pDBIN*
pWR*
pHLDA

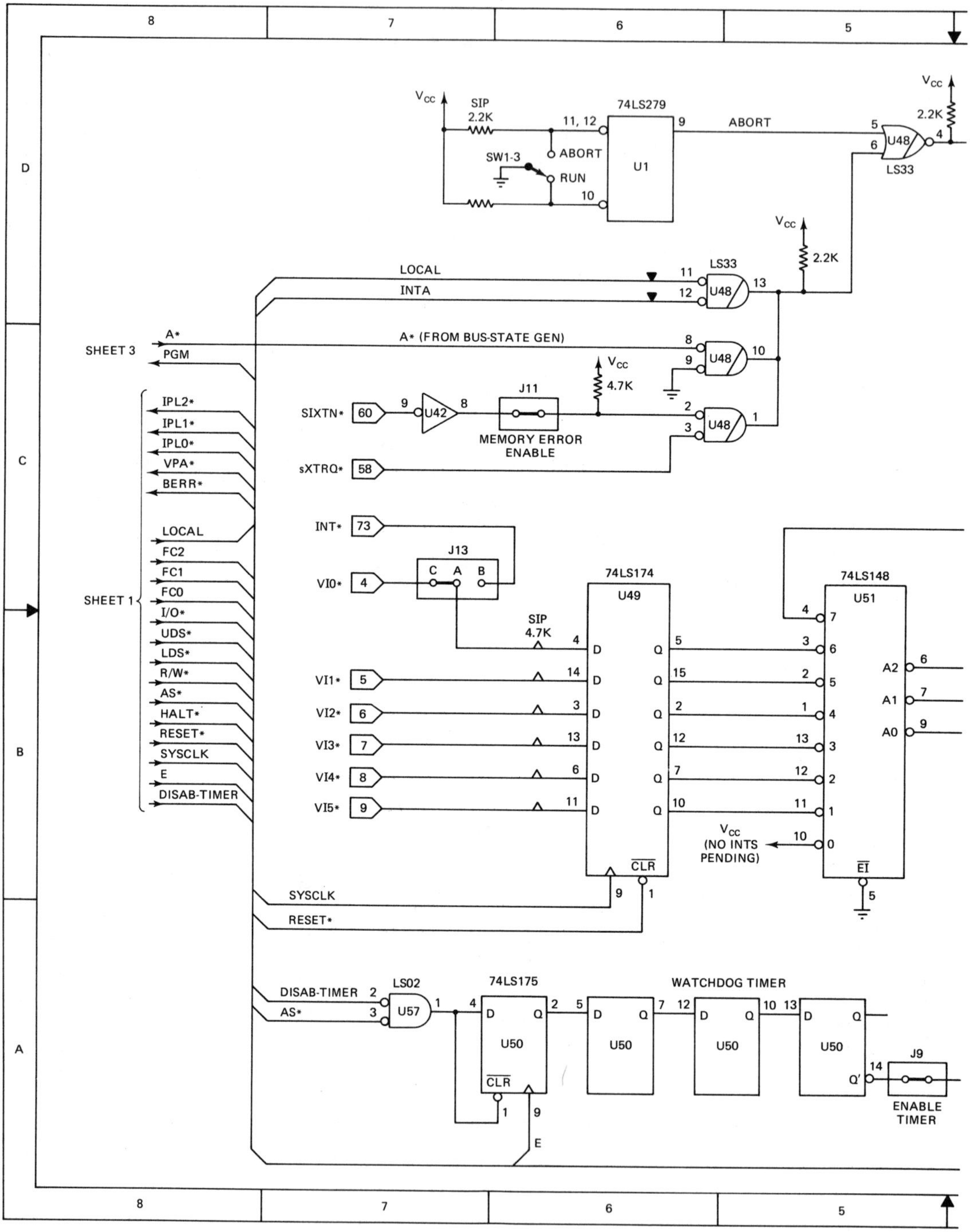
ABORT
SW1-3
RUN
74LS279
U1
SIP 2.2K
LS33
U48
LOCAL
INTA
A* (FROM BUS-STATE GEN)
SHEET 3
PGM
IPL2*
IPL1*
IPL0*
VPA*
BERR*
FC2
FC1
FC0
I/O*
UDS*
LDS*
R/W*
AS*
HALT*
RESET*
SYSCLK
E
DISAB-TIMER
SHEET 1
SIXTN*
sXTRQ*
U42
J11
MEMORY ERROR ENABLE
INT*
VI0*
VI1*
VI2*
VI3*
VI4*
VI5*
J13
74LS174
U49
SIP 4.7K
74LS148
U51
(NO INTS PENDING)
LS02
U57
74LS175
U50
WATCHDOG TIMER
J9
ENABLE TIMER

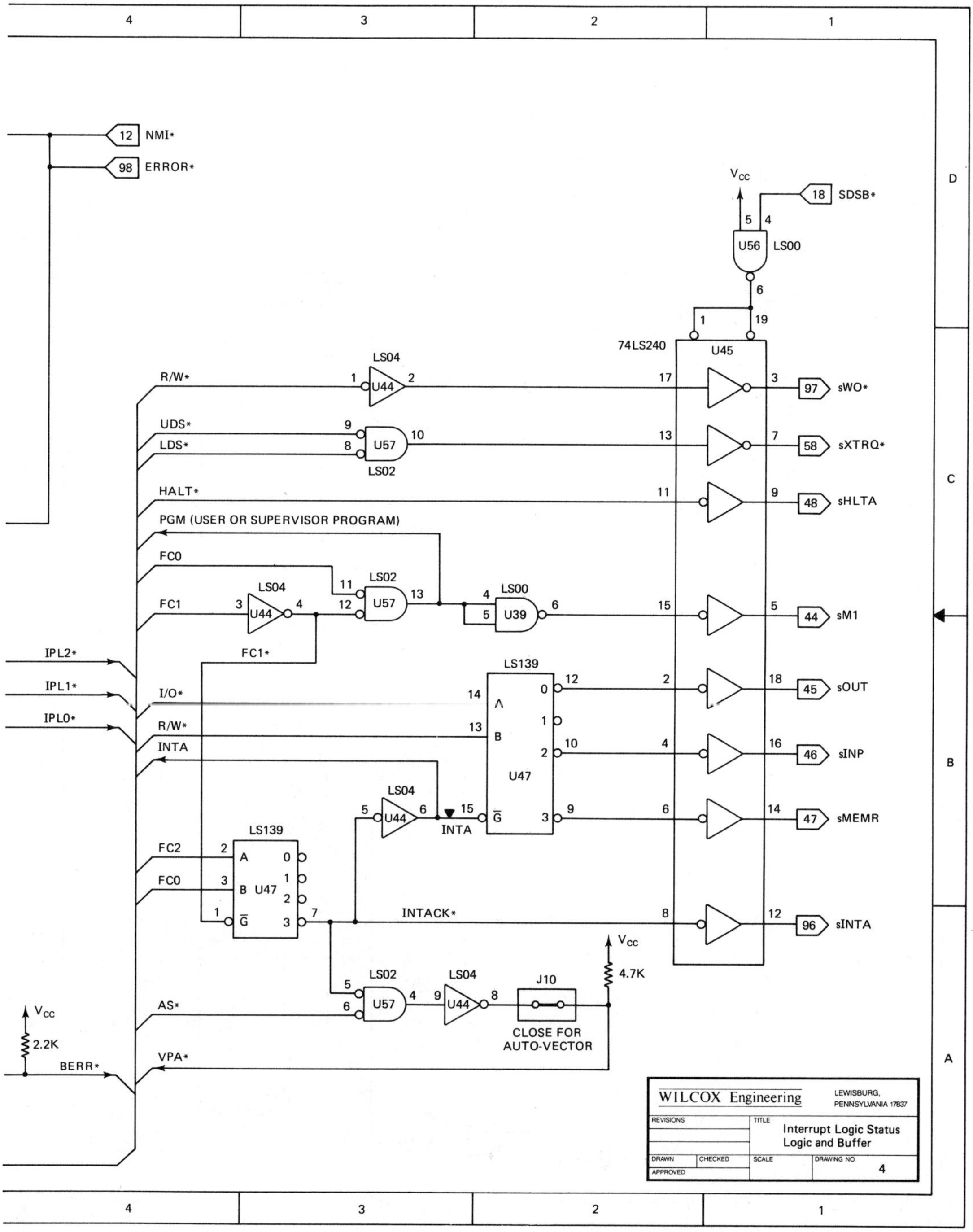

NMI*
ERROR*
SDSB*
U56 LS00
74LS240
U45
R/W*
UDS*
LDS*
HALT*
PGM (USER OR SUPERVISOR PROGRAM)
FC0
FC1
FC1*
IPL2*
IPL1*
IPL0*
I/O*
INTA
INTACK*
FC2
AS*
VPA*
BERR*
LS04
LS02
LS00
LS139
U44
U57
U39
U47
J10
CLOSE FOR AUTO-VECTOR
4.7K
2.2K
sWO*
sXTRQ*
sHLTA
sM1
sOUT
sINP
sMEMR
sINTA
WILCOX Engineering
LEWISBURG, PENNSYLVANIA 17837
Interrupt Logic Status Logic and Buffer
DRAWING NO. 4

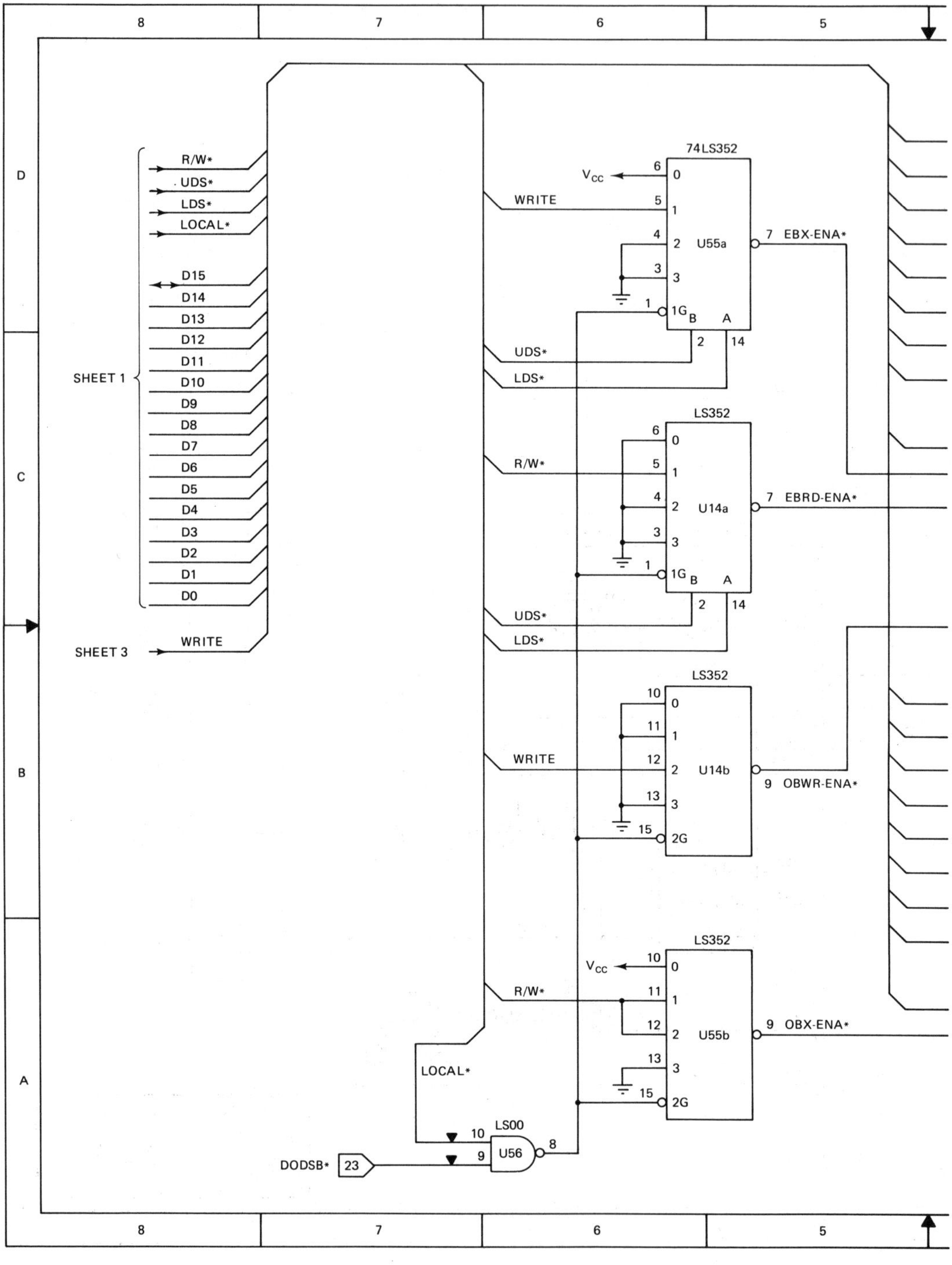
8
7
6
5
D
C
B
A
SHEET 1
R/W*
UDS*
LDS*
LOCAL*
D15
D14
D13
D12
D11
D10
D9
D8
D7
D6
D5
D4
D3
D2
D1
D0
SHEET 3
WRITE
74LS352
U55a
EBX-ENA*
LS352
U14a
EBRD-ENA*
LS352
U14b
OBWR-ENA*
LS352
U55b
OBX-ENA*
LS00
U56
DODSB*
23
LOCAL*
UDS*
LDS*
R/W*
V_{CC}

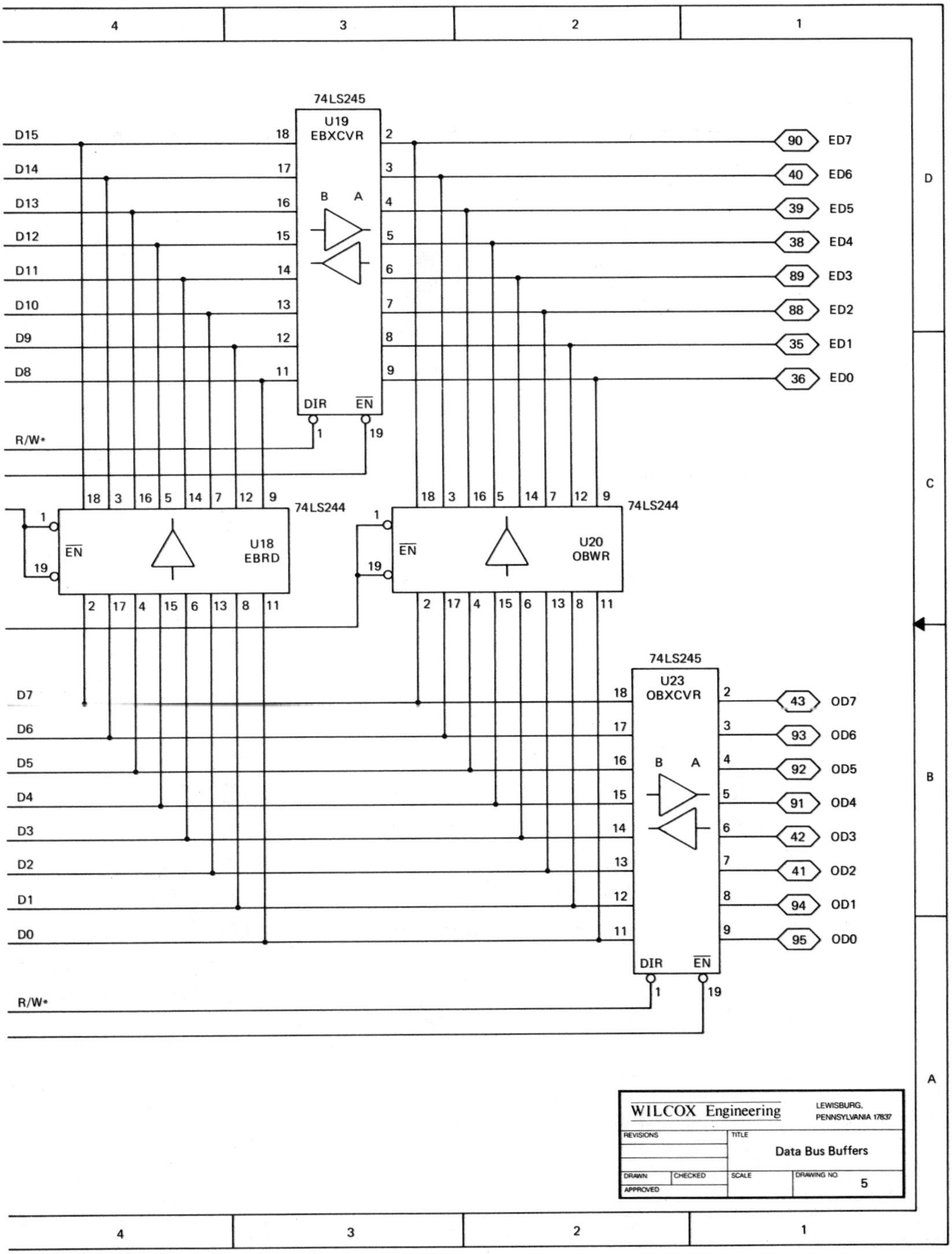
74LS245
U19
EBXCVR
D15
D14
D13
D12
D11
D10
D9
D8
R/W*
ED7
ED6
ED5
ED4
ED3
ED2
ED1
ED0
74LS244
U18
EBRD
74LS244
U20
OBWR
74LS245
U23
OBXCVR
D7
D6
D5
D4
D3
D2
D1
D0
R/W*
OD7
OD6
OD5
OD4
OD3
OD2
OD1
OD0
WILCOX Engineering
LEWISBURG, PENNSYLVANIA 17837
REVISIONS
TITLE
Data Bus Buffers
DRAWN
CHECKED
SCALE
DRAWING NO.
5
APPROVED

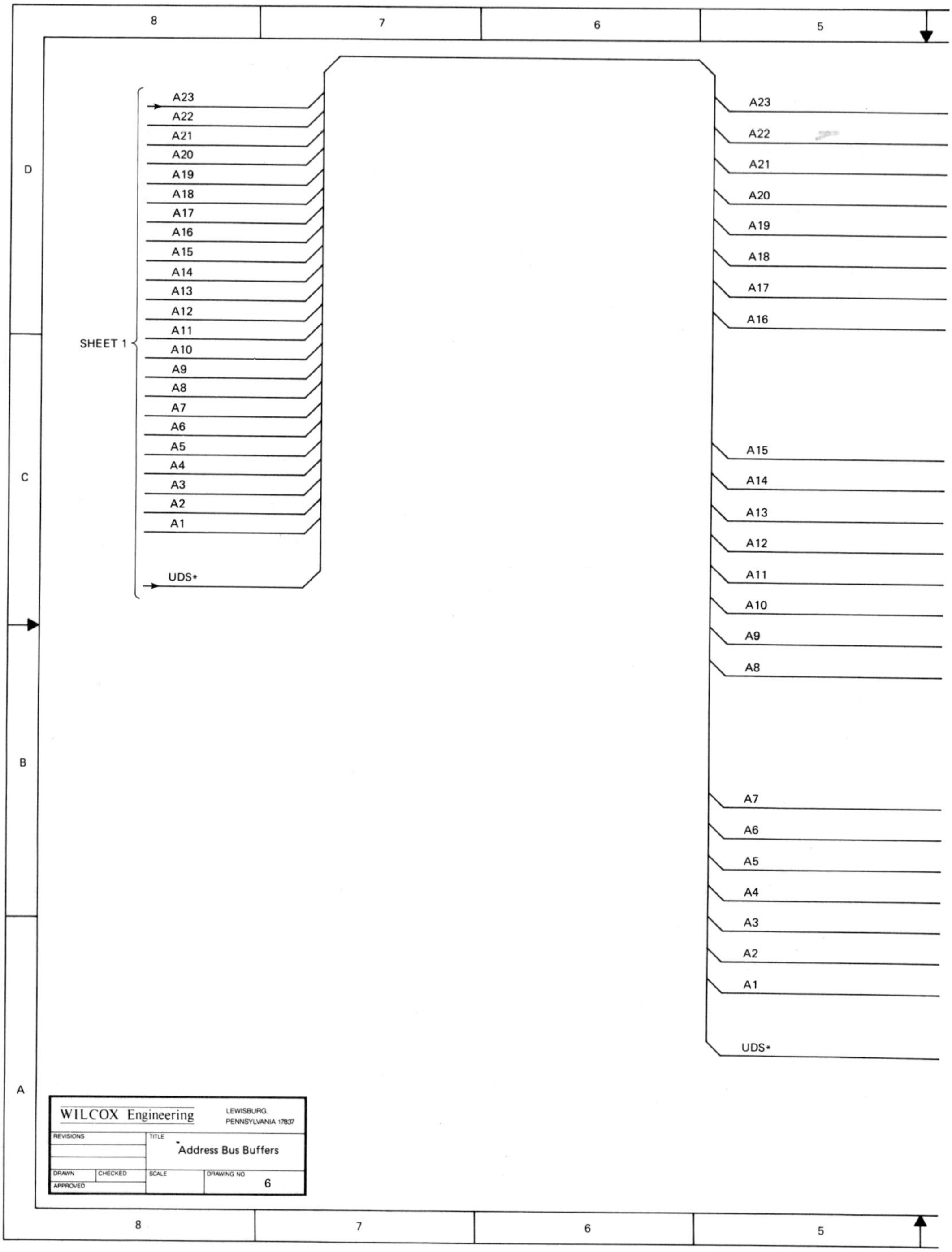
8
7
6
5
D
C
B
A
SHEET 1
A23
A22
A21
A20
A19
A18
A17
A16
A15
A14
A13
A12
A11
A10
A9
A8
A7
A6
A5
A4
A3
A2
A1
UDS*
A23
A22
A21
A20
A19
A18
A17
A16
A15
A14
A13
A12
A11
A10
A9
A8
A7
A6
A5
A4
A3
A2
A1
UDS*
WILCOX Engineering
LEWISBURG, PENNSYLVANIA 17837
REVISIONS
TITLE
Address Bus Buffers
DRAWN
CHECKED
SCALE
DRAWING NO
6
APPROVED

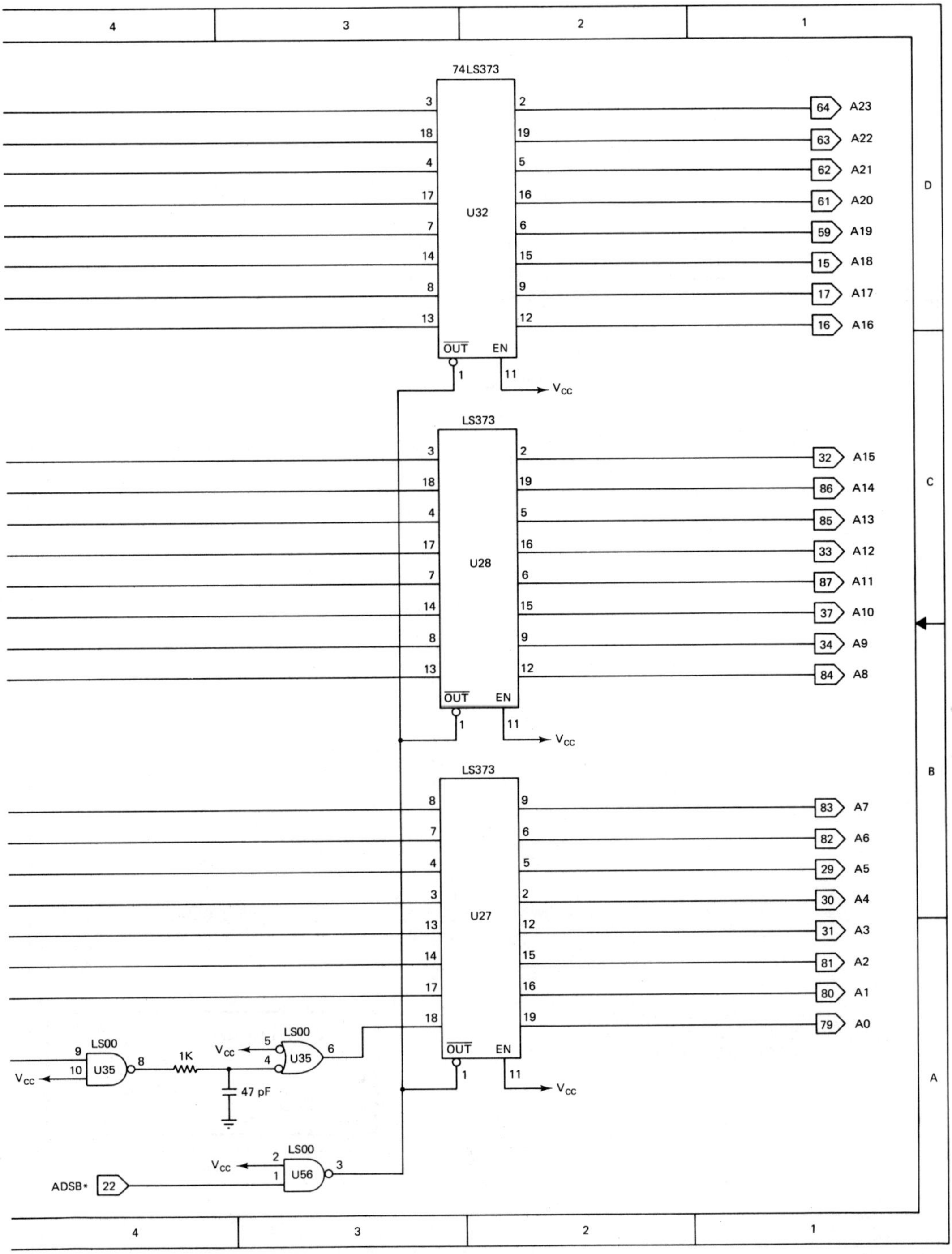
74LS373
U32
LS373
U28
LS373
U27
OUT
EN
Vcc
A23
A22
A21
A20
A19
A18
A17
A16
A15
A14
A13
A12
A11
A10
A9
A8
A7
A6
A5
A4
A3
A2
A1
A0
LS00
U35
1K
47 pF
U56
ADSB*
D
C
B
A

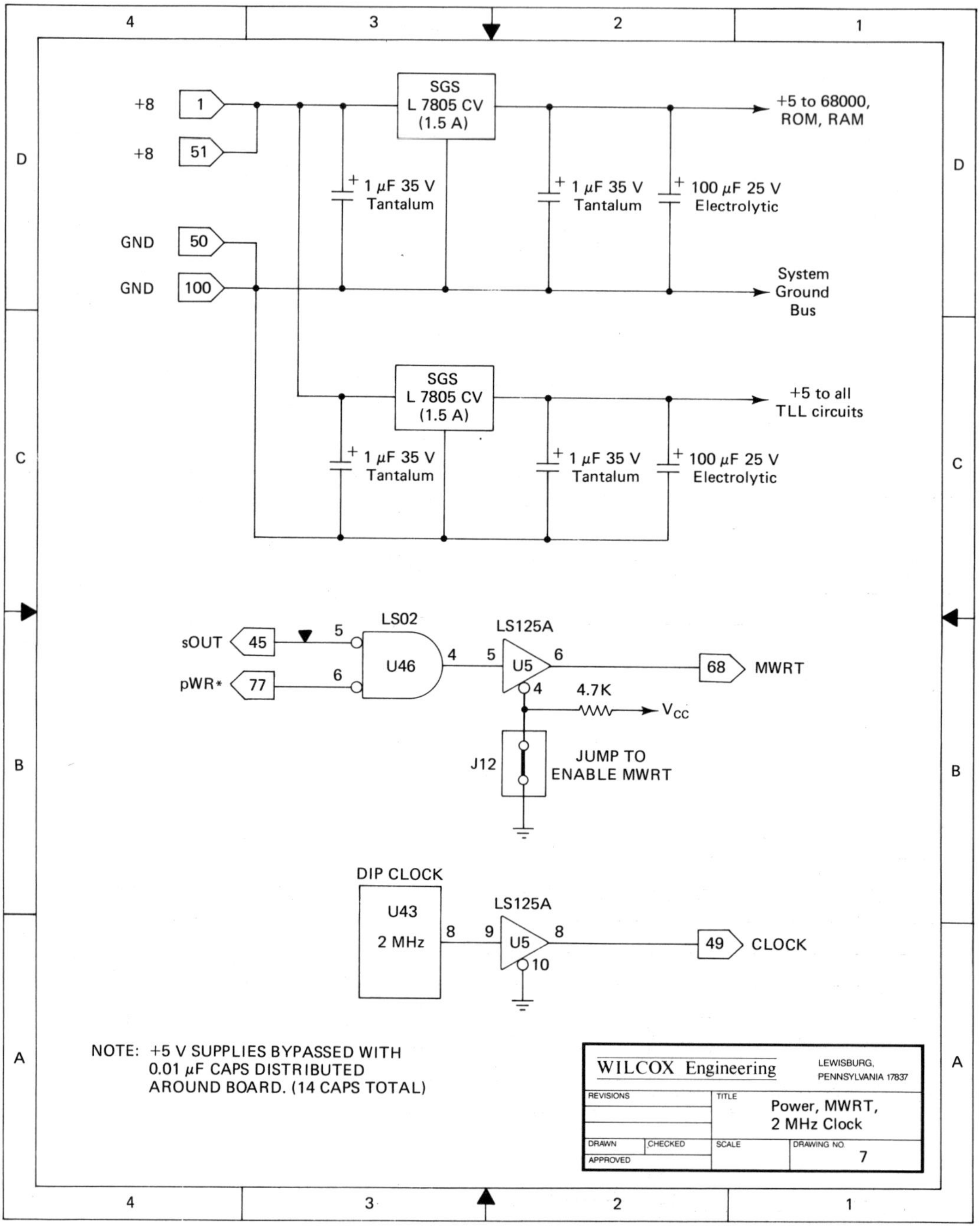
+8
1
+8
51
GND
50
GND
100
SGS
L 7805 CV
(1.5 A)
+5 to 68000,
ROM, RAM
1 μF 35 V
Tantalum
1 μF 35 V
Tantalum
100 μF 25 V
Electrolytic
System
Ground
Bus
SGS
L 7805 CV
(1.5 A)
+5 to all
TLL circuits
1 μF 35 V
Tantalum
1 μF 35 V
Tantalum
100 μF 25 V
Electrolytic
sOUT
45
pWR*
77
LS02
U46
LS125A
U5
68
MWRT
4.7K
Vcc
J12
JUMP TO
ENABLE MWRT
DIP CLOCK
U43
2 MHz
LS125A
U5
49
CLOCK
NOTE: +5 V SUPPLIES BYPASSED WITH
0.01 μF CAPS DISTRIBUTED
AROUND BOARD. (14 CAPS TOTAL)
WILCOX Engineering
LEWISBURG,
PENNSYLVANIA 17837
REVISIONS
TITLE
Power, MWRT,
2 MHz Clock
DRAWN
CHECKED
SCALE
DRAWING NO.
7
APPROVED

APPENDIX E

Data Sheets

National Semiconductor

July 1984

MM58167A Microprocessor Real Time Clock

General Description

The MM58167A is a low threshold metal gate CMOS circuit that functions as a real time clock in bus oriented microprocessor systems. The device includes an addressable real time counter, 56 bits of RAM, and two interrupt outputs. A $\overline{\text{POWER DOWN}}$ input allows the chip to be disabled from the rest of the system for standby low power operation. The time base is a 32,768 Hz crystal oscillator.

Features

- Microprocessor compatible (8-bit data bus)
- Milliseconds through month counters
- 56 bits of RAM with comparator to compare the real time counter to the RAM data
- 2 INTERRUPT OUTPUTS with 8 possible interrupt signals
- $\overline{\text{POWER DOWN}}$ input that disables all inputs and outputs except for one of the interrupts
- Status bit to indicate rollover during a read
- 32,768 Hz crystal oscillator
- Four-year calendar (no leap year)
- 24-hour clock

Functional Description

Real Time Counter

The real time counter is divided into 4-bit digits with 2 digits being accessed during any read or write cycle. Each digit represents a BCD number and is defined in Table I. Any unused bits are held at a logical zero during a read and ignored during a write. An unused bit is any bit not necessary to provide a full BCD number. For example tens of hours cannot legally exceed the number 2, thus only 2 bits are necessary to define the tens of hours. The other 2 bits in the tens of hours digit are unused. The unused bits are designated in Table I as dashes.

The addressable portion of the counter is from milliseconds to months. The counter itself is a ripple counter. The ripple delay is less than 60 μs above 4.0V and 300 μs at 2.0V.

RAM

56 bits of RAM are contained on-chip. These can be used for any necessary power down storage or as an alarm latch for comparison to the real time counter. The data in the RAM can be compared to the real time counter on a digit basis. The only digits that are not compared are the unit ten thousandths of seconds and tens of days of the week (these are unused in the real time counter). If the two most significant bits of any RAM digit are ones, then this RAM location will always compare.

The RAM is formatted the same as the real time counter, 4 bits per digit, 14 digits, however there are no unused bits. The unused bits in the real time counter will compare only to zeros in the RAM.

Interrupts and Comparator

There are two interrupt outputs. The first and most flexible is the INTERRUPT OUTPUT (a true high signal). This output can be programmed to provide 8 different output signals. They are: 10 Hz, 1 Hz, once per minute, once per hour, once a day, once a week, once a month, and when a RAM/real time counter comparison occurs. To enable the output a one is written into the interrupt control register at the bit location corresponding to the desired output frequency *(Figure 1)*. Once one or more bits have been set in the interrupt control register, the corresponding counter's rollover to its reset state will clock the interrupt status register and cause the interrupt output to go high. To reset the interrupt and to identify which frequency caused the interrupt, the interrupt status register is read. Reading this register places the contents of the status register on the data bus. The interrupting frequency will be identified by a one in the respective bit position. Removing the read will reset the interrupt.

The second interrupt is the $\overline{\text{STANDBY INTERRUPT}}$ (open drain output, active low). This interrupt occurs when enabled and when a RAM/real time counter comparison occurs. The $\overline{\text{STANDBY INTERRUPT}}$ is enabled by writing a one on the D0 line at address 16_H or disabled by writing a zero on the D0 line. This interrupt is not triggered by the edge of the compare signal, but rather by the level. Thus if the compare is enabled when the $\overline{\text{STANDBY INTERRUPT}}$ is enabled, the interrupt will turn on immediately.

Connection Diagram

Dual-In-Line Package

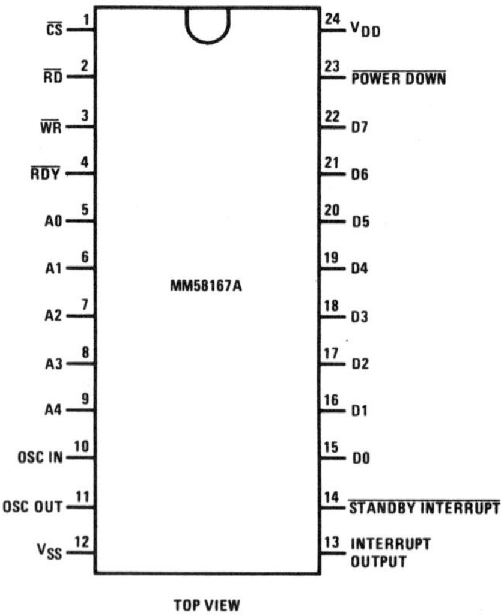

TL/F/6148-1

TRI-STATE® is a registered trademark of National Semiconductor Corp.

IM-B30M74/Printed in U.S.A.

Absolute Maximum Ratings

Voltage at All Pins	$V_{SS}-0.3V$ to $V_{DD}+0.3V$	$V_{DD}-V_{SS}$	6.0V
Operating Temperature	0°C to 70°C	Lead Temperature (Soldering, 10 seconds)	300°C
Storage Temperature	−65°C to 150°C		

Electrical Characteristics $V_{SS}=0V$, $0°C \le T_A \le 70°C$

Parameter	Conditions	Min	Max	Units
Supply Voltage				
V_{DD}	Outputs Enabled	4.0	5.5	V
V_{DD}	$\overline{POWER}$ $\overline{DOWN}$ Mode	2.0	5.5	V
Supply Current				
I_{DD}, Static	Outputs TRI-STATE® $f_{IN}=DC$, $V_{DD}=5.5V$		10	μA
I_{DD}, Dynamic	Outputs TRI-STATE $f_{IN}=32$ kHz, $V_{DD}=5.5V$ $V_{IH} \ge V_{DD}-0.3V$ $V_{IL} \le V_{SS}+0.3V$		20	μA
I_{DD}, Dynamic	Outputs TRI-STATE $f_{IN}=32$ kHz, $V_{DD}=5.5V$ $V_{IH}=2.0V$, $V_{IL}=0.8V$		5	mA
Input Voltage				
Logical Low		0.0	0.8	V
Logical High		2.0	V_{DD}	V
Input Leakage Current	$V_{SS} \le V_{IN} \le V_{DD}$	−1	1	μA
Output Impedance	I/O and INTERRUPT OUT			
Logical Low	$V_{DD}=4.5V$, $I_{OL}=1.6$ mA		0.4	V
Logical High	$V_{DD}=4.5V$, $I_{OH}=-400$ μA	2.4		V
	$I_{OH}=-10$ μA	0.8 V_{DD}		V
TRI-STATE	$V_{SS} \le V_{OUT} \le V_{DD}$	−1	1	μA
Output Impedance	$\overline{RDY}$ and $\overline{STANDBY}$ INTERRUPT (Open Drain Devices)			
Logical Low, Sink	$V_{DD}=4.5V$, $I_{OL}=1.6$ mA		0.4	V
Logical High, Leakage	$V_{OUT} \le V_{DD}$		10	μA

Functional Description (Continued)

TABLE I. Real Time Counter Format

Counter Addressed		Units D0	D1	D2	D3	Max BCD Code	Tens D4	D5	D6	D7	Max BCD Code
1/10,000 of Seconds	(00_H)	-	-	-	-	0	D4	D5	D6	D7	9
Hundredths and Tenths Sec	(01_H)	D0	D1	D2	D3	9	D4	D5	D6	D7	9
Seconds	(02_H)	D0	D1	D2	D3	9	D4	D5	D6	-	5
Minutes	(03_H)	D0	D1	D2	D3	9	D4	D5	D6	-	5
Hours	(04_H)	D0	D1	D2	D3	9	D4	D5	-	-	2
Day of the Week	(05_H)	D0	D1	D2	-	7	-	-	-	-	0
Day of the Month	(06_H)	D0	D1	D2	D3	9	D4	D5	-	-	3
Month	(07_H)	D0	D1	D2	D3	9	D4	-	-	-	1

(−) indicates unused bits

Functional Description (Continued)

TABLE II. Address Codes and Functions

A4	A3	A2	A1	A0	Function
0	0	0	0	0	Counter—Ten Thousandths of Seconds
0	0	0	0	1	Counter—Hundredths and Tenths of Seconds
0	0	0	1	0	Counter—Seconds
0	0	0	1	1	Counter—Minutes
0	0	1	0	0	Counter—Hours
0	0	1	0	1	Counter—Day of Week
0	0	1	1	0	Counter—Day of Month
0	0	1	1	1	Counter—Month
0	1	0	0	0	RAM—Ten Thousandths of Seconds
0	1	0	0	1	RAM—Hundredths and Tenths of Seconds
0	1	0	1	0	RAM—Seconds
0	1	0	1	1	RAM—Minutes
0	1	1	0	0	RAM—Hours
0	1	1	0	1	RAM—Day of Week
0	1	1	1	0	RAM—Day of Month
0	1	1	1	1	RAM—Months
1	0	0	0	0	Interrupt Status Register
1	0	0	0	1	Interrupt Control Register
1	0	0	1	0	Counters Reset
1	0	0	1	1	RAM Reset
1	0	1	0	0	Status Bit
1	0	1	0	1	GO Command
1	0	1	1	0	$\overline{\text{STANDBY}}$ $\overline{\text{INTERRUPT}}$
1	1	1	1	1	Test Mode

All others unused

The comparator is a cascaded exclusive NOR. Its output is latched 61 μs after the rising edge of the 1 kHz clock signal (input to the ten thousandths of seconds counter). This allows the counter to ripple through before looking at the comparator. For operation at less than 4.0V, the thousandths of seconds counter should not be included in a compare because of the possibility of having a ripple delay greater than 61 μs. (For output timing see Interrupt Timing.)

Power Down Mode

The POWER DOWN input is essentially a second chip select. It disables all inputs and outputs except for the STANDBY INTERRUPT. When this input is at a logical zero, the device will not respond to any external signals. It will, however, maintain timekeeping and turn on the STANDBY INTERRUPT if programmed to do so. (The programming must be done before the POWER DOWN input goes to a logical zero.) When switching V_{DD} to the standby or power down mode, the POWER DOWN input should go to a logical zero at least 1 μs before V_{DD} is switched. When switching V_{DD} all other inputs must remain between $V_{SS} - 0.3V$ and $V_{DD} + 0.3V$. When restoring V_{DD} to the normal operating mode, it is necessary to insure that all other inputs are at valid levels before switching the POWER DOWN input back to a logical one. These precautions are necessary to insure that no data is lost or altered when changing to or from the power down mode.

Counter and RAM Resets; GO Command

The counters and RAM can be reset by writing all 1's (FF) at address 12_H or 13_H respectively.

A write pulse at address 15_H will reset the thousandths, hundredths, tenths, units, and tens of seconds counters. This GO command is used for precise starting of the clock. The data on the data bus is ignored during the write. If the seconds counter is at a value greater than 39 when the GO is issued, the minute counter will increment; otherwise the minute counter is unaffected. This command is not necessary to start the clock, but merely a convenient way to start precisely at a given minute.

Status Bit

The status bit is provided to inform the user that the clock is in the process of rolling over when a counter is read. The status bit is set if this 1 kHz clock occurs during or after any counter read. This tells the user that the clock is rippling through the real time counter. Because the clock is rippling, invalid data may be read from the counter. If the status bit is set following a counter read, the counter should be reread.

The status bit appears on D0 when address 14_H is read. All the other data lines will be zero. The bit is set when a logical one appears. This bit should be read every time a counter read or after a series of counter reads are done. The trailing edge of the read at address 14_H will reset the status bit.

Oscillator

The oscillator used is the standard Pierce parallel resonant oscillator. Externally, 2 capacitors, a 20 MΩ resistor and the crystal are required. The 20 MΩ resistor is connected between OSC IN and OSC OUT to bias the internal inverter in the linear region. For micropower crystals a resistor in series with the oscillator output may be necessary to insure the crystal is not overdriven. This resistor should be approximately 200 kΩ. The capacitor values should be typically 20 pF–25 pF. The crystal frequency is 32,768 Hz.

The oscillator input can be externally driven, if desired. In this case the output should be left floating and the input levels should be within 0.3V of the supplies.

A ground line or ground plane between pins 9 and 10 may be necessary to prevent interference of the oscillator by the A4 address.

Control Lines

The READ, WRITE, and CHIP SELECT signals are active low inputs. The READY signal is an open drain output. At the start of each read or write cycle the READY line (open drain) will pull low and will remain low until valid data from a chip read appears on the bus or data on the bus is latched in during a write. READ and WRITE must be accompanied by a CHIP SELECT (see *Figures 3 and 4* for read and write cycle timing).

During a read or write, address bits must not change while chip select and control strobes are low.

Test Mode

The test mode is merely a mode for production testing. It allows the counters to count at a higher than normal rate. In this mode the 32 kHz oscillator input is connected directly to the ten thousandths of seconds counter. The chip select and write lines must be low and the address must be held at $1F_H$.

Functional Description (Continued)

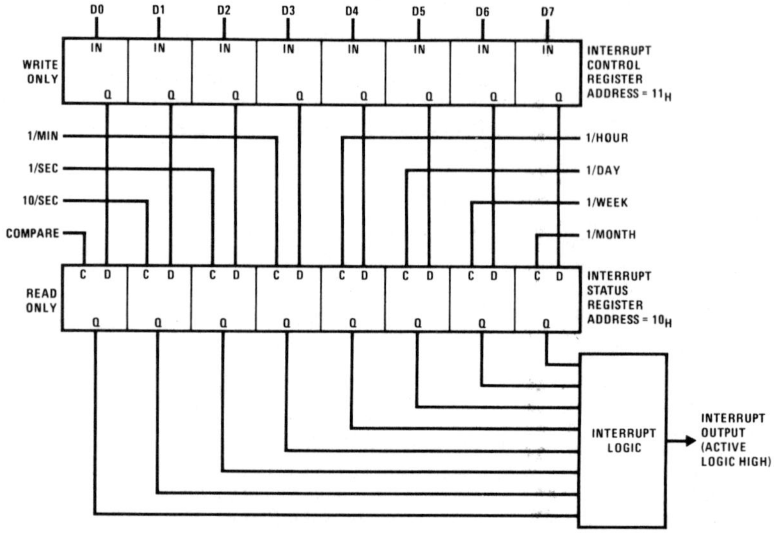

FIGURE 1. Interrupt Register Format

TL/F/6148-2

Standby Interrupt Typical Characteristics

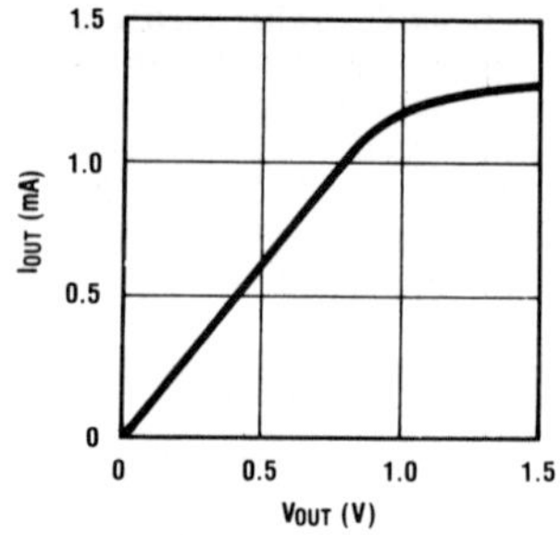

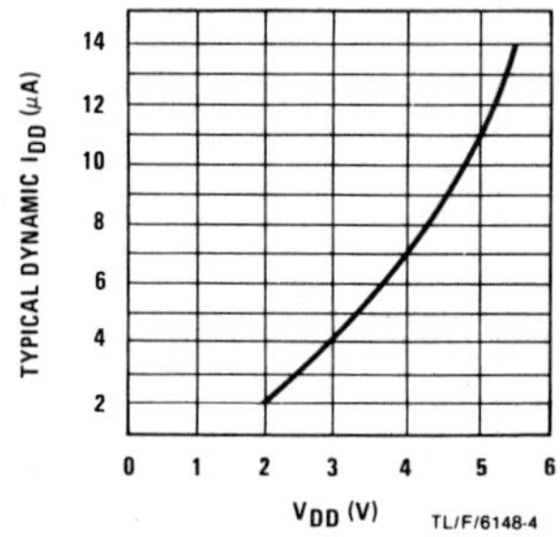

TL/F/6148-4

FIGURE 2. Typical Supply Current vs Supply Voltage During Power Down

Interrupt Timing $0°C \le T_A \le 70°C$, $4.5V \le V_{DD} \le 5.5V$, $V_{SS} = 0V$

Sym	Parameter	Min	Max	Units
t_{INTON}	Status Register Clock to INTERRUPT OUTPUT (Pin 13) High (Note 1)		5	µs
t_{SBYON}	Compare Valid to $\overline{\text{STANDBY}}$ $\overline{\text{INTERRUPT}}$ (Pin 14) Low (Note 1)		5	µs
t_{INTOFF}	Trailing Edge of Status Register Read to INTERRUPT $\overline{\text{OUTPUT}}$ Low		5	µs
t_{SBYOFF}	Trailing Edge of Write Cycle (D0 = 0; Address = 16_H) to $\overline{\text{STANDBY}}$ $\overline{\text{INTERRUPT}}$ Off (High Impedance State)		5	µs

Note 1: The status register clocks are: the corresponding counter's rollover to its reset state or the compare becoming valid. The compare becomes valid 61 µs after the 1/10,000 of a second counter is clocked, if the real time counter data matches the RAM data.

Read Cycle Timing $0°C \le T_A \le 70°C$, $4.5V \le V_{DD} \le 5.5V$, $V_{SS} = 0V$

Sym	Parameter	Min	Max	Units
t_{AR}	Address Bus Valid to Read Strobe	100		ns
t_{CSR}	Chip Select to Read Strobe	0		ns
t_{RRY}	Read Strobe to Ready Strobe		150	ns
t_{RYD}	Ready Strobe to Data Valid		800	ns
t_{AD}	Address Bus Valid to Data Valid		1050	ns
t_{RH}	Data Hold Time From Trailing Edge of Read Strobe	0		ns
t_{HZ}	Trailing Edge of Read Strobe to TRI-STATE Mode		250	ns
t_{RYH}	Read Hold Time after Ready Strobe	0		ns
t_{RA}	Address Bus Hold Time from Trailing Edge of Read Strobe	50		ns
t_{RYDV}	Rising Edge of Ready to Data Valid		100	ns

Note 2: If $t_{AR} = 0$ and Chip Select, Address Valid or Read are coincident then they must exist for 1050 ns.

Write Cycle Timing $0°C \le T_A \le 70°C$, $4.5V \le V_{DD} \le 5.5V$, $V_{SS} = 0V$

Sym	Parameter	Min	Max	Units
t_{AW}	Address Valid to Write Strobe	100		ns
t_{CSW}	Chip Select to Write Strobe	0		ns
t_{DW}	Data Valid before Write Strobe	100		ns
t_{WRY}	Write Strobe to Ready Strobe		150	ns
t_{RY}	Ready Strobe Width		800	ns
t_{RYH}	Write Hold Time after Ready Strobe	0		ns
t_{WD}	Data Hold Time after Write Strobe	110		ns
t_{WA}	Address Hold Time after Write Strobe	50		ns

Note 3: If data changes while $\overline{CS}$ and $\overline{WR}$ are low, then they must remain coincident for 1050 ns after the data change to ensure a valid write.

Data bus loading is 100 pF.

Ready output loading is 50 pF and 3 kΩ pull-up.

Input and output AC timing levels:

Logical one = 2.0V

Logical zero = 0.8V

Read and Write Cycle Timing Diagrams

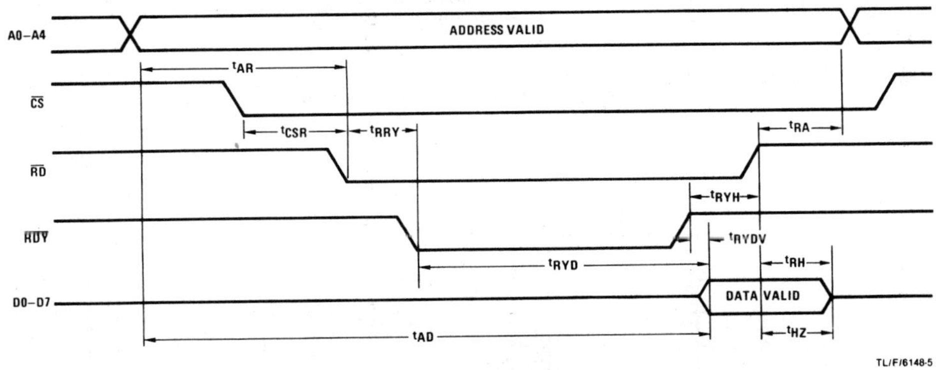

FIGURE 3. Read Cycle Timing

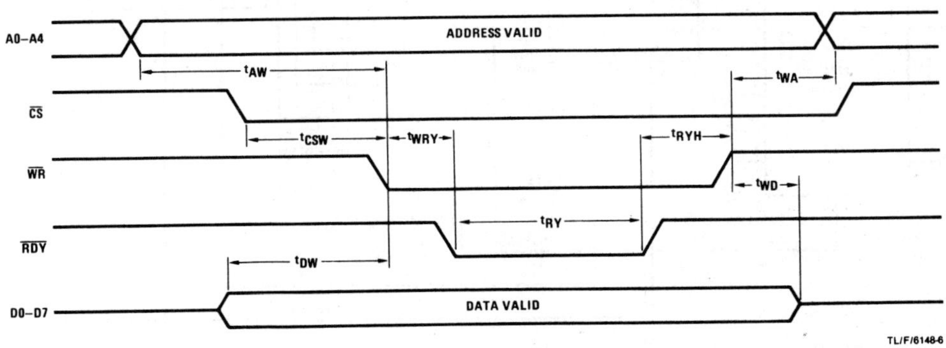

FIGURE 4. Write Cycle Timing

Typical Applications

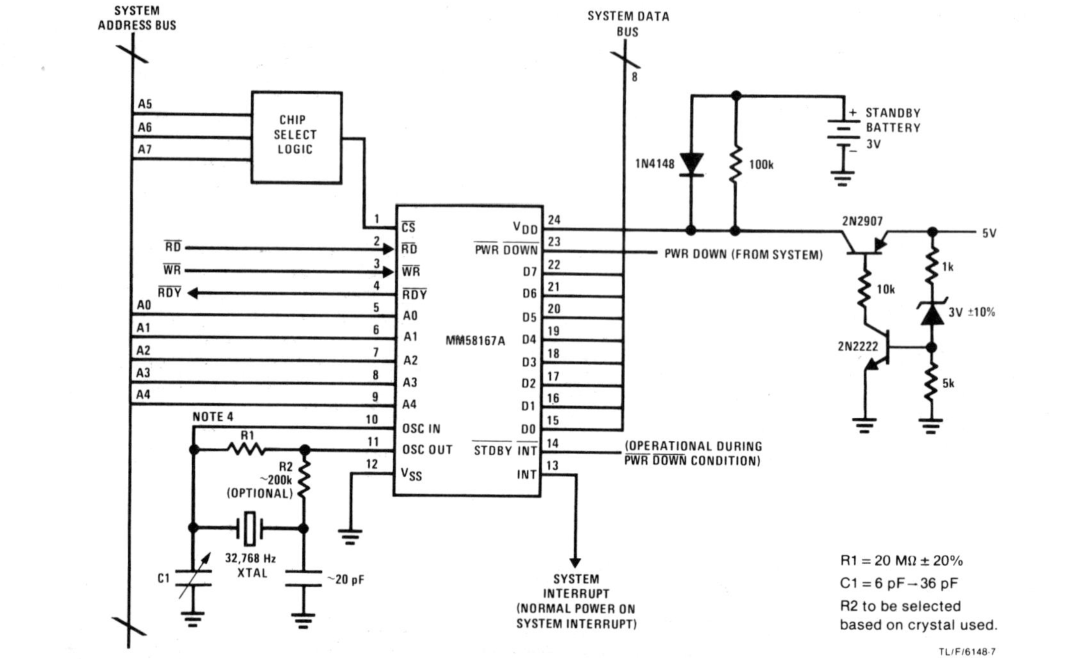

Note 4: A ground line or ground plane guard trace should be included between pins 9 and 10 to insure the oscillator is not disturbed by the address line.

FIGURE 5. Typical Connection Diagram

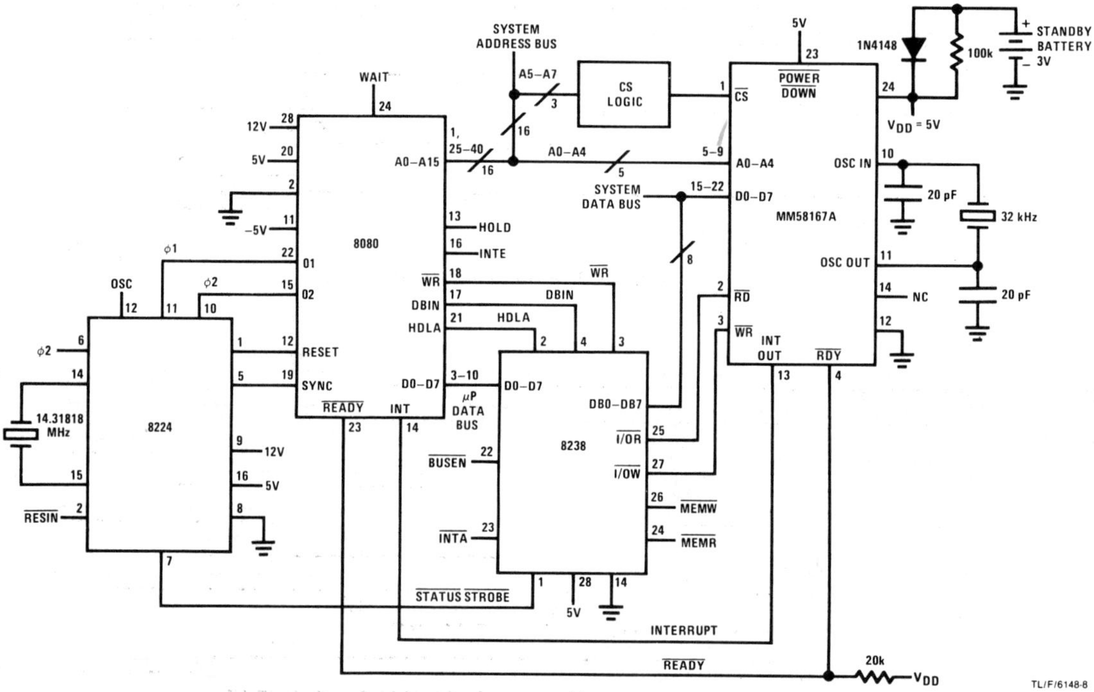

Note 5: Must use 8238 or equivalent logic to insure advanced I/OW pulse; so that the ready output of the MM58167A is valid by the end of $\phi2$ during the T2 microcycle.

Note 6: $t_{\phi2} \geq t_{RS8080} + t_{DL8238} + t_{WRY58167A}$.

FIGURE 6. 8080 System Interface with Battery Backup

Block Diagram

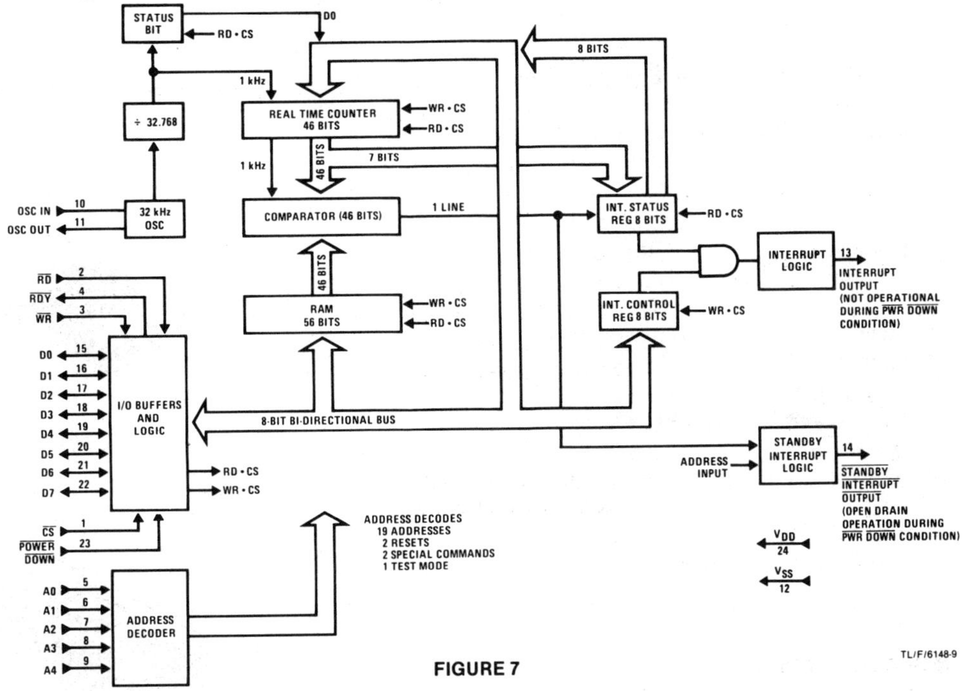

FIGURE 7

Physical Dimensions inches (millimeters)

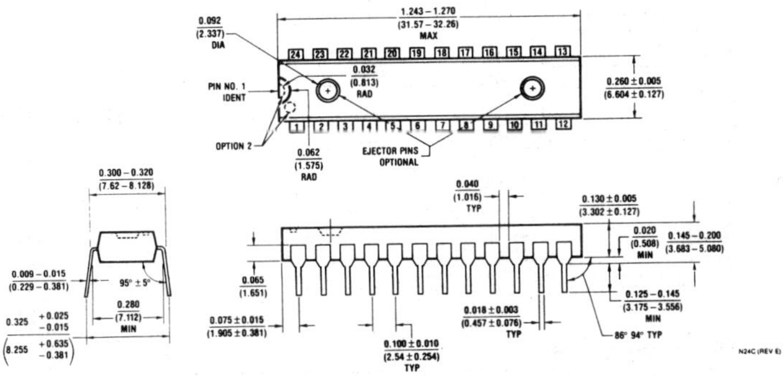

Molded Dual-In-Line Package (N)
Order Number MM58167AN
NS Package Number N24C

National Semiconductor Corporation
2900 Semiconductor Drive
Santa Clara, California 95051
Tel: (408) 721-5000
TWX: (910) 339-9240

National Semiconductor GmbH
Furstenriederstrasse Nr.5
D8000 Munchen 21
West Germany
Tel: (089) 5 60 12-0
Telex: 522772

NS Japan K.K.
4-403 Ikebukuro, Toshima-ku
Tokyo 171, Japan
Tel: (03)988-2131
FAX: 011-81-3-988-1700

National Semiconductor Hong Kong Ltd.
Southeast Asia Marketing
N.H.K. Sales
Austin Tower, 4th Floor
22-26 Austin Avenue
Tsimshatsui, Kowloon, Hong Kong
Telephone: 3-7231290, 3-7243645
Cable: NSSEAMKTG
Telex: 52996 NSSEA HX

National Semiconductores Do Brasil Ltda.
Avda Brigadeiro Faria Lima 830
8 ANDAR
01452 Sao Paulo, Brasil
Tel: 212-1181
Telex: 1131931 NSBR

NS Electronics Pty. Ltd.
Cnr. Stud Rd. & Mtn. Highway
Bayswater, Victoria 3153
Australia
Tel: 03-729-6333
Telex: 32096

HN462716, HN462716G

2048-word × 8-bit U.V. Erasable and Electrically Programmable Read Only Memory

The HN462716 is a 2048 word by 8 bit erasable and electrically programmable ROMs. This device is packaged in a 24-pin, dual-in-line package with transparent lid. The transparent lid allows the user to expose the chip to ultraviolet light to erase the bit pattern, whereby a new pattern can then be written into the device.

- Single Power Supply ···· +5V ±5%
- Simple Programming ···· Program Voltage: +25V DC
  Programs with One 50ms Pulse
- Static ··············· No Clocks Required
- Inputs and Outputs TTL Compatible During Both Read and Program Modes
- Fully Decoded-on Chip Address Decode
- Access Time ········· 450ns Max.
- Low Power Dissipation ·· 555mW Max. Active Power
  161mW Max. Standby Power
- Three State Output····· OR-Tie Capability
- Interchangeable with Intel 2716

HN462716

(DC-24C)

HN462716G

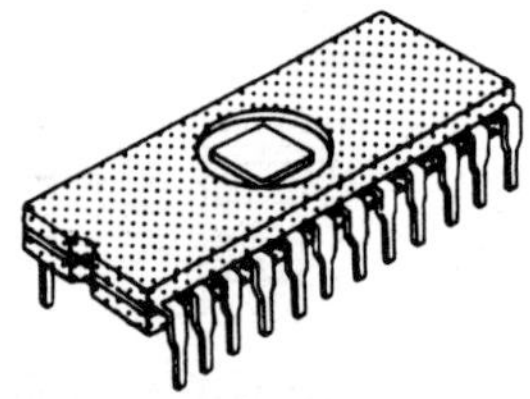

(DG-24B)

■ BLOCK DIAGRAM

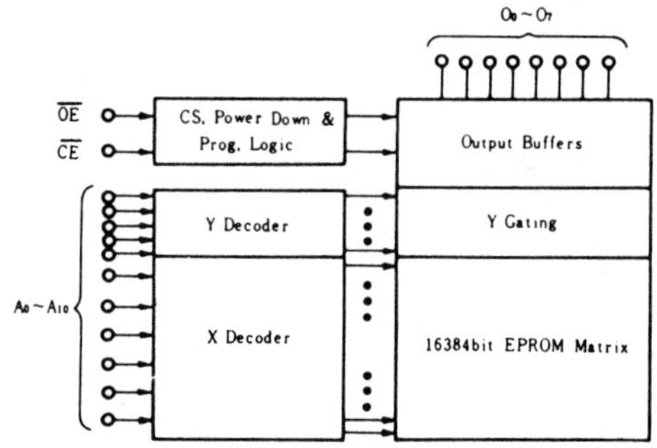

■ PIN ARRANGEMENT

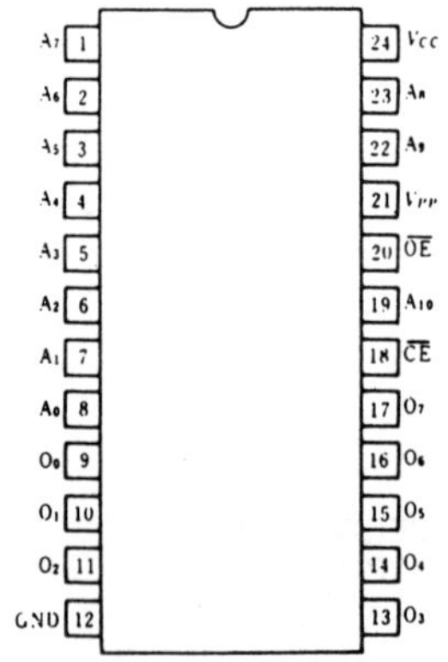

(Top View)

■ PROGRAMMING OPERATION

Mode \ Pins	$\overline{CE}$ (18)	$\overline{OE}$ (20)	V_{PP} (21)	V_{CC} (24)	Outputs (9~11, 13~17)
Read	V_{IL}	V_{IL}	+5	+5	Dout
Deselect	Don't Care	V_{IH}	+5	+5	High Z
Power Down	V_{IH}	Don't Care	+5	+5	High Z
Program	Pulsed V_{IL} to V_{IH}	V_{IH}	+25	+5	Din
Program Verify	V_{IL}	V_{IL}	+25	+5	Dout
Program Inhibit	V_{IL}	V_{IH}	+25	+5	High Z

■ ABSOLUTE MAXIMUM RATINGS

Item	Symbol	Value	Unit
Operating Temperature Range	T_{opr}	0 to +70	°C
Storage Temperature Range	T_{stg}	−65 to +125	°C
All Input and Output Voltages*	V_T	−0.3 to +7	V
V_{PP} Supply Voltage*	V_{PP}	−0.3 to +28	V

* With respect to Ground

■ READ OPERATION

● DC AND OPERATING CHARACTERISTICS ($Ta=0$ to $+70°C$, $V_{CC}=5V\pm5\%$, $V_{PP}=V_{CC}\pm0.6V$)

Item	Symbol	Test Condition	min.	typ.	max.	Unit
Input Leakage Current	I_{LI}	$V_{IN}=5.25V$	—	—	10	μA
Output Leakage Current	I_{LO}	$V_{OUT}=5.25V/0.4V$	—	—	10	μA
V_{PP} Current	I_{PP1}	$V_{PP}=5.85V$	—	—	5	mA
V_{CC} Current (Standby)	I_{CC1}	$\overline{CE}=V_{IH}$, $\overline{OE}=V_{IL}$	—	13	25	mA
V_{CC} Current (Active)	I_{CC2}	$\overline{OE}=\overline{CE}=V_{IL}$	—	56	100	mA
Input Low Voltage	V_{IL}		−0.1	—	0.8	V
Input High Voltage	V_{IH}		2.0	—	$V_{CC}+1$	V
Output Low Voltage	V_{OL}	$I_{OL}=2.1mA$	—	—	0.4	V
Output High Voltage	V_{OH}	$I_{OH}=-400\mu A$	2.4	—	—	V

Note : V_{CC} must be applied simultaneously or before V_{PP} and removed simultaneously or after V_{PP}.

● AC CHARACTERISTICS ($Ta=0$ to $+70°C$, $V_{CC}=5V\pm5\%$, $V_{PP}=V_{CC}\pm0.6V$)

Parameter	Symbol	Test Condition	min.	typ.	max.	Unit
Address to Output Delay	t_{ACC}	$\overline{OE}=\overline{CE}=V_{IL}$	—	—	450	ns
$\overline{CE}$ to Output Delay	t_{CE}	$\overline{OE}=V_{IL}$	—	—	450	ns
$\overline{OE}$ to Output Delay	t_{OE}	$\overline{CE}=V_{IL}$	—	—	120	ns
$\overline{OE}$ High to Output Float*	t_{DF}	$\overline{CE}=V_{IL}$	0	—	100	ns
Address to Output Hold	t_{OH}	$\overline{OE}=\overline{CE}=V_{IL}$	0	—	—	ns

* : t_{DF} defines the time at which the output achieves the open circuit condition and is not referenced to output voltage levels.

● CAPACITANCE ($Ta=25°C$, $f=1MHz$)

Item	Symbol	Test Condition	typ.	max.	Unit
Input Capacitance	C_{in}	$V_{IN}=0V$	—	6	pF
Output Capacitance	C_{out}	$V_{OUT}=0V$	—	12	pF

● SWITCHING CHARACTERISTICS

Test Conditions

Input Pulse Levels:	0.8V to 2.2V	
Input Rise and Fall Times:	≤ 20 ns	
Output Load:	1TTL Gate + 100 pF	
Reference Level for Measuring Timing:	Inputs	1V and 2V
	Outputs	0.8V and 2V

READ MODE ($\overline{CE}=V_{IL}$)

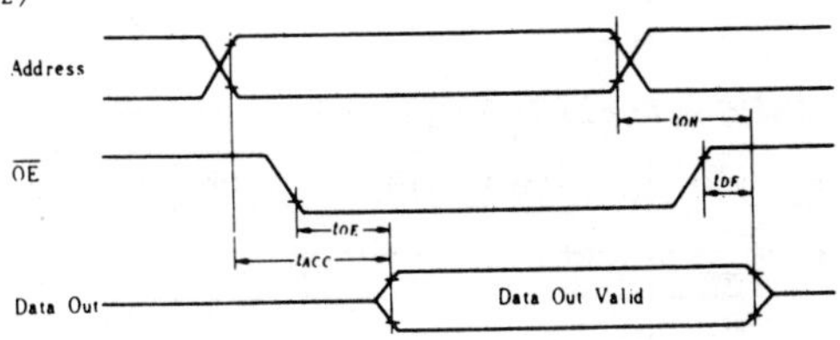

STANDBY MODE ($\overline{OE}=V_{IL}$)

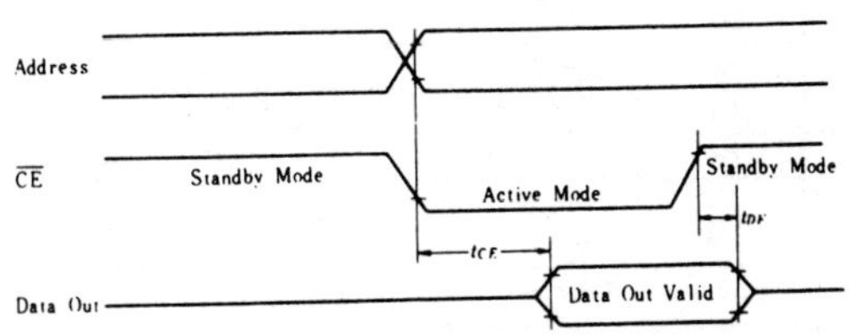

● TYPICAL CHARACTERISTICS

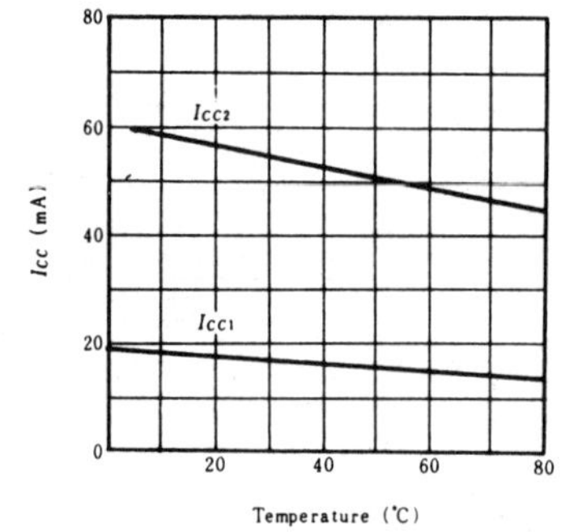

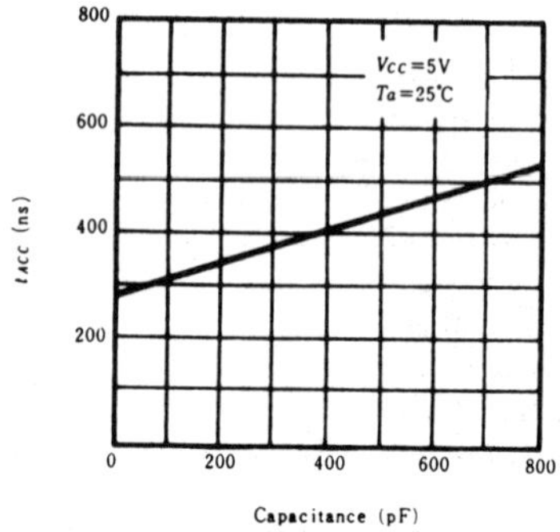

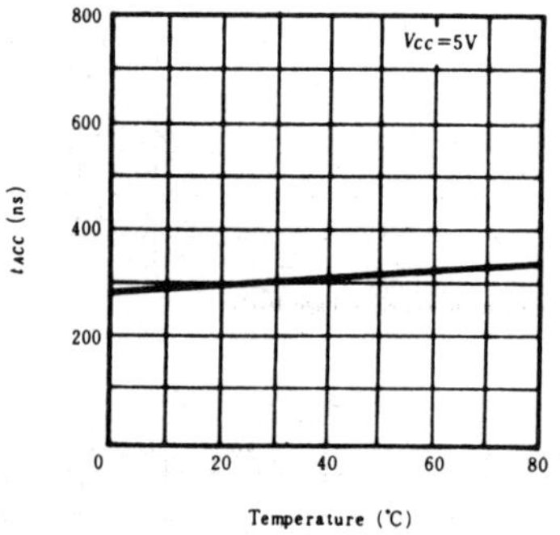

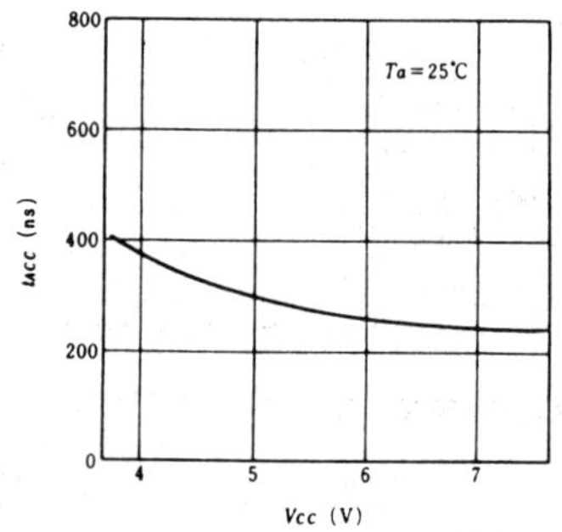

● DC PROGRAMMING CHARACTERISTICS (Ta=25°C±5°C, V_{CC}=5V±5%, V_{PP}=25V±1V)

Parameter	Symbol	Test Condition	min.	typ.	max.	Unit
Input Leakage Current	I_{LI}	V_{IN}=5.25V	—	—	10	μA
V_{PP} Supply Current	I_{PP1}	$\overline{CE}=V_{IL}$	—	—	5	mA
V_{PP} Supply Current During Programming	I_{PP2}	$\overline{CE}=V_{IH}$	—	—	30	mA
V_{CC} Supply Current	I_{CC}		—	—	100	mA
Input Low Level	V_{IL}		−0.1	—	0.8	V
Input High Level	V_{IH}		2.0	—	V_{CC}+1	V

● AC PROGRAMMING CHARACTERISTICS (Ta=25°C±5°C, V_{CC}=5V±5%, V_{PP}=25V±1V)

Parameter	Symbol	Test Condition	min.	typ.	max.	Unit
Address Setup Time	t_{AS}		2	—	—	μs
$\overline{OE}$ Setup Time	t_{OES}		2	—	—	μs
Data Setup Time	t_{DS}		2	—	—	μs
Address Hold Time	t_{AH}		2	—	—	μs
$\overline{OE}$ Hold Time	t_{OEH}		5	—	—	μs
Data Hold Time	t_{DH}		2	—	—	μs
$\overline{OE}$ to Output Float Delay*	t_{DF}	$\overline{CE}=V_{IL}$	0	—	120	ns
$\overline{OE}$ to Output Delay	t_{OE}	$\overline{CE}=V_{IL}$	—	—	120	ns
Program Pulse Width	t_{PW}		45	50	55	ms
Program Pulse Rise Time	t_{PRT}		5	—	—	ns
Program Pulse Fall Time	t_{PFT}		5	—	—	ns

Notes: V_{CC} must be applied simultaneously or before V_{PP} and removed simultaneously or after V_{PP}.

* : t_{DF} defines the time at which the output achieves the open circuit condition and is not referenced to output voltage levels.

●SWITCHING CHARACTERISTICS

Test Conditions

Input Pulse Level: 0.8V to 2.2V

Input Rise and Fall Times: ≤ 20 ns

Output Load: 1 TTL Gate + 100 pF

Reference Level for Measuring Timing:

Inputs; 1V and 2V, Outputs; 0.8V and 2V

●PROGRAMMING WAVEFORMS

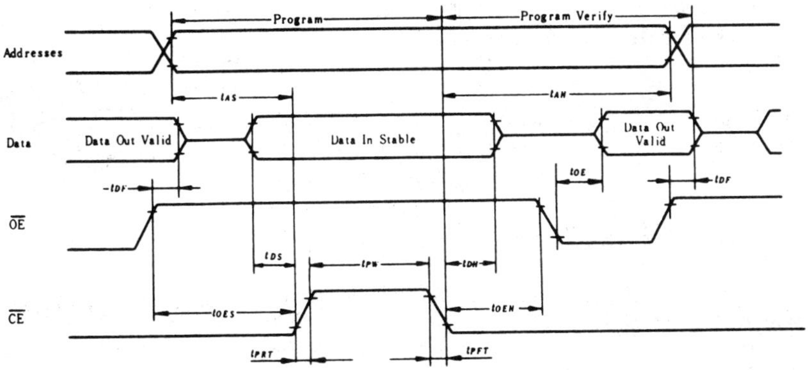

●ERASE

Erasure of HN462716 is performed by exposure to ultra-violet light with a wavelength of 2537Å, and all the output data are changed to "1" after this erasure procedure.

The minimum integrated close (i.e., UV intensity x exposure time) for erasure is 15W · sec/cm²

■DEVICE OPERATION

● READ MODE

Dataout is available 450ns (t_{ACC}) from addresses with $\overline{OE}$ low or 120ns (t_{OE}) from $\overline{OE}$ with addresses stable.

● DESELECT MODE

The outputs may be OR-tied together with the other HN462716s. When HN462716s are deselected, the $\overline{OE}$ inputs must be at high TTL level.

● POWER DOWN MODE

Power down is achieved with $\overline{CE}$ high TTL level. In this mode the outputs are in a high impedance state.

● PROGRAMMING

Initially, and after each erasure, all bits of the HN462716 are in the "High" state (Output High). Data is introduced by selectively programming "low" into the desired bit locations. In the programming mode, Vpp power supply is at 25V and $\overline{OE}$ input is at high TTL level. Data to be programmed are presented 8-bits in parallel, to the data output lines (O0 to O7).

The addresses and inputs are at TTL levels.

After the address and data setup, a 50 ms, active high program pulse is applied to the $\overline{CE}$ input. The $\overline{CE}$ is at TTL level.

The HN462716 must not be programmed with a DC signal applied to the $\overline{CE}$ input.

● PROGRAM VERIFY

The HN462716 has a program verify mode. A verify should be performed on the programmed bits to determine that they were correctly programmed. In this mode Vpp is at 25V.

● PROGRAM INHIBIT

Programming of multiple HN462716s in parallel with different data is easily accomplished by using this mode. Except for $\overline{CE}$, all like inputs of the parallel HN462716s may be common.

A TTL program pulse applied to a HN462716's $\overline{CE}$ input will program that HN462716. A low level $\overline{CE}$ inhibits the other HN462716s from being programmed.

HN4827128G-25, HN4827128G-30, HN4827128G-45

Preliminary

16384-Word x 8-bit UV Erasable and Programmable Read Only Memory

The HN4827128 is a 16384 word by 8 bit erasable and electrically programmable ROM. This device is packaged in a dual-in-line package with transparent lid. The transparent lid allows the user to expose the chip to ultraviolet light to erase the bit pattern, whereby a new pattern can then be written into the device.

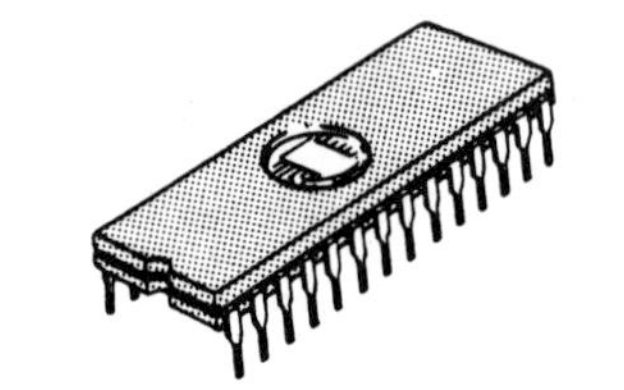

(DG-28)

■FEATURES

- Single Power Supply . . . . +5V ± 5%
- Simple Programming . . . . Program Voltage: +21V DC
  Program with One 50ms Pulse
- Static . . . . No Clocks Required
  Inputs and Outputs TTL Compatible During Both Read and Program Mode.
- Access Time 250ns/300ns/450ns
- Absolute Max. Rating of Vpp Pin 26.5V
- Low Stand-by Current 35mA
- High Performance Programming Available
- Compatible with INTEL 27128

■PIN ARRANGEMENT

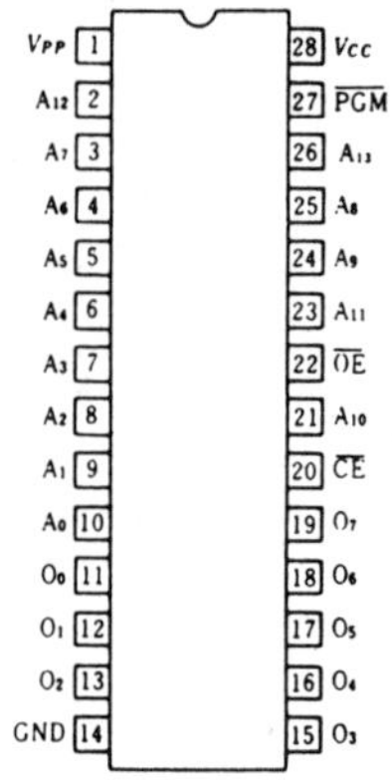

(Top View)

■BLOCK DIAGRAM

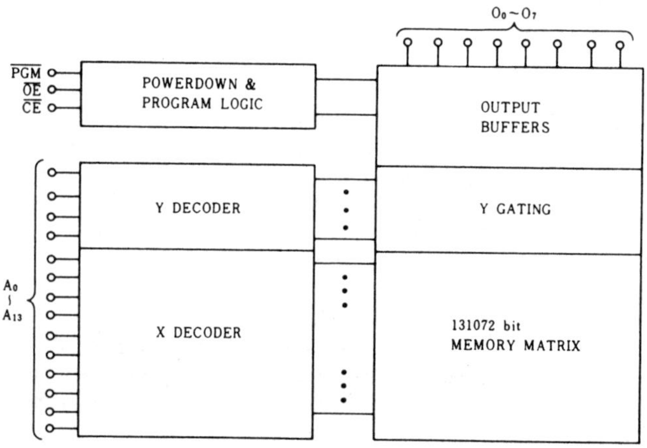

■MODE SELECTION

MODE \ Pins	$\overline{CE}$ (20)	$\overline{OE}$ (22)	$\overline{PGM}$ (27)	V_{PP} (1)	V_{CC} (28)	Outputs (11~13, 15~19)
Read	V_{IL}	V_{IL}	V_{IH}	V_{CC}	V_{CC}	Dout
Stand by	V_{IH}	×	×	V_{CC}	V_{CC}	High Z
Program	V_{IL}	×	V_{IL}	V_{PP}	V_{CC}	Din
Program Verify	V_{IL}	V_{IL}	V_{IH}	V_{PP}	V_{CC}	Dout
Program Inhibit	V_{IH}	×	×	V_{PP}	V_{CC}	High Z

Note) The specifications of this device are subject to change without notice.
Please contact your nearest Hitachi's Sales Dept. regarding specifications.

■ABSOLUTE MAXIMUM RATINGS

Item	Symbol	Value	Unit
Operating Temperature Range	T_{opr}	0 to +70	℃
Storage Temperature Range	T_{stg}	−65 to +125	℃
All Input and Output Voltages*	V_{IN}, V_{out}	−0.3 to +7	V
V_{PP} Voltage*	V_{PP}	−0.3 to +26.5	V
V_{CC} Voltage*	V_{CC}	−0.3 to +7	V

* with respect to GND

■READ OPERATION

●DC AND OPERATING CHARACTERISTICS (Ta=0 to +70℃, V_{CC}=5V±5%, V_{PP}=V_{CC}±0.6V)

Parameter	Symbol	Test Conditions	min	typ	max	Unit
Input Leakage Current	I_{LI}	V_{CC}=5.25V, V_{IN}=5.25V	—	—	10	μA
Output Leakage Current	I_{LO}	V_{CC}=5.25V, V_{out}=5.25V/0.4V	—	—	10	μA
V_{PP} Current	I_{PP1}	V_{PP}=V_{CC}+0.6V	—	—	5	mA
V_{CC} Current (Standby)	I_{CC1}	$\overline{CE}$=V_{IH}	—	—	35	mA
V_{CC} Current (Active)	I_{CC2}	$\overline{CE}$=$\overline{OE}$=V_{IL}	—	60	100	mA
Input Low Voltage	V_{IL}		−0.1	—	0.8	V
Input High Voltage	V_{IH}		2.0	—	V_{CC}+1	V
Output Low Voltage	V_{OL}	I_{OL}=2.1mA	—	—	0.45	V
Output High Voltage	V_{OH}	I_{OH}=−400μA	2.4	—	—	V

●AC CHARACTERISTICS (Ta=0 to 70℃, V_{CC}=5V±5%, V_{PP}=V_{CC}±0.6V)

Parameter	Symbol	Test Condition	HN4827128G-25		HN4827128G-30		HN4827128G-45		Unit
			min	max	min	max	min	max	
Address to Output Delay	t_{ACC}	$\overline{CE}$=$\overline{OE}$=V_{IL}	—	250	—	300	—	450	ns
$\overline{CE}$ to Output Delay	t_{CE}	$\overline{OE}$=V_{IL}	—	250	—	300	—	450	ns
$\overline{OE}$ to Output Delay	t_{OE}	$\overline{CE}$=V_{IL}	—	100	—	120	—	150	ns
$\overline{OE}$ High to Output Float	t_{DF}	$\overline{CE}$=V_{IL}	0	85	0	105	0	130	ns
Address to Output Hold	t_{OH}	$\overline{CE}$=$\overline{OE}$=V_{IL}	0		0	—	0	—	ns

* t_{DF} defines the time at which the output achieves the open circuit condition and is not referenced to output voltage levels.

●SWITCHING CHARACTERISTICS

Test Condition

Input Pulse Levels:	0.8V to 2.2V
Input Rise and Fall Time:	≤20 ns
Output Load:	1 TTL Gate + 100 pF
Reference Level for Measuring Timing:	Inputs; 1V and 2V Outputs; 0.8V and 2.0V

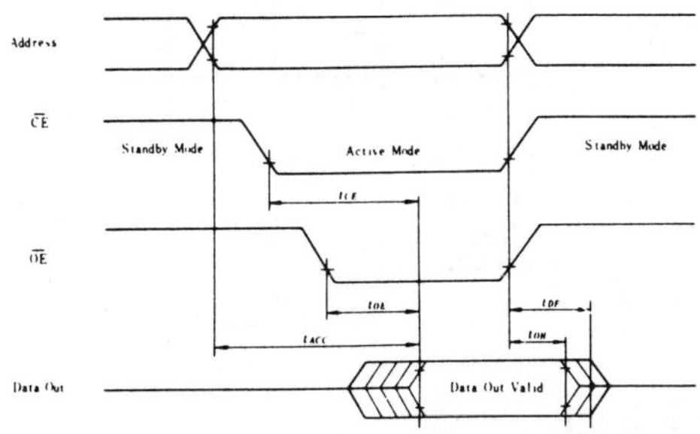

●CAPACITANCE (Ta=25℃, f=1 MHz)

Parameter	Symbol	Test Condition	min	typ	max	Unit
Input Capacitance	C_{in}	V_{in}=0V	—	4	6	pF
Output Capacitance	C_{out}	V_{out}=0V	—	8	12	pF

PROGRAMMING OPERATION

● DC PROGRAMMING CHARACTERISTICS ($Ta=25°C \pm 5°C$, $V_{CC}=5V \pm 5\%$, $V_{PP}=21V \pm 0.5V$)

Parameter	Symbol	Test Condition	min	typ	max	Unit
Input Leakage Current	I_{LI}	$V_{IN}=5.25V$	—	—	10	μA
Output Low Voltage During Verify	V_{OL}	$I_{OL}=2.1mA$	—	—	0.45	V
Output High Voltage During Verify	V_{OH}	$I_{OH}=-400\mu A$	2.4	—	—	V
V_{CC} Current (Active)	I_{CC2}		—	—	100	mA
Input Low Level	V_{IL}		−0.1	—	0.8	V
Input High Level	V_{IH}		2.0	—	$V_{CC}+1$	V
V_{PP} Supply Current	I_{PP}	$\overline{CE}=\overline{PGM}=V_{IL}$	—	—	30	mA

● AC PROGRAMMING CHARACTERISTICS ($Ta=25°C \pm 5°C$, $V_{CC}=5V \pm 5\%$, $V_{PP}=21V \pm 0.5V$)

Parameter	Symbol	Test Condition	min	typ	max	Unit
Address Setup Time	t_{AS}		2	—	—	μs
$\overline{OE}$ Setup Time	t_{OES}		2	—	—	μs
Data Setup Time	t_{DS}		2	—	—	μs
Address Hold Time	t_{AH}		0	—	—	μs
Data Hold Time	t_{DH}		2	—	—	μs
$\overline{OE}$ to Output Float Delay	t_{DF}		0	—	130	ns
V_{PP} Setup Time	t_{VS}		2	—	—	μs
$\overline{PGM}$ Pulse Width During Programming	t_{PW}		45	50	55	ms
$\overline{CE}$ Setup Time	t_{CES}		2	—	—	μs
Data Valid from $\overline{OE}$	t_{OE}		—	—	150	ns

Note : t_{DF} defines the time at which the output achieves the open circuit condition and is not referenced to output voltage levels.

● SWITCHING CHARACTERISTICS

Test Condition

Input Pulse Level:	0.8V to 2.2V
Input Rise and Fall Time:	≤ 20 ns
Reference Level for Measuring Timing:	Input; 1V and 2V
	Output; 0.8V and 2V

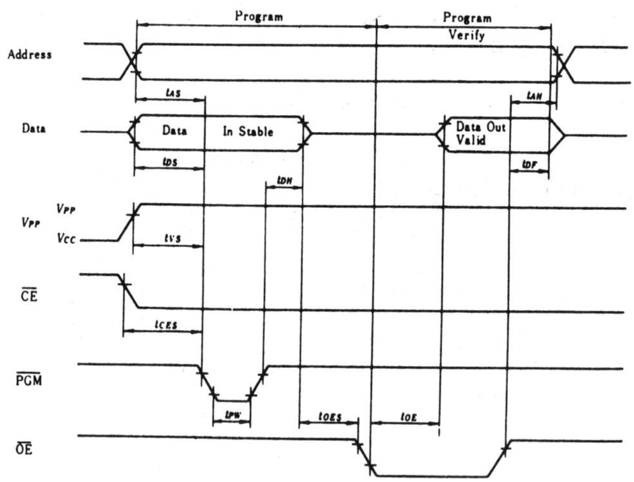

● ERASE

Erasure of HN4827128 is performed by exposure to ultraviolet light of 2537Å and all the output data are changed to "1" after this erasure procedure. The minimum integrated dose (i.e. UV intensity x exposure time) for erasure is 15 W·sec/cm².

■HIGH PERFORMANCE PROGRAMMING

This device can be applied the High Performance Programming algorithm shown in following flow chart. This algorithm allows to obtain faster programming time without any voltage stress to the device nor deterioration in reliability of programmed data.

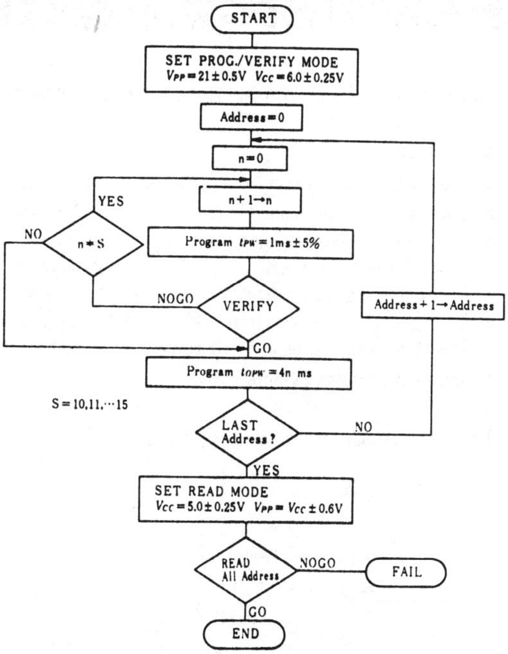

High Performance Programming Flowchart

● AC PROGRAMMING CHARACTERISTICS (Ta=25°C±5°C, V_{CC}=6V±0.25V, V_{PP}=21V±0.5V)

Parameter	Symbol	Test Condition	min	typ	max	Unit
Address Setup Time	t_{AS}		2	—	—	μs
$\overline{OE}$ Setup Time	t_{OES}		2	—	—	μs
Data Setup Time	t_{DS}		2	—	—	μs
Address Hold Time	t_{AH}		0	—	—	μs
Data Hold Time	t_{DH}		2	—	—	μs
$\overline{OE}$ to Output Float Delay*	t_{DF}		0	—	130	ns
V_{PP} Setup Time	t_{VPS}		2	—	—	μs
V_{CC} Setup Time	t_{VCS}		2	—	—	μs
$\overline{PGM}$ Pulse Width during Initial Program	t_{PW}		0.95	1.0	1.05	ms
$\overline{PGM}$ Pulse Width during Over Program**	t_{OPW}		3.8	—	63	ms
$\overline{CE}$ Setup Time	t_{CES}		2	—	—	μs
Data Valid from $\overline{OE}$	t_{OE}		—	—	150	ns

* t_{DF} defines the time at which the output achieves the open circuit conditions and is not referenced to output voltage levels.

** t_{OPW} is defined as mentioned in flow chart.

● SWITCHING CHARACTERISTICS

Test Condition

- Input Pulse Level: 0.8V to 2.2V
- Input Rise and Fall Time: ≤20 ns
- Reference Level for Measuring Timing: Input; 1V and 2V
  Output; 0.8V and 2V

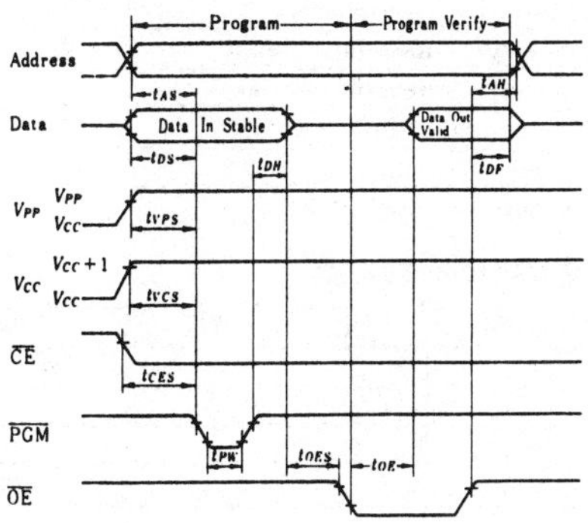

HM6116-2, HM6116-3, HM6116-4
HM6116P-2, HM6116P-3, HM6116P-4

2048-word × 8-bit High Speed Static CMOS RAM

■FEATURES

- Single 5V Supply and High Density 24 Pin Package
- High speed: Fast Access Time 120ns/150ns/200ns (max.)
- Low Power Standby and Low Power Operation — Standby: 100μW (typ.); Operation: 180mW (typ.)
- Completely Static RAM: No clock or Timing Strobe Required
- Directly TTL Compatible: All Input and Output
- Pin Out Compatible with Standard 16K EPROM/MASK ROM
- Equal Access and Cycle Time

HM6116-2, HM6116-3, HM6116-4

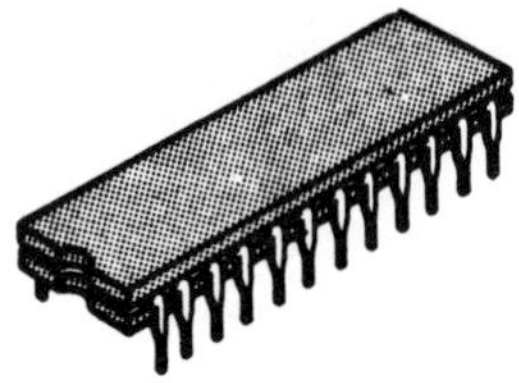

(DG-24)

HM6116P-2, HM6116P-3, HM6116P-4

(DP-24)

■FUNCTIONAL BLOCK DIAGRAM

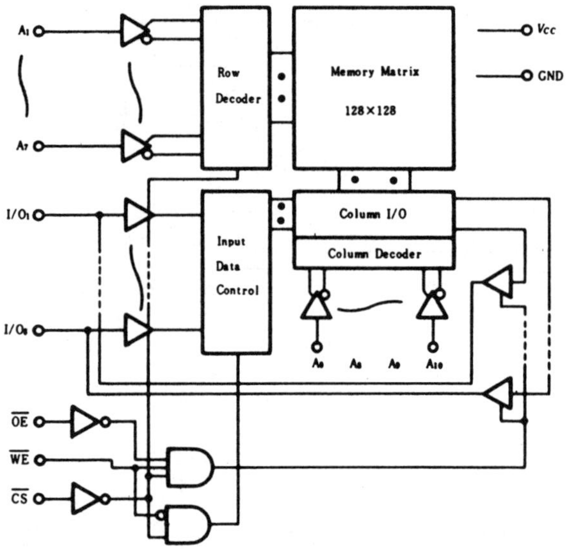

■PIN ARRANGEMENT

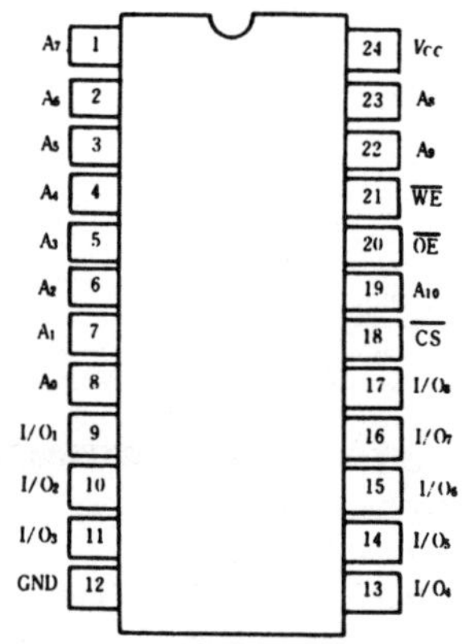

(Top View)

■ABSOLUTE MAXIMUM RATINGS

Item	Symbol	Rating	Unit
Voltage on Any Pin Relative to GND	V_T	−0.5* to +7.0	V
Operating Temperature	T_{opr}	0 to +70	°C
Storage Temperature (Plastic)	T_{stg}	−55 to +125	°C
Storage Temperature (Ceramic)	T_{stg}	−65 to +150	°C
Temperature Under Bias	T_{bias}	−10 to +85	°C
Power Dissipation	P_T	1.0	W

* Pulse Width 50ns : −1.5 V

■TRUTH TABLE

$\overline{CS}$	$\overline{OE}$	$\overline{WE}$	Mode	V_{CC} Current	I/O Pin	Ref. Cycle
H	×	×	Not Selected	I_{SB}, I_{SB1}	High Z	
L	L	H	Read	I_{CC}	Dout	Read Cycle (1)~(3)
L	H	L	Write	I_{CC}	Din	Write Cycle (1)
L	L	L	Write	I_{CC}	Din	Write Cycle (2)

■RECOMMENDED DC OPERATING CONDITIONS (Ta=0 to +70°C)

Item	Symbol	min	typ	max	Unit
Supply Voltage	V_{CC}	4.5	5.0	5.5	V
	GND	0	0	0	V
Input Voltage	V_{IH}	2.2	3.5	6.0	V
	V_{IL}	−1.0*	—	0.8	V

* Pulse Width : 50ns, DC : V_{IL} min = −0.3V

■DC AND OPERATING CHARACTERISTICS (V_{CC}=5V±10%, GND=0V, Ta=0 to +70°C)

Item	Symbol	Test Conditions	HM6116/P-2			HM6116/P-3/-4			Unit
			min	typ*	max	min	typ*	max	
Input Leakage Current	$\|I_{LI}\|$	V_{CC}=5.5V, V_{in}=GND to V_{CC}	—	—	10	—	—	10	μA
Output Leakage Current	$\|I_{LO}\|$	$\overline{CS}=V_{IH}$ or $\overline{OE}=V_{IH}$, $V_{I/O}$=GND to V_{CC}	—	—	10	—	—	10	μA
Operating Power Supply Current	I_{CC}	$\overline{CS}=V_{IL}$, $I_{I/O}$=0mA	—	40	80	—	35	70	mA
	I_{CC1}**	V_{IH}=3.5V, V_{IL}=0.6V, $I_{I/O}$=0mA	—	35	—	—	30	—	mA
Average Operating Current	I_{CC2}	Min. cycle, duty=100%	—	40	80	—	35	70	mA
Standby Power Supply Current	I_{SB}	$\overline{CS}=V_{IH}$	—	5	15	—	5	15	mA
	I_{SB1}	$\overline{CS}\geq V_{CC}-0.2V$, $V_{in}\geq V_{CC}-0.2V$ or $V_{in}\leq 0.2V$	—	0.02	2	—	0.02	2	mA
Output Voltage	V_{OL}	I_{OL}=4mA	—	—	0.4	—	—	—	V
		I_{OL}=2.1mA	—	—	—	—	—	0.4	V
	V_{OH}	I_{OH}=−1.0mA	2.4	—	—	2.4	—	—	V

* V_{CC}=5V, Ta=25°C
** Reference Only

■AC CHARACTERISTICS (V_{CC}=5V±10%, Ta=0 to +70°C)

●AC TEST CONDITIONS

Input Pulse Levels: 0.8 to 2.4V
Input Rise and Fall Times: 10 ns
Input and Output Timing Reference Levels: 1.5V
Output Load: 1TTL Gate and C_L = 100pF (including scope and jig)

●READ CYCLE

Item	Symbol	HM6116/P-2		HM6116/P-3		HM6116/P-4		Unit
		min	max	min	max	min	max	
Read Cycle Time	t_{RC}	120	—	150	—	200	—	ns
Address Access Time	t_{AA}	—	120	—	150	—	200	ns
Chip Select Access Time	t_{ACS}	—	120	—	150	—	200	ns
Chip Selection to Output in Low Z	t_{CLZ}	10	—	15	—	15	—	ns
Output Enable to Output Valid	t_{OE}	—	80	—	100	—	120	ns
Output Enable to Output in Low Z	t_{OLZ}	10	—	15	—	15	—	ns
Chip Deselection to Output in High Z	t_{CHZ}	0	40	0	50	0	60	ns
Chip Disable to Output in High Z	t_{OHZ}	0	40	0	50	0	60	ns
Output Hold from Address Change	t_{OH}	10	—	15	—	15	—	ns

● **WRITE CYCLE**

Item	Symbol	HM6116/P-2		HM6116/P-3		HM6116/P-4		Unit
		min	max	min	max	min	max	
Write Cycle Time	t_{WC}	120	—	150	—	200	—	ns
Chip Selection to End of Write	t_{CW}	70	—	90	—	120	—	ns
Address Valid to End of Write	t_{AW}	105	—	120	—	140	—	ns
Address Set Up Time	t_{AS}	20	—	20	—	20	—	ns
Write Pulse Width	t_{WP}	70	—	90	—	120	—	ns
Write Recovery Time	t_{WR}	5	—	10	—	10	—	ns
Output Disable to Output in High Z	t_{OHZ}	0	40	0	50	0	60	ns
Write to Output in High Z	t_{WHZ}	0	50	0	60	0	60	ns
Data to Write Time Overlap	t_{DW}	35	—	40	—	60	—	ns
Data Hold from Write Time	t_{DH}	5	—	10	—	10	—	ns
Output Active from End of Write	t_{OW}	5	—	10	—	10	—	ns

■ **CAPACITANCE** (f=1MHz, Ta=25°C)

Item	Symbol	Test Conditions	typ	max	Unit
Input Capacitance	C_{in}	V_{in}=0V	3	5	pF
Input/Output Capacitance	$C_{I/O}$	$V_{I/O}$=0V	5	7	pF

Note) This parameter is sampled and not 100% tested.

■ **TIMING WAVEFORM**

● **READ CYCLE (1)** (1)

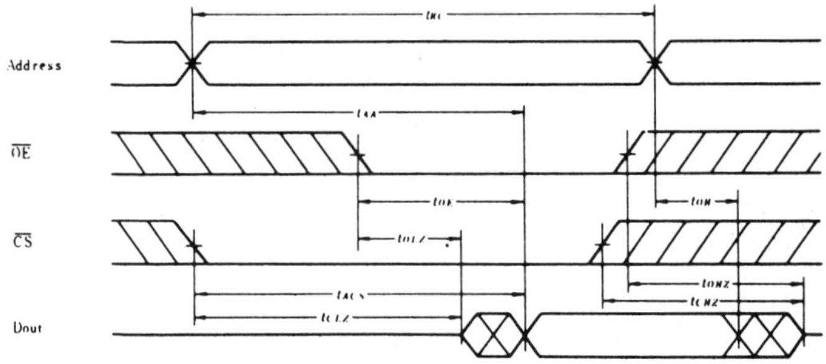

● **READ CYCLE (2)** (1)(2)(4)

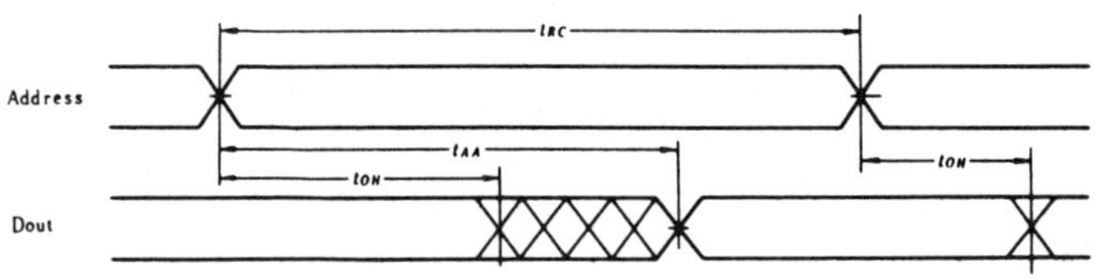

● **READ CYCLE (3)** (1)(3)(4)

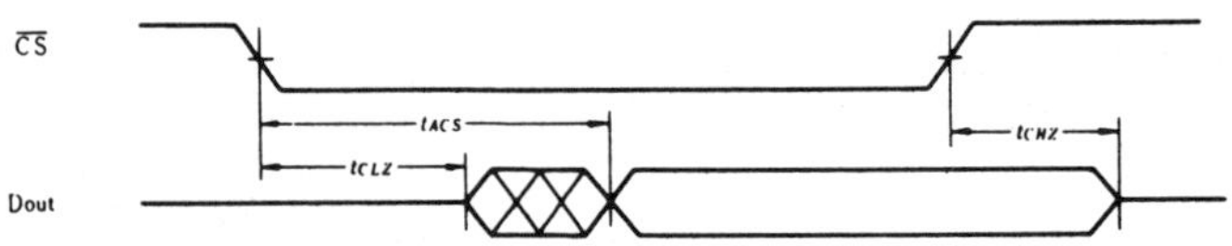

NOTES: 1. $\overline{WE}$ is High for Read Cycle.
2. Device is continuously selected, $\overline{CS} = V_{IL}$.
3. Address Valid prior to or coincident with $\overline{CS}$ transition Low.
4. $\overline{OE} = V_{IL}$.

WRITE CYCLE (1)

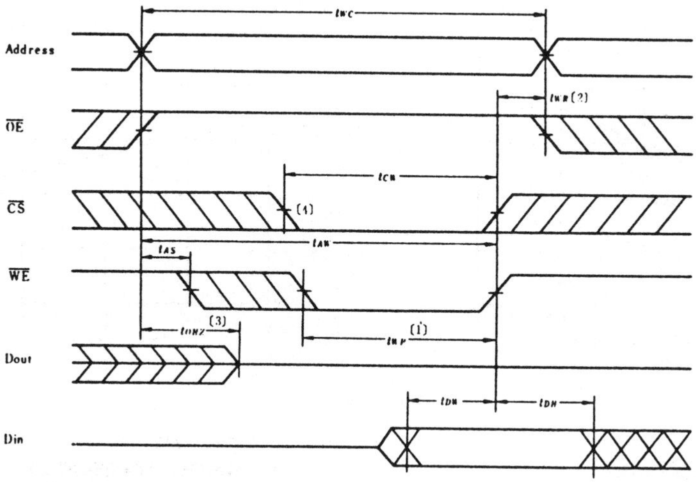

● WRITE CYCLE (2) [5]

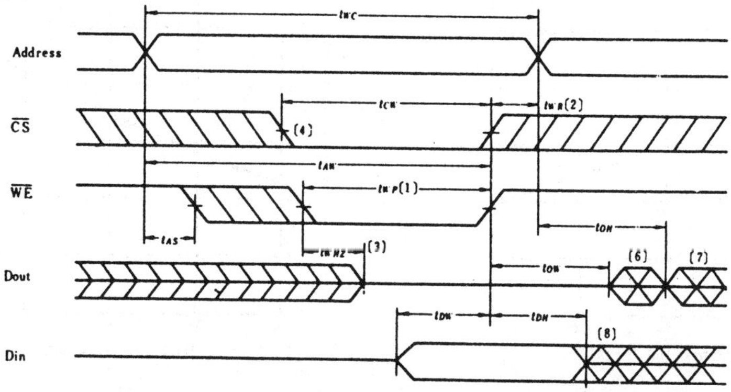

NOTES:

1. A write occurs during the overlap (t_{WP}) of a low $\overline{CS}$ and a low $\overline{WE}$.
2. t_{WR} is measured from the earlier of $\overline{CS}$ or $\overline{WE}$ going high to the end of write cycle.
3. During this period, I/O pins are in the output state so that the input signals of opposite phase to the outputs must not be applied.
4. If the $\overline{CS}$ low transition occurs simultaneously with the $\overline{WE}$ low transitions or after the $\overline{WE}$ transition, output remain in a high impedance state.
5. $\overline{OE}$ is continuously low. ($\overline{OE} = V_{IL}$)
6. D_{out} is the same phase of write data of this write cycle.
7. D_{out} is the read data of next address.
8. If $\overline{CS}$ is Low during this period, I/O pins are in the output state. Then the data input signals of opposite phase to the outputs must not be applied to them.

SUPPLY CURRENT
vs. SUPPLY VOLTAGE

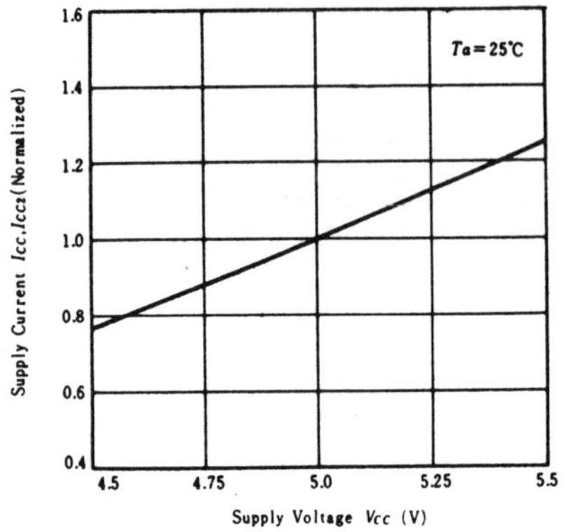

SUPPLY CURRENT
vs. AMBIENT TEMPERATURE

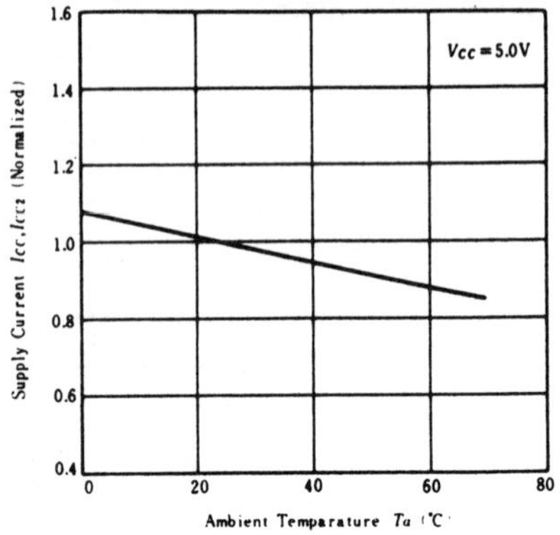

ACCESS TIME
vs. SUPPLY VOLTAGE

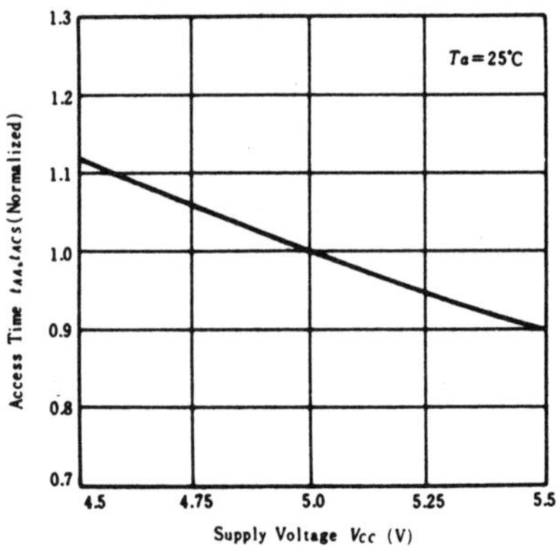

ACCESS TIME
vs. AMBIENT TEMPERATURE

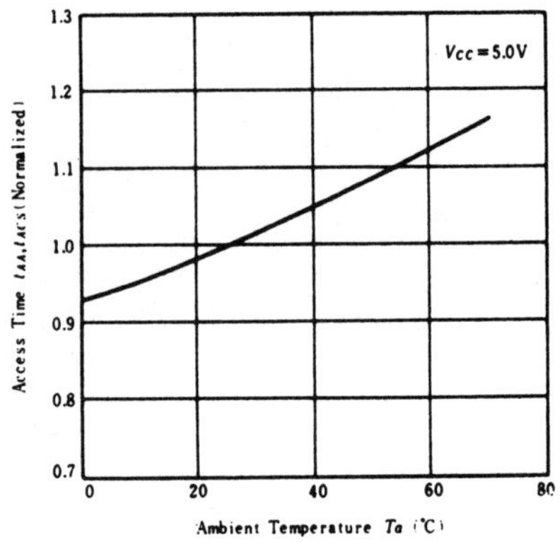

ACCESS TIME
vs. LOAD CAPACITANCE

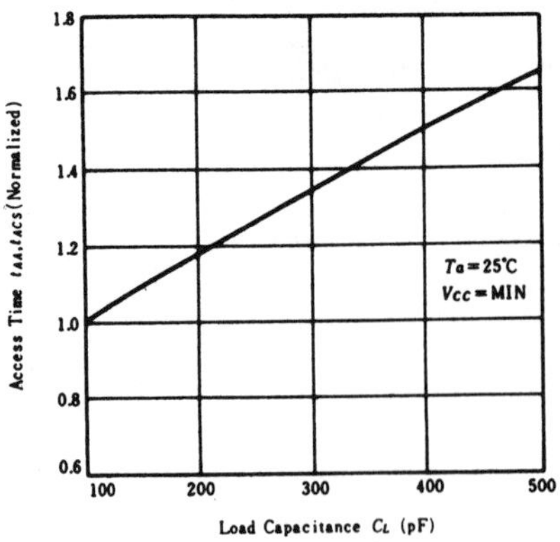

SUPPLY CURRENT
vs. FREQUENCY

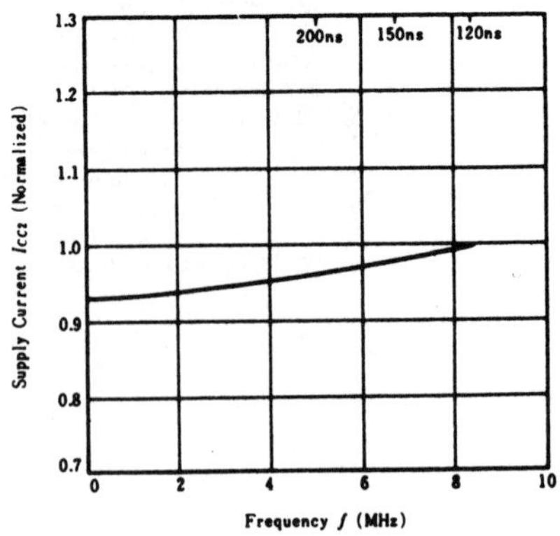

LOW INPUT VOLTAGE vs. SUPPLY VOLTAGE

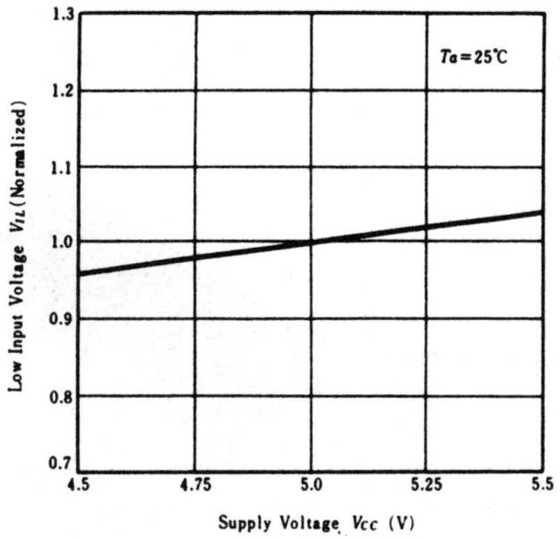

HIGH INPUT VOLTAGE vs. SUPPLY VOLTAGE

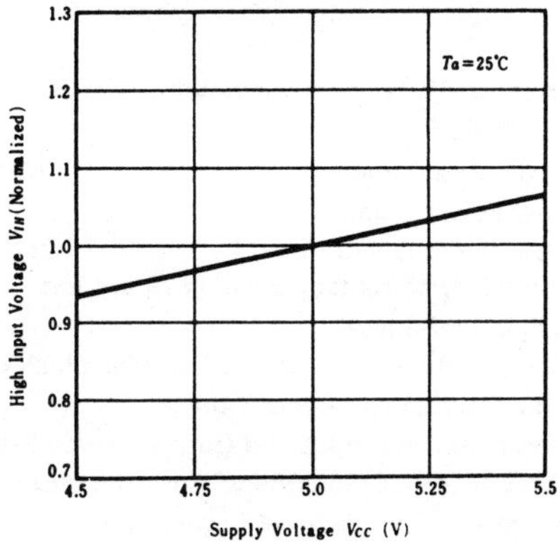

OUTPUT CURRENT vs. OUTPUT VOLTAGE

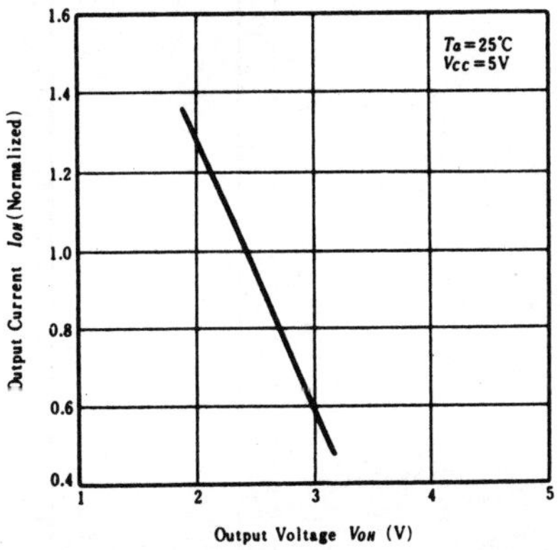

OUTPUT CURRENT vs. OUTPUT VOLTAGE

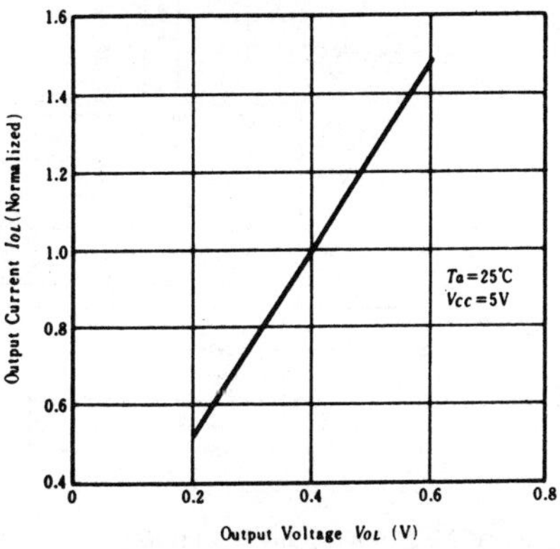

HM6264LP-10, HM6264LP-12 HM6264LP-15

8192-word x 8-bit High Speed Static CMOS RAM

■ FEATURES

- Fast access Time — 100ns/120ns/150ns (max.)
- Low Power Standby — Standby: 0.01mW (typ.)
  Low Power Operation — Operating: 200mW (typ.)
- Capability of Battery Back-up Operation
- Single +5V Supply
- Completely Static Memory. . . . . No clock or Timing Strobe Required
- Equal Access and Cycle Time
- Common Data Input and Output, Three State Output
- Directly TTL Compatible: All Input and Output
- Standard 28pin Package Configuration
- Pin Out Compatible with 64K EPROM HN482764

(DP-28)

■ BLOCK DIAGRAM

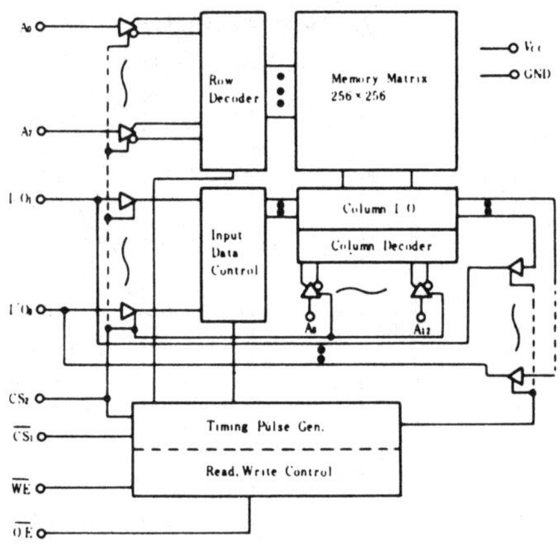

■ PIN ARRANGEMENT

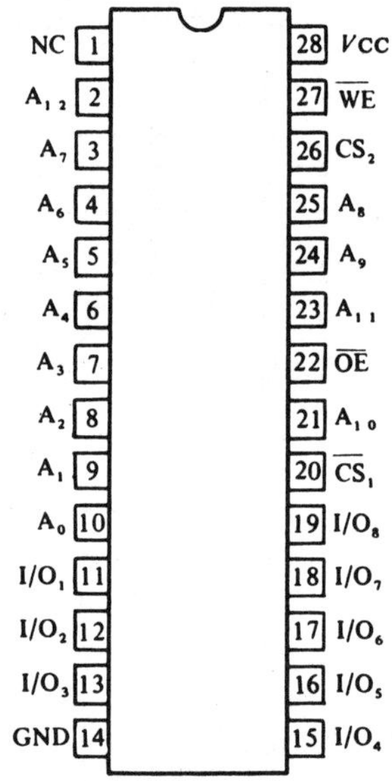

(Top View)

■ ABSOLUTE MAXIMUM RATINGS

Item	Symbol	Rating	Unit
Terminal Voltage *	V_T	–0.5 ** to +7.0	V
Power Dissipation	P_T	1.0	W
Operating Temperature	T_{opr}	0 to +70	°C
Storage Temperature	T_{stg}	–55 to +125	°C
Storage Temperature (Under Bias)	T_{bias}	–10 to +85	°C

* With respect to GND. ** Pulse width 50ns: –3.0V

■ TRUTH TABLE

$\overline{WE}$	$\overline{CS_1}$	CS_2	$\overline{OE}$	Mode	I/O Pin	V_{CC} Current	Note
X	H	X	X	Not Selected (Power Down)	High Z	I_{SB}, I_{SB1}	
X	X	L	X		High Z	I_{SB}, I_{SB2}	
H	L	H	H	Output Disabled	High Z	I_{CC}, I_{CC1}	
H	L	H	L	Read	Dout	I_{CC}, I_{CC1}	
L	L	H	H	Write	Din	I_{CC}, I_{CC1}	Write Cycle (1)
L	L	H	L		Din	I_{CC}, I_{CC1}	Write Cycle (2)

× : Don't care.

■ RECOMMENDED DC OPERATING CONDITIONS (T_a = 0 to +70°C)

Item	Symbol	min	typ	max	Unit
Supply Voltage	V_{CC}	4.5	5.0	5.5	V
	GND	0	0	0	V
Input Voltage	V_{IH}	2.2	–	6.0	V
	V_{IL}	−0.3*	–	0.8	V

* Pulse Width 50ns: −3.0V

■ DC AND OPERATING CHARACTERISTICS (V_{CC} = 5V±10%, GND = 0V, T_a = 0 to +70°C)

Item	Symbol	Test Condition	min	typ*	max	Unit
Input Leakage Current	$\lvert I_{LI}\rvert$	V_{in}=GND to V_{CC}	–	–	2	μA
Output Leakage Current	$\lvert I_{LO}\rvert$	$\overline{CS1}=V_{IH}$ or $CS2=V_{IL}$ or $\overline{OE}=V_{IH}$, $V_{I/O}$=GND to V_{CC}	–	–	2	μA
Operating Power Supply Current	I_{CC}	$\overline{CS1}=V_{IL}$, $CS2=V_{IH}$, $I_{I/O}$=0mA	–	40	80	mA
Average Operating Current	I_{CC1}	Min. cycle, duty=100%, $\overline{CS1}=V_{IL}$, $CS2=V_{IH}$	–	60	110	mA
Standby Power Supply Current	I_{SB}	$\overline{CS1}=V_{IH}$ or $CS2=V_{IL}$, $I_{I/O}$=0mA	–	1	3	mA
	I_{SB1}**	$\overline{CS1}\geqq V_{CC}-0.2V$, $CS2\geqq V_{CC}-0.2V$ or $CS2\leqq 0.2V$	–	2	100	μA
	I_{SB2}**	$CS2\leqq 0.2V$	–	2	100	μA
Output Voltage	V_{OL}	I_{OL}=2.1mA	–	–	0.4	V
	V_{OH}	I_{OH}=−1.0mA	2.4	–	–	V

* Typical limits are at V_{CC}=5.0V, T_a=25°C and specified loading.
** V_{IL} min=−0.3V

■ CAPACITANCE (f= 1MHz, T_a = 25°C)

Item	Symbol	Test Condition	typ	max	Unit
Input Capacitance	C_{in}	V_{in} = 0V	–	6	pF
Input/Output Capacitance	$C_{I/O}$	$V_{I/O}$ = 0V	–	8	pF

Note) This parameter is sampled and not 100% tested.

■ AC CHARACTERISTICS (V_{CC} = 5V±10%, Ta = 0 to +70°C)

● AC TEST CONDITIONS

Input Pulse Levels: 0.8 to 2.4V
Input Rise and Fall Times: 10ns
Input and Output Timing Reference Level: 1.5V
Output Load: 1TTL Gate and C_L = 100pF (including scope and jig)

● READ CYCLE

Item		Symbol	HM6264LP-10 min	HM6264LP-10 max	HM6264LP-12 min	HM6264LP-12 max	HM6264LP-15 min	HM6264LP-15 max	Unit
Read Cycle Time		t_{RC}	100	–	120	–	150	–	ns
Address Access Time		t_{AA}	–	100	–	120	–	150	ns
Chip Selection to Output	$\overline{CS1}$	t_{CO1}	–	100	–	120	–	150	ns
	CS2	t_{CO2}	–	100	–	120	–	150	ns
Output Enable to Output Valid		t_{OE}	–	50	–	60	–	70	ns
Chip Selection to Output in Low Z	$\overline{CS1}$	t_{LZ1}	10	–	10	–	15	–	ns
	CS2	t_{LZ2}	10	–	10	–	15	–	ns
Output Enable to Output in Low Z		t_{OLZ}	5	–	5	–	5	–	ns
Chip Deselection to Output in High Z	$\overline{CS1}$	t_{HZ1}	0	35	0	40	0	50	ns
	CS2	t_{HZ2}	0	35	0	40	0	50	ns
Output Disable to Output in High Z		t_{OHZ}	0	35	0	40	0	50	ns
Output Hold from Address Change		t_{OH}	10	–	10	–	15	–	ns

NOTES: 1 t_{HZ} and t_{OHZ} are defined as the time at which the outputs achieve the open circuit condition and are not referred to output voltage levels.
2 At any given temperature and voltage condition, t_{HZ} max is less than t_{LZ} min both for a given device and from device to device.

• **READ CYCLE**

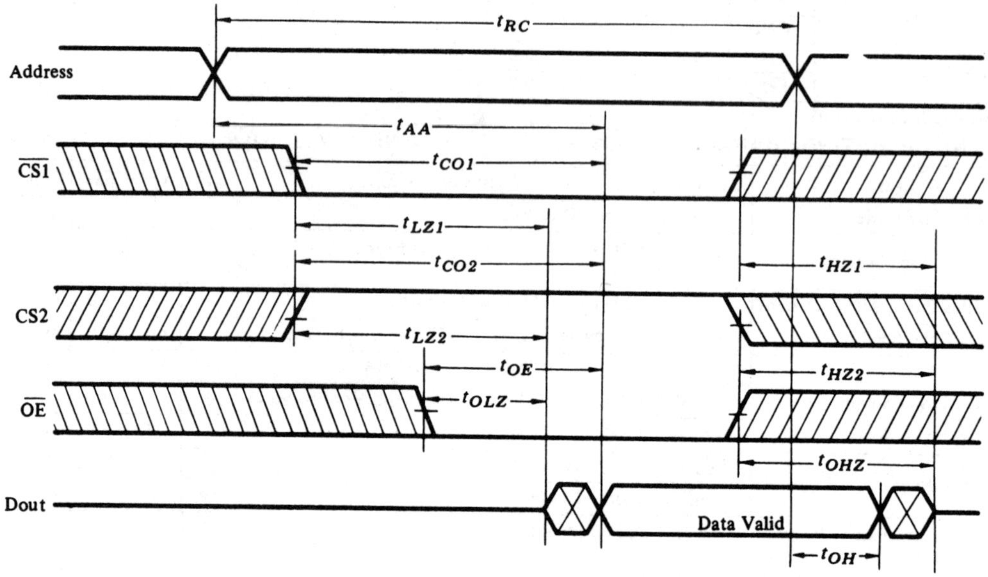

NOTE : 1) $\overline{WE}$ is high for Read Cycle

• **WRITE CYCLE**

Item		Symbol	HM6264LP-10		HM6264LP-12		HM6264LP-15		Unit
			min	max	min	max	min	max	
Write Cycle Time		t_{WC}	100	–	120	–	150	–	ns
Chip Selection to End of Write		t_{CW}	80	–	85	–	100	–	ns
Address Setup Time		t_{AS}	0	–	0	–	0	–	ns
Address Valid to End of Write		t_{AW}	80	–	85	–	100	–	ns
Write Pulse Width		t_{WP}	60	–	70	–	90	–	ns
Write Recovery Time	$\overline{CS1}$, $\overline{WE}$	t_{WR1}	5	–	5	–	10	–	ns
	CS2	t_{WR2}	15	–	15	–	15	–	ns
Write to Output in High Z		t_{WHZ}	0	35	0	40	0	50	ns
Data to Write Time Overlap		t_{DW}	40	–	50	–	60	–	ns
Data Hold from Write Time		t_{DH}	0	–	0	–	0	–	ns
$\overline{OE}$ to Output in High Z		t_{OHZ}	0	35	0	40	0	50	ns
Output Active from End of Write		t_{OW}	5	–	5	–	10	–	ns

• **WRITE CYCLE (1) ($\overline{OE}$ clock)**

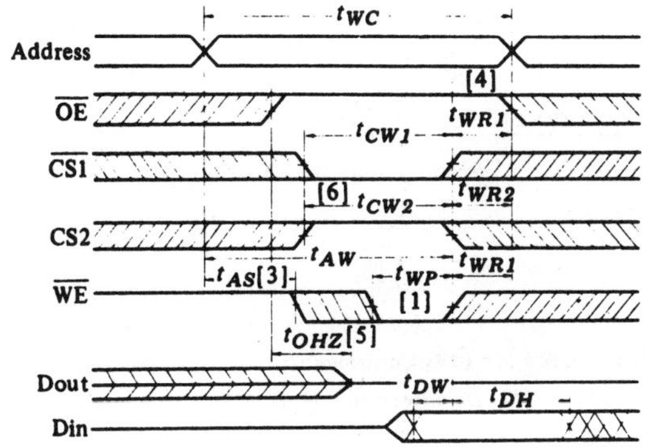

• **WRITE CYCLE (2) ($\overline{OE}$ Low Fix)**

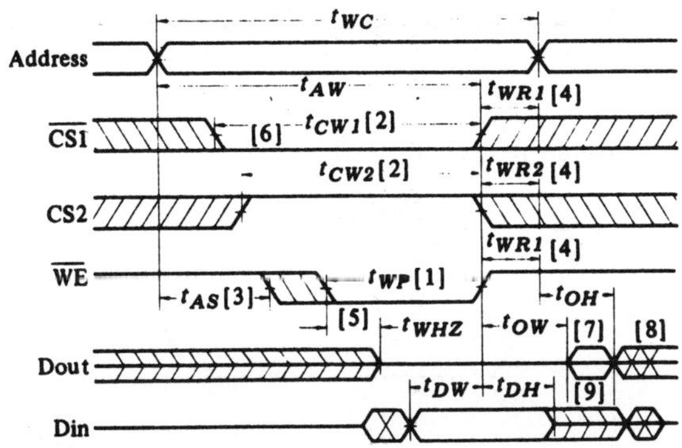

NOTES: 1) A write occurs during the overlap of a low $\overline{CS1}$, a high CS2 and a low $\overline{WE}$. A write begins at the latest transition among $\overline{CS1}$ going low, CS2 going high and $\overline{WE}$ going low. A write ends at the earliest transtion among $\overline{CS1}$ going high, CS2 going low and $\overline{WE}$ going high. t_{WP} is measured from the beginninng of write to the end of write.

2) t_{CW} is measured from the later of $\overline{CS1}$ going low or CS2 going high to the end of write.

3) t_{AS} is measured from the address valid to the beginning of write.

4) t_{WR} is measured from the end of write to the address change. t_{WR1} applies in case a write ends at $\overline{CS1}$ or $\overline{WE}$ going high. t_{WR2} applies in case a write ends at CS2 going low.

5) During this period, I/O pins are in the output state, therefore the input signals of opposite phase to the outputs must not be applied.

6) If $\overline{CS1}$ goes low simultaneously with $\overline{WE}$ going low or after $\overline{WE}$ going low, the outputs remain in high impedance state.

7) Dout is in the same phase of written data of this cycle.

8) Dout is the read data of the new address.

9) If $\overline{CS1}$ is low and CS2 is high during this period, I/O pins are in the output state. Therefore, the input signals of opposite phase to the outputs must not be applied to them.

■ LOW V_{CC} DATA RETENTION CHARACTERISTICS (T_a = 0 to +70 °C)

Item	Symbol	Test Condition	min	typ	max	Unit
V_{CC} for Data Retention	V_{DR1}	$\overline{CS1} \geq V_{CC} - 0.2V$, $CS2 \geq V_{CC} - 0.2V$ or $CS2 \leq 0.2V$	2.0	–	–	V
	V_{DR2}	$CS2 \leq 0.2V$	2.0	–	–	V
Data Retention Current	I_{CCDR1}	$V_{CC} = 3.0V$, $\overline{CS1} \geq V_{CC} - 0.2V$, $CS2 \geq V_{CC} - 0.2V$ or $CS2 \leq 0.2V$	–	1	50*	μA
	I_{CCDR2}	$V_{CC} = 3.0V$, $CS2 \leq 0.2V$	–	1	50*	μA
Chip Deselect to Data Retention Time	t_{CDR}	See Retention Waveform	0	–	–	ns
Operation Recovery Time	t_R		t_{RC}**	–	–	ns

* V_{IL} min = −0.3V

** t_{RC} = Read Cycle Time

• LOW Vcc DATA RETENTION WAVEFORM (1) ($\overline{CS1}$ Controlled)

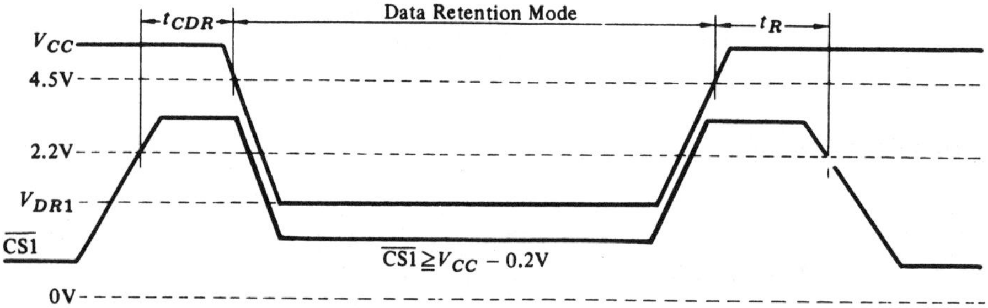

• LOW Vcc DATA RETENTION WAVEFORM (2) (CS2 Controlled)

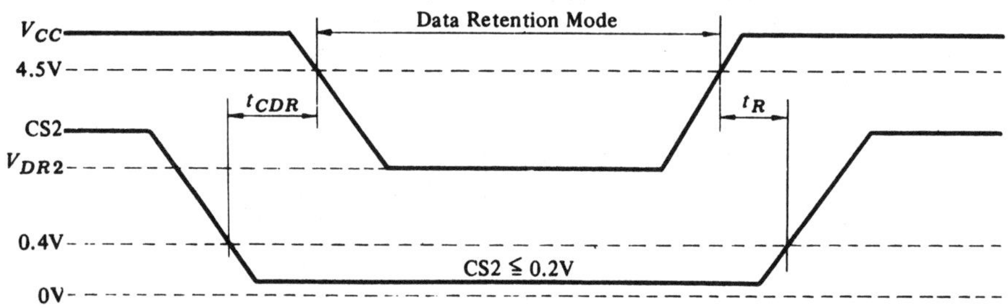

NOTE: CS_2 controls Address buffer, $\overline{WE}$ buffer, $\overline{CS}_1$ buffer and Din buffer. If CS_2 controls data retention mode, Vin level (Address, $\overline{WE}$, $\overline{CS}_1$, I/O) can be in the high impedance state. If $\overline{CS}_1$ controls data retention mode, CS_2 must be $CS_2 \geq Vcc - 0.2V$ or $CS_2 \leq 0.2V$. The other inputs level (address, $\overline{WE}$, I/O) can be in the high impedance state.

MOTOROLA

MCM2147

4096-BIT STATIC RANDOM ACCESS MEMORY

The MCM2147 is a 4096-bit static random access memory organized as 4096 words by 1-bit using Motorola's N-channel silicon-gate MOS technology. It uses a design approach which provides the simple timing features associated with fully static memories and the reduced standby power associated with semi-static and dynamic memories. This means low standby power without the need for clocks, nor reduced data rates due to cycle times that exceed access times.

$\overline{E}$ controls the power-down feature. It is not a clock but rather a chip select that affects power consumption. In less than a cycle time after $\overline{E}$ goes high, deselect mode, the part automatically reduces its power requirements and remains in this low-power standby mode as long as $\overline{E}$ remains high. This feature results in system power savings as great as 85% in larger systems, where most devices are deselected. The automatic power-down feature causes no performance degradation.

The MCM2147 is in an 18 pin dual in-line package with the industry standard pinout. It is TTL compatible in all respects. The data out has the same polarity as the input data. A data input and a separate three-state output provide flexibility and allow easy OR-ties.

- Fully Static Memory — No Clock or Timing Strobe Required
- Single +5 V Supply
- High Density 18 Pin Package
- Automatic Power-Down
- Directly TTL Compatible—All Inputs and Outputs
- Separate Data Input and Output
- Three-State Output
- Access Time — MCM2147-55 = 55 ns max
  MCM2147-70 = 70 ns max
  MCM2147-85 = 85 ns max
  MCM2147-100 = 100 ns max

BLOCK DIAGRAM

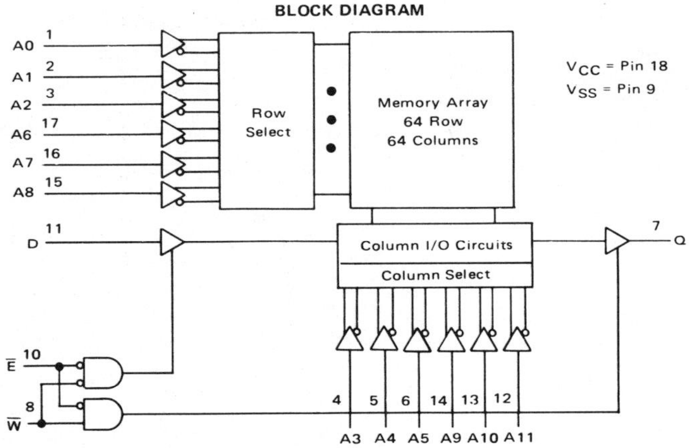

MOS

(N-CHANNEL, SILICON-GATE)

4096-BIT STATIC RANDOM ACCESS MEMORY

C SUFFIX
FRIT SEAL
CERAMIC PACKAGE
also available

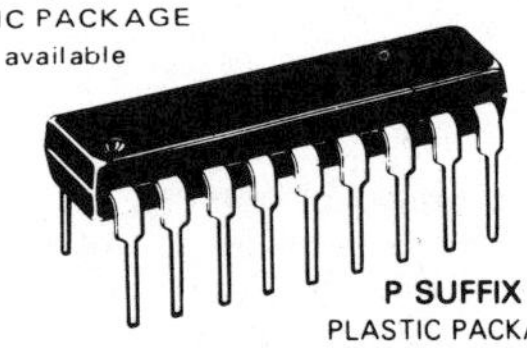

P SUFFIX
PLASTIC PACKAGE
CASE 707

PIN ASSIGNMENT

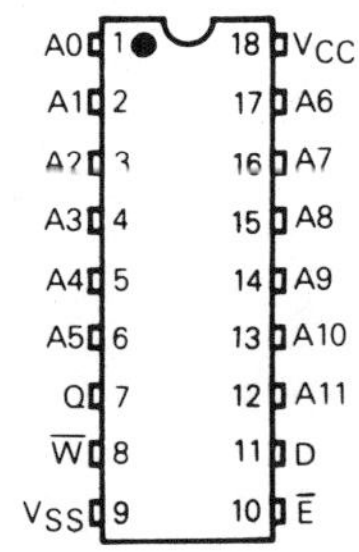

PIN NAMES	
A0-A11	Address Input
$\overline{W}$	Write Enable
$\overline{E}$	Chip Enable
D	Data Input
Q	Data Output
V_{CC}	Power (+5 V)
V_{SS}	Ground

TRUTH TABLE

$\overline{E}$	$\overline{W}$	Mode	Output	Power
H	X	Not Selected	High Z	Standby
L	L	Write	High Z	Active
L	H	Read	Data Out	Active

ABSOLUTE MAXIMUM RATINGS (See Note)

Rating	Value	Unit
Temperature Under Bias	-10 to +85	°C
Voltage on Any Pin With Respect to V_{CC}	-0.5 to +7.0	Vdc
DC Output Current	20	mA
Power Dissipation	1.0	Watt
Operating Temperature Range	0 to +70	°C
Storage Temperature Range	-65 to +150	°C

Note: Permanent device damage may occur if ABSOLUTE MAXIMUM RATINGS are exceeded. Functional operation should be restricted to RECOMMENDED OPERATING CONDITIONS. Exposure to higher than recommended voltages for extended periods of time could affect device reliability.

This device contains circuitry to protect the inputs against damage due to high static voltages or electric fields; however, it is advised that normal precautions be taken to avoid application of any voltage higher than maximum rated voltages to this high-impedance circuit.

DC OPERATING CONDITIONS AND CHARACTERISTICS

(Full operating voltage and temperature range unless otherwise noted)

RECOMMENDED OPERATING CONDITIONS

Parameter	Symbol	Min	Typ	Max	Unit
Supply Voltage	V_{CC} V_{SS}	4.5 0	5.0 0	5.5 0	V
Logic 1 Voltage, All Inputs	V_{IH}	2.0	–	V_{CC}	V
Logic 0 Voltage, All Inputs	V_{IL}	−0.3	–	0.8	V

DC CHARACTERISTICS

Parameter	Symbol	MCM2147-55			MCM 2147-70			MCM2147-85			MCM2147-100			Unit
		Min	Typ	Max	Min	Typ	Max	Min	Typ	Max	Min	Typ	Max	
Input Load Current (All Input Pins, V_{in} = 0 to 5.5 V)	I_{IL}	–	0.01	10	–	0.01	10	–	0.01	10	–	0.01	10	μA
Output Leakage Current ($\overline{E}$ = 2.0 V, V_{out} = 0 to 5.5 V)	I_{OL}	–	0.1	50	–	0.1	50	–	0.1	50	–	0.1	50	μA
Power Supply Current ($\overline{E}$ = V_{IL}, Outputs Open, T_A = 25°C)	I_{CC1}	–	120	170	–	100	150	–	95	130	–	90	110	mA
Power Supply Current ($\overline{E}$ = V_{IL}, Outputs Open, T_A = 0°C)	I_{CC2}	–	–	180	–	–	160	–	–	140	–	–	120	mA
Standby Current ($\overline{E}$ = V_{IH})	I_{SB}	–	15	30	–	10	20	–	15	25	–	10	20	mA
Input Low Voltage	V_{IL}	-0.3	–	0.8	-0.3	–	0.8	-0.3	–	0.8	-0.3	–	0.8	V
Input High Voltage	V_{IH}	2.0	–	6.0	2.0	–	6.0	2.0	–	6.0	2.0	–	6.0	V
Output Low Voltage (I_{OL} = 8.0 mA)	V_{OL}	–	–	0.4	–	–	0.4	–	–	0.4	–	–	0.4	V
Output High Voltage (I_{OH} = −4.0 mA)	V_{OH}	2.4	–	–	2.4	–	–	2.4	–	–	2.4	–	–	V

Typical values are for T_A = 25°C and V_{CC} = +5.0 V.

CAPACITANCE

(f = 1.0 MHz, T_A = 25°C, periodically sampled rather than 100% tested.)

Characteristic	Symbol	Max	Unit
Input Capacitance (V_{in} = 0 V)	C_{in}	5.0	pF
Output Capacitance (V_{out} = 0 V)	C_{out}	10	pF

Capacitance measured with a Boonton Meter or effective capacitance calculated from the equation: $C = \frac{I\Delta_t}{\Delta V}$.

FIGURE 1 – OUTPUT LOAD

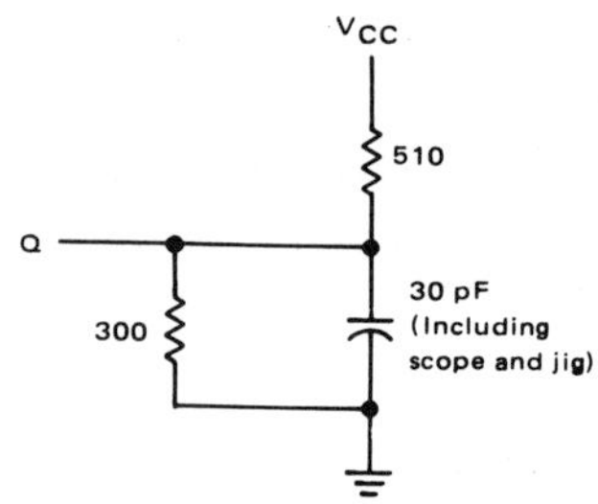

AC OPERATING CONDITIONS AND CHARACTERISTICS

(Full operating voltage and temperature unless otherwise noted)

Input Pulse Levels..0 Volt to 3.5 Volts
Input Rise and Fall Times..10 ns
Input and Output Timing Levels..................................1.5 Volts
Output Load...See Figure 1

READ, WRITE CYCLES

Parameter	Symbol	MCM2147-55		MCM2147-70		MCM2147-85		MCM2147-100		Unit
		Min	Max	Min	Max	Min	Max	Min	Max	
Address Valid to Address Don't Care (Cycle Time When Chip Enable is Held Active)	t_{AVAX}	55	–	70	–	85	–	100	–	ns
Chip Enable Low to Chip Enable High	t_{ELEH}	55	–	70	–	85	–	100	–	ns
Address Valid to Output Valid (Access)	t_{AVQV}	–	55	–	70	–	85	–	100	ns
Chip Enable Low to Output Valid (Access)	t_{ELQV1}*	–	55	–	70	–	85	–	100	ns
	t_{ELQV2}*	–	65	–	80	–	95	–	110	ns
Address Valid to Output Invalid	t_{AVQX}	10	–	10	–	10	–	10	–	ns
Chip Enable Low to Output Invalid	t_{ELQX}	10	–	10	–	10	–	10	–	ns
Chip Enable High to Output High Z	t_{EHQZ}	0	40	0	40	0	40	0	40	ns
Chip Selection to Power-Up Time	t_{PU}	0	–	0	–	0	–	0	–	ns
Chip Deselection to Power-Down Time	t_{PD}	0	30	0	30	0	30	0	30	ns
Address Valid to Chip Enable Low (Address Setup)	t_{AVEL}	0	–	0	–	0	–	0	–	ns
Chip Enable Low to Write High	t_{ELWH}	45	–	55	–	70	–	80	–	ns
Address Valid to Write High	t_{AVWH}	45	–	55	–	70	–	80	–	ns
Address Valid to Write Low (Address Setup)	t_{AVWL}	0	–	0	–	0	–	0	–	ns
Write Low to Write High (Write Pulse Width)	t_{WLWH}	35	–	40	–	55	–	65	–	ns
Write High to Address Don't Care	t_{WHAX}	10	–	15	–	15	–	15	–	ns
Data Valid to Write High	t_{DVWH}	25	–	30	–	45	–	55	–	ns
Write High to Data Don't Care (Data Hold)	t_{WHDX}	10	–	10	–	10	–	10	–	ns
Write Low to Output High Z	t_{WLQZ}	0	30	0	35	0	45	0	50	ns
Write High to Output Valid	t_{WHQV}	0	–	0	–	0	–	0	–	ns

*t_{ELQV1} is access from chip enable when the 2147 is deselected for at least 55 ns prior to this cycle. t_{ELQV2} is access from chip enable for 0 ns < deselect time < 55 ns. If deselect time = 0 ns, then t_{ELQV} = t_{AVQV}.

TIMING PARAMETER ABBREVIATIONS

t X X X X

signal name from which interval is defined
transition direction for first signal
signal name to which interval is defined
transition direction for second signal

The transition definitions used in this data sheet are:

H = transition to high
L = transition to low
V = transition to valid
X = transition to invalid or don't care
Z = transition to off (high impedance)

TIMING LIMITS

The table of timing values shows either a minimum or a maximum limit for each parameter. Input requirements are specified from the external system point of view. Thus, address setup time is shown as a minimum since the system must supply at least that much time (even though most devices do not require it). On the other hand, responses from the memory are specified from the device point of view. Thus, the access time is shown as a maximum since the device never provides data later than that time.

READ CYCLE TIMING 1
(Ē Held Low)

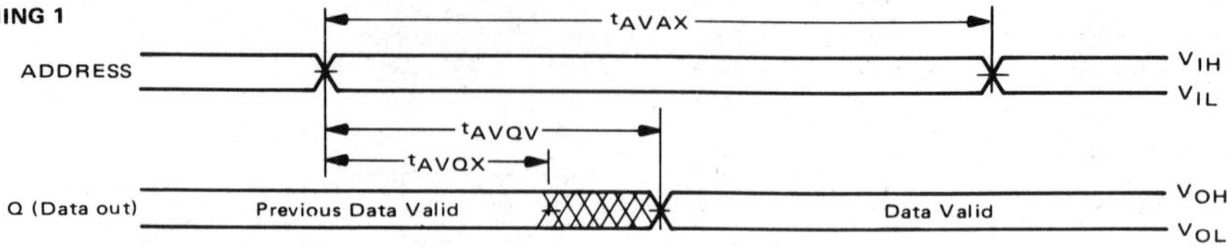

READ CYCLE TIMING 2

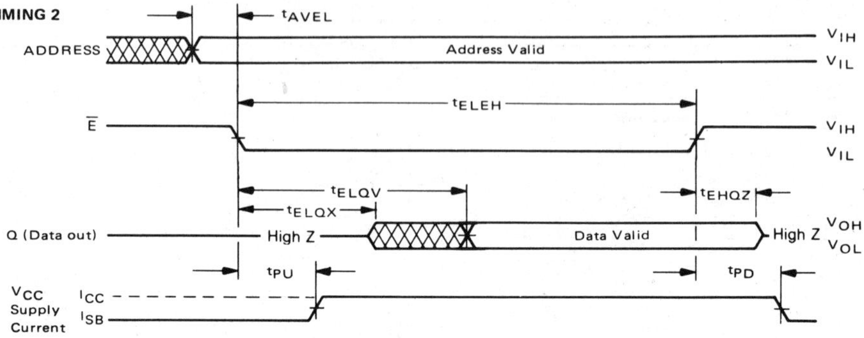

NOTE: $\overline{W}$ is high for Read Cycles.

WRITE CYCLE TIMING

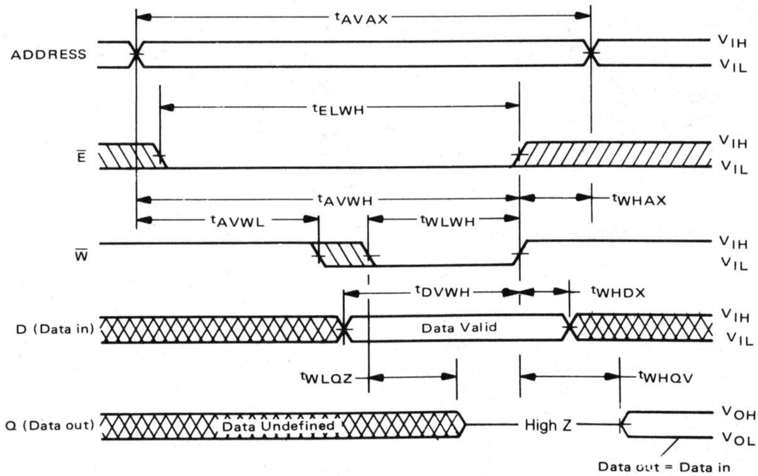

WAVEFORMS

Waveform Symbol	Input	Output
	MUST BE VALID	WILL BE VALID
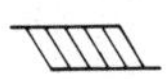	CHANGE FROM H TO L	WILL CHANGE FROM H TO L
	CHANGE FROM L TO H	WILL CHANGE FROM L TO H
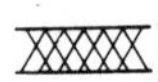	DON'T CARE: ANY CHANGE PERMITTED	CHANGING: STATE UNKNOWN
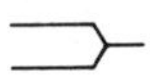		HIGH IMPEDANCE

DEVICE DESCRIPTION

The MCM2147 is produced with a high-performance MOS technology which combines on-chip substrate bias generation with device scaling to achieve high speed. The speed-power product of this process is about four times better than earlier MOS processes.

This gives the MCM2147 its high speed, low power and ease-of-use. The low-power standby feature is controlled with the $\overline{E}$ input. *$\overline{E}$ is not a clock and does not have to be cycled.* This allows the user to tie $\overline{E}$ directly to system addresses and use the line as part of the normal decoding logic. Whenever the MCM2147 is deselected, it automatically reduces its power requirements.

SYSTEM POWER SAVINGS

The automatic power-down feature adds up to significant system power savings. Unselected devices draw low standby power and only the active devices draw active power. Thus the average power consumed by a device declines as the system size increases, asymptotically approaching the standby power level as shown in Figure 2.

The automatic power-down feature is obtained without any performance degradation, since access time from chip enable is ⩽ access time from address valid. Also the fully static design gives access time equal cycle time so multiple read or write operations are possible during a single select period. The resultant data rates are 14.3 MHz and 18 MHz for the MCM2147-70 and MCM2147-55 respectively.

DECOUPLING AND BOARD LAYOUT CONSIDERATIONS

The power switching characteristic of the MCM2147 requires careful decoupling. It is recommended that a 0.1 μF to 0.3 μF ceramic capacitor be used on every other device, with a 22 μF to 47 μF bulk electrolytic decoupler every 16 devices. The actual values to be used will depend on board layout, trace widths and duty cycle.

Power supply gridding is recommended for PC board layout. A very satisfactory grid can be developed on a two-layer board with vertical traces on one side and horizontal traces on the other, as shown in Figure 3. If fast drivers are used, terminations are recommended on input signal lines to the MCM2147 because significant reflections are possible when driving their high impedance inputs. Terminations may be required to match the impedance of the line to the driver.

FIGURE 2 – AVERAGE DEVICE DISSIPATION versus MEMORY SIZE

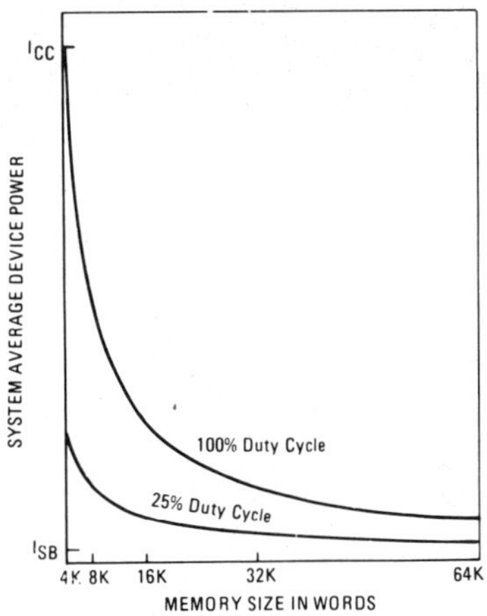

FIGURE 3 – PC LAYOUT

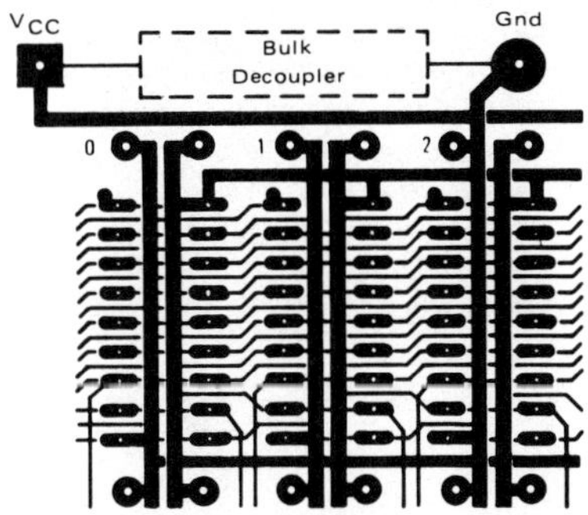

MOTOROLA
SEMICONDUCTORS
3501 ED BLUESTEIN BLVD., AUSTIN, TEXAS 78721

MC6850

ASYNCHRONOUS COMMUNICATIONS INTERFACE ADAPTER (ACIA)

The MC6850 Asynchronous Communications Interface Adapter provides the data formatting and control to interface serial asynchronous data communications information to bus organized systems such as the MC6800 Microprocessing Unit.

The bus interface of the MC6850 includes select, enable, read/write, interrupt and bus interface logic to allow data transfer over an 8-bit bidirectional data bus. The parallel data of the bus system is serially transmitted and received by the asynchronous data interface, with proper formatting and error checking. The functional configuration of the ACIA is programmed via the data bus during system initialization. A programmable Control Register provides variable word lengths, clock division ratios, transmit control, receive control, and interrupt control. For peripheral or modem operation, three control lines are provided. These lines allow the ACIA to interface directly with the MC6860L 0-600 bps digital modem.

- 8- and 9-Bit Transmission
- Optional Even and Odd Parity
- Parity, Overrun and Framing Error Checking
- Programmable Control Register
- Optional ÷1, ÷16, and ÷64 Clock Modes
- Up to 1.0 Mbps Transmission
- False Start Bit Deletion
- Peripheral/Modem Control Functions
- Double Buffered
- One- or Two-Stop Bit Operation

MOS
(N-CHANNEL, SILICON-GATE)

ASYNCHRONOUS COMMUNICATIONS INTERFACE ADAPTER

S SUFFIX
CERDIP PACKAGE
CASE 623

P SUFFIX
PLASTIC PACKAGE
CASE 709

L SUFFIX
CERAMIC PACKAGE
CASE 716

MC6850 ASYNCHRONOUS COMMUNICATIONS INTERFACE ADAPTER BLOCK DIAGRAM

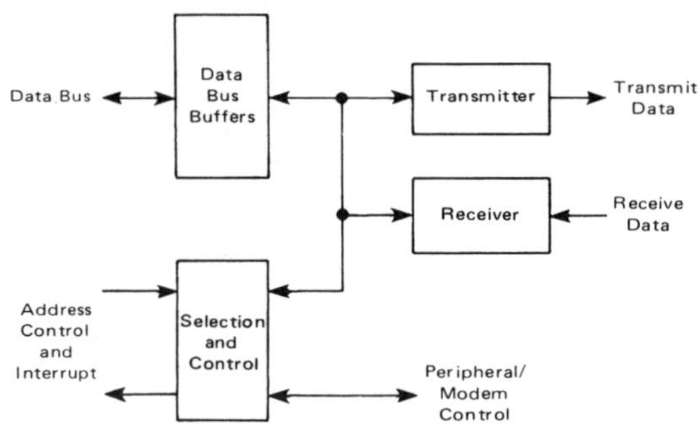

PIN ASSIGNMENT

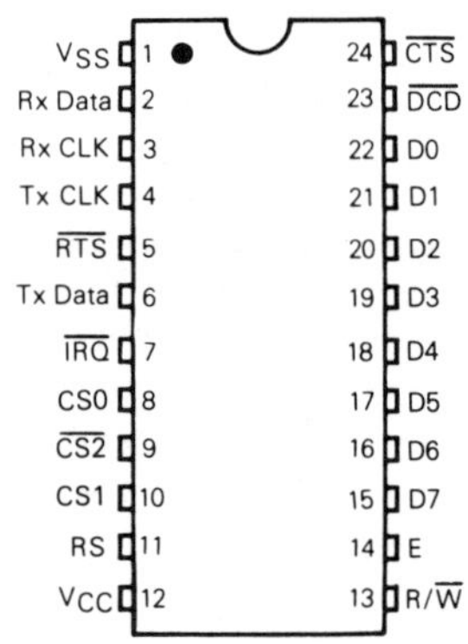

DS9493R4

MAXIMUM RATINGS

Characteristics	Symbol	Value	Unit
Supply Voltage	V_{CC}	−0.3 to +7.0	V
Input Voltage	V_{in}	−0.3 to +7.0	V
Operating Temperature Range MC6850, MC68A50, MC68B50 MC6850C, MC68A50C	T_A	T_L to T_H 0 to 70 −40 to +85	°C
Storage Temperature Range	T_{stg}	−55 to +150	°C

This device contains circuitry to protect the inputs against damage due to high static voltages or electric fields; however, it is advised that normal precautions be taken to avoid application of any voltage higher than maximum rated voltages to this high-impedance circuit. Reliability of operation is enhanced if unused inputs are tied to an appropriate logic voltage level (e.g., either V_{SS} or V_{CC}).

THERMAL CHARACTERISTICS

Characteristic	Symbol	Value	Unit
Thermal Resistance Plastic Ceramic Cerdip	θ_{JA}	 120 60 65	°C/W

POWER CONSIDERATIONS

The average chip-junction temperature, T_J, in °C can be obtained from:

$$T_J = T_A + (P_D \bullet \theta_{JA}) \quad (1)$$

Where:

$T_A \equiv$ Ambient Temperature, °C

$\theta_{JA} \equiv$ Package Thermal Resistance, Junction-to-Ambient, °C/W

$P_D \equiv P_{INT} + P_{PORT}$

$P_{INT} \equiv I_{CC} \times V_{CC}$, Watts — Chip Internal Power

$P_{PORT} \equiv$ Port Power Dissipation, Watts — User Determined

For most applications $P_{PORT} \ll P_{INT}$ and can be neglected. P_{PORT} may become significant if the device is configured to drive Darlington bases or sink LED loads.

An approximate relationship between P_D and T_J (if P_{PORT} is neglected) is:

$$P_D = K \div (T_J + 273°C) \quad (2)$$

Solving equations (1) and (2) for K gives:

$$K = P_D \bullet (T_A + 273°C) + \theta_{JA} \bullet P_D^2 \quad (3)$$

Where K is a constant pertaining to the particular part. K can be determined from equation (3) by measuring P_D (at equilibrium) for a known T_A. Using this value of K, the values of P_D and T_J can be obtained by solving equations (1) and (2) iteratively for any value of T_A.

DC ELECTRICAL CHARACTERISTICS (V_{CC} = 5.0 Vdc ±5%, V_{SS} = 0, $T_A = T_L$ to T_H unless otherwise noted.)

Characteristic		Symbol	Min	Typ	Max	Unit
Input High Voltage		V_{IH}	V_{SS}+2.0	–	V_{CC}	V
Input Low Voltage		V_{IL}	V_{SS}−0.3	–	V_{SS}+0.8	V
Input Leakage Current (V_{in} = 0 to 5.25 V)	R/$\overline{W}$, CS0, CS1, $\overline{CS2}$, Enable RS, Rx D, Rx C, $\overline{CTS}$, $\overline{DCD}$	I_{in}	–	1.0	2.5	μA
Hi-Z (Off State) Input Current (V_{in} = 0.4 to 2.4 V)	D0-D7	I_{TSI}	–	2.0	10	μA
Output High Voltage (I_{Load} = −205 μA, Enable Pulse Width < 25 μs) (I_{Load} = −100 μA, Enable Pulse Width < 25 μs)	 D0-D7 Tx Data, $\overline{RTS}$	V_{OH}	 V_{SS}+2.4 V_{SS}+2.4	 – –	 – –	V
Output Low Voltage (I_{Load} = 1.6 mA, Enable Pulse Width < 25 μs)		V_{OL}	–	–	V_{SS}+0.4	V
Output Leakage Current (Off State) (V_{OH} = 2.4 V)	$\overline{IRQ}$	I_{LOH}	–	1.0	10	μA
Internal Power Dissipation (Measured at T_A = 0°C)		P_{INT}	–	300	525*	mW
Internal Input Capacitance (V_{in} = 0, T_A = 25°C, f = 1.0 MHz)	 D0-D7 E, Tx CLK, Rx CLK, R/$\overline{W}$, RS, Rx Data, CS0, CS1, $\overline{CS2}$, $\overline{CTS}$, $\overline{DCD}$	C_{in}	 – –	 10 7.0	 12.5 7.5	pF
Output Capacitance (V_{in} = 0, T_A = 25°C, f = 1.0 MHz)	RTS, Tx Data $\overline{IRQ}$	C_{out}	– –	– –	10 5.0	pF

*For temperatures less than T_A = 0°C, P_{INT} maximum will increase.

SERIAL DATA TIMING CHARACTERISTICS

Characteristic		Symbol	MC6850 Min	MC6850 Max	MC68A50 Min	MC68A50 Max	MC68B50 Min	MC68B50 Max	Unit
Data Clock Pulse Width, Low (See Figure 1)	÷16, ÷64 Modes	PW_{CL}	600	—	450	—	280	—	ns
	÷1 Mode		900	—	650	—	500	—	
Data Clock Pulse Width, High (See Figure 2)	÷16, ÷64 Modes	PW_{CH}	600	—	450	—	280	—	ns
	÷1 Mode		900	—	650	—	500	—	
Data Clock Frequency	÷16, ÷64 Modes	f_C	—	0.8	—	1.0	—	1.5	MHz
	÷1 Mode		—	500	—	750	—	1000	kHz
Data Clock-to-Data Delay for Transmitter (See Figure 3)		t_{TDD}	—	600	—	540	—	460	ns
Receive Data Setup Time (See Figure 4)	÷1 Mode	t_{RDS}	250	—	100	—	30	—	ns
Receive Data Hold Time (See Figure 5)	÷1 Mode	t_{RDH}	250	—	100	—	30	—	ns
Interrupt Request Release Time (See Figure 6)		t_{IR}	—	1.2	—	0.9	—	0.7	μs
Request-to-Send Delay Time (See Figure 6)		t_{RTS}	—	560	—	480	—	400	ns
Input Rise and Fall Times (or 10% of the pulse width if smaller)		t_r, t_f	—	1.0	—	0.5	—	0.25	μs

FIGURE 1 — CLOCK PULSE WIDTH, LOW-STATE

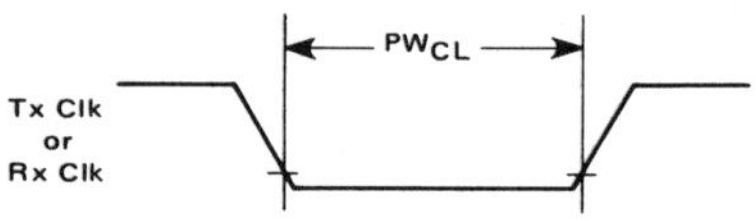

FIGURE 2 — CLOCK PULSE WIDTH, HIGH-STATE

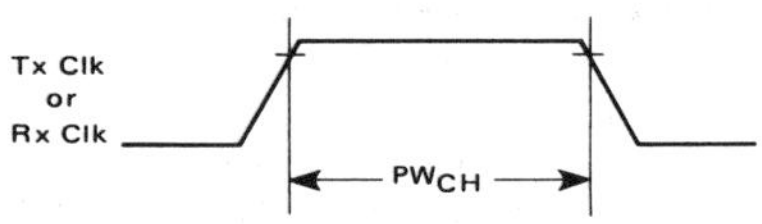

FIGURE 3 — TRANSMIT DATA OUTPUT DELAY

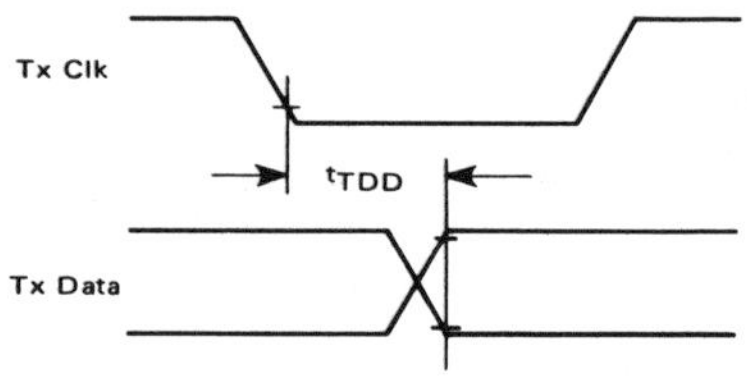

FIGURE 4 — RECEIVE DATA SETUP TIME (÷1 Mode)

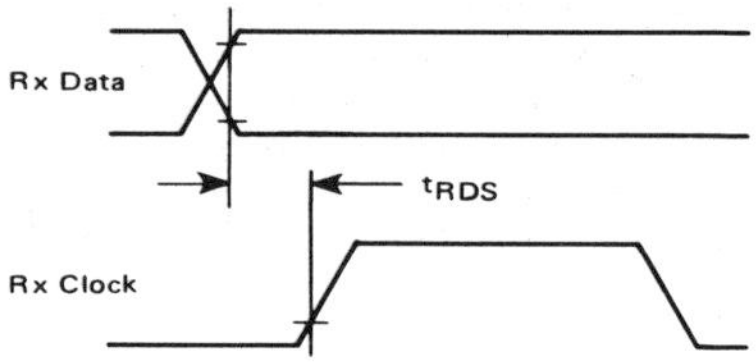

FIGURE 5 — RECEIVE DATA HOLD TIME (÷1 Mode)

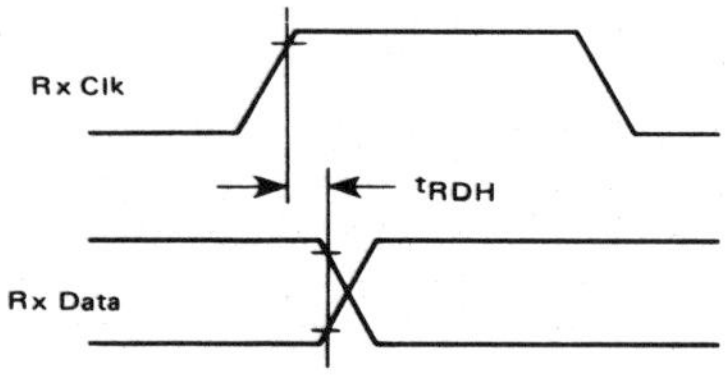

FIGURE 6 — REQUEST-TO-SEND DELAY AND INTERRUPT-REQUEST RELEASE TIMES

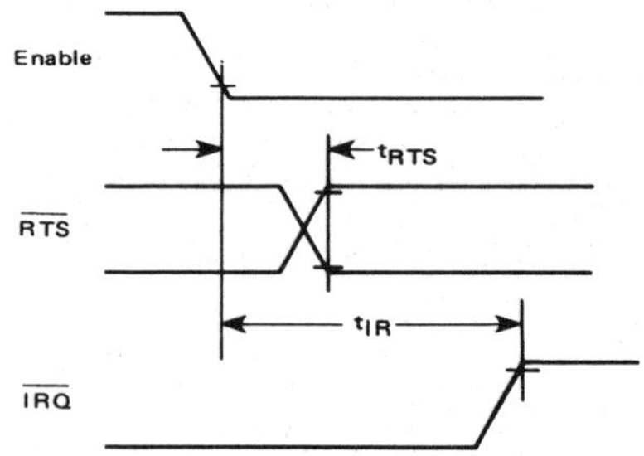

Note: Timing measurements are referenced to and from a low voltage of 0.8 volts and a high voltage of 2.0 volts, unless otherwise noted.

BUS TIMING CHARACTERISTICS (See Notes 1 and 2 and Figure 7)

Ident. Number	Characteristic	Symbol	MC6850		MC68A50		MC68B50		Unit
			Min	Max	Min	Max	Min	Max	
1	Cycle Time	t_{cyc}	1.0	10	0.67	10	0.5	10	µs
2	Pulse Width, E Low	PW_{EL}	430	9500	280	9500	210	9500	ns
3	Pulse Width, E High	PW_{EH}	450	9500	280	9500	220	9500	ns
4	Clock Rise and Fall Time	t_r, t_f	–	25	–	25	–	20	ns
9	Address Hold Time	t_{AH}	10	–	10	–	10	–	ns
13	Address Setup Time Before E	t_{AS}	80	–	60	–	40	–	ns
14	Chip Select Setup Time Before E	t_{CS}	80	–	60	–	40	–	ns
15	Chip Select Hold Time	t_{CH}	10	–	10	–	10	–	ns
18	Read Data Hold Time	t_{DHR}	20	50*	20	50*	20	50*	ns
21	Write Data Hold Time	t_{DHW}	10	–	10	–	10	–	ns
30	Output Data Delay Time	t_{DDR}	–	290	–	180	–	150	ns
31	Input Data Setup Time	t_{DSW}	165	–	80	–	60	–	ns

*The data bus output buffers are no longer sourcing or sinking current by t_{DHR}max (High Impedance).

FIGURE 7 — BUS TIMING CHARACTERISTICS

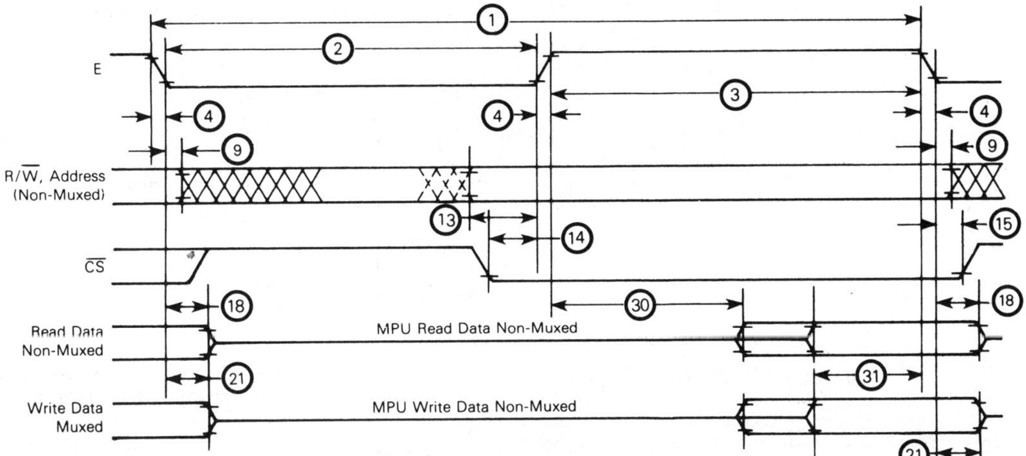

1. Voltage levels shown are $V_L \leq 0.4$ V, $V_H \geq 2.4$ V, unless otherwise specified.
2. Measurement points shown are 0.8 V and 2.0 V, unless otherwise specified.

FIGURE 8 — BUS TIMING TEST LOADS

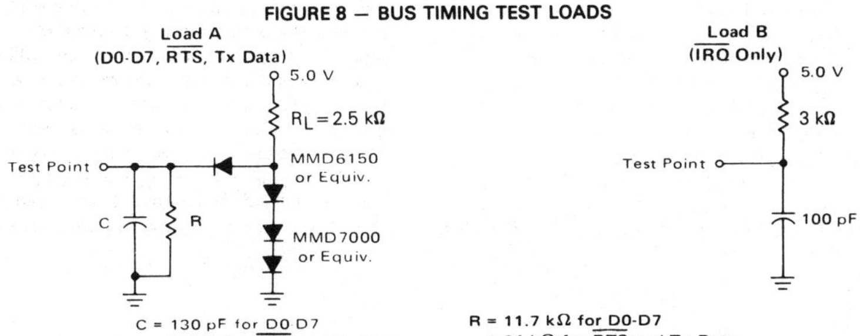

C = 130 pF for D0-D7
= 30 pF for RTS and Tx Data

R = 11.7 kΩ for D0-D7
= 24 kΩ for RTS and Tx Data

FIGURE 9 — EXPANDED BLOCK DIAGRAM

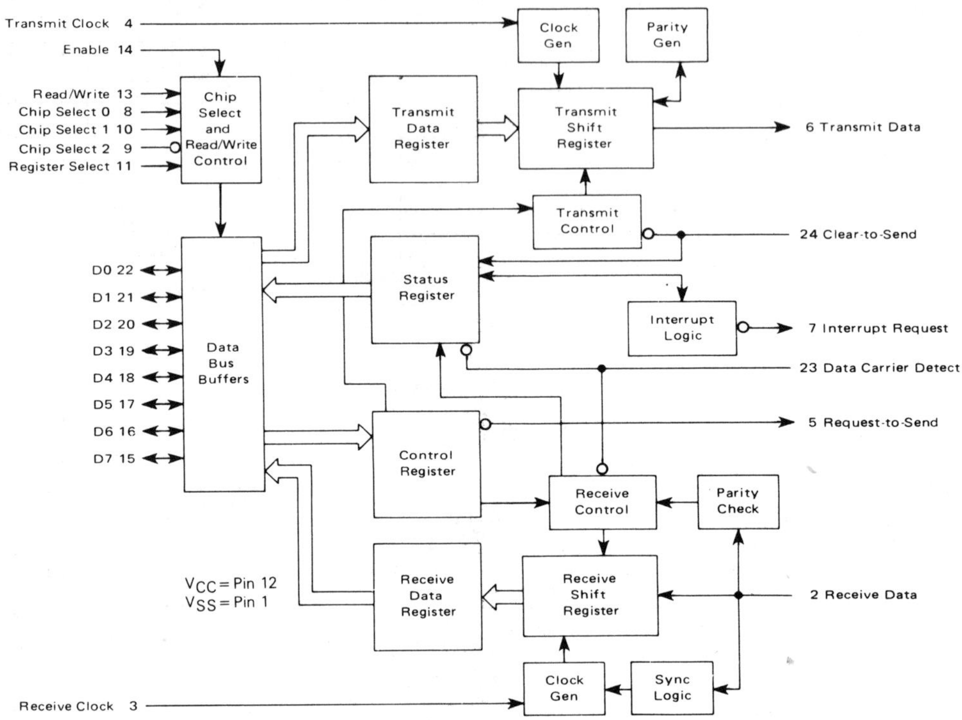

DEVICE OPERATION

At the bus interface, the ACIA appears as two addressable memory locations. Internally, there are four registers: two read-only and two write-only registers. The read-only registers are Status and Receive Data; the write-only registers are Control and Transmit Data. The serial interface consists of serial input and output lines with independent clocks, and three peripheral/modem control lines.

MASTER RESET

The master reset (CR0, CR1) must be set immediately after power-up to insure the reset condition and prepare for programming the ACIA functional configuration when the communications channel is required. During the first master reset, the $\overline{IRQ}$ and $\overline{RTS}$ outputs are held at level 1. On all other master resets, the $\overline{RTS}$ output can be programmed high or low with the $\overline{IRQ}$ output held high. Control bits CR5 and CR6 should also be programmed to define the state of $\overline{RTS}$ whenever master reset is utilized. After master resetting the ACIA, the programmable Control Register can be set for a number of options such as variable clock divider ratios, variable word length, one or two stop bits, and parity (even, odd, or none).

TRANSMIT

A typical transmitting sequence consists of reading the ACIA Status Register either as a result of an interrupt or in the ACIA's turn in a polling sequence. A character may be written into the Transmit Data Register if the status read operation has indicated that the Transmit Data Register is empty. This character is transferred to a Shift Register where it is serialized and transmitted from the Transmit Data output preceded by a start bit and followed by one or two stop bits. Internal parity (odd or even) can be optionally added to the character and will occur between the last data bit and the first stop bit. After the first character is written in the Data Register, the Status Register can be read again to check for a Transmit Data Register Empty condition and current peripheral status. If the register is empty, another character can be loaded for transmission even through the first character is in the process of being transmitted (because of double buffering). The second character will be automatically transferred into the Shift Register when the first character transmission is completed. This sequence continues until all the characters have been transmitted.

RECEIVE

Data is received from a peripheral by means of the Receive Data input. A divide-by-one clock ratio is provided for an externally synchronized clock (to its data) while the divide-by-16 and 64 ratios are provided for internal synchronization. Bit synchronization in the divide-by-16 and 64 modes is initiated by the detection of 8 or 32 low samples on the receive line in the divide-by-16 and 64 modes respectively. False start bit deletion capability insures that a full half bit of a start bit has been received before the internal clock is synchronized to the bit time. As a character is being received, parity (odd or even) will be checked and the error indication will be available in the Status Register along with framing error, overrun error, and Receive Data Register full. In a typical receiving sequence, the Status Register is read to determine if a character has been received from a peripheral. If the Receiver Data Register is full, the character is placed on the 8-bit ACIA bus when a Read Data command is received from the MPU. When parity has been selected for a 7-bit word (7 bits plus parity), the receiver strips the parity bit (D7=0) so that data alone is transferred to the MPU. This feature reduces MPU programming. The Status Register can continue to be read to determine when another character is available in the Receive Data Register. The receiver is also double buffered so that a character can be read from the data register as another character is being received in the shift register. The above sequence continues until all characters have been received.

INPUT/OUTPUT FUNCTIONS

ACIA INTERFACE SIGNALS FOR MPU

The ACIA interfaces to the M6800 MPU with an 8-bit bidirectional data bus, three chip select lines, a register select line, an interrupt request line, read/write line, and enable line. These signals permit the MPU to have complete control over the ACIA.

ACIA Bidirectional Data (D0-D7) — The bidirectional data lines (D0-D7) allow for data transfer between the ACIA and the MPU. The data bus output drivers are three-state devices that remain in the high-impedance (off) state except when the MPU performs an ACIA read operation.

ACIA Enable (E) — The Enable signal, E, is a high-impedance TTL-compatible input that enables the bus input/output data buffers and clocks data to and from the ACIA. This signal will normally be a derivative of the MC6800 $\phi 2$ Clock or MC6809 E clock.

Read/Write (R/$\overline{W}$) — The Read/Write line is a high-impedance input that is TTL compatible and is used to control the direction of data flow through the ACIA's input/output data bus interface. When Read/Write is high (MPU Read cycle), ACIA output drivers are turned on and a selected register is read. When it is low, the ACIA output drivers are turned off and the MPU writes into a selected register. Therefore, the Read/Write signal is used to select read-only or write-only registers within the ACIA.

Chip Select (CS0, CS1, $\overline{CS2}$) — These three high-impedance TTL-compatible input lines are used to address the ACIA. The ACIA is selected when CS0 and CS1 are high and $\overline{CS2}$ is low. Transfers of data to and from the ACIA are then performed under the control of the Enable Signal, Read/Write, and Register Select.

Register Select (RS) — The Register Select line is a high-impedance input that is TTL compatible. A high level is used to select the Transmit/Receive Data Registers and a low level the Control/Status Registers. The Read/Write signal line is used in conjunction with Register Select to select the read-only or write-only register in each register pair.

Interrupt Request ($\overline{IRQ}$) — Interrupt Request is a TTL-compatible, open-drain (no internal pullup), active low output that is used to interrupt the MPU. The $\overline{IRQ}$ output remains low as long as the cause of the interrupt is present and the appropriate interrupt enable within the ACIA is set. The $\overline{IRQ}$ status bit, when high, indicates the $\overline{IRQ}$ output is in the active state.

Interrupts result from conditions in both the transmitter and receiver sections of the ACIA. The transmitter section causes an interrupt when the Transmitter Interrupt Enabled condition is selected ($CR5 \bullet \overline{CR6}$), and the Transmit Data Register Empty (TDRE) status bit is high. The TDRE status bit indicates the current status of the Transmitter Data Register except when inhibited by Clear-to-Send ($\overline{CTS}$) being high or the ACIA being maintained in the Reset condition. The interrupt is cleared by writing data into the Transmit Data Register. The interrupt is masked by disabling the Transmitter Interrupt via CR5 or CR6 or by the loss of $\overline{CTS}$ which inhibits the TDRE status bit. The Receiver section causes an interrupt when the Receiver Interrupt Enable is set and the Receive Data Register Full (RDRF) status bit is high, an Overrun has occurred, or Data Carrier Detect ($\overline{DCD}$) has gone high. An interrupt resulting from the RDRF status bit can be cleared by reading data or resetting the ACIA. Interrupts caused by Overrun or loss of $\overline{DCD}$ are cleared by reading the status register after the error condition has occurred and then reading the Receive Data Register or resetting the ACIA. The receiver interrupt is masked by resetting the Receiver Interrupt Enable.

CLOCK INPUTS

Separate high-impedance TTL-compatible inputs are provided for clocking of transmitted and received data. Clock frequencies of 1, 16, or 64 times the data rate may be selected.

Transmit Clock (Tx CLK) — The Transmit Clock input is used for the clocking of transmitted data. The transmitter initiates data on the negative transition of the clock.

Receive Clock (Rx CLK) — The Receive Clock input is used for synchronization of received data. (In the ÷1 mode, the clock and data must be synchronized externally.) The receiver samples the data on the positive transition of the clock.

SERIAL INPUT/OUTPUT LINES

Receive Data (Rx Data) — The Receive Data line is a high-impedance TTL-compatible input through which data is received in a serial format. Synchronization with a clock for detection of data is accomplished internally when clock rates of 16 or 64 times the bit rate are used.

Transmit Data (Tx Data) — The Transmit Data output line transfers serial data to a modem or other peripheral.

PERIPHERAL/MODEM CONTROL

The ACIA includes several functions that permit limited control of a peripheral or modem. The functions included are Clear-to-Send, Request-to-Send and Data Carrier Detect.

Clear-to-Send ($\overline{\text{CTS}}$) — This high-impedance TTL-compatible input provides automatic control of the transmitting end of a communications link via the modem Clear-to-Send active low output by inhibiting the Transmit Data Register Empty (TDRE) status bit.

Request-to-Send ($\overline{\text{RTS}}$) — The Request-to-Send output enables the MPU to control a peripheral or modem via the data bus. The RTS output corresponds to the state of the Control Register bits CR5 and CR6. When CR6 = 0 or both CR5 and CR6 = 1, the $\overline{\text{RTS}}$ output is low (the active state). This output can also be used for Data Terminal Ready (DTR).

Data Carrier Detect ($\overline{\text{DCD}}$) — This high-impedance TTL-compatible input provides automatic control, such as in the receiving end of a communications link by means of a modem Data Carrier Detect output. The $\overline{\text{DCD}}$ input inhibits and initializes the receiver section of the ACIA when high. A low-to-high transition of the Data Carrier Detect initiates an interrupt to the MPU to indicate the occurrence of a loss of carrier when the Receive Interrupt Enable bit is set. The Rx CLK must be running for proper $\overline{\text{DCD}}$ operation.

ACIA REGISTERS

The expanded block diagram for the ACIA indicates the internal registers on the chip that are used for the status, control, receiving, and transmitting of data. The content of each of the registers is summarized in Table 1.

TRANSMIT DATA REGISTER (TDR)

Data is written in the Transmit Data Register during the negative transition of the enable (E) when the ACIA has been addressed with RS high and R/$\overline{\text{W}}$ low. Writing data into the register causes the Transmit Data Register Empty bit in the Status Register to go low. Data can then be transmitted. If the transmitter is idling and no character is being transmitted, then the transfer will take place within 1-bit time of the trailing edge of the Write command. If a character is being transmitted, the new data character will commence as soon as the previous character is complete. The transfer of data causes the Transmit Data Register Empty (TDRE) bit to indicate empty.

RECEIVE DATA REGISTER (RDR)

Data is automatically transferred to the empty Receive Data Register (RDR) from the receiver deserializer (a shift register) upon receiving a complete character. This event causes the Receive Data Register Full bit (RDRF) in the status buffer to go high (full). Data may then be read through the bus by addressing the ACIA and selecting the Receive Data Register with RS and R/$\overline{\text{W}}$ high when the ACIA is enabled. The non-destructive read cycle causes the RDRF bit to be cleared to empty although the data is retained in the RDR. The status is maintained by RDRF as to whether or not the data is current. When the Receive Data Register is full, the automatic transfer of data from the Receiver Shift Register to the Data Register is inhibited and the RDR contents remain valid with its current status stored in the Status Register.

TABLE 1 — DEFINITION OF ACIA REGISTER CONTENTS

Data Bus Line Number	Buffer Address			
	RS • $\overline{\text{R/W}}$ Transmit Data Register (Write Only)	RS • R/$\overline{\text{W}}$ Receive Data Register (Read Only)	$\overline{\text{RS}}$ • $\overline{\text{R/W}}$ Control Register (Write Only)	$\overline{\text{RS}}$ • R/$\overline{\text{W}}$ Status Register (Read Only)
0	Data Bit 0*	Data Bit 0	Counter Divide Select 1 (CR0)	Receive Data Register Full (RDRF)
1	Data Bit 1	Data Bit 1	Counter Divide Select 2 (CR1)	Transmit Data Register Empty (TDRE)
2	Data Bit 2	Data Bit 2	Word Select 1 (CR2)	Data Carrier Detect ($\overline{\text{DCD}}$)
3	Data Bit 3	Data Bit 3	Word Select 2 (CR3)	Clear-to-Send ($\overline{\text{CTS}}$)
4	Data Bit 4	Data Bit 4	Word Select 3 (CR4)	Framing Error (FE)
5	Data Bit 5	Data Bit 5	Transmit Control 1 (CR5)	Receiver Overrun (OVRN)
6	Data Bit 6	Data Bit 6	Transmit Control 2 (CR6)	Parity Error (PE)
7	Data Bit 7***	Data Bit 7**	Receive Interrupt Enable (CR7)	Interrupt Request ($\overline{\text{IRQ}}$)

* Leading bit = LSB = Bit 0

** Data bit will be zero in 7-bit plus parity modes.

*** Data bit is "don't care" in 7-bit plus parity modes.

CONTROL REGISTER

The ACIA Control Register consists of eight bits of write-only buffer that are selected when RS and R/$\overline{W}$ are low. This register controls the function of the receiver, transmitter, interrupt enables, and the Request-to-Send peripheral/modem control output.

Counter Divide Select Bits (CR0 and CR1) — The Counter Divide Select Bits (CR0 and CR1) determine the divide ratios utilized in both the transmitter and receiver sections of the ACIA. Additionally, these bits are used to provide a master reset for the ACIA which clears the Status Register (except for external conditions on $\overline{CTS}$ and $\overline{DCD}$) and initializes both the receiver and transmitter. Master reset does not affect other Control Register bits. Note that after power-on or a power fail/restart, these bits must be set high to reset the ACIA. After resetting, the clock divide ratio may be selected. These counter select bits provide for the following clock divide ratios:

CR1	CR0	Function
0	0	÷1
0	1	÷16
1	0	÷64
1	1	Master Reset

Word Select Bits (CR2, CR3, and CR4) — The Word Select bits are used to select word length, parity, and the number of stop bits. The encoding format is as follows:

CR4	CR3	CR2	Function
0	0	0	7 Bits + Even Parity + 2 Stop Bits
0	0	1	7 Bits + Odd Parity + 2 Stop Bits
0	1	0	7 Bits + Even Parity + 1 Stop Bit
0	1	1	7 Bits + Odd Parity + 1 Stop Bit
1	0	0	8 Bits + 2 Stop Bits
1	0	1	8 Bits + 1 Stop Bit
1	1	0	8 Bits + Even parity + 1 Stop Bit
1	1	1	8 Bits + Odd Parity + 1 Stop Bit

Word length, Parity Select, and Stop Bit changes are not buffered and therefore become effective immediately.

Transmitter Control Bits (CR5 and CR6) — Two Transmitter Control bits provide for the control of the interrupt from the Transmit Data Register Empty condition, the Request-to-Send ($\overline{RTS}$) output, and the transmission of a Break level (space). The following encoding format is used:

CR6	CR5	Function
0	0	$\overline{RTS}$ = low, Transmitting Interrupt Disabled.
0	1	$\overline{RTS}$ = low, Transmitting Interrupt Enabled.
1	0	$\overline{RTS}$ = high, Transmitting Interrupt Disabled.
1	1	$\overline{RTS}$ = low, Transmits a Break level on the Transmit Data Output. Transmitting Interrupt Disabled.

Receive Interrupt Enable Bit (CR7) — The following interrupts will be enabled by a high level in bit position 7 of the Control Register (CR7): Receive Data Register Full, Overrun, or a low-to-high transition on the Data Carrier Detect ($\overline{DCD}$) signal line.

STATUS REGISTER

Information on the status of the ACIA is available to the MPU by reading the ACIA Status Register. This read-only register is selected when RS is low and R/$\overline{W}$ is high. Information stored in this register indicates the status of the Transmit Data Register, the Receive Data Register and error logic, and the peripheral/modem status inputs of the ACIA.

Receive Data Register Full (RDRF), Bit 0 — Receive Data Register Full indicates that received data has been transferred to the Receive Data Register. RDRF is cleared after an MPU read of the Receive Data Register or by a master reset. The cleared or empty state indicates that the contents of the Receive Data Register are not current. Data Carrier Detect being high also causes RDRF to indicate empty.

Transmit Data Register Empty (TDRE), Bit 1 — The Transmit Data Register Empty bit being set high indicates that the Transmit Data Register contents have been transferred and that new data may be entered. The low state indicates that the register is full and that transmission of a new character has not begun since the last write data command.

Data Carrier Detect ($\overline{DCD}$), Bit 2 — The Data Carrier Detect bit will be high when the $\overline{DCD}$ input from a modem has gone high to indicate that a carrier is not present. This bit going high causes an Interrupt Request to be generated when the Receive Interrupt Enable is set. It remains high after the $\overline{DCD}$ input is returned low until cleared by first reading the Status Register and then the Data Register or until a master reset occurs. If the $\overline{DCD}$ input remains high after read status and read data or master reset has occurred, the interrupt is cleared, the $\overline{DCD}$ status bit remains high and will follow the $\overline{DCD}$ input.

Clear-to-Send ($\overline{CTS}$), Bit 3 — The Clear-to-Send bit indicates the state of the Clear-to-Send input from a modem. A low $\overline{CTS}$ indicates that there is a Clear-to-Send from the modem. In the high state, the Transmit Data Register Empty bit is inhibited and the Clear-to-Send status bit will be high. Master reset does not affect the Clear-to-Send status bit.

Framing Error (FE), Bit 4 — Framing error indicates that the received character is improperly framed by a start and a stop bit and is detected by the absence of the first stop bit. This error indicates a synchronization error, faulty transmission, or a break condition. The framing error flag is set or reset during the receive data transfer time. Therefore, this error indicator is present throughout the time that the associated character is available.

Receiver Overrun (OVRN), Bit 5 — Overrun is an error flag that indicates that one or more characters in the data stream were lost. That is, a character or a number of characters were received but not read from the Receive Data Register (RDR) prior to subsequent characters being received. The overrun condition begins at the midpoint of the last bit of the second character received in succession without a read of the RDR having occurred. The Overrun does not occur in the Status Register until the valid character prior to Overrun has

PACKAGE DIMENSIONS

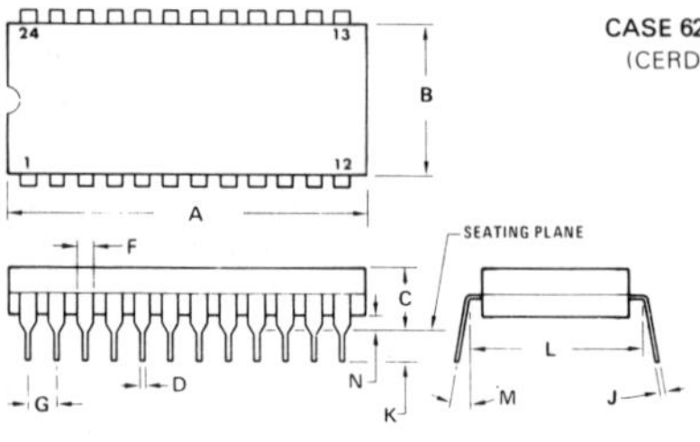

CASE 623-03
(CERDIP)

DIM	MILLIMETERS MIN	MILLIMETERS MAX	INCHES MIN	INCHES MAX
A	31.24	32.77	1.230	1.290
B	12.70	15.49	0.500	0.610
C	4.06	5.59	0.160	0.220
D	0.41	0.51	0.016	0.020
F	1.27	1.52	0.050	0.060
G	2.54 BSC		0.100 BSC	
J	0.20	0.30	0.008	0.012
K	2.29	4.06	0.090	0.160
L	15.24 BSC		0.600 BSC	
M	0°	15°	0°	15°
N	0.51	1.27	0.020	0.050

NOTES:
1. DIM "L" TO CENTER OF LEADS WHEN FORMED PARALLEL.
2. LEADS WITHIN 0.13 mm (0.005) RADIUS OF TRUE POSITION AT SEATING PLANE AT MAXIMUM MATERIAL CONDITION. (WHEN FORMED PARALLEL)

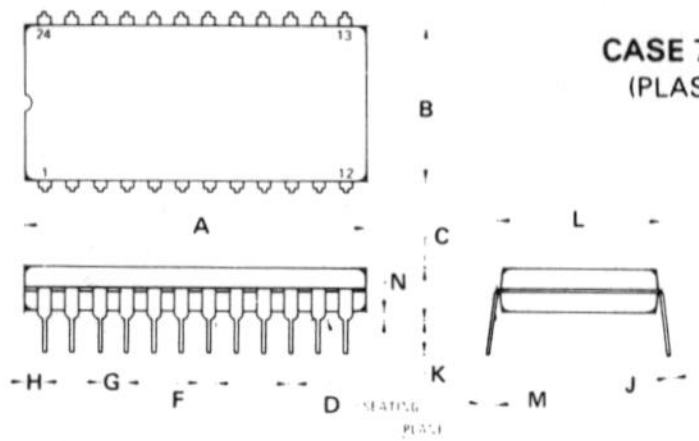

CASE 709-02
(PLASTIC)

DIM	MILLIMETERS MIN	MILLIMETERS MAX	INCHES MIN	INCHES MAX
A	31.37	32.13	1.235	1.265
B	13.72	14.22	0.540	0.560
C	3.94	5.08	0.155	0.200
D	0.36	0.56	0.014	0.022
F	1.02	1.52	0.040	0.060
G	2.54 BSC		0.100 BSC	
H	1.65	2.03	0.065	0.080
J	0.20	0.38	0.008	0.015
K	2.92	3.43	0.115	0.135
L	15.24 BSC		0.600 BSC	
M	0°	15°	0°	15°
N	0.51	1.02	0.020	0.040

NOTES:
1. POSITIONAL TOLERANCE OF LEADS (D), SHALL BE WITHIN 0.25 mm (0.010) AT MAXIMUM MATERIAL CONDITION, IN RELATION TO SEATING PLANE AND EACH OTHER.
2. DIMENSION L TO CENTER OF LEADS WHEN FORMED PARALLEL.
3. DIMENSION B DOES NOT INCLUDE MOLD FLASH.

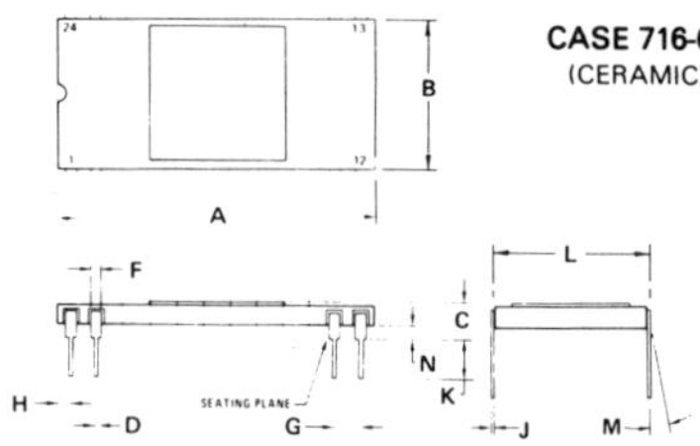

CASE 716-06
(CERAMIC)

DIM	MILLIMETERS MIN	MILLIMETERS MAX	INCHES MIN	INCHES MAX
A	27.64	30.99	1.088	1.220
B	14.73	15.34	0.580	0.604
C	2.67	4.32	0.105	0.170
D	0.38	0.53	0.015	0.021
F	0.76	1.40	0.030	0.055
G	2.54 BSC		0.100 BSC	
H	0.76	1.78	0.030	0.070
J	0.20	0.30	0.008	0.012
K	2.54	4.57	0.100	0.180
L	14.99	15.49	0.590	0.610
M	–	10°	–	10°
N	1.02	1.52	0.040	0.060

NOTE:
1. LEADS TRUE POSITIONED WITHIN 0.25mm (0.010) DIA (AT SEATING PLANE) AT MAXIMUM MATERIAL CONDITION.
2. DIM "L" TO CENTER OF LEADS WHEN FORMED PARALLEL.

MOTOROLA *Semiconductor Products Inc.*

3501 ED BLUESTEIN BLVD., AUSTIN, TEXAS 78721 • A SUBSIDIARY OF MOTOROLA INC.

A11225-7 PRINTED IN USA 4-85 IMPERIAL LITHO C30469 18,000

DS9493R4

been read. The RDRF bit remains set until the Overrun is reset. Character synchronization is maintained during the Overrun condition. The Overrun indication is reset after the reading of data from the Receive Data Register or by a Master Reset.

Parity Error (PE), Bit 6 — The parity error flag indicates that the number of highs (ones) in the character does not agree with the preselected odd or even parity. Odd parity is defined to be when the total number of ones is odd. The parity error indication will be present as long as the data character is in the RDR. If no parity is selected, then both the transmitter parity generator output and the receiver partiy check results are inhibited.

Interrupt Request ($\overline{IRQ}$), Bit 7 — The $\overline{IRQ}$ bit indicates the state of the $\overline{IRQ}$ output. Any interrupt condition with its applicable enable will be indicated in this status bit. Anytime the $\overline{IRQ}$ output is low the $\overline{IRQ}$ bit will be high to indicate the interrupt or service request status. $\overline{IRQ}$ is cleared by a read operation to the Receive Data Register or a write operation to the Transmit Data Register.

ORDERING INFORMATION

Package Type	Frequency (MHz)	Temperature	Order Number
Ceramic L Suffix	1.0	0°C to 70°C	MC6850L
	1.0	−40°C to 85°C	MC6850CL
	1.5	0°C to 70°C	MC68A50L
	1.5	−40°C to 85°C	MC68A50CL
	2.0	0°C to 70°C	MC68B50C
Cerdip S Suffix	1.0	0°C to 70°C	MC6850S
	1.0	−40°C to 85°C	MC6850CS
	1.5	0°C to 70°C	MC68A50S
	1.5	−40°C to 85°C	MC68A50CS
	2.0	0°C to 70°C	MC68B50S
Plastic P Suffix	1.0	0°C to 70°C	MC6850P
	1.0	−40°C to 85°C	MC6850CP
	1.5	0°C to 70°C	MC68A50P
	1.5	−40°C to 85°C	MC68A50CP
	2.0	0°C to 70°C	MC68B50P

MOTOROLA

SEMICONDUCTORS

3501 ED BLUESTEIN BLVD., AUSTIN, TEXAS 78721

MC14411

CMOS LSI

(LOW-POWER COMPLEMENTARY MOS)

BIT RATE GENERATOR

BIT RATE GENERATOR

The MC14411 bit rate generator is constructed with complementary MOS enhancement mode devices. It utilizes a frequency divider network to provide a wide range of output frequencies.

A crystal controlled oscillator is the clock source for the network. A two-bit address is provided to select one of four multiple output clock rates.

Applications include a selectable frequency source for equipment in the data communications market, such as teleprinters, printers, CRT terminals, and microprocessor systems.

- Single 5.0 Vdc (±5%) Power Supply
- Internal Oscillator Crystal Controlled for Stability (1.8432 MHz)
- Sixteen Different Output Clock Rates
- 50% Output Duty Cycle
- Programmable Time Bases for One of Four Multiple Output Rates
- Buffered Outputs Compatible with Low Power TTL
- Noise Immunity = 45% of V_{DD} Typical
- Diode Protection on All Inputs
- External Clock May be Applied to Pin 21
- Internal Pullup Resistor on Reset Input

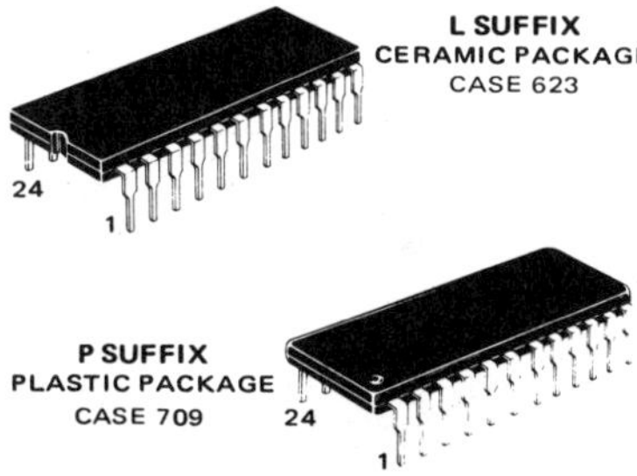

L SUFFIX
CERAMIC PACKAGE
CASE 623

P SUFFIX
PLASTIC PACKAGE
CASE 709

MAXIMUM RATINGS (Voltages referenced to V_{SS}, Pin 12.)

Rating	Symbol	Value	Unit
DC Supply Voltage Range	V_{DD}	5.25 to −0.5	V
Input Voltage, All Inputs	V_{in}	$V_{DD}+0.5$ to $V_{SS}-0.5$	V
DC Current Drain per Pin	I	10	mA
Operating Temperature Range	T_A	−40 to +85	°C
Storage Temperature Range	T_{stg}	−65 to +150	°C

PIN ASSIGNMENT

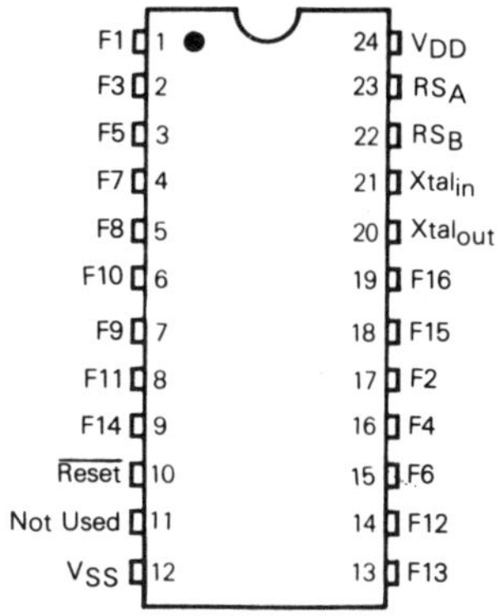

V_{DD} = Pin 24
V_{SS} = Pin 12

BLOCK DIAGRAM

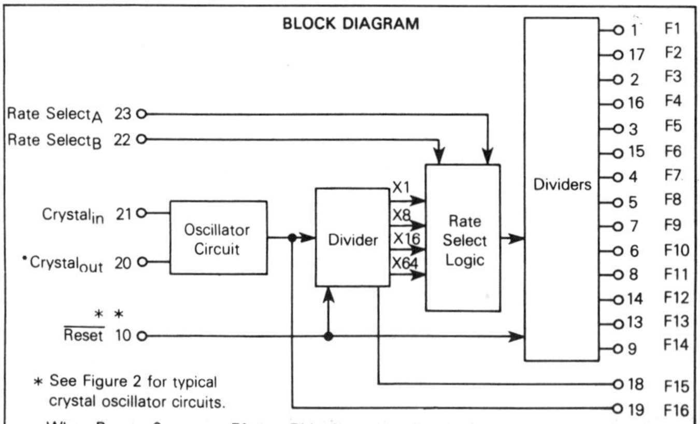

* See Figure 2 for typical crystal oscillator circuits.

* * When Reset = 0, outputs F1 thru F14 = 0, outputs F15 and F16 = 1.

This device contains circuitry to protect the inputs against damage due to high static voltages or electric fields; however, it is advised that normal precautions be taken to avoid application of any voltage higher than maximum rated voltages to this high impedance circuit. For proper operation it is recommended that V_{in} and V_{out} be constrained to the range $V_{SS} \leq (V_{in}$ or $V_{out}) \leq V_{DD}$.

Unused inputs must always be tied to an appropriate logic voltage level (e.g., either V_{SS} or V_{DD}).

DS-9386-R2

ELECTRICAL CHARACTERISTICS

Characteristic	Symbol	V_{DD} Vdc	−40°C Min	−40°C Max	25°C Min	25°C Typ	25°C Max	+85°C Min	+85°C Max	Unit
Supply Voltage	V_{DD}	–	4.75	5.25	4.75	5.0	5.25	4.75	5.25	V
Output Voltage "0" Level	V_{out}	5.0	–	0.05	–	0	0.05	–	0.05	V
"1" Level		5.0	4.95	–	4.95	5.0	–	4.95	–	V
Input Voltage ($V_O = 4.5$ or 0.5 V)	V_{IL}	5.0	–	1.5	–	2.25	1.5	–	1.5	V
($V_O = 0.5$ or 4.5 Vdc)	V_{IH}	5.0	3.5	–	3.5	2.75	–	3.5	–	V
Output Drive Current ($V_{OH} = 2.5$ V) Source	I_{OH}	5.0	−0.23	–	−0.20	−1.7	–	−0.16	–	mA
($V_{OL} = 0.4$ V) Sink	I_{OL}	5.0	0.23	–	0.20	0.78	–	0.16	–	mA
Input Current Pins 21, 22, 23	I_{in}	–	–	±0.1	–	±0.00001	±0.1	–	±1.0	μA
Pin 10		5.0	–	–	−1.5	–	−7.5	–	–	μA
Input Capacitance ($V_{in} = 0$)	C_{in}	–	–	–	–	5.0	–	–	–	pF
Quiescent Dissipation	P_Q	5.0	–	2.5	–	0.015	2.5	–	15	mW
Power Dissipation**† (Dynamic plus Quiescent) ($C_L = 15$ pF)	P_D	5.0			$P_D = (7.5\ \text{mW/MHz})\ f + P_Q$					mW
Output Rise Time** $t_r = (3.0\ \text{ns/pF})\ C_L + 25$ ns	t_{TLH}	5.0	–	–	–	70	200	–	–	ns
Output Fall Time** $t_f = (1.5\ \text{ns/pF})\ C_L + 47$ ns	t_{THL}	5.0	–	–	–	70	200	–	–	ns
Input Clock Frequency	f_{CL}	5.0	–	1.85	–	–	1.85	–	1.85	MHz
Clock Pulse Width	$t_{W(C)}$	–	200	–	200	–	–	200	–	ns
Reset Pulse Width	$t_{W(R)}$	–	500	–	500	–	–	500	–	ns

†For dissipation at different external capacitance (C_L) refer to corresponding formula:

$P_T(C_L) = P_D + 2.6 \times 10^{-3}(C_L - 15\ \text{pF})\ V_{DD}^2 f$

where: P_T, P_D in mW, C_L in pF, V_{DD} in Vdc, and f in MHz.

**The formula given is for the typical characteristics only.

TABLE 1 — OUTPUT CLOCK RATES

Rate Select B	Rate Select A	Rate
0	0	X1
0	1	X8
1	0	X16
1	1	X64

Output Number	Output Rates (Hz) X64	X16	X8	X1
F1	614.4 k	153.6 k	76.8 k	9600
F2	460.8 k	115.2 k	57.6 k	7200
F3	307.2 k	76.8 k	38.4 k	4800
F4	230.4 k	57.6 k	28.8 k	3600
F5	153.6 k	38.4 k	19.2 k	2400
F6	115.2 k	28.8 k	14.4 k	1800
F7	76.8 k	19.2 k	9600	1200
F8	38.4 k	9600	4800	600
F9	19.2 k	4800	2400	300
F10	12.8 k	3200	1600	200
F11	9600	2400	1200	150
F12	8613.2	2153.3	1076.6	134.5
F13	7035.5	1758.8	879.4	109.9
F14	4800	1200	600	75
F15	921.6 k	921.6 k	921.6 k	921.6 k
F16*	1.843 M	1.843 M	1.843 M	1.843 M

*F16 is buffered oscillator output.

FIGURE 1 — DYNAMIC SIGNAL WAVEFORMS

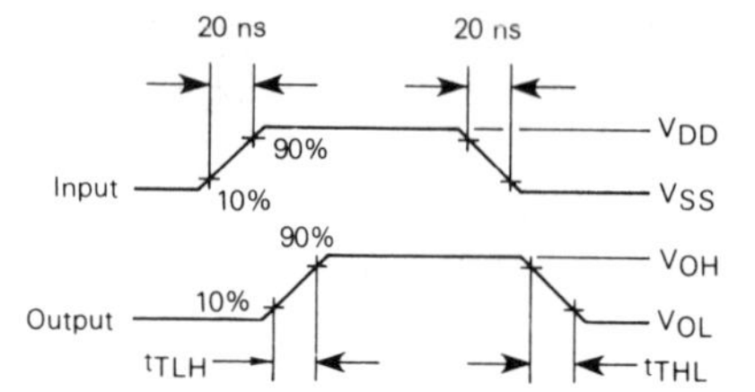

FIGURE 2 — TYPICAL CRYSTAL OSCILLATOR CIRCUIT

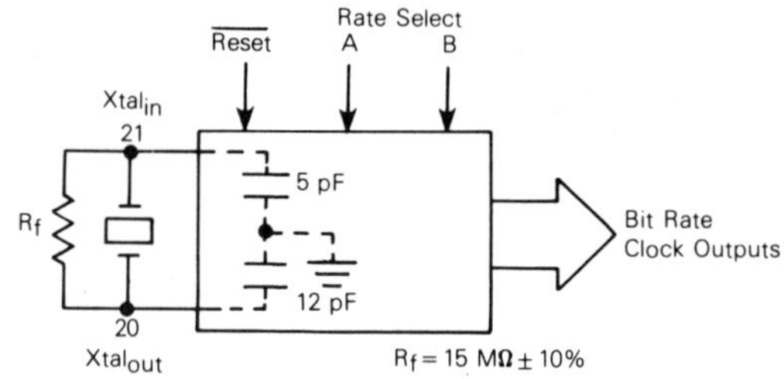

Crystal Specifications

Crystal Mode	Parallel
Frequency	1.8432 MHz ±0.05%@13 pF
R_S	540 Ω max
C_O	7.0 pF max
Temperature Range	0 to 70°C
Test Level	1 mW
Test Set	TS — 330/TSM or Equivalent

*Suggested Crystal Suppliers:
Tyco, CTS Knights

Circuit diagrams utilizing Motorola products are included as a means of illustrating typical semiconductor applications; consequently, complete information sufficient for construction purposes is not necessarily given. The information has been carefully checked and is believed to be entirely reliable. However, no responsibility is assumed for inaccuracies. Furthermore, such information does not convey to the purchaser of the semiconductor devices described any license under the patent rights of Motorola Inc., or others.

MOTOROLA
SEMICONDUCTORS
3501 ED BLUESTEIN BLVD., AUSTIN, TEXAS 78721

MCM68364

64K-BIT READ ONLY MEMORY

The MCM68364 is a mask-programmable byte-organized memory designed for use in bus-organized systems. It is fabricated with N-channel silicon-gate technology. For ease of use, the device operates from a single power supply, and is TTL compatible. The addresses are latched with the Chip Enable input — no external latches required.

The memory is compatible with the M6800 Microcomputer Family, providing read only storage in byte increments. The Chip Enable input deselects the output and puts the chip in a power-down mode.

- Single ±10% 5-Volt Power Supply
- Automatic Power Down
- Low Power Dissipation
  - 150 mW active (typical)
  - 35 mW standby (typical)
- High Output Drive Capability (2 TTL Loads)
- Three-State Data Output for OR-Ties
- TTL Compatible
- Maximum Access Time
  - 200 ns — MCM68364-20
  - 250 ns — MCM68364-25
  - 300 ns — MCM68364-30
- Pin Compatible with 8K — MCM68A308, 16K — MCM68A316E, and 32K — MCM68A332 Mask-Programmable ROMs
- Pin Compatible with 24-pin 64K EPROM MCM68764

MOS

(N-CHANNEL, SILICON-GATE)

8192 × 8-BIT READ ONLY MEMORY

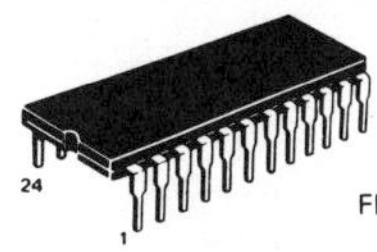

C SUFFIX
FRIT-SEAL PACKAGE
CASE 623

P SUFFIX
PLASTIC PACKAGE
CASE 709

PIN ASSIGNMENT

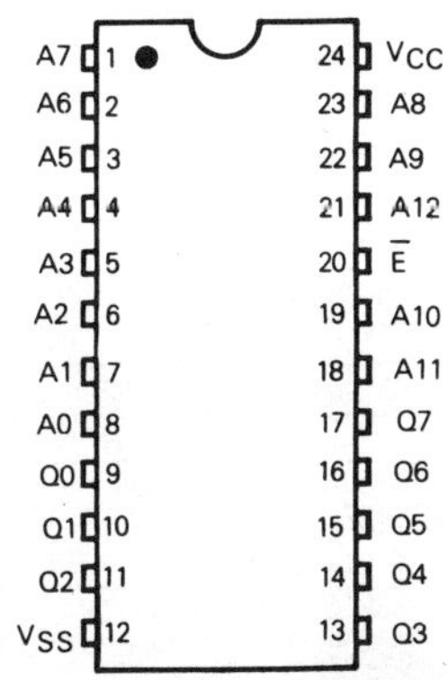

PIN NAMES	
A0-A12	Address
$\overline{E}$	Chip Enable
Q0-Q7	Data Output
V_{CC}	+5 V Power Supply
V_{SS}	Ground

MOTOROLA'S PIN COMPATIBLE ROM FAMILY

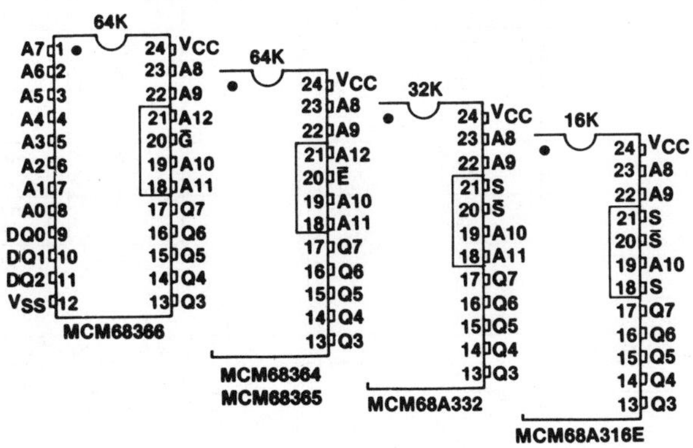

INDUSTRY STANDARD PIN-OUTS

This device contains circuitry to protect the inputs against damage due to high static voltages or electric fields; however, it is advised that normal precautions be taken to avoid application of any voltage higher than maximum rated voltages to this high-impedance circuit.

DS-9805-R2

BLOCK DIAGRAM

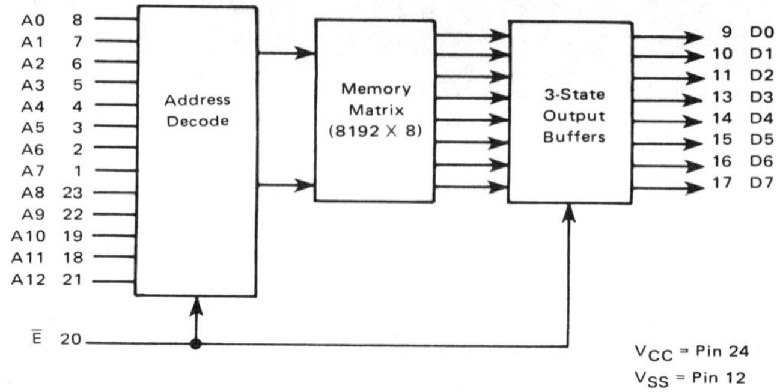

ABSOLUTE MAXIMUM RATINGS (See note)

Rating	Symbol	Value	Unit
Supply Voltage	V_{CC}	−0.5 to +7.0	Vdc
Input Voltage	V_{in}	−0.5 to +7.0	Vdc
Operating Temperature Range	T_A	0 to +70	°C
Storage Temperature Range	T_{stg}	−65 to +150	°C

NOTE: Permanent device damage may occur if ABSOLUTE MAXIMUM RATINGS are exceeded. Functional operation should be restricted to RECOMMENDED OPERATING CONDITIONS. Exposure to higher than recommended voltages for extended periods of time could affect device reliability.

DC OPERATING CONDITIONS AND CHARACTERISTICS

(Full operating voltage and temperature range unless otherwise noted.)

RECOMMENDED OPERATING CONDITIONS

Parameter	Symbol	Min	Nom	Max	Unit
Supply Voltage (V_{CC} must be applied at least 100 μs before proper device operation is achieved, $\overline{E}=V_{IH}$)	V_{CC}	4.5	5.0	5.5	V
Input High Voltage	V_{IH}	2.0	—	V_{CC}	V
Input Low Voltage	V_{IL}	−0.3	—	0.8	V

DC OPERATING CHARACTERISTICS

Characteristic	Symbol	Min	Typ	Max	Unit
Input Current (V_{in} = 0 to 5.5 V)	I_{in}	-10	—	10	μA
Output High Voltage (I_{OH} = -220 μA)	V_{OH}	2.4	—	—	V
Output Low Voltage (I_{OL} = 3.2 mA)	V_{OL}	—	—	0.4	V
Output Leakage Current (Three-State) ($\overline{E}$ = 2.0 V, V_{out} = 0 V to 5.5 V)	I_{LO}	-10	—	10	μA
Supply Current — Active* (Minimum Cycle Rate)	I_{CC}	—	25	40	mA
Supply Current — Standby ($\overline{E}$ = V_{IH})	I_{SB}	—	7	10	mA

*Current is proportional to cycle rate.

CAPACITANCE (f = 1.0 MHz, T_A = 25°C, periodically sampled rather than 100% tested)

Characteristic	Symbol	Max	Unit
Input Capacitance	C_{in}	8	pF
Output Capacitance	C_{out}	15	pF

AC OPERATING CONDITIONS AND CHARACTERISTICS

Read Cycle

RECOMMENDED AC OPERATING CONDITIONS

(T_A = 0 to 70°C, V_{CC} = 5.0 V ± 10%. All timing with $t_r = t_f$ = 20 ns, loads of Figure 1)

Parameter	Symbol		MCM68364-20		MCM68364-25		MCM68364-30		Unit
	Standard	Alternate	Min	Max	Min	Max	Min	Max	
Chip Enable Low to Chip Enable Low of Next Cycle (Cycle Time)	t_{ELEL}	t_{CYC}	300	–	375	–	450	–	ns
Chip Enable Low to Chip Enable High	t_{ELEH}	t_{EW}	200	–	250	–	300	–	ns
Chip Enable Low to Output Valid (Access)	t_{ELQV}	t_{EA}	–	200	–	250	–	300	ns
Chip Enable High to Output High Z (Off Time)	t_{EHQZ}	t_{EHZ}	10	60	–	60	–	75	ns
Chip Enable Low to Address Don't Care (Hold)	t_{ELAX}	t_{AH}	60	–	60	–	75	–	ns
Address Valid to Chip Enable Low (Address Setup)	t_{AVEL}	t_{AS}	0	–	0	–	0	–	ns
Chip Enable Precharge Time	t_{EHEL}	t_{EP}	100	–	125	–	150	–	ns

TIMING DIAGRAM

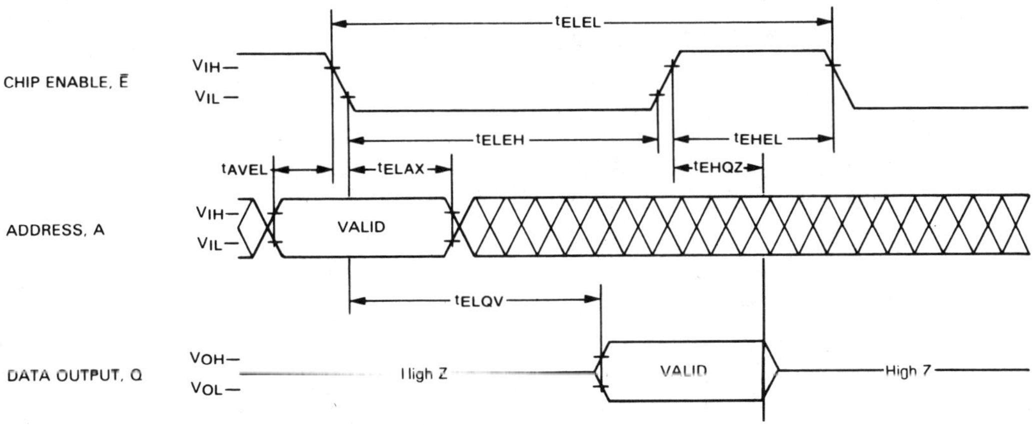

FIGURE 1 – AC TEST LOAD

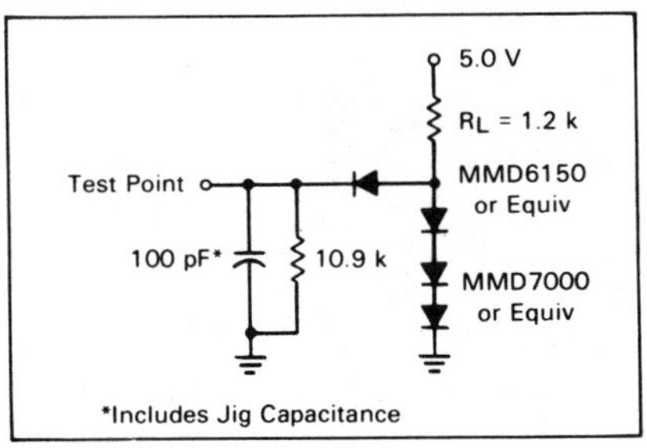

WAVEFORMS

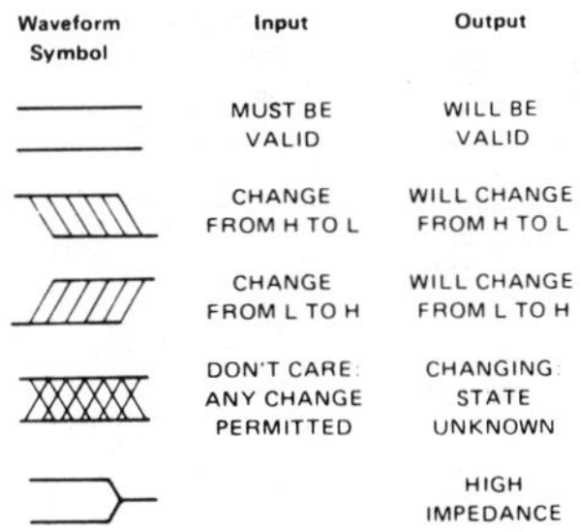

PRODUCT DESCRIPTION

This Motorola MOS Read Only Memory (ROM), the MCM68364, is a clocked or edge enabled device. It makes use of virtual ground ROM cells and clocked peripheral circuitry, allowing a better speed-power product.

The MCM68364 has a period during which the non-static periphery must undergo a precharge. Therefore, the cycle time is slightly longer than the access time. It is essential that the precharge requirements are met to ensure proper address latching and avoid invalid output data. Once the address hold time has been met, new address information can be supplied in preparation for the next cycle.

CUSTOM PROGRAMMING

By the programming of a single photomask for the MCM68364, the customer may specify the contents of the memory.

Information for custom memory content may be sent to Motorola in one of two forms (shown in order of preference):

1. EPROMs – one 64K (MCM68764), two 32K, or four 16K (MCM2716 or TMS2716).
2. Magnetic Tape – 9 Track, 800 bpi, odd parity written in EBCDIC character code. Motorola's R.O.M.S. format.

PRE-PROGRAMMED MCM68364P25-3

The –3 standard ROM pattern contains log (base 10) and antilog (base 10) lookup tables for the 64K ROM.

Locations 0000 through 3599 contain log base 10 values. The arguments for the log table range from 1.00 through 9.99 incrementing in steps of 1/100. Each log value is represented by an eight-digit decimal number with decimal point assumed to be to the left of the most significant digit.

Antilog (base 10) are stored in locations 4096 through 8095. The arguments range from .000 through .999 incrementing in steps of 1/1000. Each antilog value is represented by an eight-digit decimal number with decimal point assumed to be to the right of the most significant digit.

Locations 3600 through 4095 and 8096 through 8191 are zero filled.

All values are represented in absolute decimal format with eight digit precision. They are stored in BCD format with the two most significant digits in the lower byte and the remaining six digits in the three consecutive locations.

Example:
$\log_{10}(1.01) = .00432137$ decimal

Address	Contents	
4	0000	0000
5	0100	0011
6	0010	0001
7	0011	0111

M6800 MICROCOMPUTER FAMILY
BLOCK DIAGRAM

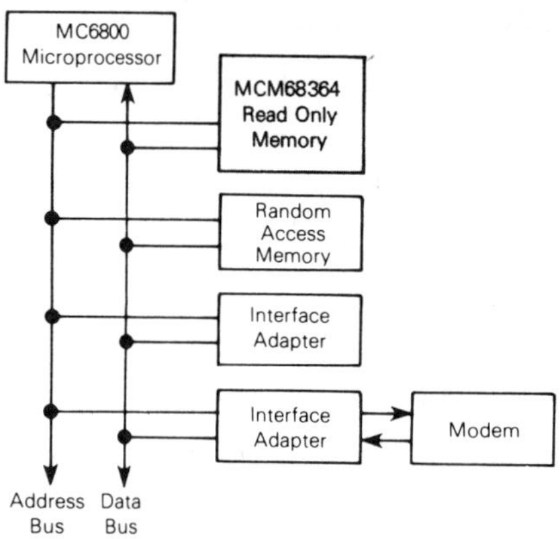

READ ONLY MEMORY
BLOCK DIAGRAM

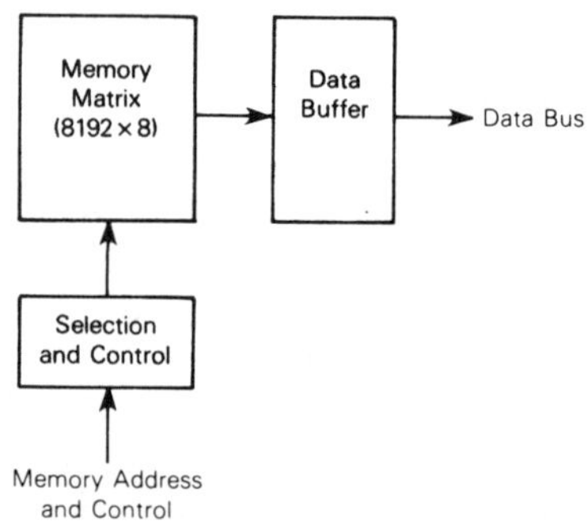

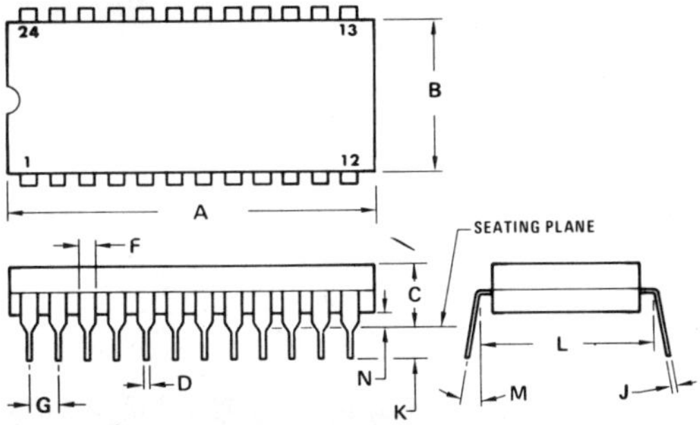

C SUFFIX
FRIT-SEAL
CERAMIC PACKAGE
CASE 623-05

DIM	MILLIMETERS MIN	MILLIMETERS MAX	INCHES MIN	INCHES MAX
A	31.24	32.77	1.230	1.290
B	12.70	15.49	0.500	0.610
C	4.06	5.59	0.160	0.220
D	0.41	0.51	0.016	0.020
F	1.27	1.52	0.050	0.060
G	2.54 BSC		0.100 BSC	
J	0.20	0.30	0.008	0.012
K	3.18	4.06	0.125	0.160
L	15.24 BSC		0.600 BSC	
M	0°	15°	0°	15°
N	0.51	1.27	0.020	0.050

NOTES:
1. DIM "L" TO CENTER OF LEADS WHEN FORMED PARALLEL.
2. LEADS WITHIN 0.13 mm (0.005) RADIUS OF TRUE POSITION AT SEATING PLANE AT MAXIMUM MATERIAL CONDITION. (WHEN FORMED PARALLEL).

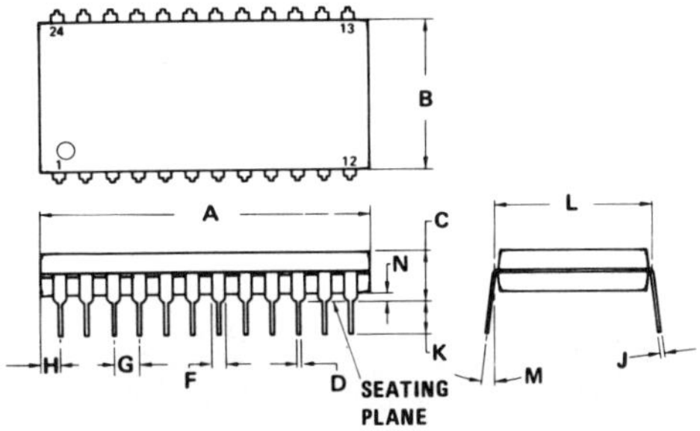

P SUFFIX
PLASTIC PACKAGE
CASE 709-02

DIM	MILLIMETERS MIN	MILLIMETERS MAX	INCHES MIN	INCHES MAX
A	31.37	32.13	1.235	1.265
B	13.72	14.22	0.540	0.560
C	3.94	5.08	0.155	0.200
D	0.36	0.56	0.014	0.022
F	1.02	1.52	0.040	0.060
G	2.54 BSC		0.100 BSC	
H	1.78	2.03	0.070	0.080
J	0.20	0.38	0.008	0.015
K	2.92	3.43	0.115	0.135
L	15.24 BSC		0.600 BSC	
M	0°	15°	0°	15°
N	0.51	1.02	0.020	0.040

NOTES:
1. POSITIONAL TOLERANCE OF LEADS (D), SHALL BE WITHIN 0.25 mm (0.010) AT MAXIMUM MATERIAL CONDITION, IN RELATION TO SEATING PLANE AND EACH OTHER.
2. DIMENSION L TO CENTER OF LEADS WHEN FORMED PARALLEL.
3. DIMENSION B DOES NOT INCLUDE MOLD FLASH.

APPENDIX F

Interrupts for the MC68000

(Courtesy Motorola Inc.)

MOTOROLA

EB-97

Engineering Bulletin

By Mitchell B. Taylor
Microprocessor Applications Engineer
Austin, Texas

A DISCUSSION OF INTERRUPTS FOR THE MC68000 (DL6, CC1, AND GN7 MASK ONLY)

A DISCUSSION OF INTERRUPTS FOR THE MC68000 (DL6, CC1, AND GN7 MASK ONLY)

INTERRUPT LEVELS

The MC68000 16-Bit Microprocessing Unit (MPU) provides seven levels of interrupts, all of which are recognized and serviced based upon the state of the $\overline{IPL0}$-$\overline{IPL2}$ interrupt control pins and the priority set by the interrupt mask. The interrupt mask consists of three interrupt mask bits (I_0, I_1, I_2) which are part of the 16-bit status register shown in Figure 1. These three bits indicate the current processor interrupt priority level which ranges between zero and seven.

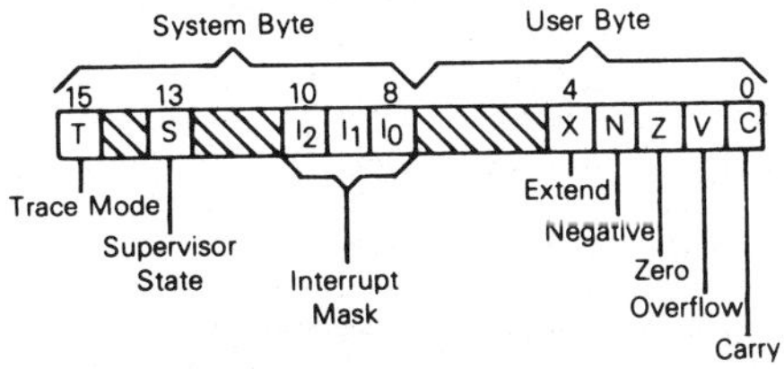

FIGURE 1 — Status Register

Interrupt request level zero (IPL0-IPL2 all high) indicates that no interrupt service is requested. When an interrupt level from one through six is requested via $\overline{IPL0}$-$\overline{IPL2}$, the processor compares the interrupt request level to the interrupt mask to determine whether the interrupt should be processed. Interrupt requests are ignored for all interrupt request levels that are less than or equal to the current processor priority level as determined by the interrupt mask bits. Level seven interrupts are non-maskable and are discussed separately under the **LEVEL SEVEN INTERRUPTS** heading. Table 1 shows the relationship between the actual requested interrupt level and the state of the interrupt control lines ($\overline{IPL0}$-$\overline{IPL2}$), plus the interrupt mask levels required for recognition of the requested level.

TABLE 1 — Interrupt Control Line Status for Each Requested Interrupt Level and Corresponding Interrupt Mask Levels

Requested Interrupt Level	Control Line Status IPL2	IPL1	IPL0	Interrupt Mask Level Required for Recognition
0*	High	High	High	N/A*
1	High	High	Low	0
2	High	Low	High	0-1
3	High	Low	Low	0-2
4	Low	High	High	0-3
5	Low	High	Low	0-4
6	Low	Low	High	0-5
7	Low	Low	Low	0-7

*Indicates no interrupt requested.

RECOGNITION OF INTERRUPTS

To ensure that an interrupt will be recognized, the following interrupting level rules should be considered:

1. The incoming interrupt request level must be at a higher priority level than the mask level set in the interrupt mask bits (except for level seven, the non-maskable interrupt).
2. The $\overline{IPL0}$-$\overline{IPL2}$ interrupt control lines must be held at the interrupt request level until the MC68000 acknowledges the interrupt by initiating an interrupt acknowledge (IACK) bus cycle. The processor indicates that it is executing an IACK bus cycle by placing the interrupt acknowledge code (all high) on the three processor status function code pins (FC0-FC2) and also asserting $\overline{AS}$.

These rules guarantee that the interrupt will be processed; however, the interrupt could also be processed if the request level is taken away before the IACK bus cycle.

The MC68000 samples the $\overline{IPL0}$-$\overline{IPL2}$ interrupt control pins and compares the level of these three inputs to the interrupt mask level once during the execution of every instruc-

The information in this Engineering Bulletin is not applicable to early MC68000 mask sets; i.e., R9M, T6E, and BF4.

tion. The exact step in the execution of an instruction which samples the interrupt control pins is instruction dependent. It is possible that an interrupt held for as short a time as two clock periods of the system clock could be recognized. For example, assume that: (1) the interrupt mask is set at level two and a level three interrupt request is present on the interrupt control pins for two system clock periods; and (2) a level six interrupt request is then requested and remains applied to the interrupt control pins. Which interrupt request will be recognized?

The level three interrupt request may be recognized but it is not guaranteed since it is not held until the IACK bus cycle is initiated. The level six interrupt request will be recognized assuming that it remains applied to the interrupt control pins until its IACK bus cycle begins. Again, to ensure that an interrupt request will be recognized, the level must be held until: the three function code outputs are high; $\overline{AS}$ has fallen (start of IACK bus cycle); and A1, A2, and A3 reflect the interrupt level requested.

The maximum time from interrupt request to the execution of the interrupt handling routine (interrupt latency period) occurs when the processor is executing the following instruction sequence: MOVEM.L (An)+,D0-D7/A0-A7; and DIVS. At the beginning of the MOVEM.L (An)+,D0-D7/A0-A7 instruction, the interrupt control pins are sampled; whereas, they are sampled at the end of the DIVS instruction. Thus, if an interrupt is present on the interrupt control pins immediately after the MOVEM instruction samples these lines, it would not be recognized until the end of the DIVS instruction. This maximum interrupt latency period would include a maximum of 146 clock periods plus wait states for the MOVEM instruction, 174 clock periods plus wait states for the DIVS instruction, and 58 clock periods for a worst-case autovector IACK sequence. Therefore, the maximum interrupt latency period for a no wait-state system is 378 clock periods.

INTERRUPT ACKNOWLEDGE SEQUENCE

The purpose of the interrupt acknowledge (IACK) bus cycle is to indicate to the processor the starting location of a particular interrupt handling routine. The following occurs during an IACK bus cycle and are qualified by the assertion of AS: (1) the MC68000 echoes the interrupt level on address lines A1, A2, and A3 which was recognized on the interrupt control lines; and (2) the function code output pins (FC0-FC2) are then driven high. This information is used by external hardware to generate an interrupt acknowledge ($\overline{IACK}$) signal to the interrupting device.

If the interrupting device has a vector register, it will then place a vector number on data lines D0-D7, and perform a data transfer acknowledge ($\overline{DTACK}$) handshake to terminate the IACK bus cycle. The MC68000 uses the vector number for indexing into the exception vector assignment table to determine the starting address of the interrupt handling routine for that particular device. Refer to Table 2 for the exception vector assignment table.

If the interrupting device does not have a vector register, then external hardware should recognize the IACK signal and assert $\overline{VPA}$ (valid peripheral address) to terminate the IACK bus cycle. When $\overline{VPA}$ is asserted, the MC68000 automatically directs itself to the proper interrupt vector; this is called an autovectored interrupt. There are seven autovectors and there is one autovector corresponding to each of the seven interrupt levels. The MC68000 selects the autovector for the interrupt level which was recognized.

The final way to terminate an interrupt acknowledge ($\overline{IACK}$) bus cycle is with the $\overline{BERR}$ (bus error) signal. Even though the interrupt control pins are synchronized to enhance noise immunity, it is possible that external system interrupt circuitry may initiate an IACK bus cycle as a result of noise. Since no device is requesting interrupt service, neither $\overline{DTACK}$ nor $\overline{VPA}$ will be asserted to signal the end of the nonexisting IACK bus cycle. When there is no response to an IACK bus cycle after a specified period of time, the system "watchdog timer" should assert $\overline{BERR}$. This indicates to the processor that it has recognized a spurious interrupt. Since a spurious interrupt is an exception, the MC68000 will go to the spurious interrupt vector to fetch the starting address for this exception handling routine.

INTERRUPT SEQUENCE

For a vectored interrupt the MC68000 executes the following sequence:

1. Make an internal copy of the current status register.
2. Set S bit, clear T bit, and replace the I_0, I_1, I_2 bits of the interrupt mask with the level of the interrupt which was recognized. (Items 1 and 2 take a total of six clock periods.) There is no bus activity during this time.
3. Stack program counter (low word) on system stack (four clock periods with no wait states).
4. Run an IACK bus cycle for vector number acquisition (four clock periods with no wait states, between 10 and 18 clock periods for autovectored interrupts).
5. Justify the vector number for vector acquisition (four clock periods and no bus activity during this time).
6. Stack former (internal copy) status register on system stack (four clock periods with no wait states).
7. Stack program counter (high word) on system stack (four clock periods with no wait states).
8. Read exception vector (high word) (four clock periods with no wait states).
9. Read exception vector low word (four clock periods with no wait states).
10. Fetch first word of instruction of the interrupt handling routine (four clock periods with no wait states).
11. Two non-bus clock periods (dead cycles).
12. Fetch second word of instruction of the interrupt handling routine and check the interrupt control pins for a valid interrupt. If a higher priority interrupt is present, the MC68000 begins an interrupt acknowledge sequence for that higher priority interrupt (four clock periods with no wait states).

Item 12 sheds more light on the interrupt example discussed in **RECOGNITION OF INTERRUPTS** paragraph. In that example, the interrupt mask is set at level two and a level three interrupt is present for two clock periods on the interrupt control pins. If the level three is then removed from the interrupt control pins and a level six interrupt is now pending, which interrupt will be recognized?

The level three interrupt will be recognized, only if the level three interrupt is present during the instruction step which samples the interrupt control pins. Assuming that the level three interrupt is recognized, the interrupt control pins will be sampled again during sequence 12 (described above) of the level three IACK sequence. At this time the processor will recognize the level six interrupt as a pending interrupt. The MC68000 will fetch the second word of the first instruction of the level three interrupt handling routine but this instruction will not be executed; instead, the processor begins the level six interrupt sequence. At the end of the level six interrupt handling routine a return from exception (RTE) instruction should be executed. The processor then fetches the

TABLE 2 — Exception Vector Assignment Table

Vector Number(s)	Address			Assignment
	Dec	Hex	Space	
0	0	000	SP	Reset: Initial SSP
—	4	004	SP	Reset: Initial PC
2	8	008	SD	Bus Error
3	12	00C	SD	Address Error
4	16	010	SD	Illegal Instruction
5	20	014	SD	Zero Divide
6	24	018	SD	CHK Instruction
7	28	01C	SD	TRAPV Instruction
8	32	020	SD	Privilege Violation
9	36	024	SD	Trace
10	40	028	SD	Line 1010 Emulator
11	44	02C	SD	Line 1111 Emulator
12*	48	030	SD	(Unassigned, reserved)
13*	52	034	SD	(Unassigned, reserved)
14*	56	038	SD	(Unassigned, reserved)
15	60	03C	SD	Uninitialized Interrupt Vector
16-23*	64	04C	SD	(Unassigned, reserved)
	95	05F		—
24	96	060	SD	Spurious Interrupt
25	100	064	SD	Level 1 Interrupt Autovector
26	104	068	SD	Level 2 Interrupt Autovector
27	108	06C	SD	Level 3 Interrupt Autovector
28	112	070	SD	Level 4 Interrupt Autovector
29	116	074	SD	Level 5 Interrupt Autovector
30	120	078	SD	Level 6 Interrupt Autovector
31	124	07C	SD	Level 7 Interrupt Autovector
32-47	128	080	SD	TRAP Instruction Vectors
	191	0BF		—
48-63*	192	0C0	SD	(Unassigned, reserved)
	255	0FF		—
64-255	256	100	SD	User Interrupt Vectors
	1023	3FF		—

*Vector numbers 12, 13, 14, 16 through 23 and 48 through 63 are reserved for future enhancements by Motorola. No user peripheral devices should be assigned these numbers.

first instruction of the level three handling routine and samples the interrupt control lines. If there is no higher interrupt present on the interrupt control lines then the level three handling routine will be executed.

IACK GENERATION

Peripherals of the MC68000 Family with vector number registers have an $\overline{IRQ}$ output and an $\overline{IACK}$ input. The $\overline{IACK}$ signal should be derived from address lines A3, A2, and A1 during the $\overline{IACK}$ vector number acquisition. A circuit to generate $\overline{IACK1}$ through $\overline{IACK7}$ is shown in Figure 2, and a representation of the $\overline{IRQ4}$ output and $\overline{IACK4}$ input is shown in Figure 3.

Interrupt request lines $\overline{IRQ1}$ through $\overline{IRQ7}$ are encoded and prioritized by U1 before being presented to the MC68000 on the interrupt control lines ($\overline{IPL0}$-$\overline{IPL2}$). When the MC68000 recognizes a valid interrupt, it echoes the interrupt level on address lines A3, A2, and A1. The three-to-eight decoder (U2) decodes the interrupt level when the function code lines (FC0-FC2) are all high and $\overline{AS}$ is low. To maintain compatibility with future M68000 Family processors, A4-A23 being driven high (along with FC0-FC2) should be used to enable the E1 input of U2. This separates the IACK space of the MC68000 from the CPU space of the MC68020. By comparing the decoded interrupt acknowledge level with the $\overline{IRQ1}$-$\overline{IRQ7}$ lines, only the recognized interrupt request is acknowledged instead of all pending interrupt requests.

"DAISY-CHAINING" OF INTERRUPTS

Several interrupting devices may share a common interrupt level. These devices may be prioritized by "daisy-chaining" their interrupt request ($\overline{IRQ1}$-$\overline{IRQ7}$) lines and interrupt acknowledge ($\overline{IACK1}$-$\overline{IACK7}$) pins. Figure 3 shows two interrupting devices, each with an $\overline{IRQ}$ output and an $\overline{IACK4}$ input. Any device is allowed to interrupt the MC68000; however, lower priority devices (device 2) only receives an $\overline{IACK}$ if higher priority devices (device 1) are not requesting an interrupt. In this manner, devices at the beginning of the "chain" are serviced first.

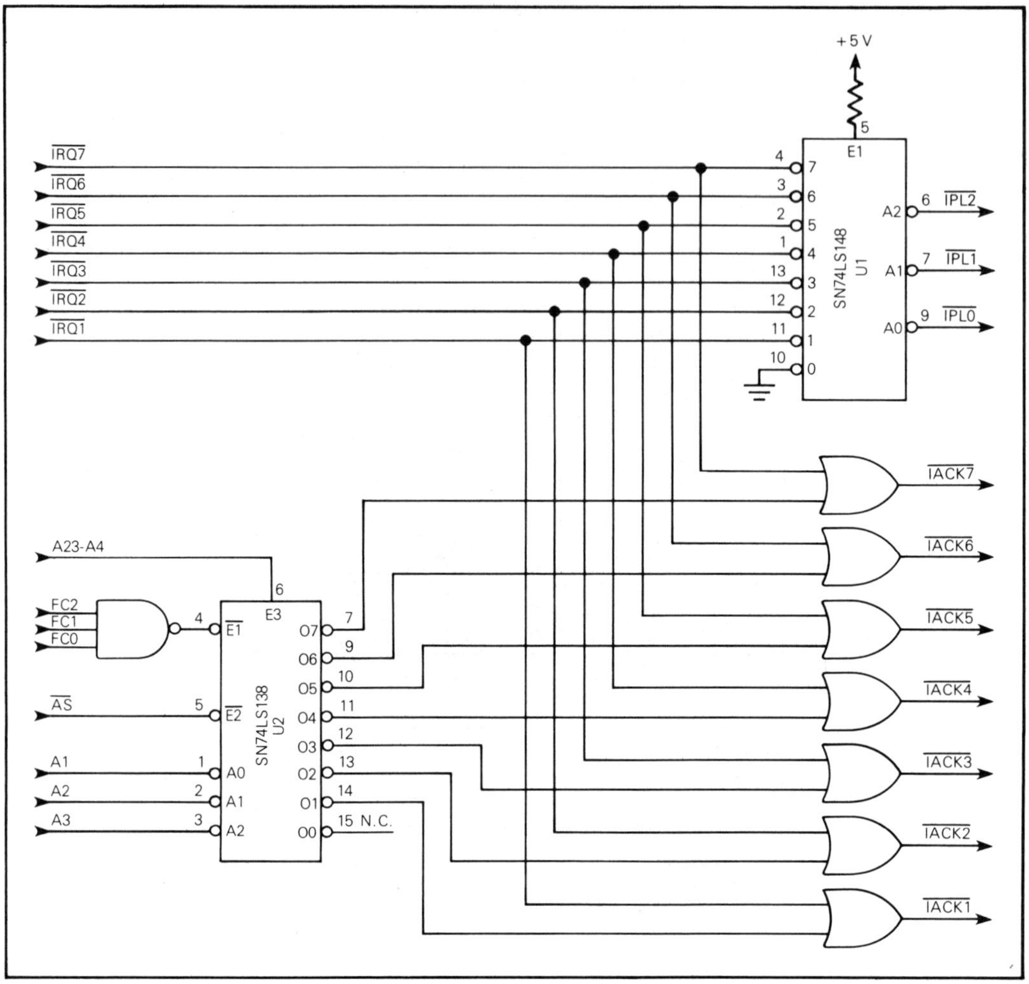

FIGURE 2 — IACK Generation Circuit Functional Diagram

When a level four interrupt is recognized, the MC68000 drives the FC0-FC1 function codes high (so that the preset on both U4a and U4b are negated) and asserts $\overline{AS}$. The interrupt acknowledge circuit of Figure 2 will then assert $\overline{IACK4}$. This causes U6 (Figure 3) to clock in the current state of the $\overline{IRQ}$ output line of each device to drive its respective $\overline{IACK}$ input pin. Clocking is inhibited for an interrupting device if a higher priority device in the chain has its $\overline{IRQ}$ line asserted. This also ensures that devices at the beginning of a chain are serviced first.

When the interrupting device receives its $\overline{IACK}$ input, it will place its vector number on the data bus and assert $\overline{DTACK}$. The MC68000 uses the vector number to acquire the starting address of the interrupt handling routine for that particular device. The $\overline{IACK}$ pins for all devices are negated when the FC0-FC2 function codes change, signaling a new bus cycle.

LEVEL SEVEN INTERRUPTS

Level seven interrupts are handled differently than interrupt levels one through six. A level seven interrupt is a nonmaskable interrupt; therefore, a seven in the interrupt mask does not disable a level seven interrupt. Again, a level seven interrupt should be maintained on interrupt control pins IPL0-IPL2 until the IACK bus cycle is initiated to guarantee that the interrupt will be recognized.

Level seven interrupts are edge triggered by a transition from a lower priority request to the level seven request, as opposed to interrupt levels one through six which are level sensitive. Therefore, if a level seven interrupt persists, the processor will only recognize this level seven interrupt once since only one transition (from lower priority request to level seven request) on the interrupt control line has occurred. For the processor to recognize a level seven interrupt followed by another level seven interrupt, one of two following sequences must occur:

1. Interrupt control pins must have a lower priority interrupt request level than level seven; i.e., level zero through six. Then, the interrupt request level on the interrupt control pins changes to level seven and remains at level seven until the IACK bus cycle begins. Later, the interrupt request level returns to a lower interrupt request level and finally back to level seven, causing a second transition on the interrupt control lines.
2. Interrupt control pins have a lower priority interrupt request than level seven; i.e., level zero through six. Then, the interrupt request level on the interrupt control pins changes to level seven and remains at that level. If the interrupt handling routine for the level seven interrupt lowers the interrupt mask level, a second level seven interrupt will be recognized even though no transition has occurred on the interrupt control pins and the interrupt mask will be set back to level seven. Note that the level on the interrupt control pins only had one initial level transition (from lower priority request to level seven request) and then was held at level seven until the second level seven interrupt acknowledge (IACK) bus cycle.

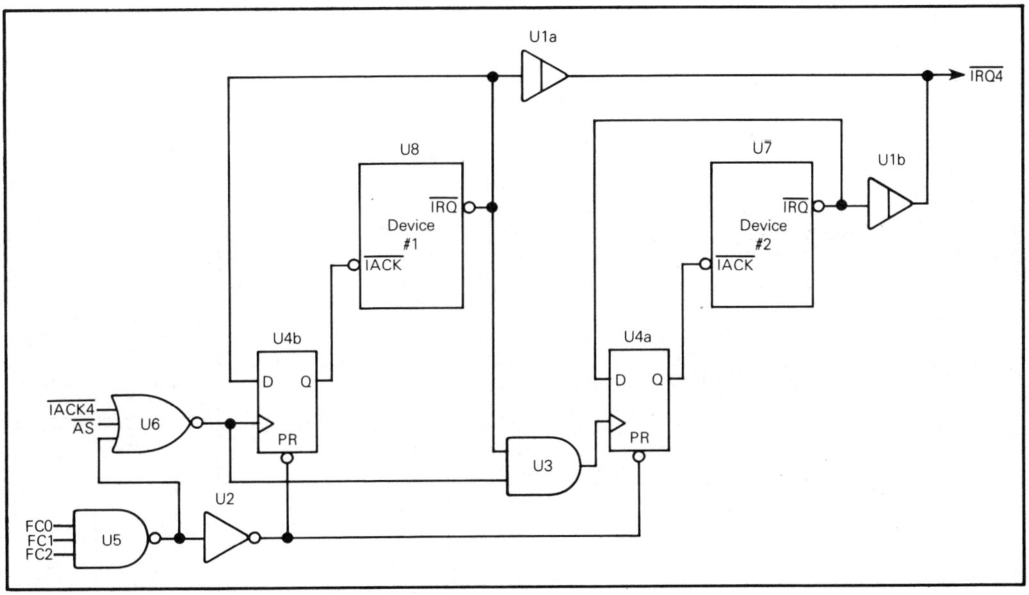

FIGURE 3 — "Daisy-Chain" Interrupts Functional Diagram

APPENDIX G

M68000 Family Fact Sheet

MOTOROLA

BR249
REV 1

	DEVICE #	DEVICE NAME	DESCRIPTION	SOURCES	SPEEDS	PACKAGE TYPE
PROCESSORS	MC68000	16/32 bit MPU	16 bit external/32 bit internal MPU. 17 general purpose 32 bit registers. 16 MB linear address space.	M, H, MK, R, S, T	8, 10, 12.5 MHz	64 lead L, LC, P 68 lead R, ZB FN (2Q85)
	MC68008	8/32 bit MPU	8 bit external/32 bit internal MPU. 17 general purpose 32 bit registers. 1 megabyte linear address space (4 MB with FN package option).	M, MK, S, T	8, 10 MHz	48 lead L, P 52 lead FN (2Q85)
	MC68010	Virtual Machine 16/32 bit MPU	16 bit external/32 bit internal MPU. 17 general purpose 32 bit registers. Virtual memory/machine. 16 megabyte linear address space.	M, S	8, 10, 12.5 MHz	64 lead L, LC, P 68 lead R, RC
	MC68012	Extended Virtual 16/32 bit MPU	16 bit external/32 bit internal MPU. 17 general purpose 32 bit registers. Virtual memory/machine. 2 gigabyte linear address space.	M	8, 10, 12.5 MHz	84 lead RC
	MC68020	32 bit MPU	Complete 32 bit microprocessor. 4 gigabyte linear address space. Coprocessor Interface. Instruction Cache. Dynamic Bus Sizing. 2-3 MIPS performance.	M	12.5, 16.67 (1Q85) MHz	114 lead RC
	MC68881	Floating Point Coprocessor (FPCP)	Meets full IEEE spec for advanced floating point calculations. Single, double and extended precision.	M (1Q85)	12.5, 16.67 MHz	68 lead RC
MEMORY MGMT	MC68451	Memory Management Unit (MMU)	Ideal MMU for non-demand paged MC68000, 68010 systems.	M, MK	8, 10 MHz	64 lead L, LC 68 lead R, RC
	MC68851	Paged MMU (PMMU)	32 bit demand virtual paged memory management unit for MC68020 based systems.	M (3Q85)	12.5, 16.67 MHz	124 lead RC
	MC68461	Memory Management Cntlr (MMC)	Gate array implementation of PMMU functional subset. Can be used with 68020, 68010, or 68012. Bipolar.	M	N/A	149 lead RC or mezz board
DMA CONTROL	MC68440	Dual DMA (DDMA)	Dual channel, high speed Direct Memory Access controller. Capable of 5 MB/sec data transfer rates.	M	8, 10, 12.5 (3Q85) MHz	64 lead L, LC, P 68 lead R, RC FN(4Q85)
	MC68450	DMA Controller (DMAC)	Four channel Direct Memory Access Controller. Capable of very complex "chained" data transfers.	M, H	8, 10 MHz	64 lead L, LC 68 lead R, RC
	MC68442	Expanded DDMA	32 bit address version of DDMA. Support for 4 gigabyte range of MC68020. Pin compatible with 68440/68450.	M (1Q85)	8, 10, 12.5 (3Q85) MHz	68 lead R
SYSTEM INTERFACE	MC68153	Bus Interrupt Module (BIM)	Routes interrupts from 4 independent sources to any of 7 M68000 MPU interrupt levels. Bipolar.	M	200 ns access time (16 MHz clock)	40 lead L, P
	MC68452	Bus Arbitration Module (BAM)	Arbitrates access of an M68000 system bus between up to 8 local masters. Bipolar.	M	50 ns arbitration time	28 lead L, P
	MC68172	VMEbus Controller (E-BUSCON)	Performs VMEbus/local bus arbitration, VMEbus requests, bus transceiver control.	S (2Q85)	N/A	28 lead L, P
	MC68173	VMSbus Controller (S-BUSCON)	Handles interface of operations between high speed serial peripheral VMSbus and controlling VMEbus.	S (2Q85)	N/A	28 lead L, P
	MC68174	VMEbus Arbiter (E-BAM)	Performs round robin and 4 level priority arbitration for VMEbus based systems. Bipolar.	M (2Q85)	N/A	20 lead L, P

M68000 FAMILY FACT SHEET

	DEVICE #	DEVICE NAME	DESCRIPTION	SOURCES	SPEEDS	PACKAGE TYPE
DATA COMMUNICATION	68561	Multi-Protocol Comm Cntlr 2 (MPCC-2)	Single channel. M68000 interface. Asynch, bisynch, SDLC.	R (1Q85)	4 Mb/s	48 lead L
	68562	Dual Universal Serial Comm Cntlr (DUSCC)	Dual channel. Asynch. Byte control (bisynch, DDCMP, X.21). Bit oriented (HDLC/ADCCP, SDLC X.25). DMA interface. Counter/timer.	S (1Q85)	4 Mb/s	48 lead L
	68564	Serial I/O (SI/O)	Dual channel. Asynch, bisynch, SDLC.	MK	1 Mb/s	48 lead L, P
	MC68652 MC2652	Multi-Protocol Comm Cntlr (MPCC)	Single channel. Byte control. Bit oriented. CRC (error correction) circuitry. (MC2652 has generic bus interface.)	M, S	2 Mb/s	40 lead L, P
	MC68653 MC2653	Polynomial Generator Checker (PGC)	Error correction, code generation/comparitor circuit. Excellent companion chip for 68652 MPCC or 68661 EPCI. (MC2653 has generic bus interface.)	M, S	4 Mb/s	16 lead L, P
	MC68661 MC2661	Enhanced Peripheral Comm I/F (EPCI)	Universal synch/asynch. Double buffered receiver/transmitter. Internal baud rate clock. (2661 generic bus I/F)	M, S	1 Mb/s	28 lead L, P
	MC68681 MC2681 MC2682	Dual UART (DUART)	Dual channel. Quad buffered receiver. Double buffered transmitter. Independent baud rate selection. 1 Mb/s. (2681 has generic bus interface; 2682 offers partial functionality in a smaller package.)	M, S	1 Mb/s	40 lead L, P (MC2682-28 lead)
LAN CTRL	68590	LAN Controller for Ethernet (LANCE)	Provides complete IEEE specified Ethernet communication control for M68000 based systems. Plus DMA controller.	MK	10 Mb/s	48 lead L
	68802	IEEE 802.3 LAN Controller (LAN)	Provides communication control between M68000 based systems and the IEEE 802.3 LAN protocol.	R	10 Mb/s	40 lead P
DISK CONTROL	68454	Intelligent Multiple Disk Controller (IMDC)	Controls up to four disks. Any combination of single/dual density, floppy or hard. 256 byte FIFO. 4 GB DMA ctlr.	S	2-10 Mb/s	48 lead L, P
	68459	Disk Phase Lock Loop (DPLL)	Companion device to 68454 IMDC. Used for interfacing more than one drive to the IMDC.	S	N/A	24 lead L, P
	68465	Floppy Disk Cntrlr (FDC)	Interfaces 2 single or double density floppy disks to the M68000 bus.	R	N/A	48 lead L, P
GENERAL I/O	MC68120/ 68121	Intelligent Peripheral Controller (IPC)	Provides peripheral control for M68000 or M6800 systems.	M, S	1, 1.25 MHz	48 lead L
	MC68230	Parallel Interface/ Timer (PI/T)	Unidirectional/bidirectional, 8/16 bit, double buffered parallel interface. 24 bit timer with 5 bit prescaler. M68000 I/F.	M, MK S, T	8, 10 MHz	48 lead L, P
	MC68901	Multi Function Peripheral (MFP)	Single channel USART. 8 source interrupt controller. 8 parallel I/O lines. Four 8 bit timers.	M, MK	4 MHz 1 Mb/s USART	48 lead L, P
GRAPHICS	MC68486 (RMI) MC68487 (RMC)	Raster Memory System (RMS)	Provides functionality required by bit mapped or object-oriented graphics systems. Features include object definition & manipulation, collision detection, light pen input, x/y capture & interrupt, 32 of 4096 colors, visual/virtual screens.	M (2Q85)	N/A	48 lead L, P (both)

Sources—M = Motorola
H = Hitachi
MK = United Technologies/Mostek
R = Rockwell
S = North American Philips/Signetics
T = Thomson CSF

Packaging: L = Ceramic DIP
LC = Ceramic DIP, Gold Lead Finish
P = Plastic DIP
R = Pin Grid Array
RC = Pin Grid Array, Gold Lead Finish
ZB = Socketable LCC
ZC = Surface Mount LCC
FN = Plastic Quad Pack

A18601-1 PRINTED IN USA 12-84 IMPERIAL LITHO C27336 10,000

APPENDIX H

RS-232C Serial Communications

E.I.A. RS-232C STANDARD

Written in 1969 by the Electronic Industries Association (EIA), RS-232C is a serial communications standard established to define electrical and mechanical requirements for interconnecting data communications equipment (DCE) and data terminal equipment (DTE). The standard describes both synchronous and asynchronous serial binary communications with data rates ranging from zero to 20,000 bits/second. Twenty-five signal lines are described by the standard, although most are not used in typical applications. Table H-1 summarizes key features of the EIA RS-232C standard.

TABLE H-1 EIA RS-232C STANDARD

Parameter	*RS-232C*
Line length (recommended maximum—may be exceeded with proper design.)	50 ft.
Input Z	3K to 7K ohm 2500 pF
Maximum frequency (baud)	20K baud
Transition time (time in undefined area between "1" and "0") tr = 10 to 90%	4% of bit period or 1 ms
dV/dt (wave shaping)	30 V/μs
Mark (Data "1")	−3 V
Space (Data "0")	+3 V
Common mode voltage (for balanced receiver)	—
Output Z	—
Open-circuit output voltage (V_o)	3 V < $\lvert V_o \rvert$ <25 V
V_t = loaded V_o	5 < $\lvert V_o \rvert$ <15 V 3k to 7K ohm load
Short-circuit current	500 mA
Power-off leakage (V_o applied to unpowered device)	> 300 ohm 2 V < $\lvert V_o \rvert$ <25 V V_o applied
Minimum receiver input for proper V_o	> ±3 V

All material in this appendix is taken from *MC68000 Educational Computer Board User's Manual, MEX68KECB/D2*. 2nd Ed. Tempe, AZ: Motorola Literature Distribution Center, 1982.

The standard connector used for RS-232C compatible equipment is a 25-signal subminiature "D" type. Table H-2 lists the pin number, signal name, and signal description.

TABLE H-2 RS-232C SIGNAL DESCRIPTION

RS-232C pin number	*RS-232C signal name*	*Description and signal direction*
1	AA	Frame ground
2	BA	Transmitted data (to DCE)
3	BB	Received data (from DCE)
4	CA	Request to send (to DCE)
5	CB	Clear to send (from DCE)
6	CC	Data set ready (from DCE)
7	AB	Signal ground
8	CF	Received line signal detector (from DCE)
9	—	Positive DC test voltage
10	—	Negative DC test voltage
11	—	Unassigned
12	SCF	Secondary received line signal detector (from DCE)
13	SCB	Secondary clear to send (from DCE)
14	SBA	Secondary transmitted data (to DCE)
15	DB	Transmitter signal element timing (from DCE)
16	SBB	Secondary received data (from DCE)
17	DD	Receiver signal element timing (from DCE)
18	—	Unassigned
19	SCA	Secondary request to send (to DCE)
20	CD	Data terminal ready (to DCE)
21	CG	Signal quality detector (from DCE)
22	CE	Ring indicator (from DCE)
23	CH/CI	Data rate selector (to/from DCE)
24	DA	Transmitter signal element timing (to DCE)
25	—	Unassigned

MEX68KECB RS-232C INTERFACE

Ports 1 and 2 of the MC68000 Educational Computer Board support asynchronous serial communications as described by the RS-232C standard. Because transmit and receive clocks are not sent out on the interface, synchronous communications are not supported. Port 1 constitutes a DCE or modem interface type; that is, data terminal equipment is connected to Port 1. Port 2 is a DTE interface and connects to data communication equipment. Baud rates at each port range from 110 to 9600 baud.

Of the 25 signal lines described in Table H-2, the educational computer supports a set of seven. These are:

BA—Transmitted data—TxDATA

BB—Received data—RxDATA

CA—Request to send—RTS

CB—Clear to send—CTS

CC—Data set ready—DSR

CF—Received line signal detector—DCD

CD—Data terminal ready—DTR

In addition, there are two ground signals:
AB—Signal ground—GND

AA—Frame ground

The frame ground is not connected to the educational computer's signal ground but can be connected externally if necessary.

The following paragraphs are a description of the signal lines supported by Ports 1 and 2. The format used is:

Signal name (RS232 pin #; signal name)
Signal direction
Signal function description

1. TxDATA Transmitted data (Pin 2; BA)
   Serial data output from terminal (DTE) to modem (DCE)
   The line/signal through which the terminal (DTE) sends data to the modem (DCE).
2. RxDATA Received data (Pin 3; BB)
   Serial data input to terminal (DTE) from modem (DCE)
   The line/signal through which the modem (DCE) sends data to the terminal (DTE).
3. RTS Request to send (Pin 4; CA)
   Control output from terminal (DTE) to modem (DCE)
   The line/signal through which the terminal (DCE) requests permission to transmit data to the modem (DCE).
   Assertion of RTS instructs the DCE to prepare to receive data from the DTE and to signify that it is ready to receive by asserting CTS. However, RTS is not monitored at Port 1; it is assumed that Port 1 is always ready to receive data. CTS is activated any time the terminal (DTE) asserts DTR, indicating that it is ready to transmit or receive data.
   RTS is asserted at Port 2 upon power-up to prepare DCE connected to Port 2 for data reception.
4. CTS Clear to send (Pin 5; CB)
   Control input to terminal (DTE) from modem (DCE)
   The line/signal through which the modem (DCE) acknowledges the acceptance of a terminal (DTE) request to send data.
   As stated above, Port 1 asserts CTS any time an active level is received from the DTE on DTR.
   Port 2 receives CTS from the DCE connected to Port 2 and will interrupt data transmission when inactive.

5. DSR Data set ready (Pin 6; CC)
   Control input to terminal (DTE) from modem (DCE)
   The line/signal through which the modem (DCE) indicates its on-line, in-service, or active status.
   Port 1 activates DSR whenever an active level is received on DTR. Port 1 is always on-line.
   Port 2 uses only the CTS input from the DCE to indicate whether data may be sent. DSR is not used in making the decision.
6. DTR Data terminal ready (Pin 20; CD)
   Control output from terminal (DTE) to modem (DCE)
   The line/signal through which the terminal (DTE) indicates its on-line, in-service, or active status.
   DTR is used by Port 1 to enable and disable the transmission of data via the CTS* input of the Port 1 ACIA—MC6850. When CTS* is driven high, transmission will stop following the completion of any in-process transmission. Port 2 activates DTR as part of the power-up/reset firmware. A write to the ACIA control register, which causes the RTS* output to go low, will activate DTR at Port 2.
7. DCD Signal Detect (Pin 8; CF)
   Control input to terminal (DTE) from modem (DCE)
   The line/signal through which the modem (DCE) indicates that the communication channel to which the modem (DCE) interfaces (the other/nonterminal side of the modem) is in an acceptable active state. This signal has meaning only in a communication channel (i.e., telephone line) context. DCD is off when no signal is being received or when the received signal is unsuitable for demodulation. While Port 1 implements a DCE or modem interface, the communication is exclusively digital. There is no need to test the suitability of the signal. DCD, at Port 1, indicates only that DTR has been received from the DTE.
   Port 2 does not monitor DCD. Again, all signals are exclusively digital.

MEX68KECB NON-COMPLIANCE WITH RS-232C

In addition to being a functional subset of the full RS-232C standard, the educational computer does not comply strictly with the signal specifications. In addition to signal definition and timing, the RS-232C standard specifies driver, receiver, and interface voltage and impedance levels (refer to Table H-1). The MC6850 ACIAs used in the serial interface are NMOS devices operating with a +5 V supply and cannot meet the interface voltage and impedance requirements. Two linear integrated circuits, the MC1488 RS-232C line driver and the MC1489A RS-232C line receiver, provide the required buffering and drive to meet the specifications.

The maximum rate of voltage change is specified as 30 V/μs in the RS-232C standard. The MC1488 line drivers have an inherent slew rate which is much too fast. The current limited output of the device can be used to control this slew rate by connecting a capacitor to each driver output. The required capacitance value is given by the formula:

$$C = I_{os} \times \frac{\Delta T}{\Delta V}$$

where C is the capacitance in picofarads, I_{os} is the output short-circuit current in microamps, and $\Delta T/\Delta V$ is 1/slew rate in microseconds per volt. A 330 pF capacitor on each output of the MC1488 will guarantee a worst case slew rate of 30 V/μs. Bear in mind, however, that this capacitance includes cabling capacitance.

These capacitors are not present on the Educational Computer Board.

APPENDIX I

Teaching Notes

68000 Microcomputer Systems: Designing and Troubleshooting can be used as the primary text in a one- or two-semester laboratory-oriented microprocessor course. As a one-semester course, the solderless-breadboard version of the 68000 system can be designed, built, and tested by each graduate student and each team of two undergraduates. By the end of the semester, the operation of each system can be demonstrated using the TUTOR EPROM set. As a two-semester course, the second semester can be used to add applications (e.g., motor controller, data-sampling system, etc.) to the basic breadboard. An alternative second semester might involve building a wire-wrap 68000 CPU board and interfacing it to the IEEE Std-696 bus.

When the book is used in a laboratory course, the teaching sequence should begin with a *brief* overview of Part I on how to do engineering design. Then move into Chapter 6 and focus on the 68000 project requirements; next, lecture on the 68000 material in Chapter 7. Lab during the first several weeks can be spent becoming familiar with the Educational Computer Board—programming it using TUTOR and testing it according to Chapter 8.[1] Then, by the end of the first two or three weeks, each team should prepare a project proposal and present it to the class. During this time, after having attempted its own project proposal, another brief discussion of Part I would be helpful.

After working with the ECB several weeks, each team can begin following their project schedule with the material in Chapters 9, 10, and 11. Coverage of this material should take until the end of the semester. Rather than straight lecturing on the topics,

[1]Motorola is very generous in donating ECBs to universities. By all means, contact them and arrange for ECBs to use in your classes.

provide for classroom dialog and general technical discussions; students should present and explain their technical design decisions to their peers. Laboratory time should be self-paced, consistent with the team project schedule. Each week may be divided between 1-3 hours classroom, 3-6 hours laboratory. At the end of the semester, each team should present its design to the class and submit a complete technical manual describing its product.

During the second semester, students can extend their 68000 systems by adding various applications to the solderless breadboards. Classroom discussions should cover the material in Chapter 12 on exception processing and then move into the software issues in Chapter 14. To have the experience of designing the 68000 system to meet bus specifications, cover Chapter 13 on interfacing to the IEEE Std-696 bus. If students want to build the 68000 CPU on an S-100 card, it will take them about 100 to 150 hours to wire-wrap the board; add about 20 to 40 hours of testing time during the construction.

68000 Microcomputer Systems: Designing and Troubleshooting can also be used to supplement a theory-only computer architecture or programming course. In this context, treat engineering design lightly and get into the construction and testing of the 68000 system on wireless protoboards. Enough hardware information is presented in each of the chapters so that the software-oriented student can build a working system. Move into the Chapter 12 material on exception processing and then into the Chapter 14 software topics. Appropriate semester projects might include writing a monitor to take the place of TUTOR, or writing boot routines for your favorite operating systems. In addition to CP/M-68K, you might want to investigate the operating system OS-9 from Microware.[2]

The Educational Computer Board is almost a necessity to make the 68000 class a rewarding experience. It is important for the student to experiment with a known-good system and learn what it should do. As the new 68000 design progresses during the semester, the student can compare the new board with the ECB and consider alternative designs. In addition, the TUTOR ROMs from the ECB (or copies of the ROMs) can be used directly in the new student systems; Motorola will license university duplications for class. If the ECB cannot be obtained, at least get the ECB manual: it is a good example of 68000 design and documentation. Note, however, that Motorola violated their own 68000 specifications at one point: see the Chapter 8 exercise on the requirement for both RESET* and HALT* assertion for a reset.

There is only a moderate equipment requirement for the 68000 course. If you have a laboratory with logic analyzers and development equipment, so much the better: you can use it to your advantage with this book. If your laboratory is somewhat more modest, you can conduct a fully effective course with only logic probes and 40 MHz dual-trace oscilloscopes. See the preface for a more detailed discussion of the support material required. Figure I-1 shows a typical lab setup.

[2]Microware Systems Corporation, 1866 NW 114th Street, Des Moines, Iowa 50322 (515) 224-1929.

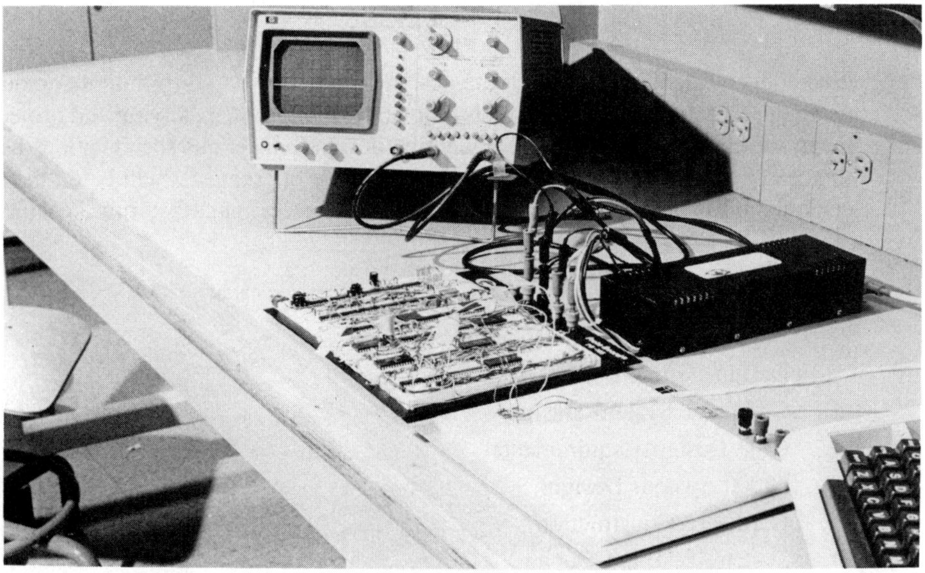

Figure I-1 A typical lab setup with student solderless-breadboard 68000 system.

TEACHING EXPERIENCE

The course is taught at Bucknell University to graduate students and upper-level undergraduates. The following outline describes the general approach to the single-semester course. The material is presented along the lines previously described; a second-semester "special projects" course is used to follow up the designs with specific applications.

The equipment used in the course at Bucknell includes a number of ECBs, logic probes, dual-trace oscilloscopes, a Fluke 9010A Troubleshhooter, and an HP-1631D logic analyzer. The Fluke is used mainly to study the operation of the ECB. Later in the course, after the 68000s are freerunning, the logic analyzer helps to provide timing diagrams. This is particularly useful (although not absolutely necessary) when EPROMs and RAM are added to the system.

The results for the first class were quite satisfactory: by the end of the first semester, six of the eight systems attempted were fully operational; the other two systems were running, but not entirely completed. The systems ran on wireless breadboards at 4 and 8 MHz clock rates. A typical student documentation package describing a semester project is in Appendix C. Student comments at the semester end remarked that this was a most enjoyable course for them: they put in many hours (an average of 20 per week) and learned the material. They stressed that keeping a neat and complete lab book was very important and that writing the final technical manual helped summarize their learning.

DESIGNING WITH MICROPROCESSORS EE-336

This course deals primarily with the design of an industrial 16-bit microcomputer system using the Motorola 68000. After a brief overview of problem solving and project management, the course will illustrate engineering design to meet bus specifications using a real-time clock example. Then the focus for the rest of the semester will be on the design and construction of a working 68000 CPU board to meet manufacturing specifications.

The following topics will be covered in the course:

Problem Solving, Project Management
Engineering Design, Documentation
Design Example: Real-Time Clock Board
Computer System Design
CPU Design Requirements
68000 System Design
Hardware Construction
System Test and Debug
System Evaluation
Software Development

Laboratory time will be used to give the engineering student bench experience in developing, building, and troubleshooting a working 68000 CPU board. Logic probes and oscilloscopes will be used to assist in bringing up the processor. Timing diagrams will be documented using the logic analyzer. All 68000 software development will be done on the 68000 Educational Computer Boards (ECBs) and then on the student CPUs.

Student Objectives

By the end of the semester, the student will be able to design and build a complete 68000 system. The student will be able to solve engineering design problems, design to specifications, document properly, and do troubleshooting.

Books Required

68000 Microcomputer Systems: Designing and Troubleshhooting. Prentice-Hall.

MC68000 16-bit Microprocessor Data Manual. Motorola.

MC68000 Educational Computer Board User's Manual. MEX68KECB/D2, 2nd Edition, 1982. Motorola.

MC68000 8/16/32-bit Microprocessor Programmer's Reference Manual, 5th Edition, 1986. Prentice-Hall or Motorola.

Lab Book: Ampad # 22-157 computation book recommended.

Index

A

B

E

F

G

H

I

K

L

M

N

O

P

T

U